A History of
Western Psychology

A History of
Western Psychology

Second Edition

David J. Murray

Queen's University at Kingston

Prentice Hall, Englewood Cliffs, New Jersey 07632

Library of Congress Cataloging-in-Publication Data

MURRAY, DAVID J.
  A history of Western psychology.

  Bibliography: p.
  Includes indexes.
    1. Psychology—History. I. Title.
BF81.M83 1988   150'.9   87–32853
ISBN 0-13-392580-3

*Editorial/production supervision and interior
design: Merrill Peterson*

© 1988, 1983 by Prentice-Hall, Inc.
A Division of Simon & Schuster
Englewood Cliffs, New Jersey 07632

Printed in the United States of America

10 9 8 7 6 5 4 3 2 1

ISBN   0-13-392580-3

Prentice Hall International (UK) Limited, *London*
Prentice Hall of Australia Pty. Limited, *Sydney*
Prentice Hall Canada Inc., *Toronto*
Prentice Hall Hispanoamericana, S.A., *Mexico*
Prentice Hall of India Private Limited, *New Delhi*
Prentice Hall of Japan, Inc., *Tokyo*
Simon & Schuster Asia Pte. Ltd., *Singapore*
Editora Prentice-Hall do Brasil, Ltda., *Rio de Janeiro*

*This work is dedicated
to the memory of my mother*

Contents

3 The Sixteenth and Seventeenth Centuries   69

4 The Eighteenth Century   102

5 1800 to 1879: The British Tradition   137

6 1800 to 1879: The Experimental Tradition   162

7 1879 to about 1910: Wundt and His Influence   199

Figures

Preface

to the First Edition

This history of Western psychology is intended as a textbook, but it will also be valuable to all who are interested in an overview of the subject. Originally, the book was intended to cover the history of psychology up to 1940, but a chapter has been added to give the reader some sense of continuity with present-day research. Any up-to-date textbook, such as Darley, Glucksberg, Kamin, and Kinchla's *Psychology*, will complement this chapter on most of the matters raised.

For reading preliminary drafts of various sections I am indebted to Páll Árdal, Neil Bartlett, Ian Hacking, P. K. Rose, and Noel Smith. Among my colleagues in the Psychology Department at Queen's University, I must particularly thank James Inglis, Andrew McGhie, and Susan Lederman for advice and the loan of materials. I am also grateful to Rizwan Kheraj and Megan Ward for discussion and to Anne Chenier and Gail Fox for research assistance in the early phases of the work. Fatima Kheraj deserves special mention for her skills and patience as my research assistant during the later stages of writing.

I should like to acknowledge the valuable help given to me by the reviewers who commented on the book at the various stages of its completion: Richard L. Blanton, Vanderbilt University; Arthur Blumenthal, University of Massachusetts—Boston; Darryl Bruce, The Florida State University; T. S. Krawiec, Professor Emeritus, Skidmore College; Abraham S. Luchins, State University of New York at Albany; Nicholas Rohrman, Colby College; and E. L. Saldanha, University of Southern Maine.

I was able to finish much of the first part of the book during the tenure of a Leave Fellowship awarded by the Social Sciences and Humanities Research Council of Canada. Auxiliary funding came from Natural Sciences and Engineering Research Council Canada Operating Grant A0-126 and a grant from Queen's University.

David Murray
Kingston, Ontario

Preface

to the Second Edition

The difficulty with rewriting any book of history is that it consists mainly of additions: New research casts new light on old personalities; one simply reads more in the interval between the first and second editions; and, as time recedes, what seemed important a few years ago gives way to new perspectives that illuminate areas previously neglected. So, for example, the research of Sulloway has necessitated extensive rewriting of the section on Freud; I have had more opportunity to read about areas, such as eighteenth-century German psychology, that were underrepresented in the first edition; and what I wrote about modern cognitive psychology only a few years ago has had to be completely rewritten in the light of new research. In fact, I have gone through the whole book, keeping the same basic framework but now trying to give more continuity to the narrative; clarifying the sources of certain ideas, particularly in antiquity; and saying more about the social background to many psychological developments. I faced a difficult problem on this last issue: To discuss fully the social and political background of all the psychology I mention would have involved extending the book to a length out of proportion to its stated use as a text. Bertrand Russell, whose *History of Western Philosophy* influenced my title, was forced to write over 800 pages to include both the background and the raw philosophy. Being unprepared to extend my book to a length that would be impossible to deal with in any reasonable course on the history of psychology, I therefore recommend that those who wish more on background refer to D. N. Robinson's *An Intellectual History of Psychology* (1981) or to T. H. Leahey's *A History of Psychology* (1987), two books giving more space to social history than I have room for here.

On the other hand, I am unrepentant about offering a history of psychology that concentrates on the discoveries themselves. I have tried to write the sort of book I wish I had had when I first started teaching the history of psychology in 1972. Back then, there were few books that neatly encapsulated ancient psychology, modern experimental psychology, and the history of applied psychology between two covers; I can well remember the sheer workload of trying to discover for myself what the great figures of the past said about mind and behavior. When I discovered that almost every major thinker from the Greeks onward had something of importance to say about psychology, I began to lose the inferiority complex so many psychologists have when they consider how unsystematic our science is compared with physics or biology. Our science is unsystematic because it is so hard; it has baffled many of the finest minds who have worked on it; but none of those minds thought that psychology was unimportant. If I convince my readers that in the history of psychology they will make contact with some of the finest and cleverest thinkers of all time, I shall feel exonerated for concentrating so much on ideas.

As I was reading these writers, I looked deliberately for discussions of three topics that pervade all our lives—emotional stress, relations between men and women, and religion. Sex, gender differences, and religion turned out to be almost taboo topics for most writers before Freud, and the topic of mental illness was left to the medical practitioners for most of that time. This lends a certain dryness, I suppose, to much of the early history of psychology, but another issue of the greatest interest in our open society, the question of empiricism versus nativism, was hotly discussed from Aristotle onward. In reading these sections, it is wise to distinguish between nativism referring to innate *knowledge* (most writers agree we have none), to innate *patterns of responding* to internal and external stimuli (as reflected in animal instincts), and to innate *capabilities* (such as the ability to remember). How far individual differences in intelligence or susceptibility to emotional stress are innate is a fourth question, still the subject of controversy.

Another topic that runs through the history of psychology is the question of what constitutes consciousness and whether animals are "conscious" in the way we are. Again, it is worth distinguishing between being "conscious" in the sense that we can *experience* pain, discriminate colors and so on, and being "conscious" in the sophisticated sense that we are aware of our own thought processes. When Romanes ascribed consciousness to sea anemones, he was thinking of the first sense; when Jaynes and Watson make an intimate link between consciousness and language, they are thinking of the second sense; and there are many gradations between these two meanings, as Bain and others have documented.

Finally, although modern psychologists think of their discipline as only beginning to make progress once experiments were done, I was surprised to find how naturally people with ideas find a place in the histories of psychology, whereas people who only do experiments tend to be neglected. As an experimentalist myself, I feel tugged in two directions. A possible way of making sure that data, rather than speculations, are given their due place in the history of psychology is to write history organized not chronologically but in terms of subject matter. Histories of twentieth-century psychology, such as those of Hearst (1979), Koch and Leary (1985), and Hilgard (1987), have been obliged to adopt this strategy, a practice that augurs for a future in which a chronological history of psychology may only be practical up to about 1930.

In preparing this second edition, I am particularly obliged to Floyd Rudmin, Kurt Danziger, Darwin Muir, Doug Mewhort, and Rod Lindsay for providing me with information I might otherwise have missed. A special word of gratitude must go to Maureen Freedman, whose cheery research assistance kept me going through the mountains of books and reprints; she was supported by Grant A8505 from the National Sciences and Research Council of Canada. Queen's University also gave generous support in the way of a microcomputer and an Advisory Research Council grant.

David Murray
Kingston, Ontario

Prologue:
Political History

The history of psychology forms a branch of history that has recently come to be known as intellectual history (Stromberg, 1975). This includes the history of ideas and of scientific discoveries and inventions; in part it tries to explain trends reflected in the history of the various arts. Other branches of history are political history, the story of the rise and fall of kingdoms, dynasties, empires, and nations and how these are affected by changes of fortune such as those imposed by economic events; and social history, the account of everyday life and conditions in various periods. In this prologue we will give a brief summary of the main political and social events of Western history, thus clearing the way for a more focused examination of the intellectual history of psychology. Maps of the Mediterranean (Fig. 1–2) and Germany (Fig. 4–2) will be given in the body of the text. The student should be familiar from the outset with terms such as *Hellenistic, medieval, Renaissance*, and *Reformation*. This section will briefly introduce these terms; they will be dealt with in more detail in later sections.

The earliest Western civilizations of which we have written records —that is, the earliest civilizations that had invented writing—were those of the Tigris and Euphrates valleys in what is now Iraq and those of the Nile Valley in Egypt. The former probably influenced the latter. We know the names and approximate dates of their kings back as far as about 3000

1

B.C.; these civilizations flourished until about 600 B.C. Their political history is mainly one of war and conquest, but their social history reveals that they had domesticated animals, grew crops in the fertile river valleys, produced metal, pottery, and cloth, had developed complicated and mainly polytheistic religions, believed in an afterlife, had slavery to some extent, and had developed systems of simple mathematics and medicine. Astronomers in both valleys kept records of the heavens, and from them the Egyptians adopted a year of 365 days. Although there were many physicians, priests, and artists during these centuries, few individual names are known to us. Hammurabi, a king of the Babylonians, caused the first known set of laws to be written down in about 1700 B.C. The Egyptians had books describing one's supposed conduct in the afterlife, and there was one king, Akhnaton (about 1379–1361 B.C.), who tried to persuade his people to worship one solar deity. There was a surge of poetry and naturalistic art during his reign, but his attempt failed and in the later periods of Egyptian civilization the people reverted to the older, polytheistic system.

Many unknown scribes, sculptors, and painters recorded the events of these centuries, often simply to satisfy the vainglory of their royal patrons. From Egypt we have certain medical documents that reveal something of primitive surgery and physiology (see Chap. 1). Although Akhnaton failed to persuade his nation of the virtues of monotheism, another tribe, the Hebrews, did come to worship one god, Jehovah, and from this belief would later spring both Christianity and, to a much lesser extent, Mohammedanism. The early history of the Jews is recorded in the Old Testament: They settled mainly in what is now Israel perhaps between 1400 and 1200 B.C. and were later joined by another group of Jews who had escaped from a slavelike existence in Egypt. The leader of this latter group was Moses who, like Hammurabi, set up a code of laws that has persisted as part of Judaism to this day.

Between 2000 and 1000 B.C. civilization was also beginning around the Aegean Sea in such areas as Crete, Mycenae, and Troy. The people of the Mycenae region, known as Achaeans, attacked Troy, and we still read of the Trojan War in the long epic poems of the *Iliad* and the *Odyssey.* Following invasions from the North, however, these civilizations died away and were replaced by many small colonies—city-states—across the areas now known as southern Greece and western Turkey. The best-known were Sparta and Athens, but intellectual life was now focused in the Turkish colonies (the region then called Ionia). Gradually, however, Athens came to dominate and founded an empire; the fifth century B.C. is the period of "classical" Greece when Athens, although somewhat tyrannical towards her subject colonies, nevertheless became a center of culture and relative freedom. It is in this period that modern drama, sculpture, philosophy, historical writing, political theorizing, physics, and other sciences originate, as will be described later.

In 338 B.C., however, Philip of Macedonia conquered Athens and the other small states and became the king of Greece. Two years later he was assassinated and his son, Alexander, who had been educated in Macedonia by Aristotle, succeeded him. Alexander began a career of new colonization when he took his Greek troops and conquered the Turkish region, the Valley of the Euphrates, most of the Middle East, including Persia, and the Nile Valley. The period that then ensued—during which all these areas learned from Greek culture and in turn contributed to Greek culture—is known as the Hellenistic period. It is also during this period that Greek thought comes into contact with Jewish thought, though the Jews were rather resistant to incorporating those aspects of Greek thought likely to turn them away from the worship of Jehovah. The Hellenistic period is also famous for its scientific achievements, many of which were recorded in the Egyptian town of Alexandria. But in turn the Hellenistic world fell to a new nation, the Romans: It is sometimes stated that the end came in 31 B.C. when Alexandria was lost to this people.

Italy during this early period had been settled by various tribes from the North and had also been colonized by the Greeks, but according to Roman tradition, Rome itself was founded at an important river crossing in 753 B.C. or thereabouts. After internal strife and wars with neighboring tribes, the Romans succeeded in conquering Italy and, later, North Africa and Greece. By the time Alexandria was taken, Rome had an empire stretching from Britain in the North to Spain in the South and to the Euphrates in the East. The power in Rome was consolidated in large part by Julius Caesar, and its cultural and political pride was at its zenith under the reign of the emperor Augustus. The Empire extended over what is now Israel, and this area thus represented a mixture of Greek, Jewish, and Roman influences: It was into this atmosphere that Jesus was born and founded a new sect dedicated to the belief that Jesus had atoned before Jehovah for the sins of man. At first this was a small Jewish sect, but St. Paul spread the new religion to non-Jews in the Middle East and Turkey, and later to Greece and Rome.

The three hundred years or so following Jesus' death are marked by a slow decline in the power of Rome and a slow rise in the acceptance of Christianity. In 313 Constantine, then emperor, declared Christianity to be a tolerated religion of the Roman state; shortly afterwards, partly because of attacks on Rome by peoples from northern Europe, he moved the capital from Rome to Byzantium (later called Constantinople; today called Istanbul). Rome fell in 410 to the Goths but still retained its importance as a bishopric; even as this was happening, St. Augustine, a bishop of the Church in North Africa, was writing his authoritative theological works. The following period, from about 500 to 1000, is known in Europe as the Dark Ages. Greek and Roman books were destroyed or lost; little progress was made in literature or science; life consisted of surviving the attack of one form of pillager or another. However, Byzantium and Rome preserved the teachings of Christianity, and at Bagdad, Cairo, Cordoba, and other centers the proponents of another new religion, Mohammedanism (Islam), kept alive the culture of the Greeks and Romans. There was a time when Islam threatened Europe: The Arabs were defeated at the battle of Poitiers (sometime called the battle of Tours) in 731. On the other hand eastern Turkey became Mohammedan after the battle of Manzikert in 1071. Also, in 1054 there was a schism in the Church between the beliefs of those centered in Byzantium and those centered in Rome. The latter came to dominate western Europe.

The period from about 1000 to 1500, known as the medieval period, or Middle Ages, is marked by the Church's being at the peak of its power; the Pope was essentially the lord of Europe, and at his instigation the various kings of the nations of Europe sent missions to the Middle East to recapture Jerusalem for Christianity. This venture had a short-lived success, but the positive result of the Crusades was to reestablish links between the Europeans and those peoples of the Middle East who had preserved classical culture. By the time of the theologian and scholar Aquinas (1225–1274), the works of classical Greece could be read again, although the real revival of classical culture took place two centuries later in the period known as the Renaissance—the rebirth. To recapture the spirit of the Middle Ages in a sentence or two is impossible, but it is during this period that the traditional structure of Western society emerges: A monarch is in charge of aristocrats who in turn both defend and are paid tribute to by an agricultural peasantry. In spiritual matters all these groups acknowledge the authority of the Church. Individual countries, often unified by a common language, begin to emerge, and cities became places where trade was carried out and where a new class, the merchant class, began to achieve power and status.

A number of isolated incidents brought about the end of the Middle Ages and the beginning of modern Europe. In 1453 Constantinople was conquered by the Turks, thus making it difficult for Europe to trade with the Far East. The result was that explorers moved out in the opposite direction, to the Atlantic; the most famous consequence was Columbus's sighting the West Indies in 1492. Gunpowder was devised during the fifteenth century, thus changing the nature of warfare, and the invention of printing allowed the propagation not only of Christian doctrine but also of classical learning and of individual opinion. By 1500 the Renaissance is associated with the rediscovery of secular scholarship and the burgeoning of art and architecture, particularly in Italy; by 1517, in Germany, Martin Luther was beginning to argue against some of the abuses of the Church. The Reformation is the name given to the movement whereby the protesters following Luther—that is, the Protestants—broke away from traditional Catholicism.

The common characteristic of both the Renaissance and the Reformation is the stress on individualism, but it must not be forgotten that the Church in the sixteenth century was still a powerful force and fought vigorously against both the propagation of secular science and the various new Christian sects who did not acknowledge the Catholic church as the arbiter of doctrine. The sixteenth century, therefore, is marked by fierce religious warfare throughout Europe, but it is also the century of Michelangelo, Shakespeare, Rabelais, and Cervantes. The major scientific events of the century were Vesalius's contributions to anatomy and Copernicus's theory that the earth moved round the sun and not vice versa. In the New World, the Spanish and Portuguese settled in and colonized California and Central and South America; on the other side of North America the coastline was known but there was little in the way of permanent settlement.

The seventeenth century is a turning point in Western history in several ways. First, there was an enormous growth of science, particularly in physics, during this period; the three major figures were Galileo, Harvey, and Newton. Second, in northern Europe, where the Catholic church was less powerful, there was a growth in free-thinking and religious toleration, an attitude that spread to many of the newly founded colonies in North America. Third, the British rebelled against the more tyrannical aspects of monarchy, and the subsequent civil war (1642–1653) led to a rule by Cromwell's military junta, later replaced by a system of checks and balances between king and Parliament that was the forerunner of many democratic governments today. Fourth, we see France at the pinnacle of power; Paris became the literary and cultural capital of Europe. However, all was not necessarily progress: The Thirty Years' War, a confused religious war, brought devastation to Germany during the first half of the century; French Protestants (Huguenots) were persecuted in France during the second half of the century and many emigrated; slavery was an institution throughout the Americas.

The eighteenth century is frequently called the Age of Enlightenment. The intellectual heroes in Paris were Newton and the philosopher Locke. Knowledge of biology and chemistry was greatly advanced, particularly when oxygen was discovered. The courts in Prussia, Austria, and Russia imitated those of France and were centers of new nationalistic movements. Nevertheless, it was also the period of three great revolutions, one social and two political. First, the Industrial Revolution began in Britain and in America. Machines were invented that could do the work of many laborers and manufacture goods of consistent quality. Factories took the place of farms, and colonization in America, Australia, and elsewhere took a new turn when it was realized that raw products could be cheaply sent back to the home country and there turned into finished goods by machines. It was in this context that Adam Smith wrote one of the pioneering economic texts, *The Wealth of Nations* (1776), in which free capitalism, with little government intervention, was advocated. Second, the settlers in the North American colonies rebelled against the laws emanating from Britain itself: At Philadelphia in 1776 a meeting of deputies from the few states then founded issued the Declaration of Independence; the American Revolution finished in 1783 with the United States being recognized as a nation in its own right.

Finally, the tyrannical power of the French monarchy became intolerable to the working classes, and in 1789 the French Revolution broke out. Its results were curiously mixed: On the one hand many archaic and unjust laws were replaced with more popular and fair ones; on the other, the various factions who had supported the revolution squabbled among themselves and there was a great deal of bloodshed. Out of this chaos arose a single leader, Napoleon Bonaparte, who attempted to revive the greatness of seventeenth-century France by founding an empire. He conquered, by force of armies, much of Europe; however, Great Britain, Prussia, and Russia resisted his advances, and he was finally defeated at Waterloo in 1815.

There was also an intellectual reaction against the emphasis on reason of the first half of the century; the reaction is generally called the Romantic movement, coinciding roughly with the period of Napoleon and a decade or so afterwards. Revolution against autocracy was one of its facets, but other facets included a reemphasis on intuition and passion, which greatly influenced the arts, and a revival of religion.

Although persons living in the nineteenth century saw it as the age of progress—the advances of technology and science led to better living conditions, the spread of democracy led to the reduction of power of the aristocrats and to a growing socialism, the opening up of trade around the world led to increased wealth among the industrialized Western nations—it was also a period of strife in many places. European powers sought to colonize the newly discovered areas in Africa, Asia, and elsewhere, often through force. In Europe many monarchies persisted in quelling revolutionary movements among intelligentsia and the working classes until a series of small and abortive revolutions broke out in 1848. In the United States the individual states were driven to civil war (1861–1865) by disagreements on states' rights and on slavery. But the final outcome was indeed a raising of living standards in the West, and in Europe many small states banded together to form the countries now known as Germany and Italy. In particular, Germany had a tradition of freedom in its universities, which gave it an academic leadership that was emulated by other countries, including the United States. By the end of the century the industrialization of the United States put it well to the front in the economic competition between nations; tragically, this competition also ultimately led to warfare between Germany and other major powers in 1914.

Social and intellectual history in the nineteenth century has many crosscurrents. The emphasis on individual freedom, a legacy of the Romantic movement, culminated in a new concern among intellectuals to illuminate social inequalities and hardships. We thus find Dickens, Hugo, Tolstoi, Dostoevsky, and Zola writing realistic novels in which the differences of class are subordinated to the depiction of the similarities in emotional needs of all classes. The theories of Darwin led directly to attempts to improve humanity's own status and to a more enlightened understanding of the place of humans in the animal kingdom. Research on electricity led to the inventions of the late nineteenth and early twentieth centuries of scientists such as Edison and Bell. Improved transport shortened travel around the globe and made people more cosmopolitan. By the end of the century the West was characterized by a technological sophistication and by an economic wealth that were the envy of the rest of the world.

But the twentieth century has, in some ways, brought us back to an eighteenth-century view of life. The power of organized religion is greatly diminished, as the eighteenth-century rationalists would have wished it. We have learned to be wary of nationalism, which, as in Germany under Hitler, can explode into war and genocide. Colonialism, once viewed as the harbinger of progress and light in undeveloped areas of the world, is now seen as economic opportunism and chauvinistic despotism. Industrialism provides jobs but pollutes the environment. And the revolutionary fervor of the nineteenth century, which had successfully been kept in control by the monarchs and police of otherwise progressive countries, broke through into reality with the Communist Revolution in Russia in 1917. The world is now divided into three segments: the Western capitalist world, the Communist world, and what has come to be known as the Third World. The West focuses on political egalitarianism; the Communist world on economic egalitarianism; the Third World on nationalistic egalitarianism. But all three are the legacy of the struggle for human rights begun in the eighteenth century.

Most of the technological and scientific advances in Western history took place in the last five hundred years or so. This forces historians to deal relatively quickly with the early period and proceed more slowly as they move towards the present. The design of this history of psychology therefore follows a similar conformation.

The Beginnings
of Psychology

1

A two-year-old child, with at best a fragile grip on language, can never-theless imagine something that is absent from the immediate purview and ask for that thing. A little girl may be in the living room and wish to go out, and so will say *park* or *grocery*, words she has associated with being taken outside by the parents. Thus, the child has developed concepts that can represent themselves in various ways such as visual images or words (cf. Paivio, 1971) and can even conjure up such representations at will. The child sometimes has images spontaneously, either when awake or when asleep. The images of sleep are called "dreaming." But a child, or a person in an unsophisticated society, does not necessarily realize that a vivid image or a dream has no external sensory referent. If a person in a primitive culture dreams he sees an enemy and wakens to tell others of it, he might persuade the others that he has really seen an enemy, and they might take measures to defend themselves.

Ancient works of literature such as the Old Testament and the *Iliad* all suggest that in those times people took dreams as having literal truth much as a child may believe that there really was a dragon when she awakens from a nightmare. If you see *yourself* in a dream (or even in a mirror), or imagine that one part of you is asleep while another part is awake, it is but a short logical step to believing that there is a part of you separate from the everyday you that makes intentions and receives impressions from the external world. A common word for this separate *you* in Western society is the *soul*, to which we shall return in a moment.

There is another aspect of imaging that needs special discussion in a chapter on ancient views of psychology. When we are awake, most of us have mild imagery and rarely experience intense imagery: For example, few of us have heard voices "in our heads," although this is a well-known symptom in certain kinds of mental illness. But Jaynes (1976) has written a book in which he suggests that in very ancient times people regularly heard voices in their heads and assumed that it was "gods" talking to them. To be more precise: Jaynes argues that in very primitive times, from about the time of the Neanderthal (about 200,000 B.C.) to the first settlement in cities (about 9000 B.C.), primitive language evolved, people used tools, and the notion of "gods" was first devised. Then writing began, although from about 9000 to about 2500 B.C. we have only a handful of written records. But during this period, Jaynes postulates, people had stronger verbal hallucinations than now: They assumed that when they heard voices their own personal gods were talking to them. Jaynes suggests that their rulers took advantage of this and gave them

Figure 1–1   The Main Figures of Ancient and Medieval Psychology Placed in Chronological Perspective.

		PSYCHOLOGY	OTHER SCIENCES
	600		The Milesians
Classical	500	The pre-Socratic writers	
Greece	400	Plato, Aristole	Hippocrates
The	300	Zeno, Epicurus	Herophilus, Erasistratus
Hellenistic	200		Archimedes
Period	100	Lucretius	Ptolemy
	A.D.1	Quintilian	Pliny
	100		Galen
The	200	The Church Fathers	
Roman	300		
Empire	400		
	500	Boethius	
The	600		
Dark	700	S. John of Damascus	
Ages	800		
of	900	Al-Farabi	Rhazes
Europe	1000	Avicenna	
	1100	Averroes	
The	1200	Aquinas, Albertus Magnus, Pedro Hispano	Bacon, Pecham
Middle	1300		
Ages	1400		Mondino
	1500		Vesalius, Copernicus

particular commands which would later be "recalled" in the shape of auditory hallucinations and carried out as if they were the commands of a god. Jaynes refers to this hallucinating kind of mind as the *bicameral mind*.

Gradually, however, between about 3000 and 1000 B.C., the bicameral mind was replaced by a new kind of consciousness more similar to that which we experience today. The greater use of writing meant that orders could be written down and less reliance had to be placed on auditory memory; overpopulation and natural disasters caused migrations, with confusion between the "gods" of various peoples; and gradually a new kind of mind emerged in which persons set up within themselves a concept of their own self, an "I." From this point on, the theory runs, thinking consisted of inner speech (not hallucinated auditory speech), by means of which we can formulate intentions for ourselves.

According to Jaynes, however, the loss of hallucinations between about 3000 and 1000 B.C. caused distress; it is as if the people felt gods had deserted them. Regarding those who still hallucinated to be "prophets," they told the old histories as if the heroes still heard voices from the gods. So, for example, we have the Hebrew prophets of the Old Testament representing the ancient voices of the gods and being given special reverence because of it; in the *Iliad* we read of the Greek and Trojan heroes who are compelled to do their actions because gods and goddesses speak to them directly. In his book, and in a useful summary article (1986), Jaynes addresses evidence from the relics and literature of the Mesopotamians, Egyptians, and Hebrews that he claims supports his opinions. It must be stressed that Jaynes's theory is still very controversial and not generally accepted by all historians.

Whether or not Jaynes is right, there is little question that from ancient times the concept of a *soul* has been made the basis of many beliefs both protoscientific and superstitious. In some societies the soul is inextricably linked with the body and dies with the body. In others the soul survives bodily death and goes to regions of varied degrees of pleasantness (compare the Judeo-Christian concepts of Heaven and Hell). In yet others the soul can return to earth as a ghost that may have to be placated. And in several societies to this day it is believed that the soul can leave the *living* body, travel about, and return to the body (Shiels, 1978). It should also be noted that within one body there can be several kinds of soul (e.g., the Laotians believe that each body has thirty-two separate and immortal souls). The reason we begin this history by pointing out that the existence of dreams and imagination (and, perhaps, hallucinations) could have given rise to the concept of the soul is that, for the first three or four millennia of psychological enquiry, much of what is believed about the *mind* is in fact the result of beliefs and speculations concerning the *soul*.

Since the concept of a soul is rather blurry and flexible, it is not surprising that in primitive Egyptian, Euphratian, and Greek civilizations there were various ideas about the soul and that these ideas determined attitudes towards conduct in life and the afterlife. Often, they used several distinct words that have rather confusing relationships to each other, much as the modern words *soul, mind, spirit,* and *consciousness* are not always as easy to delineate accurately as we would like. Much of the early history of psychology consists of the explication of certain words referring to these kinds of concepts. Figure 1–2 shows a map of the ancient world.

The state of affairs in these respects in Ancient Egypt was confusing to say the least. We know about their beliefs in some detail because, in their efforts to ensure that the soul of a dead person survived its journey through the places of death as comfortably as possible, the Egyptians buried the bodies in enormous tombs (the best known being the pyramids and the tomb of Tutankhamen), mummified the bodies, and surrounded the bodies with goods and jewelry designed to accompany the soul in its voyage. Texts were inscribed on pyramids dating from 2200 B.C. and were collected and written on papyrus, the whole corpus being called the *Book of the Dead* (Budge, 1898). The book consists mainly of advice on how to overcome the dangers of the journey of the soul through the kingdom of the dead, and copies were sometimes buried with the bodies. The Egyptians had various words for different types of soul; a modern account of the meanings of several of these words will be found in Laver (1972). But one feature of these variegated types of *soul* was that they were associated with the heart and not the brain. For example, there are vignettes painted on the papyruses of the *Book of the Dead* showing a person's heart being weighed in a balance by a god—if it balances with a feather, symbolizing truth, the person will survive to be united with the gods (particularly the main deity, Osiris), but if it is not, the heart will be eaten by a monster-god. We shall see that this emphasis on the heart as the seat of the personality persists into Greek times.

In view of the complicated concepts the Egyptians had of the soul, it is worth asking whether there is anything in the *Book of the Dead* that reveals their speculations on mind or on personality. In fact there is very little. The book consists mainly of incantations to be said by the priests at various stages in a funeral ritual—they serve essentially as charms to ward off evil. One's main impression is of an enormous host of gods waiting to be appeased by the dead person in his or her voyage through the underworld. Other than remarking that the Egyptian moral code seems little different from the modern moral code, one finds none of the theorizing about psychological matters that was to characterize the later Greek civilization.

The other great focus of civilization during the period 3000–600

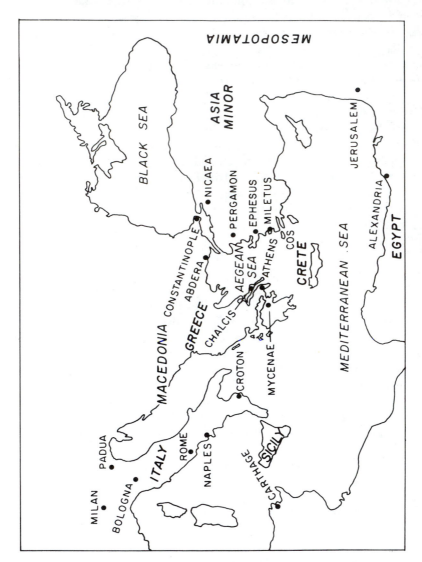

Figure 1-2 The Eastern Mediterranean.

B.C. was to the north, the region of the valleys of the Tigris and Euphrates rivers. The general name for this area is Mesopotamia, but it should be realized that over the two or three thousand years we are discussing this area was dominated at different times by different tribes or peoples. The earliest people to settle the area, and who probably developed writing as a means for recording business transactions, were the Sumerians. They were followed by the Akkadians, Babylonians, Cassites, and Assyrians, in chronological order, with other minor groups occupying the area in transitional periods. All left written records; the two best-known works are the Epic of Gilgamesh, which is probably from the Babylonian period, and the Code of Hummurabi, from the same period (the early part of the second millennium B.C.). Other writings include legends, lists of kings, records of conquests, treaties, legal contracts, many stories, books of wisdom (rather similar to those of Job and Proverbs in the Old Testament), and lists of laws other than those of Hammurabi.

From these various sources we derive quite a vivid picture of people's mentality during these centuries, but we do not find any attempt at a descriptive or explanatory psychology. However, we can hazard a guess at what such a psychology would look like. First, it must be realized that the pantheon of gods—the Mesopotamians had almost as many as the Egyptians—had a real and living presence to the individual of the time. Jaynes, it will be recalled, thought this was a reflection of hallucinations. Each person and each city had its own protective deity or deities, and any calamity that befell that person or city was held to be the direct result of the anger or neglect of the gods concerned. One document, probably written during the Cassite period and widely known to the Assyrians, is known by its first line as "I will praise the Lord of Wisdom." In it a nobleman describes his behavior when he believes his god to have deserted him. He writes,

> The omen organs are confused and inflamed for
>   me every day.
> The omen of the diviner and dream priest does not explain
>   my condition.
> What is said in the street portends ill for me.
> When I lie down at night, my dream is terrifying.
>   (translation from Lambert, 1960)

Here we see the people going to the Mesopotamian equivalent of the psychiatrist or clergy of our times, the "diviner" or the "dream priest." We see them consulting omens and trying to guess the future from the state of some more or less randomly arranged natural object. In our time people read cards, palms, and teacups; in Mesopotamian times a popular form of divination consisted in looking at the organs of dead animals, the entrails or the liver. In fact there is even a clay model of the liver that has survived from the Babylonian period. It is inscribed with magical formulas to be chanted by diviners when consulting the real liver of some dead beast. We also know from other texts that, while prophesying, priests went into a form of "trance" during which they were probably awake and seeing but allowed their speech to wander where it would (Pritchard, 1975, p. 181). Just as our own dreams may sometimes represent the result of unconscious inferences and intuitions, so may have these trance utterances.

Between the two regions of Egypt in the south and Mesopotamia in the north lay a land part desert, part fruitful, now comprising the countries of Syria, Israel, Jordan, and parts of Saudi Arabia. It was occupied by wandering tribes (the equivalent of the modern Bedouin), bandit tribes, and more settled people. The Phoenicians, who lived along the coast of the Mediterranean and traded widely with other nations by sea, also had their pantheon of gods. The two best-known were Dagon and Baal, and we read in the Old Testament how Samson and Elijah respectively fought to prevent these gods from being imposed on the Jewish cult of Jehovah.

The Jews themselves were a small nation but with a rich heritage of literature going back to Moses' time and beyond. Although the modern Old Testament was not actually written down until after 1000 B.C., the traditions on which it was based had been transmitted orally for centuries previously. What is unique about this literature is that it interweaves the political history of the Jewish people with their religious history in a way that indicates that they had selected Jehovah as their particular single deity. There are indeed elements of Mesopotamian and Egyptian culture in the Old Testament—the belief that dreams were divine messages, the possession of wives and servants, the strict codification of behavior and of the punishments for "illegal" behavior—but there are other elements that, so to speak, soften the rather hard picture painted of life. The gentler emotions such as family love or close friendship are mingled with ruder desires and passions; Jehovah is depicted not so much as a whimsical tyrant but as a wielder of justice (admittedly harsh at times). The very fact that we read the Old Testament today for edification (whereas we read the Epic of Gilgamesh for its drama) testifies that, when all the superstitious aspects of life are removed, people's emotions in the earliest civilizations were very similar to those we ourselves have.

It may be noted that the Jews were aware of mental illness—King Saul is sometimes claimed to have had paranoia—and also believed in diviners (called *witches* in Exodus 22:18 and Leviticus 20:27). Because the Jews were persecuted in those times as well as in modern times, there was a recurring plea on the part of the prophets for a "messiah" who would rescue his people. This notion played an important part in the development of Christianity some six hundred years after the Babylonian captivity. But Jaynes also argues that the early Hebrew tribes possessed a richness of hallucination that at first led them to believe in many gods, as did their neighbors; later they believed in one God, Jehovah, who spoke through the trancelike spontaneous utterances of such prophets as Amos, and even later there is a yearning for the lost gift of prophecy. Thus the witches in Leviticus are in fact gifted hallucinators, and Saul's paranoia reflects an interesting case of a nonhallucinator who feels inferior in comparison with prophets such as Samuel.

The above account does not exhaust the list of civilizations that flourished in the second millennium B.C. To the west, in the Mediterranean, was the island of Crete where a highly developed society had emerged; it is known nowadays to archaeologists as the Minoan civilization. To the north of Crete on the Greek mainland, there was another society centered on various cities such as Mycenae and therefore known as the Mycenaean civilization. The Mycenaeans seem to be identical with those persons described as Achaeans in the *Iliad* and *Odyssey.* What is curious about these works is that there is very little reference to mental activity using words we would normally employ. In the *Iliad*, when a hero has a feeling or forms an intention, it is because a god or goddess put it into his body. In the *Odyssey*, however, the heroes are more self-reliant, and Jaynes believes that the *Odyssey*, which is later than the *Iliad*, reflects the breakdown of the bicameral mind and the transition to modernity.

The period between about 1000 B.C. and 480 B.C. is often called the Dark Age of Greece. However, this is probably a misnomer; recent excavations at a town on the Greek mainland called Lefkandi have indicated the presence of a more advanced civilization there in about 900 B.C. than had previously been thought to exist. We also know that Greek peoples flourished on both sides of the Aegean Sea who, between 900 B.C. and 600 B.C., colonized areas in Sicily, North Africa, and the Black Sea area. The collected traditions of many epic poets were summarized in the work now known as Homer's and the poet Hesiod wrote a history of the origin of the world that is now recognized to be influenced by Mesopotamian myth. The Greeks, in fact, picked up many influences as they sailed around the Mediterranean, possibly the most important being the alphabet (from Phoenicia), mathematics (from Mesopotamia), and the style and sculpture of the earliest cities (from Egypt). Above all, they slowly developed a culture based on the city-state: Forrest (1986) traces the development through the period from about 1000 B.C. to 500 B.C. of a new political system in which individuals are allowed a say in government. Our modern word *democracy* is related to the Greek word *deme*, an area of land whose inhabitants had a voice in the making of decisions about the city-state as whole. The invention of coinage in the Greek cities in Asia Minor greatly facilitated trade, and not the least contributors to the preservation of Greek culture were improvements in the style of military defense, including the building of fleets of ships and a change in battle style, in which a group of soldiers formed a *phalanx* or solid block that could not easily be broken up by attackers. According to Forrest, it was in part because soldiers, in reward for their services, were given rights in political decision making, that the old system, in which a king or aristocrat had absolute power, broke down.

Nearly all scholars agree in assigning the beginning of Western thought to the city of Miletus in Asia Minor, where Thales (his dates are believed to be about 624–546 B.C.), Anaximander (about 610–547 B.C.), and Anaximenes (about 550–480 B.C.) may have written several books between them. However, all that survives of this school are a few fragments, and it is worth mentioning now that what we know of their thought is mainly based on accounts by writers several centuries later. For English translations of these fragments of the Milesian philosophers (and others coming before Socrates), Freeman's *Ancilla to the Pre-Socratic Philosophers* (1948) should be consulted first, and then for a listing of secondary sources Nahm's *Selections from Early Greek Philosophy* (1964) should be read.

It is salutary and sobering—because it makes us realize the depth of our ignorance about the Ionian writers—to consider what is left of the writings of Thales, Anaximander, and Anaximenes. Of Thales we have no extant text but learn from Herodotus and Aristotle, writing nearly two centuries later, that he apparently correctly predicted an eclipse and was able to divert the course of a river. He believed that everything in the universe was made of water. As with Hesiod, however, the theory may be related to Egyptian or Semitic myths in which the world was first made of water and later was covered by the earth (West, 1986). But however outdated Thales' hypothesis now seems we should recognize it as a very important landmark in human thought, for it is an attempt not merely to describe the world but to *explain* its phenomena. But what of psychology? We have the following statement from Aristotle's book on the soul, *De Anima:* "And Thales, according to what is related of him, seems to have regarded the soul as something endowed with the power of motion, if indeed he said that the lodestone has a soul because it moves iron" (Nahm, 1964, p. 38). From this we get the impression that the soul is not seen as something apart from or outside the body but as that which gives movement to the body.

There is a similar shortage of information on Anaximander and Anaximenes. Anaximander in particular may deserve special credit for escaping from creation myths and offering a unified system of the universe according to which there is an interruption or "injustice" in the "boundless" expanse, this interruption showing up as matter. Specifically, the matter of the universe as we know it consists of a drum-shaped earth in the center, surrounded by rings of fire enclosed in tubes of mist. But the fire shines through holes in the tubes, and these points of light are the sun, moon, and stars as we see them. West (1986) argues that this system may have been derived from Iranian mythology, but the difference is that in this mythology an act of will (by a god) created the universe, whereas for Anaximander it was an act of nature. This conceptualization represents a decisive step in the direction of a scientific explanation of the world. Unfortunately, Anaximander said little on psychological matters, but he is also reputed to have invented a sundial device for measuring time, to have been an early mapmaker, and to have suggested first, that life arose on earth because of the effect of the sun on "vapours," and second, that humans were generated from the original animals by way of fish.

Anaximenes also had a cosmology, but he believed the earth to be supported by air (not water, as Thales had it): Air surrounds and contains the earth; all other substances are derived from air by condensation and rarefaction. Otherwise, Anaximenes' cosmology is more fanciful than Anaximander's, but in one respect he contributed to psychology: namely, by suggesting that just as the air holds material substances together, so the "soul" holds the body together. Thus Anaximenes makes the "soul" a natural part of the material world:

> As our soul, being air, holds us together, so do breath and air surround the whole universe.

It is possible there are links here with an old Homeric notion that death is related to a release of "breath" or "air" from the body, and with ancient Hindu notions that a universal mind or breath determines the course of both the material world and individual living beings (West, 1986).

It is no accident that the Milesian writers are often referred to as the Ionian physicists. By offering explanations of the constitution of the world—of which the soul appears to be an instance of matter itself—they mark the escape from religious or mythological explanation into scientific or naturalistic explanation. At least one historian of psychology, Esper (1964), feels that this achievement in itself justifies their receiving a lengthy section in his book, but he is almost unique in this respect. Most histories of psychology start with Plato, born about 200 years after Thales; but it is this writer's impression that we owe an enormous debt to the Milesians, not so much for what they actually said, but for what they stood for—an attempt to use reason rather than theology as a tool for expounding the nature of the universe.

The Pre-Socratic Philosophers

The philosophers and scientists who followed the Milesian school left far more in the way of fragments. They were no longer centered on Ionia alone but were also in other areas that had been colonized by the Greeks, such as southern Italy and Sicily. They wrote on many diverse subjects but from our point of view are notable, first, because most of them followed the Milesian school in spirit, if not in detail, by looking for some singular substance of which the world could be said to be constructed and, second, because they began to speculate on matters that would form the subject matter of two new disciplines: philosophy and psychology. In matters of psychology, we find that in certain pre-Socratic philosophers of a biological bent—Alcmaeon, Empedocles, Democritus, Diogenes of Apollonia, Anaxagoras—we have the beginnings of the discussion not of what the external world might consist of, but of *how* we *know* what we do about the external world. Since such knowledge largely, if not entirely, consists of information brought to us by the five senses of touch, taste, smell, hearing, and vision, we have in the writings of these authors the first smatterings of both physiological and epistemological psychology. But before we look into this matter in more detail, the reader may find it useful to consult Figure 1–3, which shows in schematic form the names and accomplishments of the major pre-Socratic writers of interest to psychologists. Going through it quickly, from top to bottom, we note the following points.

Pythagoras left us no writings of his own but was credited with founding a school of philosophy in Italy. This school was noted for its mystical doctrines—derived from the so-called Orphic variant of early Greek religion—but more particularly for its belief that the universe was essentially logical and ordered in nature, with number being the prime unifying force. In particular, the Pythagoreans remodeled Anaximander's system of the universe to incorporate mathematics. They understood something of the mathematics of music—for example, if a vibrating

Figure 1–3   The Main Pre-Socratic Philosophers of Interest to Psychologists: Their Locations and Notes on Their Contributions.

	LOCATION	WORLD-STUFF	PSYCHOLOGICAL IMPLICATIONS
Pythagoras	Croton, S. Italy	Number	Theory of harmony
Heraclitus	Ephesus, Asia Minor	Fire, importance of change	We breathe in fire = divine reason
Alcmaeon	Croton	(?)	Theory of sensation
Empedocles	Acragas, Sicily	Earth, fire, air, water; love and strife	First extended theory of sensation and perception
Democritus	Thrace or Miletus	Atoms	Adds to Empedocles
Diogenes of Apollonia	Black Sea	4 elements, but especially air	Theory of sensation and memory
Protagoras	Abdera, N. Greece	Importance of inner experience	Subjectivism
Anaxagoras	Athens	*Nous*	Theory of sensation

string is halved in length the pitch that results when the string is plucked is an octave higher than the pitch resulting from plucking the full-length string—and discovered certain properties of the real number system. They said little about psychology but were important influences on Plato later.

Heraclitus may be said to follow the Milesians, making fire the main element of the world but also stressing that it was because changes operated on fire that fire was capable of producing the variety of phenomena we see around us. Life consists of breathing in fire—sometimes the fire is thought of as an external form of wisdom *(Logos)*—and during sleep we receive no sensory input from the fire, although we continue to breathe. But there was a religious component in Heraclitus' philosophy, insofar as he believed that a divine Intelligence (perhaps, but not necessarily, deserving the name "Zeus") controls events. This injection of change into the universe is called "strife," because it interrupts the sustained continuance of the present state. In the present state, opposites coexist and the coexistence, for example, of day and night reflect different manifestations of the divine Intelligence (West, 1986). Alcmaeon would appear to get credit for being the first of the pre-Socratic philosophers to leave us a fairly detailed account of certain aspects of human physiology. In general, he argued health results from a balance of opposites in the body, such as wet-dry, cold-hot, or bitter-sweet; an overbalance in the direction of one or other quality leads to disease. From second-hand reports we believe that Alcmaeon practiced dissection, and we shall consider his theory of sensation later.

Empedocles was perhaps the first to enunciate what would later become a standard credo of Greek science and medicine, namely, that the world consists of four elements in various mixtures and combinations. The elements are air, fire, water, and earth. The elements interpenetrate by emanations from one form of body locking into place within "pores" of another form of body. What attracts body to body is love; what repels one from another is strife.

The words "love" and "strife" are Empedocles' attempt to reconcile old religious accounts of creation with the new scientific account. In Hesiod's account of creation, we find mention of Love and Strife as forces causing disorder among the gods and men; now these forces are applied to the universe: When Love is dominant, the universe is a coherent formless whole, but Strife divides the universe into elements. The present state of the world is only temporary; at the moment the universe is on the way to becoming four distinct masses, earth in the center surrounded by spheres of water, fire, and air. Empedocles was quite ingenious in this attempt to describe natural phenomena in terms of the temporary mixture of the four elements.

Democritus, following Leucippus, employed the notion that the world consists of small particles that are indivisible (i.e., uncuttable; a-tomic, with *tom* a Greek root referring to cutting as in "lobo*tomy*"). These atoms are supposed to be of various shapes (this will have an important influence on Democritus's theory of sensation) and collide or separate in an empty space or void. "Change is the redistribution of atoms in space," as Nahm (1964) puts it.

Looking back at Figure 1–3, we have remaining Diogenes of Apollo-nia, Protagoras, and Anaxagoras. Diogenes followed Empedocles in be-lieving in four elements but insisted that air is the main "substance" maintaining life. We possess a long fragment of his concerned with the blood vessels of the body. He also anticipated Aristotle in his ideas on memory. Protagoras, one of the greatest of the so-called Sophists, stands somewhat apart from our other philosophers in so far as he does not consider the human being as a passive repository into which sensations flow but rather as an active seeker and elaborator of sensations. Esper (1964) argues that this way of considering the observer, common to such later luminaries as Kant and William James, stems ultimately from Prota-goras. Finally, Anaxagoras, whom we have placed last since there is some evidence that he flourished in Athens itself and may have taught Socra-tes, was responsible both for a theory of sensation and for a new hypothe-sis concerning the world-stuff.

Like Empedocles, Anaxagoras believed that the world started as a unified whole and that divine intervention was causing it to disintegrate into disorder. Everything is becoming mixed with everything else, except for one thing, the purest substance, Mind, which controls the process of disintegration and makes it less chaotic than it might have been. The notion of a "Mind-stuff" has continued in various forms to the present day. The Greek word Anaxogoras used for Mind was *nous*. In Homer, that word meant a power that controlled the temperament—for example, Achilles had a "merciless *nous*" (Dodds, 1951, p. 17; see also Jaynes, 1977, p. 269); later, Aristotle would use *nous* to refer specifically to human intellectual powers.

We should make special mention of the theories of the pre-Socratic philosophers concerning sensation. That the senses were indeed five in number seems to have been accepted by all the pre-Socratic writers and, we shall see, by Aristotle. But each author imposed on his somewhat simple-minded physiology a more profound philosophy of physics, which, naturally enough, led to a wide variety of theories. Democritus, for example, did not simply follow Empedocles but produced his own system. We may begin with the study of vision. The first theory of vision seems to be due to Alcmaeon. Alcmaeon was particularly impressed by the fact that if you close an eye and press with your finger at the back of the eyeball, you will see flashes of light, circular haloes, and other light phenomena—modern physiologists call these *phosphenes*, and they can be produced both by pressure and by electric currents passed through the eyeball (Brindley, 1960, p. 166). For Alcmaeon the existence of pho-phenes suggested that at the back of the eye burned a fire. The rays from the fire shot through the "water" that made up the bulk of the eye (what we now call, in a curious throwback to Greek terminology, the vitreous humor), reached the object perceived, and doubled back again to the eye. In addition, the object had an image that was reflected, as in a mirror, in the "gleaming" "diaphanous" part of the eye. It is still not clear exactly what part of the eye is meant by this—perhaps Alcmaeon was influenced by the fact that a reflection of one's own self can be seen if one looks closely into another person's pupil, but that is only a suggestion. Of more importance is the fact that Alcmaeon believed that the experience known as seeing had something to do with the connections (vascular and ner-vous) between the brain and the eye. This is one of our earliest records linking the brain with sensation—we must recall that the Egyptians and other later peoples had stressed that the heart was the center of such cognitive abilities.

But Alcmaeon's theory was elaborated on in detail by Empedocles. Some of the physiological details are maintained—such as the idea that fire rays issue from the eye—but now visual sensation is linked with Empedocles' much broader philosophy concerned with the way the four elements combine to create matter and sensation. For Empedocles, ema-nations from objects fit into "passages" or "pores" in the sense organs. The pores of the eye are held to be arranged alternatively of fire and water: By way of fire we see white, by way of water, black. Other colors are given by "effluences" from objects. These are related to the elements the objects are made of. Hearing occurs when the air, set in motion, resounds within the ear and causes the "solid parts" of the ear themselves to produce the sensation of a sound. Smell results from emanations from "subtle and light" bodies that are perceived by inhaling.

Democritus, as we would expect, bases his theory of vision on his atomic theory. He imagines that films, or replicas, of objects—the Greek word is close to our word *idol*—fly off the surfaces of objects and impress themselves on the air. In turn these impressions are transmitted to the eye, which is, as Beare calls it, "a thoroughfare for instreaming atoms." One can actually see the image formed in the eye by looking at the observer's pupil. Later scholars such as Theophrastus would object that, if Democritus were right, we should see better underwater than in the air because water is denser and would therefore carry a more sharply defined imprint. Democritus says little more about the eye but offers one of the first theories of color. Each color is an index of the surface and shape of the atoms composing the colored object. Smooth things are white; rough things are black; hot things are red; and green is a mixture of solidity and emptiness. Other colors are compounded of these primary colors. He also applies his atomic theory to hearing: Sound results when a stream of atoms sets the air in motion, a model not too far removed from the present-day notion that sound results when molecules are pushed in a back-and-forth motion in a medium such as air. Democritus suggests that taste sensations arise when atoms of a certain shape fit properly into receptacles on the tongue; he says little about smell or touch.

On one subject Democritus is more explicit than the others: He is concerned with the question of how it is that, when atoms combine, we sometimes have the experience known as sensation. He surmises that the replicas emitted by objects mix, not only with atoms in the sense organ, but also with atoms in the soul *(psyche)*. There is also a hint (see Beare, 1906, p. 207) that he was aware that some potential sensations do not actually come into consciousness because our attention is elsewhere. All knowledge, argues Democritus, results from the interaction of the atomic idols and the soul. Theories of sensation were also put forward by Diogenes of Apollonia and by Anaxagoras.

We may thus remark now that the pre-Socratic philosophers broached psychological enquiry mainly by way of a discussion of sensation and in so doing provided the beginnings of physiological psychology. In addition, they offered a variety of syntheses of religious and naturalistic explanations of the universe. The writings of pre-Socratic philosophers should be thought of as parallel and distinct contributions to science rather than as forming a simple sequence from the earliest to the latest.

Plato and Aristotle

The period of classical, or Hellenic, Greece is taken to span most of the fifth and fourth centuries B.C.—convenient peripheral dates are 480 B.C., when a Persian invasion was stopped by the Athenian navy in a great sea battle at Salamis, and 323 B.C., the date of Alexander's death. The philosopher Anaxagoras was born in about 500 B.C., so would be about twenty years old at the battle of Salamis. A pupil of Anaxagoras was probably Socrates (470–399 B.C.), who became a familiar figure during the Periclean democracy as he walked about the center of Athens discussing many different philosophical problems with as many as would listen. Socrates fought, apparently very bravely, in one of the Athenian wars, but five years after the war's end he was accused of impiety and of perverting youth. Following the custom of the time, he was obliged to commit suicide. However, his pupil Plato (c. 427–c. 347 B.C.), who was then in his twenties, spent the rest of his life teaching at a school which had been organized, the Academy, and wrote many dialogues ostensibly expounding the teachings of Socrates. The problem, of course, is to know which sayings are genuinely the opinions of Socrates and which are Plato's own, a difficulty that still obsesses students of classical Greek philosophy. Plato's most famous pupil, Aristotle (384–322 B.C.), was also in his twenties when Macedonians from the north conquered Athens; he taught in Plato's Academy until Plato's death in 347 B.C. Three years later he was invited by Philip, the king of the Macedonians, to go to Macedonia to supervise the education of Philip's son, Alexander. When Alexander set out to extend Greek/Macedonian sovereignty to the Middle East, in 334 B.C., Aristotle returned to Athens and founded his own school there, the Lyceum. He taught there until Alexander's death, when it became expedient to leave Athens because of anti-Macedonian sentiment. He died in Chalcis, a small town north of Athens, a year later.

The period at which Athens was at the height of its power, the fifth and early fourth centuries B.C., is memorable not only because of the philosophers but because during this period a system of democracy, in which a large number of Athenian citizens had votes, was put into place. A large proportion of the population, however, had no votes; these included women, slaves, and foreigners, the latter attracted to Athens because of its culture and trading opportunities. Reflecting the culture of Athens were its dramatists (such as Aristophanes, Aeschylus, Sophocles, and Euripides) and its historians (Thucydides and Herodotus). The painted pottery of this period was famous all over the Mediterranean, and of course its sculpture and architecture are still a major sight of modern Athens.

In what follows we shall make use of Jowett's (1937) translation of the complete *Dialogues* of Plato; the page numbers in the present text refer to the page numbers in that edition. But before discussing the contribution of Socrates and/or Plato to psychology, we must note immediately that the Platonic dialogues are not internally consistent; there are contradictions and logical confusions running throughout the work. (For an example of a logical error analyzed see Robinson, 1970, p. 37.) The extraction of a coherent Platonic or Socratian philosophy has been one of the major tasks of classical scholarship in modern times. Moreover, none of the dialogues is devoted to what we would now call psychology: Plato's contributions to the subject are scattered and somewhat slight. The reason for this may be imputed to an important influence that Socrates had on Plato: For Socrates philosophy was not a subject devoted to explaining or describing the universe known to the senses, as it was for the Ionian physicists and some of the other pre-Socratic philosophers; rather, it was the effort to use reason and logical argument towards the ultimate goal of making the philosopher a "virtuous" or "good" person. The contributions of Socrates/Plato to ethics and to those aspects of thought concerned with right, the good, the just, the beautiful, the true, and the temperate are of primary importance, but it can also be argued that, because of this preoccupation with the concept of the ideal person, science and to a lesser extent metaphysics were somewhat neglected.

In many ways, the *Dialogues* contain perpetuations of what we have already discussed with respect to previous generations. For example, Plato admired the Egyptians for the continuity of their culture: We saw that for centuries Egyptian civilization maintained stereotyped patterns of belief, ritual, and artistic style, and for Plato this is something to be imitated, something to be aimed for in his own ideal State *(Laws,* p. 435). Just as for the Babylonians the liver was the site wherein omens of the future could be read, so for Plato the liver is a bodily object that reflects the emotions and operations of the mind *(Timaeus,* p. 49). Following Empedocles, Plato believed that the universe is made of the four elements, earth, air, fire, and water, although he made these in turn the resultants of certain geometrical shapes—here the Pythagorean emphasis on numbers is seen. Thus, to earth is assigned the cube, to water the icosahedron, to air the octahedron, and to fire the pyramid *(Timaeus,* p. 36). Like many of the pre-Socratics, he believed that vision results when a fire sends out rays from the eye that mingle with the outside "fire" of light to render the "fires" of objects visible *(Timaeus,* p. 26).

His theories of the other senses also plainly derive from pre-Socratic doctrines. Hearing is due to a "shock" being propagated in the air to the ear *(Timaeus,* p. 46), tasting to juices being dissolved on the tongue. In this respect, he offered a more advanced classification of tastes than his predecessors *(Timaeus,* pp. 44–45), whereas, he argued, smells are difficult to classify. Like Democritus, he had a theory of color mixtures based on the idea of different kinds of "fires." Also in the *Timaeus* we read of a somewhat bizarre physiology in which Plato treated the "marrow" of the brain as being the seat of reason; elsewhere in the same dialogue, however, he spoke of taste as resulting when particles pass from the tongue through small veins to the heart. Beare (1906, p. 275) is therefore obliged to write, "From all this we can see how difficult it is to gather what Plato regarded as the common seat or organ . . . of cognition, or indeed whether he held that there was any one such seat." Other links with the pre-Socratic past include Plato's criticisms of Protagoras's theory that sensations are relative to the percipient himself—Plato thought this would lead to cognitive chaos and away from his doctrine that there was an absolute reality underlying sensations *(The aetetus,* p. 169). However, the relation between knowledge-as-given-by-the-senses and its underlying reality is described in a different way in other passages of Plato; Annas (1986) shows that he probably tried to argue from ethical ideas, such as that a real Good underlies our concept of good, to physical ideas, such as that a real world underlies our sensations of the world, and thereby was led to a doctrine (the doctrine of Forms) that Aristotle later rejected.

From Anaxagoras's teaching that *nous* underlay all material objects,

Plato would be led to the even more mysterious thesis that there was a world-soul *(psyche)* of which all human souls partook *(Cratylus,* p. 190). However, Plato's use of *psyche* also applied to the individual mind, and there are many problems with his usage of the word. These include certain inconsistencies. For example, in the *Phaedrus* (p. 257) he introduces one of his most famous images: The soul is divided into three parts, resembling a charioteer steering his horses. The charioteer is "reason," and he controls a "good" horse of spirit and ambition and a "bad" horse of greed and lust. On the other hand this purely psychological, material picture of the soul is changed when in the *Phaedo* (p. 465) we read that "the soul resembles the divine, and the body the mortal" and that "the soul . . . departs to the invisible world—to the divine and immortal and rational" and that souls tainted with immorality may, after death, enter the bodies of animals. In the *Republic* (p. 704) we have an echo of the tripartite image of the charioteer, where the soul is argued to be made of reason, desire, and passion; later (p. 839) Plato argued that individuals differ in the degree to which these different parts of the soul dominate their behavior.

Plato was, however, quite original in his treatment of memory. He offered analyses of the memory process that are still valid and analogies that are current in modern theories of the subject. In the *Theaetetus* Plato likened the impression of a datum of memory "on" the mind to the impression of a seal on wax. This metaphor would be sustained throughout the history of psychology. In particular, in the seventeenth century, it was used by Locke and others in the context of the question of whether we know anything—that is, have any memories—at birth. The theory that we do not is known as the *tabula rasa* theory. It is crucial to observe, however, that, although he used the image of a wax tablet, Plato did not himself adhere to the *tabula rasa* theory, to judge by other sources: In fact, he was one of the first to argue that at birth the soul does have certain memories in it, namely recollections from the immortal soul, put there in previous existences. The passage in which this precept is most clearly brought out occurs in the *Meno* (pp. 361–366): A slave boy is led, by the Socratic question-and-answer method, to see certain truths of geometry he had never appreciated before. It is therefore argued that Socrates has simply "brought out" innate recollections acquired by the boy in a former state of existence. Almost certainly, however, Plato also believed that persons in their present lives also acquired new information that had not been made available from previous lives. The controversy between those who believe in the *tabula rasa* theory and those who believe in the existence of innate ideas persists to the present day. It might be added that in the pages following the wax tablet image, Plato also likened the mind to an aviary in which are flying about many doves, pigeons, and other birds. Memories are like these birds; we possess them in the sense that they are already captured but cannot always take hold of just the one we are looking for. He noted that the receptacle holding the memories might have been empty in childhood, an apparent leaning towards a *tabula rasa* theory that has to be balanced against what was said in the *Meno*. In the *Philebus* Plato also observed that we particularly retain information that has excited us or moved us rather than that which is scarcely attended to; in the *Theaetetus* he anticipated the distinction between forgetting due to permanent loss of the material and forgetting due to temporary difficulty with retrieval.

Plato deals briefly with one final facet of memory theory—so briefly in fact that his contribution is often overlooked. How does one memory lead to another? Through association. Plato was well aware of this and remarked that the flow of recollection is *via* a series of images in which each image is associated with the previous one (*Phaedo,* p. 457). This assertion is only put in passing, as it were, on the topic of the preexistence of the soul before birth, but in it are the germs, of the associationist psychology of the future and also of the study of mental images. Both topics are to be of vital importance in the history of the exploration of the topic of memory. In the *Philebus* (p. 373) Plato explicitly distinguished between images arising directly from memories of perceptions and images that are the result of new syntheses, that is, imagination.

From medieval sources we know that Aristotle probably wrote over 170 books, but of these only 47 survive. They were printed in a special edition in Berlin in 1831, and it is still customary to refer to the texts in terms of the pagination of that edition. For example, *Historia Animalium*, i. 1. 488b, 25 means the book *Historia Animalium* (Aristotle's works are known by their Latin titles), book i, chapter 1, p. 488, column b in the Berlin edition, line 25. Most editions of Aristotle in English show the Berlin pagination along with the text. In what follows we shall use the Berlin pagination scheme. We shall discuss Aristotle's contributions under five headings: his views on mind and soul, his views on sensation and perception, his views on memory, his views on animal behavior, and his views on the question of whether ideas are innate or learned. However, a word about Aristotle's general opinion on physiology and philosophy is necessary first.

Like Empedocles and Plato, Aristotle believed the world to be made up of the four elements: earth, air, fire, and water (although in the *Physics*, i. 6. 189b,15 he claimed that there might be only three elements). Later in the *Physics*, ii. 2. 330a, 30, however, he stated that to the four elements can be added the four qualities hot, cold, moist, and dry. They are linked in the following way: Earth is dry rather than cold, water is cold rather than moist, air is moist rather than hot, and fire is hot rather than dry. Living things are made up of these elements, but it is the quality of *heat* that is most important for the animal body. Because it is at the center of the body, the heart is the organ for preserving heat and sending it out, mainly by way of the "veins"—the distinction between veins and arteries was little stressed by Aristotle—to the different parts of the body. Heat rises to the brain, but the brain is a cold organ that refrigerates the blood. As the blood falls back cooled to the heart, the head feels heavy and this is what engenders sleep. Death is due to the exhaustion or extinction of the fire in the heart. The heart is not only the center for the preservation of heat in the body, it is also the place to which sensations are transmitted from the sense organs and the place from which movement ability is transmitted to the limbs, much as a puppeteer controls the movements of a puppet *(De Motu Animalium* [On the Movements of Animals], 7, 70lb). It seems strange to us now that for Aristotle the heart and not the brain should be the controlling center of the body, but Aristotle considered the heart to be so dependent on the brain that they almost form a single organ. Moreover, in the field of medicine Aristotle may have been at odds with some of his contemporaries, who clearly stress the importance of the brain in psychological processes (see later).

In addition to his unusual biology, Aristotle was concerned with broader philosophical questions that might accurately be labeled "metaphysical"—that is, beyond or underlying "physics." He believed that all that existed constituted "substances" but that a substance partook of two attributes, which, it should be noted, are attributes of convenience to the thinker rather than attributes of substance in the way that color or size might be. The form attribute of a substance represents what it actually is, the reality of the substance. The matter attribute of the substance represents an embodiment of the form—thus any substance has, inseparably, both form and matter. Armstrong puts this difficult issue well when he says:

> The form is the intimate inward structure, the "thingness" of the thing; the matter is just the possibility of being that or another thing which is made actual for the time being by the reception of a particular form. If we were to speak of Pattern and Possibility instead of Form and Matter, though they would not translate accurately the Greek words Aristotle uses, they would perhaps convey a more accurate impression to modern minds. (1957, p. 79)

This distinction between form and matter is to be reflected in Aristotle's distinction between soul *(psyche)* and body. Furthermore, we see that an interesting image following from the notion that matter "receives" a form is an image of matter before and after receiving the form: Before the form is given to the matter, the matter has *potential* being; afterwards, it has *actual* being. This distinction between the actual and the potential will also enter into Aristotle's discussion of soul and body.

We turn first, then, to a discussion of Aristotle's views on the soul.

These are scattered in various books but are condensed in his major work on psychology, *De Anima*. *Psyche* is the word he used for the soul, but unlike Plato, Aristotle was relatively consistent in the way he used it. *De Anima* begins with an invaluable outline of the views of previous philosophers on the soul. For example, Aristotle considers, and rejects, Empedocles' view that the soul represents harmony between love and strife, and Democritus's view that the soul consists of spherical atoms. For Aristotle the soul is that which transforms a being into a living being—and that includes plants, though the souls of plants and animals differ in internal constitution, as we shall see. However, his most famous quotation on the difference between soul and body is in *De Anima* ii. 2. 412a, 27: "The soul is the first grade of actuality of a body having potentially in it." Aristotle did not define soul as something mystical, as Plato thought; nor was it just a synonym for *mind,* as Anaxagoras thought. Rather, he defined it as that which gave a living body life; thereby, it was the "form" for the "matter" of the body. As a consequence, it was that which rendered "actual" life to the body that was "potentially" living.

The question of interest is how mind, as we normally think of it, relates to Aristotle's very idiosyncratic use of the word *soul.* Fortunately, he was precise on the matter. *Nous*—mind—is identified with those qualities of reason possessed peculiarly by humans and to a much lesser degree by animals and to no degree by plants. So from the loftiness of "form" and "matter" we descend to the more mundane question of the chain of living being: For the first time, humanity is represented as being on a continuum representing increasing development of mind-qualities in the plant and animal kingdom. Not until Darwin will this recognition of humans' essentially "animal" nature be revived, and it is therefore of the greatest historical importance. In Aristotle's scheme, plants, animals, and people have the power of nutrition; animals and people share the powers of sensation, appetite, and locomotion; but only humans reason with their *nous.* We also note that Aristotle considered pleasure and pain to be forces driving us towards or away from environmental objects and that the sense of touch is of particular importance in this respect. As a corollary, we note that Aristotle's contribution to the mind/body problem was to assert that since everything that influences the body influences the soul and vice versa, the two cannot be separated. Thus, for practical purposes a study of the soul is possible because we can observe the behavior of the body as it is influenced by soul.

We turn now to the second topic of discussion, Aristotle's views on sensation and perception. These are treated in *De Anima,* in a short tract *De Sensu et Sensibili (On the Senses and Sensible Things),* and in other scattered places. We may state at the outset that Aristotle added relatively little to our understanding of sensory physiology, but he was more sophisticated than his predecessors on the nature of sensory stimuli, and he was much more concerned than his predecessors with the question of how sensations arise in and are integrated by what we could call the mind or perception or conscious experience.

In the case of vision, Aristotle demurred at the older theory that the eye shoots forth a ray of light, for if that were so, why should the eye not have the power of seeing in the dark (*De Sensu,* ii. 437b, 11)? Instead he thought of objects as being reflected in the eye because of its smooth surface and noted that blindness can occur if the "passages" from the eye inwards are slashed by a sword (*De Sensu,* ii. 438b, 13). Color mixtures are due to mixtures of black and white in objects themselves: The sensation of a color, however, is due to the actualization of the color itself in the seeing organ. Aristotle also noted, for the first time, the fact that a sensation does not necessarily cease when the stimulus is removed but can persist as an aftereffect. For example, if we look at the sun and then look away, we see what we now call an *afterimage* of the sun that changes colors before it disappears; if we look at a moving object such as a river and then look at something at rest such as the landscape, the landscape seems to be moving. Aristotle introduced this passage in the context of his tract on dreams (*De Somniis,* 459b): He asserted that dreams are essentially sensory aftereffects that emerge during sleep.

Aristotle's views on hearing, smell, and taste were elaborations of older theories. But on the sense of touch he truly moved ahead of the earlier writers. He had the remarkable insight that a sensation of touch arises not because there is an organ on the skin directly affected by a tactile stimulus, but because a touch is a physical effect propagated *through* the medium of the flesh to unknown underlying touch organs (*De Anima,* ii. 11. 422b, 34). Through touch we also have direct experience of the four elemental qualities hot, dry, moist, and cold. He gave an illustration of an illusion in the touch sense: "If we cross the fingers, one object placed between them so as to touch both their adjacent surfaces appears as if two" (*De Somniis,* ii. 460b, 20). This is still known as Aristotle's illusion.

The question of how a sensation arises remains. Aristotle's theory of this was that when a sense organ is affected, it sends a message through the vascular system to the heart. How? By means of a "connatural spirit" that is mixed with the blood. The Greek word for this is *pneuma*. Originally *pneuma* meant air, breath, or wind—in the quotations concerning air by Anaximenes on p. 00, the word *breath* in Greek was *pneuma*—but now it has come to mean some kind of substance or spirit that propagates sensation to the heart and also movement from the heart to the limbs. The importance of *pneuma* in physiological psychology after Aristotle will be made clear shortly; a good account of Aristotle's use of *pneuma* is given in Brett (1912, p. 117).

Possibly Aristotle's most original contribution to the study of sensation and perception was his idea that there was a "common sense" by virtue of which individual sensations from the five types of sense organs were perceived and integrated. This idea is expounded mainly in *De Anima*, iii. 2. It is through the "common sense" that we can recognize that an object is both white and sweet—as Aristotle puts it, "discrimination between white and sweet cannot be effected by two agencies which remain separate; both the qualities discriminated must be present to something that is one and single." We shall see that later physiologists ascribed a definite location in the brain to this "common sense."

The third topic on which Aristotle wrote extensively was memory. In his tract *De Memoria et Reminiscentia* he began by following Plato's distinction between *retention* (generally translated as memory) and *retrieval* (generally translated as recollection). The essence of the act of retrieving is that one has a presentation to one's consciousness that can be ascribed to a past experience. The presentation is perceived by way of the "common sense," and therefore memory is more closely allied to sense perception than to intelligence: This means that animals also have memory. The clarity or vividness of the memory depends on how well the initial perception of the stimulus was stamped on the receiving surface of the mind— here Aristotle repeated Plato's image of the wax tablet. Aristotle treats this image of a *receiving surface* rather literally and relates the reception of a memory to the moistness of the surface: If the surface is hard and dry, it will be difficult to make an impression. Aristotle suggests that the memories of very young and very old persons are poor because the surfaces are changing rapidly due to growth and decay, respectively. Recollecting itself often consists of having the experience of one movement revived as a memory and this brings with it to consciousness any other movement previously associated with that memory. He goes on to say:

> Whenever, therefore, we are recollecting, we are experiencing certain of the antecedent movements until finally we experience the one after which customarily comes that which we seek. This explains why we hunt up the series, having started in thought either from a present intuition or some other, and from something either similar, or contrary, to what we seek, or else from that which is contiguous with it. (*De Memoria*, 2. 451b, 17)

The last sentence here is possibly the most influential written in the history of psychology, for it enunciates the belief that we move by association from one concept to the next depending on how similar or contrasting the first concept is with respect to the second, or on how far the two were experienced together in the past. (*Contiguous* can mean this last but also includes part-whole relationships, as a handle is part of a hammer.) Later philosophers called these the *laws of association*. But back to recollection: Although it is often easiest to retrieve a series by starting at the beginning or the end, one can also start in the middle of the series.

Aristotle also anticipated modern research on the organization of memory by pointing out that "things arranged in a fixed order, like the successive demonstrations of geometry, are easy to remember, while badly arranged subjects are remembered with difficulty" (*De Memoria*, 2. 452a, 3). He then went on to mention the mnemonic technique of *loci*. This was possibly invented by the poet Simonides prior to Aristotle's time and is a device whereby one can remember a series of items by assigning each item to a place in an imaged house or palace. Retrieval then consists of reevoking the image and "reading off" the items assigned to each locus in the image.

As Paivio (1971, p. 154) tells it, Simonides

> was chanting a lyric poem at a banquet when he was called out by a message. During his absence the roof of the banquet hall fell in, crushing and mangling the guests so that they could not be identified. Simonides remembered the places at which they had been sitting and could thus indicate to relatives which were their dead.

The end section of *De Memoria* deals in more detail with the notion that we have to understand time if we are to understand memory and closes with comments concerning individual differences in retention and recollection ability.

We turn next to a subject that has been somewhat neglected, namely, Aristotle's contributions to the study of behavior in itself and, in particular, animal behavior. The *Historia Animalium* and other books on animals are replete with anecdotes based either on direct observation (the many small sea creatures) or hearsay. To some extent Aristotle may be thought of as the first experimentalist in that he used dissection and comparative anatomy as basic tools, although Bourgey (1975) argues that to call Aristotle an experimentalist is to exaggerate his originality. Although he divided organisms into various kinds, he did not have a complete classification (Balme, 1975). Nevertheless, we find condensed in the biological texts comments on such behaviors as eating, mating, nest building, migration, hibernation, escape behavior, and social collaboration (as in ants) in hundreds of different species. Aristotle also gave detailed accounts of how different species competed with each other for food or territory. There is much on courtship behavior, and Aristotle speculated at great length on the mechanism of sexual reproduction.

Finally, we may note that hidden in some of his books on logic are remarks that lead us to believe he was concerned with the question of nature *versus* nurture—that is, of innate *versus* learned knowledge. This matter has been brought to light notably by Baumrin (1975), who points out that Aristotle disagreed with Plato, who believed that some knowledge is innate and just needs extracting by appropriate dialectic; nevertheless, Aristotle believed that the mind cannot be entirely blank because otherwise how would we make any associationistic connections at all between premises? The solution is that the mind has an innate *capacity* to understand logical demonstrations, and the capacity to sense is, of course, innate. So we accumulate knowledge of things by virtue of this innate ability of the mind to apprehend them. Aristotle was thus a nativist in the sense that he believed that the mind has certain inborn characteristics and an empiricist in the sense that he believed most actual knowledge to be dependent on memory, which in turn depends on sensation. Many later writers on innate ideas would fail to be as precise as Aristotle about the distinction between an idea itself and the capacity to have that idea. Elsewhere (in the *Physics*, ii. 1. 193a, 7), Aristotle notes that a man blind from birth might nevertheless reason about colors because he could know the words without having the "thoughts" to correspond.

It should be noted that the students of the Lyceum who learned directly from Aristotle continued in the naturalist tradition, notably in their advanced view that the soul was intimately connected with *pneuma* and with the nervous system, which was at the time just beginning to be discovered by the medical scientists (see following). The most important students of the peripatetic school, as Aristotle's group was called, were Theophrastus (who wrote a book on the senses and who also wrote a tract called the *Characters*, discussing different kinds of personality) and Strato (who argued that, by attending, we convert sensations into the objects of consciousness).

Hellenistic and Roman Psychology

The six hundred years following Aristotle's death, from about 300 B.C. to A.D. 300, may conveniently be divided into two periods, the Hellenistic, when the Eastern Mediterranean was dominated by Greek thinkers and scientists and the great library at Alexandria was formed, and the Roman period, from about 30 B.C. onwards, when the center of learning shifted to Italy. In many ways the two periods show a strong continuity. The authorities to which people turned for knowledge of the world continued to be Greek.

When Alexander moved his armies out from Greece, he left Greek settlements in a vast area including what are now Turkey, Iran, Afghanistan, and India to the east and Syria, Israel, and Egypt in the south. Following Alexander's death, this empire was broken into large parts in which power was given to kings, but in which individual cities had a fair amount of independence. In particular, the city of Alexandria in Egypt, ruled over by a succession of kings each named Ptolemy, became famous for its museum and library, and many scholars settled there. During the Hellenistic period, from about 330–30 B.C., Alexandria became renowned for its scientists and, we shall see later, its physiologists in particular. Many of the peoples subjugated by Alexander accepted Greek domination, but some did not, and to this day Jews remember the war between Judas Maccabeus and the Greek colonizers in the second century A.D. During this period various philosophies, all of which arose shortly after Aristotle's death, came into competition and, during the Hellenistic and later Roman periods, preoccupied the major thinkers. Four views predominated: Cynicism, Skepticism, Stoicism, and Epicureanism.

Even during Alexander's reign there had been a group of philosophers known as Cynics who rejected the society they lived in, saw in the decline of Athens proof of their own belief in the corruption of humanity, and doubted the speculations of the physicists and metaphysicians. Another group were known as the Skeptics; they doubted the validity of inferences based either on sensory experience or on the principles of logic enunciated by Aristotle. The Skeptics, who were a fairly continuous school for six hundred years, left a legacy of philosophical doubt, and we may note that the seventeenth-century writers who question how far we can rely on the senses sometimes referred back to ancient Skeptic texts, in particular those of Pyrrho of Elis (c. 365–c. 270 B.C.) and the Roman writer Sextus Empiricus (died c. 200 A.D.).

It is generally accepted that the founder of the Stoics was Zeno of Citium (336–264 B.C.), who was a boy when Aristotle was organizing the Lyceum in Athens. Zeno has left little writing, but we know of his life and teachings through the biography written of him by Diogenes Laertius in the third century A.D. The latter declared that Zeno wrote books on many subjects, including appetite, the passions, and sight—if we had these books Zeno would probably be counted a major figure in the history of psychology. He was highly respected as a teacher in Athens but was himself of a humble and abstinent temperament. He wrote much on logic and grammar, but for the Stoics the chief function of the philosophers was to teach on matters of ethics and proper behavior: To this extent they are in the lineage of Socrates rather than Aristotle, and Zeno himself stressed that the chief good in life was virtue, towards which nature steers us of her own accord. There is thus a great stress on moderation, justice, equanimity, self-control, and even the eradication of disturbing emotions, whence our use of the word *stoic* referring to the power to endure misfortune.

But these ethical principles were based on a broader view of nature in general: Most knowledge is based indirectly on sensations but added to such knowledge is that based on reason. Sensations themselves can leave memories reflected in experience as images, but more important are "conceptions," that is, abstract ideas based on inferences made in thought. As would be expected, the Stoics analyzed the emotions in particular: For Zeno the four chief "passions" were grief, fear, desire, and pleasure. We know little of what the Stoics thought about sensation, but apparently they viewed vision as resulting from "a body of luminous air which extends from the organ of sight to the object in a conical form"; hearing as resulting from the air between speaker and the hearer being agitated in "waves"; and sleep as resulting from the "relaxation" of the senses. The soul is given to man directly as being a fiery breath, or *pneuma*, instilled in man by Divine Reason. *Pneuma* was thought of as an active "breath" that pervaded the universe and was itself a living thing, like a personal God; hence Stoic science would concern itself mainly with the purpose of events and things, and not be concerned with simple mechanistic explanations. The Stoics, however, believed that since our bodies were composed of water into each fragment of which was blended *pneuma*, the soul died with the body. But since *pneuma* itself, as the active principle governing the course of the universe, was immortal, the immortality of the soul became a point of contention. One solution was to assert that this universe went in cycles of destruction and reconstruction, and that during a later rebuilding our bodies were also rebuilt; in this way, we could be said to expect another life after death (Barnes, 1986). Thus, just as Plato elevated *psyche* from a thing within the body into a world-soul, the Stoics elevated *pneuma* from a bodily contained substance mixed with blood into a Universal Principle.

Epicurus, the founder of Epicureanism, was about twenty when Aristotle died. He first organized schools in various parts of the Aegean region but eventually settled in Athens, where he taught both men and women from 306 B.C. onwards. According to Diogenes Laertius, he was a controversial figure: His friends praised his generosity, wisdom, and moderation; his enemies accused him of immorality and irreverence towards the gods. On the latter issue they may have been correct, for it was one of Epicurus's chief doctrines that fear of death is an unnecessary and hampering emotion. Since fear of death arises often from fear of the gods and possible punishment in an afterlife, it is best, argued Epicurus, not to believe in divinity at all. This meant that dreams were not divine in origin.

The main doctrine of Epicurus is based on the atomic theory of Democritus. The world consists of atoms scattered through a void. The atoms fall downwards but occasionally swerve in their courses and collide; from these collisions emerges matter. Epicurus also believed that free will could be explained in terms of the swervings of atoms from set trajectories: Events are not predestined of absolute necessity by the courses of the atoms, but can be changed by the will of a free agent. This issue raised the question of the nature of causation: Do the moving atoms cause the will to make them swerve, or is the will independent of them? Barnes (1986) shows that a lively controversy between the Skeptics and the Stoics ensued on this matter, originally raised by the Epicureans. The soul is composed of very fine atoms. The ethics of Epicurus stress the goodness of the state of pleasure (which often means absence of pain or discomfort); behavior should be directed to achieving this end. The Epicurean school continued into Roman times and died out largely because of a confusion between Epicureanism and sensualism, a confusion Epicurus himself wished to avoid.

Among Epicurus' later Roman supporters we find the poet Horace, the statesman Pliny the Younger, and the poet Lucretius. Lucretius has more to say on psychological matters than is available from the remains of Epicurus, so we shall now consider his long and striking poem *De Rerum Natura (On the Nature of Things)*. Lucretius was born in 99 B.C. and died in 55 B.C. His philosophical views would therefore be known to educated Romans at the time of Christ's ministry. He wrote particularly on the body/soul relationship, sensations, and thinking and volition. On the body/soul relationship Lucretius was quite specific: Both are made of atoms and both are inseparably conjoined; when the one dies, the other dies too. The two are seen at their most undivided in the case of sensation, which involves the joint motion of both soul and body.

On sensation, Lucretius repeated Epicurus, who in his turn modified Democritus. From the surface of all objects it is assumed that emanations—images or "idols"—fly off in all directions. These emanations are filmlike entities that retain the shape and color of the surface in question with much the same accuracy as a mirror reflects the shape and color of a surface. In contrast to Democritus, who believed that the atomic surfaces imprinted themselves on the air, Epicurus and Lucretius believed that the "idols" are transmitted directly through the air and into the eyes. For color to exist, light is necessary, as Aristotle had said; Lucretius elsewhere noted the existence of visual illusions due to distance. Hearing, taste, and smell are likewise due to emanations consisting of atoms of various shapes.

On thought, Lucretius believed that the idols are diffused and scattered everywhere in the atoms of both body and soul. To think of something is to capture an idol that is latently there. Just as we often have to strain our eyes to see something elusive, so we strain our mind to capture the idol we are seeking. From the evocation of an idol in the mind's eye we make responses that are called *voluntary*. Another feature of the idols underlying mental images is that without the competition of idols pouring through the senses, they can combine in strange ways: A man and a horse can combine to form a centaur. Since the senses are most quiescent during sleep, it is during dreams that we have these idol-amalgamations at their most bizarre. Sleep itself is caused by a confusion and irregularity of the body.

We may briefly consider other Roman contributions to psychology. The treatise *Rhetorica ad Herennium (Rhetorics, written to Herennius)* was once ascribed to Cicero (106–43 B.C.) but is probably by an unknown author. We do not know who Herennius was, but the book is a detailed account of techniques of rhetoric and persuasion. It is mainly on the art of preparing and delivering a speech and shows strong Stoic influence; however, in Book III there is a long section on memory, the cultivation of which is supposed to make it easier to learn a speech by heart. The writer begins by distinguishing between natural memory ("that memory which is embedded in our minds, borne simultaneously with thought") and artificial memory, the result of training by the method of loci and other devices. Images of events that are easily pictorialized are more readily formed than images of words. But then the writer asks why mental images should differ so much in the ease with which they are awoken, and he concludes that banal or everyday events are not well remembered whereas events that are "exceptionally base, dishonourable, extraordinary, great, unbelievable or laughable" are the best remembered. Since such events often occur in childhood, childhood memories are particularly strong, and although we do not recall much of what happens to the sun each day, we easily recall a solar eclipse. From this it is inferred that the images to be set up in a mnemonic situation should be vivid and exceptional. Thus the author argues from nature to art. The section on memory in the *Ad Herennium* concludes with an assertion of the opinion that one should practice memorizing in order to train oneself for the delivery of speeches and the oration of poetry.

Quintilian (35–118 A.D.) made the teaching and practice of rhetoric a career. He wrote his *Institutes of Oratory*, a long work, towards the middle and end of his life. What renders Quintilian's work unique to us is his emphasis on the importance of early education—making him perhaps the father of educational psychology—and his further remarks on memory. On education he struck a modern note: He favored learning of the liberal arts, both literary and mathematical; he stressed that the teacher should take account of individual differences in learning ability; he was against corporal punishment; and he saw the function of education as that of producing a good citizen. After discussing education he treated rhetorical techniques after the manner of Cicero, whom he greatly admired. But Book XI, Chap. II, is devoted to memory. Quintilian particularly stressed the importance of order and structure if verbal material is to be memorized.

The Romans, of course, adopted much from the Greeks; even Quintilian recommended that young children learn Greek as well as Latin. Although they were not great innovators in science, they were fine encyclopedists and collators of information. For example, Celsus (25 B.C.–? A.D.) and Galen (131–200 A.D.) collected medical and biological data. Varro (116–27 B.C.), a contemporary of Lucretius and Cicero, wrote books on the language and arts of the ancients. From our point of view, the most notable collection of the Roman period was the *Natural History* of Pliny the Elder (23–79 A.D.). This is a very long work—37 books—and is an attempt to list as many facts as were known about "natural" objects such as animals, plants, rocks, and places. This book formed the basis on which much later zoological and botanical scholarship would be founded and is particularly valuable for its list of drugs used for medical purposes. One such drug, for instance, was taken from the black or white hellebore plant, and we shall see that this was widely employed for psychiatric purposes. Pliny described in detail the dangers of overdose—this we find acceptable—but also remarked that it should not be used on cloudy days—this enters the world of quaint and curious lore. Throughout the *Natural History* we have this mixture of learning and myth. For the historian of psychology, the most interesting books are Books VII to XI. These deal with zoology and often with animal behavior and constitute the natural successors to Aristotle's book on animals. So, again, we find described many instinctive acts such as nest building and bee foraging. In Book X Pliny notes that many creatures have more acute senses than humans; the mixture of fact and fancy is seen in the following quotation: "Eagles have clearer sight, vultures a keener sense of smell, moles acuter hearing—although they are buried in the earth . . . they can overhear people talking and it is actually said that if you speak about them they understand and run away."

We may close this section by noting that the influence of Greek philosophy persisted into late Roman times despite the inroads made by Christianity. In particular, Plotinus (about 205–270 A.D.) presented an extremely complicated philosophy based on a belief that the soul partook of a world-spirit, the One, and thereby influenced the body. Plotinus's psychology is of some interest to the specialist, for in his assertions concerning the interactions of the various levels of the soul, Plotinus came close to distinguishing between conscious and unconscious levels of functioning and to delineating the difference between sensation and perception (H. J. Blumenthal, 1971).

Ancient Physiological Psychology

We turn now to a consideration of what was known about physiological psychology in antiquity: This essentially means that we shall be concerned with the knowledge of the nervous system acquired during that period. The sources are scattered in medical texts, anatomical and physiological texts, and texts of a more philosophical nature. But it should be realized that the period from the early Ionian physicists to 300 A.D. saw the beginnings of real advances in almost every science. The Egyptians and Babylonians had elementary systems of mathematics, but the Greeks, notably Euclid (330?–260? B.C.), who may have been trained by a pupil of Plato, Archimedes (287–212 B.C.), well-known for his mechanical devices, and Apollonius (flourished about 220 B.C.) all added to our knowledge of geometry in particular. Following on from Babylonian records of events in the heavens, a surprisingly detailed astronomy was worked out in which the earth was conceived as being at a center around which revolved the moon, sun, and planets; this theory reached its peak in the system of Ptolemy (flourished about 140 A.D.) and would dominate thinking about the universe until the Renaissance. Nevertheless, at least one Greek astronomer of the time of Euclid, Aristarchus, argued that the earth went round the sun and attempted to measure the distances of the sun and moon from the earth. Eratosthenes of Alexandria (276?–194? B.C.) tried to measure the size of the earth, which he conceived of as round. Both he and, later, Ptolemy and Strabo (born 63 B.C.) did much to extend our knowledge of geography. An excellent short history of science in ancient times is given by C. Singer (1959).

The first studies of the human body were made by the Egyptians and Babylonians, both of whom have left texts on the subject. But it is to the early schools of medicine in the Greek world that we are indebted for the beginnings of modern physiology and anatomy. From the Homeric period we have the name of Asclepios, probably a real figure later deified. Ill people frequently retreated to temples devoted to Asclepios, and there were such temples at Athens and also on the island of Cos—the latter is important because it was here that the first major figure of classical medicine, Hippocrates (about 400 B.C.), taught his pupils. Many writings were left by the school of Cos, but they are usually described as the Hippocratic collection. Some indication of the scope of the interests of the group may be given by considering the subjects of those works thought of as written by Hippocrates himself: They deal with ancient medicine, "airs, waters, and places," prognosis, regimen, epidemics, head injuries, surgery, fractures, joints, ulcers, fistulae, hemorrhoids, and epilepsy. Of these works the most interesting to psychologists is that on epilepsy, *On the Sacred Disease.* Here Hippocrates takes to task those who believe that epilepsy is the result of visitation from a devil or an evil spirit and argues that it is a malady of the brain. In so doing he makes it clear that he conceives of the brain as the center of mental activity. Hippocrates is also known for putting forward the theory that to the four elements there correspond four bodily fluids or "humors": Blood corresponds to fire; phlegm, to water; black bile, to earth; and yellow bile, to air. But this doctrine was first expounded in a book by Hippocrates' son-in-law, Polybius: Its title is *On the Nature of Man.* This doctrine was mixed by later writers with another notion put forward by Aristotle, probably not original with him: It is argued that there are four primary and opposite basic qualities, hot/cold and wet/dry. According to Singer (1957, p. 27) these qualities were related to the four elements (and thereby the four humors) as follows: Fire was hot and dry, water was cold and wet, earth was dry and cold, and air was hot and wet. From now on, illnesses would be characterized as caused by imbalances in the four humors that could be treated by letting the fluids out (e.g., by bloodletting) or by medications possessing the characteristics of any humors that were lacking. These views persisted in medicine until the seventeenth century.

The great transition to a more modern point of view came with the anatomists of Alexandria, notably Herophilus (about 270 B.C.), Erasistratus (about 260 B.C.), and, later, Rufus of Ephesus (flourished about 98–117 A.D.). Probably Herophilus was the first to dissect the *human* body, and some believe that the kings of Egypt gave him criminals to dissect alive; up to then the Greeks had a great reverence for corpses and found the idea of dissection impious. We have no writings of Herophilus or Erasistratus extant, but from the later writer Galen we learn of their discoveries (incidentally, Galen was rather inimical to Erasistratus). Herophilus was the first to realize the importance of nerves. Up till then the nerves, because of their whitish appearance, had been confused with bone marrow or, more often later, with tendons. Herophilus, however, treated them as a separate kind of tissue and suggested that they were of two kinds, motor and sensory. Only in the nineteenth century would his surmise be confirmed. He also distinguished between arteries and veins, thus paving the way for Harvey. Like physiologists throughout the later ancient and medieval periods he was struck by the presence of the ventricles in the human brain and exaggerated their importance. The ventricles are hollows in the middle and base of the brain—easily visible if you look at a section through a preserved brain—that are filled with cerebrospinal fluid. This fluid is believed to be important in the brain's metabolism and in cushioning the brain from shock. But Herophilus thought the ventricles were the seat of the soul. He noticed that nerves led away from the brain and considered that they were hollow and contained a special form of *pneuma* called "animal spirits." This theory would dominate thinking until the eighteenth century. Erasistratus continued with these ideas but elaborated them into a more complete picture. He thought of air as being taken in by the lungs and going to the heart where it was changed to what we might call *pneuma* type I—"vital spirit." This was propagated via the blood in the arteries all over the body but particularly to the brain. Here it was changed to *pneuma* type II—"animal spirit"—which was then propagated down hollow nerves to the muscles. When one flexed a muscle, the animal spirits filled the muscle and caused it to expand, causing the typical bulge one sees. Again, this notion that muscular "contraction" consisted of a muscle's being blown up like a balloon with animal spirits would persist until the eighteenth century. According to Erasistratus the working of the nerves could be adversely affected by abnormal conditions of the four humors. Erasistratus is also famous for guessing that the blood vessels got thinner and thinner as they moved away from the heart until eventually they became invisible—that is, he guessed at the existence of capillaries. Later, Harvey was also obliged to speculate on their existence and it was only with the invention of the microscope that the "missing link" in the circulatory system would be authenticated. For convenience, a diagram comparing Erasistratus's theory with modern theory is shown in Figure 1–4. Later, Rufus of Ephesus would demonstrate that the nerves, the brain, and the spinal cord formed one anatomical entity; he also described the structure of the eye in detail. Extracts from Rufus and from Galen on these anatomists will be found in English translation in Clarke and O'Malley (1968). The story of how philosophers and physiologists interacted or disagreed in their accounts of the nervous system is told by Solmsen (1961).

The next great physician of antiquity was Galen (about 130–200 A.D.). Galen wrote over a hundred treatises on medical matters in Greek (in some cases, where the original Greek has been lost, we have Arabic translations available); of these only a few have been translated into English. Notably these include *On Anatomical Procedures, On the Natural Faculties, On the Usefulness of the Parts of the Body,* and *The Diagnosis and Cure of the Soul's Passions.*

In contrast to what we know of Erasistratus's theory, Galen began his account of the vascular system by assuming that when food is ingested, it is turned into *chyle.* By chyle we mean the milk-colored substance that is found in the small intestine after the vessels there have absorbed fat from the foodstuff. The liver, according to Galen, then turns the chyle into blood plus natural spirit, a new kind of *pneuma.* The blood and natural spirit are then transported by veins to the right side of the heart; here some of the "impure" fluid is exhaled through the lung and the artery leading to the lung (pulmonary artery is the modern term) while the purer part of blood and natural spirit are transferred through a hole to the left side of the heart. (One of the reasons Galen's physiology was abandoned in the seventeenth century was that anatomists showed there was no hole in the thick membrane dividing the left from the right side of the heart.) Here the blood and natural spirit were joined by *pneuma* breathed in from the air through the windpipe and pulmonary vein (modern term). From this combination is formed vital spirit, a kind of *pneuma* that had been suggested by Erasistratus. This vital spirit is then transferred by the blood, through the arteries, to a network of blood vessels at the base of the brain known as the *rete mirabile.* The brain here changes the vital spirit into animal spirit, a third kind of *pneuma.* This is sent down hollow nerves to swell the muscles. Galen also thought that *pneuma* from the external world could go directly into the brain by being inhaled through the nose and into the olfactory region of the brain. The rete mirabile is actually found only in certain animals, not in humans, and this is typical of an error frequently found in Galen, namely that he based his theories on animal rather than human dissection. Most of his research was carried out on living or dead animals, and there are several

I. THE MODERN VIEW

NERVOUS SYSTEM

STIMULI ⟶ sensory ⟶ chemical ⟶ blood supplies ⟶ chemical ⟶ muscles
receptors   propagation   central nervous   propagation   contract
excited   of sensory   system   of motor
             nerve impulses   nerve impulses

CIRCULATORY SYSTEM

blood oxygenated ⟶ left auricle ⟶ left ventricle ⟶ arteries ⟶ capillaries ⟶ veins
                                                                            ↓
lungs ⟵ right ventricle   right auricle

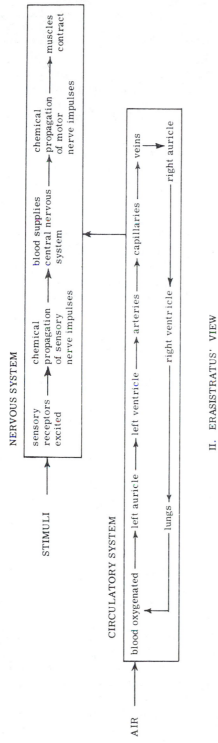

II. ERASISTRATUS' VIEW

NERVOUS SYSTEM

blood and vital ⟶ sent down ⟶ animal spirit
spirit changed   hollow nerves   expands muscles
to animal spirit
in brain

According to
Aristotle, sensing
affects 'pneuma'

BLOOD SYSTEM

AIR ⟶ lungs ⟶ heart, where changed ⟶ vital spirit and ⟶ guessed at ⟶ ?
               to 'vital spirit'   blood in arteries   capillaries

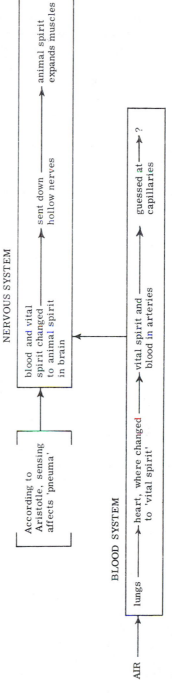

Figure 1–4 Interaction between the Vascular System and the Nervous System: The Modern View and Erasistratus's View.

AIR

41

other examples in his anatomical writings where he is misled on these grounds.

We have seen that the Alexandrians surmised that the brain was the controlling region of the body and that to it came sensory nerves while from it went motor nerves. Galen strongly reaffirmed this view. He tried to distinguish between sensory and motor nerves in terms of their "hardness"—sensory nerves were softer than motor nerves. Modern anatomy shows this to be a vain attempt (Siegel, 1970, p. 159). But his anatomical dissections indicate that he had a fairly good grasp of the way the cranial nerves left and entered the base of the brain. Nowadays we speak of there being twelve cranial nerves; Galen recognized seven pairs (see Siegel, 1970, p. 9, for a table comparing modern with Galenic nomenclature). He performed a number of experiments on the spinal cord showing, both by vivisection and clinical studies, that sensation and movement in various parts of the body depended on the cord's being intact. In another experiment he showed that by squeezing a thread round the nerve leading to the larynx, he could "shut off" sound production in the larynx. He clearly distinguished, as earlier investigations had not, among nerves, ligaments, and tendons. He was aware of the vagus nerve and followed its course in detail and castigated Aristotle for thinking that the brain was merely a blood-cooling agent. Like Herophilus, Galen imagined that the ventricles were particularly important in cerebral functioning. Galen's contributions to neurology are mainly concerned with the cord and base parts of the brain; he said little about cerebral localization, a topic that would only come to the fore in the nineteenth century. He also wrote much on the anatomy of the sense organs (Siegel, 1970). A detailed modern account of Galen's neurophysiology is given by Siegel (1973).

On more psychological matters, Galen talked about differences between individuals in terms of either the four humors or the four primary qualities. One's personality was determined by how much of a particular humor one had, but in addition each humor partook of the primary qualities as follows: Blood was warm and moist, phlegm was cold and moist, yellow bile was warm and dry, and black bile was cold and dry. Persons with a superfluity of blood were known as sanguine, those with excess of phlegm were phlegmatic, those with excess of yellow bile were choleric, and those with excess of black bile were melancholic. In *modern* parlance, such as Eysenck (1964) describes, the sanguine and phlegmatic types are essentially stable, the sanguine more extroverted and the phlegmatic more introverted; the choleric and melancholic are less stable and more volatile, with the choleric tending to anger and the melancholic to depression. But for Galen matters were actually more complicated because, as Siegel (1973, Chap. 3) describes, individual organs within the individual could have different balances of moist/dry and warm/cold; and Galen, as well as other ancient writers, paid far more attention to the melancholic type than to the other types. Not only was an increased propensity to mental illness ascribed to the melancholic person with his excess of black bile, but so also were artistic sensitivity, intelligence, and statesmanship. Later writers, right down to the Renaissance, elaborated on these schemes; according to Irwin (1947) the allotment of moist/dry and warm/cold to the temperaments was not always consistent from author to author.

Galen's book *The Diagnosis and Cure of the Soul's Passions* is mainly an attempt to persuade readers that self-control is vital to happiness, a Stoic ideal that Galen arrived at from seeing the contrast between his dispassionate father and his highly strung mother. But in this work he divides the "passions," or emotions, into two main kinds, the *irascible*, concerned with anger or frustration, and the *concupiscible*, those in which the subject has a strong desire for food, sex, or other bodily pleasures. This distinction arises from a passage in Plato's *Republic* (section 440A) in which it is argued that there are three principles in the soul, a concupiscent principle representing nutritional and sensual desires, a passionate principle that is felt if a desire is frustrasted, and a reason controlling both. Often reason and irascible passion work together, because reason can make a person object, say, to being mistreated, and irascible passion will then be evoked in a rebellion against this mistreatment. Plato's distinction between the irascible and the concupiscent was propagated via Galen into Christian psychology, the topic of our next chapter.

Galen also wrote extensively on the soul, including discussions of attempts to link reason with the brain, the irascible passion to the heart, and the concupiscent principle (for nutrition, reproduction) to the liver (Siegel, 1973, pp. 126–130). He formulated the idea that after messages from the five senses reached the "common sense," Aristotle's device for correlating the information from the senses, these data were then changed into a form more suitable for use in the processes of thinking. The Greek word for this new form was *phantasia*, which Siegel (1973, p. 150) translates as "sense data." Galen also wrote on dreams, abnormal sense perceptions such as illusions and hallucinations, and mental illness generally. He seems to have made little systematic attempt to localize different psychological functions in different parts of the brain or ventricles.

Summary

Although the ancient peoples of the Near East were acquainted with mental illness and had complex notions about the "soul," the first writings concerned with psychology as we normally think of it were produced by the Greeks. The pre-Socratic philosophers had a number of suggestions to make about the nature of the mind, and Alcmaeon, Empedocles, and Democritus wrote on the nature of sensation and perception. In classical Greece, Plato also wrote on the senses and contributed to the study of memory. Aristotle's contributions to psychology, which were in part based on his physiology and philosophy, included an extensive discussion in his *De Anima* of the nature of the soul; discussions of sensation, including the notion that a "common sense" combines messages from the separate senses; a book on memory that includes three famous laws of association; studies of instinctive behavior in animals; and discussion of the roles of heredity and environment.

During the Hellenistic period, both Stoic and Epicurean philosophers offered scattered writings on psychology. In Roman times Lucretius gave a detailed theory of sensation and the texts *Ad Herennium* and Quintilian's *Institutes of Oratory* had much to say on memorization, including discussions of mnemonic systems.

Hippocrates offered a theory of "humors" and argued that epilepsy was a brain disease. Nevertheless, other authors ascribed the seat of intellect to the heart. The transition to the modern view came with Herophilus and Erasistratus, who offered theories of how the nervous system interacted with the circulatory system. These were in turn revised by the Roman author Galen. Galen also elaborated the humoral theory into a theory of personality.

Early Christian and
Medieval Psychology 2

The Church Fathers

According to Bainton (1967, p. 109) Plotinus and other adherents of the old Greek philosophies were not friendly towards the new religion of Christianity which, in the previous two hundred or so years, had spread from the area we now know as Israel to most parts of the Roman Empire. But the attacks of the neo-Platonic philosophers did little to harm Christianity, for in the Christian world had arisen many writers whose main concern was with defending the Christian faith against attack. To the extent that Christianity became an official religion of the Roman Empire in the fourth century A.D., Christianity was more successful than was any other philosophy; however, it must be realized that between the time of Jesus and that of Constantine persecution of the Christians was a steady and persistent device whereby the emperors tried to stamp out the new faith. It is probable that many people were converted to Christianity because of their admiration for the courage of the adherents of Christianity in the face of torture and execution.

Most histories of Christianity say little about the writings of the Church Fathers, as they came to be known. The most famous was St. Augustine (354–430), but many earlier Christian philosophers paved the way for him. Their writings mainly consist of attempts to clarify aspects of Christian dogma or ritual in the face of heresies; defenses of Christianity against philosophy or the pagan religions of the Empire; and, what is of most interest to us, attempts to place Christianity into a broader context of philosophy generally. Among the earliest such writers were St. Justin Martyr and Irenaeus; later writers include, in approximately chronological order, Clement of Alexandria, Tertullian, Origen, Hippolytus, Gregory, Thaumaturgus, Arnobius, Lactantius, Athanasius, Nemesius, and Gregory of Nyssa. Figure 2–1 charts these various authors in time and in relation to Plotinus and St. Augustine. Much of our knowledge of these writers comes from two early historians of Christianity, Eusebius and St. Jerome; the latter also translated the Greek Bible into Latin. A key date in the early Christian period was 325, when a Council of the Church was held at Nicaea, near what is now Istanbul. At this Nicene council it was agreed that the concept of the Trinity should be adopted, according to which God (the Father), Jesus (the Son), and the Holy Spirit (the word *pneuma* is used here) should be seen as three Persons or Entities in One. This effectively countered such heresies as Gnosticism (which stressed the divine nature of Jesus and denied him even a human nature) and Arianism (which stressed the human nature of Jesus at the expense of his Divinity). It may also have pulled together the

Figure 2–1   The Chronological Relationships of the Major Early Christian Writers to Each Other.

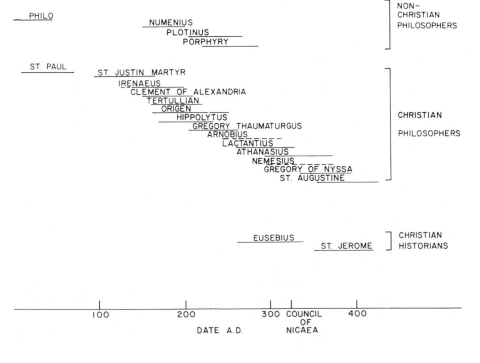

Hebrew tradition of one god, Jehovah, with the Greek tradition that there were many gods. It is thus customary to divide the Fathers of the Church into those who were Ante-Nicene, Nicene, and Post-Nicene. In the late nineteenth century a fairly complete collection of the writings of the Fathers was translated into English in two works of several volumes each entitled *The Ante-Nicene Fathers* and *The Nicene and Post-Nicene Fathers,* respectively. In what follows, with occasional exceptions, references will be made to these texts in abbreviated form. For example, "ANF, VII, 162" means "The Ante-Nicene Fathers, volume VII, p. 162." The full reference is given under the names of the editors, Roberts and Donaldson (1885–1896).

Christianity represents a world view that may be called transcendental as opposed to naturalistic (Kantor, 1963). It assumes that humans, by virtue of possessing a soul, are on a different plane from animals; it assumes that God can intervene directly in human affairs; and it assumes that a study of the body is insufficient for a study of the mind or soul, which is presumed to be immortal and immaterial. How did the Church Fathers deal with these topics?

First, what was Christianity's view of the relation between humanity and the animals? Aristotle, we have seen, stressed that humanity was superior to the animals only by virtue of having reason. Was this also the view of the Church Fathers? To some extent, yes; nearly all stress that reason is what makes humans dominant over the beast. Origen argued indeed that humans were similar to the beasts in having both a body and a soul (Origen, *On First Principles,* p. 11); and Arnobius (ANF, VI, 441) stressed how humans and animals had many physiological mechanisms in common. On the other hand, humans are different from animals insofar as they have something of God in them (as the Bible says, made in God's "image," although most theologians agreed that this refers not to bodily form but to modes of thought). So, for example, Lactantius (ANF, VII, 288) considered that humans walk erect in order that they may contemplate God's work in the heavens. Nemesius (in Telfer's edition of *Of the Nature of Man,* p. 244) thought that humans differ from animals in having the emotion of repentance over wrong deeds, thus allowing them to appreciate the sacrifice of Jesus in a way no animal can. And for Gregory of Nyssa (NPNF, V, 405) humans stand on a level between God and the animals.

On the question of the human soul versus the animal soul, there is some mild disagreement among the authors, which in turn hinges on their various definitions of *soul* and of related terms such as *mind* and *spirit.* For Lactantius, for example, the animal has a soul but it merely instills life into the animal; the human's soul, on the other hand, is immortal. Athanasius said much the same thing. Almost all the theologians follow Genesis in believing that God first created the animals and then later formed humans by "breathing" life into clay. An interesting side issue that results from this belief is discussed by Tertullian (ANF, III, 212): A human soul is so different from that of animals that Plato's notion that a human soul after death can enter into an animal becomes preposterous. To summarize, humans have much in common with animals but are different because they possess a "soul" such that they and only they can appreciate both the greatness of God and the goodness of Jesus' sacrifice. Such an attitude can only lead to a concentration on humans rather than animals.

The second transcendental assumption is that God can intervene directly into the lives of humans, thus making causal accounts of behavior that do *not* include Divine intervention incomplete. Since the very life of Jesus itself is held to be of this kind, the assumption is taken for granted by most of the Church Fathers. Jesus' miracles are held to be manifestations of the truth of Christianity; and it is recognized that God may instruct humans by way of visions and dreams. There is a legend that Constantine was converted to Christianity by a vision, as was St. Paul. The importance of revelation as a source of knowledge becomes a major issue, however, later in Christianity, with Aquinas and others.

The third transcendental assumption is that a study of the body is not adequate for a study of the mind or the soul: Mind is not just an epiphenomenon of brain. On this matter, there are a variety of opinions on the parts of the Church Fathers, but the common ground between them is their reliance on the Scriptures. Again Gregory of Nyssa puts the matter in perspective for us: In NPNF, V, 394, he points out that St. Mark's Gospel urges us to love God with "heart and soul and mind," and St. Paul, in his first letter to the Thessalonians, prays that their "body and soul and spirit" may be preserved at the "coming of the Lord." Thus we have a trichotomy of body/heart, soul, and spirit/mind. For Gregory, the body was the nutritive part of humans, the soul is the sensitive part, and the spirit is the intellectual part by which God is known.

But not all authors agreed with this. Tertullian, for example, thought of soul as being *above* the mind. It is the soul that puts opinions into the mind and not the other way round (ANF, III, 195). On the relationship between soul and body there was also some diversity of belief. For Tertullian the soul is corporeal, breathed into the body at the moment of *conception* (ANF, III, 207).

Still others believed the soul entered the body at the moment of birth, and there was a controversy between a Christian school centered at Alexandria, which said the soul entered the body at conception, and one centered at Antioch (in Turkey), which said the soul entered the body at birth. A church council was held at Ephesus in 431 to debate the matter; the school of Antioch lost, and their leader Nestorius and his followers seceded from the Church. We shall say more on this later. Apart from these two schools, Gregory Thaumaturgas wrote an invaluable short text, *On the Subject of the Soul* (ANF, VI, 54–56), in which he stressed that the soul itself is incorporeal, without color, quantity, or shape. Another problem concerns the question of whether a soul needs a body: Lactantius, for example, felt that blood nourishes the soul, and Tertullian stressed that souls can sense; the cliche that the body dies but the soul survives becomes tricky to maintain if you believe that the soul feels pain in Hell—how, if it does not have a body? All these matters are discussed at length by the Church Fathers.

Since this is not a book on theology, we shall summarize by saying that although the words *body, soul, mind,* and *spirit* are *used* casually by most of us, they offered serious problems of interpretation to the Church Fathers. But all concurred in saying that *something* survives death, be it the soul or the spirit. A much more detailed account of these early views is given in Brett (1912). Insofar as the Christians stressed the immortality of the soul, they were against Aristotle's more restricted view as expounded in his *De Anima* (Hippolytus, ANF, V, 102), but we shall see shortly that later Christians also absorbed much of Aristotle's psychology into their theological system. The innovations of the Church Fathers were not restricted to these issues, however. In many respects they showed particular individuality and insight on certain psychological matters. In particular, they had opinions on the *tabula rasa* question and on physiology, which may be specially mentioned here.

The question of what was contained in the soul—what concepts, what memories—also has a history going back to Plato. Plato had considered the soul, at birth, to contain memories ("reminiscences") of previous existences and in the *Meno* had shown how to bring out certain intuitive logical concepts by judicious questioning. He had also believed that the soul was immortal and that each person partook of the Creator-God, the Demiurge. The Christians on the other hand believed each soul to be unique to each person. Its survival—or fate—after bodily death hinged on the person's acknowledging the grace of God and the sacrifice of Christ. It was therefore necessary to attack the Platonic notion of the soul. Several theologians offered cogent arguments against the doctrine of the transmigration of souls (e.g., Irenaeus, ANF, I, 409; Tertullian, ANF, III, 207; Nemesius, p. 288).

One writer, Arnobius, was concerned to show that the Platonic elevation of humanity as a reflection of the Demiurge is wrong because humans, since the fall of Adam, have been lonely humble creatures not far removed from the beasts and whose immortality is bequeathed only by Jehovah's grace. In his work *Against the Heathen* he attacked various pagan beliefs—partly by referring to the miracles of Jesus and the failure of Jupiter and the Roman deities to produce similar miracles—but in Book II he was particularly concerned with attacking Plato's semi-deification of humankind. For example, he argued that no abstract knowledge is inborn: At birth the soul is a *tabula rasa*. To support this point, he suggested a controlled experiment in which a newborn human baby is reared from birth with no contact with other humans. That such a child would have little or no knowledge of language, fashion, or custom had already been suggested by a story—reported by the Greek historian Herodotus— that a certain king of Egypt had in fact reared a child in this way. But Arnobius is more detailed on the matter. He describes how the child should be brought up in a quiet cave with controlled temperature and with a constant cycle of light and darkness. A child is allowed to grow in this controlled environment until he is forty, being fed with the minimum of accessory sensory information and with always the same food. Will such a person, when asked questions at the age of forty, not "stand speechless, with less wit and sense than any beast, block or stone?" Only by learning and education are humans capable of rising above the beasts, and indeed, in some respects beasts are superior to humans, as when a bird seems innately to know how to build a nest. Arnobius, then, in order to prove humanity's need of grace, stressed its helplessness, its lack of innate knowledge of how to cope.

On the physiology of the body, the Church Fathers—with certain exceptions—were not particularly prolific. But Tertullian, Lactantius, Nemesius, and Gregory of Nyssa all felt that the body influenced the soul and should therefore be discussed. Tertullian (ANF, III, 230) referred to the animal spirits as the body's "charioteer," controlling movement by the soul. Lactantius (ANF, VII, 289 ff.) stressed how the mind along with the five senses is involved in perception. Being the creation of a perfect God, the senses do not deceive us: All perceptions result from the interaction of the senses and the soul and the mind. Illusions such as double vision result when the mind is "impaired by poison and the powerful influence of wine." There is a long account of the "beauty" of the body, including mention of the idea that our having two eyes, ears, nostrils, and so on is because the brain is divided into two parts. The "mind" is placed in the brain rather than the heart. Nemesius had an exceptionally detailed description of the physiology of the whole body, but he added little to what Galen had already said. Imagination is localized in the front part of the brain, the intellect in the middle of the brain, and the memory in the hindmost part of the brain. He followed Galen in asserting that sensory nerves are soft and motor nerves hard; he had a historically valuable account of theories of blood flow in ancient times and concludes that Galen's system is essentially correct. Like Galen, he believed the body to be, in its turn, compounded of the four Greek elements. An explicit distinction is made between voluntary and involuntary movement.

Finally, Gregory of Nyssa stressed the bodily components entering into disturbances of the "soul," as in dreams and fever. He likened *sensations*—not memory—to a stamping of impressions on a surface. Dreams result from the operation of the irrational part of the soul while the senses are at rest; the exception is that some dreams, as described in the Bible, are of divine origin (see also Lactantius, ANF VII, 298).

The reader will probably feel that these accounts of physiology add little to what Galen said, and this is probably a fairly accurate impression. Quite often when reading the Church Fathers we come across statements to the effect that many details of how the body works and of what the universe is constructed are deliberately kept secret from humans by God (see, e.g., Arnobius, ANF, VI, 457). That Christianity encouraged contemplation rather than experiment and observation is a notion sporadically foreshadowed in the writings of the Church Fathers.

St. Augustine

In many ways, the writings of St. Augustine can be seen as the culmination of the attempts to link together the secular thoughts of the great philosophers and the new beliefs of Christianity with their emphasis on Jehovah's grace and the saving power of Jesus. St. Augustine's early life, as described in his *Confessions* (1886, 35–207), shows him as a person of great ability and ambition: He was of strong intellectual bent but at the same time deeply concerned with attaining things of the world, such as a position of respectability and a socially valuable marriage. He was educated near Carthage in North Africa but in his late twenties went to Rome and thence to Milan in pursuit of a career in rhetoric, a skill we have already seen was highly valued in antiquity. But, partly at the urging of his mother (who was later canonized as Saint Monica), partly because of his dissatisfaction with a certain Persian religion of which he was at one time an adherent (Manichaeanism), he was led to contemplate Christianity seriously. His conversion to Christianity came when he realized that his previous concentration on earthly things was vain and unlikely to lead to happiness. He then studied Christianity and, following his conversion, wrote about it. Eventually he was made Bishop of Hippo, near Carthage, to which he had returned from Rome. His later years were filled with exemplary activity in both pastoral and exegetical matters.

St. Augustine's psychology is widely scattered and has to be teased out from the mass of his writings. All his comments on mental activity are subservient to his pedagogical purpose of instruction in Christian thinking. Here are some of the ways in which he concurs with, but also adds to, those writings of the earlier Fathers on the same subjects. On the relation between humans and animals, St. Augustine was explicit: Humans have a faculty of reason that can understand, to some extent, its own workings and can be used to contemplate God; animals do not have this. This faculty is part of the soul—"that soul, I mean, by which, as men, we differ from the brutes" (1888, 263). This soul is immortal because it is unchangeable (*On the Immortality of the Soul,* in Oates, 1948). An attractive way in which St. Augustine distinguished humans not only from animals but also from inanimate objects was to say that an inanimate object such as a stone *is;* an animal or a plant *lives;* but a person is, lives, *and* understands (1964, p. 40; 1887, p. 484 ff.).

On the question of whether "mind" is just an epiphenomenon of brain, St. Augustine said little, nor had he much to say on the physiology of the body generally. Nevertheless, he recognized that the "soul," or "mind," is influenced by the body, as in dreams or abnormal states of consciousness, and the soul itself can influence the body in its turn. The two-way flow of influences is exemplified in the following example: Too much bile can make a person irritable; on the other hand, a person made irritable by external events will himself create more bile. St. Augustine gave this Galenic account in a letter in which he answered a friend's query concerning the origin of certain dreams (1886, p. 227). Finally, St. Augustine also agreed with not only the Church Fathers, but also Aristotle, in maintaining that to the five senses there is added a sixth element, a "common sense," which he termed an "inner sense." The inner sense makes judgments about sensory information from the five outer senses; reason makes judgments on the contents of the inner sense. But, in turn, God is more "excellent" than reason. St. Augustine's emphasis on the inner sense thus served a religious rather than a physiological goal (1964, p. 46 ff.).

St. Augustine divided the faculties of the soul into three: memory, understanding, and will. For St. Augustine, memory constituted a marvel of God's creation. In the *Confessions* (1886, p. 145 ff.) he says how he will soar above the power of the senses, "ascending by degrees unto Him who made me. And I enter the fields and roomy chamber of memory where are the treasures of countless images, imported into it from all manner of things by the senses. . . ." In this ecstatic vein he goes on to describe how these images are deposited there by the senses; how he can search and call up an image as he wishes; how memory contains not only recollections of things sensed and experienced but also literary, mathematical, and emotional concepts; how forgetting is a versatile and flexible phenomenon, allowing us to pass over the unimportant; and, how we can exercise memory in such a way as to learn that which will be fruitful in a happy life devoted to God. He also asked the difficult question of how much we can know about God when all we have to go on is what our memory contains (on this, see Mora, 1978). Perhaps to a greater extent than his predecessors St. Augustine took account of the fact that mental life can be described as a sequence of memory images experienced either spontaneously or as the result of a conscious search; but it is not only in the *Confessions* that we find St. Augustine's most interesting remarks on memory. In his *Homilies on the Gospel of St. John* (1887, p. 155), St. Augustine likened the experience of a recollection of a visual experience to the perceiving of an external object: The only difference is that the former resided in memory prior to the experience. He also grappled with the question of whether *all* our memories must be in image form (1886, p. 223).

On the matter of the understanding, we may mention again that it distinguishes humans from the animals, and it can contemplate *itself*. St. Augustine, however, often gives the impression that within the broad category of understanding he distinguishes between the *inner sense* and *reason,* which operates on the inner sense. Through reason we can acquire certain concepts not directly given by the senses, notably the concepts of *number* and of *wisdom.* Higher even than these is the concept of *truth.* Since wisdom and truth are concepts inseparable from the contemplation of God, the understanding, which gave rise to them, is the part of the mind whereby we are in contact with Him. These matters are discussed particularly in St. Augustine's treatise *On Free Choice of the Will.*

On will itself, we cross the dividing line between psychology and theology. For St. Augustine the will was probably the most important "faculty" of the mind, for the following reason. We assume that God created the world, is all-knowing, all-powerful, and good. But evil exists. As Epicurus put it, if evil exists because God *cannot* destroy it, then He is not all-powerful. If it exists because God wants it to exist, then He is not good. To these we may add that if it exists because God did not know that it would be there when He created the world, then He is not all-knowing. All of his life, St. Augustine pondered on these problems. The Manichaean religion had given him an easy answer in saying that good and evil were created together. But when he left Manichaeanism, St. Augustine had to look for a better solution. He found his answer when he realized that evil was not something in itself, but simply the absence of good. When humankind was created, it was created good. But since the "absence of good" exists, men and women must have been created with the ability to do good rather than not good—that is, they must have free will. Free will, in other words, was given in order that people could choose to do the good. This includes electing to accept God and Jesus as they were revealed in the New Testament. Take away free will, and this answer to the problem of evil loses much of its force; hence St. Augustine's emphasis on the will. But he did not try to analyze it in depth. Instead he stressed its importance in maintaining memories and in determining to what we attend in the external world. A good introductory account of the place of the will in St. Augustine's theology is given by Oates (1948) in the foreword to his edition of selected works of the saint. One could perhaps credit St. Augustine with being one of the first to ask questions about selective attention, but some would probably feel this was stretching a point.

But St. Augustine is probably best remembered to psychologists for the observations on psychological experiences contained in his *Confessions*, one of the earliest autobiographies in our possession. In the course of his account Augustine mentioned his experiences as an infant and child: For example, he described himself as having once been a baby who only knew how to suckle, be satisfied with enjoyable things, and cry when injured. Later, he says, he learned to smile and only later still did he become self-aware and able to communicate his desires to others. If they did not accede to his request, he cried further. This simple description of the growth of the infant's control of his environment is matched by modern psychoanalytic and behavioristic accounts, and for this reason St. Augustine is seen as one of the first to write about child psychology.

Augustine also describes his later feelings of grief and melancholy at the death of his mother Monica. Mora (1978, p. 348) calls this an "autobiographical anticipation" of Freud's writing on melancholia. Most important, however, is the fact that the *Confessions* contain extensive self-observation, or *introspection*, as it came later to be called. From this time onward, introspection was recognized as one way in which psychology could be studied, although we shall see that when *experimental* psychology began at the end of the nineteenth century there was considerable disagreement about how useful introspection actually was for understanding, as opposed to describing, psychological events.

Following St. Augustine's death, which coincided roughly with the demise of the Roman Empire, the list of names of intellectuals who wrote on the mind becomes indeed sparse. In fact, we are lucky to have any writings at all from this period, and we owe what we have largely to the foundation of monasteries. The idea of retreating into seclusion and escaping the temptations of life goes back to the Middle East in the second and third centuries; the great founder of the European monastic system was St. Benedict (480–543), who founded the monastery of Monte Cassino near Naples in 529. This was followed by the founding of monasteries in Ireland, where the monks did particularly noble service in preserving ancient manuscripts, and in other countries. Two Christian writers were especially important during the Dark Ages. These were St. Isidore of Seville (560–636), whose encyclopedic *Etymologies* included detailed definitions of words such as *anima* (soul), *spiritus* (spirit), and others (see Sharpe, 1964); and St. John of Damascus (645?–750?), whose *Exposition of the Christian Faith* included detailed discussions of psychological functions. He localized imagination in the anterior ventricle, thought in the mid-ventricle, and memory in the posterior ventricle of the brain; this outline is similar to that of Nemesius. St. John also wrote on the "passions," by which he meant emotions felt at the consideration of something good or bad. The monasteries also preserved the meditations of the non-Christian philosopher Boethius (480–524), who elaborated on Aristotle's ascription of various kinds of mentality to various species.

During the Dark Ages, little more was written on psychology or other disciplines, although a few texts, usually entitled *De Anima*, continued to be produced (Castonguay, 1963). But we should note that Christianity became an increasingly powerful political force during this period, and that Charlemagne (742–814), who crowned himself "Holy Roman Emperor" in 800, employed the English monk, Alcuin, to teach him to read and write and to set up schools in the Empire. But the sequence of Christian writing does not take on new life until about 1200. Before dealing with this period, we must turn to the place where the old Greek and Roman texts continued to be studied and commented on—namely, the Arab Middle East—and discuss Arabic contributions to psychology.

Arabic Psychology

During the early period of the Christian era most of the missionary work, the spreading of the new religion, took place in a westerly and northerly direction from Jerusalem, its founding place. St. Paul and the Apostles took Christianity to Asia Minor, Greece, and Rome; from there it spread out to cover the then Roman Empire, including what are now known as France, Germany, Britain, and North Africa. By the time of Charlemagne most of western Europe was part of the Holy Roman Empire. But Christianity also spread eastward from Jerusalem. By the time of the council of Nicaea (325) there were churches in Syria, Mesopotamia, and even in Persia. Particularly in the Syrian churches, many Greek manuscripts such as those of Aristotle and the Church Fathers were translated into Syriac, a language of the Semitic family, which also includes Arabic and Hebrew.

In 428 occurred the controversy we have already mentioned: whether the soul enters the body at conception or at birth. Nestorius, the Patriarch of Constantinople, who was excommunicated for holding the latter belief (which implied that the Virgin Mary should only be considered the mother of the human body of Christ), migrated with a number of followers to Persia, and this group brought with them certain books of Aristotle, notably his logical works. In particular, their scholarship was focused at the town of Nisibis, and Nestorian missions went out from there to convert the Persians and the neighboring Arabs. At another town, Jundi-Shapur, a hospital and an observatory were founded and here the study of Greek science continued. By the year 762, over a century after Mohammed (569–632) had founded his new religion in Arabia, we have the picture of an active Nestorian church in the area bordering the Persian Gulf, while the Mohammedan Arabs were building a new capital for Islam at the nearby town of Baghdad. The Caliph of Baghdad, Harun-ar-Rashid, attracted scholars from the Nestorian church to his court, and in this way many Greek works of philosophy and medicine were transmitted to the Arab world. A more detailed account of how Greek science passed to the Arabs is given by O'Leary (1949).

The two most important Arabic scholars from the point of view of the history of psychology were Avicenna (Arabic name, Ibn Sina, 980–1037) and Averroes (Ibn Rushd, 1126–1198). In addition, Al-Kindi (died after 873) was probably the first Arabic philosopher to expand in depth on the works of Aristotle and is also noted for his theories of optics, which were to play a key part in medieval studies of vision. In this he was followed by another Arabic physicist, Alhazen (965–1038). Two famous medical men, Rhazes (al-Razi, ?860–930) and Haly Abbas (d. 994), propagated the theories of Galen, including his ideas on animal spirits in the nervous system and his analysis of the humors. More details on Arabic physiology will be found in E. R. Harvey (1975).

Avicenna was probably the most brilliant scholar in the Arab constellation, but in the eleventh century the unity of the Arab world was being somewhat fragmented so that Avicenna, of Persian derivation, spent his life going from court to court, being well paid for his services, but often having to escape retribution from jealous courtiers and others. He wrote an enormous number of books, including works on logic, metaphysics, Moslem theology (which shares many concerns with Christian theology), astronomy, mathematics, politics, linguistics, and other subjects. To psychologists, however, he is best known for the part of his large book *Kitab al-Najat (The Book of Salvation),* which is concerned with the soul; and for his large *Canon* of medicine. An engrossing account of Avicenna's life and work will be found in Afnan (1958); his chapter on the soul has been translated into English by Rahman (1952); and the First Book of the *Canon* has been translated into English by Gruner (1970).

What is striking is that Avicenna's views on the soul are wholly bound up with his views on the body: Thus, in the book on the soul we find a certain amount of physiology, and in the medical work we find much about the human faculties and emotions. We may begin with the *Canon.* After defining the nature of the disciplines of medicine itself, Avicenna describes the four elements and thus discusses the varieties of human temperament, which are influenced by race and climate and show greater "equability" in humans than in animals. If the proportions of these qualities are uneven, we get the "inequable" temperaments, which often require medical treatment. The balance of the four qualities changes with age and Avicenna quotes Galen on this matter. There is then a long section on the four humors, previously discussed by Hippocrates and Galen. One learns from this section the detail with which the ascription of humors to bodily organs was carried out. Then he briefly mentions that we have five external senses (or eight, if, as defined in his book on the soul, the touch-sense is subdivided into four senses: perception of the hot *versus* the cold, the dry *versus* the moist, the hard *versus* the soft, and the rough *versus* the smooth).

On the other hand there are five groups of interior faculties or "internal senses." This term, according to Wolfson (1935), is first found in the works of St. Augustine and other Church Fathers and was immediately adopted by the Arabs, so that by the time Avicenna came to write, this was a standard term. For Avicenna, the five internal senses are: (1) the common sense of Aristotle, sometimes translated as *fantasia:* Avicenna describes this as "that which receives all forms and images perceived by the external senses, and combines them (into one common mental picture)" (Gruener's translation, p. 136). According to the book on the soul, this faculty is located in the forepart of the front ventricles. In the rear part is located (2) the faculty of representation, or *imaginatio,* which preserves the inputs from the five senses after they have been processed by the common sense. In the middle ventricle of the brain is located (3) a faculty known as *cogitativa,* which corresponds roughly with the *cogitation* or *understanding* of earlier writers. Avicenna, however, divides this into different powers, one possessed by animals and one possessed by humans. In animals the power is known as (4) *estimativa;* it is the power that allows an animal to know *instinctively* what stimuli should be approached and what stimuli should be avoided. Thus, the sheep would approach its own lamb and avoid the wolf.

This is something quite new, and we may briefly give the background history of this "estimative" internal sense. According to Wolfson, Aristotle did not deal in depth with instinctive animal responses and patterns of behavior in his *De Anima.* On the other hand, in his *Historia Animalium,* he does mention that animals have a sort of wisdom or sagacity, exemplified, for example, in the building of a nest by a swallow or a web by a spider. Aristotle never really gave this instinctive knowledge a name, but the Arabs had a word, *wahm,* which roughly corresponded to Aristotle's intended meaning. The first to use *wahm* in this way was Al-Farabi (?870–950). Avicenna apparently therefore owes his estimative faculty to earlier Arabic sources, which in turn could be traced to certain passages of Aristotle (on this matter see also Rahman, 1952, pp. 79–83). It is important that we recognize that here, with the estimative faculty, we have the beginnings of a theory of instinctive behavior. What of "innate knowledge" of the good or harm of perceived objects on the part of humans? Avicenna gave this the different name of *cogitativa* or *imaginativa* (not to be confused with *imaginatio,* the second internal sense). In humans this is controlled by the rational soul and, while admitting that it is sometimes less valuable for the preservation of the species than is the animal's estimative power, Avicenna grants that it does something the animal power cannot—namely, combines memories of sense impressions into new conglomerates, such as an "emerald mountain" or a "flying man." As mentioned earlier, both the estimative and cogitative faculties were located in the middle ventricle. In the hindmost ventricle is located (5) the fifth internal sense, memory (*memorialis*). This faculty retains the results of the estimative and cogitative faculties and includes both retention and recollection, both storage and retrieval as we might now say.

In his book on the soul, Avicenna dealt with some new problems concerning the highest of human capacities, reason. He introduced a term that ultimately went back to Aristotle and was to be treated further by later writers, namely the notion of an *active,* or *agent, intellect.* This is a new notion to us, but it can be traced back to a passage in Aristotle that received extended treatment from a long line of commentators on *De Anima.* One of the reasons this passage excited so much interest was simply its obscurity, which thus opened it to a variety of interpretations:

> Since in every class of things, as in nature as a whole, we find two factors involved, (1) a matter which is potentially all the particulars in the class, (2) a cause which is productive in the sense that it makes them all (the latter standing to the former as e.g. an art to its material), these distinct elements must likewise be found in the soul.
>
> And in fact mind as we have described it is what it is by virtue of becoming all things, while there is another which is what it is by virtue of making all things: this is a sort of positive state like light; for in a sense light makes potential colours into actual colours. (Book 111, Chap. 5, 430a)

Here Aristotle seems to be arguing that mind is like all other objects in nature, having a potential or possible nature and an actual or "patterned" nature. But his image at the end—of the light shining on a potential color to make it an actual color—seized the imagination of later commentators, who came to think of knowledge, after it had been processed through the chain of the internal senses, as then being transformed by a kind of "mental" light into a more actual form.

The two types of knowledge became known as the *possible* or *potential* intellect, and the *agent* intellect, the latter behaving like the transforming light. But individual commentators had individual opinions, particularly about the relationships of these kinds of intellect to what we now call reason and about the relationship of the active intellect to the nonbodily soul. Some postulated more than two kinds of intellect, and some identified the agent intellect with God or a "first cause" (a few lines, from scattered books of Aristotle, led to this belief). The commentator who did most to distinguish between the potential intellect as laid down by the senses and the agent intellect that is immaterial and Godlike was Alexander of Aphrodisias (d. 211); other commentators criticized and amended Alexander's views. By Avicenna's time the notion had crystallized that an agent intellect was an extra power acting on knowledge after the latter had been laid down in memory. For Avicenna, the agent intellect acted to transmute sensory knowledge into a kind of knowledge that was not "material"—that is, not associated with any body part such as a ventricle—but he actually distinguished the agent intellect from four other types of intellect. The most comprehensive survey of ancient theories of the intellect is by Hamelin (1953); the most useful source in English on the history of the agent intellect from Aristotle to Aquinas is by Fotinis (1979, esp. pp. 320–339).

The second Arabic philosopher of interest in the history of psychology is Averroes. Avicenna had flourished in the Moslem courts of the area around Persia; Averroes worked in southern Spain, which had been under Arab rule from 756 onwards. Although Averroes, unlike Avicenna, left little in the way of medical writings, he left much in the way of commentary on Aristotle. Unfortunately his legacy was double-edged: On the positive side, he was most responsible for bringing the Aristotelean corpus back into the scholarly spotlight in the Western world. On the negative side, he added much to or changed the original meanings of Aristotle, with the result that "Averroism"—seen by Christians as bad for being both Islamic and based on the pagan Aristotle—was severely attacked by the Church in the early thirteenth century.

About Averroes we may first note that in his *Epitome of Aristotle's Parva Naturalia* he commented on Aristotle's treatises on the senses, memory, sleep and waking, and dreams in such a way as to show how Avicenna, Galen, and others had added to Aristotle. He discussed the Avicennian chain of common sense → imagination → cogitation → memory and the localization of these faculties in the ventricles; he pointed out how interdependent the various faculties are. Averroes' comments on the senses add to Aristotle what Galen and others had said on the structure of the eye. But Averroes also put forward the notion, which had been foreshadowed by certain earlier commentators on Aristotle, that the agent intellect could be seen as a power external to the individual, indeed as a power pervading the universe. This almost Godlike agent intellect did not appeal to Christian writers, and it was the great thirteenth-century theologian St. Thomas Aquinas who did most to prevent this Averroistic doctrine from affecting orthodox Christian theology.

Medieval European Writers

We now turn back to Europe. Since the Dark Ages, Europe had become much more unified thanks to the fact that certain kings, following Charlemagne in the ninth century, carried the banner of the Pope throughout a wide area of Europe. The barbarism of the Dark Ages gave way to a more peaceful type of existence usually characterized as "feudal": The peasants would work the fields under the watchful eye of a nobleman, who in return for their produce would protect them with an army of knights. As the monasteries grew rich in land, book, and art treasures partly through the donations of believers, more and more young people joined the Church, probably because it was the only place they could indulge in intellectual activities. (It was also at this time that celibacy became a requirement of priesthood; prior to the eleventh century, many clergy had been married.) In order to train people for the Church, but also for careers in law and medicine, monastic schools were started, and in 1088 a school was founded at Bologna in Northern Italy that specialized in the teaching of both Roman law and church law. This example led to the founding of other schools, first in Italy, then in other countries, which became known as universities. Particularly important examples were the University of Paris (founded in 1160), Oxford (founded in 1190), Cambridge (founded informally in 1209), and Naples (founded in 1224).

At these universities theology was one of the main subjects taught, but so was philosophy, under which were included the theories of the soul. But it must be realized that at the end of the Dark Ages many of the works of Aristotle and of the Arabic scholars were unknown, partly because they had not been translated. The beginning of the rediscovery of Aristotle, through the Arabic legacy, came in 1088 when the Spanish city of Toledo was reconquered by the Christians from the Arabs, and Christian scholars began translating Aristotle from the Arabic into Latin.

The greatest teacher of the thirteenth century was Albertus Magnus (1193?–1280), who brought the new Latin translations of Aristotle to the University of Paris and who was considered the most learned man of his time. It was through meeting Albertus Magnus in Paris that a more famous scholar, St. Thomas Aquinas was to become preoccupied with Greek philosophy. It should be stressed, however, that although Acquinas is usually considered the main thinker of the Middle Ages, other excellent philosophers emerged before or during the thirteenth century. These included Pierre Abelard (1079–1142), whose writings were important in demystifying the notion of a "concept": According to Abelard, if I refer to "Socrates," I am merely using a verbal label with a referent to a real person, I am not naming an entity that has a reality of its own (or is like a Platonic Form).

As one of the most astute commentators on Aristotle's psychology, Albertus Magnus himself played a crucial role in medieval psychology and persuaded the young Aquinas also to study Aristotle. An account of Albertus Magnus's integration of Aristotle's concept of the soul into a Christian framework is given by Craemer-Ruegenberg (in Kovach & Shahan, 1980). Michaud-Quantin (1966) gives the most complete account of the psychology of Albertus Magnus, which is based on the latter's extensive reading of the classical writers as well as the Church Fathers and the Arabs. He attempted to make a synthesis of all these writings and this he transmitted to Aquinas: When we deal with Aquinas's psychology, it must be realized that much of it is an elaboration and commentary on Albertus's synthesis.

Albertus Magnus took over from the Arabs the notion of the flow of information from the common sense through the estimative sense to memory; he also adopted an analysis of the emotions, an analysis that had a checkered history summarized by Michaud-Quantin (1966, p. 85). We recall that Galen, basing his views on the *Republic* of Plato (and probably also *Timaeus*, 70A, 77B), had distinguished between the irascible and concupiscent passions. By the Middle Ages this distinction became confounded with Aristotle's writings on the appetitive part of the soul, which, for Aristotle, gave rise to "desire, passion and wish" as three "species" of a "genus." The essence of desire was to seek what was pleasant (*De Anima*, II, 3, 414b). After disagreements among Christian scholars as to how to analyze the appetites/passions, by the time of Albertus Magnus it became conventional to identify Plato's "concupiscence" with Aristotle's "desire for what was pleasant," and to identify Plato's "irascibility" with the various emotions that were aroused when a concupiscent desire was thwarted in some way. We shall say more on this subject when we come to Aquinas. Michaud-Quantin also points out that Albertus Magnus added to Aristotle in his treatment of the highest powers of the soul: Besides the human powers of practical intellect and voluntary actions corresponding to Aristotle's rational soul, for Albertus Magnus there were also "theological" faculties leading the human to the highest good, God, including an innate knowledge of the basic principles of morality.

Another important influence on medieval cultural history was the founding of various monastic orders. We saw that the Benedictine order, stressing seclusion and isolation from society, had been founded in the Dark Ages, but in 1208 St. Francis founded the Franciscan order, in which the friars took a vow of poverty and begged for the essentials of life in return for giving spiritual counsel. In 1215, a Spaniard, Dominic de Guzman, founded the Dominican order expressly for the establishment of an orthodox theology. This event was to have a doubled-edge effect: On one hand, Aquinas joined the order, as did many other eminent theologians, and the Dominicans became responsible for the preservation of a great deal of scholarship. On the other hand, the Dominicans instituted the Holy Inquisition, a group for suppressing heresy that was feared everywhere because it used torture to extract confessions. Many controversies of the Middle Ages centered around the place of these orders within the Church, and Aquinas played an important part in arguing against those who wished to abolish the begging friars and scholar monks.

Thomas Aquinas (1225–1273) was born to aristocratic parents in

Italy. Schooled at the Benedictine monastery of Monte Cassino, he showed great early talent; he then studied at the University of Naples but astonished his parents and teachers by joining the Dominicans. The Dominicans had set up schools of theology at Paris, Cologne, and Naples, and Thomas Aquinas was sent to Paris, where he met Albertus Magnus; later the two traveled together to Cologne. After they parted, Thomas worked on various theological projects, including the defense of the friars, and wrote various treatises. In 1264, Thomas retired to a Dominican place of study in Naples where for the first time he read Aristotle in Latin translated, not from the Arabic, but from the original Greek. Here he began his great *Summa Theologica*, the main work of his career. In 1268, he went again to Paris, this time to take part in a controversy against the Averroists, but also to counteract a growing trend to accept Aristotle's naturalism and to reject the Christian theology. It was crucial for Aquinas to be able to show that Aristoteleanism and Christianity did not necessarily clash and could be reconciled. It is during this rise of Aristoteleanism, represented by such thinkers as Siger of Brabant, that we may discern the first crack in the theological structures that had dominated European thought for the previous thousand years. After this controversy, Aquinas was given the chair of Theology at Naples, but died shortly afterwards with his *Summa Theologica* still unfinished.

Aquinas's psychology is most clearly put forward in the first and second parts of the *Summa*. This book, like his book on the soul, *De Anima*, adopts a question-and-answer dialectic. We see plainly revealed his reliance on Aristotle for his concept of the relationship between body and soul and for the structure of the soul. To Aristotle, however, he adds many extra remarks on the emotions and on the will. We see at various points the influences of Galen and St. John of Damascus on the subject of the passions (the emotions); on the will Aquinas is influenced by St. Augustine.

It is difficult to extract a comprehensive but simple picture from this wealth of material, but Brennan (1941), in his book *Thomistic Psychology*, makes a fine attempt to do so. The essence of Thomistic psychology is rooted in two basic premises: Everything in the soul is built up from the senses; and the soul, in all its facets, vegetative, sentient, and rational, is indissolubly linked with the body, with the exception of the agent intellect. Not only is this an Aristotelean viewpoint, it is consistent with many more modern and materialistic models of the mind. As Chesterton (1933) points out, Aquinas represents the triumph of good sense in the face of transcendental idealism or bizarre and abstract philosophies. The contents of the mind are in what Aquinas calls the possible intellect, which derives them from the senses by way of the agent intellect. The five outer, or external, senses present material to the common sense, which extracts a datum or percept. The percept is processed by the imagination, the memory, and cogitation (animals, we saw, have the estimative power at this point); the result is a *phantasm*. The agent intellect abstracts the "form" or "nature" of the phantasm and places it in the possible intellect, where it resides as an idea. In one sweep we have Aristotle revised by Avicenna retranslated back into Aristotle. In the *Summa Theologica* (1948) Aquinas clearly acknowledged the contribution of Avicenna and argued against Plato's theory of innate ideas and in favor of Aristotle's *tabula rasa*.

In his discussions of the emotions Aquinas considered that to each emotion is attached a fundamental desire or appetite. Taking his vocabulary from Plato and thence Galen, Aquinas divided appetites based on the senses into two kinds, the *concupiscible* and the *irascible*. The concupiscible appetite is that which desires pleasure of any kind and in particular wants to conserve what is to the good of the individual's existence; the irascible appetite is that which is called into play when the concupiscible appetite is for some reason thwarted. As Brennan (1941, p. 150) puts it, "man and the animals are equipped with sensitive appetites whose objects are the goods of sense. Some of these goods are simply good, and as such are objects of concupiscible appetite. Others are arduously good, and as such are objects of irascible appetite. In the former there is pleasure for pleasure's sake." The avoidance of evil is subsumed under both headings.

Brennan summarizes this standpoint by asserting that the concupiscible appetite for good results in the passions of love, desire, and joy; the concupiscible repugnance for evil results in hatred, aversion, and sorrow. The irascible appetite, when concerned with arduous good, results in hope or despair, depending on the attainability of the good. The irascible appetite confronted with evil gives rise to courage, fear, or anger, depending on the vincibility of the evil. Later (Part I–II, Q. 25, Art. 1) Aquinas asks whether the irascible passions "precede" the concupiscible passions or vice versa. His conclusion is that one frequently begins with a concupiscible desire for a good; it is blocked or prevented from being attained, whence we feel an irascible desire of, say, anger; when the block is removed, we attain the concupiscible passion of joy in the pleasure of obtaining the good object. Long passages deal with the psychology of the various passions such as love, sorrow, and fear. This is perhaps the most systematic approach to the emotions that we have yet encountered and is noteworthy for its emphasis on feelings of pleasure and pain as being the basic substrates of the more global emotions.

Aquinas also wrote much on the will. Like St. Augustine, he considered it necessary that humans be endowed with free will in order to be able to recognize and pursue that which is good. The irascible and the concupiscible are two sensitive appetites, appetites based on feelings; will is an intellectual appetite, following not a particular sensory good but an intellectually derived universal notion of good. Humans differ from animals partly insofar as they can use their will to control their passions to a greater degree than can animals and partly because animals have only an imperfect knowledge of the end of an action and can therefore perform only imperfect voluntary acts. In humans the will is moved by the intellect and by the sensory appetites; Aquinas is at pains to point out that heavenly bodies cannot influence the will directly.

Even Aquinas's staunchest supporters admit that his role was less that of an explorer and more that of a synthesizer, one who pulled together all existing knowledge into a Christian edifice structured on Aristotelian logic. Almost all the writers we have hitherto mentioned are referred to or quoted by Aquinas: We may stress his influence on Catholic psychology by indicating that at least two histories of psychology written in the twentieth century take the position that psychology went astray after Aquinas (Mercier, 1918; Brennan, 1945).

Aquinas, of course, was only one of many eminent intellectuals of the thirteenth century revival of learning. Several of his contemporaries also wrote on psychology but, like the work of Aquinas, much of their theorizing is derived from Aristotle, Avicenna, and other predecessors. Another scholar contemporary of Aquinas and Albertus Magnus, who also joined with them in support of the friars, was St. Bonaventure, who argued that we know God by a sort of innate knowledge not dependent on the senses: Leahey (1987) claims this reflects the tradition of Plato and St. Augustine that was ultimately defeated, in Catholic theology, by the neo-Aristoteleanism of Aquinas.

Another eminent scholar of the time was Duns Scotus (1266–1308). He wrote a book entitled *Concerning Human Knowledge* and another on *The Spirituality and Immortality of the Human Soul.* This latter is heavily Aristotelian but also maintains the imperishability of that part of the soul known as the intellect. In the former work, however, there is a recognition of the existence of illusions. The illusion that a stick is bent if it is placed in water is recognized as an illusion, claimed Duns Scotus, because the intellect knows that soft substances, such as water, do not break hard substances, such as the stick. According to Duns Scotus, "there is always some proposition to set the mind or intellect aright regarding which acts of the senses are true and which are false" (1962, p. 115). Elsewhere in the same work he argued that people differ in their ability to abstract concepts and principles, a foretaste of later theories of the reasons underlying individual differences in intelligence.

A third great scholar of this period was the English Franciscan friar Roger Bacon (1220–1292). In his *Opus Majus* he gave a detailed account of many aspects of natural science, including astronomy, geography, chemistry, and comparative linguistics. On the thorny question of the agent intellect, he suggested that Aristotle may have been misinterpreted by his commentators. He argued that certain illnesses are of natural rather than demonic origin. His plea for the importance of experiment and mathematics in scientific research is well known and must be mentioned here; however, it led him into trouble with other Church authorities. Bacon's freedom was restricted and his book suppressed. He briefly discussed the nervous system and the brain and adopted Avicenna's ascription of the faculties (including the estimative) to the ventricles. His most original writing, however, concerns optics, and we may briefly describe here important developments in physiological psychology since Galen. The Arabs—notably al-Kindi and Alhazen—had argued that light travels in straight lines and thus enters the eye; the old theory that the eye shot out a ray was largely, though not entirely, abandoned. The main organ for sensation was believed to be the crystalline lens with the other coatings of the eye surrounding the lens, such as the cornea and the sclera, there to "enclose, darken, moisten, and protect" the crystalline lens (Lindberg, 1970). It was known by this time that light rays were refracted when they entered a new medium, though the laws of refraction were not known. It was assumed that only unrefracted rays affected the crystalline lens. Beyond this, however, the rays were believed to be refracted in the vitreous humor and stimulate the optic nerve. Bacon elaborated this theory and is particularly interesting in his accounts of experiments demonstrating double vision (e.g., by pushing one eye or by focusing on a very near object). This he explains as a failure of the optic nerve to combine the stimulations from the two eyes into one impression. Bacon's book was not the only important text on vision and perspective; an archbishop of Canterbury, John Pecham (1230?–1292), drawing partly on Bacon, wrote a book entitled *Perspective Communis* that was used as a source on optics for the next two or three centuries. It has been translated into English by Lindberg (1970). Lindberg (1976) gives a detailed account of theories of vision from the Arabs through the Middle Ages.

We may also mention the Emperor of the Holy Roman Empire, Frederick II (1194–1250). He encouraged learning and culture at his court, although he was accused of certain barbaric experiments such as raising two children without their ever hearing speech in order to discover what language they would first utter. But Frederick II is of interest to psychologists for his own *Art of Falconry*, a large book in which he not only described the training of falcons to hunt but also described the habits and behavior of many species of birds. It is a major work on natural history: An account of it which brings out the relations between medieval training procedures and modern operant conditioning and the modern concept of imprinting has been given by Mountjoy, Bos, Duncan, and Verplank (1969). An inexpensive full-color facsimile of this book is now available (see References, "Frederick II," 1980); it is copiously illustrated with pictures of different species of birds.

Finally we must make special mention of one book on the soul written in the thirteenth century which by virtue of its length and detail constitutes probably the single most useful source on medieval psychology. Its author, Peter of Spain, or Pedro Hispano (1215?–1277), was born in what is now Portugal and became an eminent professor of medicine at the Italian University of Siena. He wrote on eye diseases and anatomy as well as offering commentaries on Hippocrates, Galen, and Aristotle's biological works. Nevertheless, he is best known for his book on logic, the *Summulae Logicales,* and his main contribution to psychology was his text *De Anima* which, in a modern edition, is about five hundred pages long. It is divided into thirteen books. Book 1 is on the nature of the soul. In Book 2 he discusses the Aristotelian division of the soul into vegetative, sensitive, and intellective (rational). Book 3 discusses the functions of the vegetative soul, particularly nutrition, growth and generation. Book 4 is on regimen. Book 5 deals with the vital functions of the heart and breathing. Book 6 is a long treatise on the senses, comprehending discussions of apprehension, abstraction, touch (he distinguishes eighteen kinds of touch experience), taste (there are nine basic taste qualities), smell, vision (with more on color than is usual in early texts), and hearing and speech.

Book 7 discusses the division of the internal senses into the common sense, *imaginatio,* fantasia, estimation, and memory; the latter depends in particular on the moistness of the brain. Book 8 is on the emotions. Book 9 deals with the immortality of the soul. Book 10 discusses the possible and agent intellects and other subdivisions of the intellect. Book 11 is on the will and the passions again, with an interesting section in which mental illnesses are related to exaggerated or deficient emotions. Book 12 is on the organs of the body. Book 13 is on ancient theories of the soul, with particular reference to the pre-Socratic philosophers. The work, although elaborate, is not overwhelmingly original. The year before he died, Pedro Hispano was made Pope John XXI. It is worth recognizing that almost all medieval intellectuals were members of the Church and that their intellectual accomplishments were often the foundation for advancement into senior and responsible positions in the Church hierarchy.

The next two centuries, from 1300 to 1500, offer lean pickings for the historian of psychology. Some late medieval philosophers such as William of Ockham (1290–c. 1349) and Nicholas of Autrecourt (born 1300) stressed, as Abelard had, that thinking is essentially a *psychological* event: When we think of Socrates, it does not imply an ideal form of Socrates exists; when we wish to move our arm, it does not imply an abstract faculty of Will with an existence of its own. There were also some important developments in physics, in which Aristotle's science was challenged by writers such as Jean Buridan (c. 1300–1358) and Nicholas Oresme (1320–1382). The poetry of Dante and Chaucer also dates from the fourteenth century. But otherwise the fourteenth and early fifteenth centuries constituted a period of disasters such as the Black Death and lengthy wars; it saw a revival of old superstitions such as astrology and the belief that certain persons consorted with the devil or were possessed by him. In 1450, however, printing was developed, and many of the classical and thirteenth-century manuscripts were then made available in printed form. Also during the thirteenth century medical schools had been founded in several places in Europe, and medicine was often taught by Jewish doctors. Their teaching was heavily dependent on Galen and Avicenna, but in 1316, Mondino of Bologna wrote an anatomy that was based on dissection of dead humans (usually criminals); an intriguing account of this book is given by C. Singer (1957). But the teachings remained traditional. It is not, for example, until Vesalius's dramatic discoveries of the sixteenth century that the *rete mirabile* will disappear from diagrams of the human brain. It should be stressed, however, that there is a dearth of accounts and translations of medieval psychology in English and that our knowledge of the subject might substantially change as a result of further research.

Summary

Christianity brought a new world-view in which humankind was seen as central in Creation. It was believed that God could intervene directly in human affairs and that the soul is immortal and immaterial and therefore not as closely connected with the body as Aristotle had suggested. The early Church Fathers had varied and sometimes conflicting opinions on these matters, but they were united in their arguments against Plato's belief that one was born with memories from the soul's previous existences: This led Arnobius, for example, to stress that adult behavior is almost entirely a matter of learning. Nemesius followed Galen in many matters but crystallized into Christian thought a simple schema whereby mental faculties were localized in the ventricles of the brain. St. Augustine divided the faculties of the soul into memory, understanding, and will and wrote in some detail on each of these topics. His stress on the will arose directly from his theology, and his *Confessions* represents the start of the modern introspective tradition.

During the Dark Ages in Europe, classical learning was kept alive by the Arabs in the Middle East. Avicenna in particular elaborated Nemesius's localization scheme to include instinctive behavior; the Arabs also developed the notion of an immaterial agent intellect acting to extract and preserve key concepts from the flow of thoughts. Averroes made the intellect a near-divine entity. Among the achievements of medieval scholars such as Albertus Magnus and Aquinas were criticisms of these new notions; therefore, they attempted to rediscover Aristotle in the original. Aquinas's psychology is still built on the Arabic framework, however, but is much more detailed on the interplay of motives and emotions. Other thirteenth-century contributors to psychology included, Duns Scotus, Bacon (particularly important for his emphasis on scientific method and his theory of the eye), Frederick II (who wrote on falconry), and Pedro Hispano, author of a text summarizing medieval psychology. Between 1300 and 1500 there was little original psychology.

The Sixteenth and
Seventeenth Centuries   3

The Sixteenth Century

The period from about 1450 to 1550 is generally known as the Renaissance period, though we have seen that its origin can be traced back to the thirteenth century and may say that some scholars would extend the word *Renaissance* to include the late sixteenth century. There have been many attempts to characterize the Renaissance, that of Kristeller (1961) being perhaps the best known. As a result of the invention of printing and the growth of a wealthy patronage among the merchant classes, the aristocracy, and the clergy, there was an outburst of invention and scholarly activity, reflected in an increasingly large number of books being printed for general circulation. Many works of Aristotle that had not been well known in the Middle Ages were now made available in Latin and some even in the vernacular languages French, German, English, and Italian. Plato, many of whose works had been neglected in the medieval period, was now made more accessible, and editions were printed of the writings of the Romans and of the Church Fathers, which greatly extended the available sources of the thought of antiquity. For example, the works of Lucretius and of Plotinus had been hardly known in the Middle Ages; editions were now made of these authors. As a result of all this activity, separate strands of Aristotelian, Platonic, and Scholastic thought can be seen to influence the philosophers and thinking of the Renaissance period: An excellent account of these separate influences is given by Kristeller. But there is no one single metaphysical system that might be called Renaissance "philosophy." The predominant philosophy of the time in fact was Christianity; what was new about the Renaissance was essentially an attitude rather than a thought system—an attitude that stressed aspects of the person other than that of his or her role as a Christian. A useful word summarizing this attitude is *humanism:* A human is seen in his or her whole aspect, and values are placed on this person's emotions and creative activity that a strict Christian ethos would perhaps treat otherwise, namely, as less important than piety. To some extent this humanism was reinforced by the discovery of the non-Christian classics of pagan antiquity—the plays, the poetry, the rhetoric, and the history of the Greeks and Romans. The slow erosion of the political power of the Church, particularly in the northern countries of Europe, made it easier to be a humanist. Artistic ability gave one license to observe and treat in a naturalistic manner the themes both of Christianity and of classical mythology by an aristocracy desirous of building and preserving a culture by which they would be remembered. Probably the best-known productions of the Renaissance are the great paintings, sculpture, and architecture created in Italy by Michelangelo, Leonardo da Vinci, Raphael, and others sponsored both by the aristocracy and by a wealthy Church.

These great works of art, however, were paid for in part by the sale of indulgences (pieces of paper that "guaranteed" a person less time in Purgatory after death), and the various countries of Europe were separately striving for an independent existence, free from the influence of Rome. Hence it came about that in Germany, Martin Luther (1483–1546) broke away from the Catholic Church and urged the return to simple faith, in which the individual enjoyed a one-to-one relationship with God without need of the intercession of saints or priests; in England, Henry VIII (1491–1547) broke away from the Church for the much less elevated reason that he wished to divorce his wife, Kathleen of Aragon. Henry later dissolved the English monasteries and divided the spoils among his noblemen.

Learning, in fact, was no longer the prerogative of the Catholic clergy, and simultaneously with the Reformation more and more laypeople wrote literature and became interested in science. The universities, however, were still largely dominated by the Church, with the theology faculties firmly in power and enforcing Aristotle and Galen as the main classical authorities. Many of the scientists we will meet in this chapter functioned, as a consequence, outside the university system.

Against this background emerged two scientists of major importance, Vesalius and Copernicus, and many others who through experiment and observation prepared the way for such giants of the seventeenth century as Harvey, Galileo, and Newton. Vesalius (1514–1564) started as a believer in Galen's anatomy but after dissecting both animals and humans for himself, came to disconfirm many of Galen's beliefs. From the point of view of psychology, perhaps his most important achievements were to show that the *rete mirabile* did not exist in humans and to argue that the brain and the nervous system, as opposed to the heart, were the seats of psychological activity. He published his anatomy in 1543 in the magnificent illustrated volume *De Corporis Humani Fabrica (On the Structure of the Human Body)*. It should be observed that Vesalius made a number of errors, but these are minor in comparison with the general accuracy of his anatomical studies. His physiology of the vascular system remained, however, Galenic to a great extent.

Also in 1543 a book appeared in which the monk Copernicus (1473–1543) published, at the very end of his life, his theory that the earth moved in a wide circle round the sun. This theory accounted for many problems raised by the Ptolemaic world system but unfortunately clashed with the views both of Luther and of the Catholic church—namely, that the sun moved round the earth. Later scientists such as Kepler (1571–1630) were able to show that Copernicus's theory was probably correct, particularly if the paths traced by the earth and the planets around the sun were not circles, as Copernicus had thought, but ellipses.

Figure 3–1 Chronological Order in Which Most of the Major Sixteenth-Seventeenth-, and Eighteenth-Century Works on Psychology Were Written.

	PSYCHOLOGICAL WORKS	SCIENTISTS
1500	Vives' *De Anima* 1538	Vesalius
1550	Huarte's *Men's Wits* 1575	Copernicus
		Bruno
1600		Galileo, Kepler
		Harvey
	Descartes' *Discourse* 1657	
1650	Descartes' *Passions* 1650	Willis, Duverney
	Hobbes's *Leviathan* 1651	
	Spinoza's *Ethics* 1677	Newton
	Locke's *Essay* 1692	
1700	Leibniz's *New Essays* written 1700–1705	Swedenborg
	Berkeley on vision 1709	
	Wolff's psychology books 1731–1734	
	Hume's *Treatise* 1737	Haller, Whytt
	Hartley's *Observations* 1749	
1750	Condillac's *Treatise* 1754	
	Reid's works 1764–1788	
	Kant's *Pure Reason* 1781	Lavoisier
	Kant's *Anthropologie* 1798	Cabanis
1800		

Nevertheless Copernicus's book was placed on the list of forbidden books by the Church and so exercised less influence in the sixteenth century than its quality warranted.

Other scientists of some importance in the sixteenth century were Leonardo da Vinci (1452–1519), whose anatomical drawings foreshadowed those of Vesalius; Agricola (1494–1555), the father of mineralogy; Paré (1510–1590), a pioneer of surgery; Mercator, the mapmaker (1512–1594); Gesner (1516–1565), who listed not only all the animals and plants known to him but catalogued all books known to him in Hebrew, Greek, and Latin; Gilbert (1544–1603), a pioneer in magnetism; and Brahe (1546–1601), an astronomer whose observations provided the link among Copernicus, Kepler, and Newton. Nor should we forget the explorers: Columbus (1451–1506) first sighted the beaches of the Bahamas in 1492, and the crew of Magellan (1480–1521) were the first men to sail round the world.

During the sixteenth century several hundred books concerned with psychology were printed. Most of them are only available in certain libraries; only a few gained enough renown for later students of the history of psychology to consider their being worth reissuing or translating in a modern format. However, Schüling (1967) has done a great service by listing most of these sixteenth-century books in a bibliography and the discussion that follows is based mainly on a consideration of this work. First, we may immediately note that Aristotle's *De Anima* was reprinted by many different authors and often with a new commentary; Schüling lists no fewer than forty-six commentaries on *De Anima* written in this century. Naturally, earlier commentaries (such as those of Averroes and Aquinas) were also printed for general use. Commentaries were also written on other classical works such as Aristotle's *De Memoria*, Theophrastus's book on the senses, and Galen's book on the temperaments.

Second, many books appeared on two topics of interest to both psychologists and theologians: the immortality of the soul and the question of free will. As we hinted earlier, this last question was influential in the Reformation, for both Luther and Calvin believed that the fates of our souls in the afterlife were predestined, whereas the Catholic church, basing its reasoning partly on the work of Augustine and Aquinas, held to a belief in free will. Schüling's bibliography lists sixty-nine works with titles indicating that the books dealt with the soul's immortality and forty-eight with titles indicating that the books discussed the question of free will. We shall rest content with simply pointing out that these two questions absorbed many scholars and writers of the sixteenth century.

But, third, many of these sixteenth-century works were original books with a title such as *De Anima* or a variation thereof, such as *De Homine* (on man). Of these, only one has reached any great fame among historians of psychology, and that is the book entitled *De Anima et Vita (On the Soul and on Life)* by Juan Luis Vives (1492–1540). Vives was a Spanish Catholic of Jewish origin who became famous in his time as an educator; he believed particularly in the education of women. During the Middle Ages, women had borne the brunt of a misogyny engendered by a celibate clergy who saw sex as a threat to their mental complacency; even the women who joined the Church (and there were many competent and literate nuns) did not enjoy all the privileges of priests. Sometimes women reacted by joining heretic movements, and sometimes women who allowed their feelings to show were persecuted as witches. But, as Leahey (1987, p. 68) points out, the Middle Ages also saw the birth of the convention that a romantic passion that thoroughly preoccupies one or both parties is a natural state and one to be desired; romantic love, as we think about it in popular song, is a concept that seems to have arisen at this period. The situation of women was still second class at the time of the Renaissance; with the advent of humanism, however, women were permitted to seek higher education, and certain enlightened noblewomen founded schools and colleges. Vives was a friend of Katherine of Aragon and was also acquainted with a coterie of English women of high birth, including the family of the Catholic Sir Thomas More. It was in this environment that Vives wrote a book on the education of women. When Henry VIII divorced Katherine, however, it was no longer safe for Vives to stay in England (and indeed Sir Thomas More was executed, for which he is still remembered with veneration in the Catholic Church). Vives moved with his family to Bruges in Belgium, where he wrote his main work, *De Anima*.

Vives' *De Anima* is divided into three books. The first, which deals with the nature of the soul and with the senses, relies heavily on Aristotle. The five internal senses of the medieval writers are allocated to the ventricles in the usual way. Galen's humoral theory is described. The second book is more original. Dividing his subject matter into memory, understanding, and will—Augustine's classification—he treated each separately. His remarks on memory (translated by Murray and Ross, 1982) are particularly famous: Although he adopted the old theory that retentiveness is in part due to the degree of moisture in the brain, he also argued that it depends on the way the learner organizes the material and that forgetting can occur either because the information is erased or because it is temporarily occluded. In searching for an item, the seeker makes use of various types of association—Vives' list of associative rules is longer than Aristotle's and includes part-whole and cause-effect relationships. He also noted how a trivial sensation or idea can evoke an important idea associated with it: For example, the sight of cherries reminded Vives of a fever he had in childhood, during which he had eaten cherries. The remainder of the second book is concerned with reasoning, will, sleep, and other topics. The third book is mainly an extensive discussion of the emotions. Clements (1967) points out how Vives related emotional experiences to physiological changes, a feature that makes Vives a predecessor of Descartes (see following). It is also customary to think of Vives as the link between Aristotle and later writers on the association of ideas—F. Watson (1915) has called him the father of modern psychology.

A fourth theme of considerable popularity among sixteenth-century writers on psychology was the question of how far one's psychological characteristics were reflected in one's facial features, bodily build, gait, and so on—the so-called art of physiognomy. Closely related to it is the pseudoscience of cheiromancy, or palmistry as it is now known, and books combining physiognomy with cheiromancy were quite common. Among the authors responsible for such works were Cocles (1467–1506), Indagine, who published an introduction to physiognomy, cheiromancy, and astrology in 1522, and Rio (1551–1608), who added dream interpretation to this list. Dream interpretation had been a popular activity ever since the Roman Artemidorus (second century A.D.) had written a highly successful guide to divining the secret meaning of dreams; although these dream guides often asserted that dreams are premonitions of future events, they also agreed with Freud that a dream reflects a feeling or emotion not easily accessible to the conscious mind.

To return to physiognomy: This field of study had a lineage going back to classical times. The first known such work was for a time attributed to Aristotle but is now considered to be perhaps the work of a contemporary. Entitled the *Physiognomonika*, it discussed the way in which character may be interpreted from various bodily characteristics: Courage, for example, is considered to be revealed by coarse hair, strong bones, a flat stomach, a sturdy neck, a gleaming eye, and a not too large nor too wrinkled forehead. Often animal characteristics are transferred to a person if certain features are common to him or her and that animal. Thus, the panther is both brave yet furtive and tricky, and people with small faces, long and thin necks, and mottled complexions are thought to share the panther temperament. Character is also indirectly related to physique if one considers that a flow of blood and other humors is related to physique; thus, men of normally small height are quick and active, it was argued, because the blood moves rapidly, in the small space, to the heart, the Aristotelian seat of intelligence.

Other influential handbooks on physiognomy appeared in Roman times; a full account of classical sources on the subject, including references to literary works of the period, is given by E. C. Evans (1969). In the Middle Ages the best-known work was the so-called *Secreta Secretorum*, a book of "secrets" designed to aid a king in securing the trust of his subjects and political power. After general advice on the virtues that should become a king, there is a section on physiognomy, designed to aid the king in his choice of wise and loyal counsellors. The book passed itself off as a genuine work of Aristotle but is clearly of much later origin and is an interesting example of how the exponents of pseudoscience seek the mantle of "authority" for their precepts. Michael Scotus, of the thirteenth century, wrote another popular physiognomy. The *Physiognomonika* and the *Secreta* were published in several different cities in the sixteenth century.

Nevertheless there was a book that was probably influenced by this literature but advanced far beyond it in scope and in quality. Juan Huarte (1529–1588) was a Spanish doctor, well acquainted with the physiological writings of Aristotle, Galen, and Nemesius, who in 1575 wrote *The Examination of Men's Wits*. This work was rapidly translated into several European languages and was something of a best seller. In it Huarte focused on the question of "wit," or as we should now say, intelligence. He attempted to show what bodily signs and behavior patterns correlate with different types of intellectual ability and to suggest ways in which the intellect may be cultivated. It is thus a pioneering work both on individual differences and on educational theory, in the latter respect probably being influenced by Vives. Individual differences, however, he saw as mainly depending on the qualities hot, moist, and dry. In a particularly original passage, Huarte argued that the traditional ascription of the faculties to the ventricles is probably erroneous: The powers of memory, imagination, and understanding are probably all contained in each of the first three ventricles (that is, the two anterior ventricles and the central ventricle). The fourth ventricle serves as the site where vital spirits are changed into animal spirits, a role previously assigned to the *rete mirabile.* Huarte, having discussed the relations between the qualities and the intellect in some detail, then asserted that different kinds of intellectual activity require imagination, understanding (reason), and memory in different proportions. Language learning, law, divinity, cosmography, and arithmetic require memory above all. Physics, eloquence, music, astrology, art, and literature require imagination. Since these faculties are unequally assigned to different individuals, each individual will have to find the career best suited to his or her gifts. Since so much depends on the qualities and the spirits, good intelligence in the adult is the result of wise nutrition and hygiene in infancy and childhood. A fuller account of Huarte's arguments, and a fuller description of his influence on later writers, is given by Mora (1977).

A fifth topic of some popularity in sixteenth-century psychology was that of mnemonics, or memory training. We have seen how the author of *Ad Herennium* and Quintilian advocated the method of loci for memorization: Each item to be retrieved is set in an imagined place in an imaginary house or palace or other such locale. A fascinating account of the development of these mnemonic schemes from classical times to the Renaissance is given by Frances Yates in her book *The Art of Memory* (1966). She describes how, after being apparently lost during the Dark Ages, the Roman writings were rediscovered and utilized by Albertus Magnus and Aquinas, who assimilated to it Aristotle's remarks in *De Memoria*. Aquinas recommended that memory be cultivated perhaps by something like the method of loci, and this recommendation led to a number of books on mnemonics being written and printed in the late fifteenth and sixteenth centuries. In many of these books actual representations are shown of rooms and places that should themselves first be memorized, then used for the storage of new material. To palaces and houses may be added churches and abbeys as sources of mnemonic loci, or even quasi-Ptolemaic pictures of the spheres of the universe.

Possibly the most ostentatious mnemonic scheme was that of Camillo (1480–1544) who may actually have built a model of a large theater in each of whose many locations were to be stored various items of information. Concepts from classical mythology, Christianity, Neoplatonism, and Jewish mysticism mingle to serve as extra aids in visualization. Later we find that Giordano Bruno (1548–1600), known in the history of science as a martyr burned by the Inquisition for his espousement of the idea that the earth was just one of many heavenly bodies and for his belief in heliocentrism, also invented a vast mnemonic system that was very popular at the time. Bruno's scheme was larger and more versatile than that of Camillo and may have been influenced by an earlier medieval scheme of Ramon Lull (1235–1316). In Lull's scheme loci were laid out on concentric wheels that could be revolved so as to yield many different combinations of objects to be imagined. Mnemonic schemes continued to be devised well beyond the sixteenth century—they are still being devised by those who would have you train your memory—but it was in the sixteenth century that they became particularly popular.

Many other topics of psychological interest were discussed in works that have not been particularly remembered by historians of psychology. There were a number of books on sleeping and dreaming. There were a few on the special senses. The humors and the temperaments were common topics. There were a number of books on the "passions." Later, we shall deal with works on psychiatry. There were several books on the topic of love, influenced by such literary classics as Ovid's *Art of Love* (12 B.C.) and the medieval work *The Romance of the Rose* by Jean de Meung and Gilbert de Lorris. But of all the books published on psychological topics we may note one in particular, Goclenius's *Psychologia, hoc est de hominis perfectione (Psychology, or on the improvement of man)*. It appeared in 1590. Goclenius, whose German name was Rudolf Goeckel (1547–1628), was an eminent scholar who wrote on many topics and was best known for an encyclopedia written in the early seventeenth century. According to the *Allgemeine Deutsche Biographie* (the *General German Biography*, Vol. 9), Goclenius's psychology has become famous . . . , but the only thing to praise in it is its uniting of physiological with psychological observations; for he follows, quite dependently, the Aristoteleans of the Middle Ages and the sixteenth century, whose endless and fruitless investigations into the origin, determination and future of souls, on the faculties of the soul, and on the various kinds of intellect, excite his greatest interest and evoke little contradiction.

We mention it here simply because this is the first time we have met the word *psychology* in a book title. It would seem that the earliest known use of this made-up word was in a manuscript by Marulic (1450–1524): Boring (1966) shows a facsimile of the title as it appears in a contemporary listing of Marulic's writings. A rough guess at the date of its appearance would be 1520. A history of the early appearances and use of the word *psychology* is given by Lapointe (1972).

Early Seventeenth-Century Science

We turn now to the beginning of the seventeenth century. This century is, above all, the century in which modern concepts of physics and astronomy displaced the outmoded concepts of Aristotle and Ptolemy and in which the modern view of the circulation of the blood displaced the old Galenic notion of the ebb and flow of blood mixed with the various kinds of "spirits." From the point of view of psychology the century opens with the name of Descartes, generally held to be the first of the moderns, as opposed to the ancients. But before we discuss the work of Descartes it is worth pausing to consider the writings of three men most famous for their contributions to sciences other than psychology but who nevertheless contributed in significant ways to the growth of that discipline: Galileo (1564–1642), Harvey (1578–1657), and Kepler (1571–1630).

Galileo is well known for discovering, with the aid of a telescope, the mountains of the moon, the sunspots, the satellites of Jupiter, and the fact that the Milky Way is made up of many stars not normally visible to the naked eye. His cosmology was that of Copernicus rather than Ptolemy, and this unfortunately led him to be in conflict with the Inquisition in his later life. But his contributions to more mundane matters of mechanics were equally important. In addition, Galileo's contributions to psychology were twofold. First, he was able to show that the pitch of a sound depended on the frequency of vibration of the object causing the sound. Apparently, he discovered this by accident when he scraped a brass plate with a chisel (though some scholars now doubt this story). He was able to show that strings of different lengths vibrated at different frequencies when plucked; although the ancients had recognized that a string half as long as another, when plucked, gave a tone an octave higher than the other, they had not appreciated that it was the frequency of the vibration rather than the length of the string that was most directly responsible for this phenomenon. Recognizing that pitch was mediated by frequency was a major step forward in the development of our understanding of sound and hearing.

Galileo's second contribution to psychology was his assertion, in a book called *The Assayer*, that objects have two kinds of qualities, *primary qualities* that can be measured and that enter into a physicist's account of the behavior of objects—examples are size, position, shape, speed, and number—and *secondary qualities* that are known to the senses but are not obviously measurable—examples are color, smell, taste, and sound. This distinction is now treated less seriously then previously because in fact the latter can be measured, but in the history of science it was useful in stressing the difference between the world of the physicist, concerned with primary qualities, and the world of the psychologist, whose basic data are mental and arise from sensory experience. Later, Locke and Berkeley would try to clarify the relations between primary and secondary qualities in the context of a scientific psychology. A more detailed account of Galileo's views on this matter is given by Martinez (1974).

William Harvey is best known, of course, for his argument that the blood circulates around the body. In Harvey's system the heart's function is not to produce any special kind of spirits, nor is the liver there to manufacture the blood. Instead the heart is a large pump, sending blood into the arteries, then into the veins, then into the lungs, then back into the arteries (see Figure 1–3). He was aided by previous discoveries: Fabricius, Harvey's teacher, had emphasized the importance of the valves in the veins, which allowed only a one-way flow, and Servetus had indicated the existence of the circulation through the lungs. But it was Harvey who, by a number of elegant experiments, was able to demonstrate the true picture. The main feature missing from this model was a way by which the blood got from the arteries to the veins, but Malpighi, with the aid of a microscope, was able to show the existence of the capillaries about four years after Harvey's death. Galen had thought that the blood went from one side of the heart to the other through pores in the septum, the thick membrane dividing the heart lengthwise; Harvey showed that in fact the only route from one side of the heart to the other was by way of the roundabout pulmonary circulation. But Harvey's role in the history of psychology is more direct than might be imagined; for he became very skeptical about the actual existence of anything like the vital or animal spirits. In his *Circulation of the Blood*, he asserted: "Medical schools admit three kinds of spirits: the natural spirits flowing through the veins, the vital spirits through the arteries, and the animal spirits through the nerves . . . but we have found none of these spirits by dissection, neither in the veins, nerves, arteries nor other parts of living animals" (W. Harvey, 1847, p. 116).

Johan Kepler was most famous for showing the paths of the planets around the sun; but he also wrote two books on optics. In the first, a volume that appeared in 1604 with a title indicating that he was commenting on a medieval work on optics by Witelo, he dealt extensively with refraction, particularly of the light from the sun and the moon but prefaced this treatment with a discussion of the human eye. Light, according to ancient theories, spread out like a cone; according to Kepler each object could be seen as the base of a pyramid of light whose apex was in the eye. But whereas the medieval writers had thought of the image of an object as being in the lens, then translated by animal spirits from the lens to the center of the common sense, Kepler argued that the lens served to refract and thereby focus the light at a place deep within the eyeball. For reasons discussed by Crombie (1964), the medieval scholars had thought of the image as being focused in the lens at the center of the eyeball; Kepler said, on the contrary, that the lens was just on the periphery of the eyeball and focused the image, through the humors of the eye, onto the netlike structure at the back of the eyeball we now call the retina. Furthermore, argued Kepler, the light had to enter the lens itself through the small hole of the pupil, and this had the effect of making the image on the retina upside down. From the angle the two eyes formed with respect to the two pyramids of light emitted from an object, the subject could judge the distance of the object. In a later work, the *Dioptrics* (1610), Kepler added that the image was conveyed by animal spirits from the retina to the seat of common sense in the brain. In a single sweep Kepler thereby laid the foundations for the modern view of the process of vision, foundations on which Descartes and others were soon to build. A comprehensive account of the medieval background to Kepler's achievement, and a summary of the ways in which Kepler came to realize that the retina was the crucial part of the eye for subserving vision, is given by Lindberg (1976).

Descartes

Perhaps the most self-conscious rebel against ancient or medieval beliefs was René Descartes (1596–1650). A precocious child, he received a classical education at a Jesuit school and to the end of his life maintained he was a devoted Catholic; several of his correspondents in later life were priests such as Father Mersenne, who evinced a keen intellectual curiosity concerning matters of science. He spent a few years in Army service, and he tells us that it was in this time that he devoted himself to mathematical and philosophical meditation. His best-known claim to fame is in fact the system of rigorous doubt he inculcated in himself. Tearing away everything of whose factuality he was not completely persuaded, he eventually arrived at the one datum of which he felt absolutely sure—namely, his certainty that, while meditating, he was actually thinking and that therefore something must exist which did the thinking—that is, himself. All this is encapsulated in his famous sentence, "I think, therefore I am." Basing his thought structure on this dictum, he built up a philosophical system in which a belief in the almost mechanical regularity of external phenomena was combined with more metaphysical thought on the nature and importance of God. Most of these ideas were expounded in such books as *The Discourse on Method* (1637), the *Meditations* (1641), and the *Principles of Philosophy* (1644). He wrote most of these works while living in the country in Holland, a region he retired to after leaving the army.

Descartes' fame had soon spread across Europe, and he was invited to the court of Queen Christiana of Sweden in 1649. Possibly because he was forced to break a life-long habit of rising late, and thus became ill in the frosty winter dawns of Stockholm, he died a short while after arriving there. But his contributions to knowledge were by no means limited to philosophical disquisitions. He wrote books on geometry, meteorology, optics, cosmology, and physiology, which placed him in the foremost rank of seventeenth-century scientists. In particular, his theory of the universe was an important steppingstone between those of Copernicus and Newton and, because of its reliance on reasoned mathematics, represented still another breakaway from faith and authority as reliable guides to our understanding of the world. One of Newton's primary aims was to show that Descartes' theory that the universe could be described in terms of circular motions should be replaced by a theory making uses of "forces." But Carter (1983) has argued that Descartes' cosmology played a much broader role in his "overall" thinking than is usually realized: Descartes drew the analogy between movements in a universe undergoing the process of growth and those of a living organism undergoing the process of growth. Because both were subject to natural law, the physical body of an animal or human had to be considered as a natural object like others; and since, as we shall see, Descartes believed that mental events were tied one to one with physical events (particularly brain events), this meant that psychology too could be based on a mechanistic system of natural law. Carter stresses that although Descartes continually refers to the "soul," he really means by "soul" what is now meant by "mind"; and although he apparently toned down his mechanistic account of "mind" to appease the Church, Carter suggests that in fact Descartes was in complete opposition to its teaching and to its reliance on the authority of Aristotle on scientific matters. One of Descartes' last writings, for instance, is *The Passions of the Soul*, a detailed mechanistic analysis of the physiology of the emotions along with ethical lessons to be drawn from this analysis. It was written probably four years before his death but was only published after his arrival in Sweden. His physiological theories are found mainly in a treatise, *On Man,* published fourteen years after his death. In discussing his contribution to psychology we shall concentrate first on his physiology as expounded in that book, then turn to the theory of the emotions he founded on his physiology, and finally deal with his comments on thought and the nature of the mind.

Descartes' physiology is an amalgam of the new and the old. In physiological matters he accepted Harvey's theory of the circulation of the blood but added to it a theory of animal spirits clearly derived from Aristotle and Galen. For Harvey, the muscles of the heart, when they contracted, forced or squeezed the blood out of the arteries. For Descartes, the heart was filled with a kind of innate heat. As droplets of blood entered the heart the heat led them to expand, forcing the blood out into the arteries. In his treatise *On Man* he then goes on to say:

> As for those portions of the blood which penetrate as far as the brain, they serve not only to nourish and maintain its substance, but principally also to produce a certain very subtle wind, or rather a very lively and pure flame, which we call "animal spirits." For it must be understood that the arteries which carry these from the heart, after having divided into an infinity of little branches and having formed little tissues which are spread out carpet-like at the bottom of the brain cavity, cluster around a certain little *gland,* situated in about the middle of the brain substance, right at the entrance to its cavities. (1618–1637 / 1963, p. 388)

This gland we now call the pineal gland. Descartes actually mislocalized it; its function seems to be to mediate between light changes in the external world and certain kinds of motivated behavior related to light changes; it probably plays a very small part in human behavior. But Descartes explained, in a later work, the *Passions of the Soul,* why he laid such emphasis on the gland: It is the only part of the brain, he said, which seems a unit in itself. Most other parts of the brain, such as the great cerebral hemispheres, are divided into two. In *On Man,* Descartes then went on to describe how the pineal gland is moved and shaken by incoming animal spirits, which are then discharged by the gland into a system of tubules or "pores" that ultimately terminate in nerves. The animal spirits are carried down the nerves to muscles; as the spirits run into the muscles, they are inflated, thus causing contractions of the body region in question.

One of the most interesting sections in *On Man* concerns involuntary actions. Suppose you put a foot near a fire. According to Descartes messages are sent via the animal spirits in the nerves of the foot to the brain, where the pineal gland shunts them into those pores leading most directly to the nerves controlling leg movements. All this happens very quickly and mechanically without our exercising strong control over it: The end effect is that the foot is rapidly withdrawn from the fire.

Many historians of physiology have not hesitated to describe this mechanism as the first sound treatment of what we now call the *reflex*. But its implications, for the philosophically minded Descartes, were much greater, for it led him to assert, at various places in his works, that the animal body was nothing but a machine whose parts were operated by the ebb and flow of animal spirits. There is some reason to believe that Descartes was influenced in this notion by watching certain automatic machines that had been invented more or less as toys. A statue could move an arm, for example, by way of a system of tubes inside it through which water ran. By seeing the animal as a machine Descartes essentially demystified it, but for the seventeenth century Descartes' notion was somewhat shocking, for it forced people to ask whether they, like animals, were not also machines. To divest humanity of its special status as a soul carrier bordered on heresy, and Descartes, fully aware of the dangers to himself from the Church, took special pains, in ways we shall shortly consider, not to be accused of arguing that humans were only machines. It is a quirk of intellectual history, however, that Descartes led some to believe that the *animal* was a machine literally, arguing that since machines cannot feel anything, not having souls, neither can animals, so one need not feel guilty about kicking the cat! Rosenfield (1968) has an account of some of the other ways Descartes' mechanistic biology was interpreted at the time. In *On Man,* and in another work, the *Dioptrics,* Descartes also elaborated on Kepler's theory of the eye and was actually able to report seeing an image on the retina of a dead bull's eye from which the outer coatings had been stripped.

We have seen how his mechanical physiology can be applied to the matters of the reflex muscle action and of the eye. But for Descartes himself another most important application, to judge by the length with which he wrote on it, was to the problem of the emotions. One of his later books, the *Passions of the Soul,* is devoted to showing that an emotion or "passion" is felt as the result of complex mechanistic interactions between blood flow, the animal spirits, and the functions of certain viscera. When we imagine something we love, for instance, the animal spirits in the nerves from the brain influence the blood to flow into the heart in such a way that the heat of the heart gives a particularly strong push of spirits into the brain. This in turn causes the excitement and obsessiveness associated with thinking of a loved object or person. He gives similar explanations of other emotions such as hatred, joy, and sadness.

Nevertheless, Descartes was not wholly original in his description of the emotions. Ever since Aquinas and Vives, many minor authors had written on the emotions, usually with a view to propounding some ethical precept. According to Levi (1964), who has written an account of such works produced in France prior to Descartes' *Passions of the Soul,* many relied on the old distinction between the concupiscible and the irascible, which we discussed earlier when talking of Aquinas. One such writer, Cureau de la Chambre (1594–1669), however, was more inclined to physiology. He was a medical man, impressed with physiognomy and cheiromancy, who wrote a long work entitled *Characters of the Passions*, the first volume of which appeared just before Descartes' *Passions of the Soul*. La Chambre's work makes much mention of animal spirits—and, it may be added, La Chambre rejected Harvey's theory of the circulation of the blood. There is reason to believe that Descartes was strongly influenced by La Chambre (Diamond, 1968, p. 48). On the other hand Descartes rejected the division between the concupiscible and the irascible because "this seems to me to signify nothing but that the soul has two faculties, the one of desire, and the other of anger . . . " whereas for Descartes there was much more. Yet one wonders whether Descartes was fully acquainted with the subtleties of the concupiscible and the irascible as described by Aquinas.

Descartes believed there were six fundamental passions, each of which could be subdivided into others. These six were wonder, love, hatred, desire, joy, and sadness. The latter five could all be derived from the basic emotion of love, whereas wonder (or "admiration") was an emotion aroused by new experiences. Each had its own physiological mechanism, each intermingled with the others to form complex emotions such as jealousy, and it is rare to find one in pure form without a mixture of another (e.g., hatred is rarely devoid of sadness). The third part of the *Passions* is an attempt to base advice or counsel on observations of how these separate passions affect those around one. Like his predecessors, he was also concerned to show that we can control our emotions by the will. Perhaps nowhere in Descartes' writings is his combination of the new scientific outlook with remnants of an older lore more clearly evinced than in his doctrine of the emotions.

But did Descartes go too far? What we have in the *Passions of the Soul* are accounts for the passions that remind us of exactly those automatic machines to which Descartes had earlier assimilated animals. Are not, then, men and women equally "mechanical"? The answer, according to Descartes is no; in fact, much of the first part of *Passions of the Soul* is devoted to explaining that we each have a soul, which is not a material thing, not a mechanical object to be dissected or analyzed, but which nevertheless *interacts* with the mechanistic body. "The soul," he writes, "has its principal seat in the little gland which exists in the middle of the brain, from whence it radiates forth through all the remainder of the body by means of the animal spirits, nerve, and even the blood, which, participating in the impressions of the spirits, can carry them by the arteries into all the members" (1955, p. 347). The words *principal seat* in the above extract should be especially noted; the soul is in fact united to all parts of the body, but *particularly* to the pineal gland. To understand Descartes' distinction between the soul and the body we must, however, go back some ten years to his first great work, the *Discourse on Method*.

After describing his various interests and various rules of intellectual exercise, Descartes tells us why he arrived at his notion that "I think, therefore I am" is a foundation stone on which to erect a larger system. He began by rejecting the view that sensations could be trusted; in so doing, he followed the skeptical tradition, which, from ancient beginnings, had grown in the sixteenth and early seventeenth centuries into something of an intellectual movement (Popkin, 1960). Descartes, however, was not concerned with agreeing with skepticism, but essentially with outflanking it by seizing on self-evident truths other than those derived from sensations. In fact, philosophers of skeptical bent were among the first opponents of Cartesianism. He also rejected certain kinds of reasoning and asserted that "everything that ever entered into my mind was no more true than the illusions of my dreams." He was left with little more than the knowledge that, in doing all this, he is actually thinking, whence he infers his own existence: "I think, therefore I am." But from this he went on to assert something with which many of us would be less inclined to agree: He asserted that because his existence is certain from the fact that he thinks, his "substance" has an "essence" or "nature" of "thinkingness." For its existence there is not need for a body: This "soul" is "entirely distinct from body." Later he explained that the main characteristic a body has is that of being extended in space; his soul, on the other hand, is not so extended. Thus Descartes was led to the theory known as dualism: There are separate entities known as "body" and "soul." They interact, however, and we have seen that the chief seat of this interaction is the pineal gland. Thus, even though the soul moves the pineal gland to cause the mechanisms of the reflexes and the emotions, it has an existence apart from the body and, Descartes later argues, is immortal.

Dualism is therefore a species of transcendentalism and one that raises problems of its own, which later seventeenth-century philosophers such as Malebranche, Spinoza, and Leibniz would criticize on various grounds (see Radner, 1971). The most immediate problem raised by dualism is that it renders any mechanistic account of mental phenomena implausible. By believing in an incorporeal soul whose essence was "thinking," Descartes could, in other words, defend himself from being charged with holding that human beings were nothing but machines. But it also opens a way to an account of that great psychological problem with which Descartes eventually had to grapple—namely, the problem of memory and knowledge.

Morris (1969) has carefully examined all the available evidence on Descartes' theories of memory and concludes that he abandoned an early physical theory of memory storage (he imaged memories to be stored in the folds of the brain) for a dualistic theory in which he recognizes "still another memory, completely intellectual, which depends on the soul alone." This, of course, is a revival of our old friend, the agent intellect. Morris shows how, in his correspondence, Descartes argues that human memory is mainly based on intellectual memory whereas animal memory is mainly based on physical memory. But as soon as one admits an incorporeal memory, one asks whether knowledge could not be gained from outside one's experience. Descartes asserted that in fact, in our intellectual memory, we do have certain ideas that are not the result of sensory experience but are "innate." Among innate ideas are those of God and of certain geometrical truths. The idea of perfection may possibly, if I interpret the *Discourse* correctly, also be innate.

In a late defense of his philosophy in a work called *Notes Directed Against a Certain Programme,* he carefully remarked, however, much as Aristotle had done (see Chap. 2), that by *innate* he does not necessarily mean that a baby has an innate idea at the moment of birth but that the baby has an innate tendency to develop such an idea: "In the same sense we say that in some families generosity is innate, in others certain diseases like gout or gravel, not that on this account the babes of these families suffer from these diseases in their mother's womb, but because they are born with a certain disposition or propensity for contracting them" (1955, p. 442).

Many historians would have placed Descartes at the start of a new chapter. Yet it is surprising how derivative he was, as we have tried to make clear. His most original feats, we suggest, were his mechanistic approach to living things and his desire to break with the past and found a new science of human beings based on his own introspection. But even these were in the current of his time: Francis Bacon (1561–1626) had also argued for a naturalistic approach in the study of behavior. Certainly, for the Aristotelians and theologians of the early seventeenth century, Cartesianism was controversial enough to be a threat: In 1663 his works were placed on the Catholic Index of banned books. And with some reason: Over the next hundred years certain individuals would take the idea of the beast-machine and argue—despite Descartes' dualism—that there is also a man-machine (Rosenfield, 1968). His doctrine of innate ideas would continue to be a subject of controversy right to the present time. His dualism would be countered by alternative theories of the mind-body problem. His errors on nervous physiology would have to be corrected. Nevertheless, the picture remains of a brilliant, dedicated, concentrated individual who saw clearly—as even in the present century some do not—that living things and their behavior should be the object of a scientific inquiry and who applied, as best he could, scientific methods to the answering of some of the questions raised thereby. A more detailed evaluation of Descartes' role in the history of psychology is given by R. I. Watson (1971); a classic biography of the man has been written by Haldane (1905). The most extensive treatment of Descartes' psychology and its relationship to his other scientific work is found in Carter (1983).

Late Seventeenth-Century Physiologists

The influence of Descartes on science and philosophy in the remaining years of the seventeenth century cannot be underestimated. While the influences of Aristotle on philosophy and Galen on physiology were quietly being eroded, Descartes' own suggestions on philosophy and physiology were taken up and discussed by the leading intellects of the century. Some, the so-called Cartesians, agreed with their mentor to the extent that they may almost be accused of lack of originality; others, including many clergymen, fought fiercely against his mechanistic notions on the grounds that the essentially spiritual side of human nature was not being properly appreciated. But added to the groundswell of dissatisfaction with the systems of antiquity were other voices. Understanding of mathematical and physical principles was sharpened by an illustrious line of scientists from all countries of Europe. The inquiry as to the behavior of people in groups became the foundation stone of several new theories of political science. Underpinning all was the desire of thinking people to be free of the annoyances—both petty and major—of the flux of religious contentions, the disputes between King and the Parliament, and the restraints imposed by ecclesiastical or governmental censorship. If we look back at the seventeenth century from our present standpoint, it can be viewed as a time of turmoil in which, despite all the confusion, certain individual thinkers stand out whose influence would penetrate deep into the following decades. Furthermore, these thinkers were not isolated. They formed scientific and philosophical societies to communicate with each other; examples were the French Academy of Sciences (founded in 1665) and the British Royal Society (founded in 1663). These societies were formed in part because their members wished to be independent of the university system, still dominated by government and church.

Scientific journals were published for the propagation of new information. Books became cheaper and more readily accessible to all. The seventeenth century finishes in a kind of crescendo with two books that would forever change our thinking on scientific matters: Newton's *Mathematical Principles of Natural Philosophy* (1687) showed, among other things, that many of the movements of the celestial bodies could be explained in terms of three fairly simple laws of motion; and Locke's *Essay concerning Human Understanding* (1690) raised, more explicitly than even Descartes had done, the question of how much the knowledge of an adult human being can be seen as the result of the sum total of his or her experiences. Newton and Locke became focal points of discussion for the European intelligentsia of the eighteenth century, and both were able to achieve what they did by building on the foundations laid by more minor figures who preceded them. But the *questions* they asked had been posed most explicitly—and, it must be admitted, answered somewhat confusedly—by Descartes.

Concerning the growth in knowledge of physiological processes during the seventeenth century, we may remark that one of the primary aims of research in this area was to validate (or disconfirm) Harvey's theory of the circulation of the blood. Apart from this, however, we also see the beginnings of modern neurology.

We mentioned that Harvey was somewhat skeptical of the existence of "animal spirits" because he could not detect them. Leeuwenhoek, in 1677, had suggested that a nerve was made up of very small vessels "lying by one another" but still wondered whether animal spirits ran through the vessels. Borelli (1608–1679), however, suggested that nerves were more solid and consisted of a moist, spongy substance. Briggs (1642–1704) taught Newton some anatomy and may have persuaded Newton that nerves were solid objects that transmitted "vibrations." But these observations were not really assimilated, and the term *animal spirits* is found in various contexts right to the end of the century. There was, however, one set of experiments that pointed to a rejection of the doctrine of the spirits. Descartes, it will be recalled, like Galen, had thought the spirits, in a fluid state, ran down a nerve into the muscle. By way of the reflex mechanism and the pineal gland, the spirits were supposed to flood into the muscle and expand it like a balloon. Jan Swammerdam (1637–1680) immersed a frog's muscle in water. When he pinched the nerve leading to the immersed muscle, the muscle *contracted,* as we now say, but the level of the water didn't change, as it should have if the muscle's volume had increased. In another experiment he was able to show that the muscle actually thickened and shortened. More was also learned about nervous anatomy in general. Of the many who dissected the brain and the nervous system to demonstrate their structures, the best known was Thomas Willis (1621–1675).

Willis was the center of a notable group of physicians living at Oxford—he knew Sydenham, the most famous medical practitioner of his time, and also John Locke, who studied medicine at Oxford. Willis's book, *The Anatomy of the Brain* (1664), which contained plates drawn by the architect Wren, corrected the account of the cranial nerves given by Galen; named many of the basal ganglia, that is, those clearly visible centers in the middle part of the cerebral hemispheres, which we now know are concerned particularly with the control of the motor system; and invented the words *thalamus* and *neurology.* He was instrumental in stressing the role of the *brain's* substance, as opposed to the ventricles, and from this time on the ventricles take a back seat, so to speak, with respect to their presumed importance for psychological functioning. He described the blood vessels of the brain in detail, and the circle of Willis, a ring of blood vessels at the base of the brain, preserves his name, although he was not the first to observe it. (Sometimes this circle was given the name *rete mirabile*, causing confusion.) He was also responsible for producing a number of theories that, though mistaken in detail, were highly innovative and anticipated later discoveries. For example, he thought muscle contraction occurred from an "explosion" of nerve substance and blood substance, and that epileptic seizures were also the result of "explosions" within the nerve substance of the brain; this was erroneous, but anticipated the modern doctrine of nervous discharge. He thought that a painful stimulus excited a flight of animal spirits to the region we now think of as the upper brain stem, where the spirits were "reflected" down to the muscles that moved the limb away from the painful stimulus: The physiology was wrong, but in his use of the word *reflected* Willis anticipated the modern term *reflex*. He thought that the cerebral hemispheres controled voluntary movement and the cerebellum involuntary movement; again, this identification is fallacious, but he was correct in looking for separate kinds of nervous activity involved in "voluntary" versus "involuntary" acts. He thought that sensation was encoded in a region of the brain stem he called the *corpus striatum*. If a sensory impulse was carried further, into the corpus callosum, it became an imagination; and if it was carried even further, into the cerebral cortex, it became a memory.

This allotment of abilities to brain areas is now known to be wrong, but it represents one of the first modern attempts at localization of function in the brain substance, as opposed to the ventricles. Willis was also ahead of his time in discovering the nerves of the *autonomic* nervous system, that is, those nerves concerned with the involuntary control of heartbeat, emotions, and other bodily functions; and he suggested that certain body areas, including the testes, *secreted* substances, a clear anticipation of the modern doctrine of hormones. He also did important work on nervous diseases and on psychiatric illness, which will be mentioned again in Chapter 11. Willis's work was underestimated for centuries, but Spillane (1981) has recently given a summary of Willis's contribution to our understanding of the nervous system.

Other contributors to neuroanatomy included Vieussens (1641–1716), who did much original research on the basal ganglia; Sylvius (1614–1672), whom we still remember when we speak of the great fissure of Sylvius at the side of the brain; and Blasius (1625–1692), who first showed that you could see an H-shaped configuration of grey matter in a cross-section of the spinal cord. An important contributor to our under-

standing of brain disease was Wepfer (1620–1695), who first clearly demonstrated, in his 1658 book on apoplexy, that a "stroke" was the result of
damage to the blood flow in the brain. In so doing he adopted Harvey's
theory of the circulation of the blood. Valsalva (1666–1738) demonstrated that in cases of paralysis of one side of the body, the brain damage
in question would be found on the opposite side of the brain. This is one
of the first—and most important—observations on laterality effects in the
nervous system. And what of the pineal gland, so emphasized by Descartes? Jaynes (1973) points out that various observers noted that an
animal such as a snake or tortoise continued to move even hours after the
brain and other organs had been excised. It was therefore assumed that
many movements, including what we now call reflex movements, did not
require the mediation of the pineal gland. From this time onward, the
pineal gland would be more or less ignored until the present century.

The other area of biology to which Descartes contributed was, of
course, the study of the special senses. In the seventeenth century a fair
amount was added to our knowledge of the functions of the sense organs,
notably the eye and the ear. Concerning the mechanism of the eye itself,
it became realized that the focusing of light onto the retina by the lens
was not fixed but variable. Descartes had observed that when the excised
eye of a bull was squeezed, the image on the retinal surface changed.
Some investigators therefore argued that the focusing of an image on the
retina was achieved by elongating or compressing the eyeball itself
through its external musculature. Others, including Mariotte (1620–
1684), believed that it was the lens, rather than the eyeball, that changed
so as to sharpen the derived image on the retina. The ciliary muscles
controlling the lens were known, but their function was obscure. The
correct alternative was not really established until 1801 by Thomas
Young: When we focus on something, the curvature of the lens is
changed by involuntary contractions of the ciliary muscle. Mariotte, in
the course of his dissections of the eye, also noted that the optic nerve left
the retina, not at its center but over to one side, towards the nose. He
therefore predicted that an object whose image fell on that point of exit
of the optic nerve would not be visible. He was able to demonstrate this
by the now familiar experiment of concentrating the gaze on one dot on a
piece of paper, with another dot just visible to one side. By moving
backwards or forwards one finds the point at which the second dot becomes invisible. This demonstration of the "blind spot" was given with
great success to both the French Academy in 1666 and the British Royal
Society in 1668.

The main breakthrough in optical research came with Newton's
theory of color. Theories of color go back to the Greeks: The general
opinion, still held by some even as late as the nineteenth century, was that
colors arose by appropriate mixtures of light and dark. In 1664 Robert

Boyle (1627–1691) wrote a book entitled *Experiments and Considerations concerning Colors.* According to Boring (1942, p. 122), "Boyle, although presenting a great mass of casual information and opinion, seems to have had no great influence, presumably because he lacked a central idea that would give significance to his facts." It fell to Sir Isaac Newton (1642–1727) to conceive this central idea, possibly as a result of reading Boyle's book, possibly because, with his interest in telescopes, he wished to know more about the annoying colored edges that formed around the images in a refracting telescope.

Newton obtained a prism in 1666 and described the results of his experiments in his first published paper, which appeared in the *Philosophical Transactions of the Royal Society* in 1672. A somewhat unpleasant controversy then arose with Hooke on certain matters to do with the nature of light, and Newton only published his full researches and opinions on light and color in his *Opticks* of 1704 (Hooke had died the previous year). What Newton, following Francis Bacon's terminology, called his crucial experiment was simple and elegant. A beam of white light (Newton used sunlight) is passed into a prism. The result is that the white light is split up into the colors of the rainbow. This in itself suggested to Newton that white light was a mixture of all the colors. This rainbowlike band of colors is cast onto a convex lens that focuses the band onto yet another prism, and out of the other prism comes a ray of light. This prism has served to reconstitute the spectrum into the original form of white light. To bring back the spectrum, a third prism is placed in the path of the white light and the colors can then be displayed on a screen.

It was Newton who named the separate colors of the spectrum as red, orange, yellow, green, blue, indigo, and violet; there have been speculations that he did so by analogy with sound, where there are seven notes in the diatonic scale from a starting note to its octave; but it is certain that this division was of little scientific value either for physics (there are an infinite number of wavelengths in the spectrum) or for optical physiology (the eye probably responds directly to only three colors, red, green, and blue, not seven).

Much more important was Newton's realization that the colors resulted because the white light was differentially refracted by the prism. We now know that different wavelengths of light are differentially refracted; Newton only knew that something was differentially refracted and, with his belief that light was particlelike rather than wavelike, he missed seeing the simple equation between wavelength and perceived color. Nevertheless, before he adopted the particle theory of light, he did suggest that perhaps light of different colors might be associated with light rays having different "vibrations," much as the sensation of different tones is associated with different vibrations of the air. On the other hand he was able to explain the origin of the colors of bodies: By a series of experimental observations, he showed that their various colors arise because light is reflected by their surfaces in different proportions. He was also able to use his theory to explain the colors of the rainbow (Descartes had been able to account for the shape but not the colors of the arc), and he was able to show how the colored rings arose in refracting telescopes and devised a reflecting telescope that did not require the operator to worry about this "chromatic aberration."

Most of the above is described in Book One of the *Opticks*. Book Two deals with colors as they result from reflection from surfaces or lenses, and Book Three grapples with the problems of diffraction.

From a psychological point of view, the last part of Book Three, consisting of various *queries,* is still rewarding reading. In Query 12, Newton wondered whether rays of light might not excite "vibrations" in the retina, which are "propagated along the solid fibres of the optick Nerves into the Brain." Here Newton, probably following Briggs, did not talk of animal spirits but rather of solid fibers that vibrate: This opinion would be taken up in detail by Hartley in the next century. In the next query, Newton asked whether vibrations of different "bignesses" in the nerves might give rise to different color sensations. He then raised the question of how the messages from the two eyes might combine to form one unified picture, and he discussed the "persistence" of vision, as when, a lighted coal is whirled rapidly in a circle and one sees not a moving spot of light but a coherent glowing ring. It is enough to say that Boring, in his classic *Sensation and Perception in the History of Experimental Psychology,* treats the subject of vision by discussing the topic as it was before Newton and then as it was after Newton: For Boring, Newton was the dividing line between the ancients and the moderns of visual science.

On subjects connected with audition, we may distinguish between research on the nature of sound and research on the auditory mechanism. On the nature of sound, we recall that Galileo had established that the pitch of a note correlated with the frequency of vibrations of the inducing medium (such as a string). Mersenne, a close colleague and supporter of Descartes, did a number of experiments in which he was able to derive equations relating rates of vibrations to other physical variables such as the lengths of different strings and the weights of objects pulling on them. These equations were simplified to what is essentially the modern form by Brook Taylor in 1713 (see T. H. Wolf, 1935, p. 282). Overtones and other forms of sympathetic vibrations were explored in the seventeenth century, as was the velocity of sound. It was Newton who, in his *Mathematical Principles,* proved on theoretical grounds that the velocity of sound varied with the elasticity and the density of the conducting medium—and since these vary from day to day it is not surprising that in the seventeenth century many different results were given for the velocity of sound in air. But most were in the right region, just over 1000 feet per second. That sound needs a medium of propagation, such as air, was proved when Guericke (1602–1686), using the air pump he had invented, showed that no sound was audible if a bell was struck in a vacuum. As more and more air was let into the vessel enclosing the bell, the sound became increasingly audible. Discoveries on auditory functioning in the seventeenth century were less imposing. Various anatomists from Galen onwards, including Willis, had described the appearance of the ear, both external and internal, but the most comprehensive treatise of the century was written by Duverney (1648–1730) in 1683. Willis had argued that the organ of hearing was the cochlea rather than any other part of the middle ear. Duverney, however, came much closer to realizing how the ear worked than any predecessor—Crombie (1964) has called him "the Kepler of hearing." For Duverney, vibrations set up in the air caused the eardrum to vibrate. The vibrations were transmitted to the small bones, the ossicles, of the middle ear and then to the cochlea, which Duverney thought was filled with air. He made the far-reaching speculation that different parts of the cochlea responded, by a sort of sympathetic vibration, to sounds of varying pitches. Crombie (1964) reproduces some of Duverney's elegant drawings of the auditory system.

Little of importance was apparently published in the seventeenth century on smell, taste, or touch, although we should point out that it was not long before the microscopists of the early eighteenth century were detecting certain bodies in the tissue of the skin that we now know to subserve tactile sensation.

Late Seventeenth-Century Philosophers

The philosophical successors to Descartes in this century may be divided into those who followed him in many matters, the Cartesians, and those who were concerned either with non-Cartesian matters or who criticized him outright. One major Cartesian was Louis de la Forge (1632–1666), who followed Descartes' dualism faithfully but who also offered an account of animal learning in terms of the flow of animal spirits. When two stimuli have been experienced together, he argued, then two streams of animal spirits are conjoined in the brain, one corresponding to each stimulus. When one of the stimuli is reexperienced, the first stream of spirits rearouses the second stream, forming the basis of a learned association. Other French writers stressed similar ideas, and Diamond (1969) has called this group the *connectionists*.

Another great Cartesian was Nicholas Malebranche (1638–1715). Malebranche was essentially concerned with reconciling Cartesianism with Christianity and devised the theory known as *occasionalism*, according to which, since the soul's events are in unextended substance and the body's events in extended substance, the two could not influence each other without the intervention of a third party, God. As Mercier puts it, "the soul's volitions became an *occasion* for God's causal operation upon the body, and the movements of the animal spirits became the *occasion* of an operation of God upon the soul" (1918, p. 38). But there is no direct causation between soul and body. In developing his theory Malebranche expressed his skepticism about the existence of an agent intellect and also about innate ideas, but he was also deeply interested in the phenomena of erroneous reasoning and perceptual illusions because they seemed to be inconsistent with the role of God in the operations of the soul-body system. He is particularly well known for arguing that we are prevented from making serious misinterpretations of the world around us because we make use of cues, largely learned by experience, concerning the real nature of objects. If, for example, we see a tree on the horizon that looks as small as our thumbnail, we are prevented from concluding that it really is that small because we have learned to use cues that allow us to correct for the effect of distance. Among cues to distance are (1) the angle of vision subtended, with distant objects subtending smaller angles, (2) the mechanism of visual accommodation, allowing for focusing, (3) the relative size of objects, with distant objects looking smaller than near objects, (4) our knowledge of the original size, for example, of trees, (5) texture, with near objects showing more detail on their surfaces, and (6) the presence of intermediary objects that, for example, can cut off part of the tree, indicating it is further away than the object blocking it.

Our discussion of non-Cartesians will focus on Hobbes (1588–1679), Spinoza (1632–1677), and Locke (1632–1704). Each is notable for being very individualistic in his thought, courting unpopularity and calumny as a result. Hobbes, despite his own written protestations, was accused of atheism because of the strongly materialistic tone of many of his writings: To be called a Hobbesian in the late seventeenth century was to be insulted. Spinoza, while dealing in great detail with the concepts of nature and God, said little about Divine Revelation, thereby earning the criticism both of his fellow Jews and of Christians. Locke, by his continued expression of his Christian beliefs, escaped much condemnation from the churches but ran afoul of political enemies in England and was forced to leave the country for some time.

If only by virtue of their intellectual courage these men are to be remembered, but what is important from our point of view is the fact that they each had something to say about psychology. True, it is usually agreed that Hobbes, Spinoza, and Locke were primarily philosophers, but we shall see that each in his own way forced his readers to consider psychological matters as well.

Hobbes studied at Oxford and traveled widely in Europe as a gentlemen's companion; he met Galileo and may have had a brief meeting with Descartes. He had a good knowledge of mathematics, and this partly led him to see the universe as almost a machine in itself, in which matter was endlessly in motion following just those laws that Hobbes himself did not know but that would later be described by Newton. His most important writing was political: His *Leviathan* (1651) dealt with the question of how far a sovereign should be seen to reflect the general will of his subject people. But to do this the sovereign should have some idea of the general workings of people's minds, and so the first portion of *Leviathan* is a short account of human psychology in general. Almost the first sentence is: "The original of all thoughts is that which we call SENSE, for there is no conception in a man's mind, which hath not at first, totally, or by parts, been begotten upon the organs of sense." With this sentence we have the beginnings of the movement that would come to be called British empiricism. The word *empiricism* is derived from the use of *empirical* that implies all knowledge is based on experience: There are no innate ideas.

Hobbes was not the first to state that all our knowledge was the result of sense experiences. According to Cranefield (1970) there is a Latin phrase *"Nihil est in intellectu quod non prius fuerit in sensu"* (there is nothing in the intellect which was not first in the senses) which is found as far back as the Dark Ages as a description of something Aristotle might have believed. It recurs in Aquinas; we shall meet it again in Leibniz. The basic idea that all knowledge is based on memories laid down by the senses is also found in the *Syntagma philosophicum* of Pierre Gassendi (1592–1655), a work not yet translated into English but that, on the basis of secondhand accounts, would appear to precede Hobbes as an example of modern empiricism. But whereas the catch phrase had previously been used to *expound* an idea, Hobbes actually *asserted* it. Each perceived sensation, argued Hobbes, leaves an image that gradually decays, but it can form an "imagination" while it is fairly new or a "memory" when it is fairly old. Thus, he argued, "imagination and memory are but one thing" (1651/1839, p. 6). This represents a blow against the medieval faculty psychology, which had allotted imagination and memory to different places in the ventricles. The results of the process of imagining or remembering we call thoughts. Hobbes then distinguished between unguided thought processes, which often seem random as in daydreaming, and regulated thoughts, where an underlying desire or goal determines what thoughts will next come to mind. In a later work, entitled *Human Nature* (1658), this flow of thought was vividly described in a passage that represents the introduction of the notion of a flow of associations into the empirical tradition:

> The cause of the *coherence* or consequence of one conception to another, is their first *coherence* or consequence at that *time* when they are produced by a sense: as for example, from St. Andrew the mind runneth to St. Peter,

because their names are read together; from St. Peter to a *stone*, for the same cause; from *stone* to *foundation*, to *church*, and from church to *people*, and from people to *tumult*: and according to this example, the mind may almost run from anything to anything.

Baruch Spinoza was born of a Spanish-Portuguese-Jewish family in Amsterdam in 1632, at a time when the small republic of Holland was just shaking itself free from the tyranny of Spanish Catholic rule. Holland became independent in 1648 and until the end of the century was a center of trade, exploration, culture, and intellectual freedom. This period justly deserves the name of the Golden Age of Dutch history. We recall that Descartes settled there for much of his life; Leeuwenhoek worked with his microscopes there; Locke would eventually reside there for several years to escape certain political troubles in his native England. In this stimulating atmosphere Spinoza studied both Christian and Jewish writings but was particularly excited by the novel ideas of Hobbes and Descartes. Ousted by the Jewish community from Amsterdam because of his "free thinking," he ground lenses for a living for a few years, but his writings soon became known and admired to the extent that he was offered certain university positions, which he did not accept.

One of Spinoza's earliest works was an account of Descartes' philosophy, but his main work, published three years before his death in 1677, was a book entitled *Ethics Demonstrated with Geometrical Order*. Following Euclid's method, the book starts with certain definitions and axioms from which all later propositions are deductively derived. The *Ethics* is in five parts: Part I is on God, Part II on the mind, Part III on the affects or emotions, Part IV on the strength of the affects, and Part V on the intellect. The general gist of the book is as follows: First Spinoza showed how the concept of God is related to the two "attributes" of extension and thought; this dichotomy probably is derived from Descartes. It is a short step from this beginning to the discussion of the nature of mind and body in themselves. The underlying goal of the activity of mind is self-preservation, and to this end our behavior is adapted in such a way that each idea we have is followed by, and related to, a bodily experience known as an affect. All affects in turn rest on three primary affects, joy, sorrow, and desire. The book's final sections relate the contents of this striving mind to its control over the affects and to an understanding and love of God. From these remarks it can be seen that the beginning of the book is concerned with metaphysics, the middle with psychology, and only the end with what we would now call ethics.

The reader should be aware that the preceding discussion has been quite cavalier in its skimming and avoidance of the difficulties of the work. For a start Spinoza argued that extension and thought are the only two attributes of the substance of the universe that our minds are able to apprehend and that in turn God's own nature is itself characterized by extension and thought. Wolfson (1934), after a brilliant and scholarly account of Spinoza's indebtedness not only to Descartes but also to medieval philosophy, comments that the idea that God is extended marks a daring leap forward, abolishing the distinction between nature (the universe) and God. Spinoza, claims Wolfson, made other such identifications, all in the direction of breaking down the artificial distinctions of dualism (and other systems) among the material, the mental or spiritual, and the divine. A second daring leap was Spinoza's belief that since God and the universe follow the identical laws of nature, we cannot think of God as a purposeful being meddling with those laws at a whim. A third daring leap was for Spinoza to argue that since God is extended and material any concept of the soul as somehow divine and immaterial must be replaced. Soul is inseparable from body: Whatever affects the body affects the soul and vice versa. This is a fundamental breakaway from Cartesian dualism and allows Spinoza to build up his theory of emotional behavior without having to hedge himself by arguing for an immaterial soul or spirit that interferes with the operation of the natural laws of the emotions.

A final daring leap is to assert that, since the aim of behavior is self-preservation, each element of our behavior is determined by a previous action and therefore there is no need to postulate something called a will. To be more precise, Spinoza argued that the concept of *will* is subsumed in the concept of *intellect* and that this in turn is merely a word we use to say that we have a conscious awareness both of our own bodily sensations and of our thoughts. Spinoza explicitly condemned the medieval doctrine of the agent intellect and labeled all such faculties as "fictitious," mere names for "metaphysical . . . entities which we are in the habit of forming from individual cases" (1930, p. 195).

Spinoza's most highly developed contribution to our understanding of behavior was his account of the emotions. Starting with joy, sorrow, and desire, he showed how as many as forty-eight emotions could be derived by the interplay of these three fundamental emotions with the array of pleasant or painful stimuli we encounter in everyday life. Wolfson, however, has demonstrated that forty-three of these are taken almost directly from Descartes' *Passions of the Soul*; the other five are probably from some unknown source, perhaps classical. There are hints that we can hate or love objects for reasons not obvious to us; Spinoza stressed the individual differences in the causes and intensities of our emotional feelings; he gives an interesting discussion of socially motivated affects such as commiseration, emulation, and benevolence.

John Locke followed, in his empiricism, in the line of Hobbes, though apparently he was little influenced directly by Hobbes (R. I. Watson, 1968, p. 181). He studied medicine and other sciences at Oxford and was also learned in Greek and philosophy. He joined the Royal Society and throughout his life kept notebooks of medical observations and other scientific matters. Dewhurst (1963) reports that Locke may have tried to distill blood to see whether it could be reduced to Aristotle's four elements; at the end of his life he wrote, in a letter, that "I fear the Galenists four Humours . . . will upon Examination be found to be but so many learned empty sounds, with no precise, determinate Signification" (Dewhurst, 1963, p. 310). Nevertheless, he referred to animal spirits which he suggested might be "exhausted" by epileptic seizures (Dewhurst, 1963, p. 136). His life, then, spanned the period in which ancient medical lore was being replaced by the new scientific discoveries mentioned earlier in this chapter. Possibly Locke's most interesting contribution to neurological medicine was his account of a case of trigeminal neuralgia (a painful inflammation of the facial nerve, usually on one side of the face), which he asserted was indeed the result of "mischief" done to a nerve (Dewhurst, 1963, p. 95). His physician's practice, however, took up only part of his time, and for many years he was also confidante and secretary to the Earl of Shaftesbury. Shaftesbury had to flee to Holland to escape retribution for his part in a plot against Charles II, and Locke, perhaps himself under suspicion, followed him there. Locke returned to England in 1689 and began publishing his major works on politics and education. His most important work from our point of view was the *Essay Concerning Human Understanding*, which appeared twelve years before his death in 1704. He rewrote and enlarged this book in 1700, and it is to this fourth edition that we refer in what follows.

Hobbes had argued that all knowledge was built up on the basis of sensory information, but he had not tackled, in any explicit way, the question of innate ideas. In fact, even before Descartes' espousal of these the question had become one of fashionable importance. Descartes' concept of innate ideas fell on fertile ground in England in the first part of the century, for several thinkers had argued that conscience was implanted in man by God, and for the remainder of the century a steady stream of works appeared, often written by clergymen, which claimed that God had instilled humans with innate ideas of morality. In particular, a group of writers led by Ralph Cudworth (1617–1688), known as the Cambridge Platonists, were concerned to integrate orthodox theology with the analytical power of the new philosophies. Some authors have argued that Locke, by beginning his *Essay* with an attack on the doctrine of innate ideas, was as concerned with criticizing these persons as much as with criticizing Descartes. The question of *whom* Locke was attacking— he named few persons in particular—is discussed in detail by Yolton (1956). Whoever it was, there is no question that, like Hobbes, Locke believed that all the concepts in adult thought are the result of two processes, sensation and reflection. By sensation the mind receives data from the external world. The sensations vanish, but memories are left. We can observe these memories with our minds and by reflecting on them can lay down further memories and, moreover, give ourselves certain concepts by the process of mental abstraction. A single word symbolizing a unit of content of the mind at any time is "idea": Ideas for Locke, then, arose either from sensation or reflection.

Locke's "ideas" tell us about reality, but certain concepts, such as those of "extension" or "time," would seem off-hand to be the result of more intuitive knowledge. Locke, however, asserted at length that these concepts *do* arise by way of experience. Our concept of space (extension), he argued, is not based on sight alone, is not the result of some innate grasp of the way the world should appear visually: It is construed from a synthesis of sight and touch. That learning plays a role in our normal perception of the world was, we saw, mooted by Malebranche: Locke discussed it explicitly and, as an example, dealt with a question raised by his friend Dr. Molyneux. The question is whether a blind man who has learned to distinguish, by touch, a cube from a sphere, could, if he regained his sight, say by sight alone which is the cube and which the sphere. Locke suggested that the proponents of an innate sense of space would answer yes to this question; Locke himself, however, answered no and maintained that the man would have to be taught which was which by linking his new visual experiences with his previously learned tactile experiences.

Locke also argued that our concepts of time and God were not innate but the result of intellectual, albeit unconscious, construction. Our ideas, for Locke, are either simple or complex, the latter being essentially amalgamations of the former; included as complex ideas might be those such as the idea of the metal "gold," which is constructed from simple ideas such as yellow, metal, hard, and so on. In turn, these simple ideas allow us to represent to ourselves certain qualities in the external world: Sense data, for Locke, result from the "secondary qualities" of objects. It is not *necessary* that gold be yellow or hard: The matter is of secondary importance if we ask what the essence of an object is. On the other hand, almost by definition, all objects have, necessarily, certain "primary qualities" such as those of being extended, solid, movable, and shaped. The primary qualities are "inseparable" from the bodies in question. A third quality is the *power* of a body to exert an influence on another body, as fire had the power to make lead fluid. Locke's distinction between primary and secondary qualities was, we noted earlier, foreshadowed by Galileo.

The first two books of the *Essay* are replete with other assertions worthy of discussion here. Forced to make a choice, we shall mention only Locke's conception of what is meant by the self and Locke's contribution to the associationist tradition. It is possible to read into Descartes' dictum "I think, therefore I am" the following assumption: "Because I think, there must be a self which thinks, and that self is me." The awareness that one is oneself, or has *a* self, seems intuitive and unlearned. For Locke this was not so: Like the concepts of extension and duration, the concept of one's self is an acquired one, the result of abstractions and cognitions during one's lifetime. The essence of an assertion that one is or has a self is that one is conscious of experiencing, sensing, perceiving, thinking, and so on. One's knowledge of a continuously existing self is the result of comparing the present objects of which one is aware with one's memory of objects of which one was previously aware. It is the continuity of consciousness that is the criterion of asserting that one has a continuing self or identity, and Locke looked ahead to nineteenth-century psychiatry when he pointed out that part of oneself can carry out an act of which another part is unaware: The self is more fragile than we like to think. Locke's argument has been criticized many times since its inception; Allison (1966) nevertheless calls it "the earliest systematic treatment of the problem of personal identity in the history of modern philosophy" (p. 41) and reviews the background and subsequent history of Locke's views on the matter.

The second issue is Locke's role as an associationist. We have seen that the line of associationists goes back to antiquity—the peaks were Aristotle, Vives, and Hobbes—but we have not yet encountered an author who explicitly discussed the matter using the word *association*. Locke, however, has a whole chapter entitled "Of the Association of Ideas," but it is less concerned with the reasonable flow of ideas we presume to be guided by contiguity, similarity, and so on as with the unreasonable flow of ideas we find both in certain kinds of illness and in the more relaxed moments of everyday life. His prime examples of unreasonable associations are what we would now call conditioned emotional responses. He recounts the story of a friend who had a surgical operation without anesthetic: The friend, though grateful to the surgeon, could never bear to look at the surgeon afterwards, so strong was the association between the surgeon and the pain the friend had suffered. He also tells of a man who learned complicated dance steps in a room in which there happened to be a trunk, then found he could only dance well if that or a similar trunk was present, so strongly had the memory of the steps linked itself with the sight of the trunk. People can be put off books because they are associated with unpleasant memories of school. All sorts of absurd conceptions of God can arise if one's idea of God is associated with a particular picture of God. An ignorant person can inculcate ideas of goblins and sprites in a child's mind at bedtime and as a result he or she learns to fear the dark. These anecdotal examples illustrated the importance in our lives of the associations between events and emotions, but Locke did not attempt a systematic analysis of other kinds of association. The chapter on the self and the chapter on the association of ideas were late additions to Book II of the original text of the *Essay*. Book III is about language and Book IV about truth and how knowledge of the truth can be obtained. The interest of these two books is essentially philosophical rather then psychological.

So far we have seen that both physiology and philosophy contributed much to the history of our hybrid discipline. Was there any pure psychology? Books on mnemonics, physiognomy, dream interpretation, and so on continued to be published, but we may close this chapter by a brief mention of three works on behavior that do not fit obviously into the categories of pure physiology or philosophy. In 1672 Willis published a book entitled *Two Discourses Concerning the Soul of Brutes*. In this he offered an account of how memory is subserved, in both animals and humans, by the flow of animal spirits, which can arouse memory images. This wide-ranging book also discusses the differences between humans and animals in terms of differences between their brains; makes the suggestion that the intensity of a stimulus determines how much of the brain is affected; offers a theory of sleep and dreaming in terms of animal spirits; and discusses both neurological and psychological illnesses, among other topics. It refers to its topic as a "Psycheology" of the soul. Christian Thomasius (1655–1728) proposed to use a questionnaire to rate the degree to which different individuals possessed different personality attributes; this possibly represents the first use of numbers to measure something psychological (Ramul, 1963). Finally, Hooke in 1682 gave a lecture on memory that raised a number of questions, such as the role of interference in retrieval, anticipating modern research (B. R. Singer, 1976).

A listing of other seventeenth-century works in psychology is given by Schüling (1964). Commentaries on Aristotle continued to appear in this century, and there was a revival of interest in the *Characters* of Theophrastus. The word *psychology* appears rarely, but several works have titles containing the words *anthropology* (the science of humans) and *pneumatology*. This last was the name given particularly to studies of the soul, including its theological connotations.

Summary

Following some general remarks on the achievements of the Renaissance, a survey was given of the major topics written about by psychologists in the sixteenth century. Although Vives continued to propagate certain medieval ideas, his treatment of memory and the emotions was more modern; Huarte, however, questioned the medieval localization of function, even though he continued to argue that intelligence was associated with humoral physiology. Other books of the century were concerned with physiognomy and mnemonic systems.

At the start of the seventeenth century, Galileo contributed to our understanding of sound and Kepler to our understanding of vision. Harvey, who overturned Galen's theories by his discovery of the circulation of the blood, was also skeptical of the existence of animal spirits in the nervous system. Standing at the crossroads between ancient and modern times was Descartes, who, however, offered mechanistic accounts of reflexes and emotions based on older notions about animal spirits. Descartes was also the founder of modern dualism, a corollary of which is that certain ideas might be present in the individual at birth. Later physiological contributions of the century included explicit criticisms of the theory of animal spirits and attempts at localization of function in the brain were no longer restricted to the ventricles. The understanding of visual functioning also grew, particularly following Newton's analysis of the nature of color. Duverney began modern research on audition.

In the late seventeenth century, many philosophers followed Descartes, but others were more original. Hobbes began the tradition of British empiricism, which held that psychological activity is determined by the flow of associations linking memories laid down by sensations. Spinoza offered an alternative to Cartesian dualism and built up a theory of the interplay of the emotions. Locke attacked the notion of innate ideas and argued for an empiricist account of our ability to interact with the visually perceived world; he also offered an analysis of the concept of the self and an account of how emotional associations can determine much of our behavior.

The chapter closed with mention of some minor writings of the seventeenth century.

The Eighteenth
Century

4

Introduction

The eighteenth century represents the beginning of the modern period in a number of ways, including the first signs of popular uprisings against tyrannical regimes (the French Revolution, the American War of Independence). Although these political upheavals took place at the end of the century, their groundwork was laid in the writings of many literary men and women, particularly philosophers—in fact, the French writers were known collectively as *les philosophes*. Newton and Locke had put England at the center of the new skepticism about the true value of the old teachings based on Aristotle and the Bible; their example inspired writers such as Berkeley and Hume in England, Voltaire, Diderot, Condillac, and La Mettrie in France, and Wolff and Kant in Germany, to erect in place of standard Christian doctrine a variety of independent systems that had in common empiricism and optimism. They believed that because much of adult behavior was based on experience, that is, education, individuals had the right to make enquiries for themselves and not placidly accept what they were told by the Church. Moreover, they should not passively accept their place in a hierarchical society, but should work actively to remodel it for the general good. The democracy of Athenian Greece became a standard to be emulated: Gay (1966) has traced in detail how the *philosophes* and others moved away from Church teachings to a rediscovery of "pagan" virtues widely praised in Greek and Roman times, notably the simple virtue of happiness; the American Declaration of Independence is essentially a crystalization of eighteenth-century optimism and distrust of authority. But it must be realized that many of the writers of the eighteenth century were threatened with prison by the censors and that the "Enlightenment" took place against a background of antagonism from Church and monarchy in many of the countries of Europe. Moreover, only a few, such as d'Holbach, argued for an unfettered atheism; a preferred solution to the dilemma of faith versus reason was deism, a belief in a Supreme Being who was not necessarily the personal God of Christianity. The role of deism in eighteenth-century thought is discussed particularly by Hazard (1946/1973).

Furthermore, toward the end of the eighteenth century, a reaction set in against the emphasis on reason typical of the middle eighteenth century, and many followers of thinkers like Jean-Jacques Rousseau (1712–1778) in France argued that often we should follow our feelings rather than our reason. This was the beginning of the Romantic movement, which reached its zenith in the first decades of the next century.

In psychology, the most important result of this free spirit of inquiry was that it forced writers to ask where morality and religious beliefs fitted in, given an empirical account of the growth of the mind. Different writers such as Hume, Reid, and Kant gave different answers. We shall say more later on how psychology as a university discipline gradually emerged from this confusion of opinion, but it is important to note that when writers on psychology were associated with universities, such as Wolff in Germany or Reid in Scotland, they had to tread carefully, given the power of the theological faculties.

Another growing trend was the belief that all mental states ultimately depend on bodily states, and throughout the century quite ambitious attempts were made to link psychological moods and feelings with events in the nervous system. Nevertheless, discoveries about how the nervous system *worked* were rather meager in the eighteenth century. We shall begin our coverage by first examining these discoveries, then move on to the writings of the philosophers in Britain, France, and Germany.

Physiological Advances

Knowledge of the anatomy of the brain and central nervous system was advanced considerably in the eighteenth century: Among three major summaries of these topics were books entitled *The Brain* (Swedenborg, 1741–1744), *The Elements of the Physiology of the Human Body* (Haller, 1757–1766, eight volumes), and a *Dissertation on the Function of the Nervous System* (Prochaska, 1784). The first and last of these are available in modern reprints. In these books diagrams of the brain look like modern diagrams, the main brain parts were named much as they are today, and Emmanuel Swedenborg (1688–1772) in particular made enlightened guesses about the functions of the various brain regions. But all this speculation remained curiously inconclusive; our understanding of nervous activity and brain localization of function really began in the nineteenth century.

Two aspects of neurology, however, were of particular interest to the eighteenth-century pioneers. One question concerned the general nature of nervous tissue and how it related to what we may loosely call *soul* or *mind*. The second concerned reflexes. We shall deal with these in turn.

Throughout the eighteenth century attempts were made to offer grand syntheses of neurology, psychology, and theology. For example, Swedenborg wrote an ambitious book entitled *On the Soul*, in which he tried to imitate Aristotle by first describing how the body, and especially the senses, worked, then postulating how the soul was related to the body. But his account was essentially Christian and almost mystical, and gave God a direct role in the integration of body and soul. Apart from Swedenborg, it was generally argued that the soul was the vague entity that controlled rational as well as emotional or instinctive behavior. The person who most strongly argued along these lines was G. E. Stahl (1660–1743). Reacting against the growing mechanistic approach to the body, he argued that bodily tissue itself produces a "soul" whose function it is to protect that tissue against deterioration and decay. Flesh and other bodily substances are therefore themselves ensouled, so to speak. A move away from this quasi-mystical approach was made by Albrecht von Haller (1708–1777), probably the greatest physiologist of his time. One of Haller's most innovative achievements was to argue against Stahl's "soul" in favor of the notion that certain tissues in the body had particular properties that made them *appear* ensouled but that in fact could be described mechanistically. He distinguished "sensible" parts of the body—namely, those supplied with nerves—from "irritable" parts—parts consisting of muscular tissue. The word *irritability* had been introduced by Glisson (1597–1677). On certain matters of detail Haller was criticized: For example, he thought that tendons were insensible, and he did not recognize that for a muscle to be irritable—that is, contractile—it had to have a nervous supply just as did sensible parts. Nevertheless this opinion, as expressed in a short treatise of 1755, was of great importance in convincing researchers that even such soullike activities as feeling and moving could be talked about in terms of straightforward physiology.

A further step forward was taken by J. F. Unzer (1727–1799), who, in a long work entitled the *Principles of Physiology* (1771), attempted to reconcile the views of Stahl and Haller by suggesting that there was a special kind of "life" or "force" intrinsic to the nervous system—following

Haller, he called it a *vis nervosa*. This in itself does not seem to say much, but Unzer elaborated the argument so as to show that complex behavior patterns such as instincts, passions, and voluntary acts all derived from the action of the *vis nervosa* in the brain and the nervous system. The action of the *vis nervosa* could continue even when the organism was without a brain: A decapitated frog would continue to show certain responses to particular stimuli (see following), and there had been reports for decades of decapitated tortoises and snakes "living" for some time after the operation. As late as the middle of the nineteenth century the argument still maintained enough of the mystery of the "soul" to render controversial the question of whether certain tissues were imbued with "life"; on the other hand, the notion that nerves were characterized by a particular property not shared by other tissues (such as blood vessels) prepared the way for the discovery of the electrical properties of nerves at the end of the eighteenth century. A final point worth noting is that, during the eighteenth century, efforts were made actually to examine "animal spirits" by squeezing nerves. These attempts to show that the nerves were filled with fluid failed—a marrowy exudate is what usually emerged—nevertheless, the term *animal spirits* is still found in writings throughout the century. But *vis nervosa* increasingly came to replace *animal spirits*. It was only in 1781 that Fontana asserted definitely that there was no apparent canal inside a nerve fiber along which the supposed animal spirits could flow.

Probably the century's main contribution to neurophysiology was the elaboration of the theory of reflexes. Descartes had first mooted the general principle, but it was Stephen Hales (1677–1761) who showed (1) that a decapitated frog would "kick" its leg if a foot were stimulated, but moreover (2) that if the spinal cord were destroyed, such reactions could no longer be elicited. His experiments were repeated and elaborated by Robert Whytt (1714–1766), who added the information that some reactions could be elicited even if only parts of the spinal cord were left intact. Whytt also did some interesting research on the pupillary response to light. Descartes' theory that the pineal gland mediated these reactions fell into abeyance; and other authors, such as Unzer and Prochaska, began to discuss these responses as fundamental elements in the account of animal and human behavior. There was still some mystery about these reactions: Whytt thought the soul was necessary for their production and argued that the existence of these responses after removal of the brain supported the notion that the spinal cord had a soul of its own (see Liddell, 1960, pp. 60–73 on the persistence of the notion of a "spinal cord soul" well into the nineteenth century).

Unzer, on the other hand, was content to use the concept of the *vis nervosa* and was largely responsible for the introduction of the words *stimulus* and *response* to refer to the sensory and motor elements of the total reaction. Like Willis, he thought that messages from the stimulus were somehow reflected into motor messages much as light is reflected from a mirror, but it was not until an article by Marshall Hall in 1833 that the noun *reflex* started being used. A corollary of these early hypotheses on reflexes was that the spinal cord took on a more important role in physiological thinking: It was no longer just a big nerve extending from the brain.

Prochaska summarized much of the early knowledge on reflexes in the 1784 book mentioned earlier and introduced the term *sensorium commune* to refer to the presumed locus of interaction between the influence of the stimulus and the initiation of the response. Many reflex responses, such as limb withdrawal from a painful stimulus, sneezing when the nostrils are irritated, choking when food particles enter the windpipe, and blinking if something comes near the eye, are, Prochaska argued, useful to the preservation of the health of the organism.

A final step in applying the knowledge acquired from studying reflexes was taken by Cabanis (1757–1808) in 1799: He postulated that some reflexes were carried out at a purely spinal level (e.g., the continued movements of an animal after decapitation or even a human after being guillotined); other responses were carried out at "higher" levels by means of the brain. The concept of one's own self was the result of the highest level of brain activity. Murphy and Kovach (1972) suggest that Cabanis's hypothesis was a forerunner of more elaborate theories of "levels of nervous organization" expounded in the following century.

Research on the special senses in the eighteenth century had little of the pioneering appeal of seventeenth-century and little of the sheer weight of nineteenth-century research. On vision, we may note that two major books were written during the century, both by Englishmen. William Porterfield's large book of 1759, *A Treatise on the Eye, the Manner and Phaenomena of Vision,* dealt with the optics of the retina, the still-unsolved problem of the accommodation of the eye in distance perception, the convergence of the eyes (a point on which Berkeley wrote, see following), the various cues to the perception of distance, why we see only one field of vision when we have two eyes, adaptation, and color. On adaptation, we may note only that it was recognized throughout the century that bright lights can fatigue us and that we can become accustomed to the dark after a few minutes; the experimental treatment of these topics, however, was not really begun until the late nineteenth century.

As for color, we might record in particular the suggestion of the mathematician Euler (1707–1783) that light—which he believed, in opposition to Newton, to be wavelike rather than corpuscular—had frequencies of vibration just as sound did. Color, he suggested, was therefore related to the frequency of the waves per unit of time. Euler's theory was largely ignored during his life, and it was only much later that color was related to wavelength.

A second major work of the period was Joseph Priestley's *The History and Present State of Discoveries Relating to Vision, Light and Colours* (1772). This book was mainly about the physics of light but included mention of some phenomena of vision that were explored experimentally in the eighteenth century. These included afterimages, whose duration was measured (Ramul, 1963) and whose interplay of color was described, and color and brightness contrast. The main development in the physics of light in the eighteenth century concerned the measurement and study of light intensity. Both Bouguer (1698–1758) and Lambert (1728–1777) invented devices for measuring how bright one light was in comparison with another. Posterity remembers Lambert's name in the word *millilambert,* a unit of reflected light intensity; he also introduced the term *albedo* to refer to the fraction of light reflected from an object.

Bouguer did what is probably the first experiment on just noticeable differences among light intensities. He found that if a shadow of an object was made just noticeably different from the background illumination, this difference could be preserved provided the absolute values of intensity of the lights (candles) illuminating the object and the background were kept in a constant ratio. This is an early foreshadowing of what would later be called *Weber's Law.* Perhaps the most striking contribution of the eighteenth century to visual science was the observation made particularly by John Dalton (1766–1844) that some persons—Dalton himself included—could not distinguish among certain colors. Dalton himself had difficulty distinguishing red and green. It was not long before color blindness, as it is now called, became one of the main phenomena that had to be explained by any theory of color vision.

The study of sound got off to a good start in 1700 when Joseph Sauveur (1653–1716), using organ pipes, suggested that the deepest note a human subject could detect had a frequency of about 12 cycles per second and the note of highest pitch a frequency of about 6400 cycles per second. (The modern account usually gives values of about 20 and 20,000 cycles, respectively, for these two limits.) Furthermore, Sauveur made the first measurement of differential sensitivity, arguing that a difference in pitch of only about one-hundredth of a semitone could be detected. This he estimated using a single string whose length could be varied by very small degrees. A year later Sauveur clarified the matter of overtones, which had been known since the time of Descartes. He used the word *fundamental* to refer to the basic frequency and talked of the other tones as *harmonics.* He understood that these overtones resulted from vibrations from parts of the string added to the basic vibration of the whole string. In the course of this research he discovered that if notes of slightly different pitches were sounded together, the observer could detect a sort of pulsation in the total chord, *beats* as they came to be known. Sauveur showed that the beats were due to vibrations alternately reinforcing and canceling each other out and that the rate of beats corresponded to the difference in original frequency of the two notes. The tuning fork was invented by Shore in 1714. On the working of the ear itself, little was added to previous knowledge, largely because microscopes were not yet good enough to permit close examination of the cochlea. Nevertheless, Haller, in his treatment of hearing in *Elementa,* suggested that the sensations of different pitches may have something to do with the length of the fibers of the cochlea, a theory that adumbrated Helmholtz's later resonance theory.

On the senses of smell, taste, and touch we may note simply that all received chapters in Haller's treatise but that little of positive importance was added. At the end of the century, Erasmus Darwin (1731–1802) described how a certain patient had anesthesia in his legs for touch and pinpricks, yet he could detect heat if a hot object was brought near one of his legs. This is one of the earliest indications that there might be separate receptor systems for touch and heat perception.

We cannot leave eighteenth-century neurophysiology, however, without considering certain persons who attempted to base fairly comprehensive systems of psychology on fundamental physiological principles. The persons in question are David Hartley (1705–1757) and Charles Bonnet (1720–1790). Both argued that an understanding of animal and human behavior rested ultimately on an understanding of the nervous system; even though there was so much left to be known about nerves and the brain, they felt that enough knowledge was available to allow them to build a psychological superstructure on a physiological foundation.

Hartley studied theology and mathematics at Cambridge before pursuing a medical career. Over the course of several years he wrote a long work with the title *Observations on Man, His Frame, His Duty, and His Expectations;* it finally appeared, after some delay, in 1749. The book is in two parts. The first concerns an individual's "Frame" and is the section of greatest interest to psychologists. The second concerns "Duty and Expectations" and is almost purely theological: A person's expectations are held to include mixed pleasure and pain in life but finally happiness later. However, Part I of the *Observations* is quite avowedly an attempt to draw together Newton's speculation on the nature of matter, particularly the matter of the nervous system, and Locke's speculations on the association of ideas. Locke had never explicitly attempted to reduce *all* human complex behavior to associations, but a certain Reverend Doctor Gay had apparently tried to do so, and Hartley followed his example.

The gist of Hartley's theory is easy to understand because it essentially corresponds to our present fashion of thinking. For Hartley each sensory input leaves a mark on the nervous system. Synchronous and successive sensory inputs leave synchronous and successive marks, respectively. These marks persist for a while in what we would now call short-term memory. In so doing they are subject to more complicated processes, and ultimately we have a brain full of marks or vestiges left by previous experiences. These in various combinations underlie our mental life. We may be more precise about the marks: Following Newton's theory that the nerves were solid and conducted vibrations, Hartley argued that for each sensory input there was a corresponding vibration in the nerves. The marks left in brains by these vibrations were miniature vibrations or *vibratiuncles*. If stimuli A, B, and C were perceived in succession, they left miniature vibrations a, b, and c successively in the "medullary" substance of the nerves and the brain. The extent to which the solid nerves were loose enough to vibrate freely depended in part on the pressure exerted on the brain by the blood vessels. In states such as sleep or drunkenness the veins were expanded, resting more heavily on the brain, and thus attenuating the vibrations. Hence unconsciousness would be experienced in these states. Animals were held to have simpler brains than humans, hence simpler thought experiences. Hartley was very much a naturalist in his belief that humans and animals shared much in common in their mental lives and in his belief that brain events underlay mental events. He remained a transcendentalist, however, in his faith in divine revelation, with its corollary that God could directly reveal his intentions to the individual's mind.

Hartley devoted many pages to developing his idea that most mental life results from the interplay of associations. In particular, he applied associationistic analysis to the study of how children learn languages. But, ultimately, complex mental experiences such as reasoning or emotion depend on memories of sensations, hence Hartley has a long section on the special senses. The experience of different pitches, he said, depends on the frequency of different vibrations, as does the experience of different colors: In his chapters on vision Hartley almost slavishly followed Newton's misguided attempt to base the range of colors on the range of notes in the octave (see Chap. 3). On the other hand he argued that pain can result from excessive vibrations: Touch and other stimuli affecting the skin, if too intense, result in pain. Since all stimuli are stored as miniature vibrations along with those vibrations mediating pleasure or pain, our mental lives are closely determined by pleasure or pain. For example, we learn to *love* the things that give us pleasure, then to *desire* what we love, then to *hope* for what we desire, and experience *joy* if we obtain it. Contrariwise, we learn to *hate* the things that give us pain, feel *aversion* for such things, *fear* their coming, and experience *grief* if they do arrive. Thus, many of the emotions arise by association from the two basic feelings of pleasure and pain.

Charles Bonnet, a Swiss naturalist and philosopher, had very similar ideas. He believed that from a few basic functions many more sophisticated functions could be built up by association, but underlying his associationism was the view that for each cognitive experience there were corresponding changes in the nerve fibers. Like Hartley, he acknowledged his debt to Newton; but he was less emphatic that the change in the fibers consists of vibrations. Instead he spoke of movements in a fiber, with these elicited by stimulation. Once a fiber has been stimulated, its "disposition" to respond again to the same stimulus is changed. A stimulus in the external world causes the fibers to move more freely than does stimulation from another bundle of fibers; thus, the experience of a sensation is more intense than the experience of a memory image. The movements imparted by stimuli to nerves die away slowly, thus leaving aftereffects. Throughout his book exposing these views, the *Essai Analytique sur les Facultés de l'Âme (Analytic Essay on the Faculties of the Soul,* 1760), Bonnet stressed that the mind was essentially mechanical. He made comparisons between humans and artificial models and clocks, but at the end of the work he insisted that the soul itself is immaterial. To this extent Bonnet remained a Cartesian dualist and even attempted to localize the seat of the soul in the brain: He suggested, but did not completely espouse, the notion that this seat is in the corpus callosum.

The Philosophical Tradition: Britain and France

Our organization of this section will focus first on the main empirical tradition common to both Britain and France. This tradition rests on the notion that adult mental processes are the result of memories laid down by sensations and interacting by virtue of the laws of association. Then we will deal with the German tradition, which, although it too absorbed the influence of British and French empiricism, was more ready to accept the notion that certain of our "ideas" were not acquired by experience.

Locke's immediate successor in the empiricist tradition was George Berkeley (1685–1753). As a student he read and discussed Locke's *Essay* at Trinity College, Dublin, the main university of Berkeley's native Ireland. At the early age of twenty-four he published an *Essay towards a New Theory of Vision* in which he examined Locke's thesis in the light of a close examination of certain aspects of sight. The following year he published his *Treatise concerning the Principles of Human Knowledge* in which a broader philosophy was based, in part, on the conclusions drawn in the book on vision. Three years later, in 1713, while he was still a scholar at Trinity College, he published three *Dialogues between Hylas and Philonous,* an attempt to make more comprehensible some of the more difficult assertions of the earlier books. By the time he was twenty-eight, then, he had produced most of his philosophy and psychology. After this, he traveled extensively in Europe and America before finally settling down in Ireland. He preached for a while at a church in Newport, Rhode Island, where a memorial to him can still be seen.

Berkeley's book on vision is mainly concerned with three aspects of vision: distance perception, magnitude perception, and location perception. Although not explicitly stated at the start of the work, it becomes clear that for Berkeley the initial data of vision consist entirely of dots and splotches of color of varying shades of brightness. This is all the eye offers us. But, as we mature, we learn to make various kinds of judgment based on the interplay of these dots and splotches of color with each other and with our other sensations, particularly those of touch. It is not always realized, however, that he maintained that the associations of the world of vision remain separated from the associations of the touch sense. He thus had an answer to Dr. Molyneux's question: If a blind man is given sight and asked to identify a cube and a sphere, items he had previously known only to touch, would he be able to identify the cube and sphere given visual information alone? According to Berkeley, he would not, because there would be no association between the old memories of touch and the new experiences of vision.

Berkeley argued that experience is necessary to use visual angle as a cue to depth: It is only through experience that we associate near objects with large angles and far objects with small angles. This association in turn depends on our observing that when we focus on a near object, it is because the large angle it subtends can, if the object is very near the eye, elicit a fuzzy appearance because the apex of the angle actually falls behind the retina. Furthermore, by focusing on the object so as to make it less fuzzy, we receive sensations from the eye muscles as the two eyes converge. Thus, while it is true that the subtended angle is related to distance judgments, it is because these in turn are associated with experiences of fuzziness and sensations of the movements of our eyes. Berkeley listed a number of other visual cues to distance, such as the number of interjacent objects, a list that often coincides with Malebranche's list: How far Berkeley may have been indebted to Malebranche is discussed in detail by Luce (1934). He also elaborated on how learned cues were used in the estimation of magnitude and location.

Given, then, that for Berkeley the visual world consisted entirely of sensations to which learned responses were appended to permit us to judge distance, magnitude, and location, we must ask whether any other concepts typifying our visual experiences need explication. Yes, answered Berkeley. The perceptual world consists only of what Locke called secondary qualities: color, pitch, and so on; Locke's primary qualities—such as extension, solidity, and number—are the result of associations based on experiences with the secondary qualities. Berkeley went even further:

Since extension, solidity, and number are mere extrapolations from experiences of color and intensity, he argued, we cannot *assume* that there is an underlying substrate called *matter,* which has these so-called primary qualities. Matter is purely a mental conception. Faced with the difficult problem of how to explain our sensations if there is no such thing as matter causing them, Berkeley argued that the cause of sensations resides in another *mind,* namely that of God. We will not follow him further into this intriguing theory; we would simply point out that in these assertions Berkeley strikes yet another blow at an Aristotelian assumption, namely, that there is a definite "substance" that elicits sensations. For the history of psychology, and of philosophy, the import of Berkeley's argument is that we have been making logical leaps from assertions about experiences to assertions about facts concerning the external world, leaps that are not strictly justified. Berkeley's philosophy may be controversial, but his psychology was profoundly stimulating.

Berkeley's successor in the empirical tradition was David Hume. Hume was born in 1711 in Edinburgh, where a thriving university had been in existence for over a century. He studied law and commerce at that institution but was more interested in a literary career. Given relative freedom, thanks to a legacy, Hume went into seclusion at La Flèche in France, where Descartes had similarly studied as a young man. Here, before the age of twenty-eight, Hume wrote his first and greatest work of philosophy/psychology, *A Treatise of Human Nature,* a long and difficult work that seemed to make little impact on the public. But the *Enquiry concerning Human Understanding* was published in 1748 and the *Enquiry concerning Principles of Morals* in 1751. These works, generally speaking, condensed many of the points made in the earlier work. In later life he became a historian and diplomat. He died in Edinburgh in 1776.

We mentioned earlier that Newton and Locke were the contemporary authors most respected in the early eighteenth century. But we also mentioned that Cudworth and other Cambridge Platonists had been deeply concerned with the problem of the relationship between religion and ethics: In particular, they had been concerned with whether morality was based on innate ideas. In the early eighteenth century a number of new writers on morals appeared in Britain, notably Bishop Butler (1692–1713). It almost forced itself on Hume's maturing mind that human knowledge could be expanded if he were to try to base a theory of morals on first principles of science—essentially psychological science—using as he went the deductive systematic approach that had proved so successful in Newton's hands.

This was not too different from what Locke had attempted, but Hume's goal was more obviously ethical than Locke's had been. If we adopt this viewpoint, the outline of Hume's philosophy becomes more transparent, for it must be realized that Hume's philosophy has, from the time of its publication, been seen as difficult and as capable of varying interpretations. To show the line of his reasoning: If he was to discuss morals, he was forced to discuss the concepts of vice and virtue. In turn, he saw that vice and virtue were terms that made sense only in the light of human feelings—the passions, as he called some of them. How the passions operated was admittedly connected with the issues of reason and will, but these could be seen as tangential to the main question of how the passions could be defined and how the several passions followed on one from the other. This question in turn forced him to consider the question of the associations between the passions: Clearly one passion led to another because the ideas connected with the one passion gave rise by some sort of association mechanism to the ideas connected with the subsequent passion. So Hume was forced to consider the association of ideas. Incidental to this consideration were the questions of how the flow of ideas determined our concepts of the self and how events could be talked about in terms of causes and effects. But how could the association of ideas be discussed unless *idea* was defined? The most elementary step in the progression from initial postulate to final ethical assertion must be the definition of an *idea*—Hume in fact distinguished mental ideas from sensory impressions. This of course is very similar to Locke's initial distinction between reflection and sensation and, although Hume is not as explicit as Locke in rejecting the concept of innate ideas, he is explicit in arguing that our ideas result from memories left by sensory impressions. For this reason Hume may be considered as being in the tradition of British empiricism. Thus we see that the logical flow of the argument in the *Treatise* can be put in perspective if we consider it all as tending in the direction of an analysis of ethical values and behavior.

In order to expound Hume's position, it is better to start, as Hume did, with the concepts of impressions and ideas and build up from there. Our main contention here will be that Hume's unique contributions to psychology were his analysis of causality and his later analysis of how the association of ideas could be extended to cover the association of the emotions. This last gives a unity to the flux of behavior of greater psychological interest than a unity imposed by the bland assertion that we have a "soul." Hume, in fact, only rarely talked about the soul. From his remark that "bodily pains and pleasure are the source of many passions both when felt and considered by the mind; but arise originally in the soul, or in the body, whichever you please to call it" (1739–1740/1955, p. 276), we are probably entitled to infer that he thought the soul a term likely to induce confusion rather than clarity.

Hume began by asserting that the only difference we *experience* between sensory impressions and mental ideas is in terms of their liveliness or intensity as subjectively felt. However, impressions are not restricted to sensations derived from objects in the external world; our internal feelings also count as impressions. Hume later remarked that all ideas are derived from impressions which "are correspondent to these, and which they exactly represent." Among the evidence Hume cited to support this view were his observations that children learn concepts in the order in which they first perceive the originating sensory impressions, and that persons without certain sensations, such as the blind or deaf, never attain any ideas corresponding to those sensations.

Hume then considered the association of ideas. Since chance alone does not join ideas in a haphazard sequence, Hume argued that there must be some "uniting principle." This led him to state that "the qualities, from which this association arises, and by which the mind is after this manner convey'd from one idea to another, are three, VIZ. RESEMBLANCE, CONTIGUITY in time or place, and CAUSE and EFFECT" (*Treatise*, p. 11). Like Aristotle, Hume offered three laws, but whereas both agree in suggesting *resemblance* and *contiguity*, Aristotle had suggested *contrast*, which Hume replaced by *cause and effect*. In his later *Enquiry* (1751/1800, p. 24), Hume gave his reason for not including *contrast*: "Where two objects are contrary, the one destroys the other; that is, the cause of its annihilation, and the idea of the annihilation of an object, implies the idea of its former existence." Thus for Hume *contrast* was the result of a mixture of causation and resemblance. Two of the most interesting implications that Hume drew from his laws of association concerned (1) the causal relation and (2) the application of those observations to an account of the flow of emotional experience. We shall discuss these in turn.

One of the longest sections in the *Treatise* concerns Hume's analysis of exactly what occurs when we make the inference that A causes B. This analysis is of great importance in the history of philosophy of science, but we cannot stress this aspect here. What we stress is that Hume's analysis consisted of a list of the observations we make about A and B that allow us to say that A causes B. That is, when we ourselves judge that A causes B we do so as the result of certain observations, and we can plausibly— but wrongly—infer that A causes B when some of those observations seem to gibe with each other. What observations are these? Hume asserted that causative inferences are the result of *experience* and are therefore not innate.

First, A and B have to occur contiguously if we are to say that A causes B. Second, A must be prior to B in time. Third, there must be what Hume called a necessary connection: We assume B would not happen without A. Fourth, there must be a constant conjunction between A and B: The two must always happen together. When all these observations are made we are then at liberty to infer that A causes B. However, when some of these elements are present, we sometimes make a wrong inference that A causes B. The classic example in philosophy texts is the case of the town with two factories. One has a factory whistle that sounds for lunchtime at noon, the other a whistle that goes off five minutes later. The first occurs contiguously with the second, is prior in time to the second, and is constantly conjoined with the second. But I would be wrong to infer that the first sound *causes* the second sound. For one thing, I do not know that the two sounds are necessarily connected; for another, both events may be said to have occurred as effects of a single primary cause, the time of day. Psychologists have also shown experimentally that persons will make wrong causal inferences if most of Hume's cues to causation are present. Michotte has written a book entitled *The Perception of Causality* (1946/1963) in which it is shown through many experiments that if one event is regularly followed by another in time subjects will in fact infer that the first event caused the second.

The second area is Hume's classification of the various emotions. His starting point was that differences in intensity existed between the emotions aroused from reflecting on sensations, pleasure or pain, or memories. He divided the emotions into relatively unintense, or "calm" emotions and relatively intense emotions, or "passions." The calm emotions are the sense of virtue and vice, and the sense of beauty. Some passions are evoked directly by being associated with objects of pleasure or pain; these include desire and aversion, joy and grief, and hope and fear, respectively. Others are evoked indirectly by persons or objects *associated* with pleasure or pain; these include love and hatred for persons or objects, and pride and humility. Hume's system has its similarities to Hartley's, but it is original in an important respect. Although excessive pride or vanity had been castigated as a fault since the time of the ancients, Hume showed that modest pride or self-respect was involved in many human endeavors, including those of finding careers, spouse, and property; and he was also aware of the serious effects humiliation can have on mental health. The achievement of self-respect and the avoidance of humiliation are prime goals in Hume's ethical system.

There is no space here to elaborate on Hume's treatment of moral behavior in Book III of the *Treatise,* but Árdal's 1966 book on this subject is an important commentary on how Hume's theory of the passions underlay and propped up his system of ethics. We might also note that whereas, for most previous writers on the emotions, reason and will were faculties whose function was to control the emotions, Hume treated the passions as primary. Reason, he argued, rarely controls one's emotions, though it may control the *expression* of those emotions; will, he maintained, was just a convenient word to describe yet another feeling or impression. "By will" he said, "I mean nothing but the internal impression we feel that we are conscious of when we knowingly give rise to any new motion of our body or new perceptions of our mind" (1739–1740/1955, p. 399). But despite Hume's reductionist account of the will, others in the eighteenth century would persist in maintaining the will as a particular "faculty," so Hume's effect on that particular fashion was rather small. Hume also had a reductionist argument of the concept of the self: He argued that the logic that leads to such a concept is based on the notion of identity. In turn this notion, in the case of our personal identity, depends on observing that our thoughts have a certain resemblance to each other and cause each other. Thus the concept of self is another outcome of the operation of the laws of association.

The empiricist tradition of British philosophy continued to influence British thinkers, particularly those of the associationist school, to be discussed in a later chapter. But the most striking influence of Locke, other than on Berkeley, Hartley, and Hume, was on a group of French intellectuals who flourished around the middle of the eighteenth century. The most important names are La Mettrie (1709–1751), Diderot (1713–1784), Condillac (1715–1780), Helvétius (1715–1771), and d'Holbach (1721–1789); to this list may be added the names of Bonnet and Cabanis, already mentioned. It would be wrong to call this group a school; there were too many differences of opinion among them. However, they are often bracketed together in scholars' minds because they shared that nontranscendentalist outlook that is encapsulated in various degrees in such terms as naturalism, mechanism, sensationism, empiricism, and materialism. In fact, La Mettrie and d'Holbach were avowed atheists, among the first to have any important impact on modern thought, and all shared the Lockeian belief that most psychological experience is built up on a foundation of sensations. Locke, to these men, was a hero of the stature of Newton or Harvey. In what ways, then, did they add to what Locke had said?

La Mettrie, whose *Traité de l'Ame (Treatise on the Soul*, 1745) may be considered the first major work of the French empiricist tradition, had a varied career, beginning first as a student for the priesthood but moving quickly from that vocation to an apprenticeship as a medical student under the Dutch doctor Boerhaave (1668–1738), perhaps the most famous clinical teacher of the time. Returning to France, La Mettrie was made physician to the military corps of the guards, and while at war he fell ill of a fever. His observations that his thoughts during his fever seemed to be directly the outcome of his bodily illness reinforced the materialistic attitude he had acquired from Boerhaave; but when he expressed this in his treatise on the soul, written shortly thereafter, the French clergy aroused such violent feelings against him that he went into exile into Holland. Here his book *Man a Machine* (1748) caused the Dutch clergy, in turn, to denounce him. But the king of Prussia, Frederick the Great, always anxious to acquire intellectuals at his court in far-off Berlin, offered him refuge and a pension. Here he wrote medical texts on dysentery and on asthma before his death at the age of forty-one.

In the treatise on the soul, La Mettrie argued that all ideas arise from combinations of sensations. Using the concept of the *sensorium commune,* he claimed that there are four laws concerning sensation: (1) the more an object acts on the *sensorium,* the clearer and more distinct the resulting ideas; (2) the more an object acts on the same part of the *brain,* the clearer the idea; (3) the more often a sensation is renewed, the clearer the idea; and (4) the more striking and differentiated the sensation, the clearer the idea. Underlying these laws is the presumed action of the animal spirits: The locus of this interplay between sensation and idea—La Mettrie here revived the Aristotelian term of the sensitive "soul"—might be in the corpus callosum, which joins the two hemispheres. He went on to discuss memory and emotion and was at pains to stress that "all the faculties of the soul, even consciousness, are only dependencies of the body" (1954, p. 98). The exception—one that marks La Mettrie off from some of his more empirically minded compatriots—is instinct. For La Mettrie animals are possessed of certain innate fears and desires that express themselves through complicated chains of what we now call reflexes. As evidence for the importance of learning in establishing human ideas, however, La Mettrie cited the case of a ten-year-old boy found in 1694 in a forest on the borders of Lithuania. This boy had apparently been abandoned—the legend ran that he was reared by bears—and had no speech, walked on all fours, and "did not have the use of his reason" (1954, p. 120). La Mettrie also describes the *tabula rasa* experiment of Arnobius (see Chap. 2) with approval. The treatise finishes with the remark "no sensations—no ideas."

La Mettrie's more famous second book, *Man a Machine,* has been seen by certain commentators as the logical extreme to which Descartes' mechanistic philosophy had pointed. For Descartes, animals were machines, but humans were not; for La Mettrie, even humans are machines. All our most complicated thoughts, he argued, are the results of bodily operations; the word *soul* is now described as "empty"—he does not even accept Stahl's use of *soul* in its particular reference to the properties of living tissues. Human beings are compared with mechanical models such as were made by one Vaucanson, an inventor known for his automated toys. As evidence for human dependence on the body, La Mettrie mentioned the influences of illness, climate, and diet on psychological processes.

The most painstaking effort to build up the complex psyche from elementary sensations was due to Etienne Bonnot, the Abbé of Condillac. Only nominally a clergyman, Condillac spent most of his life as a tutor and a scholar. His first work along empiricist lines was his *Essai sur l'Origine des Connaissances Humaines (Essay on the Origin of Human Knowledge),* which appeared one year after La Mettrie's treatise on the soul. His doctrine was a little more precise than that of other empiricists insofar as he argued that we do not remember all sensations, but only those to which we pay particular attention. Underlying the buildup of a corpus of ideas is brain physiology, and he considered the most powerful function of the soul to be that of reasoning, in which concepts are abstracted and compared. He reaffirmed Locke's distinction between simple and complex ideas. On Dr. Molyneux's question, however, he differed from Locke: Locke had assumed that the person who had just been made to see for the first time would perceive a globe as a flat circle; Condillac believed that three-dimensional vision is more immediately given. Against his own argument, it would seem, was the evidence from a true case of cataract removal reported by Cheselden in 1728. A fourteen-year-old boy had cataracts removed surgically and behaved much as Locke and Berkeley had predicted: He could not immediately denote the objects he saw, and he related all his new visual experiences to his preexisting memories of touch. Condillac asserted, however, that this apparent evidence favoring Locke's view was only a result of the fact that it takes the eye a long time to adjust to its new sensations: The boy's perception, he argued, was too "confused" for this case to be taken as evidence for or against Locke's answer.

Eight years later, in 1754, Condillac devoted a whole book to showing how complex cognitive activity could be based entirely on sensations. That, at least, is what the *Treatise on the Sensations* claims to do: It starts by assuming that we have a statue endowed with only a sense of smell, but it becomes clear in the first few pages that the statue is also endowed with (1) memory and (2) feelings of pleasure and pain.

A statue thus furnished with the capacities of smelling, retaining, and feeling will readily develop the complex emotion of desire. Still basing his argument on the one sense of smell, Condillac, with some virtuosity, went on to show that from desire we build up the emotions of love and hate; from memory, we learn to compare, whence we make judgments. Also, the sensations laid down in time will form a chain of ideas, which if they flow in our experience in the same order, may be said to constitute a retrieval. If, however, they flow in a different order, we may be said to be imagining. Dreaming is a form of imagining, and from our imagination we can derive the concepts of number, possibility, and duration. If we imagine what we hate, we have the passion of fear. I have drawn a diagram of this logical argument so that the reader may more fully appreciate its quality (see Figure 4–1).

Having established that such complex activities as desiring, imagination, and certain emotions can be based on one sense only (smell), Condillac went on to add hearing as a second sense, then taste as a third sense. Sight is the fourth sense to be added, and from sight we learn to derive the concept of an extended surface. None of these senses, however, gives rise to the concept of one's own body or of movement. For that, asserted Condillac, we need touch. Given a sense of touch, we can feel by the way

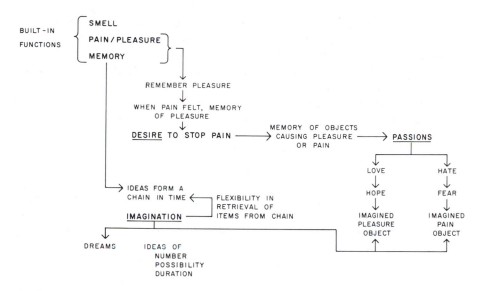

Figure 4–1 Condillac's Scheme of Cognitive Activity Derived from Sensations.

our hand, let us say, touches our chest that there is a self. Gradually we learn to distinguish between touch sensations felt by our own body in two places (e.g., hand and chest) and single touch sensations resulting from contact with outer objects. These, combined with the evidence of our other senses, lead to a construction of an "outside world." If we then imagine this outside world, we can form, using memory, an abstract concept of space, or "extension."

Condillac's statue represented a speculation about what mental capacities *could* evolve, given senses, memory, and feelings of pleasure and pain. But at the end of the *Treatise on the Sensations* Condillac did not identify that statue with an adult human; instead, he asserted that the statue was a creature of "habit" roughly on a plane with the Lithuanian bear-boy. For the statue to reflect on its own self, to *reason* about general ideas such as "dog" (which themselves could be derived from seeing similarities between, e.g., two dogs and were therefore possessed by the statue), and to communicate with others, it was necessary for the statue to add a system of *signs* representing external objects. Such signs, for Condillac, were given by the words and grammar of language. Since these signs could only be acquired by learning them from other people, society plays the first role in determining what we learn, and this takes us out of the world of the statue subject only to sensations. In fact, his earlier book, the *Essay on the Origin of Human Knowledge*, had as its main thesis the ideas that abstract, reflective reasoning as exemplified in philosophy, literature, and the sciences could not have emerged without the development of language in the human species; it is language that differentiates the human, not only from the animals but from Condillac's statue as it is presented at the end of the *Treatise on the Sensations*.

Condillac believed that, just as memory was innately one of our abilities, so was the *liaison* of ideas—by this meaning that those sensations we had attended to together would be linked together in memory but would also be linked with needs and emotions at that point in time. This chain of ideas could be formed, linked together by common motives, and these links would form the basis of imagining, thinking, and remembering. Language, he believed, emerged naturally as a consequence of the liaison of ideas. In particular, liaisons would be made between natural vocal sounds, such as cries, and stimuli related to those cries. In primitive times, the sound the child made naturally demanding something may have been copied by the parents, and this sound came to stand for, or to be a sign of, the object in question.

Condillac was not the only writer of the period to imagine a statue slowly endowed with sophisticated characteristics as more and more sensory experiences are added; in his *Analytic Essay on the Faculties of the Soul*, discussed earlier in this chapter, Bonnet repeated the analogy of the statue but this time was more specific than Condillac on the need for a neural substrate. He also attempted to show that even more could be "derived" from a single sense, smell, than Condillac himself had derived.

The other writers of this group did not attempt to build up such a concise model of experience as Condillac had offered. While retaining his sensationism, their remarks were more limited. In 1749 Diderot, famed as the editor of the great *Encyclopédie,* wrote a work entitled *Lettre sur les Aveugles (Letter on the Blind)*. Taking examples from blind friends and from the evidence relating to a blind mathematician named Saunderson, Diderot showed that the blind have learned to interpret their remaining sensations with an accuracy that can often astonish seeing persons; they can use the touch sense even to thread a needle. Saunderson did his calculations on a machine designed to represent numbers by the location of different pins on a board. There is a discussion of the Cheselden cataract case, and Diderot expressed his agreement with Condillac's reservations on the relevance of the results for Locke's theory. The *Letter* is partially translated by Morgan (1977), who stresses its importance as a historical catalyst in focusing interest on the question of how our "internal" world of reasoning and understanding is influenced by the nature of the sensations we can receive.

Helvétius was not particularly concerned with sensationism as a psychological theory but was most impressed with the fact that, if sensationism were valid, it would imply that social skills and even genius were the result of education. Since education in turn is an outcome of the structure and *mores* of society, Helvétius built a political structure on a theory he quite openly asserts to be Locke's. Helvétius's theory was put forward in his *De l'Esprit (Essays on the Mind,* 1758) and his posthumous *A Treatise on Man* (1772–1773). The implications of sensationism for philosophy—in particular, religious philosophy—were discussed at length in d'Holbach's *Système de la Nature (System of Nature,* 1770). For d'Holbach the concept of a soul as something immortal and immaterial was a Christian corruption resulting from the notion that humanity was set apart from nature. But humanity must be seen as an element *in* Nature. Like animals, human beings have no *innate* moral ideas: Moral behavior is the result of experience and must be learned. Descartes is castigated for the dualism in which he preserved the notion of human separateness from the animals.

Finally, we may mention a book that in many ways summarized both the physiological and the psychological contributions made by Britons and Frenchmen to eighteenth-century thought. Cabanis's *Rapports de Physique et du Moral de l'Homme (Relations of the Physical and the Moral in Man,* 1799) elaborated La Mettrie's arguments on the importance of physical (physiological) changes on mental and moral processes. We mentioned earlier that Cabanis was among the first to establish that the nervous system had a hierarchy of levels of functioning; in this book Cabanis interweaved this general notion with discussions of the effects of such variables as age, sex, temperament, disease, climate, and sleep habits on psychological activity. He believed, however, that many of our personality characteristics and certain "instincts" are inherited and in passing offered some criticisms of Condillac's empiricism on these grounds. The book is replete with observations on physiological processes and is a fittingly materialistic finale to this episode in French psychological thought.

The British empiricist outlook propagated itself, then, particularly in the writings of French savants in the middle and late eighteenth century. But there was another aspect of the philosophy of Berkeley and Hume that was not so well received either in the British Isles or on the European continent. We refer to that aspect of their philosophy called skeptical. Berkeley denied that the existence of matter could be proved deductively. Hume, like Locke, had reduced the self to a set of observations, had analysed cause in such a way as to make the analysis a branch of psychology as much as of philosophy, and had raised serious questions as to whether there was an absolute code of ethics that could be propounded from first principles. The reaction against skepticism involved a number of writers, but two in particular concern us because they wrote on psychology as well as on philosophy. These were Thomas Reid (1710–1796), a Scottish divine who held professorships in philosophy successively at the universities of Aberdeen and Glasgow, and Immanuel Kant (1724–1804), a German of Scottish descent.

To discuss Kant properly we must go back to those sources in German philosophy to which he was originally most indebted, so we shall first consider the several writings of Reid. His main contributions to psychology were contained in his *Inquiry into the Human Mind* (1764), his *Essays on the Intellectual Powers of Man* (1785), and his *Essays on the Active Powers of the Human Mind* (1788). All three works are contained in *The Works of Thomas Reid* edited by Sir William Hamilton (Reid, 1852). Hamilton's footnotes and appendices to his collection are valuable essays on the history of psychology in their own right and will be mentioned where appropriate later. All quotations refer to this edition.

Reid's chief objection to Berkeley and Hume (and to some extent to Descartes and Locke) was that by the use of reason they had undermined belief in the existence both of one's own self and of the external world. To redress the matter Reid argued that we are born with certain intuitively understood beliefs; the fact that these beliefs are difficult (but not impossible) to justify rationally is beside the point. The point is that we are endowed with a "universal sense" *(Essays on Intellectual Power,* p. 298), "instinctive presciences" *(Inquiry,* p. 199), or, the term Reid uses most often, a "common sense" understanding of how we relate to the world. Berkeley's and Hume's arguments went against common sense, contended Reid; it is time, he said, for philosophers to stress that certain beliefs that we have are part of our natural constitution, put there by our Maker. The argument is put forward fairly closely in the *Inquiry* but most explicitly in the sixth *Essay* on the intellectual powers. Here Reid listed twelve beliefs that he asserted we possess and need not question. There is not room to list them all here but among them are the following:

2. "That the thoughts of which I am conscious, are the thoughts of a being which I call MYSELF, my MIND, my PERSON" (p. 443). In this proposition, Reid struck at Hume's reductionist argument of the self.
5. "That those things do really exist which we distinctly perceive by our senses, and are what we perceive them to be" (p. 455). Here Reid criticized the arguments of Berkeley and Hume concerning the validity of sensory experience.
11. "There are many events depending upon the will of man, in which there is a self-evident probability, greater or less, according to circumstances" (p. 451). Here Reid asserts that men do have "a" will according to which—except in cases of insanity—they act and according to which the rules of society are drawn up.

The reductionist arguments of Locke and Hume, both of whom had argued that *will* is just a name for the feeling we have of being in control of our actions, are not highly estimated by Reid: In fact in his last book there is a long discussion of the necessity of "free will." The arguments are theological and moral in nature, as befitted Reid's avowed Christianity. Reid may then be considered the founder of a common sense, or realist, school of philosophy. Among his successors were Dugald Stewart (1753–1828), Thomas Brown (1778–1820), and Hamilton. Hamilton's Appendix A to the collected works contains a scholarly history of the origins of the term *common sense* as used by Reid.

In the course of his discussion of our belief that what we sense is actually caused by external objects affecting the sense organs, Reid had much to say on sensation itself. In particular, Reid is perhaps best known for being the first to distinguish explicitly between the meanings of *sensation* and *perception* and define them as we still do. He was, of course, not the first to *hint* at the distinction; Hamilton's Appendix D to the collected works traces the distinction back to Aristotle and Plotinus and shows it to be present in the writings of several Cartesians. But Reid is usually given the credit for establishing the modern usage. Again, a hint of the distinction is given in his earliest book, the *Inquiry* (see especially p. 182), but it is in the second *Essay* on the intellectual powers that the dichotomy is firmly laid down. The sensation is the actual datum of experience; the perception is the "cognitive surround," one might say, of the sensation, the inferences and implications we draw from the sensation. Morgan (1977) stresses that for Reid, a "perception" involved above all the identification of objects sensed, an identification based on evidence from various senses combined that can be influenced by an innate understanding of qualities such as shape and extension.

Although this distinction is easy enough to understand in the abstract, there are passages in the *Inquiry* where Reid becomes concerned about whether certain experiences of sensation are as "immediate" as they seem. He discussed at length whether our eyes move in parallel natively, or only as the result of practice; whether we see the world right side up natively, given that the image representing the world is inverted on the retina; and why we usually only see one thing at a time, given that the eyes receive slightly different images of the same object. There is a historically important discussion of the meaning of the term *corresponding points*—that is, those points on the two retinas that, when stimulated, give rise to the sensation of seeing a single point; and there are comments on Cheselden's cataract case and also on the problem of single vision when it is associated with squint (strabismus). Reid's general conclusion is that experience is added to our native intuition in determining both what we sense and what we perceive, but he is far more of a nativist in bias than were his predecessors, the empiricists.

Reid's three books cover just about all the topics of psychology popular in the eighteenth century, save physiological psychology. They present, in fact, an epitome of late eighteenth-century thought on the mind. We may note three points of particular interest from the many we might discuss. First, Reid firmly believed in the concept of instinct—that is, complex actions carried out by organisms with no previous experience of those actions. In the *Essays on the Active Powers,* Reid stated that sucking and swallowing are two instincts humans possess at birth; animals have a much richer repertoire of innate behavior patterns, including nest building and patterns of maternal and sexual behavior. He defined instinct as a natural blind impulse. Much of what is instinctive in animals humans learn by imitation.

Second, Reid used the word *faculty* quite frequently to refer to the different abilities of the mind: He in fact compared his own use of *faculty* to the word *power* as used by Locke and Hume. A faculty, such as that of memory or judgment or reason, is innate. Nevertheless, he was skeptical of earlier divisions of the faculties: The only one he explicitly approved of was that between the understanding and the will. He dealt with the former in the essays on *intellectual* powers, the latter in the essays on *active* powers of the mind. It is possible to extract from the skein of his later books as many as forty-three mental faculties, however (Brooks, 1976). Finally, he asserted that associations in the train of thought do follow according to certain rules, but he felt that Hume's three laws were inadequate. What guides the sequence of thoughts, Reid argued, is the underlying emotion or passion or intention, and this is too extensive a matter to be neatly squeezed into a few headings such as "contiguity" or "similarity." In Hamilton's edition of Reid's works, Appendix D is perhaps the first attempt to show in detail how Aristotle, Vives, and others were placed in the long history of the "laws" of association.

The Philosophical Traditions in Germany

To aid the reader in following the next few chapters, Figure 4–2 shows the main university towns in Germany of importance in the early history of modern psychology. The boundaries shown are the modern boundaries between West Germany and East Germany (now part of the Soviet bloc).

The writings of Kant were in many ways anticipated by earlier German scholars from the late seventeenth century onwards. We must therefore turn back in time to that period and consider the first major German author concerned with psychological matters, Gottfried W. Leibniz (1646–1716). Not only was Leibniz one of the greatest mathematicians in history—independent of Newton, it would appear, he devised calculus and his notation is the one we still use—but he was an inventor who constructed an early calculating machine, a writer on law, history, and politics, and a major philosopher.

We have said little about Germany since remarking in the Prologue that the Reformation was started there by Luther and that printing had been invented there; in fact, in the Middle Ages and early Renaissance

Figure 4-2 Some Principal German University Towns.

period Germany had been a thriving center of commerce and culture. But in the late sixteenth and early seventeenth centuries religious warfare turned Germany into a dreadful battlefield where minor princelings fought continuously and where it was almost impossible for cultural activity to survive. The Thirty Years' War (1618–1648) almost exhausted the economy of the country, and from that time onwards what is now geographically modern Germany was a scattered agglomerate of small states, some of which eventually became independent kingdoms. The largest such independent kingdom was Prussia, constituted in 1701.

Leibniz was two years old when that war ended and for most of his adult life he served as representative of, or librarian to, some of the key figures in those small states. He traveled to Paris and Holland, where he met some of the leading intellectuals of the seventeenth century and studied in detail, with a view of expounding and criticizing them, the works of Descartes, Spinoza, Malebranche, and others of his period. One writer who particularly struck his attention was Locke, and between 1700 and 1705 Leibniz wrote a book whose title imitated Locke's, namely the *New Essays concerning Human Understanding.* The work consists of a dialogue in which Locke's viewpoints are taken by one speaker and Leibniz's views by the second speaker. Just after it was written, however, Locke died, and Leibniz did not feel he should publish the book: In fact it was first made public in 1765. It is therefore one of Leibniz' s latest works and incorporates a number of concepts that Leibniz had worked out in the many years between his earliest writings and the *New Essays* and that were expounded in a wide variety of scattered texts. These concepts were to become vital and essential in much later psychology, German and otherwise.

Most philosophers before Leibniz had taken the old viewpoint, refurbished by Descartes, that the world consisted of two disparate elements: mind and matter. Mind differed from matter in not being extended in space. Leibniz adopted what at first sight is almost a transcendental opinion—namely, that mind was a fundamental entity or composite from which the world was constituted, with matter being secondary to mind rather than the other way around. But when we look more closely at Leibniz's argument, we find that this relation is not the insubstantial thing it might appear to be. For Leibniz the crucial question was whether a substance had consciousness or not—that is to say, whether it was aware of the surrounding world or not. In the human, consciousness is developed to a high degree; in the animal, to a medium degree. A plant or even a stone has consciousness to a very low degree. This whole approach requires that we sidestep as it were: Instead of seeing mind as an epiphenomenon, albeit a mysterious one, of brain substance, we should see brain substance as substance associated with a "lot of" consciousness and plants and stones as substances associated with little or imperceptible "amounts of" consciousness.

From the notion that all substances can be classified in terms of the degree to which they possess consciousness, Leibniz was led in two directions of thought that are unique to him. First, for Leibniz there is no *sharp* division between substances in the degree to which they possess consciousness. He formulated what has been called a law of continuity, according to which all nature moves from state to state, quality to quality, in a smooth and uninterrupted fashion. Cases of apparent discontinuity only reflect our inability to detect the underlying continuous changes.

Second, since the world consisted of substances with consciousness, Leibniz conceived of the "fundamental units" of such a world as being conscious entities *not* extended in space and by definition indivisible. These he called *monads:* Leibniz's *Monadology,* written two years before his death, describes them in detail. The theory of monads is extremely difficult and according to some writers self-contradictory (Russell, 1900) or untenable (Hacking, 1972); however, it is not necessary to understand the monadology to appreciate Leibniz's psychology.

From the law of continuity, it follows that consciousness varies in *degrees* from states equivalent to wide-awake self-awareness to states in which one is hardly aware of anything, such as when one is sleeping. For Leibniz, however, awareness is still present in sleep to a small degree: We awaken if stimuli become too loud—that is, if they exceed a certain level. One voice might not awaken us, many voices will. The contents of consciousness are fairly unitary but this is the outcome, the emergent phenomenon, of many small sensations we hardly notice. We hear the waves pounding on the shore: This is a unitary roar. But that roar is made up of countless small sensations, each of which scarcely reaches conscious awareness. Leibniz called these individual experiences *petites perceptions,* minute perceptions. From the mass of minute, barely conscious perceptions emerges that strong perception of which we are certainly conscious through a process for which Leibniz had to coin a new word: *apperception.* Apperception is the process of making aware to the self the outcome of many unconscious perceptions.

From the *New Essays* we learn that the process of apperception is unique to those substances that are self-aware: Thus, for Leibniz, apperception applies more to humans than to animals. Animals have perceptions but are not self-aware, hence lack much of the apperceptive ability. (This remark is somewhat oversimplified; a more detailed commentary on the way animals relate to humans, according to Leibniz, is given by McRae, 1976, pp. 30–36.) Not only perceptions can be unconscious, that is, exercise an effect on thought and behavior even though we are not aware of them. In the *New Essays,* Leibniz describes how memories can exist in unconsciousness (1776/1949, p. 106), and how motives can be unconscious (p. 195). The latter explains how we often feel a certain uneasiness that we cannot readily account for. Often we do something to escape from a "painful" sensation of which we are not consciously aware. The reader will appreciate, of course, that this notion of an active continuum of consciousness, from the unconscious to the fully aware, would be the wellspring of the latter psychoanalytic school. It might be noted that Diamond (1972) asserts that Leibniz may have been indebted to a Jesuit mathematician, Pardies (1637–1673), for the general idea of apperception.

In view of the fact that our mental activity consists largely of apperception abetted by the unconscious, Leibniz was led to assert that the human perceiver is always acting on sensations. But to do this a person must have certain patterns of apperceptive activity, certain beliefs, before sensations even begin to enter consciousness. Leibniz is therefore against the *tabula rasa* theory: Many of the first chapters of the *New Essays* are directed against Locke's view that there are no innate ideas. Two ideas in particular are inborn, even though we may not consciously enunciate them. One is that "whatever is, is"; the other is that "it is impossible for a thing to be and not to be at the same time" (p. 72). The "truth" of these propositions is known to us innately: They constitute part of the armament of the inborn "intellect." This led Leibniz to remark at one point: *"Nihil est in intellectu, quod non fuerit in sensu,* exipe: *nisi ipse intellectus"* ("nothing is in the intellect which was not in the senses, *except* the intellect itself") (p. 111). Elsewhere (p. 78), Leibniz quoted with approval Plato's demonstration in the *Meno* that geometrical truths may be taught even to the uneducated; the truths of mathematics are based on an unlearned understanding of certain logical principles, argued Leibniz. In fact, Leibniz foreshadowed modern symbolic logic, on which mathematics can be argued to be based, by over two hundred years: The germs of a logical calculus are to be found as early as 1679 (see P. P. Wiener, 1951, p. 26). It should be noted that Leibniz asserted both that innate principles may not be self-evident to introspection and that they may be obscured, though not effaced, in children. Note, however, this is a nativism concerning the way we understand; it is not a nativism asserting that a particular concept such as "God" or "extension" is innate.

Two other aspects of the *New Essays* of interest to the historian of psychology may be briefly mentioned. Throughout the work Leibniz used the word *ego* to refer to that constellation of mental experiences we associate with our personal identity. Also, one must not get the impression that Leibniz was at odds with Locke on all matters: He agreed with Locke on the association of ideas and added a number of further instances of conditioned emotional responses to those given by Locke. The best known is his mention of Descartes' tendency to be attracted to persons with a squint, this being the outcome of an adolescent affection for an individual with this characteristic. Finally, on the matter of the mind-body relation, Leibniz argued for what has come to be called psychophysical parallelism: The mind and body run their separate courses but in absolute unison, much as two clocks wound up at the same time will continue both to show the same time afterward (P. P. Wiener, 1951, p. 118). This theory ultimately has its roots in the notion that a "pre-established harmony" has been set up by God so that the monads can work in unison, even though each is independent and does not interact with others (on this, see Russell, 1945, pp. 583–588).

Even though Leibniz considered the mind highly conscious and the body a substance with less consciousness, he still felt the necessity to speculate on how the two entities were related. In Leibniz's multifarious writings, however, somewhat conflicting opinions are to be found on other details of the mind-body relationship: The reader is referred to Russell (1900, Chap. 12) for a discussion of the matter.

Leibniz is generally recognized to be the first great modern thinker of Germany, the advance guard of the Enlightenment in that country. His successors in that region nearly all occupied university positions; in fact, Leibniz was the exception in not holding such a post. The first professor in such an institution to follow Leibniz in his interest in psychology was Christian Wolff (1679–1754). Leibniz recommended to the King of Prussia that Wolff be appointed professor of mathematics at the University of Halle. Here he wrote not only on that subject but on philosophy in general; in fact, he had a grand scheme according to which all knowledge could be divided into related areas, and he himself contributed to many of those disciplines. Unfortunately, in 1723 Wolff fell foul of opposition from members of the faculty of theology, who accused him of irreligion, and, on pain of death, he was forced to leave Halle. He quickly found a position at the University of Marburg, where in 1731 he wrote a book in Latin entitled *Psychologia Empirica* and in 1734 a sequel, entitled *Psychologia Rationalis*. It is normally maintained that these are the first books with the word *psychology* in the title since Goclenius's work of 1590.

The distinction between empirical and rational psychology would be widely adopted by many of Wolff's successors. The difference is a little strange to us now, but will be clarified when we consider the contents of Wolff's two books. By *empirical* psychology is meant the collection of data concerning mental and behavioral phenomena. Since we only know what we do about the mind by observing ourselves and others, our "teacher," as Wolff put it, is "experience." By *rational* psychology is meant the interpretation or explanation of the mass of data we collected when doing empirical psychology. To do rational psychology, we need reason. Wolff used two terms extensively that Kant and other eminent writers would also use: *a posteriori* knowledge, knowledge acquired through experience that is never innate (most of the knowledge listed under empirical psychology is *a posteriori*) and *a priori* knowledge, knowledge we possess that has not been taught to us or acquired by experience. The task of empirical psychology is to establish *a posteriori* what applies to the soul; the task of rational psychology is to explain this empirical knowledge in terms of our knowledge of what is correct reasoning, much of which Wolff believed to be *a priori*. A translation of the sections from Wolff's books describing his distinction between empirical and rational psychology is given by Richards (1980a).

Wolff had an enormous influence on the German thought of his time, and his ideas were spread into France. For example, in France a great Encyclopedia was published by Diderot and others between 1751 and 1772; the article on "psychology" is very short and consists of an account of the distinction between empirical and rational psychology. Later encyclopedias propagated the distinction until well into the nineteenth century, when the terms fell into disuse.

The contents of Wolff's *Psychologia Empirica* can be divided into two main sections, one on the properties of the soul in general, and one on the properties of the soul in interaction with the body. In the first section, Wolff adopts a notion found in Leibniz, namely, that the senses give us a vague or obscure idea of what exists in external reality, whereas the operation of the intellectual faculties makes these ideas clearer. When information pertaining to an event is laid down in the soul, it can be reproduced by memory and imagination. In particular, Wolff suggested that when we retrieve the memory of an event, it is associated with the total general context in which the event was embedded. For Wolff, this was the major *law of association*.

In the second part of the book, Wolff relates mental and physical characteristics. He argues that there are degrees of pleasure and discomfort (*taedium*) arising from bodily feelings and even suggests that since they are graded, we could have the basis of a science of measurement, a *psychometrics*, which could possibly be applied to the soul. Pleasurable and unpleasurable feelings lead us to formulate the notions of "good" and "bad" things, and in turn these concepts give rise to appetites and aversions. He classifies the emotions into pairs of opposites (such as happiness-sadness); the final passages of this section concern how we use the intellectual faculty of reason to make decisions between good and bad. Here Wolff touches on the topic of how "free" we are, in fact, to choose, and the *Psychologia Empirica* closes with a statement that the soul and the body are often interdependent in ways we do not as yet fully understand.

In his sequel, the *Psychologia Rationalis*, Wolff essentially tries to explain the system set out in *Psychologia Empirica*. The purpose of sensation is to present us with a picture of the external world, and the purpose of other faculties, such as attention, memory, and imagination, is to allow us to obtain clear ideas about the world. Because we are born with the power to represent objects (in sensation or in memory), Wolff would alter Locke's sensationism to include mention of this inborn power, although, like Locke and Gassendi, Wolff is sympathetic to the general notion that most of our knowledge is acquired *a posteriori*. The power to represent objects also allows us to form the desires, appetites, and aversions discussed in the second part of *Psychologia Empirica*. One of the reasons this power is so effective is that mind and body are deeply interconnected; after discussing Cartesian dualism and Malebranche's occasionalism, Wolff concludes that the best account of the mind–body relationship is

Leibniz's doctrine of pre-established harmony. It will be seen from this short summary that empirical psychology asks, "What?" and rational psychology asks, "Why?"

Wolff's writings were followed rather slavishly in many German universities, and one of the ambitions of our next great eighteenth-century German writer, Immanuel Kant (1724–1804), was to offer a system of general philosophy that took over some of Wolff's notions but replaced his system by one that examined much more closely the *a priori* and *a posteriori* content of the human mind. Kant's psychology cannot be understood without a general account of his system of philosophy, in which psychology had a particular position, so we must first make some remarks about Kant's ideas in general. Kant himself spent most of his life in the city of Königsberg in East Prussia (now known as Kaliningrad) and intensely preoccupied himself with lecturing not just on philosophy but on "anthropology" (to be defined later), geography, logic, and pedagogy. But Kant's great love was philosophy and his main efforts were directed at erecting a system in which all the phenomena of the natural world, as well as human phenomena such as ethics and taste, were subsumed within a single logical framework.

In some ways Wolff's psychology provided a forerunner for Kant's system. Wolff had constructed a rational psychology into which an empirical psychology could naturally fit. Kant wanted, in essence, a rational physics (or *metaphysics*) with which an empirical physics could be integrated, a rational ethics into which an empirical or practical ethics could be fitted, and a rational aesthetics from which practical judgments about beauty and taste would follow. It turned out that the metaphysics most directly influenced his evaluation of psychology, so we shall concentrate on that; furthermore, Vleeschauwer (1939/1962) has shown how, once the metaphysics was arrived at, in Kant's most famous book, the *Critique of Pure Reason* (first edition, 1781; second revised edition, 1787), the rational ethics and rational aesthetics followed without too much difficulty. So we proceed with a discussion of the metaphysics. Note, however, that after the *Critique of Pure Reason* had been published, Kant produced a shorter and more popular exposition of his philosophy. Psychologists will probably get a better grasp of Kant's main points from this shorter work, entitled *Prolegomena to Any Further Metaphysics* (1786).

Like others before him, Kant started with the notion that the primary data of our experience are sensations, which are then processed by the perceiving subject. According to his empiricist predecessors, we had, over the years, learned to interpret our visual and other sensations within the context of space and time; according to Kant, the mind knew innately that sensations were ordered in space and time, and therefore the usual empiricist account of our understanding of how our sensations related to each other was not necessary. He gave five arguments for believing that space and time were innately understood. One was that space and time seemed to be necessary for understanding the very concept of matter: You can imagine space without any matter in it, but it is impossible, he said, to imagine matter not somehow distributed in space. Space and time seemed to be the necessary conditions or substrates for any phenomena being possible at all. Another argument was that space was not a concept that was abstracted from our noticing that objects stood in certain relationships to each other: This, thought Kant, would lead to the notion that there were several "spaces," whereas only one space exists around us. Kant listed three other arguments, and on the basis of all five he proposed that we do not learn that objects have to be located in space or time, although of course he would not deny that we do learn to find our way about in space to some degree (as Condillac explained) and that only when we acquired language do we acquire the words "space" and "time" and an understanding of them.

But for Kant one aspect of our processing of sense data was still innate, and that was our understanding that all objects are located in space and time. Kant gave a special name to this understanding: He called it an *intuition* (German *Anschauung*, a "looking at"). So the observing subject organizes sense experiences into the frameworks of space and time intuitively, so that objects have relations to each other in space and come before or simultaneously with each other in time. It is *a priori* knowledge.

Kant's arguments that we innately know about space and time are, however, not always grasped by students, and we may note here that Bertrand Russell (1945), in his *History of Western Philosophy*, also ran into difficulties in trying to explain why Kant believed what he did. Russell's solution was to look very carefully at Kant's arguments, and he concluded that the reason they are hard to grasp is that they are open to query. To be precise, Russell argues (pp. 712–718) that Kant's five arguments supporting an innate intuition of space and time are all faulty, and that the empiricist account of such writers as Berkeley is more likely to be correct. For example, Russell's objection to the first argument—that we cannot imagine a world with no space—was that we cannot deny the existence of something merely because we cannot imagine it. He also objected to Kant's assertion that we can imagine space with nothing in it—"you can imagine looking at the sky on a dark cloudy night, but then you yourself are in space" (p. 715). But let us move on to complete Kant's own line of argument.

Kant went on to argue that we make other judgments about our sense data, once they have been organized in space and time: We see immediately their quality and their quantity, and conceive of certain relations between them, such as cause and effect. Kant actually listed a total of twelve *concepts* of the understanding which he believed operate automatically on sense data; these are sometimes called *categories*. He suggested, then, that a considerable armory of unlearned organizings and understandings of sense data are brought to bear at the time the data are received.

The human mind not only organizes inputs into unities that form the contents of a given moment of consciousness, it also has the power to reproduce past inputs (the power of memory); in particular, it can recognize that a given reproduction is the same as a sense datum recently experienced. That is, by seeing X and then thinking about X, we can acquire the abstract concept of X. In this way the mind can construct a synthesis of experience, but all of this experience is organized in time. What space is for matter, a matrix in which elements are organized, time is for the mind or "soul." At this point, however, Kant goes on to assert that physics and psychology part company insofar as the possibilities of a rational and an empirical science are concerned.

As concerns physics, we only know what is given to us by experience, that is, phenomena. We cannot go beyond to know the objects of the extended world in themselves, as *noumena*, to use Kant's term: We are restricted to our knowledge of the sense data representing external objects. So in rational physics, there are limits to what we can say about things in themselves, but we know, through our intuitions of space and time, how phenomena relate to each other, and hence we can expound an empirical physics about these relationships. When we come to psychology, however, we have no intuitions about the soul corresponding to our intuitions of space and time; all we know is that experience is organized in time. Kant dealt particularly with the problem of the unknowability of the soul in the *Prolegomena* and, after refuting several arguments that seemed on the surface to suggest we do know something about the soul, came to the conclusion that since we had no basic intuitions about the soul, there was no possibility of a valid rational psychology. These arguments, too long to present here, are given extensive scholarly discussion by Ameriks (1982). Kant also gave a second reason why a rational psychology could not be developed: Space and time, the substrates in which physical events occur, can be measured. But the "soul" does not have properties that can be measured. Hence a rational psychology would not have numbers in it, and Kant felt that this made it impossible to develop a valid science of the soul.

Kant also objected to the possibility of an empirical psychology. Such a psychology, he said, had to be based on our own experience, that is, on introspection. But we can only introspect what has already passed, and therefore there is room for error. Later, in his *Anthropology*, he also expressed the view that introspection that was carried out in order to understand mental illness could itself interfere with the natural workings of the soul to such an extent one could become ill oneself.

Is there, then, any hope of a science of psychology? Kant believed something could be salvaged from these criticisms: He believed that by studying the behavior of others, we could formulate valid concepts about them that would allow us to predict, or even control, their future behavior. He called this near-science "anthropology." He felt that in his time too little was known about the brain to allow of a "physiological anthropology," but he did feel that from everyday experience one could develop a "pragmatic anthropology" that might be of practical use. Kant lectured on pragmatic anthropology for many years and at the end of his life allowed the lectures to be published in *Anthropology from a Pragmatic Point of View* (1797/1974), whose contents we may briefly consider.

The book is divided into two parts. The first has some parallels to Wolff's *Psychologia Empirica*: Kant begins by discussing the cognitive powers, then goes on to discuss pleasure and pain and finally the appetites. In his account of the cognitive powers, he repeats the notion of Leibniz and Wolff that the function of the intellect is to develop clear ideas from obscure ones and stresses that the imagination, which allows new ideas to result from the combination of old ideas, is an important component of the intellectual faculty. Imagination was also discussed in the *Critique of Pure Reason* and Kant's interest in this may have derived from a reading of a large work on psychology by J. N. Tetens (1736–1807), who had also stressed the importance of creativity, as opposed to passive recall, in the flow of thought. Kant also discussed abnormalities of cognition and made a sharp distinction between mental illness and mental retardation. We also noted earlier that the "self," for Kant, is a learned concept: In the *Anthropology* he offers a sketch of how the child develops a sense of self. In his account of pleasure and pain, Kant discusses the problem of "good taste," which would also form a foundation for his theory of aesthetics, and stresses that avoidance of pain is a prime motivator of behavior. His discussion of the appetitive powers involves a distinction between shallow *affects* and deep *passions*—he divides the passions into *ardent* (desires for freedom and sex) and *cold* (desires for honor, power, and possessions).

The second half of this work concerns anthropological characterization, or, as we should now say, individual differences. Individual differences arise from personal constitution (here Kant uncritically repeated Galen's theory of the four temperaments), sex, national origins, and the human species itself. On sex differences, Kant suggested that the basic difference between men and women was the degree of timidity, women being more timid because they would need to be more protected during childbearing periods: He also argued that marriage was more of a preoccupation with women than with men, and had a number of suggestions for what would make a good marriage. On national differences, Kant makes amusing reference to differences between nationals from different

European countries. On the human species, he is skeptical: He believes that humans have the capacity for evil but also have a strong desire towards good, which shows itself particularly in a desire for good government. Good government, for Kant, was essential if the species were to survive.

It can be seen that Kant's anthropology is discursive and less systematic than perhaps we would wish. But it also shows what he believed to be the one positive virtue of anthropology, namely, that its study permitted better value judgments about how to function in a society.

Leibniz, Wolff, and Kant were not the only major figures of the German enlightenment. Others included H. S. Reimarus (1694–1768), who argued that animals and humans are endowed with a large number of "drives" or "impulses" (German *Trieb*) and listed forty-seven of these (Jaynes & Woodward, 1974a, 1974b), and Moses Mendelssohn (1729–1786), who divided the subject matter of psychology into knowing, feeling, and willing. This distinction, propagated into the nineteenth century, has a loose connection with Kant insofar as Kant's metaphysics was about knowing, his aesthetics was about feeling, and his ethics was about willing. The most useful historical summaries of eighteenth-century German psychology are found in Carus (1808), Dessoir (1897, 1912), and Brett (1921).

Summary

In the eighteenth century there was considerable controversy over the question of whether nervous tissue could be said to have a "soul." The resolution of the conflict marked the beginning of a more naturalistic account of nervous physiology. Reflex behavior was also studied in detail, and understanding of vision and audition advanced. Hartley and Bonnet offered associationistic accounts of behavior based on premises about the functioning of the nervous system. The empiricist/associationist tradition was also maintained, in Britain, by Berkeley and Hume, Berkeley being especially concerned with the role of experience in depth perception and Hume with linking his theory of associations to accounts of causal judgments and the growth of the "passions." In France La Mettrie, Condillac, and Diderot maintained the tradition, with Condillac in particular offering a detailed account of how higher mental functioning could result from the mere possession of sensation, feelings of pleasure and pain, and retentiveness.

However, the British empiricists had raised doubts about the validity of inferences that could be made on the basis of assertions about one's own experience. The Scottish philosopher Reid attempted to counter this skeptical tradition with his "common sense" philosophy. In Germany,

Kant's response to skepticism was to maintain that some of our knowledge is not learned but is the result of intuitions. Kant's psychology was, however, essentially based on writings of German predecessors such as Leibniz (seventeenth century) and Wolff (eighteenth century). Leibniz began the German tradition of analyzing the contents of consciousness (along with the concomitant view that there was mental activity that was unconscious); Wolff distinguished between rational and empirical psychology. Kant was skeptical that either could be developed into a valid science.

1800 to 1879:
The British Tradition

5

This and the next chapter will examine developments in psychology from approximately 1800 to 1879. Why this particular date? As many readers probably know, 1879 was the year in which Wundt, a professor at Leipzig University in what is now East Germany, was able to found an institute for the experimental study of psychological matters. His "institute" was not a large and well-funded establishment of the kind we speak of in a contemporary Western university; it was essentially a small unit of four or five rooms, and it was devoted to "seminars," that is, to the teaching of experimental psychology, as much as to research. There are quibbles in the literature about whether 1879 should really mark the beginning of modern psychology as a recognized science: Wundt himself, in earlier days in Heidelberg and in Zürich, had possessed university-owned space for experimentation or storage; at Harvard University in the United States, William James had a room for psychological experimentation and taught a course called psychology as early as 1875. But since 1879 is the traditional date of the founding of psychology as a discipline in itself, we shall follow convention and treat 1879 as a convenient dividing line in our account of nineteenth-century psychology, taking Wundt as a focus towards whom psychological speculation and experimentation led and who in turn was responsible for spreading the new psychological learning both by publications and by his training of young psychologists who propagated that learning.

Wundt's work was anticipated, particularly in Germany. Following the writings of Kant, in the early 1800s several seminal books on mental processes appeared by Herbart and by Beneke, some with the word *psychology* in the title. At about the same time research by Weber on the touch senses initiated experimentation on the psychological aspects of sensation and perception, and later, following a hint laid down by Weber, Fechner experimented on the variables affecting the accuracy of judgments about various kinds of sensory stimuli. These early decades also saw rapid progress in neurology, so that when Wundt came to write, enough was known about the nerve cell, the central nervous system, and the special senses for him to title his large handbook *Principles of Physiological Psychology*. Moreover, Donders, in Holland, had begun the experimental study, not so much of the *accuracy* as of the latency or *quickness* of judgments concerning sensory stimuli.

Having finished the previous chapter by discussing the origins of German psychology, it would seem an obvious next step to deal in more detail with the matters just outlined. But to do so would be to ignore another tradition of pre-1879 psychology, essentially a speculative rather than an experimental tradition—namely, that tradition in British psychology that can be shown without too much strain to derive from the empiricist writings of Locke, Berkeley, Hartley, Hume, and particularly Reid. Since it would be awkward to deal with the German experimental work then suddenly shift back to the British tradition before discussing Wundt, we shall deal first with the British tradition, thus paving the way for the clear run from Herbart to Wundt that most historians of psychology acknowledge to exist.

There is another reason for devoting a special, and preliminary, chapter to early nineteenth-century British psychology. While it is true that some of the earliest experimental studies of associative processes were carried out in Wundt's laboratory, there is no very obvious sign in Wundt's own writing that he was greatly indebted to the British ideas on association that, as we shall shortly see, were such a dominant feature of pre-1879 British psychology. He *was* indebted to Leibniz and Herbart in particular for his opinions on associations. We are therefore left with the rather curious situation that those persons who devoted most attention to the implications of associations for the development of the total psyche were in fact not very influential in determining the bulk of later experimental research on the subject. British associationism, as it came to be called, has even been seen by some writers as a dead end, a promising movement that actually made little impression on modern experimental psychology.

It would seem good didactic policy therefore to consider this movement as the culmination of the philosophical tradition, and then move from it to the initiation of the experimental tradition that was to be so

BRITAIN	EUROPE
1802 Young on color vision	
	1810–1819 Gall's *Anatomy and Physiology*
	1816 Herbart's *Textbook*
1820 Brown's *Lectures*	
	1824 Flourens's *Researches*
	Herbart's *Psychology as Science*
1829 J.Mill's *Analysis*	
1833 Hall on reflexes	1833 Beneke's *Textbook*
	1834 Weber's *De tactu*
	1838 Müller's *Handbook*
	Wheatstone's stereoscope
1843 J. S. Mill's *Logic*	
	1846 Weber's *Tastsinn*
	1850 Helmholtz on speed of nervous conduction
	1852 Lotze's *Medical Psychology*
1855 Bain's *Senses and Intellect*	
Spencer's *Principles of Psychology*	
	1856–1866 Helmholtz's *Physiological Optics*
1859 Bain's *Emotions and Will*	
Darwin's *Origin of Species*	
Hamilton's *Metaphysics*	
1860 Laycock's *Mind and Brain*	1860 Fechner's *Psychophysics*
	1863 Helmholtz's *Sensations of Tone*
	Wundt's *Beiträge*
	Sechenov's *Reflexes of the Brain*
1865 J. S. Mill on Hamilton	
	1868 Donders on reaction time
1869 J. Mill's *Analysis* reprinted	
1872 Darwin's *Expression of Emotions*	
	1873 Wundt's *Physiological Psychology*
1874 Carpenter's *Mental Physiology*	1874 Brentano's *Psychology*
	1878 Sechenov's *Elements of Thought*
	1879 Wundt's Institute at Leipzig

Figure 5–1   The Main Psychological Works Written in Britain and Europe between 1800 and 1879.

much more fruitful in terms of establishing a body of *knowledge* for the fledgling "science" of psychology. On the other hand, anybody who takes the trouble to read the works of the British school, voluminous though they are, cannot fail to be impressed with the insight and conscientiousness with which almost all the problems of psychology are discussed. It is quite possible that the long-term verdict of historians will be that the British school furnished a body of theoretical *attitudes* that, far from being outmoded, were ahead of their time in the broadness and intellectual sweep with which the total subject of psychology was examined. The reader will be in a better position to make his or her own decision after reading this chapter.

Let us remind ourselves of the main thrust of the British empiricist tradition. From Hobbes onwards, the argument was made that the total corpus of our knowledge, up to the point of death, could be shown to consist either of sensations or of memories or complexes of memories left by those sensations. The flow of sensations and ideas, as the memories were often called, was not random but followed certain rules, the rules of association. Hobbes had stressed how the flow was based on similarity between the various elements; Locke had stressed how our emotional attitudes to otherwise neutral stimuli were the result of association; Berkeley had particularly focused on how, by the association of vision and touch, we acquired concepts as advanced as those of space and matter. Hume had suggested that similarity, contiguity, and cause and effect were the three basic principles of association; Hartley had offered a picture of how one's adult behavior and thought rested on the interplay of ideas, which in turn rested on the interplay of vibrations in the nervous system. Reid, admittedly, had reservations both about empiricism and associationism: He believed that many of our judgments were not the result of learning and considered associations to be as much the results of a plan or emotion as the result of simple "similarity" or "contiguity." But Reid held a vital position in the history of British *academic* psychology: His lectures were widely read and his beliefs, while not always upheld by his successors, were at least discussed seriously by them. He taught, it will be recalled, at Aberdeen and Glasgow.

Reid's best-known disciple was Dugald Stewart (1753–1828), who taught moral philosophy at Edinburgh from before Reid's death. Stewart wrote, almost in emulation of Reid, an *Elements of the Philosophy of the Human Mind* in three volumes: The first appeared in 1792, the next in 1814, and the last in 1827. Like Reid, Stewart was critical of the *tabula rasa* theory and upheld an emphasis on "instinctive" behavior. With one or two exceptions, notably a discussion of the historical origins of language, he dealt with the same subject matter as Reid. When he was temporarily forced to give up teaching duties because of ill health in 1808, Stewart's replacement was the young Thomas Brown (1778–1820), a student of law and medicine who had become fascinated with philosophical psychology. Brown's lectures, numbering one hundred, were published as *Lectures on the Philosophy of the Human Mind* in 1820. He gave a greater precision to the classification of associations than had anybody previously (see following) and made certain original contributions on sensation in the muscles.

After Brown's early death, Sir William Hamilton (1788–1856), whose notes on Reid we mentioned in the last chapter, obtained the chair of logic and metaphysics at Edinburgh in 1836. He taught there for twenty years, and his *Lectures on Metaphysics* were published in 1859, three years after his death. They are particularly notable for adding to the discussion of the empiricists a considerable account of German psychology: Kant and Leibniz were mentioned along with Locke and Hume as contributors to psychological speculation. This attempt to integrate the Scottish and German traditions fell on stony ground, however; in fact, in 1865 John Stuart Mill, a scholar best known for his contributions to logic and to political economy, roundly criticized Hamilton's efforts in his *Examination of Sir William Hamilton's Philosophy.* We thus see a continuous tradition where each writer amends, criticizes, or applauds his successor's speculations. The Scottish School, then, runs from Reid through Stewart through Brown to Hamilton. They shared, incidentally, a position friendly to revealed religion that would be missing from the other British writings now to be mentioned.

The critic of Hamilton, John Stuart Mill (1806–1873), was himself in the tradition of empiricism. His father, James Mill (1773–1836), was a Scotsman who studied under Dugald Stewart but who, at the age of twenty-nine, left Edinburgh to spend the rest of his life in London. He wrote a classic *History of India,* which allowed him to obtain a position with financial security and a certain amount of leisure. In 1829 he published a major work on psychology entitled *Analysis of the Phenomena of the Human Mind.* This is the most important comprehensive attempt to build up experience from associations since Condillac, though the French sensationists are hardly mentioned in the *Analysis.* In his book we see clear influences of the Scottish School and Hartley, but there are also others.

James Mill was a friend of Jeremy Bentham (1748–1832), best known for his development of the theory that moral behavior should be such as to ensure the greatest good for the largest number of people (a theory later named *utilitarianism*). In turn, however, this precept of ethics and politics depended on Bentham's belief that our basic motivations are to avoid pain and pursue pleasure; in fact, McReynolds (1968a, 1968b) has shown that Bentham made a number of original contributions, scattered through various works, to the development of the general concept of motivation as now conventionally used by psychologists.

James Mill was also influenced by a number of minor writers on association who obtained most of their ideas from earlier authors such as Locke and Hartley; among these may be listed Abraham Tucker (1705–1774), Joseph Priestley (1733–1804), Archibald Alison (1757–1839), and Erasmus Darwin (1731–1802). Tucker and Priestley were particularly notable for arguing that two ideas may so fuse in an association as to form a new complex idea very different from the simple concatenation of the two original ideas: The analogy was made with color mixing, with a mixture of several colors giving rise to a new color, white. This suggested that the mixture of associations could be like mixtures of chemicals, an analogy hinted at by James Mill and more specifically praised by Thomas Brown. James Mill's *Analysis* met with considerable interest, and some of its doctrines were reassessed by his son in the latter's *System of Logic* (1843). Much later, in 1869, John Stuart Mill, along with others, produced a new edition of the *Analysis* with lengthy footnotes, which are important in their own right as contributions to the British associationist tradition.

But the person who served as the summarizer of both these twin lines of tradition—the Scottish School and the associationists such as the two Mills—was Alexander Bain (1818–1903). Bain brings us back to the Scottish lineage: He was born and lived for most of his life in Aberdeen, the city of Reid. From an impoverished working class background, Bain rose by industry and dedication to obtain a scholarship at the University in Aberdeen. He wrote extensively on a variety of topics and thus became friends with John Stuart Mill. His fascination with psychological matters led him to compose two large books on the subject, *The Senses and the Intellect* (1855) and *The Emotions and the Will* (1859). These books established his reputation, and in 1860 he obtained a chair of logic and English at Aberdeen. He wrote on grammar, philosophy, and education as well as on psychology, but it is as a psychologist that he is mainly remembered. The two books mentioned went through several editions and effectively became the first generally adopted textbooks of psychology in the English language. They dealt with the nervous system as well as with more purely mental phenomena; they included references to Weber and Wundt, the German experimentalists; but their major portion was a speculative attempt to build all knowledge on certain simple associationistic laws combined with emotions and with a theory of the development of the voluntary control of the motor system. We shall discuss the details shortly; it may simply be noted now that these two books appeared well over a decade in advance of Wundt's *Principles of Physiological Psychology* (1874).

Bain's combination of physiology and philosophy in an attempt at a synthetic psychology is felicitous in places, strained in others, but that the synthesis should be attempted at all marks one of the culminating points in the history of embryonic psychology. Bain also helped to found the journal *Mind* in 1876, an early outlet for experimental psychological studies, and he assisted John Stuart Mill with the 1869 footnotes to James Mill's *Analysis*. He also wrote books on the two Mills. When Bain died, psychology was flourishing as a discipline in its own right; when he had started, even the word *psychology* was hardly known in the English-speaking world (among those who helped to make it an acceptable term were the poet Coleridge and then John Stuart Mill and Hamilton; see Hearnshaw, 1964, p. 2).

Finally, we have recently become aware of a line of medical men in

Victorian Britain who became intrigued with the relationship between mind and brain; only now are their insights being appreciated. In particular, we mention Thomas Laycock (1812–1876), who was a lecturer at a medical school at York until 1855, after which he was Professor of Medicine at the University of Edinburgh. In 1845, Laycock wrote an article on the reflex that had little impact at the time but heralded the late nineteenth-century view that some voluntary acts can become automatic or unconscious. In 1860, he wrote an ambitious book entitled *Mind and Brain* in which he offered a general synthesis of philosophy with psychology and showed that he had been influenced by German psychology. And there was W. B. Carpenter (1813–1885), who worked at the University of London. Following his successful *Textbook of Human Physiology* (first edition, 1852), he became increasingly interested in the role of brain activity in determining behavior and, particularly influenced by Laycock, gave unusual attention to unconscious functioning. G. H. Lewes (1817–1878), best known as the husband of the novelist George Eliot, also wrote several books on psychology as it related to physiology, in particular, the five-volume series, *Problems of Life and Mind* (1872–1879).

These various lines of development may seem confusing, but they can be conceptualized as shown in Figure 5–2.

It would be not only tedious but logistically awkward to attempt a summary of each book. Instead we shall treat the group as a whole—fully recognizing that some members were very critical of others—and discuss them in two ways. First, we shall attempt to establish the common threads that justify our treating this variegated list of savants as a single group. Then we shall take four key topics on which the group wrote and consider their various opinions on those issues. The four key topics are knowing, feeling, willing, and consciousness. The perceptive reader will note that this choice of subject matter essentially derives from the pre-Kantian German tradition: Several eighteenth-century German authors had argued that mental life should be divided into the classes of knowing, feeling, and willing; and of course consciousness was a subject whose importance was first brought out, in an influential way, by Leibniz. Is there any justification for imposing this classification on the works of the British tradition? The answer is yes: After Hamilton's championship of the German psychology, Bain found it appropriate to divide his textbooks into the topics of the senses, followed by the intellect, emotion, and will— that is, the study of knowing, feeling, and willing. His book *The Emotion and the Will* ends with a discussion of consciousness. In this respect eighteenth-century German psychology may indeed be said to have influenced the British tradition.

Apart from their interlocking life histories, the British group may be seen to have four key interests in common. Where one or more of the group diverged from the consensus, this will be stated.

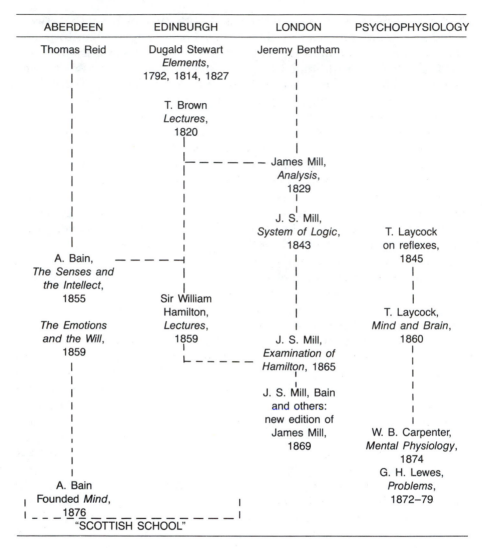

ABERDEEN	EDINBURGH	LONDON	PSYCHOPHYSIOLOGY
Thomas Reid	Dugald Stewart *Elements*, 1792, 1814, 1827	Jeremy Bentham	
	T. Brown *Lectures*, 1820		
		James Mill, *Analysis*, 1829	
		J. S. Mill, *System of Logic*, 1843	T. Laycock on reflexes, 1845
A. Bain, *The Senses and the Intellect*, 1855	Sir William Hamilton, *Lectures*, 1859		T. Laycock, *Mind and Brain*, 1860
The Emotions and the Will, 1859		J. S. Mill, *Examination of Hamilton*, 1865	
		J. S. Mill, Bain and others: new edition of James Mill, 1869	W. B. Carpenter, *Mental Physiology*, 1874 G. H. Lewes, *Problems*, 1872–79
A. Bain Founded *Mind*, 1876			
	"SCOTTISH SCHOOL"		

Figure 5–2   Connections Among the British Psychologists of the Nineteenth Century.

First, they were strongly in the empiricist tradition; that is, they stressed learning at the expense of innate intuitions. The two Mills best exemplify this trend: James Mill's *Analysis* attempted to show, for example, that all language is based on learned associations between visual and spoken stimuli and that much of our thought is simply internal speech. John Stuart Mill devoted much of his *Examination of Sir William Hamilton's Philosophy* to a critique of Hamilton's apparent sympathy for Kantian intuitions. Bain spent almost the whole of the second half of *The Senses and the Intellect* arguing that the complex cognitive activities of the adult, including the creative, inventive, and artistic endeavors, are founded on the operations of simple associationistic laws. These in turn operate on ideas, which are the result of electric "currents" in the nervous system, currents mainly initiated by experience. For Bain the concept of extension is built up from vision and touch: There is little mention of the Kantian categories. We also learn, he added, to control our movements with increasing facility. Nevertheless, Bain admitted, with earlier members of the Scottish School such as Reid and Stewart, that animals are born with certain instincts, so that not *all* capacities are the result of learning. Bain observed a newborn lamb and related how each new stimulus seemed to elicit a specific behavior that culminated in the lamb's finding and sucking on the ewe's teat. Stewart (1829, Vol. III, p. 248) revived an old experiment described by Galen. A baby goat was extracted from its mother's uterus and taken immediately to a room with many vessels, each containing a different foodstuff, including one with goat's milk. The kid, when it could walk, smelled at each vessel, then drank the contents of the one containing milk. From this Stewart concluded that, in this case, an "instinctive determination is attached" to the smelling of milk. The study of instinct would be further developed by later British psychologists (see Chap. 11); but in the earlier nineteenth century the discussion of animal instincts was kept separate from the question of whether human cognitive ability depends on innate intuitions. Most of the group were empiricists, on the latter question, and it should be noted that both Stewart and Brown were critical of, but did not reject outright, Reid's concept of "common sense" knowledge.

Second, the British group were not only against intuitions, they were against a simple "faculty" psychology of the kind that is often imputed to Reid. The mind is not, they asserted, a filing cabinet with little boxes labeled *memory, judgment, kindness,* and so on. In the early nineteenth century, in fact, a movement known as *phrenology* tried to allocate different faculties to different parts of the head. Hamilton in particular sought to throw calumny on phrenology. Reid's analysis of different abilities was not adopted by his successors. Each member of the British group had his own ideas on how the mind should be divided; they concurred, however, that a psychology with an arbitrary large number of faculties was of little value. Brown (1820/1830, p. 101) preferred to speak of "states" of the mind and resolved them into only three classes: external powers or susceptibilities (sensations, including internal sensations such as hunger pangs); intellectual powers or susceptibilities; and susceptibilities of emotion. Hamilton (1859, p. 125) was content to divide the "facts" of mind into cognitions, feelings, and conative powers (will and desire). Bain explicitly supported Hamilton and extended the critique of faculty psychology to include current ideas about brain localization. Faculty psychology was not merely inapplicable as a classification of mental phenomena but could no longer serve as a model for brain phenomena. It should be noted, however, that Hamilton argued that the word *faculty* could be used in a more rigorous sense to mean a "capacity" or "ability." He suggested that the mind possesses six such abilities or faculties: the presentative (enabling us to sense); the conservative (for retention); the reproductive (for retrieval); the representative (giving us images); the elaborative (for comparing, which leads to generalization, judgment, and reasoning); and the regulative (which provides the basic lines along which we think, much as Reid argued for common sense laws determining how we judge). This last operates according to *a priori* principles; the other five are designed to build up a bank of knowledge *a posteriori.*

A third thread uniting the group was their interest in associations. Those most dogmatically asserting the necessity of an associationistic analysis were James Mill, John Stuart Mill, and Bain, but Brown and Hamilton also made important contributions to our understanding of how associations operated. These contributions will be discussed later.

A fourth thread uniting the group was their belief that there could be a branch of science concerned with establishing the laws of mental phenomena. As mentioned earlier, the word *psychology* was not really popular until Hamilton expressly asserted its value. Other terms such as *mental philosophy* were used, and even Hamilton thought of what we now call psychology as a branch of, indeed the very kernel of, *metaphysics.* Brown was particularly hopeful that the laws of the mind and the classification of mental phenomena could be made so deductively appealing and accurate that a science analogous to the physics—or more particularly, chemistry—could be founded. John Stuart Mill, in his *Logic,* believed that the laws of inference and probability that gave rigor to the other sciences could be applied with equal validity to the workings of mind. He even proposed a separate branch of science, concerned with the development of character, or personality, to be called *ethology.* This term now means something quite different—the study of animal behavior in natural surroundings—but the point is that John Stuart Mill saw the subject matter of mental phenomena and behavior as fit for a scientific discipline. Hamilton, in *Metaphysics* (1859, p. 43), talked of psychology as "pre-eminently a philosophical *science*" (italics added). Bain, it goes without saying, wrote as if he took it for granted that the study of mind was to be pursued with the same dedication as was being devoted to the other sciences.

The British group accepted, then, that psychology was a discipline in its own right. Still, a word of caution is necessary on one issue: The final and most influential member of the group, Bain, had no hesitation in assuming that a knowledge of the nervous system underlay, and constituted part of, this discipline. But it would be wrong to think of all the others as agreeing with Bain. Brown, despite his medical training, explicitly asserted that the study of mental phenomena could be carried out with little or no reference to physiology; the editor of Hamilton's lectures points out *(Metaphysics,* 1859, p. 264) that Hamilton was in the habit of occasionally adding lectures on the nervous system to this course with the avowed intent of showing that "no assistance is afforded to Mental Philosophy by the examination of the Nervous System." In the late nineteenth and early twentieth centuries, British psychology was, partly for this reason, essentially a stepchild of philosophy; some hold that this was, pragmatically speaking, a less successful aspect of the British tradition. The psychophysiologists, such as Laycock, Carpenter, and Lewes, did stress the physical basis of mind. Nevertheless, Laycock and Carpenter, with their Christian beliefs, shied away from a pure materialism and instead thought of mind as ultimately connected with brain substance but as nevertheless having a transcendental aspect, Mind, in tune with God (on this, see Danziger, 1982).

We turn therefore to a summary of the opinions of these writers on knowing, feeling, willing, and consciousness.

Knowing

The empiricist tradition of Locke and others had led to the notion that each sensation leaves behind it a trace, or impression, which can potentially be experienced as a revival of the sensation. This revival, however, is much less intense than the original sensation and was usually termed an *idea*. Ideas remained the key elements of psychic experience for the nineteenth-century writers, but they also held, perhaps as a result of German influence, that we also experience "feelings." *Ideas* are essentially intellectual entities; *feelings* are like *sensations* in that they arise from direct bodily experiences. Brown and Bain were the two writers who most emphasized feelings, partly because they both believed that earlier speculators on psychological matters had ignored those feelings we experience on moving muscles. Given, then, this broadening of the spectrum of the contents of experience, we may ask how the authors in question considered ideas and feelings to flow one from the other. The answer of course was that the laws of association determined the flow, but there were some disagreements as to precisely what these laws were.

For Stewart, Hume's three laws (contiguity, similarity, cause and effect) were inadequate. He argued, however *(Elements,* 1792/1829, p. 213), that the distinction should be made between association flows whose source is obvious to introspection and association flows where the source is less obvious. In the first group he placed "Resemblance and Analogy, Contrariety, Vicinity in time and place, and those which arise from accidental coincidences in the sound of different words." In the latter group he placed "Cause and Effect, Means and End, Premises and Conclusion; and those others which regulate the train of thought in the mind of the Philosopher, when he is engaged in a particular investigation." This last remark led him to note that individuals differently skilled in logical thought have different trains of associations and that these in turn rest on the individual's acquired habits of thought. Stewart also pointed out that when we make errors in an attempt at logical thought, it is because association by similarity or the like can divert our thoughts from the desired or proper sequence.

Brown was more precise on associations; in fact, he may be said to have come to grips with the whole problem more courageously than most of his predecessors. In his *Lectures* (1820/1830, p. 216 ff.) he argued that the intellectual states of mind we experience arise either by *simple sugges-tion* or by *relative suggestion*. Simple suggestions are essentially spontane-ous revivals of ideas; relative suggestions are those concerned less with the past than with the present. If we notice that our feelings elicited by two external events co-occur, or occur in close succession, we speak of relative suggestion. But simple suggestions, which underlay mental activi-ties as diverse as memory, conception, and imagination, flow from each other according to rules. Aristotle, remarked Brown, made the earliest proposal for the list of rules when he said that in searching for an idea we hunt for it using resemblance, contrariety, and contiguity. Brown also listed Hume's laws but disapproved of Hume's rejecting contrast in favor of cause and effect. In their place Brown distinguished between sugges-tions that arise one from the previous one because of the relations of the objects or feelings underlying them and the variables that decide *which* laws shall be operative at any given time. The former he called *primary* laws of suggestion; the latter, *secondary* laws of suggestion. The primary laws are essentially Aristotle's: similarity, contrast, and nearness in place or time; the secondary laws, however, are more numerous and Brown may be quoted directly, as they are essentially self-explanatory:

> In addition, then, to the primary laws of suggestion, which are founded on the mere relations of the objects or feelings to each other, it appears that there is another set of laws, the operation of which is indispensable to account for the variety in the effects of the former. To these I have given the name of *secondary laws of suggestion*—and we have seen, accordingly, that the suggestions are various as the original feelings have been, 1st, Of longer or shorter continuance; 2dly, More or less lively; 3dly, More or less fre-quently present; 4thly, More or less recent; 5thly, More or less pure, if I may so express it, from the mixture of other feelings; 6thly, That they vary according to differences of original constitution; 7thly, According to differ-ences of temporary emotion; 8thly, According to changes produced in the state of the body; and 9thly, According to general tendencies produced by prior habits. (1820/1830, p. 240)

Examples of how these variables influence the revival of new ideas and feelings were drawn from history and literature, including some anecdotes taken from Stewart; another example, of interest to American readers, was an anecdote related by the doctor Benjamin Rush of Philadelphia, one of the signatories of the Declaration of Independence. Rush described how he was able to revive the spirits of a patient suffering from typhus fever by enunciating a few simple words that reminded her of happy times of her childhood. But although these secondary laws of suggestion are of great interest to a modern memory theorist, Brown passed over them rather quickly, preferring to stress that the laws of suggestion underlay what previous writers had called the "faculties" (such as memory or imagination) and to argue that intellectual and moral character is reflected in the individual's trains of suggestions. Brown's main reason for preferring to use the word *suggestion* rather than *association* was as follows: If we consider A and B to be *associated* and coexperienced in the real world, and then later find that the idea of A gives rise to the idea of B, we are not justified in asserting that the idea of A is *associated* with the idea of B in the same way that A and B were associated in the real world. All we can properly infer is that A, according to some primitive law of the mind, *suggested* B. Brown elaborated on this argument in depth but did not succeed in displacing the word *association* from the pedestal it has continued to occupy to the present.

James Mill opened his chapter on the association of ideas with an approving nod to Brown and went on to stress that the flow of our *ideas*— a word he had earlier carefully defined—follows the flow of the sensations initially setting them up. Sensations occur either synchronically (simultaneously) or successively. In turn the ideas representing those sensations, when revived, will be occurring synchronically or successively. The best example of successive associations is seen when we learn something by heart; just as the poem or prose passage is first read in a particular order, we retrieve it in that order. To go against this order is difficult: James Mill observed (1829/1869, p. 80), "How remarkably this is the case, any one may convince himself, by trying to repeat backwards, even a passage with which he is as familiar as the Lord's Prayer."

From this basic assumption James Mill proceeded to explain how we build up complex ideas from simple sensations perceived in succession, but like Brown, he was concerned with the question of the *quality* of the idea as well as its origin. He introduced the concept of the *strength* of an association: "One association, we say, is stronger than another: First, when it is more permanent than another: Secondly, when it is performed with more certainty: Thirdly, when it is performed with more facility." But then James Mill went on to reduce the *causes* of these variations of associative strength to two: "the vividness of the associated feelings; and the frequency of the association." No mention here, it will be noted, of the importance of reward or punishment in setting up an association, but we may remark (1) that the effect of a reward or punishment may be to render the associated feelings more vivid and (2) that much later in the *Analysis* James Mill related aversions and desires to the feelings of pleasure and pain *associated* with the objects of aversion or desire. The importance of frequency of association, for Mill, was exemplified in the effects of practice in learning a language, playing a musical instrument, or performing arithmetic. However, Mill then made an assertion of some importance in the later development of his theory: He argued that some ideas are so strongly connected by association as to be inseparable or indistinguishable. The analogy, probably drawn from earlier associationists, is made between such a strong association and the sensation of white that results when a wheel with the seven prismatic colors painted on it is rapidly revolved.

Towards the end of the chapter on association, James Mill spoke critically of previous "laws" of association. For Mill synchronicity and successiveness were subsumed under the heading of contiguity. He stated, without much elaboration, that "resemblance" can be reduced to "contiguity" in so far we can perceive, and learn, that two objects are similar by perceiving them simultaneously or in close succession—that is, contiguously. John Stuart Mill has a long footnote at this point in which he argues that, according to his father's notion, everything that is *unlike* should also be associated by contiguity; in fact, he states the converse of his father's theory, namely that association by resemblance actually underlies many cases of association by contiguity, for by *recognizing* that two things near in place or time are similar, we thereby associate them.

In his *System of Logic*, John Stuart Mill nevertheless defended his father's stress on the simplicity and primitivity of the laws of association as underlying the flow of mental phenomena. Most of this book is concerned indeed with logic and with the validity of various kinds of inference and is of only indirect interest to the historian of psychology. But at the end, when he asserted that a science of mental phenomena is possible, even though it may not be an "exact" science like physics, he stated that what makes psychology a science is the uniformity with which the various laws of association operate. He stressed, in particular, the laws of similarity and contiguity as well as what we might call a law of intensity, according to which "greater intensity in either or both of the impressions is equivalent, in rendering them excitable by one another, to a greater frequency of conjunction" (1843/1893, p. 557). He went on to praise his father's *Analysis* as the paradigm of an associationistic work.

Nevertheless, he also attempted to correct James Mill on the matter of "new" complex ideas arising from the fusion of simple ideas. Complex ideas, he argued, are *generated* from simple ideas but do not *consist* of them: White is generated by a rapid succession of colors, it does not *consist* of them. In John Stuart Mill's later work on Hamilton's philosophy, he said, however, that if two sensations are associated in every single case that they are experienced, then their representative ideas may be so strongly associated as to be "inseparable." Boring (1929/1950), in reviewing John Stuart Mill's contribution to associationism, summarizes the matter by saying that in 1843 he had three laws of association—similarity, contiguity, and intensity—whereas in 1865 he had four laws—similarity, contiguity, frequency, and inseparability.

As we might expect, Sir William Hamilton showed a certain originality in his assessment of the value of the various laws of association. Associations are introduced in the context of the discussion of the reproductive faculty. Aristotle gave his three laws, argued Hamilton, but St. Augustine, in Book 10 of the *Confessions,* asserted that only one law was necessary—namely, "thoughts which have once coexisted in the mind are afterwards associated" (Hamilton's words). This law, which Hamilton named the law of redintegration, was repeated by Malebranche and, as we saw in Chap. 4, by Wolff. After listing the classification of Hume, Stewart, and Brown, Hamilton maintained that the two most commonly designated laws were those of contiguity in time and of similarity. Both of these he then tried to reduce to the law of redintegration: Things coexperienced in time or space are associated, and things whose resemblance is salient are also coexperienced. The emphasis is on the whole, the total constellation of coexperienced ideas. One such idea, when revived, will serve to bring up the other idea or ideas that made up the original constellation. John Stuart Mill, in the *Examination of Sir William Hamilton's Philosophy,* contended that this law could not explain how, when we think of a sweet taste of today, we are reminded of the similar sweet taste of a week ago, since the two had not been coexperienced. For him, a separate law of similarity was still needed. He had other arguments against Hamilton's notion and accused Hamilton of misunderstanding certain aspects of James Mill's *Analysis.*

Bain's associationism was perhaps the simplest of all. In discussing the intellect, or thinking function of the mind, Bain argued that its fundamental attributes were the consciousness of difference, the consciousness of agreement, and retentiveness. When two simultaneous or successive events are retained in such a way as to revive the corresponding ideas simultaneously or successively, we have association by contiguity. When we are conscious of the agreement or likeness between two things, we have association by similarity. On the basis of these two laws, Bain built a superstructure showing how most of our linguistic, voluntary, and creative activity results from the joint operation of the laws. The law of contiguity, he argued, underlay many of the phenomena of our perception of the external world. The law of similarity was reflected in intellectual achievements of various kinds. Associations could combine into various conjunctions. The importance of the emotional tone of a conjunction was emphasized, as was the fact that the trend of volitions or desires we experience is determined by association.

Before leaving the contributions of this group of theories concerning knowledge, we may note two other undercurrents of interest that can be picked out from the total corpus. First, we recall that one of the questions of importance for James Mill was the notion that two ideas could so fuse as to form a new "inseparable" idea: The analogy was made with the several colors' melding to produce white. In 1820 (Lecture 10) Brown, in trying to justify the existence of a branch of knowledge devoted to mental phenomena, had argued that, just as chemical elements interact and fuse to produce new mixtures and compounds, so ideas could be thought of as interacting to form new complex ideas. John Stuart Mill, in his *Logic,* combined these two suggestions and proposed that there could in fact be a mental chemistry just as there was a physical chemistry. The concept of extension, for example, could be seen as a mental compound resulting from the associations of various sensations and memories acquired in the course of experience. This notion of mental chemistry became quite popular, and Wundt would eventually—with little reference to the British movement—speak of mental *elements* and *compounds.*

Second, one issue hotly debated in the nineteenth as well as in previous centuries was the general question of how we do arrive at our knowledge of space and extension. Berkeley, we recall, had argued for empiricism; Kant had argued for native intuitions. In the case of the present writers, we may summarize the course of arguments for and against empiricism and nativism in the acquisition of spatial concepts as follows: Brown repeated many of the empiricist arguments of the eighteenth century but felt that, when talking of sight combining with touch, previous writers had been rather vague on just how touch helped us to derive concepts both of matter and of space. He observed that if he touched, say, a table, he not only felt sensations in his fingertips but also felt sensations in his arm muscles, these sensations growing in intensity if he actually pushed the table. From these experiences, Brown argued, we not only developed notions of thereness and solidity but also of *resistance.* Our knowledge of external objects, he claimed, was based on concepts of resistance as well as spatial extension. Moreover, when acquiring new motor skills such as dancing, we attend to sensations from the muscles to a great degree. This kind of organic sensation was also stressed by James Mill, who allowed sensation of resistance to play an important part in the development of our concepts of extension and motion.

Bain also stressed the importance of resistance in the development (by way of contiguity associations) of our concepts of externality. The one writer who took exception to this kind of argument was Hamilton, with his sympathy for Kantian intuitionism. One of his reasons for believing that the sense of extension was native to the observer was his observation that if we ever see more than one color at a time, there must be a line of demarcation between the two colors. This fact of itself tells the subject, Hamilton asserted, that the colors are extended in space. John Stuart Mill's answer in the *Examination* was that to see extension at all you also need eye movements, which Hamilton's example ignores. Muscular sensations from the eye muscles combine with the visual sensations of color to give the "feeling" of extension. Many more detailed empirical arguments on the matter will be found in the *Examination*.

There is an interesting footnote concerning this aspect of John Stuart Mill's critique of Hamilton. According to his *Autobiography* (1873), Mill was not merely disappointed in Hamilton's *Lectures on Metaphysics* when they appeared, he was worried that the opinion expressed in them might have practical consequences. To argue that one's corpus of knowledge was based on unchangeable intuitions, as Hamilton did, was to deny that character and ability could be molded by education. As a social reformer Mill felt obliged to attack Hamilton's nativism.

Feelings

In all their attempts at comprehensive systems of psychology, the writers of the British tradition gave a large role to the feelings and, in particular, to emotional feelings. But organic feelings, such as muscular or visceral sensations, were also included. Hamilton, reviewing earlier theories in his *Metaphysics,* listed authors from the Greeks onward according to whom the touch sense should be supplemented with another sense comprising sensations of hunger, thirst, and so on. In the 1790s several German authors suggested that a *Vital* sense be distinguished from an *Organic* sense: The latter comprised the usual five senses, whereas the former encompassed sensations of heat and cold, shuddering, hunger, thirst, visceral sensations, and the like. The distinction was in fact adopted in Kant's *Anthropologie* (1798) and the Vital Sense was sometimes given the synonym "common sensibility" or "coenaesthesis" (German, *Gemeingefühl*). Brown adopted a similar classification *(Lectures* 17 and 18: We noted earlier that Brown subsumed internal sensations under the first of his types of susceptibility). We shall see in the next chapter that the nineteenth century opened with some attempt at a physiological account of common sensibility.

But in the British tradition, apart from the emphasis on the relevance of the feelings of resistance to the growth of concepts such as extension and externality, the main kinds of feelings of interest were those connected with the emotions: The classification of the emotions, the importance of emotions in determining our associations, the roles of pain and pleasure in determining our habits, and the old question of whether there was a moral sense—all these issues were discussed in detail by the members of the movement, and we may briefly indicate their positions on these matters.

How to classify the emotions had been a long-standing question in the history of psychology. The British school added some more classifications: In an appendix to the *Emotions and the Will* Bain summarized the divisions of Reid, Stewart, Brown, and Hamilton. Brown's classification has some ingenuity to it insofar as he divides the emotions into those concerned with the present (such as love and hate), the past (such as regret and gratitude), and the future (the desires). These three main genera are each divided into subclasses. Hamilton's account was also quite orderly and made more mention of the *aims* of the various emotions than had earlier authors; for example, he saw each of the emotions as related to five basic practical desires—namely, self-preservation, the enjoyment of existence, the preservation of the species, the tendency towards self-development, and the "moral law."

On the other hand, Bain, who devoted three hundred pages to the discussion of the emotions, was skeptical of any classification: He spoke of the "permanent and insuperable difficulty of expounding the Emotions in a strict order of sequence. . . . there is no one absolutely preferable arrangement" (*The Emotions and the Will*, 1859/1880, p. 74). His set of chapters on the emotions treats them in the following order: emotions of relativity (novelty, wonder, etc.), emotions concerned with memories ("ideal" emotions), sympathy, tender emotions (including sexual and parental feelings), fear, anger, power, emotions regarding oneself (e.g., self-esteem), emotions of intellect, pursuit, and aesthetic emotions, and the ethical emotions (under which is subsumed a discussion of the moral sense). In contrast with the orderliness of the treatment by predecessors such as Hume or Brown, Bain's discussions tend to be disjointed and at times trite. It seems to be a general opinion that Bain was least successful in his discussions of the emotions.

The other questions concerning emotion may be dealt with more sketchily. On the role played by emotion in determining the flow of association, James Mill was perhaps the most specific, although Bain also discussed what we now call *conditioned emotional responses* in the sections on association by contiguity and similarity in *The Senses and the Intellect*. Mill pointed out how learned fears, such as fears of thunderstorms or of small animals such as spiders, can originate in some early fright and be very persistent. Hamilton raised the issue of emotions such as fear and anger that originate in the unconscious, a matter we shall return to shortly.

On the importance of pain and pleasure, we may recall the importance of utilitarianism in the thought of James Mill, and he emphasized the key role of these feelings in determining learned behavior. But Hamilton, in his *Metaphysics* (Lecture 42), made a bold attempt to say *why* some feelings are pleasurable and others painful. He asserted that conscious existence involves energy, with "the energy of each power of conscious existence having, as its reflex or concomitant, an appropriate pleasure or pain." Each such energy has a degree of "perfection" by relation (1) to the power of which it is the exertion and (2) the object about which it is conversant. The more "perfect" the energy, the more pleasurable the associated feeling; the more imperfect the energy, the more painful the associated feeling. After elaborating on this theory, Hamilton discussed older historical views concerning pleasure and pain, one of the many passages in the *Metaphysics* that are both fascinating and educational to read in the light of their author's erudition. However, Hamilton's difficult and rather vague hypothesis was roundly criticized by John Stuart Mill in Chap. 25 of the *Examination:* In particular, Mill argued, it is hard to understand how Hamilton could explain "passive" pain, such as a toothache, where no exertion of a "power" seems to take place. Hamilton's theory has therefore had little influence on the progress of psychology.

Finally, the matter of the "moral sense" was given approving attention by those members of the Scottish school concerned with reconciling "mental science" with theology: Bain, however, came to grips more rigorously with the question of why we tend to behave according to moral rules. He stressed the importance of punishment—by society or an individual—as a major force determining what we do and do not consider immoral. "Utility" and sentiment, for Bain, determine the growth of conscience and ethical behavior. He stated categorically, "I entirely dissent from Dugald Stewart and the great majority of the writers on the Theory of Morals, who represent Conscience as a primitive and independent faculty of the mind" *(The Emotions and the Will,* 1859/1880, p. 285).

Willing

We have come a long way from the Middle Ages where "the Will" was presumed to be a sort of "soul above a soul," controlling the body and essentially "free." We have mentioned how Locke and Hume explicated the notion of a free will in such a way as to make *will* the name for a kind of feeling—namely, the feeling that we are in control of our destinies. This essentially bifurcates the general topic of the will into two aspects: a subjective aspect where we simply study feelings related to such activities as planning and intending and voluntarily moving; and an objective aspect, the province of philosophers rather than psychologists, concerned with the general question of whether "choice" can be allowed to be a variable in the description of behavioral events. In the early nineteenth century, however, practitioners of mental science still felt obliged to deal with this philosophical question of "liberty" and "necessity": We find, for example, chapters on the subject in Bain's *The Emotions and the Will* and in John Stuart Mill's *System of Logic.* We shall discuss the two matters separately.

On the first question, the nature of willing itself, we may note that we are forced to discuss the relation between involuntary and voluntary behavior, between reflexes and intentional acts. We saw in the previous chapter that Cabanis in particular had talked of levels of performance, with the simplest performances being mediated by the spinal cord and the most complex by the cerebral cortex. We may now add that Reid, Stewart, and Brown recognized the importance of unlearned, involuntary reponses such as sucking in the development of the child: They argued that from this reflexive behavior the child acquired "ideas" from the resulting sensations and feelings of movement, and that from these ideas the child made associations such that he voluntarily began to make movements eliciting the appropriate sensations. However, in Reid, Stewart, and Brown these notions are not greatly developed; it was James Mill who, in the final chapter of the *Analysis,* gave coherent shape to this developmental theory of the acquisition of voluntary behavior and sharpened it by linking this acquisition with feelings of pleasure and pain. Furthermore, he argued, as facility in the revival of ideas develops, the individual begins to form plans and intentions and to narrow down the range of his voluntary movements to those essential for the fulfillment of those intentions.

James Mill saw the subject of the will as the *final* topic in a synthetic psychology, but also as a crucial one. Bain would be even more emphatic that the development of voluntary control was a subject of great importance to psychology. To James Mill's notion that associations of movements with sensations led to the acquisition of voluntary movements, Bain added that the body, from birth, possessed the power of *spontaneous* movement and that voluntary control was fashioned by imposing order on these spontaneous movements. He did not successfully answer the question of what caused the spontaneous movements in the first place, but Kuo (1932) much later studied movements in chick embryos and argued that most movements were responses to the extraembryonic environment, although they occasionally arose as a consequence of the heartbeat. Kuo therefore argued against the idea that movements arose "spontaneously." Tempting as it is to discourse at length on this kind of theorizing, this is not the place to do so; we simply related these facts as further supporting the contention that nineteenth-century associationism could never be accused of being narrow-minded in its choice of topics worthy of a psychologist's attention.

The most original writers on the will were perhaps Laycock and

Carpenter. In early Victorian England there was a great deal of interest in topics such as hypnosis, communications with "spirits" by way of mediums, who often claimed to be able to spell out messages using a small writing machine called a planchette, and the claim that some persons could see lights shining round the poles of magnets. Laycock, as a doctor, was also interested in the complaint of *hysteria*, at that time predominantly female, which in the 1840s seems to have been a very general term used to describe excessive emotional upset, but which even then could involve disturbances of the body with no obvious physical cause. In an article on the reflex (1845) and a book on hysteria, Laycock came to the view that the distinction between involuntary and voluntary behavior was not hard and fast, but involved gradations: It was possible, he argued, that a reflex action of the body could be evoked not only by an external stimulus but by activity in the mind itself. The subject was not always aware of this, but it meant that movements could occur even if he did not deliberately will them, as in the movements of the hypnotized subject or the writing of the planchette. There could even be a loss of the ability to will to move a limb, as in the apparent paralysis of a hysterical patient. Even sensations might be influenced by unconscious mental activity; a hysterical subject could experience extra-intense sensations (as well as stronger sexual feelings). Laycock (and later, Carpenter) thought that those who could see lights round the ends of magnets were being unduly suggestible. However, these intriguing ideas are only given scant mention in Laycock's book *Mind and Brain*, which predominantly concerns the mind/body problem.

It was Carpenter, in his *Principles of Mental Physiology*, who first made precise the relationship between involuntary and voluntary behavior. He distinguished three levels of behavior: First was *reflex* behavior, unlearned and automatic, which had as its purpose the maintenance of bodily well-being. Second was *involuntary* behavior, behavior originally learned that had become so routine that no conscious thought was given to it: Examples are walking or writing without having to think deliberately about every single letter. Third was *volitional* behavior, in which conscious effort was directed to the actions produced: Although my writing is fairly involuntary, I am using considerable effort in deciding what words to write and how to phrase my thought.

Carpenter's recognition that many skilled acts are automatic led naturally to an inquiry into the role of automatic behavior in unusual mental states, such as hysteria, hypnosis, and the effects of drugs such as alcohol; he believed that in all three states there was a loss of *volitional* behavior without a loss of *involuntary* behavior. Carpenter related these different levels of will to different degrees of control by the higher centers of the brain, and we shall see shortly that his study of involuntary behavior led him to believe in an active "unconscious" mind.

On the second question—whether humans could truly be said to possess "free will"—there was a variety of answers, but it should be said now that the issue was of interest not only to psychologists but even to physicists. At the start of the nineteenth century, it was felt that physicists like Newton and Laplace (1749–1827), who had been almost as ingenious as Newton in providing a mathematics for predicting the movements of heavenly bodies, were laying the groundwork for a picture of the universe in which all motions followed precise scientific laws and in which there was no room for "chance." Contemporaneously, as we shall see in the next chapter, the physiologists were showing the dependence of mental events on brain events. For both groups, the notion that there was a "free agent" capable of determining the next mental event independent of what had just preceded it, that is, of a truly "free will," threatened the assumptions of natural law. Daston (1982) has written a detailed account of various Victorian solutions to the dilemma. Some writers were simply unembarrassed by the loss of "freedom" a psychophysiological account seemed to offer and stressed, particularly in the context of the theory of evolution, that "free will" was essentially a feeling that the higher animals were aware of when they were making decisions. Others, such as Laycock and Carpenter, invented different metaphysical systems, attempting to integrate the new psychophysiology with traditional Christian beliefs (see also Danziger, 1982). The physicists themselves were forced to take a closer look at the meanings of the concepts of "chance" and "freedom," one important outcome of this inquiry being the understanding that by "chance" we often mean that a small change at some level in a system can have effects that multiply into very large changes in the total behavior of the system. In the history of science, then, the problem of "free will," as it was being raised in the context of accounts of the dependence of mind on brain, represented a major challenge, with ramifications on many disciplines ranging from physics to theology. In psychology itself, the general problem of willing was a central one in the nineteenth century, and as a result the two psychological giants of the end of the century, Wilhelm Wundt and William James, were both intensely preoccupied with the position of the will in their new science.

Consciousness

Stewart did not pay particular attention to the topic of consciousness, even though, at the time he was writing, German successors to Leibniz were giving consciousness special prominence, and even though Reid had considered it one of the "intellectual powers." Brown devoted two lectures to consciousness, essentially commenting on Reid and stressing that a consciousness of one's "self" underlay the concept of one's own identity.

James Mill gave it a chapter of three and a half pages and offers a definition: *Consciousness,* he argued, is a generic word under which "all the names of the subordinate classes of the feelings of a sentient creature are included." For James Mill, *consciousness* was a word to be used or not used as a speaker felt fit. Bain felt obliged to add a chapter on consciousness at the end of *The Emotions and the Will* and enumerated thirteen different ways the word could be used. From this verbal analysis of the word, he led into a discussion of the distinction between one's self and the external world, that is to say, subject and object. For most writers of the British tradition, *consciousness* was, if anything, a word to be analyzed rather than a phenomenon to be studied in its own right.

Hamilton, with his profound knowledge of the German tradition, tried to bring the topic of consciousness into contemporary psychological thought. He devoted some earlier lectures to an analysis of the meaning of the word, to a history of theories about it, and to an enumeration of rules to be followed in discussing it. He also offered a speculation about it: He argued that the fewer objects we are conscious of at once, the clearer and more distinct will be our knowledge of them. There is, he argued, a limit to how much can be attended to at once. If one throws a handful of marbles on the floor, it is difficult to view at once more than six or seven without confusion. This observation has been taken by Glanville and Dallenbach (1929) to be the first "experiment" concerned with what is now called the *span of apprehension.* Hamilton also speculated elsewhere *(Metaphysics,* 1859, p. 99) that sensation and perception, while always coexistent, were in inverse ratio to each other. The stronger the sensation, the less strong the perception and vice versa. This argument Hamilton derived from a sentence in Kant's *Anthropologie.*

Putting his remarks on attention span together with this law, we get the impression that Hamilton perceived consciousness as a kind of receptacle of limited capacity in which individual feelings and ideas struggle for attention. This is precisely the model that Herbart wrote so much about, as we shall see. Furthermore, Hamilton not only discusses the contents of consciousness, he discusses the unconscious. Memories can be unconscious and perceptions can be unconscious, along the lines Leibniz had suggested; the flow of our thoughts is influenced by the unconscious. In a word, Hamilton tried to introduce into British thought a concept of consciousness far broader than that typically adopted by his contemporaries. Was the effort a success? Hardly. In his *Examination* John Stuart Mill took Hamilton to task for certain inconsistencies in his use of the word *consciousness* and reiterated the value of his father's analysis of how the word should be used. In many ways Mill's rejection of Hamilton's espousal of consciousness foreshadowed Watson's later rejection of consciousness as a variable to be included in establishing the laws of behavior.

On the other hand, the psychophysiologists, probably because of their medical experience, went in the opposite direction and stressed that far more of our everyday behavior was the result of unconscious activity than had hitherto been realized. We have already mentioned that Laycock stressed "unconscious" reflex activity and that Carpenter distinguished involuntary from volitional determinants of even complicated movements and sensory judgments. Carpenter gave the name *unconscious cerebration* to the activity that took place in the mind even when no conscious awareness of such activity was present; he also invented the term *ideomotor* to refer to the possibility that an idea, conscious or unconscious, could be the origin of a movement. One of the main spurs to Carpenter's thinking along these lines was his observation that awareness of sensations themselves could fluctuate: He gave examples of professors who were in great pain at the start of a lecture, seemed not to notice their pain during the heat of delivery, then felt it again after the lecture. If awareness of sensations was so variable, it could also be that awareness of movements was variable: Sometimes we consciously carry out a movement, but at other times we are hardly aware of volition at all, as in sleepwalking (somnambulism). Carpenter went on to assume that thought processes themselves can be carried out unconsciously, as when we achieve the solution to a problem in a dream.

Another aspect of unconscious cerebration was that it could explain experiences and feelings that the subject could not understand himself. For example, Lewes (1872–1879) reports the case of a fifteen-year-old who entered a room at an inn and found himself "suddenly surprised and pursued by a pack of strange, shadowy, infantile images . . . a wild reverie of early childhood, half-illusion, half-reality seized me" (vol. 3, p. 127). It turned out that the room had the same wallpaper as the nursery the subject had occupied as a four- and five-year-old, wallpaper he had not seen since then. Carpenter (1874) tells how a judge dreamed one night that lizards were crawling over him, then noticed that the room in which he had passed the previous evening had a clock with figures of crawling lizards on the base. As Carpenter puts it, "This he must have *seen* without *noticing* it; and the sight must have left a "trace" in his brain, though it left no record in his conscious memory" (p. 587).

This concludes our survey of the opinions of the writers of the British tradition. We have tried to emphasize not only the points of agreement between them but also the many points of disagreement. Associationism was not only a British movement. In his invaluable survey of the history of associationism, H. C. Warren (1921) reviews additional associationistic writings of France, Italy, and Germany. The most famous non-British writer on associations was H. A. Taine (1828–1893), whose book *De l'Intelligence* (*On Intelligence*, 1870) in some ways did for French psychology what Bain's books did for British. Taine's book is a synthesis of the associationism of the two Mills and Bain with the new findings on exceptional mental states such as hypnosis, but he is more concerned with the explanation of high-level reasoning ("intelligent" reasoning) than he is with emotion or personality. In particular, Taine has detailed association-istic analyses of how we learn to ascribe causes to explain events and how we are able to correctly interpret confusing sensory information.

It may be surmised, however, that it was a feeling of frustration with armchair theorizing, coupled with a promise of hope in the experimental method as it was being applied to the study of sensation, perception, and simple reactions, that led to the origins of a truly *experimental* psychology in the 1860s and 1870s. For an account of the development of this movement, we must turn back to Germany as it was in 1800.

Summary

Although the main developments in experimental psychology took place in Germany in the early nineteenth century, there was a strong tradition of "mental philosophy" in Great Britain at the time. The Scottish school, heavily influenced by Reid, included Stewart, Brown, and Hamilton. In England, James Mill and his son John Stuart Mill wrote extensively on psychology, and Alexander Bain anticipated the beginnings of modern psychology with his influential texts *The Senses and the Intellect* (1855) and *The Emotions and the Will* (1859). All members of this group were united in their bias towards empiricism, with Hamilton, who favored Kant, being the main dissenter. They were united in their resistance to a single "fac-ulty" psychology, their interest in associations, and their belief that there could indeed be a "science" of psychology. Nevertheless, there were many disagreements among the members of the group—on the subject of knowing, they differed in the kinds and numbers of "laws" of association they promulgated, and they differed in their beliefs concerning the fu-sion of ideas and the degree to which learning determined the success with which the individual found his or her way about in space. On the subject of feeling, they had various classifications of the emotions and some disagreement as to the existence of a "moral sense." On the subject of willing, we may note particularly Bain's attempts to give a chronology of the growth of voluntary behavior. On consciousness, Hamilton in par-ticular tried to introduce German concepts of the topic into British thought but was strongly criticized by John Stuart Mill. Two doctors, Laycock and Carpenter, proposed the existence of unconscious cerebra-tion, differentiating acts over which we have conscious control from acts and feelings that seem to be determined by unconscious factors.

1800 to 1879:
The Experimental Tradition

6

In this chapter we shall consider the origins of psychology as an experimental science, as opposed to a branch of philosophy. The first sparks of encouragement that led thinkers to believe that mental phenomena could be explored experimentally came from studies of the special senses, particularly Weber's work on touch. That psychological phenomena could be closely related to physiological phenomena was demonstrated in various ways in the early nineteenth century, but we may single out particularly the discovery that the different parts of the brain exercised specific influences on specific forms of behavior. The origins of psychophysics were laid down by Fechner; the origins of reaction time studies, by Donders. A comprehensive integration of perception and learning, as seen in our ability to find our way about in space, was offered by Lotze, although it is of course possible to trace this line of thought back to Malebranche and Berkeley. When Wundt founded his laboratory in 1879 there lay before him a series of well-beaten paths leading into the unknown land of experimental psychology: It was he who extended those paths and set a large number of explorers onto them. By 1900 enough was known about the new country for the theorists to attempt the first fine-scale maps, the first comprehensive theories that relied on experimental evidence for their support.

Herbart and Beneke

The first claims on our attention, therefore, are the discoveries about the brain and the special senses that were made in the first two-thirds of the nineteenth century. But we cannot pass directly to them without mentioning two professors of philosophy in Germany, each of whom wrote a book claiming to be a "textbook" of psychology and each of whom sought to offer a comprehensive system of psychology in its own right. Johann Friedrich Herbart (1776–1841) and Friedrich Eduard Beneke (1798–1854) are often paired in people's minds because of the similarity of their careers and interests and because some critics of Beneke have argued, misleadingly, that he was merely a follower of Herbart. Another reason for pairing them together is that both men believed that the fundamental phenomenon for psychology to describe is the interplay of "presentations" *(Vorstellungen)* in conscious experience.

But there is another, more fundamental reason for considering both these thinkers in the same section. It will be recalled that Kant had denied the possibility of a scientific psychology, partly because he could not see how to bring mathematics into psychology, partly because he felt we had no direct knowledge of the soul. The first German of note to revolt against Kant's pessimism was Jacob Friedrich Fries (1773–1843). Instead of arguing that our knowledge of our own experiences was fallible because we could easily make mistakes about our own mental processes, Fries argued that the fact we have at least some knowledge of our experiences should serve as a foundation on which to build. And even though Fries allowed that introspection could be fallible, he could not see that this drawback warranted the abandonment of a hope for an empirical psychology; we do not reject physics because sometimes our measurements are in error. After Fries had reacted against Kant, Herbart and Beneke went on to formulate their own psychological systems, with Herbart also arguing to his own satisfaction that mathematics *could* be brought into psychology. The story of this rebellion against Kant is told in more detail by Leary (1978).

Herbart was a precocious child who, like John Stuart Mill, was educated in boyhood mainly by his parents, particularly his mother. At the age of eighteen he attended the University of Jena, where he was exposed to Kant's philosophy; then at the age of twenty-one he went to Switzerland, where he tutored the three sons of the governor of Interlaken. He became slightly acquainted with J. H. Pestalozzi (1746–1827), the foremost theorist of education of his time. He then moved to Göttingen, a small German town with an excellent university; here he obtained his doctorate and wrote his first books. These included works on metaphysics and logic as well as education. Then in 1809 he was delighted to receive a call to a chair of philosophy at Königsberg: the chair Kant had occupied. He spent twenty-four years there and, while continuing to write on philosophy and education, now added psychology to his armament. His short *Textbook in Psychology* appeared in 1816; the formidable and lengthy *Psychologie als Wissenschaft (Psychology as Science)* appeared in 1824–1825. Despite his duties at the university, Herbart also taught in a boys' school in Königsberg. This gave him the opportunity to put some of his educational principles into practice. In 1833, however, he went back to Göttingen as professor of philosophy. Eight years later he died there unexpectedly of a stroke. His successor in the Göttingen chair was Lotze, whose work we shall presently discuss.

Posterity has seen Herbart primarily as an educator, secondly as a psychologist, and only finally as a philosopher, but in his own mind philosophy was primary and his educational theories and psychological ideas were the offshoot of a grand scheme of metaphysics that shows the influences of Leibniz and Kant. From this scheme fell out various principles of aesthetics and ethics, and Herbart saw the goal of education as the inculcation of a sophisticated morality and of a "many-sidedness" capable of properly evaluating the finest things of life, notably artistic productions. This in turn, it would seem, led him to ask how one idea dominates another in consciousness, and we have the seed from which his psychology would develop. It is sometimes thought that Herbart first devised a psychology, then applied it to education; in fact, he probably worked the other way round, devising his psychology from his pedagogy. For more details of how Herbart's philosophy, psychology, and pedagogy were related to each other, Dunkel (1970) may be consulted.

In Herbart's educational philosophy, new learning should always be built on the foundation of previous learning. Moreover, one of the aims of education is to teach children to concentrate, to focus their interest. In Herbart's psychology, therefore, a major question is how new information, which is carefully attended to, is integrated with old. The way to do this, argued Herbart, is to build up from a fundamental set of presentations *(Vorstellungen)* a total mass of presentations into which new presentations are integrated according to habits of self-control and the laws of association. Mental life is the interplay of presentations, some of which come from the outside world, others from internal memories. The interplay is experienced as a flow of events in consciousness. The task of psychology is to predict (1) the order of flow of presentations in consciousness and (2) the *clarity* of the presentations as consciously experienced.

In his *Textbook of Psychology* Herbart offers the beginnings of a deductively derived system according to which the clarity of each experimental presentation is directly described as its "strength" in consciousness. The basic picture is that there is a *threshold*—Herbart invented this term deliberately—separating that which is experienced now (i.e., is in consciousness) from that which is not experienced now (i.e., is unconscious). A given presentation is at its clearest when it is fully in consciousness, and its strength can vary with the amount of it that persists above the threshold of consciousness. Because of the ceaseless impinging of new sensory information on the contents of consciousness, a presentation, while at its strongest when it forms the focus of conscious experience, gradually fades away until it is entirely below the threshold of consciousness. The disappearance process is held to occur rapidly at first, then more slowly; in fact, Herbart offers an equation that describes how the strength of a presentation decreases to zero as the item vanishes below the threshold. The equation is derived from first principles and, like the physics Herbart so wished to imitate, involves the calculus that had been invented by Newton and Leibniz.

Coming back to the interplay of presentations: A presentation that is strong (i.e., above the threshold of consciousness) can fuse with other presentations or can help other presentations up from below the threshold or can hinder or inhibit other presentations, pushing them down below the threshold. Thus mental experience is the outcome of a battle of "forces" just as physics has its dynamics of forces. In *Psychology as Science* Herbart devotes some two hundred pages to an account of the mathematics of his "mental mechanics." Boring's evaluation of this noble but relatively uninfluential exercise is that Herbart's assumptions are often questionable but that his mathematics is valid, given these assumptions (Boring, 1929/1950, p. 260). Leary (1980) shows that Herbart was not the first to introduce mathematics into psychology: Sir Frances Hutcheson (1694–1746) had tried to quantify the amount of good in an action, and Pierre L. M. de Maupertuis (1698–1759) had tried to quantify the intensity of pleasure and pain.

The second half of *Psychology as Science* is nonmathematical and has been successfully summarized by Stout (1888). Here Herbart applied his flow-of-presentations scheme, with the accompanying mechanisms of fusion, helping, and inhibition, to the wider range of human experience, including the flow of emotional feelings, the revival of memories, and the development of the self or ego. The feelings include the passions; in the *Textbook* Herbart noted how emotional pressures can affect the contents of various otherwise emotionally neutral presentations. Memories are revived in the order in which they appeared: The memory train ABC is revived because presentation A helps presentation B above consciousness, and the fusion of A with B helps presentation C in turn to rise above the threshold. This implies that A will be strongly associated with B, less with C, and so on; we shall see later that Ebbinghaus actually devised an experiment to test Herbart's assumption of "remote associations."

As for the growth of the ego, Herbart argued that at any given time a new incoming presentation will fuse with the *total* complex of previous presentations, some of which will be above the threshold of consciousness at that particular moment. This total complex is given the name *apperceptive mass*. The growth of the self is the growth of the apperceptive mass, but it is a continuously evolving structure because new presentations are either fused with previous ones or inhibited from being assimilated. Herbart argued that the child only gradually formulates the distinction between himself-as-an-object-like-others and himself-as-an-object-"I"-can-control. Note how Herbart here was not content to analyze the meaning of *self* in the way Locke and Hume had done; he believed there is also an *explanation* to be given. The reader will also observe how Herbart stands at a sort of crossroads between Leibniz (the introducer of the concepts of consciousness and apperception) and Freud (the delineator of the emotional forces battling to construct the adult personality).

Beneke was rather a tragic figure. Like Herbart, he saw the science of psychology as being that of a description of the dynamics of conscious experience but also viewed psychology as the fundamental science on which ethics, religion, metaphysics, and educational theory should be based. There was even a name given to this point of view: *psychologism*. But psychologism was not popular in those German universities where the faculties of theology were still powerful and where the faculties of philosophy were becoming dominated with the idea that there was an absolute "good," and absolute "reality," not to be explained away on psychological grounds. Beneke, in fact, having studied at Berlin, was not allowed to teach there after the publication of his *Foundations of a Physics of Morals* (1822): The work was said, unreasonably, to be "Epicurean," still a term of opprobrium after more than two thousand years. After a few years teaching at Göttingen, however, he was reinstated at Berlin, where he wrote his main psychology texts. There were several of these, the best known being the *Lehrbuch der Psychologie als Naturwissenschaft (Textbook of Psychology as a Natural Science)* of 1833. The 1877 edition of this book, edited by Dressler, contains valuable cross references to Beneke's other psychological works. Two years after the textbook, he wrote *Erziehungs und Unterrichtslehre (Textbook of Education and Instruction)*, in which he applied his psychological theories to pedagogy. In 1845 he published his *Die Neue Psychologie (The New Psychology)*, in which he defended himself against the accusation that he merely imitated Herbart. In 1854 he died by drowning in Berlin. It might have been suicide.

Beneke's view, as summarized in the textbook, might be characterized as Lockeian in the sense that he tries to build up an account of knowledge on the basis of sensory experience, but Kantian in the sense that he believes that when we are born, we are not a *tabula rasa* but rather have innate dispositions to develop particular abilities. The dispositions are given the name *Urvermögen,* which means roughly "original faculties"; Beneke denotes such abilities as the ability to sense, the ability to seek stimulation, and the ability to retain as original faculties. The newborn child, argues Beneke, actively seeks stimulation. When a stimulus affects the child, it will leave a memory trace, but the child is still not yet "conscious" in the usual sense of the word. But gradually over time the child builds up a system of interrelated traces such that some stimuli, when received, excite a subsystem of traces that in turn revive other traces according to a principle that Beneke calls the "mutual attraction of similars." This principle asserts that traces of the same kind unite together. Thus a stimulus can excite traces similar to itself, which in turn can lead to an "experience" underlain by a chain of traces operating independently of the original stimulus. Such an experience has come to be called *conscious.* Consciousness, then, is something the child develops. The child's later life will consist of alternations between consciousness (being awake) and nonconsciousness (sleep), and during the conscious periods external stimuli and internal representations will rival each other as to which is most effective in reviving new traces—that is, bringing them from the unconscious to the conscious state.

At this point, Beneke introduced a new concept for which other psychologists have criticized him (see, e.g., Stout, 1889). He imagined that when presentation A brings presentation B into consciousness, it does so by way of intermediary devices that were originally associated with the *Urvermögen.* He calls them *movable* or *transferable* elements. These elements flow or are transferred perpetually from one presentation to the next, which it brings into consciousness. The transferable elements also become attached to pleasurable feelings, so that a desire can arouse an unconscious trace system through the transference of these elements to it. Stimuli or presentations that are coexperienced in time become fused by way of an appropriation of movable elements that bind them together; the strength of the association will still be marked, though reduced, if the events occur successively in time.

From this basic principle of the binding of simultaneous or closely successive events, Beneke derived other "laws" of association such as the laws of similarity, contrast, and cause and effect. The subjective value or importance of a presentation varies directly with the number of traces associated with presentations. Given these assumptions, Beneke was then able to develop a comprehensive theory in which the various emotions, feelings, and desires all have their place in the ebb and flow of conscious experiences mediated by the movable elements. Differences in the *Urvermögen* determine later differences in temperament and ability, so that Beneke was able to deal with individual differences and even certain mental aberrations. The most comprehensive account in English of Beneke's psychology will be found in Raue (1871).

Physiological Psychology

At the end of the eighteenth century nervous function was still hardly understood. Haller's *vis nervosa* was almost as mystical as the animal spirits it was supposed to replace. Over a period from about 1780 to 1850 it was gradually discovered, however, that nerves and muscles displayed properties such that electricity might be thought of as forming the basis of a *vis nervosa*. First, Galvani (1737–1798) observed that electricity could serve as a stimulus for nervous action; he then went on to assert, erroneously, that there was a force in the nerves, which he called "animal electricity" and treated as if it were a fluid. His errors were corrected by Volta (1745–1827), the inventor of the battery.

The problem for these early pioneers was to measure the very small current we now know to be produced by the nerves and muscles in action; eventually this was achieved, notably by du Bois-Reymond (1878–1896) of Berlin. Helmholtz, of whom we shall say more later, showed that the propagation of the impulse down a nerve was relatively slow, about 25 to 43 meters a second in the frog's motor nerve. Hermann (1838–1914) discovered that the nerve impulse was a "wave of negative excitation" propagated from point to point along the nerve or muscle structure. By 1879 a rough picture was emerging of the manner in which the nervous impulse ran down the nerve fiber, although a more detailed account was not to emerge until the present century (see Chap. 12).

Nerves, however, consist of many individual nerve cells: The typical nerve cell has a body centered about a nucleus, as do other cells, but it differs from most other cells insofar as there is one long appendage, known as the *axon,* reaching out from the cell body. The axon can be as long as a few feet. It is usually surrounded by a sheath of a substance known as *myelin.* Small gaps at regular intervals along the myelin sheath serve to sustain the nerve impulse as it travels from the cell body to the end of the axon. The axon terminates near, but does not actually touch, smaller appendages at the receiving end of another cell body. These appendages, which are usually not as long as the axon, are called *dendrites.* The gap between the cells is the *synapse.*

But none of this was known in the early nineteenth century. It was then thought that the nervous system was like a network of wires all connected together—this was known as the *reticular* theory from the Latin word for *net.* Even the concept of a cell had not been arrived at, although individual cells in plants, and unicellular animals, had been described, with the aid of the microscope, as early as the late seventeenth century. Since the concept of a cell was missing, no clear account could be given of why some parts of the brain and cord looked white while others looked gray. The nerve was thought of as a single unit, whereas a nerve is in fact a bundle of axons that can be either sensory or motor in function: Some nerves contain both kinds of axons.

Within the first forty or so years of the nineteenth century, however, this picture was greatly changed. A German botanist, Schleiden (1804–1881), put forward the view in 1838 that plants were made of individual units with nuclei; he called the units *cells*. The Berlin physiologist Schwann (1810–1882) went on, in the next year, to argue that all animal tissues also consisted of cells. He did fundamental studies on the ways cells reproduce by successive divisions and discovered one kind of cell in the nervous system, still called the *Schwann cell;* the myelin sheath, which Schwann was the first to describe, develops from it. Prior to his time individual nerve fibers (axons) had been identified. In 1843 Valentin (1813–1883) was able to demonstrate that there were nerve cells with nuclei, but he was not able to show that the fibers actually came from the cell bodies. In 1838 Purkinje (1787–1869), using new techniques of cutting very thin slices of brain tissue and fixing and embedding them, also described cells in the cerebellum with nuclei and what we now call dendrites. These are still known as *Purkinje cells.*

Deiters (1834–1863) was the first to present a fully rounded description of a nerve cell not only with a nucleus and dendrites but also with a fiber, or axon, actually attached to the cell body. The *idea* that fibers and cell bodies were connected was not new—it had been in the air for the preceding two or three decades—but Deiters, in a book published after his untimely death, was able to establish the connection decisively, particularly with the aid of new techniques that had been invented for staining the whole cell. Another item of evidence supporting the idea that nerve fibers originated in nerve cells was the discovery of Waller (1816–1870) in 1850 that if a nerve is cut, the part away from (distal to) the cell body of the nerve degenerates, whereas the part near the cell body remains intact as if being nourished from the cell body. This "Wallerian degeneration" was also used by neuroanatomists as a means of tracing out pathways in the nervous system. As a final touch to this picture, in 1878 Ranvier (1835–1922) described the gaps of the myelin sheath, which are still known as the *nodes of Ranvier.* One essential feature of the description of the nerve cell was still lacking: In 1879 many experts still believed the reticular theory—that is, that the axon of one nerve cell actually connects with the cell body or dendrites of another cell. The word *neuron,* which now denotes the isolated nerve cell, was coined by Waldeyer in the context of the controversy over the reticular theory, which was still debated as late as 1891.

Schwann, the cofounder of the cell theory, did his work in the Berlin physiology department, where du Bois-Reymond was later to be professor. But in Schwann's time the professor was Johannes Müller

(1801–1858). Müller played a role in the development of neurophysiology very similar to the role Wundt would play in the development of psychology. His students included not only Schwann, but also du Bois-Reymond, Helmholtz, Sechenov (see following), and Virchow (1821–1902), a pathologist who argued that many diseases were the result of abnormalities developing in otherwise normal cells. Müller's best-known publication was the large *Handbook of Physiology* (1833–1840), in which, apart from summarizing most of the then available knowledge on physiology, he amplified an idea he had first offered in 1826: A given sensory nerve, no matter how it was stimulated, would always yield the same kind of sensation. For example, the optic nerve yields sensations of light not only when stimulated by a visible object but also when the eye is hit or when an electric current is passed through it. This came to be known as the doctrine of *specific nerve energies*. In fact Müller listed ten laws, all amplifying the general idea that each nerve is associated with one kind of conscious experience. Law VI, for example, asserts that a nerve of one sense cannot take the place and perform the function of a nerve of another sense; Law VII suggests that the end-location of the nerve in the brain might be what determines the kind of conscious sensation unique to that nerve.

Partly because of Müller's prominent position in the academic world, his doctrine was discussed at length by his contemporaries, and Boring has claimed (1950, Chap. 5) that without the favorable accord given to the doctrine, the development both of brain-localization studies and of sensory physiology might have been delayed. It need only be noted that today we should probably refer to it as the doctrine of specific nerve *qualities*, rather than *energies*, and that soon after the *Handbook* appeared the question would be raised as to whether individual fibers *within* a nerve would be uniquely associated with specific color experiences. Helmholtz would come to reply that they would.

Next, we move up the scale to the simplest behaviors produced by small sets of neurons, or reflexes, particularly reflexes mediated by the spinal cord. We now know that the typical reflex results when an input from a sensory neuron is transmitted either directly to a motor neuron in the cord or via intermediary neurons known as *internuncial* neurons. The former are called *monosynaptic* reflexes, the latter *polysynaptic*. But at the beginning of the nineteenth century, little more was known about reflexes than that the spinal cord played a crucial part in their elicitation (see p. 105). Nor was the anatomy of sensory and motor nerves vis-a-vis the spinal cord known, although the general speculation that nerves could be distinguished into sensory and motor went as far back as Herophilus and Galen (see pp. 39–42). The distinction between sensory and motor nerves and the discovery that sensory nerves enter the spinal cord posteriorly whereas the motor nerves emerge from the anterior side of the cord were made essentially by Francois Magendie (1783–1855), although Sir Charles Bell (1774–1842) came very close to anticipating him. A modern account of the controversy between the two over priority of the discovery is given by Cranefield (1974). Further research by various workers traced the pathways in the spinal cord, including the discovery that some pathways from the left side of the body crossed to the right side of the brain and vice versa.

But our main interest is in the reflex. It is generally agreed that the most fundamental discoveries about reflexes in this period were made by Marshall Hall (1790–1857). It appears that Hall did not concern himself greatly with the controversy between Bell and Magendie, nor did he pay much attention to the eighteenth-century research on reflexes by Whytt, Prochaska, and others. But he was interested in a demonstration in 1812 by Legallois (1770–1814), who had shown that if one damaged a section of spinal cord, both feeling *and* movement were lost in the corresponding bodily regions. Hall himself was a doctor who had practiced in Edinburgh and Nottingham before moving to London: He was noted for his disapproval of the widespread practice of bloodletting. He was made a Fellow of the Royal Society in 1832 and in the following year presented an extremely influential paper entitled "On the reflex function of the medulla oblongata and medulla spinalis." The very title is innovative: Although eighteenth-century writers such as Prochaska had talked of a touch being "reflected" from the cord into a movement, nobody had coined the noun *reflex.* The "medulla spinalis" of the title is simply what we now call the spinal cord.

The starting point of Hall's paper was that there were four kinds of movements. Three were well known to physiologists: ordinary voluntary movement, respiratory movement, and movement resulting from the application of a stimulus to the "neuromuscular fiber" itself. The fourth kind of movement, Hall argued, had been ignored. It was movement that survived intact so long as the spinal cord was intact, even if the cerebrum and medulla oblongata were missing. Moreover, the movement was excited, not from the central part of the nervous system, but from a remote region "whence the impression is carried to the medulla (spinalis), *reflected,* and reconducted to the part impressed, or conducted to a part remote from it, in which muscular contraction is affected." We may quickly give other characteristics of this new "reflex," as recounted in later papers and books of Hall. It was essentially spinal, and independent of the "psychic" activity associated with the cerebrum. As evidence for the latter, he pointed to reflexes elicited from decapitated reptiles and also from children born without a cerebrum or cerebellum. Nevertheless, although the spinal system was capable of operation when the higher centers were absent, the higher centers could exert a modifying influence on the reflexes. Drugs could also modify reflex action. He insisted that there was a clear-cut distinction between "unconscious" reflexes and "consciously willed activity": Each had its own independent subsystem. He devised many terms to describe various characteristics of reflex movement, and although nearly all have disappeared, his term *reflex arc* has persisted.

Partly because of a certain egotism, Hall found himself involved in a controversy about whether he had plagiarized his ideas from Prochaska: Some of the details of the story are given by Fearing (1930). Müller, on the other hand, was favorably impressed with Hall's work and quoted it at length in his *Handbook*. Neither Hall nor Müller speculated very much about the mechanism whereby the reflex was initiated in the spinal cord. More positively, Hall's view of *what* constituted reflex behavior was very broad and included reflexes associated with respiration, eating, sex, excretion, vision, and even emotion.

From Hall's time onwards reflexes came under increasingly detailed examination. The greatest name in reflexology is probably that of Sherrington, whose first paper on reflexes was written in 1892, one year after Waldeyer had invented the term *neuron*. Between the times of Hall and Sherrington, however, some useful discoveries were made about reflexes. Grainger (1801–1865) found, partly by studying reflexes in collaboration with spinal lesions, that the white matter of the cord was essentially for conduction. He also helped to clear up a problem that intrudes like a sour note into much of this early literature, the idea of special respiratory nerves. For Grainger all nervous action was either sensory or motor. Pflüger (1829–1910) drew up what he called laws of reflex action, such as "if the peripheral stimulus causes contraction in only one half of the body, the contraction, always occurs on the same side as the stimulus" (quoted by Fearing, 1930/1964, p. 163). Sherrington would later show some of these laws to be invalid.

The most important, and at the time puzzling, discovery was that stimulation of a nerve could sometimes lead not to the movement but to the *cessation* of movement of a muscle; that is, nerves could not only excite action, they could inhibit it. In 1846 the brothers Eduard and Ernst Weber described how stimulation of the vagus nerve could inhibit the heartbeat; in 1863 Sechenov, a Russian who studied at Berlin, reported that stimulation of certain *brain* regions in the frog, such as the thalamus, could inhibit reflex motions. The full importance of inhibition for reflex action would be brought out by Sherrington. We shall meet Ernst Weber and Sechenov again, the former in the next section of this chapter, the latter when we examine the origins of behaviorism (Chap. 10).

The middle 1800s were also the years of what was probably the most tedious controversy of the several we have had to mention. The question was whether the spinal cord was "conscious"—to be more precise, did it have a "soul"? Pflüger argued it did; Lotze, whose psychology we shall consider shortly, argued that it did not. One off-shoot of the controversy was an interest in the behavior of animals without a cerebrum, but this takes us beyond 1879. Nevertheless, it was discovered early that some simple animals, when rendered brainless, can perform surprisingly complicated acts. If a brainless frog is placed under water, it will, for instance, rise to the surface to breathe. More details about the Pflüger-Lotze controversy and the research it left in its wake are given in Fearing (1930/1964) and E. G. T. Liddell (1960).

The first half of the nineteenth century was crucially important in the history of physiological psychology, for the first research on the functions of different parts of the brain took place then. One of the first persons to assert that various faculties might be localized in specific areas of the brain, particularly the cerebral hemispheres, was Franz-Josef Gall (1758–1828), and the first animal research on cerebral localization was carried out by Luigi Rolando (1773–1831) and Marie Jean-Pierre-Flourens (1794–1867).

Gall was German, but after obtaining his medical degree from Strasbourg he moved to Vienna in 1785. In his early years he carried out much fundamental research on the anatomy of the brain. For example, he was aware that white matter was essentially the conductor of messages between the various areas of gray matter; in addition, he noted certain similarities between the organization of the spinal cord and the cerebral hemispheres. He did fundamental research on the origins in the brain of the cranial nerves and worked on the anatomy of the basal ganglia, the cerebellum, and the cerebral convolutions. He established that certain tracts crossed over from one side of the body to the other in the lower brain stem. But his chief claim to originality was his assertion that one was born with certain innate faculties or propensities and that these were reflected in the degree of development of the various parts of the cerebral hemispheres. This development was shown in turn in the conformation of the skull.

There were antecedents for this notion that somehow character was reflected in appearance. Just before Gall's time, Lavater (1741–1801) had boosted the old pseudoscience of physiognomy with a comprehensive and profusely illustrated treatise on the subject of how facial appearance, both in people and in animals, is supposed to reflect personality characteristics (*Essays on Physiognomy,* 1775–1778). This best seller opened the door for Gall's more scientific-sounding "cranioscopy," or study of character through the analysis of the development of the skull—bumps on the head, to be precise. Another antecedent resided in Gall's own history; he recounts how even as a boy he observed that certain characteristics were associated with certain physical features in his schoolmates. He thought, for example, that boys with good memories tended to have protruding eyes. In later years, he would relate this to the growth of the skull in the eye region; this in turn was shaped, he argued, by the development in the cerebral hemispheres of the organ associated with verbal memory. By an often amusing collection of observations of this kind, Gall built up an elaborate system that came to be called *phrenology,* in which twenty-seven faculties were associated with different organs in the cerebral hemispheres. His followers, of whom he had a great many, notably J. C. Spurzheim (1776–1832) and George Combe (1788–1858), added a few more faculties. The allotment of faculties to skull areas was based on the kind of casual observation described previously and on sheer arbitrariness; the choice of faculties may possibly have owed something to Reid (Spoerl, 1935). After his promotion of phrenology, Gall traveled extensively throughout Europe, eventually settling in Paris, where he was admired by the populace and disapproved of by the academic hierarchy. A history of the phrenological movement is given by Cooter (1984).

Rolando was one of the first to use experimental animals to study localization in the brain. Later, he examined in detail the anatomy of the fissure we still call the *fissure of Rolando.* He noted in particular, in work reported in 1809, that cutting the fibers in various parts of the cerebrum led to disorders and anomalies of movement. He inferred, too sweepingly, that the cerebrum, particularly its internal fibers, was associated with voluntary movement. Excising parts of the cerebellum or cutting it also had profound effects on movement, and he suggested that the cerebellum was the "organ controlling locomotion." But the most successful experiments, insofar as they permanently influenced our conception of the brain's functions, were those of Flourens. In 1824 Flourens published a short monograph in which he described the results, not so much of cutting across fiber tracts, as of ablating (removing) relatively circumscribed regions of brain in conscious animals. He also stimulated various parts of the brain by pricking. It is mainly to Flourens that we owe the picture that is frequently used to introduce the brain to novices—that picture showing three main parts of the brain: the medulla oblongata, which controls life functions such as breathing; the cerebellum, whose main function is to coordinate movements; and the cerebrum, which is the site of perception, cognition, and "intelligent" behavior.

Flourens was not the first to discover the role of the medulla oblongata as a vital knot, a *noeud vital:* It had been known for some years that damage to this area caused death. On the cerebellum, he had been anticipated in some respects by Rolando, but at the end of his studies, Flourens was able to be more precise than Rolando had been: The cerebellum, he argued, *controls* the various movements. As he stated it: "All movements persist following ablation of the cerebellum, all that is missing is that they are not regular and coordinated." Removal of the cerebral lobes, on the other hand, left a pigeon still able to right itself after being put on its back, to fly if it was thrown in the air, to walk if it was pushed. What was missing was the initiation of such actions in the first place. Flourens described the bird as "an animal condemned to perpetual sleep." In other experiments he showed that removal of the lobes led to loss of sight and hearing. It was Flourens's opinion that the lack of sensation automatically entailed a lack of memory and judgment, which would lead to a lack of volition. "The cerebral lobes are, therefore," he related, "the exclusive site of all sensations and of all the intellectual faculties."

To this extent, Flourens might have agreed with Gall. But he would have nothing to do with Gall's ascription of each of twenty-seven different faculties to different parts of the cerebrum. This was partly on common sense grounds, given the arbitrariness of Gall's allocations, but there was also an experimental basis. When Flourens restricted his ablations to specific sites on the cerebral hemispheres, he was unable to localize particular sensations or faculties. He therefore argued that "there are no different sites for the different faculties nor for the different sensations . . . none the less each of the various special sense organs have [sic] a distinct origin in the cerebral mass."

But Gall's hypotheses were not completely ignored. Bouillaud (1796–1875), in particular, observed that many of his patients with brain damage had impediments to or loss of speech. The loss of speech was not simply due to a loss of control of the tongue, for the brain damage could leave intact the tongue movements involved in eating. In particular he observed that loss of speech was associated with lesions in the anterior lobes of the brain and argued that Gall may have been correct in allotting verbal memory to a site near the eyes. Although this work was reported in 1825, because of Gall's disrepute and Flourens's authority it was ignored. But in 1861 Auburtin (1825–1893) revived interest in Bouillaud's paper by finding a patient with a frontal skull lesion that made it possible to press the frontal lobe with a spatula. When this was done, the patient's speech was disrupted. The only reason that the patient could speak at all with such a lesion was, said Auburtin, because the anterior lobe on the other side of the brain was still undamaged.

In the same year Broca (1824–1880) presented one of the most famous cases in all medical history. This concerned a man nicknamed "Tan" because this was the only word he could express. He had been aphasic for twenty-one years. After Tan's death, autopsy revealed that there was indeed damage to the left anterior lobe, not near the eyes, as Gall would have claimed, but further back, along the fissure of Sylvius. This area is still known as *Broca's area*. Broca's discovery had a great impact on the neurologists of the time: Even though later writers felt that Broca had given too precise an interpretation to the import of Tan's lesion, it revived interest in cerebral localization with far-reaching results in the late nineteenth century (see Chap. 12).

The Special Senses: The Origins of Psychophysics

Let us first treat the senses of smell, taste, and touch. Cloquet wrote a large book on the subject of smell in 1821 but not until after 1862 was much progress made in our understanding of olfaction. In that year the anatomist Schultze (1825–1874) was able to pinpoint the olfactory epithelium high up in the nasal cavity as the sense organ responsible for smell. Here he found the olfactory receptors, special cells with small "hairs" embedded in the tissue and surrounded by other types of cells. But further knowledge of how smell operated had to wait until after 1879. On *taste,* Haller in the eighteenth century had known of the papillae (ridges) on the tongue and both Bell and Johannes Müller later subscribed to the belief that the papillae were the taste organs. But it was not until 1867 that Schwalbe and Löven independently described small structures embedded in and around the papillae that seemed to be the true mediators of taste sensations. Löven named these structures *taste buds* and Schwalbe indicated that there might be as many as four hundred taste buds in a single papilla. Classifications of the different kinds of taste were rife in the eighteenth century but not until 1880 did von Vintschgau decide in favor of only four: salty, sweet, sour, and bitter. A description of these early classifications of taste is given by Boring (1942, p. 453). Research on the chemical foundations of smell and taste and on the neurophysiology of smell and taste has essentially been a twentieth-century endeavor.

Touch, on the other hand, received extensive attention in the early 1800s, and the study of touch led indirectly to Fechner's new science of "psychophysics." The great name in early touch research is Ernst Heinrich Weber (1795–1878), who taught at the University of Leipzig for most of his life. But for Weber the sense of touch in the skin was intimately linked with what Kant had called common sensibility (see p. 153), a catch-all term for such sensations as pain, hunger, and thirst as well as sensations from internal organs and possibly from muscles. We say *possibly* because in Weber's time it was not known for certain whether the muscles did indeed possess sense organs.

Aside from the question of the muscle sense, it was also known to Weber that there were small onion-shaped receptors deeply embedded in tissue below the skin, the so-called Pacinian corpuscles. These were first observed by Vater in 1741, and rediscovered by Pacini in 1835. We now know they are also dispersed in the linings of various organs of the body and in the neighborhood of tendons and joints. They mainly subserve sensations of deep pressure, but for Weber, writing in 1846, their function was still conjectural. Pain, a third aspect of this common sensibility, seemed to Weber the result of overintense stimulation: He showed experimentally, for example, how increasing heat led from sensations of "warm" through "hot" to "painful." But he did not suspect that pain might have its own receptors in the skin; it was only in 1895 that von Frey theorized that pain might be the outcome of stimulation of the so-called free nerve endings in the skin. That pain might be mediated by separate pathways in the spinal cord was first suggested in 1858 by Schiff. Common sensibility, as Weber discussed it, was therefore a mixture of problems, many of which would only be answered long after 1846.

On the skin senses, in contrast, Weber himself was not merely a reviewer of other people's writings but an active experimenter and innovator. His belief in experimentation was the direct outcome of an early interest in physics and in biology. His research in physics, in which he cooperated with his brother Wilheim, a famous physicist, included studies of hydrodynamics and musical instruments. Later, he applied his knowledge of physics to the study of blood flow. His biological research included investigations of human and animal audition, and he is perhaps most famous to historians of science for his observation, already mentioned (p. 172), that stimulation of the vagus nerve could inhibit heartbeat.

But his research on touch is what has immortalized him among psychologists. In an early work in Latin, *De Subtilitate Tactus* (1834), often referred to as just *De Tactu (On Touch)*, he described a series of experimental investigations of the touch sense, some of which were carried out with the aid of his brothers. Later, in a contribution to a handbook of physiology, he wrote a more theoretical work, *Der Tastsinn und das Gemeingefühl (The Sense of Touch and Common Sensibility,* 1846). Both these works are now available in one volume in English.

De Tactu opens with the direct question of whether sensitivity to touch varies over the different regions of the body. As a means of measuring touch sensitivity, Weber devised the so-called two-point threshold test, and possibly his choice of the word *threshold* was related to Herbart's propagation of the concept. In this test, the legs of a pair of compasses are stretched out and the subject's skin is lightly touched with both compass points at once. The subject will usually report two touches. But as the legs of the compass are gradually brought closer together, the subject finds it increasingly difficult to distinguish between two touches and one touch, and when the compass points are very close together he or she feels only one touch. Clearly, the closer together the compass points are which continue to elicit sensations of two touches, the more sensitive the skin will be to separate touches at such a location.

In *De Tactu* Weber provides tables charting the sensitivity of the whole body in respect of the two-point threshold: The tip of the tongue and the tips of the fingers are very sensitive according to this measure, whereas much of the trunk, and the back in particular, is very insensitive. In fact, Weber shows numerical data that to elicit a sensation of two touches the compass points have to be spread out sixty times as far in the middle of the back as they do at the tip of the tongue.

But the skin does not only receive passive stimulation. To estimate the size, shape, and texture of the objects we move our tactile surfaces over them or lift them. In so doing, we can add to the sensations of the skin sensations from the muscles and related tissues concerned in the movements. We can estimate weight better by lifting the object than by feeling the object pressing on a passive body area. Weber briefly discusses the elusive muscle sense at this point and then reports another experiment. Subjects from various walks of life were given two weights and told to report when one was "just noticeably different" (Weber's exact term) from the other. In one condition, the weights were placed on the subjects' hands resting on the table; in another, the subjects actually lifted their hands with the weights on them. In the latter condition the subjects were aware of smaller differences in weight than in the former condition. For example, one subject, a merchant, could tell with hands resting on the table that two weights in the ratio 32:26 were just noticeably different; when he lifted the weights, however, he could tell that two weights in the ratio 32:31 were just noticeably different. In further research Weber showed how the sensitivity to differences in weight varied with the body part on which the weights were placed. Thus Weber had now mapped tactile sensitivity over the body in respect of acuity (the two-point threshold, or what Weber called the place sense, *Ortsinn*) and of pressure (just noticeable differences in weight, or what Weber called the pressure sense, *Drucksinn*). He noticed, incidentally, that areas with a well-developed localization sense tended to often, but not always, have a well-developed pressure sense.

In *De Tactu,* Weber then examined a third kind of sensation found in the skin, the temperature sense. Although objective temperature can be measured on a continuum varying from a few or a negative number of degrees to a large positive number of degrees (on any of the usual temperature scales), Weber felt that warmth and cold might be discrete aspects of experience. He also argued that sensations of temperature could summate and merge—as he put it in referring to summation, "a smaller degree of heat received by a larger surface of the skin arouses the same sensation as a greater degree of heat stimulating a smaller surface of the skin" (1834/1978, p. 83). In *Der Tastsinn,* Weber's discussion of the temperature sense was elaborated to include a discussion of the effects of the duration of the stimulation, the thickness of the skin, and the body area concerned upon temperature sensations. One of the most unusual of Weber's demonstrations was to show that the pressure sense and the temperature sense can interact: He demonstrated that a cold coin placed on the forehead felt heavier than a warm coin of the same size put in the same place. J. C. Stevens and B. G. Green (1978) have replicated this result under a variety of conditions and discuss various possible reasons why it occurs. Weber's contributions to our knowledge of temperature sensitivity in itself were rather limited, but he must be given credit for broaching topics that would later turn out to be of the greatest importance in sensory physiology—that is, neural interactions such as are involved in summation and fusion—and he had already demonstrated inhibition via the vagus nerve.

The last thing Weber mentioned in his discussion of the temperature sense is the fact that different temperatures of liquids are more easily discriminated if a finger is first put into one liquid and another finger into a second liquid immediately afterwards than if both fingers are immersed in the two liquids simultaneously. He observed that weights were judged to be just noticeably different more readily if first one weight then another was lifted, rather than if both weights were lifted simultaneously. He put the disadvantage of simultaneous comparison down to the unwanted fusion of information from the two sources and showed how successive comparisons could be correctly made even after a few seconds had elapsed. This observation led Weber to consider the more general question of how acute the various senses were in comparison to one another: He remarked, at the end of *De Tactu,* that vision is more acute than touch because the visual sense can distinguish the hundredth part of a line, whereas the touch sense can distinguish only a thirtieth part of a weight—to put it another way, two lines can differ by only one-hundredth of the length of one of them to be just noticeably different. Discussing the limits of acuity in the various senses, Weber later remarked:

> I have shown that results for weight-judgements (sic) are the same whether ounces or half-ounces be used: for the results do not depend on the *number* of grains making up the extra weights, but upon whether the extra weight is 1/30 . . . of the weight to be compared with the second weight. It is the same with the comparisons of the lengths of two lines or the pitches of two tones. (1846/1978, p. 221)

The key words have been italicized for they stress what Fechner would come to call Weber's Law: The intensity of an increment ΔI that needs to be added to a stimulus of intensity I to make I just noticeably different is a constant *fraction* of I. It is not a constant *number.* Mathematically,

$$\Delta I \ = \ kI$$

where k is a fraction. To give an example in words, if I can just tell the difference between a stimulus of intensity 100 and another of intensity 101 (so that the fraction is 1/100) then I can predict that I will be able to just tell the difference between a stimulus of intensity 1000 and another of intensity 1010 (i.e., one that is 1/100 bigger than the first, and not just one unit). It might be added that Weber's Law was soon discovered to be invalid at the extremes of a range of intensities. Fechner soon made use of the law in deriving his new psychological law.

Gustav Theodor Fechner (1801–1887) was precocious as a child and entered the University of Leipzig at the age of sixteen to study medicine. One of his physiology professors was Weber, who apparently made a profound impression on him. Like Helmholtz, Fechner also studied mathematics and the biological sciences. However, he seems to have become disenchanted with the medical profession and at the same time enchanted with the writings of a group of philosophers associated with the Romantic movement, a group that expounded what has been called nature philosophy. This movement endeavored to demonstrate the unity of nature by showing how parallels exist that reveal in themselves the systematic order and beauty of nature. At its best, this approach would lead the poet Goethe to notice affinities between the vertebrae and the skull of various species and thus provide history with a slight nudge in the direction of evolutionary theory. At its worst, it provided writers such as Oken (1779–1851) with outrageous and so-called meaningful analogies between such diverse objects as the blood (which circulates) and the earth (which rotates).

Fechner would appear to have been ambivalent in his attitude to nature philosophy. Under the pen name of Dr. Mises, he satirized it in an 1825 article entitled "The Comparative Anatomy of Angels" (see Marshall, 1969, and Corbet and Marshall, 1969, for an English translation). The piece piles analogy upon analogy in such a way as to "prove" that since the sphere is a perfect shape, and angels are perfect, so angels must be spherical, but so are planets; therefore, angels are living planets, etc., etc. But in 1823 he also wrote a serious thesis entitled "Premises Toward a General Theory of Organisms" (summarized by Marshall, 1974) in which he accepted the unifying attitude of nature philosophy and, among other theses, hypothesized that "one and the same law prevails throughout the entire universe and its individual parts" and that hence, "reasoning by analogy must not be rejected as empty and unworthy of science."

His satirical articles under the pen name of Dr. Mises continued to be produced for almost thirty years and included diatribes against the medical profession he himself soon abandoned. His serious articles, on the other hand, can be fairly firmly divided into the experimental and the quasimystical. Among his experimental writings were a classic paper on electric batteries, which led to his being appointed professor of physics at Leipzig in 1834, and a few papers on vision, including one on afterimages. During his research on vision he had stared at the sun through colored glasses, and this may have affected his sight. But years of overwork on dull translations and the like, which had provided him with a living, added to his visual problems. In 1839 he retired from his chair of physics and became a recluse, showing various psychotic and autistic symptoms. He spent some three years wearing bandages over his eyes. In 1843 he dared to remove the bandages and was struck by the variety and intensity of his newly recovered visual world. He may have believed that he had a new insight into the unity underlying all nature, which had always intrigued him.

At any rate, over the next ten years he wrote his quasi-mystical works, such as *Nanna* (1848) and *Zend-Avesta* (1851), in which he preached that all the world was "besouled" and that the duality between mind and matter that had become ingrained into psychological thinking since Descartes could be replaced by a monistic view with mind and matter indissolubly linked because they represented two sides of nature. Consciousness, that is, could be seen as an indissoluble property of all things, so that instead of only viewing mind as an epiphenomenon of body, bodies could also be viewed as epiphenomena of mind. The usual name given to Fechner's notion is *panpsychism;* a detailed account of how he expressed his views in terms of various analogies is offered by Woodward (1972). His panpsychism may have been influenced by an earlier acquaintance with Spinoza's writings. Marshall (1982), however, has recently shown that in the *Zend-Avesta* Fechner may have had an insight into how series of numbers can be related to each other and this may have suggested to him the law we will discuss later. He did not abandon physics completely; in 1855, he wrote a thesis on atoms that has considerable historical importance and that also argues that metaphysics should be founded on sound physics. Marshall claims that this paper should be seen in the context of Fechner's general endeavor to link the mental and the material.

According to Fechner himself, on October 22, 1850, at the age of forty-nine, well recovered from his illness, he awoke with the idea of scientifically proving that mind and matter were two aspects of nature: He would show how an increase in the material world (an increase in stimulus intensity) would be paralleled by an increase in mental experience (an increase in sensation intensity). For the next ten years, Fechner worked out some of the mathematical implications of his idea and carried out various experiments, mainly with visual and weight stimuli. His large *Elements of Psychophysics* appeared in 1860; in it Fechner claimed to have founded a new science, which in its turn had two aspects. *Outer psychophysics* was concerned with the relationship between stimuli and sensations; *inner psychophysics* was concerned with the almost unexplorable relationship between sensations and matter—that is, the nervous system. Volume I of the *Elements* is available in English (Adler's translation; Fechner, 1966); it introduces the basic concepts of outer psychophysics and the methods by which the topic may be experimentally investigated. Volume

II gives the generalization emerging from the experimental work of Volume I—namely, Fechner's Law—then reviews various problems of sensation and perception. It closes with a long discussion of the problems raised by inner psychophysics and with a historical chapter. In this last, Fechner acknowledges the importance of Weber's Law but also points out that he was influenced by work in the early 1700s of the mathematician Daniel Bernoulli, who tried to relate the subjective value of money to its objective value; by Herbart's general attempt to bring mathematics into psychology; and by some work of early nineteenth-century astronomers relating the magnitude of a star to its perceived brightness (on this, see Pliskoff, 1977).

After some preliminary remarks on inner and outer psychophysics, and on the relationship of the concept of energy to outer psychophysics, Fechner in Volume I made an important distinction between the *absolute threshold* and the *differential threshold*. The absolute threshold represents the smallest intensity value of a stimulus that can just be detected by the human senses—that is, the quietest sound or the dimmest light. The differential threshold represents that increment that must be added to (or subtracted from) an intensity value to make the sensation just noticeably different. Fechner thought of the just noticeable difference as a *unit* of sensation. The way to determine the magnitude of a sensation, therefore, is to determine the differential threshold, or just noticeable difference (j.n.d.), and then sum the j.n.d.s. If we accept this logic, it follows that as a sensation increases in magnitude in steps each consisting of a j.n.d., the stimulus that causes each new increment in magnitude must change by some factor related to the j.n.d. But what is this factor? Let us take some imaginary numbers to illustrate the point we wish to make. Let us assume a starting intensity I of 8 units and assume that k in Weber's Law, $\Delta I = kI$, is $\frac{1}{2}$. Then the j.n.d. $\Delta I = \frac{1}{2}$ of 8 = 4. To make I just noticeably different we must add ΔI (= 4) to I (= 8), giving a new intensity I_2 of 12. Now to make I_2 just noticeably different, we must add ΔI again—i.e., $\frac{1}{2}$ of I_2, or 6. The new intensity I_3 will be $I_2 + 6$—that is, 12 + 6, or 18. The argument continues in the same vein, but a pattern begins to emerge. The three intensity values I_1, I_2, and I_3 that need to be used to yield successive just noticeable increments in sensation strength are 8, 12, and 18. The reader may possibly note that each number here is the previous number multiplied by $1\frac{1}{2}$. This is not an accident, for we can infer from Weber's Law, that adding a j.n.d. ΔI to a starting intensity I means that kI is also increased by I:

$$I + \Delta I = I + kI$$
$$= I(1 + k)$$

To get a just noticeable increment in I, we must multiply I by $1 + k$; in this example, with k = ½, we multiply each I by 1½. It is not hard to show that to increase this new intensity by a further j.n.d. we should multiply it by $(1 + k)$ again and that, in general, to increase a sensory intensity by n j.n.d.s we should multiply the starting intensity by $(1 + k)^n$. Thus, we see that if we are to increase sensation intensities by equal magnitudes, we must multiply each stimulus intensity in question by a constant number (which turns out to be $1 + k$). A sequence of numbers that increases by equal steps (such as 2, 4, 6, 8, . . . , where each number is the previous number *plus* two) is called an arithmetic progression. A sequence of numbers that increases by multiplying each number by a constant amount (such as 2, 4, 8, 16 . . . , where each number is the previous number *times* two) is called a geometric progression. According to Fechner's argument, therefore, an arithmetical increase in sensation magnitude must be the result of a geometric increase in stimulus magnitude. This is one way of expressing Fechner's Law; another way is described later. One effect of this generalization is that in order to double the *apparent* brightness of a light, you would have to more than double the physical intensity of the light.

Fechner, with his preoccupation with the j.n.d. as a unit of sensation strength, was most concerned with estimating the j.n.d. by experimental means. He described three psychophysical methods that could be used to determine either differential thresholds (j.n.d. estimations) or absolute thresholds. The names he gave them have not survived unchanged, and in Woodworth and Schlosberg's 1954 handbook, they are described by names more commonly used today. The chart in Figure 6–1 shows Fechner's names and their modern equivalents and briefly describes each method. In Volume I of the *Elements* Fechner went into detail on some of the experimental problems associated with each of the methods. He then discussed how Weber's Law fit the results obtained from experiments using weights, visual luminosities, tones of various pitches and intensities, and visual size. We may mention here a particularly convincing confirmation of Weber's Law that Fechner pointed out. If you look at the sky through a medium dark glass, you can pick out a cloud that is just noticeably different from the background. If you now look at the same area through a still darker glass, the cloud in question does not disappear; it remains just noticeably different. This is because the *ratio* of intensities between cloud and sky-background has remained constant even though the absolute intensities of both cloud and sky are much lower when viewed through the darkest glass. Fechner's detailed accounts of how to carry out psychophysical experiments remained a standard source for decades, being superseded perhaps only when Titchener's *Experimental Psychology* appeared, between 1901 and 1905.

Volume II of the *Elements* is much more theoretical and less practical than Volume I. It opens with the account of how sensation strength grows arithmetically as stimulus strength grows geometrically. But Fechner now expresses the law in a simpler way by introducing the concept of logarithms. If $10^2 = 100$, we say that the log to the base 10 of 100 is 2. Similarly, if $10^3 = 1000$, we say that the log to the base 10 of 1000 is 3. As we run through the geometric series 10, 100, 1000 . . . , the respective logarithms are 1, 2, 3 . . . , that is, they increase arithmetically. So as sensation strength grows arithmetically, the fact that the relevant stimulus strength grows geometrically implies that the *logarithms* of the relevant stimulus strengths in fact grow arithmetically. If we call sensation strength S and stimulus strength R (from the German *Reiz,* meaning "stimulus") we can then say that S varies directly with log R, or

$$S = c \log R \qquad (1)$$

where c is a constant to be established and whose value also depends on the base the logs are taken to. (Fechner actually elaborated this equation to include the absolute threshold, but this law is best known in the simplified form given here).

The *Elements of Psychophysics* appeared when Fechner was fifty-nine years old. He lived to be eighty-six, and during his final twenty-seven years he continued to follow actively the fate of his new science, which was almost immediately assailed on various grounds: Some persons offered alternatives to equation (1) that they felt were better warranted on theoretical grounds; the very concept of "sensation strength" is invalid, some objected, because only things in space or time can be measured, and sensation is not one of those things. It was further objected that Weber's Law was not valid, an objection strenuously fought by Fechner. Fechner replied to his critics one by one, and at length, in two books, *In Sachen der Psychophysik (In Matters of Psychophysics)* (1877) and *Revision der Hauptpuncte der Psychophysik (Review of the Main Points of Psychophysics)* (1882). He produced numerous articles, both on theory and on the psychophysical methods, and also wrote on the new topic of statistics: Fechner was among the first to show that the *variability* of data can be as informative as measures of central tendencies such as means, medians, or modes. In addition, he was a founder of experimental aesthetics, but his book on the subject, *Vorschule der Aesthetic* (1872)—*An Elementary Course in Aesthetics* might be a possible translation—is devoted to a discussion of aesthetics in general as much as it attempts to found aesthetics on scientific principles. Nevertheless, he did attempt to measure people's preferences by counting the number of votes given a stimulus such as a painting or a rectangle. Arnheim (1985), however, in his review of Fechner's book, considers that aesthetic taste is too complicated to be measured by ratings of pleasantness alone.

FECHNER'S NAME	METHOD OF JUST NOTICEABLE DIFFERENCE	METHOD OF AVERAGE ERROR	METHOD OF RIGHT AND WRONG CASES
MODERN NAME	METHOD OF LIMITS	METHOD OF ADJUSTMENT	METHOD OF FREQUENCY, OR METHOD OF CONSTANT STIMULI
Technique for finding absolute threshold	Present single stimuli; each time S says yes or no he detected it. Usually in ascending or descending steps.	E or S manipulates the stimulus until it disappears (or appears).	Have stimuli in the transition zone: find percent of yeses out of all responses. "Doubtful" responses sometimes permitted.
Technique for finding differential threshold	Present pairs of stimuli, a *standard* (St) and a *comparison* (Co). Co differs from St by small steps. Find what Co is just noticeably different from St.	E or S manipulates Co until it seems just noticeably different from St.	Present a few Co's falling close to St many times: find percent of yeses. "Doubtful" or "equal to" responses sometimes permitted.

Figure 6–1   The Three Psychological Methods of Fechner (1860).

Fechner died in 1887, the center of controversy as much for his metaphysics as for his psychology. He had seen psychophysics become the center of active *experimentation* in Wundt's laboratory and elsewhere. Not everyone approved of psychophysics: William James, for example, found it a dreary topic. But of one thing we may be sure: Fechner's views were not neglected by his contemporaries. Above all, Fechner brought the experimental tradition of physiology into psychology. His law has been revised by many writers since Fechner's time, particularly by S. S. Stevens. But psychophysics still remains a major branch of psychology: Gescheider's *Psychophysics: Method and Theory* (1976) gives an overview of modern theory and methods.

The Special Senses: Audition and Vision

The study of hearing and vision was revolutionized by the work of Hermann von Helmholtz (1821–1894), whose *Sensations of Tone* (1863) and *Physiological Optics* (3 vols.; 1856–1866) remain to this day standard reference works on audition and vision, respectively. Helmholtz studied medicine with J. Müller and du Bois-Reymond but soon extended his interests into physics and chemistry as well as physiology. From 1857 to 1870 he taught at Heidelberg; from 1870 to his death he was at Berlin. His background in the other sciences made him particularly well prepared to undertake research in the special senses.

We begin with investigations of hearing in the early and middle nineteenth century. Part I of Helmholtz's *Sensations of Tone* summarizes much earlier work, particularly concerning sound as a stimulus. It also has a relatively short section on the anatomy of the auditory system; the historical importance of this section cannot be underestimated, for it introduces a theory of hearing that formed the basis for most subsequent research on audition. Part II is concerned with combinations of tones and included Helmholtz's own discoveries on overtones and related phenomena. Part III explores questions concerning the nature of harmony and the development of the various musical scales. Musicians will find this last part perhaps more to their taste than will psychologists.

Part I of the *Sensations of Tone* revealed Helmholtz at his most ingenious: Helmholtz knew that the ear was constructed to detect many tones sounding simultaneously. He also knew of current theories of acoustics, and he knew of recent research, carried out in the 1850s, on the microscopic structure of the cochlea. His achievement was to combine acoustic theory with anatomy so as to yield a plausible picture of how the ear transformed air vibrations into sensations and, in particular, of how it was able to detect the individual sounds within a complex of sounds. Let us examine these physical and physiological aspects of early nineteenth-century auditory theory separately.

On acoustic theory, it had long been known that if the ratio of the frequency of a tone A to the frequency of a simultaneous tone B could be expressed as a ratio of whole numbers, the chord that resulted formed a consonance, that is, was an acceptable chord in the usual music of the West. One outcome of Helmholtz's interest in this relationship of whole numbers to musical consonances was extensive work on the question of consonance and dissonance. But another outcome was his questioning how the auditory system analyzed such a complicated stimulus as a musical chord. The work of two physicists gave him a clue as to where to begin his investigations. First, J. B. Fourier (1768–1830), a brilliant mathematician, discovered in the course of his investigations into heat flow that any complicated wave form can be analyzed into a set of simple wave forms, each of which may vary in frequency and amplitude from the others. The curve of $y = \sin x$ is wave shaped: To be more precise, Fourier showed how a complicated wave form could always be analyzed into a sum of sine waves. Second, G. S. Ohm (1787–1854) studied Fourier's work on heat and tried to apply it to the flow of electricity. His name is famous for the consequent discovery, usually called *Ohm's Law*, that electric flow depends in part on the resistance of the conductor. But there are two "Ohm's Laws," and the second concerns hearing: It says that any sound, no matter how complicated, can be decomposed by the auditory system, via a Fourier analysis, into a sum of "simple vibrations."

Helmholtz's achievement was to work out how the ear could indeed perform the analysis as required by Ohm's Law. He realized that a machine could respond selectively to certain tones and not to others by sympathetic vibration. If a tone is sounded into a piano, the strings corresponding to the appropriate frequencies (that is, the fundamental frequency plus the frequencies of the overtones) will vibrate. Arguing by analogy, Helmholtz suggested that specific fibers in the basilar membrane of the cochlea would vibrate sympathetically to certain tones—he arrived at this conclusion only after considering alternative theories of cochlear action. While modern acoustics experts, notably Von Bekesy (1899–1972), have considerably elaborated on this place theory of hearing, Helmholtz's theory still forms the basis of the modern account.

Helmholtz also wrote about the frequency analysis of vowel sounds, problems concerned with the absolute threshold for pitch, and the acoustics of different kinds of musical instruments. The reader unwilling to work through the 430 closely written pages of the *Sensations of Tone* may prefer to look at one of Helmholtz's short popular lectures, entitled "On the Physiological Causes of Harmony in Music" (1857/1962). This gives a good indication of the clarity and breadth of Helmholtz's writing style.

In discussing vision we shall take as the guiding thread Helmholtz's three-volume work, *Physiological Optics*. Volume I, *The Eye*, opens with a description of the anatomy of the eyeball and describes two optical instruments invented by Helmholtz: The *ophthalmometer* enabled the experimenter to measure the radius of curvature of various parts of the cornea, the outer transparent skin of the eye. A modern version of Helmholtz's ophthalmometer is still used by doctors to determine the degree of astigmatism, or irregularity of curvature, of the cornea. The other instrument was the *ophthalmoscope*, which allowed the observer to look directly into the eye of the subject. Normally one sees only black when one looks into somebody else's pupil; Helmholtz's ophthalmoscope shone a light into the subject's pupil so as to illuminate the retina, and the reflection of this bright image from the retina was then made visible to the observer by an arrangement of mirrors and lenses. Again, the modern opthalmoscope used by doctors to study the condition of the retina and of the blood vessels supplying it is an improved version of Helmholtz's original.

Helmholtz's description of the eye is extremely detailed and includes summaries of measurements of the eyeball, the cornea, the lens, and the iris and pupil and attached membranes. In his account of the retina he described two separate kinds of cells known as rods and cones but did not know how these functioned differentially. He gives extensive information on how light gets refracted in its passage from cornea to retina and even diffracted a little, and he includes an account, based on first principles, of the geometrical laws determining how a point of light is focused by the lens onto a particular area of retina. Sometimes the light stimulates not a point but a larger area of retina: Helmholtz called such areas, which can be of various shapes, *blur circles.* He gives an accurate description of the mechanism of accommodation, for which he was indebted to Thomas Young (1773–1829), who showed in 1800 that the eyeball does not change in length when the eye is being focused.

Volume II, *The Sensations of Vision,* explores those aspects of visual experience that can be mediated by either one or two eyes; the chief topics are color vision, sensations of intensity differences, persistence of vision, afterimages, contrast, and various subjective phenomena. We shall begin by examining Helmholtz's views on color, but first we should discuss his nineteenth-century predecessors.

Ever since Newton had shown that white light could be seen as constituted of most visible colors, there had been both interest in the nature of color and also some resistance to Newton's ideas. The poet Goethe (1789–1832), for instance, added to his literary output with some work on optics, an endeavor that resulted in his *Beiträge zur Optik (Contributions to Optics)* of 1791–1792 and his *Farbenlehre (Theory of Colors)* of 1810. Much of this later book argued against Newton: As had other writers before Newton, Goethe felt that a color was the result of a mixture of light and dark. Blue, for example, had more of dark than yellow, which had more of light. When Goethe looked through a prism at a black object on a white ground, or a white object on a black ground, he observed that the object had yellow or blue borders, leading him to the above argument. Apparently he never properly obtained Newton's splitting of white light into the spectrum. Goethe's color theory, though influential, was wrong; however, his books are full of reliable information on various phenomena of color as seen in afterimages, contrast situations, and even in dark and light adaptation. A valuable English account of the *Farbenlehre* will be found in Lewes (1855/1930). Many of Goethe's observations were supported by reports from a Czech physiologist, J. E. Purkyne, whose name is more often Germanized as Purkinje (1787–1869). He not only worked on vision but also studied vertigo, the cerebellum, the development of eggs in birds, phonetics, plants, and general histology. Historians of visual science know him best for four discoveries:

1. He found that a light shone on the outside of the eyeball could cause treelike shadows to be perceived; these were the shadows of one's own retinal blood vessels, and this observation led indirectly to a recognition that it was the rods and cones in particular that mediated sensations.
2. He found that if an object were presented at the periphery of the visual field, its color could not always be distinguished: This would lead to the post-Helmholtzian theory of the differential sensitivity of rods and cones to color.

3. He was the first to observe reflected images from the anterior and posterior surfaces of the lens, a fact Helmholtz used in this theory of accommodation.

4. He reported what is still called the *Purkinje phenomenon*, or *Purkinje shift*. As the eye becomes adapted to the dark, blue objects are more easily recognized as blue than red objects are recognized as red. Or, to put it another way, the relative luminosities of blue and red change as the overall illumination decreases.

Again, the importance of this for our understanding of rod and cone functioning was not brought out until after Helmholtz's time.

Helmholtz was also indebted to Thomas Young. In a lecture published in 1802, Young discussed Newton's speculation that the different color sensations were the result of vibrations in the optic nervous system. He argued that "as it is almost impossible to conceive each sensitive point of the retina to contain an infinite number of particles, each capable of vibrating in perfect unison with every possible undulation, it becomes necessary to suppose the numbers limited . . . to the three principal colors" (1802/1855, p. 147). For Young at this time the three principal colors were red, yellow, and blue; but later, writing in 1807, according to Helmholtz, Young preferred as principal colors, or primaries, the colors red, green, and violet. Red, yellow, and blue are indeed primaries for artists who mix pigments: Yellow paint plus blue paint, for example, yields green. But when we are mixing *lights* we find that we can obtain most colors, including white, by mixing red, green, and blue. The blue involved is almost violet in hue, hence Young's choice of violet as a primary. Red and green lights, when mixed, yield a dull yellow. It was Helmholtz who first properly accounted for the fact that the laws for mixing lights and pigments are different. In so doing, he clarified many puzzles about color mixture and the nature of primaries. He also discussed and developed the general theory of mixing colors using lights. Others who contributed to our understanding of color mixtures were Grassmann (1809–1877) and Clerk Maxwell (1831–1879). Grassmann put forward several laws of color mixture (for a modern listing, see Graham, 1965a, p. 372). Maxwell formulated the rules of color mixture taking into account the intensities of the lights as well; he also invented a device for mixing colors by very rapidly rotating discs with different colored sectors.

Chapter 3 of Volume II begins by explaining the difference between pigment mixture and light mixture and discusses the problem of representing color mixtures by diagrams. Because all the hues could be obtained by suitable mixtures of lights of only three colors, Helmholtz argued that the eye was probably provided with three kinds of fiber, one that responded mainly to red light, one to green, and one to blue-violet. This theory has since been known as the Young-Helmholtz theory. Helmholtz's evidence in support of the theory included (1) observations on color blindness, the various types of which he ascribes to a deficiency in the operation of one or more of the three fiber types; (2) the observation that a drug, santonin, seems to render the eye temporarily blind to violet; and (3) evidence from afterimages. In a later chapter he argued that if one fiber type is fatigued by overstimulation, the other two fiber types may still function when stimulated by light. Thus, if we stare at a red object on a gray ground for some time, then switch our gaze to the gray ground, the gray "light" will have no effect on the fatigued red fibers but will excite the unfatigued blue and green fibers, yielding a blue-green afterimage. It should be noted that the above account is based on the translation of the third edition of *Physiological Optics;* apparently the untranslated second edition has more on color than does the third (see Graham, 1965b, p. 447).

Helmholtz's color theory did not go unchallenged. K. E. K. Hering (1834–1918) argued against it partly on phenomenological grounds, partly on the basis of experimental data. From a phenomenological point of view, we may note that whereas a mixture of blue and green looks bluish green, and a mixture of blue and red looks bluish red (i.e., a shade of purple), a mixture of red and green, the remaining primaries, does *not* look reddish green; it looks yellow. Moreover, we all understand what is meant by *reddish yellow* and *greenish yellow* but *bluish yellow* is absent from our vocabulary. These observations led Hering to argue that yellow should in some sense be considered a primary, and furthermore, since you cannot have reddish green, or bluish yellow, that perhaps red/green and blue/yellow were pairs of "opposing" primaries.

From an experimental point of view, Hering attacked Helmholtz on his own ground by showing that certain individuals who had difficulty distinguishing red from green could nevertheless see yellow (which, on the Young-Helmholtz theory, should not be possible, since a perception of yellow demands the ability to perceive red and green). Moreover, analysis of the various kinds of color-blindness indicates that many individuals lose perception both of red and green: Why should there be this pairing, on the Young-Helmholtz theory? It is as if red and green receptors were somehow linked together. The upshot of these and other arguments was that Hering contended that there were three kinds of receptors in the retina but that each kind could respond in two ways. According to its metabolism one kind of fiber would give rise to red (under an admittedly unknown metabolic change Hering labeled *dissimilation)* or to green (under an admittedly unknown metabolic change Hering labeled *assimilation).* Another kind of fiber would yield yellow (dissimilation) or blue (assimilation). Another would yield white (dissimilation) or black (assimilation). Thus, a red-green color blind individual will have lost the use of only one kind of fiber. Unfortunately, there is more than one kind of red-green blindness, and Hering's theory cannot easily explain this (see the introduction to Hurvich and Jameson's translation of *Outlines of a Theory of the Light Sense,* Hering, 1920/1964).

For many years the Young-Helmholtz theory and the Hering opponent-processes theory were rivals in the classic mold of theory clashes. The present view is that there are probably three kinds of retinal cells (probably three kinds of cone cells) sensitive to red, green, and blue colors in particular, but that interactions between neurons just beyond the level of the rods and cones are such as to support the view that red/green and yellow/blue are indeed associated in ways not clearly accounted for by the Young-Helmholtz theory. Graham (1965b) and Abramov (1972) may be consulted for a summary of this research. At any rate, Hering's theory offered an alternative to Helmholtz's and was able to explain the occurrence of complementary colors in afterimages and in simultaneous contrast by assuming that if one metabolic process was exhausted by fixation (e.g., the process responding to red), the other metabolic process would occur in the same fiber (e.g., green would be visible).

Later chapters of Volume II of Helmholtz's book deal with luminosity, aftereffects (including afterimages), and color contrast. He argued that contrast judgments are largely the result of our experience, one of the first points at which Helmholtz's empiricism appears. Color contrast can be seen when a grey square looks greenish because it is on a red background, or when the same grey square looks reddish because it is on a green background. Helmholtz thought this effect was caused by our making unconscious allowances for the background color, that is, it was a matter of experience; but Hering did an ingenious experiment suggesting that color contrast arose from processes in the retina, and his view appears to have won wider credence than Helmholtz's.

In Volume III of the *Physiological Optics,* in which depth perception and eye movements are discussed, Helmholtz argued even more strongly that much of what we perceive is the outcome of judgments based on experience. Volume II was entitled *The Sensations of Vision;* Volume III, *The Theory of the Perception of Vision,* and Helmholtz made it clear from the outset that he considered perception to be the result of psychic processes operating on raw sensations. Again, he was indebted to certain nineteenth-century predecessors, of whom we may mention two in particular: F. C. Donders (1818–1889) and R. H. Lotze (1817–1881).

F. C. Donders studied at Leiden University in Holland for his medical degree. After serving various offices in the Dutch army he came to the University of Utrecht, where he taught and did research on various problems of physiology. He became particularly absorbed by ophthalmology and in 1864 published a book on accommodation and refraction in the eye. But earlier, in 1846, he had become interested in eye movements and postulated what Helmholtz, in his book, would later call *Donders' Law.* This asserts that if one looks in direction x with the position of the head held constant, the eye will always move to the same position as previously used for viewing objects in direction x. This implies in turn that any objects in direction x will always stimulate the same retinal point in the eye. If Donders' Law is true, then one will be able to orient oneself towards objects in space by virtue of experience both in moving one's eyes and head for the purpose of fixation and also by experience with the fact that other objects surrounding the fixated object will stimulate other retinal points whose locations are congruent with the locations of those objects in space. Over a lifetime one will come to realize that the size and distance of an external object can be estimated by (unconsciously) relating the sensations derived from it to the sensations evoked by other objects in the visual field. One learns, for instance, that if an object *looks* to be to the left of another, it *will* be to the left of another. It is as if one has learned that to each point experienced in the visual world there is a corresponding point in objective external space.

The person who most stressed this notion was R. H. Lotze. Lotze had studied medicine and philosophy at Leipzig—like Hering, influenced by Weber and Fechner—but when he was only twenty-seven he was called to succeed Herbart in the chair of philosophy at Göttingen. Most of Lotze's later writings were on philosophy, particularly metaphysics, but in 1852, in his middle thirties, Lotze wrote an ambitious work entitled *Medicinische Psychologie, oder Physiologie der Seele (Medical Psychology, or The Physiology of the Soul)*. The subtitle should give us immediate warning that such hoary questions as the faculties of the soul and the seat of the soul are likely to be discussed, and indeed they are, at the beginning. But the middle and the end of the book are much more experimental and in some ways did in Germany what Bain was doing in Britain at the same time, namely, integrate the philosophical and physiological traditions into the fledgling discipline of psychology. We read of Weber's experiments on touch and temperature; Fechner's transformation of Weber's Law is mentioned, eight years before Fechner's *Elements of Prychophysics* would appear. There are sophisticated discussions of many of the findings on hearing and vision discussed above, and such physiological discoveries as those of Flourens and of Bell and Magendie are given due attention.

But the most original section of Lotze's book (1852, pp. 325–435) concerns "spatial" perceptions. Lotze, influenced by Kant, appears to have thought his goal was to provide a model of how we learn to coordinate messages from the senses with messages to the eyes and limbs consistent with Kant's theory that our understanding of space is innate. This attempt led Lotze into confusion, as is pointed out in detail by Morgan (1977, Chap. 6), but the upshot was that Lotze invented a term that has been highly influential in theories of space perception up to the present day. The term was *local signs*: By this we mean that each place on the retina, and also each place on the skin, if stimulated, gives rise to a sensation that can be associated with sensations from other parts of the retina or skin and is also a sign of "where" the sensation comes from in external space. A child learns, for example, that her mother's eyes are *above* her mother's nose by associating sensations from the retinal sites stimulated by the eyes with the retinal sites stimulated by the nose. These in turn provide signs to the brain that if the child wishes to touch the mother's nose she should reach out in a particular direction. Since the eyes are seen as "above" the nose, the hand should then be moved *upward* to touch the eyes. Each sensation is related to other sensations in such a way that there is an inner representation of external space. An English account of the local sign theory will be found in Lotze's lecture notes, published posthumously as *Outlines of Psychology* (1886).

Armed then with Donders' Law, Lotze's local signs, and his own conviction that seeing is as much a psychological as a physiological process, Helmholtz concentrated his energies in Volume III of the *Physiological Optics* on the problem of spatial orientation and perception. The first chapter is an attempt to bring some order into the confusion of the discussion between empiricists and nativists. An idea, argued Helmholtz, is a memory image; if the memory image is accompanied by actual sensations, it is a special kind of perception *(Wahrnehmung)* that may be called *apperception (Anschauung)*. There is no abrupt transition between memory and sensation: They "continuously supplement each other, only in varying degrees." As a result of experience, we build up what might be called a "normal" use of the eyes; if we view objects in unusual ways, such as when we hold the head in an unusual position, our apperceptions are less accurate. Helmholtz was against the nativistic or "intuitionistic" theory because he considered it unnecessary. Moreover, the intuitionist is obliged to assume that the original space sensations persist even though experience is supposed to alter and change them; compared with empiristic theory, an intuitionistic theory lacks parsimony. But it is now the onus of the empiricist to explain how order is brought into the flux of sensations apperceived in accordance with experience. Helmholtz argues that we use inductive logic; that is, we infer from the fact that A has caused B in all cases hitherto that a new occurrence of A will again cause B. But we are unaware of this process; according to Helmholtz, we make unconscious inferences in these cases. Helmholtz, then, may be held to maintain that we build up our internal model of external space by continuous and multitudinous unconscious inferences.

It should be noted that even Helmholtz himself was not always happy with the term *unconscious inference;* in an 1878 address delivered at Berlin he said he wished to avoid its use, partly because it had become associated with some views of the disciples of the philosopher Schopenhauer (1788–1860), with which Helmholtz was not in sympathy. But in an article written in 1894, just before his death, he revived the concept as "admissible within certain limits since those associations of perceptions in the memory actually take place in such a manner, that at the time of their origin one is not aware of it." Both the 1878 address and the 1894 article are given in English translation in Warren and Warren (1968). Incidentally, Turner (1977) has suggested that although Helmholtz was an empiricist, he owed a debt to Kant for the idea that causality was an *a priori* intuition underlying unconscious inferences, and Helmholtz's emphasis on *inductive* processes may have derived from John Stuart Mill. Turner (1982) also notes that Wundt might have anticipated Helmholtz's espousal of unconscious inferences.

In the following chapters of Volume III Helmholtz applied his empiricist theory to the study of eye movements, the location of objects in space, visual illusions, and monocular cues to depth. He then discussed the contribution of the two eyes to depth perception. It had been known since the seventeenth century that each eye receives a slightly different image of the external world; in fact, the illusion of depth could be given by showing two slightly different views of the same flat picture, one to each eye. This could be achieved by means of the stereoscope, invented by Sir Charles Wheatstone (1801–1875). It should be mentioned that in ninenteeth-century England there was also intense interest in vision, and there was a dispute in priority between Wheatstone and Sir David Brewster (1781–1868) over who actually invented the stereoscope. On this matter Wade (1984) should be consulted; he argues that both Brewster and Wheatstone should receive more credit for their research on vision than has traditionally been accorded them. Helmholtz discussed stereoscopic vision extensively. He also discussed *binocular rivalry*, a striking phenomenon in which we see first one picture, then the other, in alternating fashion, if two pictures are presented simultaneously one to each eye.

We may note finally that Hering published a book entitled *The Theory of Binocular Vision* two years after Helmholtz's Volume III of the *Physiological Optics*. In this work he proposed what has since been called Hering's Law. It asserts that neither eye can be moved without the other eye's being affected in some way. This was a simplification with respect to some of Helmholtz's assertions of how we learn to control eye movements: It incidentally entailed a denial of the belief, to some extent maintained by Helmholtz, that we are capable of rotating the two eyes in opposite directions. The linkage between the innervations of the two eyes was innate, argued Hering, and he was the first to study eye movements in infants with a view to demonstrating that he was correct. At the end of the book he proved that Hering's Law of mutual innervation applies to the muscles controlling the lens as well as the muscles controlling the eyeball. The interactions of accommodation and convergence in cases of strabismus and ocular paralysis are worked out in such a way as to support his claim that the association between the muscles of the two eyes is inborn rather than acquired.

In every respect, Hering is as careful an experimentalist as Helmholtz, and at one point he admits to disliking being classified *only* as a nativist. His argument, he maintains, is that there are more inborn factors in binocular vision than Helmholtz would allow, but he never would deny the importance of experience. Hering made other contributions to visual science: He devised a very sophisticated color mixture apparatus and specially colored papers; he was among the first to measure color and intensity responsiveness in dark adaptation; and in 1876 he argued that Fechner's logarithmic law should be replaced by a power law (Hurvich, 1969).

When Wundt's laboratory was founded in 1879, one of the main topics of interest, therefore, was the special senses. Weber had provided a foundation for the study of the tactile sense and, of course, had formulated Weber's Law; Fechner had transmuted Weber's Law into a general law relating sensation strength to stimulus strength; Helmholtz had offered a theory of hearing and a theory of color vision, both of which were comprehensive and rigorous enough to be experimentally testable; and Helmholtz had also offered an empiricist account of spatial perception that stressed the importance of psychological processes in vision. Hering, with his color theory, his research on eye movements, and his nativistic account of spatial perception, added a countervoice to the weight of the associationistic tradition, one that would ultimately lead to the Gestalt movement.

The emerging new science of psychology also took advantage of the respectability of sensory physiology. As Turner (1982) notes:

> The new psychology borrowed much from sensory physiology during the crucial years of its institutional retrenchment between 1870 and 1895. It borrowed from physiology the experimental methods necessary to support a research program and flesh out the techniques of psychophysics, the body of facts and expertise necessary to sustain its teaching and licensing activities, much of the prestige of that well-established and powerful German science, and the methodological program necessary to differentiate itself and raise itself above its parent discipline of philosophy and the older psychological tradition rooted in it. (p. 151)

Reaction Time

It only remains to add that Donders, whose law of eye movements we described earlier, did some of the earliest experimental research on reaction times. He was not the first to note individual differences in the speed of reaction; in fact, astronomers who had been obliged to perform complex feats of eye-ear-hand coordination in recording the time of the passage of stars across the cross wires of a telescope, had known since the late 1700s that different persons performed this task with different efficiencies. The astronomer Bessel (1784–1846) studied different observers and described the differences in the times they reported stellar transits in terms of a "personal equation." Person A might report a stellar transit as occurring half a second before the time named by person B, so the personal equation would be A − B = .5. Because of the error introduced into astronomical observations by the factor of the personal equation, efforts were made to invent mechanical means of timing astronomical events. The first such invention, which still involved a human intermediary, was the chronograph; the observer tapped a key at the moment of a stellar transit. This key caused a pointer to make a jag in a continuously drawn line. By comparing the jag with the jag produced by a steadily counting clock, a fairly accurate estimation of the time of the stellar transit was obtained. One could measure the "personal equation" by arranging for an artificial star to cause one jag mechanically at the moment it crossed the cross wire, then compare that time with the time it took an observer to tap the key in response. A variety of experimental studies soon showed that the observers' reaction times varied with the nature of the stimulus, their expectancy, their degree of attention, and so on. A full account of the history of research concerned with the "personal equation" is given by Boring (1950, Chap. 8).

It was Donders who in 1868 first published the studies on reaction time in which the purpose was not simply to ascertain individual differences but to measure the time taken to perform mental acts. His method of recording reaction time was to have a struck tuning fork transmit its vibrations to a pointer that marked a track on a revolving drum, producing a continuous wavy line. A separate device, the phonautograph, allowed a single sound to cause another pointer to make a jag on a continuous straight line running parallel to the wavy line caused by the tuning fork. Reaction time was measured by having the experimenter utter a sound, causing a first jag in the output of the phonautograph, then having the subject utter another sound as quickly as possible in response to the first sound, thus causing a second jag in the output of the phonoautograph. The time elapsing between the two jags could be counted in terms of the number of waves shown on the output from the tuning fork. Knowing the frequency of vibration of the tuning fork, the elapsed reaction time in thousandths of a second (milliseconds, msec) could be derived.

Donders gave names to three kinds of variation of this basic experiment. In the *a-method*, a sound such as *ki* is given by the experimenter and the subject must repeat the *ki* sound as quickly as possible. The subject knows the sound will always be *ki*. This yields a measure of simple vocal reaction time to a heard sound. In the *b-method,* the experimenter may give one of a variety of sounds, such as *ki, ko,* or *ku,* and the subject has to imitate the sound as quickly as possible. Any difference between the results using the a-method and the b-method must, argued Donders, reflect the time it takes to discriminate the sound and choose the correct response. In the *c-method,* the experimenter can give one of a variety of sounds, such as *ki, ko,* or *ku,* but the subject must imitate only one of them, *ki* and remain silent when the others are given. Any difference between the results using the a-method and the c-method are taken to reflect the time it takes to make the discrimination between one sound and a standard sound held in memory. Summarizing, one can use the b-method to measure discrimination-plus-choice time and the c-method to measure discrimination time. A typical average result from Donders's experiments (1868/1969b, p. 431) was that a mean discrimination time (c − a) was about 39 msec, while a simple discrimination-plus-choice time (b − a) was longer, 75 msec.

Donders also invented more complicated devices for measuring reaction times to visual and tactile stimuli (for details, see Donders, 1969a, 1969b, 1969c). The methods described by Donders are usually called "subtractive" methods for estimating the times taken by simple mental processes. They were frequently used in the early research in Wundt's laboratory and elsewhere, and the first edition of Wundt's 1874 handbook describes Donders's three methods.

Summary

The German tradition in psychology was continued in the early nineteenth century by Herbart and Beneke, both of whom offered ambitious systems. Herbart attempted to describe the ebb and flow of presentations into consciousness by a mathematical model; Beneke developed an empiricist account of how adult capacities are based on certain primitive abilities present at birth.

Physiological psychology made great advances in the first half of the nineteenth century. It was gradually discovered how nervous functioning was associated with electrical charges in the nerves; the anatomy of nerve cells was elucidated; Johannes Müller formulated his doctrine of specific nerve energies; and Marshall Hall clarified the nature of reflexes. Gall was at times wildly speculative in his ascription of the various faculties to specific regions of the cerebral cortex, but Flourens, basing his findings on experiments, was able to delineate the main ways in which the medulla, cerebellum, and cerebral cortex functioned in animals. The first hint of localization of function in the cerebrum of humans came with Broca's report in 1861 of a speech deficit following a specific lesion.

Weber was able to map the sensitivity of the skin to pressure and measure two-point thresholds.

Weber had observed that the amount needed to be added to a stimulus to make it just noticeably different was a constant fraction of the stimulus. Fechner, whose interest in psychology stemmed from his philosophical inclinations, elaborated on Weber's Law in such a way as to make it possible to predict the strength of a sensation from the strength of the stimulus. He invented various ways of establishing thresholds, the so-called psychophysical methods. His *Elements of Psychophysics* (1860/1966) was the first major work on truly experimental psychology. At the same time Helmholtz established his place theory of hearing and in his works on optics put forward the view that the retina incorporated cells that responded specifically to light of particular wavelengths. He revived the empiricist account of space perception, using the term *unconscious inferences*. In so doing Helmholtz made use of important contributions to visual science by Young, Wheatstone, Donders, and Lotze. Hering, however, debated with Helmholtz both on the color theory and on the empiricist issue.

Although astronomers had known of differences in reaction time between individuals, the first attempts to use reaction times to measure the speed of mental processes were made by Donders in the 1860s.

1879 to about 1910: Wundt and His Influence

7

Wilhelm Wundt

In the late 1860s the work of Weber, Fechner, Helmholtz, Hering, and Donders was read by a scattered few who were interested in psychology in its own right, but it remained for Wilhelm Wundt (1832–1920) to establish the discipline as a unitary field of endeavor with its own department in universities, its own M.A.s and Ph.D.s, its own textbooks, and its own journals. Of course, Wundt was not alone at this time in considering psychology as a discipline separate from philosophy and physiology: Bain in Britain and, as we shall see, William James in the United States were thinking along the same lines. But Wundt was unusually single-minded and conscientious in his efforts to give the science an identity of its own. We may begin this chapter with a short account of his achievement and then discuss how psychology was propagated, from Wundt's laboratory and others, first in Germany and then rapidly in other countries.

For the English reader, a useful short biography of Wundt is given by Bringmann, Balance, and Evans (1975). Wundt was born in a small village in Germany to a family with a long history of distinction in intellectual endeavors. His father was a Protestant minister with many social contacts, but Wilhelm was a rather introverted and lonely child; one of his best friends was a retarded older boy. Apparently, Wilhelm daydreamed a good deal, which made some of his school experiences rather unhappy. But in early adolescence he went to a new school in nearby Heidelberg, where he became less shy and developed interests in history, languages, and literature that remained with him all his life. When he entered the university, first at Tübingen, then at Heidelberg, he began the study of medicine: His first experiments concerned the effects of deprivation of salt intake on the urine and, later, the effects of severing the vagus nerve on respiration. On graduation he practiced medicine for about six months, then studied physiology at Berlin for one semester with Johannes Müller and Du Bois-Reymond. He then taught for a while at Heidelberg but after a serious illness applied to work with Helmholtz as an assistant. He was accepted and this position lasted for six years. It would be useful to know more about this period in Wundt's life: Helmholtz apparently recommended Wundt highly for his skill at teaching and rigor at research, but Wundt apparently chafed at being in a very junior position.

During this period with Helmholtz, between 1858 and 1862, however, he wrote a number of articles that were ultimately published in that last year as the *Beiträge zur Theorie der Sinneswahrnehmung* (*Contributions to the Theory of Sense Perception*). Much of this concerned questions of details left unanswered by Weber (touch) or Helmholtz (vision, hearing), but the introduction to the book is a landmark in the history of psychology, for in it Wundt laid down a program for his own future and a plea for a new "psychology," which in many ways charted the remainder of his career. We shall examine this introduction more closely shortly. The following year he printed some lectures on the soul of humans and animals—*soul* being not a theological term but the conventional German word for the psyche as late as the end of the nineteenth century—and began what was to be his single most influential work, the textbook entitled *Grundzüge der physiologischen Psychologie* (*Principles of Physiological Psychology*). He left Helmholtz in 1864 but remained in Heidelberg for the next six years and taught courses in anthropology and medical psychology. The first volume of the *Grundzüge* appeared in 1873 and the second in 1874; in that year Wundt also moved to Zürich. But one year later he was called to the prestigious chair of philosophy at Leipzig; from 1875 to 1917 he taught there continuously.

When he arrived at Leipzig, he was given a room to store the apparatus he had brought with him from Zürich: This in itself is important as it indicates how much he was valued at Leipzig (obtaining extra space was difficult), but also indicates how strongly he felt about the need to do psychological experiments involving apparatus. Four years later, he received an invitation to move to the University of Breslau; in part, he was able to get better facilities at Leipzig (and a better salary) because the Leipzig authorities did not want to lose him. In 1879, then, he was given quite a large block of space in a building that had previously been used partly as a dining hall for poor students. There were two large class-rooms, a conference room, a darkroom, and two laboratories as well as a waiting room: A floor plan is shown by Bringmann, Bringmann, and Ungerer (1980), who provide a detailed description of the foundation of this first "Institute for Experimental Psychology," to give it Wundt's name. It was during this period that Wundt's first students came to Leipzig, among them a young American, James McKeen Cattell (1860–1944), who served as Wundt's first assistant. The first research to be published from the Institute, according to Wundt (1910), was a study by Max Friedrich on the duration of "apperception"; it appeared in a new journal founded by Wundt in 1881 expressly to propagate the work of the Institute. The journal was called *Philosophische Studien,* an expression of Wundt's own belief that psychology had not yet found its feet, but twenty years later he changed its title to the more appropriate *Psychologische Studien.*

For the next two decades Wundt published books and articles in a tireless stream, with the *Grundzüge* being reissued in new editions and always in a larger format incorporating the results of new research. Many students came and went, spreading the tidings of the new psychology both East and West, but particularly West. Wundt, despite a serious problem with his eyesight, which made reading difficult, continued to administer the Institute with kindness but authoritativeness. In 1897 the laboratory was given new quarters in a greatly expanded form. From Wundt's 1910 account, we know it had rooms for research on vision and audition, its own special classrooms and rooms for demonstrations, and even two rooms ostensibly for animal research.

Wundt's major work of his last years was the enormous *Völkerpsychologie* (*Folk Psychology,* 1900–1909) in several volumes. This work dealt with the borderland between social anthropology and social psychology. It did not, contrary to appearances, represent a change of interest on Wundt's part: In 1863 in his introduction to the *Beitrage* he had argued that psychological progress had to rest in part on a body of knowledge concerning society; he was simply carrying out his own plan. Wundt retired in 1917 and died three years later. We shall say more about the students he guided, but the following references are indispensable for a greater appreciation of Wundt's achievement: Titchener and Geissler (1908) offer a complete Wundt bibliography up to that year; Krohn (1892) has a detailed description of the apparatus available in Wundt's laboratory in that year. Tinker (1932) has a list of Wundt's doctorate students and the titles of their theses; Bringmann, Ungerer, and Ganzer (1980) offer a fine collection of photographs and illustrations of Wundtiana.

In discussing Wundt's own contributions we immediately confront the problem of his prolixity. From the full bibliography, I have selected what seem to me the most important works on psychology and listed them in Figure 7–1 and noted what English translations are available.

Publication details will be found in the References at the end of this book. It must be stressed that this is only a fraction of Wundt's total output: He had, for example, fifty articles in the *Philosophische Studien*. We shall discuss the first three works separately and then give an overview of Wundt's opinions on psychology, drawing mainly on the later references in the table.

As mentioned, the introduction to the *Beiträge* ranks as Wundt's program of his own intentions. It begins by arguing that psychology has scarcely advanced since Aristotle's time, despite the advances of physics. One reason for this, the argument continues, has been psychology's enslavement to philosophy and particularly to metaphysics: The study of *how* the mind works should be liberated from the traditional metaphysical questions of why the mind or soul exists or its fate after death. Moreover, the advancement of psychology has been hampered by our ignorance of the relevant facts in three important areas: childhood (i.e., we need to know more about what is now called developmental psychology); zoology (i.e., we need to know more about what is now called comparative psychology); and anthropology (i.e., we need to know more about social influences on our behavior, here Wundt pleaded for a *Völkerpsychologie*). The methods adopted by those claiming to study the mind have also been inadequate; deductions from metaphysical principles have been found unsatisfactory (one thinks of Descartes here), while too much reliance has been placed on self-observation. This last remark may come as a surprise to those who imagine that Wundt, because he flourished in the late nineteenth century, was an introspectionist, but the following quotation shows that Wundt, even at the beginning of his career, was against introspection as a "scientific" method:

> Self observation . . . is totally insufficient, when one's intention is to go back to the beginnings and to the cause of the phenomena. Self observation can never go beyond the facts of consciousness . . . for the phenomena of consciousness are composite products of the unconscious psyche. Their nature is such, that—once they have already entered the consciousness—they will seldom allow direct conclusions concerning their formation. (1862/1961, p. 57)

That is, the mind masks its own operations: Introspection is at best unreliable.

What about Herbart's brave attempt to found a psychology on mathematics? Wundt admired Herbart for treating the psyche as a whole but thought that his mathematics rested on false assumptions and hence was, in the long run, fruitless. Is all then lost for psychology? No, argued Wundt. If we broaden our observations to include the study of society, childhood, and animals, we shall have a factual basis for the development

SOME OF WUNDT'S KEY PSYCHOLOGICAL WORKS

1862	*Beiträge zur Theorie der Sinneswahrnehmung* (*Contributions to the theory of sense-perception*). Untranslated except for theoretical introduction, which will be found in T. Shipley, *Classics in Psychology* (1961). This work had appeared in installments from 1858 onwards and illustrated how crucial the study of sensory psychology was for the development of psychology.
1863	*Vorlesungen über die Menschen und Tierseele.* The second, greatly revised edition of 1892, was translated into English by Creighton and Titchener, *Lectures on Human and Animal Psychology* (1901).
1874	*Grundzüge der physiologischen Psychologie* (*Principles of physiological psychology*); 2nd ed., 1880; 3rd ed., 1887; 4th ed., 1893; 5th ed., 1902–1903; 6th ed., 1908–1911. Volume 1 of the 5th edition was translated by Titchener as *Principles of physiological psychology* (1904).
1878	Essay, "On the present state of animal psychology." Reprinted in *Essays*, 1885.
1879	Der Spiritismus. Reprinted in *Essays*, 1885.
1880–1883	*Logik.* Important for Wundt's views on the methodology of psychology.
1881	First issue of *Philosophische Studien*; included an article by Wundt on psychological methods.
1885	*Essays.*
1886	*Ethik.* Mainly philosophical but includes some psychology of morals. Translated by Titchener, Gulliver, & Washburn, as *Ethics* 1897 (3 vols.).
1887	Article on introspection in *Philosophische Studien*, Vol. 4.
1888	The divisions of the sciences, *Philosophische Studien*, Vol. 5.
1889	*System der Philosophie.* The origins of knowledge, meaning of consciousness, psychic causality.
1892	*Hypnotismus und Suggestion.* 2nd ed. of the 1863 lectures.
1894	Article on psychic causality in *Philosophische Studien*, Vol. 10.
1896	*Grundriss der Psychologie.* Translated by Judd as *Outlines of Psychology*, 1897. This was the main source in English for most of Wundt's ideas.
1900	*Völkerpsychologie* (*Folk psychology*). Not translated. Came out in four parts in 1900, 1905, 1906, and 1909. Topics are language; origin of speech, myth, and religion; primitive customs and beliefs; origins of religion.
1901	*Einleitung in die Philosophie.* Places psychology in a scientific context.
1907	Article critical of Würzburg school introspectionism, *Psychologische Studien*, Vol. 3.
1910	Description and history of Leipzig institute. *Psychologische Studien*, Vol. 5.
1911	*Einführung in die Psychologie.* Translated by Pintner as *Introduction to Psychology*, 1912.
1920	*Erlebtes und Erkanntes* (*The experienced and the learned*). An autobiography.

Figure 7–1 Wundt's Main Works.

of a general psychology, and if we avoid metaphysics and introspection and concentrate on the experimental method, we shall have a scientific basis for the development of the new science. As examples of good methodology in recent psychology, Wundt mentions the personal equation and Fechner's Law.

From this important tract, Wundt turned to more substantive matters in his next major work, the *Lectures on Human and Animal Psychology.* The topics discussed in the first volume of the 1863 edition include the history of psychology; thought and judgment; recent work on the sensations (including Helmholtz's three-color theory); the perception of space and time; consciousness; the personal equation; and the growth of our understanding of physical concepts. Topics in the second volume include feelings, including aesthetic feelings; moral judgments; society and its development down the ages; animal behavior; religious feelings; comparative religion; instincts (including a discussion of Darwin's theories); language; and will.

It was in the *Lectures* that Wundt also put forward an opinion that reached fruition in his late years. He believed that even experimentation on human psychology had its limits; much of our behavior can only be understood by references to influences from other people that have affected our personality and thought processes. Language, for example, is acquired from others and forms the basis of thinking and reasoning. Our emotions concerning what is acceptable and not acceptable social behavior are largely determined by the society we grow up in. And a study of the instincts, as expressed not only in the lower animals but also in the study of primitive societies, gives us a background against which to formulate a psychology of willing. This suggestion that a study of anthropology and history should complement what we learn in the laboratory was realized in his *Völkerpsychologie.* Here we see reflected his opinion that there are two main branches of psychology, experimental and "social" (on this, see Titchener, 1921a). A detailed account of the origins of these ideas in some earlier German writers, and of Wundt's opinions of the role of the culture in determining the individual's psychology, is given by Danziger (1983). Wundt's remarks on all these topics were greatly elaborated in the second edition of 1892, which, because it was translated, was quite influential in its time. In this edition, for example, the discussion of the personal equation is elaborated to include much new work on reaction times done in Wundt's laboratory and elsewhere.

But Wundt's most massive contribution was the *Grundzüge.* The first edition of the book is in five sections: The first concerns the physiological characteristics of the nervous system and includes much of that nineteenth-century psychophysiology we reviewed in the previous chapter. The second section is on the sensations. The third section is on *Vorstellungen* (presentations) but includes topics we would now call *percep-*

tual as opposed to sensory—for example, treatments of the two-point threshold, the hearing of harmonic intervals, the laws of eye movements and the principles of depth perception, images and dreams, and complex presentations such as abstract concepts. Aesthetic feelings are also described. The fourth section is on consciousness and the "alternation" of presentations—here we find discussions of attention and apperception, reaction times (Donders), and the laws of association (a brief mention of the British associationists but more on Herbart and Beneke). The section ends with a chapter on feelings, desires, and instincts. The fifth and final section is on movements; it discusses the differences between voluntary and involuntary behaviors and has a chapter on expressive movements.

The final chapter of the book is philosophical, with accounts of varying views on the mind-body problem and on the nature of consciousness. This sketch would be greatly elaborated in the five subsequent editions of the book of which only the first part of the fifth edition is available in English. It would be fascinating, for example, to follow the physiological sections over the forty years or so covered in Wundt's later life and see the growth in our understanding of the cerebral hemispheres in particular.

But the most important thing to realize about Wundt's *Principles* is that they constituted the main source of factual information for most young psychologists of the last decades of the nineteenth century. Bain and William James did indeed present rival texts, but for detail on experimental and neurophysiological matters Wundt's *Principles* had no rivals. Of course, it became desirable for non-German psychologists of the periods to learn German and many did so: In American universities of the late nineteenth century, German courses were almost obligatory for the budding aspirant to a doctorate in psychology.

Clearly, Wundt felt that his pioneering position in the establishment of academic psychology was a most responsible one. Although he did a few experiments himself, he preferred to leave laboratory work to his students and to concentrate instead on writing reviews (such as the *Grundzüge*), theoretical works (such as the various articles for the *Psychologische Studien* and his best-known later work, the *Outlines of Prychology*), or historical works (such as the long sections on the history of theories of the psyche in his various philosophical texts). It is difficult to encapsulate Wundt's theoretical principles in one concise picture, with one ready reference source. As William James said of him, perhaps a little sweepingly, "cut him up like a worm, and each fragment crawls; there is no *noeud vital* in his mental medulla oblongata, so that you can't kill him all at once" (quoted by Perry, 1935, Volume 2, p. 68). But it is possible to tease from his writings six characteristics of his opinions on what psychology should be and how it should be carried out; it becomes an interesting exercise, not merely to assimilate these characteristics into a unity (this simply convinces us of Wundt's independence and originality), but to discover whether there are any inconsistencies that would invalidate the assimilation. (So far the present writer has not succeeded in doing so.)

1. Wundt was quite explicit that psychology was indeed a science, but he made a distinction (apparently quite current in his time) between natural sciences (*Naturwissenschaften*) and sciences of the spirit (*Geisteswissenschaften*). We immediately correct any false impression of the acceptability of the latter by pointing out that *Geist,* while related to the English word *ghost,* is more a reference to the "spirit" in the sense of higher mental activity. The *Geisteswissenschaften,* according to the 1888 *Philosophische Studien* article, included studies of processes of the spirit in their own right—that is, individual psychology, folk psychology, social psychology, psychology, psychophysics, and anthropology; studies of phenomena created by the human spirit (philology, economics, politics, jurisprudence, theology, the arts, scientific method); and history. Other disciplines, such as physics, chemistry, and biology, are "natural" sciences. According to his later work *Einleitung in die Philosophie* (*Introduction to Philosophy*) Wundt considered that the division between the two classes of discipline arose in the early nineteenth century and was influenced by Hegel and John Stuart Mill, among others; he also considered psychology as in many ways the "science of the spirit" which underlay the others. In his *Logik* a whole section is given to a discussion of the logic of the various *Geisteswissenschaften.* More mention of his comments on the topic of psychology is given below.

2. In his self-conscious search for laws underlying psychological behavior, Wundt found himself obliged to admit that, in his opinion, the laws of psychic life are unlike the laws applying to physical objects in a number of ways. If we see one billiard ball hit another we can describe what happens by using such concepts as mass and acceleration. But if we can observe one brain process, we cannot infer what the associated psychic event is. Moreover, all psychic events differ from physiological events insofar as a psychic sequence such as "Thought A 'causes' thought B" can only adequately be described by referring to *values,* the goodness or aptness of A and B, and values have no place in the description of physical events. Another difference between physical and psychic causality, asserted Wundt, was that if two physical objects come together they do not necessarily lose their individual identity, whereas the concatenation of two psychic events often results in a new event quite different from the original conjunction. For all of these reasons, Wundt believed that description of the regularities of conjunction of mental events requires a different kind of language than description of the regularities of the conjunction of physical objects. To quote his 1894 article, "all psychic causality is a phenomenal (*anschaulich*) causality, all physical causality is a conceptual causality" (p. 109).

We immediately make two remarks. First, it would be wrong to infer from the fact that Wundt believes that different kinds of words are needed to describe psychological causal sequences as opposed to physical causal sequences that Wundt therefore believed that "mind" is a different kind of substance from "body." In fact, Wundt asserted in many places that psychological experiences are dependent on the material substrate of brain events; he is no dualist in the sense that Descartes was. But Wundt never denied that there is a problem for the objective scientist insofar as we know physics from observation, but from observation can only know the processes of our *own* minds. He nevertheless hoped that experiments would solve the problems of formulating valid laws of psychic causality. A useful discussion of this difficult matter is given by Mischel (1970/1971).

Second, Wundt himself tried to formulate actual laws about this elusive psychic causality. From the *Beiträge* onwards, there are hints that mental ontogenetic development is not haphazard but lawful; however, it is only in the *Outlines of Psychology* that we get the complete statement of Wundt's laws of mental activity. There are six: The law of psychical resultants argues, as we mentioned previously, that a new thought is not necessarily a simple sum of its constituent thoughts—a creative synthesis transmutes a conjunction of psychic experiences into a new content. The law of psychical relations argues that every psychical content receives its significance (i.e., its value) from its relation to other psychical contents. The law of psychical contrasts emphasizes the affective aspects of all thought experiences. The law of mental growth allows for continued expansion of the contents of the psyche as a result of creative synthesis. The law of heterogony of ends stresses the broadening of psychical contents from simple intentions to such mental frameworks as are implied by such words as *volition* and *ethics*. Finally, there is a law of development towards opposites according to which each phase in the sequence of childhood, adolescence, early adulthood, and so on has emotional characteristics that tend to be counterbalanced in the succeeding phase. The important thing to notice is that no attempt is made at a psychophysiological account of mental life: Mental life needs its own metalanguage for its description.

3. We mentioned previously that in the early introduction to the *Beiträge* (1863) Wundt expressed his dissatisfaction with introspection as a scientific method. This same dissatisfaction was reexpressed at various periods during his life, most notably in his 1887 *Philosophische Studien* article; but to the argument that introspection is unreliable because we are unaware of our own motives Wundt now adds the argument that introspection is unreliable because we cannot examine (observe) a *present* thought, we can only try to capture it, as it were, after it has gone. All we can do is examine a memory. For Wundt the only valid way to make a self-observation was by a psychological experiment. This article was writ-

ten twenty-four years after the *Beiträge,* and Wundt's final diatribe against introspection came yet another twenty years later, in his *Psychologische Studien* article of 1907. To appreciate this article properly, we have to know more about the writings of the Würzburg school; it will be enough to say at this point that this group studied thinking and problem solving largely by asking subjects to describe their solution processes. For Wundt this was a step backwards. Introspection, as practiced by the members of the Würzburg school, was now criticized even further on the grounds of its lack of replicability; the difficulty that observers have in initiating and modifying their own thought processes so that their "introspections" can be carried out on *controllable* events; and the effects of waxing and waning attention on the reliability of introspections.

Nevertheless, it must also be said that in several accounts of the history of psychology, notably Boring (1950), Wundt is portrayed as a believer in introspection. This is only one of a number of misconceptions about Wundt that has probably in part arisen because one of Wundt's students, Titchener, was a source for Boring's otherwise outstanding text. Danziger (1980) and Blumenthal (1980) have shown that in part this misinterpretation of Wundt lies in the fact that three different German words were all translated as "introspection"; and one of these words referred to a special case of self-observation in which a subject was asked to wait until something was clear in consciousness before responding to it. In this special sense, Wundt can be said to have used "introspection"; otherwise, he did not ask subjects to explain what was going on in their minds during an experiment. Danziger shows further that out of dozens of studies reported in the *Philosophische Studien,* only a handful used introspection in this sense. Later, when we come to Titchener, we will see that introspection *was* important in Titchener's laboratory. At the same time, Wundt did not deny that we could get *ideas* about psychological explanations from observing our own thought processes, but he stressed that these ideas had to be investigated by using objective methods of experimentation before they could be accepted as useful.

4. In various books, such as the *Ethik,* the *Logik,* and the *System der Philosophie,* Wundt gave brief sketches of historical antecedents in psychology in which he described attitudes towards psychological matters under various headings such as materialism (the belief that brain processes underlay psychical processes) and intellectualism (the belief that "mind" can be analyzed into faculties, associations, etc.).

But for one view, which had few adherents, he showed special sympathy in his own writing and gave it a name we have so far not met, *voluntarism.* We note immediately that we shall rarely meet it again: Voluntarism was lost like sand in the onslaught of the tidal currents of the Würzburg school and other twentieth-century movements. Yet if a single word has to be applied to Wundt's theoretical stance, this would be the

word. That it refers to the will may be easily inferred, but its true meaning refers not just to a theory stating that we have a will, but to a theory
insisting that the operations of the psyche cannot properly be described
without reference to the will. This stands in contrast to a simple faculty
psychology, in which labeling our various psychic potentialities is held to
be tantamount to a description of mental processes, even when the will is
listed as one of those faculties; and it stands in contrast to a simple
associationistic theory according to which presentations and ideas are
unchanging objects subject to the operation of a simple laws such as
similarity or contiguity. Voluntarism argues instead that our psychic life is
a flow of events whose order is *dependent* on the operation of our will: As
Wundt puts it in an essay on speech and thought (1895, pp. 244–285),
when we prepare a sentence we are able to deliver it intact because by an
act of will—which, Wundt argues, we often *call* an act of thought—we
pursue the sentence to the end and are not distracted by all the side
associations that try to push us off the selected track. The laws of association operate best in a daydreamlike situation: As soon as we exercise will,
we go *against* the laws. Thus I am able to write "I am thinking of Wundt"
because my will and my general efforts are being directed to this paragraph: Had I followed my natural association stream, however, I might
have written "I am thinking of dinner," a genuine impulse, but one that
by will I ignored.

   Wundt wrote of the importance of the will in various places. Its
importance in moral behavior is brought out in Volume III of *Ethics;* an
attack on associationism in the light of voluntarism will be found in pp.
164–168 of the *Logic;* in the *Essays* will be found an account of the
development of the will and its consort, consciousness, from infancy onwards; and in the second edition of the *Lectures,* will is assigned its role in
the development of personality and character. Like Bain, Wundt believed
that willing emerged in the natural course of things from the growth of
voluntary movement and the control of reflexes.

   5. Closely related to his voluntarism is the fact that, as a consequence of seeing the will as a unifying force shaping the flow of our
thought and behavior, Wundt came to dislike theories of psychology that
insisted on breaking up the psyche into fixed components such as images,
presentations, sensations, feelings, and so on. Wundt says explicitly:

> Psychic processes form a *unitary* event. The division into presentations,
> feelings, strivings, willings, etc. as it is already practised in popular con-
> sciousness and, as a result of this, in speech is a product of psychological
> analysis and abstraction; these processes however are not really distinct, but
> indivisible interconnected components of *one* event. To distinguish between
> these components is indeed inevitable in the interests of psychological anal-
> ysis; but one should never lose sight of the fact that the aim of every
> psychological investigation should remain that of ascertaining the connec-

tions between the elements of psychic events and that the outcome of such an exercise will be clouded if one elevated each product of this abstraction into an independent (psychic) content *(Logik,* 1880–1883, p. 67).

Here, Wundt uses the word *element,* but he is apologizing for it. But elsewhere, particularly in the *Essays,* he discusses *feelings* at great length. And in the *Outlines of Psychology* the various sections constitute discussions of *psychical elements* (such as sensations and feelings) and *psychical compounds (ideas* of space and time, composite feelings, emotions, and volitional processes). *Associations* are "interconnections of psychical compounds." Small wonder then that Wundt has been represented as the archanalyst of the psyche into little bits and pieces, one who attempts to put together a structure from primitive building blocks. Nor is it surprising that, because he uses the words *elements* and *compounds,* he should be claimed as an exponent of "mental chemistry" in much the same way as John Stuart Mill was. Like Mill, who argued that a new mental compound such as *white* was *generated* from simple elements of sensation like the seven prismatic colors, Wundt argued that new compounds could emerge from simple elements by the principle of "creative synthesis." But Blumenthal (1980) has argued that it is a mistake to identify Wundt's apparent elementarism with that of Mill. First, Wundt was more influenced by the line of Germans from Leibniz to his time and makes rare and usually critical mention of the British writers. Second, in his voluntarism, Wundt stressed that it was the will that led to the mind's constructing creative syntheses; new ideas did not arise from some passive concatenation of elementary ideas that happen to occur together. Nevertheless, Wundt has been categorized by some in a sort of scapegoat class, the simplifier against whom the holistic psychologists, such as the Gestalt school with their dislike of a simple atomistic approach, could conveniently rebel.

Thus it cannot be stressed strongly enough that Wundt himself was well aware of the deficiencies of an atomistic approach and of the dangers of an elementist vocabulary. He argued that the mind formed a unity in which the mortar was will; he argued that no thought or feeling could be judged in isolation from its surrounding thoughts or feelings; he insisted that one feature making psychic causality different from physical causality was the need for the former to be described in terms of values. It is perhaps in this context that we best appreciate William James's aphorism about Wundt's invulnerability. But the gist of this paragraph is to the effect that, like Helmholtz, Wundt was well aware of the dangers of seeing psychic life as a sequence of static sensations and presentations. Nevertheless, that is how he chose to organize his discussions of psychological matter, not only in the *Outlines,* but also in the *Grundzüge.*

6. Finally, we would point quickly to an article first published in

1878 and recast for the *Essays* seven years later. Its title was "Animal Psychology." In it Wundt pleaded for a genuinely experimental psychology of animal behavior in which the language of description was rigorous (avoiding such vague terms as *society, instinct,* and *purpose* when applied to lower forms of life), the observations were free of anthropomorphisms such as the ascription of human emotions to animals, and reliance was placed more on controlled observations than on anecdote (particularly in the case of the higher animals such as apes). These arguments were well ahead of their time. Wundt was responsible for little animal research, however, and his chapters on animal behavior in, for example, the second edition of the *Lectures* are methodological rather than substantive in content.

Wundt made still other original contributions to knowledge and theory. While working with Helmholtz, he carried out a careful experiment concerned with the questions of how far accommodation and convergence, operating in isolation, could yield cues to depth perception. His discussions of associations included a classification that distinguished between *outer* and *inner* forms of associations (found in the third edition of the *Grundzüge* but in most detail in an 1882 paper by his pupil Trautscholdt). By *outer* associations he meant associations between items that had been met in real life: Such associations could be between items encountered simultaneously, or successively, and would include part-whole relationships. By *inner* associations he meant associations linked by some mental activity such as a ranking in terms of some ordering (e.g., individual items in relation to a particular class), or by noticing their similarity or contrast, or by detecting cause-effect or common-purpose relationships. Trautscholdt actually gave experimental data on the frequency of these two kinds of associations, finding that about 54 percent of associations had "outer," and 46 percent "inner," origins. Wundt also distinguished among various kinds of psychic compounds such as the fusions of tones into harmonic chords and "complications" where, say, a visual sensation is linked with a tactile sensation to form the concept "cold object."

One of the ways in which Wundt was most influenced by his German predecessors was in his adoption of the Leibnizian concept of *apperception*. As Richards (1980b) has shown, Wundt assumed that the total process, from initial sensation to active recognition or identification of an object, took place in stages. Suppose a stimulus were flashed in the periphery: The sensation would yield a signal (a Lotzian "local sign") to the brain, leading to an eye movement that brought the stimulus to the fovea. This linkage of a sensation with a movement, called a *colligation* by Wundt, formed the basis of our buildup of a picture of external space. But the present colligation is linked by association with memories of previous colligations: This act is unconscious (Wundt queried Helmholtz's priority on the topic of unconscious inference) and forms part of the total process of apperception, which in turn can lead to a response to the identified stimulus. One effect of the act of apperception is to make the percept clearer, and Wundt believed that the general process was controlled by the frontal lobes acting in concert with the visual and motor centers.

Finally, in the fourth edition of the *Grundzüge* and in the *Outlines* (Chaps. 7 and 13) Wundt put forward, rather briefly, the theory that both feelings and emotions had three aspects or dimensions: pleasurable and unpleasurable feelings and emotions; arousing and subduing (or exciting and depressing) feelings and emotions; and feelings and emotions of strain and relaxation. Any one feeling or emotion could partake of one, two, or three of these dimensions. This speculation generated a fair amount of interest and research in its time, and P. T. Young (1961, p. 321d) has argued that in some ways Wundt's tridimensional theory of feeling anticipated the results of Osgood's 1952 factor analysis of *meaning* into the three dimensions of value (like Wundt's pleasantness-unpleasantness dimension), activity (like Wundt's arousing-subduing dimension), and potency (like Wundt's strain-relaxation dimension). But even one of Wundt's most admiring pupils, Titchener, came to criticize the tridimensional theory on introspective grounds (on this, see Danziger, 1979, p. 218).

In many ways Wundt, despite being such a central figure in the dissemination of psychological knowledge, was a peripheral figure in terms of the influence of his theories. His voluntarism never caught on and in fact Danziger (1979) has argued cogently that his views on the will, psychic causality, and values led him to be considered as a metaphysician by some of his younger colleagues. In rebellion, argues Danziger, they adopted a more rigorous, positivist stance that foreshadowed behaviorism. Wundt has also suffered from being misinterpreted: A. L. Blumenthal (1975) wrote an important article that tried to correct the mistaken impression that Wundt was an introspectionist and a dualist; later we shall comment on what some have called Wundt's structuralism. Blumenthal (1980) lists nine ways in which Wundt has been misrepresented, and Tweney and Yachanin (1980) and Leahey (1981) have shown in detail how this in part arose from a tendency to misidentify Wundt's ideas with those of his pupil Titchener. We might again note Wundt's many-sided interests: He wrote on every conceivable branch of psychology, including areas controversial in his time such as hypnosis and mediumship. We may finally remark that Wundt's pupils remembered him with affection as a first-rate lecturer and as a conscientious research supervisor who nevertheless gave his students considerable independence. The 1921 issue of the *Psychological Review* contains a number of entertaining reminiscences of Wundt the professor written by some of his former pupils; and

Bringmann and Tweney (1980) and Rieber (1980) have edited important collections of papers on Wundt.

The obvious matter to discuss here would be the spread of psychology from Leipzig to other universities in Germany, America, and elsewhere by students of Wundt. But other crosscurrents in the psychology of the 1880s should be mentioned first. Most notably, important laboratories of experimental psychology were set up at Berlin by Ebbinghaus and at Göttingen by G. E. Müller. Young psychologists eager to learn the new skills of psychophysics and reaction time testing would indeed make Wundt's Leipzig their Mecca, but would also try to visit Berlin and Göttingen. Moreover, a new intellectual movement was catching the imagination of precisely those young people who would be doing the grand tour of the European laboratories looking for a scientific psychology: We refer of course to the enunciation by Charles Darwin in 1859 of the theory of evolution. This theory did more than anything else finally to destroy the notion that humans were somehow special beings set apart from the other animals; it thereby indirectly contributed to the beginning of experimental comparative psychology. Clearly, we run the risk of entanglement in the thickets of these various developments. So for clarity we shall adopt the following plan: For the rest of this chapter, we shall discuss Ebbinghaus and G. E. Müller, then describe the propagation of psychology out from Leipzig, Berlin, and Göttingen. In the following chapter we shall pay special attention to the achievement of William James in founding psychology as an academic discipline in the United States, discuss the

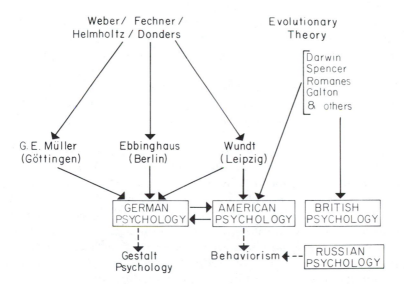

Figure 7–2 Main Developments in Experimental Psychology at the End of the Nineteenth Century.

line of mainly British psychologists influenced by the theory of evolution, and give an account of other events in German psychology that prepared the way for the twentieth-century movement of Gestalt psychology. This scheme is perhaps made clearer by Figure 7–2, which shows Wundt as a central figure influencing both German and American experimental psychology.

Ebbinghaus and G. E. Müller

Hermann Ebbinghaus (1850–1909) studied history and philosophy at various German universities before eventually obtaining his doctorate from Bonn in 1873 with a thesis on philosophical aspects of the concept of the unconscious. From 1873 to 1880 he essentially lived the life of a private scholar and tutor: It was while he was in France that he first read Fechner's *Elements of Psychophysics*. He was probably well versed in the works of the British associationists, which would have bent his interests in the direction of cognitive as opposed to sensory processes, and he almost certainly read Wundt's *Grundzüge*. The outcome of this combination of influences was a decision to attack the problem of human memory experimentally.

It has been the traditional verdict of history that Ebbinghaus single-handedly founded this important branch of experimental psychology; however, Stigler (1978) has unearthed some forgotten work by the American physicist Francis E. Nipher (1847–1926). In 1876 Nipher observed that immediate recall of the middle digits of a six-digit number was poorer than recall of the first or last digits, and he tentatively began research designed to show how recall deteriorated with the passage of time. This work, however, was completely overlooked by Nipher's contemporaries. Ebbinghaus himself knew of no predecessors to guide him, and there is no question that his was the first influential work on the topic; that is, it was immediately appreciated, was described in such texts as the later editions of Wundt's *Grundzüge*, and led to considerable research efforts by others. Some five years of rather intermittent research, using himself as a subject, preceded the publication of Ebbinghaus's *Memory* in 1885; it was his first publication other than his doctoral thesis.

Before the appearance of this work, writings on memory had been prolific but based on little in the way of deliberately collected data. Memory ran like a giant undercurrent through the works of Herbart and the British associationists. Clinical neurologists, influenced by the discovery of Broca's area, were just tentatively beginning to draw conclusions about memory deficit from studies of brain damage. Mnemonic schemes remained popular even at institutes of higher education. But it was Ebbinghaus who forced writers on memory to be rigorous both in scientific method and in terminology. On scientific method, Ebbinghaus described his results in terms of averages (arithmetic means) but also in terms of their variability. He argued that if one were to study memory in its purest form, one would not wish the data to be biased by including materials of various levels of difficulty nor should the materials remind one of other associations that might distract one from the immediate task of memorizing. So Ebbinghaus invented nonsense syllables. At first these were defined in terms of *sounds,* so that a six-letter syllable such as *cheich* (which is meaningless in German) was acceptable; much later, the convention emerged that nonsense syllables should be defined in terms of three *letters,* consonant-vowel-consonant, and these CVC trigrams, as they are called, still play a major role in modern memory research. The syllables now usually used are those listed by Noble (1961).

By dint of studiously memorizing lists of syllables of predetermined length, Ebbinghaus was able to carry out five extended experiments on memory. He discovered (1) how the difficulty of learning increased as the number of syllables to be remembered increased; (2) that once you have learned a list fairly well by heart, there is little point to overlearning it by further self-tests; (3) that recall falls off over time rapidly at first and then more slowly—the amount forgotten after a month was only slightly greater than the amount forgotten after eight hours; (4) that learning could be more efficient if spaced out over small units of study time than if condensed into one long study period; and (5) that associations in a list learned by heart such as A B C D E . . . were not merely between adjacent items such as B and C but also between remote items such as B and D or B and E. This last experiment, professed Ebbinghaus, was done directly to test Herbart's theory of remote associations (see p. 164). The best-known result of the above series was the third, and Ebbinghaus's forgetting curve is still quoted in standard modern texts. He himself fitted a logarithmic equation to the curve.

The years following the publication of *Memory* saw Ebbinghaus installed in a teaching position at Berlin. Here he helped establish a laboratory of experimental psychology and worked on problems of sensation (notably Weber's Law as applied to brightness and color vision). In 1890, with Arthur König, an expert on vision, he founded a new journal designed as an outlet for the growing mass of research for which Wundt's *Philosophische Studien* had no room. Its title was the *Zeitschrift für Psychologie und Physiologie der Sinnesorgane* (*Journal of Psychology and the Physiology of the Sense Organs*). Wundt's journal ceased publication in 1917; Ebbinghaus's journal is still perhaps the best-known current German journal of psychology. Helmholtz and Hering, among others, acted as cooperating editors during the first years of its existence.

In 1894 Ebbinghaus, for reasons which still remain a matter of speculation among historians of psychology, was not promoted to the full chair of philosophy at Berlin. Instead he accepted the vacant chair at Breslau. Here he wrote his own *Grundzüge der Psychologie* (*Principles of Psychology*, 1897–1902). The work was shorter and more readable than Wundt's enormous tome and rapidly became the standard textbook—as opposed to handbook —of psychology in the German-speaking world. The work was dedicated to Fechner. It had the usual very extended treatment of the senses and, as might be expected, was wholly experimental in its approach to memory and associations. In his *Memory* Ebbinghaus had not drawn a forgetting curve, presenting only tabular data; but in the second edition of the *Grundzüge* (1905, p. 680) appears Ebbinghaus's own version. To derive this curve Ebbinghaus memorized lists of thirteen nonsense syllables and then recalled them at time intervals up to six days. Here he also reported that learning a long list of syllables that are *not* nonsense—for example, stanzas from Byron's *Don Juan*—is much easier than learning lists of syllables. He first learned Byron at the time of writing *Memory;* eleven years later, he reports in the *Grundzüge*, he re-learned the same stanzas in about 20 percent less time than at the first learning. Ebbinghaus moved from Breslau to Halle in 1905 and there wrote a short and popular *Abriss der Psychologie* (translated as *Psychology: An Elementary Text Book*). In his later years he also pioneered in designing intelligence tests for children. He died in 1909 at the height of his personal popularity as a systematizer of the new experimental psychology.

Ebbinghaus's work on memory had laid a foundation both methodological and theoretical; but Ebbinghaus speculated little on the mechanism of forgetting. Georg Elias Müller (1850–1934) was the pioneer of what we now call the interference theory of forgetting, a term connoting the belief that much forgetting is not the result of the dying away of the material to be remembered but is rather the result of interference from other memories at the time of retrieval. His name is customarily given as G. E. Müller to avoid confusion with the Johannes Müller of the doctrine of specific nerve energies. Like Ebbinghaus, Müller was first captivated by psychophysics; like Ebbinghaus, in addition to his work on memory, he wrote on color vision, espousing a modified version of Hering's opponent process theory; and one of his last works was also a short *Abriss* (outline) of psychology. But whereas Ebbinghaus moved a great deal, Müller remained settled in one place, Göttingen, for forty years, and Müller's contributions to psychophysics were more influential than Ebbinghaus's.

Müller intended to study history but while at Leipzig was introduced to Herbart's psychology, which apparently made a strong impression on him. After a short spell in the army, he also read Helmholtz on optics and made the personal acquaintance of Lotze. In 1873 Müller received a doctorate from Lotze's university, Göttingen, for a thesis on sensory attention, a pioneering work on that most nuclear but elusive of cognitive functions. He traveled for the next three years and at this time corresponded with Fechner; the result was a thesis and an article on psychophysics. The article, published in 1879, included an elaboration of Fechner's method for fitting the data obtained from the method of right and wrong cases with a curve based on the normal distribution. This involved the use of what came to be called the Müller weights: A clear account of this fairly central issue in psychophysics is given by Woodworth (1938, p. 412).

After four more years in Göttingen, then one year at Czernowitz, Müller finally settled in Göttingen as full professor replacing Lotze from 1881 onwards. The laboratory he established was generally agreed to be second only to that of Leipzig. Moreover, Müller was more of an experimentalist than Wundt, and with his students he produced the classic work on interference in memory (which we shall describe), collaborated in important research on psychophysics with L. J. Martin, and was responsible for materially assisting the French psychologist Victor Henri (1872–1940) in his studies on the two-point threshold. In 1903 Müller condensed much of his thinking on psychophysics into his *Die Gesichtspunkte und Tatsachen der psychophysischen Methodik* (*Viewpoints and Facts of Psychophysical Method*). In his final years he was occupied with a criticism of the new Gestalt psychology, and in 1930 he wrote a 647-page monograph *Über die Farbenempfindungen: Psychophysische Untersuchungen* (*On Color Sensations: Psychophysical Investigation*). Boring (1950, p. 382) offers a bibliography of Müller's most important writings. Although Müller's penchant for introspection made his late writings seem somewhat *passé* in the surroundings of experimental studies emanating from the Gestalt and behaviorist movements, his early work on psychophysics made him second to Fechner in the estimation of his contemporaries, and his work on memory will ensure him a perpetual place in posterity.

The memory research appeared as three publications. First, in 1893 he and Friedrich Schumann (1863–1940) published a long monograph in which, acknowledging their indebtedness to Ebbinghaus, they described rules for formulating nonsense syllables and a new device, a kind of memory drum, for presenting materials to be learned by heart. Using the device, they showed that learning is facilitated if a rhythm is imposed on the sequence to be learned; they also analyzed various kinds of errors that occur during memorization. Second, in 1900 Müller and Alfons Pilzecker (1865–ca. 1920) published a long monograph as a supplement in Ebbinghaus's journal putting forth for the first time a detailed analysis of interference in retrieval from memory. By analyzing the errors obtained from the learning of lists consisting of pairs a-b, c-d, and so forth they were able to indicate various kinds of inhibitions that prevented ready recall. One of these was called *retroactive inhibition:* If one has learned first list X, then list Y, relearning of X will be hampered by the unwanted arousal of memories from list Y. It is as if memories of Y were acting "backwards" on the memories laid down by the original learning of X. For Müller and Pilzecker, however, *any* kind of interference resulting from cognitive activity between the original learning of X and its relearning was due to retroactive inhibition. They also described other kinds of inhibition that would now be called *proactive:* cases where new memorizing is hindered by the unwanted arousal of old memories. (The term *proactive inhibition* was first introduced by Whitely and Blankenship, 1936).

Müller and Pilzecker also mooted the notion that when a memory trace is first set up, it is subject to interference but nevertheless resists this attack by virtue of "perseveration" in the nervous tissue for a while. This perseveration allows the trace to be "consolidated" and thus insures that the strength of the trace remains unchanged. The term *consolidation,* like *retroactive inhibition,* would become standard.

Müller's third contribution to memory was a series of articles published in the *Zeitschrift* supplements for 1911, 1913, and 1917. These included remarks on the unusual memory capacities of the prodigy Rückle. They are little read nowadays, but summaries of the experimental findings of Müller and Schumann and of Müller and Pilzecker were widely disseminated in the English-language publications of the time and in such works as Ebbinghaus's *Grundzüge.* A modern account is given by D. J. Murray (1976).

We have therefore three important laboratories in Germany: Leipzig, Göttingen, and Berlin. Experimental research on the special senses, psychophysics, and human memory was under way in each of these places. It remains to give an indication of how young students would go from these centers and begin their own departments, particularly outside Germany. Clearly there is no place here for a complete enumeration of the doctoral students of the three laboratories; instead, we shall briefly describe the contribution of the more important alumni of these laboratories. The chart in Figure 7–3 lists the key names in question: It remains

Figure 7–3 Students Who Obtained Their Doctorates at Leipzig, Göttingen, and Berlin in the Late Nineteenth Century.

Leipzig		Göttingen	Berlin
AMERICAN	GERMAN		
Hall	Lange	Schumann	Ebbinghaus
Cattell	Dietze	Pilzecker	Stumpf (prof.)
Baldwin	Meumann	Jost	Stern
Scripture	Kraepelin		Langfeld
Judd	Münsterberg		Pfungst
Stratton	Marbe		
Warren	Külpe		
F Angell			
Titchener			

only to describe, very briefly, their achievements. The two lists under *Göttingen* and *Berlin* will be described quickly; the list of main interest is that under *Leipzig*.

At Berlin, Ebbinghaus's most famous pupil was William Stern (1871–1938). Stern went to Breslau shortly after Ebbinghaus had moved there and stayed until 1915, when he obtained the chair at a newly founded university at Hamburg. In later life he devised a personalistic psychology, but he is perhaps best known for his earlier research on children's thought processes and linguistic development. He was responsible for the concept of intelligence quotient (a matter we shall clarify in Chap. 12). He was also a pioneer in applied psychology and in 1907 founded the first German journal devoted to that topic, the *Zeitschrift für Angewandte Psychologie* (*Journal for Applied Psychology*); he made one of the first studies of the blind and deaf girl, Helen Keller.

The department at Berlin remained a key center for research after Ebbinghaus left. Its new chairman, who remained there from 1894 to 1921, was Carl Stumpf (1848–1936). Stumpf's role in the history of psychology is debatable. On the one hand he was a powerful figure in academic circles in the whole era from Lotze to the early twentieth century. He knew Weber, Fechner, and Helmholtz personally and had a dispute on tonal perception with Wundt. He worked in no fewer than five universities (Göttingen, Würzburg, Prague, Halle, and Munich) before settling in Berlin. In his days of retirement in Berlin he saw his old department become the center of the new Gestalt movement, and both Köhler and Koffka, eminent Gestalt psychologists, were his students. On the other hand, most modern psychologists would be hard put to say what Stumpf actually contributed to the substance of psychological knowledge. His main contribution was in fact a large two-volume *Tonpsychologie* (*Psychology of Tone,* the first volume from 1883, the second from 1890), which in part added the modern psychophysics to what Helmholtz had earlier said in his *Sensations of Tone* and in part was more explicit about the notion of tonal fusions. Stumpf offered several laws of tonal fusion, but modern experts on musical theory are skeptical of their value (Davies, 1978, p. 160). He also paved the way in some respects for Gestalt psychology (on this, more follows) and encouraged the development of research into child psychology at Berlin. Among students who learned under him at Berlin, we may note two in particular: The American, H. S. Langfeld (1879–1958), was best known for textbooks written with Boring and Weld in the 1930s and 1940s; he worked at Harvard and Princeton after obtaining his Ph.D. with Stumpf. Oskar Pfungst (1874–1932) wrote the best-seller *Clever Hans: The Horse of Mr. van Osten* (1907), which demonstrated how apparent "thought reading" by a horse could be explained away if it was realized that the horse noticed small unconscious cues betrayed by his master, who was watching the human subject whose thoughts the horse was supposed to be reading. G. E. Müller's colleague, Schumann, after getting his degree at Göttingen, moved to Berlin and became Stumpf's assistant for eleven years before eventually settling in Frankfurt.

The laboratory at Göttingen under G. E. Müller was possibly the best equipped in the world. Among its apparatus, according to Krohn (1893), were an elaborate chronoscope for measuring reaction times, a voice key (which recorded the time elapsing between a stimulus and the response of a human voice), Schumann's memory drum, weights based on Fechner's specifications, click-producing electrical devices for psychophysical experiments, revolving drums with paper rolls on which pointers could write to yield continuous curves for various kinds of responses, a device for mixing colors by rapidly rotating color discs, and various electrical measuring instruments and other apparatus. The equipment was made good use of in G. E. Müller's own research on psychophysics. Schumann's and Pilzecker's contributions to Müller's memory research were outlined previously; it remains to add that, following further research with the list memorization paradigm, Adolph Jost (about 1870–1920) put forward in 1897 what have come to be known as Jost's laws. These are:

1. If two associations are of equal strength but of different ages, the older gains more from a new repetition.
2. If two associations are of equal strength but of different ages, the older is less diminished during the interval.

Wundt's German Students

But it is to Leipzig that we must turn if we wish to understand the spread of psychology in the late nineteenth century. Let us first describe the work of some of the German students who worked under Wundt. Ludwig Lange (1863–1963) made a distinction that at the time became a central issue in reaction time research. He discovered that if, in a reaction time task, one attended to the sensory stimulus (e.g., a light), one's reaction time was markedly slower (about 100 msec) than if one attended to the movement itself (e.g., a key-press). The distinction was thus made between sensorial and muscular reaction times. This work was reported in Wundt's *Philosophische Studien* for 1888 and was possibly the single most controversial finding about reaction times to emerge from the Leipzig laboratory. Woodworth reviewed the subsequent literature, in which not all workers corroborated Lange's results, and concluded that:

> The best explanation for the retardation of the sensorial reaction is probably very simple: in the sensorial form (the subject) is not quite so ready to

act. The muscular attitude is a single-minded readiness to react, while attention to the coming stimulus diverts a fraction of the energy, the size of this fraction varying with the subject's understanding of the instructions. (Woodworth, 1938, p. 306)

Lange's research has been considered important not only as a contribution to the literature on reaction time but also as a pioneering paper on selective attention. Lange later went to Tübingen. Another Leipzig student to investigate attention was George Dietze, who in 1884 asked how many successive clicks could be apprehended in a single act of attention. The number turned out to vary with the rate of the clicks, but if they were spaced out at intervals exceeding four seconds, subjects found it difficult to group the clicks. Schumann (1890) then suggested that this was because an auditory memory image might fade away over the course of a few seconds; Dietze's study was therefore one of the first researches into auditory short-term memory. Three years after Dietze's experiment, in 1887, J. Jacobs in Britain undertook the first study of the limits of short-term memory for verbal materials such as digits: The term *memory span* was coined shortly after Jacobs used the term *span of prehension* to refer to these limits.

Other German students of Wundt pursued new fields after leaving the Leipzig laboratory. Ernst Meumann (1862–1915), who had worked on time estimation at Leipzig, traveled considerably before settling down at Hamburg. His best-known book was a popular *Psychology of Learning* (1903), in which the findings of Ebbinghaus, G. E. Müller, and others were integrated into a more general framework encompassing individual differences in imagery type and matters concerned with learning in a school environment. Emil Kraepelin (1856–1926) carried out pioneering studies on the effects of drugs such as caffeine and alcohol on mental efficiency in normal subjects: These appeared in the very first issue of Wundt's journal. Kraepelin later became professor of psychiatry at Munich, but his first major work on psychiatry appeared as early as 1883, and it was Wundt who actively discouraged him from a life of pure neurophysiological research and led him into full-time psychiatry. Kraepelin's categorization of the major mental illnesses formed the basis of present-day classifications and will be discussed in more detail in Chap. 11.

Hugo Münsterberg (1863–1916) studied with Wundt from 1882 to 1885 before moving first to Heidelberg, then Freiburg in 1889. Here he carried out some original research mainly concerned with the role of the motor system as a factor in consciousness; he showed, for example, that if the speech system were occupied in a trivial task, simultaneous memorization was adversely affected. This work anticipated certain tenets of behavioristic doctrine. William James invited him to take over the fledgling laboratory at Harvard in 1892. But instead of staying within the bounds laid down by the experimentalists, Münsterberg went on to write at great length on what we would now call applied psychology. He carried out experiments—for example, on the reliability of eyewitness testimony and on the factors influencing jury decisions—and wrote these up in a book entitled *On the Witness Stand* (1908). He did a number of studies on the best place to put advertising in a magazine and concluded that an advertisement in the upper righthand corner of a page was twice as likely to be read as an advertisement anywhere else on the page and that advertising on a page solely reserved for advertisements had a better chance of being remembered than if it was on a page that also contained reading material (see *Psychology and Social Sanity*, 1914, Chap. 7). His experiments on the acquisition of skills were reported in *Psychology and Industrial Efficiency* (1913). He advocated the scientific method for making decisions about teaching and psychotherapy.

In all, Münsterberg wrote well over a dozen books emphasizing the experimental psychologist's duty to apply his techniques in areas of practical importance. One of his last works, *The Film: A Psychological Study* (1916), has been acclaimed by art historians as the first attempt to analyze the psychological processes called into play by film; the potential of this medium was only just beginning to be recognized in 1916. In his day Münsterberg was both famous and notorious for his outspoken opinions; unfortunately, his advocacy of strong ties between Germany and America went sour in World War I, and he died rather embittered. A life of Münsterberg was written by his daughter (M. Münsterberg, 1922), and Hale (1980) has written a new appraisal of Münsterberg's importance in the development of applied psychology.

Another erstwhile experimentalist who fled the camp for the applied field was Karl Marbe (1869–1953). Marbe studied linguistics and psychology at various universities before spending a year at Leipzig, but he was an early contributor to the *Philosophische Studien*. He then went to Würzburg and was an important member of the Würzburg school (see p. 277). In 1901 he collaborated with the linguist Albert Thumb (1865–1915) in an experimental study of associations. This was not the first research on the topic: Credit for that must go to Galton (1879). But Marbe was enabled to enunciate what came to be called Marbe's Law: "The more common an association is, the faster it is given" (Thumb and Marbe, 1901/1978, p. 49). In 1905, however, Marbe moved to Frankfurt, where he established a psychological institute. From then on he was more interested in applied psychology and wrote on such diverse topics as advertising, vocational aptitudes, legal psychology, and psychological aspects of accidents. He wrote an interesting autobiography in 1936.

The most famous of Wundt's German students was Oswald Külpe (1862–1915). He worked with Wundt at Leipzig for a year and with G. E. Müller at Göttingen for three semesters before finally coming back to

Leipzig in 1886 and spending eight years as one of Wundt's right-hand men. He wrote on the will for *Philosophische Studien* and did research on reaction times as they reflected attentional processes. Külpe at this time felt the need for a short German textbook, more accessible than Wundt's *Grundzüge*, and in 1893 he published a highly influential *Grundriss der Psychologie*, translated into English by Titchener two years later as *Outlines of Psychology*. It is an invaluable summary of psychological knowledge as it was fourteen years after the founding of the Leipzig laboratory. The new researches on reaction time, Müller's contributions on psychophysics, Stumpf's work on tonal fusions, and Ebbinghaus's work on memory are all included. Like Wundt, Külpe adopted the strategy of dealing with sensations and feelings as elements to be combined into fusions and colligations. Also included are a rather positive evaluation of introspection as a methodological tool and accounts of recent discoveries on the senses. The reader can confidently be recommended to consult Külpe's *Outlines* as representing, in not too indigestible a form, the epitome of the official psychology of the 1890s.

But then in 1894 Külpe was offered a full professorship at Würzburg, where he offered advice and direction while Marbe and others did the research associated with the Würzburg school: Külpe's own interests, however, turned increasingly to philosophy and aesthetics. The work of the Würzburg school, which Külpe himself never quite managed to focus into a single written opus, finished at about the time he was called to Bonn in 1909. In 1913 he moved to Munich, where he died two years later.

This list—Lange, Dietze, Meumann, Kraepelin, Münsterberg, Marbe, and Külpe—by no means exhausts the important German psychologists associated with Leipzig, but as history progresses, their names seem more destined to survive than do the others. But in some ways even more influential than Wundt's German students were the young Americans who came to Leipzig to learn about the new science. Throughout the nineteenth century it had become conventional for young Americans who had an eye to an academic career, or even a career in law or medicine, to travel to Germany and spend a year or two studying with the eminent professors who taught there. The Americans did not always stay in one place; they would move around, and take exams, where the courses seemed most useful. In addition, they took advantage of the opportunity to see the great art treasures of Europe and attend concerts and operas. For example, more than 1,100 American students registered at the University of Göttingen between 1782 and 1910. One reason for the special attraction of Germany was that original research was stressed as a way of learning additional to the traditional lecture technique. Moreover, the German universities were reorganized in the nineteenth century to give more emphasis to science and scholarship, and there grew up a tradition of freedom from interference from governments or religious bodies that boded well only for an objective study of science or history. Leipzig had a much smaller American colony than Göttingen, but the fame of Wundt soon changed that picture, at least insofar as psychology was concerned.

Wundt's American Students

Wundt's first American student, taken on in 1879, was Granville Stanley Hall (1844–1924). Hall had had an active academic career before coming to Leipzig at the age of thirty-five. Born into a pious Protestant family in a farming community in Massachussetts he had intended to become a clergyman before finding that he preferred an academic career devoted to philosophy. Thanks to a grant from a wealthy benefactor, Hall spent a year in Germany studying philosophy before taking a position in Ohio teaching English literature and philosophy. It was at this period, possibly inspired by reading Darwin, that his interests veered even further into the scientific domain, and psychology began to replace philosophy as a contender for this interest. He went to the one place in America where, in 1876, one could learn this latest psychology: Harvard, where the young William James had just began offering lectures on "physiological psychology."

In 1878 Hall obtained a doctorate in psychology from Harvard with a thesis on the muscular perception of space: This was probably the first Ph.D. on a psychological topic to be granted in the United States. He immediately went to Germany, where he studied first with Helmholtz at Berlin, then with Wundt at Leipzig. At Leipzig he knew Külpe and Kraepelin and attended Wundt's lectures and seminars and also studied physiology (with special attention to the muscles). On returning to the United States he lectured on education for a while at Harvard before being offered first a lectureship in 1882, then the position of professor of psychology and pedagogy in 1884, at the recently founded graduate Johns Hopkins University in Baltimore.

It may be said that the Johns Hopkins laboratory, instituted in 1883, was the first to be consciously "founded" in the United States; unfortunately, it only survived for four years, 1883–1887, before being closed until 1903. But it formed a focus for several young psychologists who did not have the opportunity to study at Leipzig but who nevertheless made important contributions on their own to the growth of psychology in the United States. J. Jastrow (1863–1944), for example, founded the department at Wisconsin in 1888 and obtained the first *official* Ph.D. in psychology in the United States, and the young John Dewey (1854–1952), who left for Johns Hopkins from Chicago in 1894, was destined to write an article on the reflex arc that would represent a major break from the elementism of Wundt and Külpe. W. H. Burnham (1857–1941) wrote a classic series of papers on memory (1888–1889); and H. H. Donaldson (1857–1938) wrote an important work on physiological psychology entitled *The Growth of the Brain* (1895). Yujiro Motora (1858–1912) became Japan's first professor of psychology at Tokyo University, where he founded the first laboratory of experimental psychology in Japan in 1888. Clearly, then, the line of development for this sudden flowering of American psychology was: Hall with James—Hall at Berlin and Leipzig— the Johns Hopkins nucleus. But Hall did more than just found the first department of psychology in the United States. In 1887 he began the *American Journal of Psychology,* the first North American journal for the propagation of the new psychology, and in later years he founded other journals devoted to the applied topics he himself became increasingly interested in. These included *Pedagogical Seminary* (1891), the *Journal of Religious Psychology* (1904), and the *Journal of Applied Psychology* (1915).

In 1888 Hall was approached by a millionaire named Clark to become president of a new university Clark was founding in Worcester, Massachusetts. Once again Hall traveled to Europe to learn as much as he could about university administration before setting up the new psychology department at Clark University, as it was named, and devoting himself to the duties of a senior administrator. One of the reasons the Johns Hopkins department had to close temporarily was that apparently Hall took both staff and apparatus with him to Clark. Once at Clark, mutual dislike developed between Hall and the founder Clark himself. Nevertheless, Hall continued at Clark for thirty-one years and was the author of such works as *Adolescence* (2 vols., 1904), *Senescence* (1922), and an interesting *Life and Confessions of a Psychologist* (1923).

At Clark, Hall arranged two conferences that were to have wide repercussions. In 1892 he invited a number of the best-known American psychologists to a meeting at which was founded the American Psychological Association; charter members included Jastrow, Burnham, Dewey, William James, and others to be mentioned later. Then in 1909 he arranged for a number of distinguished Europeans to lecture briefly at Clark: They included William Stern and two young doctors destined to reshape psychological thinking in its entirety, Sigmund Freud and Carl Jung (see Chap. 11). Hall's interest in Freud and Jung stemmed from his dual interests in developmental psychology and sexology, interests that were evident in his careful examination of the psychology of puberty in his *Adolescence.* But later he became disenchanted with the single-minded focus on sexuality that psychoanalysis represented (Ross, 1972, p. 399). That the Clark department was particularly well known for its child psychology is also illustrated by the fact that two of its Ph.D. students went on to establish themselves among the foremost child psychologists of the early decades of the twentieth century, namely L. M. Terman (1877–

1956) and A. L. Gesell (1880–1961). It must not be forgotten that Hall, despite all his works of administration, editing, and conference organizing, was first and foremost a researcher predominantly interested in human motives as expressed (with particular force during adolescence) in sexual and religious aspirations. This preoccupation with the development of the psyche in turn rested on an acceptance of evolutionary principles. Hall professed his own aim at the height of his interest in child psychology to be as follows:

> To contribute ever so little to introduce evolutionary concepts into psychology, when they were practically unknown, and to advance the view that there were just as many rudiments and vestiges in our psychic activity and make-up as in our bodies and that the former was just as much a product of slow evolutionary tendencies as the latter, comprised about all my insight and ambitions. (1923, p. 306)

Ross (1972) has written a biography of Hall in which his contribution to the growth of the study of children in North America is clearly brought out.

Wundt's first official assistant was also American. James McKeen Cattell (1860–1944), after graduating from Lafayette College, spent the years from 1880 to 1882 studying abroad, incidentally making the acquaintance of Lotze and Wundt. He then returned to America for a year's study at Johns Hopkins. He worked under Hall for one semester. It was during this period that Cattell began to take an interest in individual differences in cognitive capacity. When he returned to Leipzig in 1883, he began experimentation on a topic dear to Wundt's heart, the measurement of the time it took to make discriminations between stimuli that were presented very briefly, along with the related topic of the time it took to identify pictures, letters, or words presented very briefly.

Cattell did a number of pioneering studies on the identification of briefly exposed stimuli, showing, for example, that a picture could be perceived with a shorter exposure time than a word, but it took longer to actually name a picture than a word. He also showed that if four or five letters formed a word, they were identified more quickly than if they did not. Cattell published some of this work in Wundt's journal, but also published some of it in English in the British journals *Brain* and *Mind*. He was also complimented by Wundt, who asked Cattell to serve as his assistant. Cattell was not only busy doing research on word identification, he also was one of the first to collect norms of word associations, establishing what were the most common associations to various stimulus words. One of the most useful sources of references for understanding Cattell's experiences at Leipzig is contained in his correspondence, recently edited by Sokal (1981). Cattell subsequently went to England, and his work there will be mentioned in Chapter 12.

After obtaining his doctorate with Wundt in 1886, Cattell lectured at the University of Pennsylvania and Bryn Mawr (1887), and after a trip to Britain he founded a laboratory of psychology at Pennsylvania in 1888. He stayed there for three years, during which he did research on psychophysics with G. S. Fullerton (1859–1925). In this research they criticized some of Fechner's methods and made a rigorous attempt to deal with the variability of subjects' responses. In 1891 he left the Pennsylvania department in charge of another Wundt student, Lightner Witmer (1867–1956), and founded a new department at Columbia University in New York City. He stayed there until 1917, watching it become one of the most important centers of experimental psychology in the world. He himself became involved in mental testing, but he also found time to organize, with Baldwin (see following), a new journal entitled *Psychological Review* in 1894. He lost his position at Columbia in 1917, partly because he aroused controversy by asserting that professors should have more of a say in the administration of the university, partly because of his pacifist stance in World War I, but he then devoted himself to editing and organizing various journals of general scientific interest, notably *Scientific Monthly* and *Science*. He became, in essence, a psychological consultant for the remaining years of his life. At his death in 1944 he could fairly be called America's "senior psychologist" (Boring 1950, p. 535). Sokal (1971) has published a short autobiographical sketch written by Cattell at the age of seventy-six.

The third great organizer in the formal development of psychology was James Mark Baldwin (1861–1934). After graduating from Princeton, he spent 1884 to 1885 at Berlin and Leipzig, where he acquired the "new psychology." But he was also a keen enthusiast of the theory of evolution and was acquainted with developments in psychopathology, particularly in France. He then became instructor at Princeton in modern languages, where he also obtained his Ph.D. in philosophy (1885–1887); professor of philosophy at Lake Forest University near Chicago (1887–1889); professor of metaphysics and logic at Toronto in Canada, where he founded the first laboratory of experimental psychology in that country (1889–1893); professor of psychology at Princeton, where he again founded what would become a famous laboratory (1893–1903); professor of psychology at Johns Hopkins, where he revived the laboratory that had lapsed after Hall's departure to Clark. He was, however, more active in philosophy than in experimentation during his years at Johns Hopkins (1903–1908). He was forced to leave Johns Hopkins and went to Mexico to advise on the founding of the National University there (1908–1913) and finally to France, where he taught at a school for social studies and where he died in 1934.

While at Princeton Baldwin founded, with Cattell, the *Psychological Review* and two related journals, the *Psychological Index* (now *Psychological*

Abstracts) and *Psychological Monographs*. In 1904, while at Johns Hopkins, he founded a journal devoted to review articles, the *Psychological Bulletin*. His early *Handbook of Psychology* in two volumes (1889 and 1891) was a highly abstract and speculative work reminiscent of Bain rather than Wundt; the second volume included a complicated classification of the "feelings." But his *Mental Development in the Child and the Race* (1895) should be recognized as a landmark work, first, because it included experiments with children in which strict experimental methodology was applied to the study of color perception and the growth of handedness in infants and, second, because it took full cognizance of the theory of evolution. We shall deal with this book in more detail in the following chapter. Another major work edited by Baldwin was a vast *Dictionary of Philosophy and Psychology* (1901–1902). He also wrote a *History of Psychology* (1913) and a popular work, incorporating much child psychology, *The Story of the Mind* (1916).

In the above we have used the term the *new psychology*. *The New Psychology* was in fact the title given by our next Wundt student, Edward Wheeler Scripture (1864–1945), to a short but widely used laboratory manual published in 1897. Scripture obtained his Ph.D. with Wundt in 1891 after having spent time not only at Leipzig but also at Berlin with Ebbinghaus. In 1892 after a year in Hall's department at Clark, he was invited to become instructor of experimental psychology at Yale in a new department founded by Ladd. Scripture's experiences with experimental research led to the publication of his manual and also to a series of *Studies from the Yale Research Laboratory*. In 1903, following a wrangle with Ladd, Scripture was obliged to resign and moved to Europe, where he took a medical degree from Munich in 1906. He then spent a short period in Cattell's department at Columbia (1909–1914); his later life was devoted to the study of the neurology, pathology, and acoustics of speech. He did research on these topics in London and Vienna.

Scripture was replaced at Yale by Charles Hubbard Judd (1873–1946). Judd had obtained his Ph.D. with Wundt in 1896. But even Judd only stayed at Yale for six years, moving to become director of the Psychological Laboratory at Chicago (which had been founded by C. A. Strong in 1892–1893). Judd in 1907 wrote a general textbook of psychology; he also did research on a variety of topics connected with learning. He is perhaps best known for his studies of transfer—that is, his studies of how prior learning can facilitate or hinder new learning. He showed in particular how the learning of a principle can facilitate the learning of even a difficult motor skill: Boys who were taught the principles of refraction were better able to hit targets lying under water than were boys not so taught (Judd, 1908). He also did fundamental research on eye movements using the new device of cinematography. From 1909 to 1938 Judd was in charge of the Department of Education of Chicago and wrote several books on educational psychology.

The new psychology was spread to California in part by George Malcolm Stratton (1865–1957). After studying at Yale and the University of California at Berkeley, he spent two years with Wundt, returning to California in 1896. In the following year he published the results of research in which subjects wore a system of lenses that made the world appear upside down (or to put it more accurately, presented the retina with a noninverted image). This work demonstrated how adaptation to unusual perceptual environments could take place; in describing his difficulties in adjusting to his new perceptual world, Stratton had frequent recourse to Lotze's concept of local signs. In 1899 he established the psychological laboratory at Berkeley and, apart from four years at Johns Hopkins (1904–1908), remained there for the rest of his life. Among his later contributions was a translation of Theophrastus on the senses.

Another Wundt student was Howard Crosby Warren (1867–1934). After study in Leipzig he returned to his old *alma mater* Princeton, where he was appointed demonstrator in psychology under Baldwin. He remained, in increasingly senior positions, at Princeton for the remainder of his life and saw an independent department of psychology first established there in 1920. He is probably best remembered for his *History of the Association Psychology* (1921), still an invaluable reference source.

We may also mention the name of Frank Angell (1857–1939), who obtained his doctorate with Wundt with a thesis on the estimation of sound intensities in 1891. He was then invited to become assistant professor at a new, but large and well-endowed college, Cornell University in northern New York state. He was only there for a year before being invited to become head of another newly established department at Stanford University near San Francisco, where he stayed from 1892–1922. He had an outstanding reputation as a scholar and lecturer and remained a close friend of Külpe, whom he had met at Leipzig.

But Wundt's most famous student was probably Edward Bradford Titchener (1867–1927). In fact, Titchener was not American, but English. He studied philosophy and related topics at Oxford, where he became acquainted with the writings of Wundt. He even translated the third edition of the *Grundzüge* into English, although this was never published. When he went to Leipzig to take his doctoral degree, he helped Külpe plan the latter's *Outlines* (later translating this into English as well) and made friends with Meumann and Frank Angell. After obtaining his doctorate in 1892 with a thesis entitled "On binocular effects of monocular stimuli," he taught biology for a summer at Oxford but then received an invitation from Angell to take over Angell's position at Cornell when Angell moved to Stanford. Titchener was to stay at Cornell from 1892 until his death thirty-five years later. He became the chief representative in North America of Wundt's experimentalism at a time when many of Wundt's other students were turning to applied psychology.

As a scholar, particularly of psychological trends in Germany, Titchener had no peer. We may quickly list some of his many books and articles. His first work was a short *Outline of Psychology* (1896), which, like the book of the same title by Külpe, was notable for its emphasis on experimental methods. But from the start Titchener makes it clear that introspection as well as measurement is crucial in experimentation. Wundt, we recall, had argued against introspection because it was of necessity contaminated by being reliant on memory. Titchener argued that one could get around this problem by working with memory at its most recent and most vivid. The main body of the book is an account of the results of recent research on sensation, feelings, intellectual processes, and reaction times; the level is fairly elementary. This was followed two years later by another general guide to the twin contributions of philosophy and experiment to psychology, the *Primer of Psychology* (1898). It is notable for its use of questions and exercises for the student and its inclusion of a chapter on abnormal psychology.

It will be recalled that Wundt had divided his treatment of the psychological elements into those of sensations, feelings, and compounds. Titchener, for most of his life, believed that the subject matter of psychology was consciousness and that the analysis of conscious processes, using the tools of introspection and measurement, was the task of a scientific psychology. In 1898 he wrote an article in the *Philosophical Review* in which he stressed the idea of this kind of analysis of the structure of consciousness and contrasted it with analysis concerned not merely with *what* was in consciousness but also with *why* it was in consciousness. This latter approach he called *functional*. It was one of his first controversies and it lasted for much of his lifetime, for others believed that the structuralist approach was sterile in comparison with the approach that related mental to other kinds of function in the organism. The chief representative of the functional outlook was Frank Angell's cousin, James Rowland Angell (1869–1949), who in 1903 published an article, also in the *Philosophical Review*, putting forward the advantage of functionalism.

The whole issue of structuralism versus functionalism, which certainly preoccupied American psychologists during Titchener's lifetime, never quite died away because the word *functionalist* came to apply very broadly to the work of many psychologists (particularly at Chicago and Columbia) during the first thirty years or so of the twentieth century. Structuralism on the other hand may be said to epitomize Titchener's approach and, with certain qualifications, the approaches of Wundt and Külpe's *Outlines*. Both Wundt and Külpe stressed sensations and feelings as elements; but Wundt, as we saw on p. 208, was hesitant about the value of this way of talking. Külpe clearly adopted the elementist language, however, and for that reason should be treated as a structuralist. The historian of this period of psychology has to make a difficult decision concerning how much emphasis to give to the structuralist-functionalist controversy. Rather than break the flow of the narrative to discuss the matter in detail, we have outlined the main events in the argument in an appendix at the end of this chapter.

In the late 1890s this was not Titchener's only controversy. There was also a dispute with Baldwin on the matter of sensorial versus muscular reaction times. Titchener wished to emphasize the generality of the superiority of the muscular reaction time; Baldwin wished to emphasize individual differences associated with the distinction. Like Wundt, Titchener had little interest in individual differences; like Cattell and other Americans, Baldwin preferred to stress them.

Titchener will perhaps best be remembered, however, for his *Experimental Psychology*. This large work in four parts treated "qualitative" and "quantitative" psychology separately for students and instructors. It appeared between 1901 and 1905. For students, Titchener gave fine details on how to perform experiments both qualitative (e.g., on color mixing, muscular sensations) and quantitative (e.g., on psychophysics and reaction times). The instructor's manuals are highly advanced discussions of the available literature on each topic; in fact, they constitute the single most erudite source on early psychology, particularly psychophysics, in the English language. If one wants to know what Fechner added to what he said in the *Elements*, how G. E. Müller, Wundt, and others elaborated on the psychophysical methods, or the exact numerical values of the various thresholds, the Instructor's Manual is the work to turn to. It is also a gold mine for the historian interested in early apparatus such as the Hipp chronoscope, the standard equipment used in reaction time studies for many years; apparatus is profusely illustrated. Titchener did a great service in making the results of contemporary psychophysics available to non-German readers. But already his isolation was beginning to show itself: Many of his colleagues were moving away from the "classical" Leipzig approach.

Titchener did keep up with events in Germany. Between approximately 1901 and 1909 there appeared many papers, notably from Külpe's Würzburg department, concerned with thought processes. These made extensive use of Titchener's own recommended method, introspection. He performed another valuable service in describing this research in detail and commenting on it, in his *Experimental Psychology of the Thought-Processes* (1909). Also, Wundt's tridimensional theory of feeling and his general concern with apperception led to a formidable amount of quasi-philosophical polemics in the literature: This Titchener summarized in his *Psychology of Feeling and Attention* (1908). In the former book, Titchener argued against some of the doctrines of the Würzburg school (see Chap. 8); in the latter book, on introspective grounds, he failed to agree with Wundt that feeling had more than the single dimension of pleasantness/unpleasantness. Thus he was caught up in two more controversies.

The old *Outline* of 1896 was considerably elaborated and revised in his *Textbook of Psychology* (1909–1911). The level is still elementary, but whereas the *Outline* had been 368 pages long, the 1911 issue of the *Textbook* has 552 pages. There is relatively little on psychophysics and reaction times but a great deal on sensations and perception. Under "attention" Titchener discusses Wundt's theory that attending involves a clear focus and a nebulous margin in the "periphery" of "conscious awareness"; an early tachistoscope is also described in this section. Under "association" Titchener asserted his belief that the usual laws of contrast, similarity, and contiguity can be reduced to a single law; in his words, "wherever a sensory or imaginal process occurs in consciousness, there are likely to appear with it (of course, in imaginal terms) all those sensory and imaginal processes which occurred together with it in any earlier conscious present" (1911 edition, p. 378). Under "retention" Titchener described experiments along the lines of those carried out by Ebbinghaus and G. E. Müller. Under "emotions" there is a critical discussion of Wundt's tridimensional theory, and under "thought" some general remarks concerning the difficulties of using the introspective method in this domain. But the basic framework for the *Textbook* remained unchanged from that of the *Outline:* The main method of psychology is still introspection; its subject matter is the analysis of conscious experience into elements, or rather, elementary processes, of which Titchener believed there were three kinds—sensations, images, and affections.

It should be said, however, that in the *Textbook* Titchener outlined in detail many developments in the areas of sensation and perception that we have not yet discussed. These matters will be raised in Chap. 12, but we may note that they include the following: the discovery that separate parts of the skin seem to subserve separate sensations of warmth, cold, pressure, and pain; the discovery that sensations such as giddiness and those generally associated with balance were related to certain parts of the inner ear; the discovery that the two kinds of cells in the retina, the rods and cones, had different functions, with the rods mediating sensations of brightness and the cones mediating sensations of color; and the beginning of retinal chemistry. These were the major new events in the history of research relating to the special senses in the period from 1879 to about 1910. It should also be noted that the *Textbook* included very little physiological or comparative psychology. However, it has been said that the *Textbook* "is the only book in which Titchener's psychology is worked out to the end and put together between two covers" (Boring, 1950, p. 416).

From 1910 to his death seventeen years later Titchener was less active in original experimentation and textbook writing. But he continued to ponder the system outlined in the *Textbook,* and there is some reason to believe that he began to shift his ground during this period. Evans (1972), for example, has documented evidence that Titchener no longer saw sensations as satisfactory elements in their own right but rather preferred to think of experience as having dimensions such as quality and intensity, with individual experiences being described in terms of attributes along such dimensions. Introspection also played less of a part in this new way of thinking. Henle (1974) has shown how Titchener became increasingly dissatisfied with the notion that feelings were elements and began to think they could be reduced to sensations. It is possible that all this might have been made clear in a large work Titchener was reputedly planning, but it never appeared. There was a short late work entitled *Systematic Psychology: Prolegomena,* which was published two years after his death. In this he critically summarized and appraised the writings of yet another group of German psychologists who otherwise might have been ignored in the English-speaking world; they are Brentano, Lipps, Witasek, and others; we shall discuss their ideas in the following chapter. The question of concern to Titchener in this book was the question also raised by Wundt in the context of his writings on psychic causality: What is it that makes a psychic experience similar to or different from an object in the external world? The persons just named gave varying answers. Here also we find an expression of the view that feelings might be reduced to sensations.

Another of Titchener's achievements in these late years was the editorship of the *American Journal of Psychology* from 1921 to 1925. Titchener was also active in organizing conferences of a group calling itself simply the "Experimentalists"; in 1929 it was transformed into the prestigious Society of Experimental Psychologists. This group was a forum for the expression of new views on psychology, but Boring (1967) tells us how animal psychology, child psychology, and social psychology were, to Titchener's mind, taboo subjects. During all his life he supervised doctoral students: His first Ph.D. student, Margaret Washburn (1871–1939), later contributed to a study of animal behavior and wrote an imporant book, *Movement and Mental Imagery* (1915), in which she tried to give a coherent account of how images are conscious events whose origin lies in a subtle development of the motor system. The book was unfairly neglected during the heyday of behaviorism. Margaret Washburn became president of the Americal Psychological Association in 1921 but was not the first woman to achieve this status—Mary Calkins, who will be discussed in the next chapter, held the position in 1905.

Edwin G. Boring (1886–1968) obtained his Ph.D. with Titchener in 1914 and went on to become the best-known historian of the origins of experimental psychology with his *History of Experimental Psychology* (1929, revised 1950). J. P. Guilford graduated in the year of Titchener's death; he later became well known for his contributions to psychological testing and the analysis of intelligence. But throughout his life Titchener maintained the standards of the older Leipzig tradition; he did indeed differ from Wundt in his emphasis on introspection, but in other respects, including his domination of his laboratory, his extraordinary scholarship, and his dedication to general experimental psychology, he was Wundt's successor.

This brings to an end our selective discussion of those who propagated the Wundtian psychology and the new experimentalism from Leipzig and other German centers. That the Americans from Leipzig exercised considerable influence on organized psychology in the United States may be seen from the fact that so many became presidents of the American Psychological Association: Hall (in 1892 and 1924), Cattell (1895), Baldwin (1897), Stratton (1908), Judd (1909), and Warren (1913). To give a bird's eye view of the beginnings of individual laboratories we may note the main foundings in chronological order: Leipzig (Wundt, 1879), Göttingen (G. E. Müller, 1881), Johns Hopkins (Hall, 1883), Berlin (Ebbinghaus, 1886), Pennsylvania (Cattell, 1887), Toronto (Baldwin, 1890), Columbia (Cattell, 1890), Cornell (F. Angell, 1891), Yale (Scripture, 1892), Stanford (F. Angell, 1893), Princeton (Baldwin, 1893), and California (Stratton, 1896). Many other laboratories were of course established in North America and Europe during this period. A more complete listing of laboratories founded before 1900 is given by Sahakian (1975, p. 138), and a listing of North American laboratories founded before 1928 is given by Garvey (1929). Hilgard (1987, p. 32) has a chart showing where the founders of the American departments obtained their degrees and under whom: The importance of Wundt and Hall are clearly demonstrated here.

The new psychology also had its effect in Great Britain, although it was some time before the tradition of philosophy was replaced by an experimental approach. James Sully (1842–1923) occupied the Chair of Logic and the Philosophy of the Human Mind at the University of London from 1892 onwards and wrote several widely read texts. He was also responsible for the founding of the British Psychological Society in 1901. James Ward (1843–1925) taught psychology at Cambridge and encouraged the foundation of a laboratory there in 1897; its first organizer was W. H. R. Rivers (1864–1922), who was joined by C. S. Myers (1873–1946) in 1904. G. F. Stout (1860–1944) also wrote influential textbooks. These men were influenced by the German quite as much as by the British associationist tradition; in fact, they were often critical of the latter.

It has been impossible to write the present chapter without reference to certain topics that must now be covered in more detail. First, there were some important U.S. psychologists, notably William James, who did not study for a doctorate in Germany at this period. Second, we mentioned the influence of the theory of evolution when we discussed Hall and Baldwin: The matter needs amplification. Third, we have indicated that there were other psychologists in Germany—notably, the members of the Würzburg school—who made important contributions to psychology in the late nineteenth and early twentieth centuries. The following chapter is devoted to these matters.

Appendix: "Structuralism" versus "Functionalism"

In 1884 William James was writing about the problem of introspection and stressed in particular that when we introspect we often seize on a small thought experience that is part and parcel of a smooth flow or stream of thought and then mentally dissect it out. This in itself, argued James, was to prepare the way for error: It gave a sort of pseudothingness to an image or a sensation, whereas images and sensations are in fact indissectible from the stream of consciousness. If we claim to be able to dissect out a mental image or sensation, we often find it seems to have a fringe of vagueness about it: It is rarely complete in itself. The fringe has meaning tone, so much that we may care to call the image plus the fringe a feeling. It is thus possible to distinguish between two aspects of mental facts, a structural aspect in which we are talking about a feeling or "peculiarly tinged segment of the stream" (1884a) and a functional aspect in which we consider the context of the mental fact, its truth, its intellectual bearing. This was the first distinction between the terms *structural* and *functional* as applied to the discussion of mental processes.

Despite James's warning, the notion that there were certain elemental processes—sensations, images, feelings—that constituted the stuff of consciousness continued to be propounded by writers of the 1890s such as Külpe, Ebbinghaus (in his *Grundzüge),* and Titchener. In 1898, at a time when psychology was self-consciously trying to emulate the other sciences, Titchener tried to show that, if we adopted a certain viewpoint, psychology could be seen as "an exact counterpart" of biology. In biology we can consider the structure of an organ or tissue and then ask what its function is in the life of the animal. In psychology, argued Titchener, we can likewise examine the structure of mind, with the aim being "to ravel out the elemental processes from the tangle of consciousness" (p. 450), or alternatively, we can study the mind as a "collective name for a system of functions of the psychophysical organism," (p. 451). Among the functions of mind are memory, recognition, imagination, conception, judgment, attention, apperception, volition, and other "verbal nouns."

Clearly, psychology studies both structure and functions, but in the case of the latter there is the risk of a reversion to the old faculty psychology and also a risk that psychological explanation will become "teleological." By this Titchener meant that investigations would fail to study, say, memory as it is but instead ask what its purpose is and sink back into those philosophical meanderings from which experimental psychology had so recently escaped. So, given the early stage of the development of the science Titchener was concerned with, he preferred the more rigorous, if slightly less thought provoking, structural approach. Most of the 1898 article was devoted to a close discussion of the number and nature of the elemental processes of mind.

But Titchener did not argue that the functional approach was useless; he argued that it was premature. In a subsequent rejoinder to a critic, Titchener (1899) amplified the distinction to include the famous sentence "Introspection, from a structural standpoint, is observation of an is; introspection, from the functional standpoint, is observation of an Is-for" (p. 291). To introspect along the latter lines, looking for meanings and values, was according to Titchener a misapplication of the useful tool of introspection. But Titchener reiterated that the distinction between structural and functional psychological approaches was simply to reinforce the analogy between psychology and biology: It was "no more than a working schema, by which one's present knowledge may be temporarily arranged: a schema to be ruthlessly discarded as soon as a better is proposed" (Titchener, 1899, p. 297).

However, Titchener's insistence that the distinction should be temporary was apparently ignored by several psychologists who, unimpressed by the attempt to dissect mind into elemental processes and unpersuaded that that should form the foundation stone of a scientific psychology, turned instead to experiment and to the broad study of such abilities as memory in developmental and comparative contexts as well as in the adult human. The spokesman for the rebellion against Titchener's belief was James Rowland Angell. In 1904 he wrote a book entitled *Psychology: An Introductory Study of the Structure and Function of Human Consciousness.* His first words in the Preface were:

> Psychologists have hitherto devoted the larger part of their energy to investigating the structure of the mind. Of late, however, there has been manifest a disposition to deal more fully with its functional and genetic phases. To determine how consciousness develops and how it operates is felt to be quite as important as the discovery of its constituent elements.

The book was a broad survey of the field, including many references to developmental aspects of mind. In the previous year Angell had also written an article in which he pointed out that a structural approach delimits the subject matter of psychology to the extent that psychology is more or less self-contained, but a functional approach relates psychology not only to the biological sciences but also, because of the questions of "truth" and "meaning" and "value" raised in the course of a functional enquiry, relates psychology to various branches of philosophy. Titchener, it would seem, was anxious to see psychology stand alone; Angell preferred to be less bounded, with links to other disciplines.

In 1906 Angell was elected president of the American Psychological Association; his presidential address was entitled "The Province of Functional Psychology." Here he outlined three aspects of functionalism, a school of thought Angell claimed had "a higher degree of self-consciousness" and "a more articulate and persistent purpose" than had hitherto been recognized. The three aspects were (1) an attempt to analyze not so much the "contents" of consciousness as the "operations" of consciousness; (2) an outlook that incorporated extrapsychological ideas such as those of the theory of evolution and brought the psychologist "cheek by jowl with the general biologist"; and (3) a stress on the interaction of body and mind; the psychology of consciousness was not to be divorced from physiological psychology. "Functional psychology," then, covered a much broader spectrum of enquiry than did the "structural" psychology of Titchener. Furthermore, Angell's remarks were welcome to many of the young experimentalists in North America who, for example, were interested in studying learning processes not only in college sophomores but also in animals, and not only by the introspection method but also by more objective methods. Insofar as a student was doing experiments, believed that the psychology of children and animals was an essential part of the total corpus of psychology, and felt somewhat skeptical about the value of the structuralist positions on sensations, images, and feelings: Insofar as he held these views, he could be called a functionalist.

Since these views characterized a very large number of psychologists, particularly in North America, there is the very real possibility that the word *functionalism* could be applied uniformly to all but a few. Certainly, historians of psychology have spoken about schools within functionalism: There was "Chicago functionalism," in which the key name was Angell, with his predecessor Dewey (who emphasised the total function of the reflex arc rather than its structure of stimulus-mediation-response) and his successor Harvey A. Carr (1873–1954), who wrote an important survey of the functionalist position in 1930. There was also "Columbia functionalism" of which Cattell has been said to be a representative; the best-known members of the Columbia group were E. L. Thorndike (1874–1949), whose work on learning theory will be discussed in Chapter 10, and R. S. Woodworth (1869–1962), author of valuable textbooks and believer in the importance of motivation as a variable influencing memory and other cognitive functions. But almost any American psychologist flourishing between 1900 and 1930 could have been called a functionalist if there is evidence that he was not a hard-line structuralist.

Titchener nevertheless resisted these trends. In 1921 he divided prevailing views of psychology that were not structuralist into two kinds: functional psychology and act psychology. Act psychology was essentially a German movement we shall discuss in the following chapter. Functional psychologies were those that both described and tried to explain such phenomena as conciousness: Angell's views were mentioned briefly in this context. For Titchener, there were four main tendencies characteristic of functionalism. First, the notion that consciousness had a function as well as a structure was incontestable, but the analogy with biology that made the distinction respectable was, for Titchener, now outdated. Second, because of their stress that consciousness reflected neurological processes, Titchener felt that the functionalists narrowed the problem of consciousness too much to its relation to such entities as reflexes, ignoring the more meditative aspects of awareness. Third, he repeated his fear that functionalism courted teleology rather than causation. Fourth, this teleological attitude in turn "threatens the stability of psychology as an independent branch of knowledge" (1921b, p. 540). The psychology of the functional systems seemed to Titchener to "always appear as a half-way house on the journey to something else and not as an abidingplace" (1921b, p. 540); for example, "textbooks of functional psychology . . . tend . . . to make of psychology either an introduction to philosophy or an aid to individual and social welfare" (1921b, p. 542). Several sections of this article were reprinted *verbatim* in Titchener's final work, the *Systematic Psychology*.

When Titchener died in 1927, so did the obsession with the division of consciousness into elements and the emphasis on introspection, which is sometimes thought of as an essential aspect of structuralism, though of course this is questionable. Later writers on the matter also labeled Wundt a structuralist because of this emphasis on elements and compounds, but as we said on p. 210, Wundt, like James, was aware of the dangers of dissection of the flow of consciousness. So the structuralist "school" of Wundt (maybe), Külpe, Ebbinghaus, and Titchener, by its very demise, turned the structuralist-functionalist controversy into a historical rather than a still-living issue.

Not all of Angell's and Titchener's contemporaries were impressed with the squabble: Stanley Hall (1923), for example, could not see that the distinction was as fundamental as others made it out to be. Moreover, Angell and Titchener were wholly agreed that the subject matter of psychology was consciousness; in 1913 J. B. Watson, who had studied under Angell, would begin the behaviorist movement with his revolutionary argument that consciousness was the one thing psychology should *not* concern itself with. The word *structure* has been revived by modern cognitive psychologists but they mean by it such putative systems as "short-term memory" or "feature detector" and not what Titchener meant by it. In reading what follows the reader will be on safe ground if he realizes that many of the Americans named have been called functionalists by some historians (e.g., Sahakian, 1975, who has a chapter of nearly one hundred pages called "Functionalism in America"), even though they did not contribute explicitly to the controversy with Titchener. Sahakian even counts behaviorism as an offshoot of functionalism. In this book we will discuss the eminent contributions of American psychologists to learning theory in a special chapter focused on behaviorism (Chapter 10), but it is undeniable that they were influenced by the general functionalist mood in America in the first forty years of the twentieth century.

Titchener's death, however, not only signaled the end of structuralism but also the end of introspection as a method of psychological enquiry in America. At the end of the nineteenth century Cattell and others had done experiments with individual subjects in a relationship where the experimenter and subject could have exchanged roles and where the subject was expected to be highly sophisticated. This situation was continued under Titchener. But in the 1890s some Americans interested in memory, following the work of Jacobs (1887), had begun testing subjects in groups classified, for example, by age or sex. A survey of these experiments is given by D. J. Murray (1976). This introduced a new element into psychology, the study of psychological performance as a function of individual differences, a topic given considerable impetus by the work of Galton and other researchers interested in intelligence (see Chapters 8 and 12).

In the early part of the twentieth century, during the height of the functionalist movement, there was increasing pressure on psychologists to study memory and other characteristics in selected groups of subjects such as groups varying in educational grade or possessing a particular clinical profile. The funding for such research often came from educational or clinical institutions. Apart from testing special groups, there was also a growing feeling that important findings about such topics as memory, fatigue, motor skills, reading, and attention could be derived by carrying out experiments in which separate groups of subjects each did one experimental condition. Although in Wundt's laboratory such experiments would have been difficult, by about 1910 so many students were taking psychology in American universities that it became normal to ask these students to cooperate as subjects. One of the direct results, therefore, of the breakaway from introspection methods by the functionalists was a rise in experiments involving separate groups of subjects; by the 1930s statistical techniques were being invented that encouraged the use of group testing even more. This shift in methodology, which had both theoretical and social origins, described in detail by Danziger (1985, 1987), is one of the most striking legacies of the rebellion against Titchener's structuralism.

Summary

In 1879 Wundt founded an "institute" for the study of experimental psychology, a few rooms at the university in Leipzig. Prior to this, Wundt had studied medicine and written three major works summarizing the knowledge then available concerning psychology. The most ambitious of these works was the *Principles of Physiological Psychology*, which incorporated much of the information obtained by Wundt's predecessors such as Helmholtz and Fechner. Another key work, the *Beiträge*, included an introduction in which Wundt laid out his ideas concerning the nature of a truly experimental psychology. Wundt's general outlook was discussed under six heads: his classification of the sciences, his beliefs as to what constituted laws of psychology, his dissatisfaction with introspection, his voluntarism, his concern about the dangers of dividing the flow of mental experience into elements (despite his own contributions along those lines), and his suggestions about animal psychology, including his remarks on associations, apperception, and his tridimensional theory of feelings.

At about the same time Ebbinghaus founded a department of psychology at Berlin and G. E. Müller headed a department of psychology at Göttingen. Both of these authors made substantial contributions to psychophysics and, more particularly, to the study of human memory.

These three departments gave doctoral degrees to a number of students who then went on to head departments of their own, including some in the United States. Among Wundt's American students were Stanley Hall, who was involved in the setting up of the American Psychological Association and the *American Journal of Psychology*, and Titchener, who became the chief representative of the Wundtian tradition in the early twentieth century. Titchener especially favored introspection as a method in psychology, but he also acted as a sounding board for many of the new movements that began in his lifetime. Titchener also played a focal role in a controversy between structuralism and functionalism; many American psychologists in the early twentieth century came to think of themselves as functionalists, despite Titchener's disapproval. One consequence of the functionalist abandonment of Titchener's structuralism was a shift to group testing in the study of human psychology.

1879 to about 1910: Other Currents of Thought

8

In this chapter we shall deal predominantly with certain currents of thought that were central to the psychological thinking of the period between the founding of Wundt's laboratory and the emergence of the Gestalt and behaviorist schools in the early twentieth century. First, we shall discuss William James and other American psychologists who were not treated in detail in the preceding chapter; then we shall consider the influence of the theory of evolution, which gave rise to a number of influential writings, particularly in the United Kingdom; and finally we shall discuss certain aspects of German and Austrian psychology of the period, in particular "act psychology" and the Würzburg school.

James and His Contemporaries

Although Stanley Hall, a Wundt student, had founded the first American department of psychology, the American Psychological Association, and the *American Joural of Psychology*, all these efforts fell on fertile ground prepared by certain Americans who had not studied at Leipzig. Among these were William James (1842–1910), George Trumbull Ladd (1842–1921), John Dewey (1859–1952), and Mary Whiton Calkins (1863–1930). But even prior to the time of James, psychology had been taught in

241

American universities and colleges as part of the curriculum in theology or philosophy. Cattell had remarked that the history of psychology in America prior to 1880 "could be set forth as briefly as the alleged chapter on snakes in a certain natural history of Iceland: 'There are no snakes in Iceland' " (1898). But more recent scholarship, notably by Fay (1939), has shown that from the time of the founding of Harvard in 1636 and Yale in 1701, psychology had not been neglected.

In the eighteenth century the American Samuel Johnson (1696–1772) knew Berkeley and wrote an *Elementa Philosophica* in 1752 that ranks as a first-rate summary of the writings on psychology known to scholars of that period. After the publication of Reid's work in Scotland, the writings of the Scottish school became widely propagated by various educators; an important writer on abnormal and normal psychology was the physician Benjamin Rush (1745–1813), one of the signatories of the Declaration of Independence. In 1812 Joseph Buchanan (1785–1872) wrote the *Philosophy of Human Nature:* This book was of a marked physiological and associationistic bent. Then in 1832 the *Mental Philosophy* of Thomas C. Upham (1799–1872) of Bowdoin College in Maine provided a synthesis of the writings of the Scottish school; the work covered the topics of the intellect, the "sensibilities" (emotions, desires, morals), and the will.

Several other scholars wrote various smaller texts in this period, but a major effort at a system was offered in the *Rational Psychology* (1849) and *Empirical Psychology* (1859) by Lawrence P. Hickok (1788–1888). Hickok was a Presbyterian minister who taught philosophy in various institutes of higher education. He felt that a science of psychology could aid the pastor in the care of his congregation: To this end, Hickok offered an introspective, philosophically oriented account of the mind, with emphasis on the higher powers of understanding and reason.

There was also at this time an intense interest in "mental hygiene," a quasi-religious, quasi-medical trend towards inculcating good habits of thought suitable to a dynamic and growing new society. One work which crystallized the ideas of this movement was *Mental Hygiene* by Isaac Ray (1807–1881); Ray was a psychiatrist with a special interest in the question of the legal responsibility of the insane. Probably the most ambitious text of the mid-nineteenth century was *Human Intellect* by Noah Porter (1811–1892). Porter was president of Yale and his text, published in 1868, revealed the influence of German philosophy added to the British empiricist tradition. He argued that there should be an "inductive science" of psychology, which he defined as the "the science of the human soul." At the same time psychology was receiving more and more attention in universities, particularly at Princeton, where James McCosh (1811–1894), who had originally come from Scotland and had taught for some time in Ireland, became president in 1868. McCosh gave the subject its full weight in his courses at Princeton and ultimately published a two-volume work, *Psychology*, in 1886, which was very much in the tradition of the Scottish school.

But things were changing. In the same year John Dewey also published a *Psychology*, also intended as an introductory text, which dealt with Weber's Law and Fechner's methods even though the bulk of the work was in the armchair introspection tradition. At the end of the chapter, for example, was a comprehensive reading list including the names not only of Bain and McCosh but also of Lotze, Wundt, and Ebbinghaus. Dewey published this book just after leaving Hall's department at Johns Hopkins and going to Michigan. Although this essentially brings our account up to date, the reader should realize that there is a great deal of contemporary research on early American psychology. Some of this is summarized in a symposium on *The Roots of American Psychology* published in the Annals of the New York Academy of Sciences for 1977.

The most prolific, persuasive, and popular psychologist of this early American period was William James. He was instrumental in teaching psychology as an experimental discipline at Harvard in the 1870s, and Stanley Hall obtained his Ph.D. in psychology from that department before going to Leipzig. James's *Principles of Psychology* (1890) was an outstanding text rivaling the works of Wundt and Titchener for the attention of students and laypeople alike in the succeeding decades. For originality of thought and clarity of writing style James stands out as unique from the crowd of personalities jostling for priority as psychological innovators in the years we are discussing. We shall first give a sketch of his life and then outline the more striking of his original contributions.

Much of James's life appears to have been an odyssey in quest of an identity. This was in part because of his many interests. From his father, Henry James, Sr., William inherited an interest in religion and the questions religion tries to answer. In his early and formative years he traveled widely with his well-off family; before he was eighteen he had spent time in New York, London, Switzerland, France, and Germany, and it was only then that Henry James, Sr., settled in the town of Cambridge, Massachusetts, the home of Harvard University. William showed affinities for both the arts and the sciences: For much of his adolescence he took art lessons and was always good at drawing, and at home he did chemical experiments. His father encouraged both activities but eventually concluded that William's bent for science outweighed his talent for art. At the same time William developed, partly through letter writing, a unique fluency with the English language. His brother, Henry James, Jr., also had outstanding writing ability, which he devoted to literature; William's writing was to be mainly devoted to science, psychology, and philosophy.

Later in life William developed a number of health complaints that may have been psychosomatic, and there is a great deal of speculation in the literature that some sort of tension existed between William and his father; the two lives contain surprising parallels. For example, both had emotional crises in early adulthood that may have in part been resolved by intense intellectual work and in part by a marriage to a domestically minded person who gave them a large family that provided responsibilities and companionship. Henry James, Sr., himself may have rebelled against his own father, a successful businessman who left the family independently wealthy and free to follow their individual intellectual interests; in turn, William may have rebelled against Henry James, Sr. Henry James, Sr., acquired a considerable reputation for his writings on religion, and William in turn was to make religion the topic of one of his finest books. There is also a suggestion that the intensely moral atmosphere of the James household had a powerful effect on William's superego: He felt driven to make the best of himself. For an exposition of the theory that much of William's character was developed against a background of possible rivalry with his father, including a hidden resentment against having to give up a career in art, Feinstein's (1984) biography of James should be consulted. There are also hints that William had some sibling rivalry with his brother Henry James, Jr. (see Myers, 1986, Chap. 1). The James family has provided plenty of material for writers of nineteenth-century American social history, in part because they traveled so widely and knew so many eminent people.

In 1861 William entered Harvard intending to study chemistry, but by 1864 he had become more interested in physiology: He enrolled in the Harvard Medical School in that year. In 1865 he traveled with Louis Agassiz (1807–1873), an eminent biologist, to South America, where he spent much of his time exploring backwaters and streams of the Amazon and collecting fish, some of which were new species. But he also contracted smallpox, which left him with eye weakness and back trouble. In those days the treatment for many medical ills was to travel to European spas, with their various cures based on their native mineral waters. But while traveling from spa to spa James also pursued his reading and at one point attended courses in physiology and psychology at Berlin, where du Bois-Reymond's lectures firmly convinced him of the need for a psychology based on physiological principles. In 1868 he made a trip to Heidelberg, where he hoped to meet Helmholtz and the young Wundt. However, he only caught a glimpse of them. He returned to Cambridge, where the combination of physical ailments and lack of direction in his career led to a period of depression and what seems to have been a very intense attack of "free-floating anxiety." In 1870, for example, upset by the death of a close relative, he had a sudden vision, which he described in his later work, *Varieties of Religious Experience*, as follows:

> There fell upon me without warning, just as if it had come out of the darkness, a horrible fear of my own existence. Simultaneously there arose

in my mind the image of an epileptic patient whom I had seen in the asylum, a black-haired youth with greenish skin, entirely idiotic, who used to sit all day on one of the benches, or rather shelves against the wall . . . moving nothing but his black eyes and looking absolutely non-human. This image and my fear entered into a species of combination with each other. That shape am I, I felt, potentially. Nothing I possess can defend me against that fate, if the hour for it should strike for me as it struck for him. (1902/1958, p. 135)

This experience, the biographers agree, was important because it forced William to consider the fragility of his own ego: If he was to overcome this fear it would be by the effort of his own will, an idea he obtained in part from the reading of the French philosopher Charles Renouvier (1815–1913). As James put it in his diary for April 30, 1870:

I see no reason why (Renouvier's) definition of free will—"the sustaining of a thought *because I choose to* when I might have other thoughts"—need be the definition of an illusion. . . . My first act of free will shall be to believe in free will. (Allen, 1967, p. 168)

From now on James, like Wundt, would make will an essential part of his psychology.

His fear had a parallel in an experience his father had undergone many years earlier, which had turned Henry Sr.'s mind in the direction of religion, but Strout (1968) suggests that the emphasis and fear of losing his "self" that William experienced also had its roots partly in his discontent with the medical career in which he felt trapped. Myers (1986, p. 468) also points out that the context in which the above experience was described, in the *Varieties of Religious Experience*, indicates that one factor that helped William preserve his sense of selfhood was an appeal to God for help, a direct outcome of William's religious upbringing. It was in part through this experience that William came to recognize the very real need individuals have for a religious faith to cling to in difficult times.

Two years later the tide turned and William James was asked to teach half a physiology course at Harvard. Over the next few years, apart from occasional travel, his teaching duties expanded until by 1875 he was teaching a graduate course titled "The Relations between Physiology and Psychology." He had students do simple experiments: Stanley Hall recalled that "in a tiny room under the stairway of the Agassiz Museum, he had a metronome, a device for whirling a frog, a horopter chart and one or two bits of apparatus" (Hall, 1923, p. 218). The "device for whirling a frog" attested to James's early interest in dizziness and the function of the inner ear. Later James would actually demonstrate that deaf-mutes, whose inner ear was probably damaged, would be less prone to becoming dizzy when rotated than would hearing persons. As for the question of the priority of this as a laboratory, James wrote to Cattell in 1895 that "I, myself, 'founded' the instruction in experimental psychology at Harvard in 1874–1875, or 1876, I forgot which. For a long series of years the laboratory was in two rooms of the Scientific School building, which at last became choked with apparatus, so that a change was necessary" (Cattell, 1928, p. 433). The change came in 1890 when a new building was provided; the following year James called Münsterberg over from Germany to become director of the laboratory.

James himself seemed to dislike teaching laboratory work or even doing "hands on" research; it was as a lecturer and writer that he made his great reputation. Some reminiscences of James as a laboratory demonstrator and lecturer will be found in the *Psychological Review* for 1943: His classes were apparently open-ended rather than authoritarian, and James spoke in a down-to-earth manner that contrasted with the power and verve of his written texts.

In 1878 James contracted to write his *Principles of Psychology*, a work he thought he would finish quickly but that in fact took twelve years to complete. He received promotions within the philosophy department at Harvard in 1885 and 1889; in 1884 he wrote two important articles, one on the dangers of introspection (in which he talked of the "structure" and "function" of consciousness) and one on the emotions. In this latter paper what became known as the James-Lange theory concerning the organic concomitants of the emotions was first put forward. Passages from both these papers, and from others written in this period, were incorporated *en bloc* in the *Principles*. After the *Principles* appeared—despite its 1377 pages of text, it was an instant success—there was pressure on James to write more accessible works both for students and for teachers with some professional interest in psychology. For students he wrote the *Textbook of Psychology: Briefer Course* in 1892; for teachers, the *Talks to Teachers on Psychology* in 1899. Both of these, again, incorporated long passages taken directly from the *Principles*. So the *Principles* is the central work in James's career, including his earlier theorizing and influencing his later popularizing.

In 1889 he was given the title of professor of psychology. During the last two decades of the nineteenth century James continued to combine work with extensive travel, the latter often for health reasons—his "neurasthenia" never quite vanished. He established a correspondence with most of the major intellectual figures of the time—the list includes such psychologists as Baldwin, Cattell, Dewey, Hall, Helmholtz, Hering, John Stuart Mill, Münsterberg, Stumpf, and Wundt and such writers as Bergson, Carlyle, G. K. Chesterton, Emerson, Longfellow, Tennyson, Thackeray, Mark Twain, H. G. Wells, and of course his brother, Henry James. He developed a strong interest in psychical research and was active in the founding of the American Society for Psychical Research; he organized sittings with some of the best-known mediums of the period. He also revived his interest in the psychological factors relating to religious belief. This last bore fruit in his *Varieties of Religious Experience* (1902), one of the most scholarly and fascinating accounts of that subject in existence. He also gave an important series of lectures in 1896 on "exceptional mental states": these were a summary of his views on such topics as mental illness, dreams, multiple personality, witchcraft, and genius that fully show the extent to which the notion of unconscious or subliminal memories and perceptions had rooted itself in psychology by the end of the nineteenth century. These lectures, of which only James's notes survived, have been reconstructed by Taylor (1982).

During this period James often spent time at a country house he had bought in New Hampshire; it was while walking in the nearby hills that he may have strained his heart in 1898. For the last twelve years of his life this restricted his energies somewhat, but he nevertheless plunged into philosophy and became, with Dewey, a founder of the philosophical movement known as *pragmatism.*

A thorough analysis of how pragmatism emerged naturally from some of James's psychological speculations on the nature of knowledge has been given by Myers (1986), whose book on James's thought is the most comprehensive currently available. James, who had been worrying about the problem of the relation between the knower, the material that was supposed to be "known," and external fact, concluded that this was not a question for psychology but for philosophers. In an essay entitled "On the Function of Cognition," James asserted that no connection between the knower and the content known can be discovered by the mind: "The only relevant connection between the two is the process by which the knower verifies what he knows" (Myers, 1986, p. 292). This led James into a general inquiry into the nature of verification and, incidentally, an analysis of what we mean by "truth." From this beginning was born the philosophy of pragmatism. It cannot be summarized in a couple of sentences, but its essence is a denial that any absolute Truth or Ethic exists; instead, one should choose what to believe or how to behave in terms of how successful the belief or behavior seems to be. James wrote several books and articles on pragmatism and other philosophical topics.

Another shift in James's thinking concerned the mind-matter problem: He came to believe that all we actually possess directly are experiences and that mind and matter are concepts arising from different interpretations of raw experiences. This view was condensed in a book published after James's death, *Essays in Radical Empiricism* (1912).

When James died in 1910, Bertrand Russell wrote, "The high value of his work on psychology is universally admitted, but his work on pragmatism is still the subject of controversy" (Allen, 1967, p. 494). At his funeral one of the casket-bearers was Ralph Barton Perry, who later would edit a large collection of James's letters with biographical commentary under the title of *The Thought and Character of William James* (1935). A shorter biography that stresses James's relationships with the other members of the family, including Henry James, Jr., is Allen's *William James* (1967); a bibliography has been provided by McDermott (1967). As mentioned earlier, more on James's life can be found in Feinstein (1984); a summary is available in Myers (1986).

In discussing James's contributions, we may distinguish between those topics on which he offered a new and self-consistent opinion that has formed part of the mainstream of psychological thought and those on which he offered varying and at times contradictory opinions. The inconsistencies in James's thought have received considerable attention from later scholars. Allport has delineated this aspect of James's writings in the following remark:

> If time allowed, we could trace the productive paradoxes that characterised his own voluminous writings. In the *Principles* alone, we find brilliant, baffling, unashamed contradictions. He is, for example, both a positivist and a phenomenologist. On Tuesdays, Thursdays and Saturdays, he points in the direction of behaviorism and positivism, although he seems more exuberantly natural on Mondays, Wednesdays, Fridays and Sundays when he writes about the stream of consciousness, the varieties of religious experience, and the moral equivalent for war. (1966, p. 146)

Allport himself had, in 1943, written an influential article pointing out that by seeing both sides of a question, James often succeeded in laying bare the kernel of a problem, thus making a paradox productive as opposed to merely tantalizing. Of those problems on which James was particularly consistent, however, we may note four: his work on the stream of consciousness, the theory of the emotions, his contributions to memory theory, and his theory of religious experience.

In the appendix to the previous chapter we mentioned James's view that introspection could scarcely be admissible as a scientific method because it assumed that somehow a thought or a feeling could be extracted as a unit from the flow of experience. This flow James likened to a stream. Even the concept of *now* is a vague and borderless one, argued James: If I try to capture the essence of what I am thinking right now, there is a blur of pastness insofar as I am aware of what I have just done or thought, and there is a hint of futureness insofar as I am aware of what I am just about to do. This lack of a hard edge to the present moment led James to describe nowness as a *specious* present, a term that has been adopted into general psychological terminology. James apparently did not change his opinion on this view as it was presented in the *Principles*. In his later *Talks to Teachers* he explicitly criticized previous writers for seeking to tease out "elementary psychical particles" from the stream of consciousness, castigating even Locke for introducing the notion of simple "ideas" of sensation and reflection. Wundt and James were agreed in the early 1890s in their dislike of the elementarism so prevalent in the laboratories of their period. On the other hand, Myers (1986, p. 64) has analyzed how James also believed that introspection was not necessarily without value. It was by introspection that James came to a number of conclusions about what is meant when we say we are "conscious" or "have a sensation." Later, however, he became skeptical of the value of these conclusions and preferred to talk about "experience" rather than "consciousness" as a framework for interpreting our sensations and feelings.

Probably the most influential of James's contributions to the mainstream of psychology is his theory of the emotions, usually called the James-Lange theory because within a year of each other James and the Dane C. G. Lange (1834–1900) propounded very similar notions. James (1884b) wrote an article in which he suggested that a given stimulus could arouse a variety of physiological concomitants, ranging from increased heartbeat to increased muscular tonus in preparation for action to a paling or blushing of the face and so on. These concomitants of a total reaction were felt *as* the emotion; we are afraid because we run, feel sorry because we cry, angry because we shiver. As James characterized it, "the bodily changes follow directly the PERCEPTION of the exciting fact, and . . . our feeling of the same changes as they occur IS the emotion" (1884b, pp. 189–190). Lange's monograph of the following year offered a broad theory of the physiological responses characteristic of each of the main emotions; of particular importance in Lange's theory was the notion that a nervous message could constrict the capillaries near the surface of the skin, causing changes in the blood supply to the skin and the muscles. This addition to or withdrawal of blood from the skin and the muscles was associated with the pallor of fear, the redness Lange thought characterized anger, and the feeling of a glow of joy.

It will perhaps be convenient to think of the James-Lange theory of the emotions as being historically important in two ways: First, there was a major concerted attempt to bring a physiological determinism into the discussions of the emotions. This was not new—Titchener (1914a) quoted Descartes and La Mettrie as predecessors in this respect—but it made use of the great advances in neurophysiology of the nineteenth century and to that extent deserves to be called the first extended modern theory of the subject. Its central importance and value has been clearly brought out by Mandler (1979) in his historical account of empirical research on emotion in this century. The second facet, and the more controversial one, concerns James's insistence that the physiological changes often precede the cognitive aspects of emotion, much as if to deny that we ever think first and respond physically second. The fact of the matter is probably that thoughts and feelings can co-occur or alternate rapidly in experience, so that sometimes what James described does occur (much as if our unconscious acted faster than our conscious mind) but at other times there may be a delay between a perception of an object and a realization of its emotional significance. That one can act as if one is afraid even when there are no obvious pallors or tremblings is suggested by the discovery that animals deprived of the activity of the sympathetic nervous system (which mediates many of the neurovascular changes of the kind outlined by Lange) nevertheless still behave as if they were afraid of a noxious object.

The details of Lange's physiology are probably wrong, although, according to Mandler, we are still not much further ahead one hundred years later in our understanding of the physiological details of an emotional reaction. Moreover James himself (1894) defended the James-Lange theory from attacks by Wundt, among others, but even James felt that Lange's details were probably mistaken; for example, anger can make one grow pale, not redden. Feinstein (1970) has drawn attention to the relevance of James's own anxiety attacks for his development of a scientific background against which to view them. One side result of the interest in the James-Lange theory was a renewed interest in the neuropsychology of sensory deficit: If a person could not feel his heart beat, would he therefore not feel certain emotions? There was some evidence from the clinical literature that James felt supported his beliefs. In a later article, James (1894) also withdrew his more extreme claim that when we say we are frightened, *all* we mean is that we are running: He admitted that emotion has a large cognitive component as well. Nevertheless, he still maintained that the cause of an emotion is a set of bodily feelings, and he used introspection to support this claim.

On the subject of memory James made a number of contributions. His chapter on memory in the *Principles* opens with the point that for a "state of mind" to survive in memory, "it must have endured for a certain length of time" (1890/1950, p. 643). James remarked that any strong sensory impression seems to persist in the nervous tissue and that this can be thought of as "primary memory." If something has survived the passage through primary memory, it may be said to enter secondary memory, or "memory proper"—defined as "the knowledge of an event, or fact, of which meantime we have not been thinking, with the additional consciousness that we have thought or experienced it before" (1890/1950, p. 648). James's distinction between primary and secondary memory is clearly related to the modern distinction between short-term and long-term memory; in fact, James's terminology was forgotten for decades before being revived, successfully, by Waugh and Norman (1965).

On secondary memory generally, James referred to the "native retentiveness" we are born with; he believed that it is not susceptible to the beneficial effects of training. He described one of his few experiments at this point: He learned 158 lines of poetry by Victor Hugo, then spent twenty minutes a day for thirty-eight days learning the first book of

Paradise Lost; then another 158 lines of Hugo. Learning of the first Hugo passage took almost 132 minutes; learning of the second passage took over 151 minutes. There was therefore no evidence of a reduction in the time needed to learn the second passage. Other similar experiments were carried out by several of his colleagues, with the same results. The prevalent belief that learning by heart enhanced memory ability (not to mention "improving the mind") was therefore strongly criticized by James. On the other hand he believed that acquiring new means of organizing material could facilitate memorizing performance. Furthermore, he ardently advocated the acquisition of good *habits* of work and thought: By the use of the will, one could consciously develop habits that could become so ingrained as to be of positive value in one's career and to one's mental health. James described habit as the "enormous fly-wheel of society, its most precious conservative agent" (1892, p. 143): Without habit society would be anarchical. He gave a number of rules for incubating good habits—the chapter on this topic in the *Briefer Course* is still a standard set-piece for anthologizers of James.

As a final original contribution to be stressed here we mention James's theory of religious belief. Although there were intense family pressures for James to be concerned with religion, and although he regularly attended church on his way to classes at Harvard, James did not leave us an explicit statement about his own beliefs. But he never denied the importance of religion as a fact of people's lives, and he stressed that it could be a constituent of people's personalities that made them feel secure and contented. In his *Varieties of Religious Experience* he reported many written descriptions of conversion or mystical experiences and concluded that the value of religion was that it provided a solution to many problems at once—the suddenness and completion of a conversion was like the snapping into place of many links in a chain of subliminally unresolved problems. James in fact explicitly believed that there was a subliminal, or subconscious, aspect of one's self with its own emotional and intellectual needs and that these needs could be satisfied to some extent by religious faith. The *Varieties of Religious Experience* was given as a set of lectures at Edinburgh and includes much of James's later thoughts on such topics as the self and altered states of consciousness.

Of course James wrote on almost all aspects of psychology, but there is no space to do other than touch on some of those themes. On the self and its fragility, James anticipated the psychodynamic writers of the twentieth century concerned with the neuroses. On associations, he said different things to different audiences: In the *Principles* he argued that there was only one law of association: the "law of neural habit," according to which a frequently repeated act or experience led to a "drainage" of energy from one particular nerve channel to another as a regular event. However, in his *Talks to Teachers,* he separately discussed the laws of similarity and contiguity. On the will he remained, like Wundt, an anti-reductionist: In the *Principles* and in the *Briefer Course* the chapter on the will serves as a kind of climax to the work, as if James was concerned with the will not only as an intellectual matter but also as a matter of welfare for the reader. Murphy (1971) has evaluated James's views on the will in the light of contemporary psychology.

Examining James's views on the unconscious we run into one of Allport's paradoxes: In long passages in the *Principles* James found reasons for disapproving of the term, particularly as Helmholtz used it in his concept of "unconscious inferences." A critical analysis of James's strictures of Helmholtz and others is given by Fishman (1968), while an apparent self-contradiction, within a few pages, in his discussion of Helmholtz has been found by Pastore (1977). On the other hand, the concept of the unconscious, or subliminal, self is central to the *Varieties of Religious Experience*. It is also fundamental as a concept for explaining such phenomena as dreams, hypnosis, automatic writing, hysteria, multiple personality, and cases of so-called "demoniacal possession"; that list represents some of the topics on which he lectured in 1896 (Taylor, 1982). Myers (1986), summarizing James's views on the unconscious, concludes that for James the word *unconscious* validly refers to cases where items are ignored because we are consciously attending to something else, but they can nevertheless be "felt"; and to the foregoing cases from abnormal psychology, where there seems to be a secondary "self" determining behavior of which the primary self is not aware. But James was not like Freud: He did not believe in a battle of unconscious sexual forces as Freud did.

On the functions of psychology in general, James felt that Fechnerian psychophysics contributed a "dreadful literature" *(Principles,* Vol. I, 1890/1950, p. 549) and in his *Talks to Teachers* remarked that "there *is* no 'new psychology' worthy of the name. There is nothing but the old psychology which began in Locke's time, plus a little physiology of the brain and senses and theory of evolution, and a few refinements of introspective detail, for the most part without adaptation to the teacher's use" (1899, p. 7). But of course James's own laboratory and courses at Harvard were the very hub of late nineteenth-century psychology in North America. Other inconsistencies discussed by Allport include James on the mind-body problem, the objective methods of psychology, and individual differences. But few questions of interest to psychologists were left untouched by James, and even now he is worth turning to as a first step to investigating almost any topic in psychology.

The *Principles of Psychology* dealt with almost all questions of importance in psychology, but it was not a factual textbook after the fashion of Wundt's *Grundzüge*. The work that took the place of the *Grundzüge* in English was probably G. T. Ladd's *Elements of Physiological Psychology,* which appeared in 1887, three years before the *Principles*. This book represented a valuable condensation of all the new research on psychophysiology and sensory physiology, including references to psychophysics and reaction times, and a long discussion of the nature of mind and consciousness. When it appeared Hall (1887) wrote "it is at last possible to read a plain statement of the facts of a good part of the field of experimental psychology in English. . . . it is likely to be for a long time indispensable to every student of the subject not familiar with German." This indeed it did become, so much so that it was revised in 1911 by Ladd with considerable collaboration from R. S. Woodworth; the revision included references to much of the new research on human and animal learning as well as other topics, becoming in essence a handbook on experimental psychology.

Ladd himself took holy orders and preached in Ohio and Wisconsin before being called to teach philosophy at Bowdoin College in 1879. As a minister he was somewhat controversial because of his enthusiasm for the new theory of evolution—as his biographer E. S. Mills puts it, "the biological and theological theories were foremost in his mind when he decided to devote his life to a mediation between the old and the new learning" (1969, p. 97). In 1881 he moved to Yale, where he taught psychology, basing his teaching in part on Lotze and in part on Porter's text (see p. 242); and, despite his lack of training in physiology, he began the arduous work that was to culminate in the writing of the *Elements*. Ladd later wrote a *Primer of Psychology* in 1894 and a *Psychology, Descriptive and Explanatory* in the same year: Psychology was defined as the study of consciousness, and Titchener was to make Ladd's analysis of consciousness the focus of one of his late discussions of the nature of psychology (Titchener, 1929). At Yale Ladd encouraged experimentation but did little himself, bringing in Scripture (see p. 228) as a manager of the laboratory; unfortunately, there was tension between the two men, and later, in 1905, only two years before he was due to retire, the University began procedures to dismiss Ladd on the grounds that the conditions in the Department of Philosophy were "unsatisfactory." Disagreements with colleagues on university policies and a feeling that Ladd's views were old-fashioned, insofar as he himself failed to move with the mainstream into experimental work in the laboratory of psychology, combined to bring about this state of affairs. Ladd spent part of his last years traveling to the Far East, where in Japan particularly he had many admirers; he was important in spreading a knowledge of Western psychology to that country. He wrote extensively on theology, politics, and philosophy as well as on psychology.

Another courageous pioneer of early American experimental psychology was Mary W. Calkins. After traveling with her parents in Europe in 1886 and 1887 Calkins began to teach Greek at Wellesley College, a newly founded women's college near Boston. But at Wellesley it was felt there was a need to teach the new experimental psychology, so Calkins, who had expressed an interest in the subject, was asked to undertake a year of study in psychology and then return to teach it. She considered working with G. E. Müller in Germany, but women were not welcomed there; she also considered studying with Dewey at Michigan, Ladd at Yale, or Hall at Worcester. But in the end she entered the seminars of William James at Harvard; this was less easily done than might be imagined, for at Harvard women had to get special permission to attend seminars. She was not in fact allowed to register at the University. When she returned to Wellesley she founded a new laboratory there. The college catalog for 1891–1892 reports that "required experiments are chiefly in sensation, space perception and reaction times, sensational and intellectual."

In 1895 Calkins presented a Ph.D. thesis titled "An Experimental Research on the Association of Ideas" at Harvard; it was passed by James, Münsterberg, and others, although she did not actually obtain the degree. Her thesis work was in fact the beginning of research using the method now known as "paired associates" and was published in 1894. In order to examine how well an association might be learned, the experimenter arranged numbers randomly with patches of color, and the subject had to learn which color went with which number. By learning a list of these pairs the effects of variables such as recency and frequency on learning could be examined. This is Calkins's best-known contribution to experimental method; her other original contributions included extensive discussions of the nature of the conscious self. In 1905 she was made the fourteenth president of the American Psychological Association—her presidential address tried to reconcile structuralism and functionalism by pointing out that both approaches are necessary to the study of the self. She spent the rest of her life teaching and writing at Wellesley. A discussion of her psychology of "self" is given by Strunk (1972); a short account of her life is given by Furumoto (1979).

Mary Calkins is generally recognized as the first woman in the history of psychology to merit special mention, but she was quickly followed by others who attained eminence both as researchers and teachers. We have cited Margaret Washburn in the previous chapter and should also mention Lillien Jane Martin (1851–1943), who collaborated on psychophysics with G. E. Müller. One of the most noticeable trends in my own psychology department at Queen's University over the last twenty years has been the growing number of women graduating with honors psychology and graduate degrees, and it is only natural that there has been renewed interest in the contributions of women to the history of psychology. G. Stevens and S. Gardner (1982) have now written a two-volume history of the roles played by women in psychology, and they give particular credit to Calkins, Washburn, and Martin as pioneers in experimental psychology. More widely known, because of their involvement in applied psychology, were Dorothea Dix (1801–1887), the prison reformer, and Maria Montessori (1870–1952), the pioneer of the view that very young children should be encouraged to learn by constructive play. Stevens and Gardner provide a full list of eminent female psychologists, and we shall see that women played particularly important parts in the propagation of psychoanalysis.

The Theory of Evolution and Its Impact on Psychology

Wundt, Hall, Baldwin, and Ladd were all concerned to some extent with the theory of evolution. It is now time to consider this epoch-making breakthrough in our understanding of natural phenomena. The key date is 1859, the year of the publication of the *Origin of Species* by Charles Darwin (1809–1882); but the notion that the universe dated back for more than the 6000 years suggested by biblical scholarship had been developing. In geology there was evidence for more than one cataclysm, or, as we now say, glacial period. In biology von Baer (1792–1876) had shown that, as the embryo grows, certain anatomical characteristics that appear and disappear remind one of analogous anatomical characteristics in more primitive types of animal, and Malthus (1766–1874) had argued that the only way population did not explode geometrically was by a system of checks and balances including natural disasters, competition between individuals, and deliberate abandonment of the physically unfit. However, it was Darwin who had the insight of seeing that the process whereby animals can be *selectively* bred for certain characteristics (horses for speed, pigeons for particular traits, etc.) could have occurred in nature; that is, that population control could be influenced by a natural selection such that only those creatures suitably adapted to their environment would survive and, in turn, breed. However, for natural selection, with its large chance factor, to operate, eons of time would be needed, and Darwin persistently argued that the geological record we had was a very incomplete one, as was the fossil record necessary to the idea that modern living creatures traced their ancestry back to archetypal forms.

Darwin's insight was in part based on his reading of Malthus and others—there are extant several notebooks in which we see the germination of the theory of natural selection in his mind. But it was also based on the famous voyage he took around the world as a scientist on the survey ship the *Beagle*. His long forages ashore around South America and the Galapagos Islands lying off Ecuador led him to fundamental discoveries about geology, including an explanation of how fossils could come to be found thousands of feet up in the Andes; to his realization that animals in a given geographical area had characteristics in common, suggesting that they derived from some primitive stock that had concentrated in that area; and to his gradual appreciation of the fact that once a species found a niche in an environment, as did the finches and tortoises of the individual Galapagos Islands, they would successfully survive for centuries in that environment without appreciable change. In more varied environments, however, chance would play a larger part in determining the survival of individual animals, and so it could come about that a "variety" would survive and breed offspring with similar characteristics, which in turn would breed new offspring and so on until in fact we had a new "species." Darwin drew the analogy of a tree: From primitive species there would develop new varieties which, assuming the processes of natural selection (including the factor of fertility) to operate, would eventually form new branches, or species.

As subsidiary evidence for the theory that species had "evolved" from other species Darwin drew upon the evidence from embryology: The embryo sometimes shows characteristics (e.g., in humans, a rudimentary tail) that had eventually vanished in the more advanced form but that had been present in the more primitive forms from which the advanced species had evolved. At the time, the great stumbling block to appreciation of the theory was knowledge of how certain favorable characteristics could be inherited in successive members of a family line, but Mendel and others later laid down the laws of heredity, which were successfully shown, in the early years of the twentieth century, to be quite consistent with Darwin's doctrine of natural selection.

But the *Origin of Species*, in which the above ideas were put forward, offered more than just a theory about the evolution of physical characteristics down the centuries. For a species to survive, its *behavior* must be adapted to its environment. Darwin called those aspects of behavior that were apparently unlearned in animals *instincts*. For Darwin, instinctive behavior also evolved—creatures that spontaneously showed certain behavior patterns that led to successful feeding or breeding would survive. At first sight, instinctive behavior patterns such as nest building seem too complex to have been the subject of an evolutionary process, but Darwin was able to analyze certain instinctive behavior patterns into components that, he argued, could easily have been inherited and thus subject to the forces of natural selection. For example—and here, we shall be overly brief and urge the reader to consult Chapter 8 of the *Origin of Species* for greater detail—Darwin showed how the instinct for the cuckoo to lay an egg in the nest of another bird could be the result of egg-laying habits that had evolved because of their success (the young survived and the mother was able to migrate earlier by not being encumbered by her own offspring); the habit of the baby cuckoo of ejecting the other nestlings from its nest could be a side effect of a particular vigor in that large bird.

Darwin went on to analyze the slave-making habits of certain ants and the comb-building instinct of the honeybee along similar lines. He carried out certain experiments on the honeybee, for example, observations to determine how bees will start building a comb in an environment foreign to them. On the basis of these experiments, he surmised that the hexagonal cells of the honeycomb could be produced if, down the centuries, bees had simply developed the habit of digging shallow circular holes at roughly equal distances from each other. In a word, Darwin pioneered the experimental study of animal behavior as well as the development of the biological theory of evolution. In his later works he was to advance his theories in both respects.

His next work of importance to us, *The Descent of Man* (1871), took more positively a position only adumbrated in the *Origin of Species*— namely, that humans evolved as a species from primitive ancestors: remotely, some species of primate, and still more remotely, primitive marine animals. His remarks on this are, however, only a few pages long; he was more concerned with buttressing the theory of natural selection by two addenda. First, he was directly concerned to show that humans share with lower species emotions, desires, and skills that have been the subject of selection down the ages. Chapters 2 and 3 of *The Descent of Man* are titled "Comparison of the Mental Powers of Man and the Lower Animals"; Darwin agreed that the most primitive human is incredibly more advanced mentally than the highest apes, but he nevertheless pointed out that apes do use tools, possess primitive systems of communication, show emotional behavior usually thought of as peculiarly human, and act in society with enough sophistication to make it believable to us that humans are on a behavioral continuum with these lower species. This is one of the most direct statements of this belief since the time of Aristotle and did more to encourage research into animal behavior as *related* to human behavior than any single writing of a psychologist.

The second addendum concerned the mechanism of sexual selection. Of all the mechanisms of natural selection, sexual selection—the choice of mate—might have exercised the dominant influence on the development of intelligence and strength as characteristics of the higher species. Darwin worked his way through the animal kingdom showing how the males with most attractive appearances, courtship skills, and fighting ability were the ones that succeeded in most readily attracting the females and therefore of having offspring. The second half of *The Descent of Man* is a rich treasury of observations on instinctive behaviors associated with mating.

The third book of interest to psychologists is *The Expression of the Emotions in Man and Animals* (1872). Its main aim is to show that different species have evolved different ways of *expressing* fear, anger, and so on, and that one can trace more primitive emotional expression patterns in the higher species. Weeping, the raising of the eyebrows in surprise, the various contortions of the facial muscles in anger and disgust, and the curious vascular change known as blushing are all described in anatomical detail and then shown either to have survival value in their own right or to be vestiges of behaviors more directly adaptive in a more primitive environment. Underlying the theory of emotions is the assumption that strong emotion (from a real cause, such as a threatening predator) excites the "cerebrospinal" system and generates "nerve force" that can affect both muscular and vascular systems—the theory is a rough sketch of what Lange would later attempt to delineate in detail. The way in which a particular emotional expression has evolved is often very complicated, and adult expressions may be modifications of infantile expressions.

The importance of this book, from the point of view of a psychologist, is that it takes a facet of thought—namely, its emotional side—and shows how its expression may have been inherited because it once had adaptive value; again, it forces us to the conclusion that humans are not beings entirely separated from animals but are psychologically as well as physiologically similar to some of them. Of course, this signaled the demise of the notion of a soul peculiar to humans from the mainstream of psychological discourse: Darwin himself, who at one time contemplated becoming a clergyman, gradually became agnostic, and it is common knowledge that the theory of evolution was immediately seen to be a threat to established Christianity.

Readers who wish for an up-to-date analysis of the findings and beliefs of modern evolutionary theory can do no better than to read *The Blind Watchmaker* (Dawkins, 1986); for a thorough evaluation of the struggle between religion and science in Darwin's lifetime, Cosslett (1984) should be consulted. Gruber (1981) traces the slow unfolding of Darwin's own beliefs on the descent of man from animals, and on its implications for religion, through an analysis of Darwin's notebooks.

Darwin's influence on the study of both human and comparative psychology was enormous. We recall that the dominant school of psychology in Britain in Darwin's time was the associationist school (discussed in Chap. 5); Bain's *The Emotions and the Will* came out in the same year as the *Origin of Species*. Notable among British writers of associationistic leanings who adopted the new evolutionary theory were Herbert Spencer (1820–1903) and George Henry Lewes (see Chapter 5). Darwin's writings on instinct initiated a lively interest in the topic. Two key representatives of the movement to study instinctive behaviors in animals were Douglas A. Spalding (1840?–1877) and Sir John Lubbock (1834–1913). In Britain George J. Romanes (1848–1894) did more than anybody to collate the growing body of knowledge on animal behavior and to amplify Darwin on the evolution of "intelligent" behavior. Baldwin made similar efforts in America with particularly influential implications for the study of child psychology. Finally, Sir Francis Galton (1822–1911) applied the notions of heredity that underlay evolutionary theory to the problem of the inheritance of human abilities; he also had much to say about other aspects of mental performance. We shall give a brief account of the contributions of these individuals.

Probably the most ambitious was Herbert Spencer, who in a series of books given the generic title of "a system of philosophy" attempted to apply the theory of natural selection to a wide gamut of phenomena—biology, sociology, ethics, anthropology, and psychology. In fact, his belief in evolution was published before the *Origin of Species:* It was from Spencer that Darwin adopted the phrase "survival of the fittest"; and the book that concerns us most, the *Principles of Psychology,* appeared four years before the *Origin,* in 1855. Spencer had started life as a skilled engineer but eventually gave this up to devote himself to his vast synthesis of the social sciences. His first important work, the *Social Statics* (1851), drew the analogy between the physiological system of an organism, with its various organs each following a particular function, and the system of a political society. His interest in physiology, incidentally, has been shown by R. M. Young (1970) to be related to an early captivation by the phrenological movement. His interest in this specialization of functions in both organisms and societies led Spencer to a consideration of evolutionary theory; he replaced his early phrenology with an associationism that owed much to the two Mills, even though he himself disagreed with John Stuart Mill on a number of matters.

Spencer's interest in evolution and associationism was focused into a fairly coherent whole in his large *Principles of Psychology:* The first volume is essentially about the evolution of mental resources; the second about the application of mental resources, via associationistic mechanisms, to the development of such advanced concepts as inference, space, time, and motion. The second volume in fact could well have been treated in Chapter 5 as an adjunct to Mill's criticism of the intuitionistic concepts of Kant and Hamilton; Spencer, like Helmholtz who was writing his *Optics* at this time, was a pure empiricist in terms of his explanation of how we orient ourselves in space. We build up a picture of the external world through associations based on the comparison of touch sensations from various parts of our body and the movements we make that influence those sensations. In none of these sections is there much reference to evolution.

But in the first volume of the *Principles,* it is clearly laid down that the task of the psychologist is first to map the course of the development of the nervous system and its related systems (e.g., the vascular system) across the various species. He discovers in so doing that simple nervous systems, such as found in sea anemones, are associated only with reflex responses. As we move higher up the scale, brains and other ganglia develop, and these are associated with the development of simple instinctive responses based on pleasure and pain and the need for survival of the species. Still higher up the scale, the instincts become too complex to be simply automatic; along with the evolution of a larger brain comes the evolution of the capacity to reason. In humans, conscious experience is of two kinds—sensations and emotional responses; both are called feelings by Spencer. When two events co-occur, or occur successively, in the external world, the feelings representing those events are likewise related. When a feeling is revived, it reminds us of like events experienced in the past—this is the main law of association and is the direct outcome of the mapping of our experience onto the nervous system. When we recognize an object it is because the object reexcites certain nervous "vesicles" that had been excited in the past: Throughout the *Principles* the psychological events discussed are given parallels in neurological terminology.

But there is another characteristic of human conscious behavior that makes it proper that evolutionary theory be mentioned in connection with it: Not only is complex behavior the result of the evolution of a complex nervous system, it also represents a growth from a primitive, undivided "homogeneous" reactivity, as in a baby, to a mature "heterogeneous" array of abilities and propensities, as in an adult. The evolution from "an indefinite, incoherent homogeneity to a definite, coherent heterogeneity" (Spencer, 1855/1890, p. 189) that occurs in the individual's life span is like the similar evolution in the development of tissues within organisms, and organisms themselves, across the centuries. As Spencer put it, "Mind rises to what are universally recognized as its higher developments, in proportion as it manifests the traits characterizing Evolution in general" (Vol. I, 1855/1890, p. 189). It should be noted that the above account in some ways oversimplifies Spencer's system: He is far more subtle on the questions of relations *between* relations external and internal and on the importance of change as a factor affecting our behavior than this short description gives him credit for.

The advent of the theory of evolution also signaled the beginning of experimental studies into animal behavior, particularly those behaviors Darwin had called instinctive. In view of the prevalence of associationistic empiricism—one thinks of Bain, Helmholtz, and Spencer in this regard—it is not surprising that some authors should turn to the study of animals in an attempt to discover to what extent such behaviors as flying or food seeking are learned as opposed to innate. In particular, Spalding argued in a series of papers that very young animals were capable of spatial orientation and motor responding, which made it doubtful that these behaviors were the result of a slow accumulation of experience. In 1872, for instance, he showed that a chicken kept in darkness for one to three days after it had hatched could successfully catch flies within minutes of seeing for the first time. It went straight towards a hen, leaping over obstacles in its path and running around larger obstacles. Spalding wrote, "It would seem that, prior to experience, the eye—at least the eye of a chicken—perceives the primary qualities of the external world, all arguments of the purely analytical school of psychology to the contrary notwithstanding" (1872, p. 485). In other studies reported in the same paper Spalding gave evidence that sounds were meaningful to chicks as soon as they could hear and that grooming and escape behaviors might be innate in some species. In 1875 he described how piglets will seek their mothers within minutes of being born and showed that swallows prevented from flying until they were fully fledged nevertheless flew quite accurately the first time they were given the opportunity. He was also aware that some very young creatures will follow moving objects, an anticipation of the later discovery of "imprinting." Spalding's work, neglected for some time, has more recently been given its due in the history of studies of animal behavior (P. H. Gray, 1967).

Another pioneer in the use of experimentation for studying comparative psychology was Sir John Lubbock. His *Ants, Bees and Wasps* (1882) is replete with experiments designed to discover how ants relate to each other and to other species, the degree to which they recognize members of the same tribe or nest (including studies of apparent "cooperation" between ants), the degree to which ants use sight, hearing, and scent, and the degree to which their behavior is "intelligent," or adaptive. He discovered, among other things, that ants were sensitive to ultraviolet light. He was not the first entomologist to do experiments, but for completeness and ingenuity Lubbock's work is outstanding. In order to study his specimens easily, he invented a way of placing ants' nests between glass plates for observation. He also invented mazes in order to study the adaptability of food-seeking behavior, and he studied the degree to which ants could modify their instinctive behavior patterns by putting obstacles in their paths—often the ants were less "intelligent" than one might expect under such circumstances. Lubbock was also eminent in geology and botany and in his capacities as a Member of Parliament and vice chancellor of London University did much to encourage scientific research in the late Victorian period.

Lubbock's work was given a great deal of attention in a book that was one of the first attempts to provide a broad overview of the range of animal behavior, the *Animal Intelligence* (1882) by Romanes. Romanes was born in Kingston, Ontario, but while he was still a child his parents moved to Britain, where he eventually graduated from Cambridge University. At Cambridge Romanes studied physiology and first read Darwin; later he became a close friend of Darwin, and Darwin, who had compiled copious notes on animal behavior partly in preparation of the chapter on instinct in the *Origin of Species,* gave Romanes full access to these notes.

From 1874 to his death in 1894 Romanes devoted himself to the study of invertebrate physiology and to an ambitious attempt to show how the development of "intelligent" behavior in the various animal species was related to the position of the species on the evolutionary scale. With respect to the former, Romanes was a pioneer in the study of very primitive nervous systems and in the case of jellyfish was able to show that the nervous system acted as a network of functionally related, though not necessarily anatomically connected, units. This foreshadowed the later discovery of the synapse. But he is better known to psychologists for his attempt to relate psychological development to evolutionary advancement. His project had three stages. First, to outline how far animal behaviors could be said to show "intelligence"—this was attempted in his *Animal Intelligence*. Then, partly covering the same ground again, he showed how, the higher an animal was on the evolutionary scale, the more adaptive and "humanlike" its behavior became—this was attempted in his *Mental Evolution in Animals* (1883). Finally, realizing that the antievolutionists were complacent in their assumption that no evolutionary theory could explain how humans had evolved that facility making them most different from animals—namely, language—Romanes tried to show that language itself could have appeared quite naturally, given certain cognitive capacities that themselves had evolved by natural selection. This thesis was put forward in his *Mental Evolution in Man* (1888).

Romanes's *Animal Intelligence* has achieved the status of a classic, but it is not without some notoriety. It is classic because it was the first major attempt to describe the full range and scope of animal behaviors, from protozoa through insects all the way up to the primates. It is short on the lowest organisms and the primates, gaps that would be filled by extensive research this century; it is long on insects, which receive almost two hundred pages. In part this is because the work of Lubbock and others had furnished experimental data, which of course was lacking for the higher animals. For information on the higher animals, Romanes had to rely on eye-witness evidence from pet owners, naturalists, and others who, often in books of travel, had described such "instinctive" behaviors as dambuilding by beavers or such "learned" behaviors as shown by domesticated elephants in India. Romanes went to great pains to avoid hearsay and to trust only the evidence of witnesses he believed reliable; yet, he was prone to ascribe human motives such as altruism or revenge to the subject of these narratives. This approach has been called the anecdotal approach, and later Romanes came to be criticized for bordering on anthropomorphism. But in his time he had no choice but to rely on anecdotal evidence, and a reading of *Animal Intelligence* will quickly persuade the skeptic that Romanes tried to be as scientifically rigorous as possible both in selecting his material and in describing its relevance. Here is an example of an anecdote submitted to Romanes by a famous logician, Venn; it appears in the section on memory in birds:

> I had a grey parrot, three or four years old, which had been taken from its nest in West Africa by those through whom I received it. It stood ordinarily

by the window, where it could equally hear the front and back door bells. In the yard, by the back door, was a collie dog who naturally barked violently at nearly all the comers that way. The parrot took to imitating the dog. After a time, I was interested in observing the discrimination association between the back-door bell and the dog's bark in the parrot's mind. Even when the dog was not there, or for any other cause did not bark, the parrot would constantly bark when the back-door bell sounded, but never (that I could hear) when the front-door bell was heard.

This is but a trifle in the way of intelligence, but it struck me as an interesting analogous case to a law of association often noticed by writers on human psychology. (Romanes, 1882, p. 268)

In a few years students of comparative psychology would come to be quite harsh in their rejection of animal anecdotes such as this, but without such narratives Romanes could not have erected the framework of his main theory, which was that evolution had advanced through a series of stages, from the reflex to the instinct to reason, which he could trace in the successions of living creatures. From his work on jellyfish, sea anemones, and similar creatures, Romanes derived the notion that the nervous system had evolved from the purpose of conveying information from one part of an organism to the other; how it had evolved was not known in detail but in very simple one-celled animals Romanes saw evidence of discrimination (e.g., going to or avoiding light) and conductibility (the influence of events in one part of even a single-celled animal on another part). Following the development of the nervous system (neurility) there evolved the ability to sense and the ability to give reflex movement— instincts appeared at this stage.

Romanes's next book, *Mental Evolution in Animals*, is now being recognized as one of the most important books in the history of psychology because it attempted to unify all the research on animal instincts and animal intelligence into a single evolutionary scheme. The contents of much of the book are summarized in Figure 8–1, which shows the evolution of emotions, will, and intellect as a function of the place of an animal in an evolutionary scale. Note, first, that modern evolutionary theory is far less likely to consider evolution as culminating in a particular "higher" species, humankind; a modern evolutionist thinks of a brain as being one organ that has evolved to a high level in humans in particular, but does not consider this as more "worthy" in any way than the evolutionary development of, say, an echolocation system in bats. Second, Romanes indicates that he has a somewhat different view of the origin of instincts than I have mentioned so far. Both Romanes and Darwin were uncertain of the role played by *acquired* characteristics in evolution: If I learn some new skill, can I in some way pass this on to my children? The modern opinion (summarized by Dawkins, 1986, Chap. 11) is that no acquired characteristics can be inherited; the mistaken view that they can is called *Lamarckism*, after an early pioneer of evolution theory. Romanes, and possibly Darwin himself, were Lamarckian in the sense that they believed that if an animal did an intelligent act or learned a skill requiring intelligence, the propensity to repeat this skill could be passed on to the offspring. But if we overlook these shortcomings, Romanes's scheme deserves our close attention because it epitomized the new perspective from which psychology was considered after Darwin.

The chart is divided into fifty levels from bottom to top: These are numbered for convenience in four of the columns. The center shows how the primitive disposition to excitability, found in protoplasmic organisms, evolved into the nervous system, a system that had the properties of discrimination and conductability. The main trunk of the tree indicates that from simple reflex actions the "higher" animals were able to develop *volition*, or control over voluntary movements: Levels 29 to 50 presumably represent the various levels of cultural development in humans. On the left of the main trunk are branches showing how the emotions may have evolved, first as a means of self-preservation as shown perhaps in insects but, in a separate branch, as a means for the proper conduct of social relations with other individuals (leading ultimately to "civilization" in humans). At the extreme left are the individual emotions, with surprise and fear classed as basic, unsophisticated emotions (level 18), and other emotions, including sympathy, entering at higher levels. Revenge, for instance, is seen at level 27, the level of monkeys and elephants; in *Animal Intelligence* Romanes had told the story of a zoo elephant that apparently took "revenge" on somebody who fed it an unpleasant-tasting sandwich by squirting water over him. (Some animal psychologists would argue that this interpretation was anthropomorphic, but this of course was the charge often made against Romanes.)

The righthand branch from the trunk shows the development of intellectual powers. Building on a base of sensations, the powers include perception, imagination, abstraction, generalization, and reflective and self-conscious thought, the last two being purely human characteristics. Apes and dogs are presumed to be close to humans in intelligence, and the beginnings of morality are held to be present in these animals. The products of intellectual development, including the abilities to retain, recognize, and associate, are shown to the right of this branch. Note that consciousness is assumed to evolve in concert with the development of pleasure and pain and memory and to be a meaningful concept in connection with very "low" animals such as sea anemones (coelenterates) and starfish (echinoderms). In this column, marked "products of intellectual development," is, of course, the germ of an entire theory of how human consciousness evolved from primitive beginnings. Finally, Romanes speculated that the growing infant recapitulated the general sequence in the first few months of life: This is shown in the column marked "Phylogenesis of Man." According to Romanes, a fifteen-month-old baby was at about the same level of "intelligence" as an adult dog or ape, though, of course, there is a great latitude of interpretation here in what is meant by "intelligence."

Whether the details of this scheme are correct is not so important a question for our purposes as whether this scheme influenced the history of psychology. There is no question that an explosion in animal research followed Romanes. This research was focused particularly on the questions of where consciousness fits in the animal kingdom and how far acquired skills interacted with instinctive, unlearned habits in determining behavior. A fascinating and well-illustrated history of this research boom, and of the way in which research on learning gradually became separated from research on instinct, is provided by Boakes (1984). We will take up this theme again in Chapter 10 but note now that Romanes's scheme was certainly not adopted in its entirety, and may have been unfairly overlooked in the early twentieth century, because of its anthropomorphic tendencies.

Romanes had attempted to show, very briefly, that the way intelligence evolves across species (that is, phylogenetically) might be recapitulated within the individual over the first fifteen months or so of life. That is, the newborn child is presumed to have only sensations, reflexes, and the power of gross motor activity, but as the nervous system develops, so do the capacities for perception, imagination, and abstraction. The theory that phylogenetic evolution is recapitulated ontogenetically—that is, within the individual's life span—was put forward in most detail by Baldwin in a trilogy of books, *Mental Development in the Child and the Race* (1895), *Social and Ethical Interpretation in Mental Development* (1897), and *Development and Evolution* (1902). Baldwin assumed that there were two main mechanisms that assured the survival of the individual: namely, habit, which is based on the tendency of the individual to repeat movements that have brought pleasure and avoid those related to pain; and accommodation, which works against habit in the sense that each accommodation is a new act that, because of its success, leads the child to new and more inventive behaviors. Accommodation acts may arise by chance, but more often they result because a habitual act that has brought pleasure also brings with it an excess of energy or motor discharge that releases itself in the form of a new act.

This concept of the *excess of energy* resulting from pleasure was derived by Baldwin from Bain and Spencer. In turn the new accommodation acts may themselves become habitual or lead to yet further accommodations. The tendency for an act to become habitual was called the *circular reaction;* the tendency for a *stimulus* to release a circular reaction increases as the child grows older in the form of the many acts of imitation the child learns to make. Speech acquisition in particular is largely a matter of imitation. In his second book Baldwin showed how children

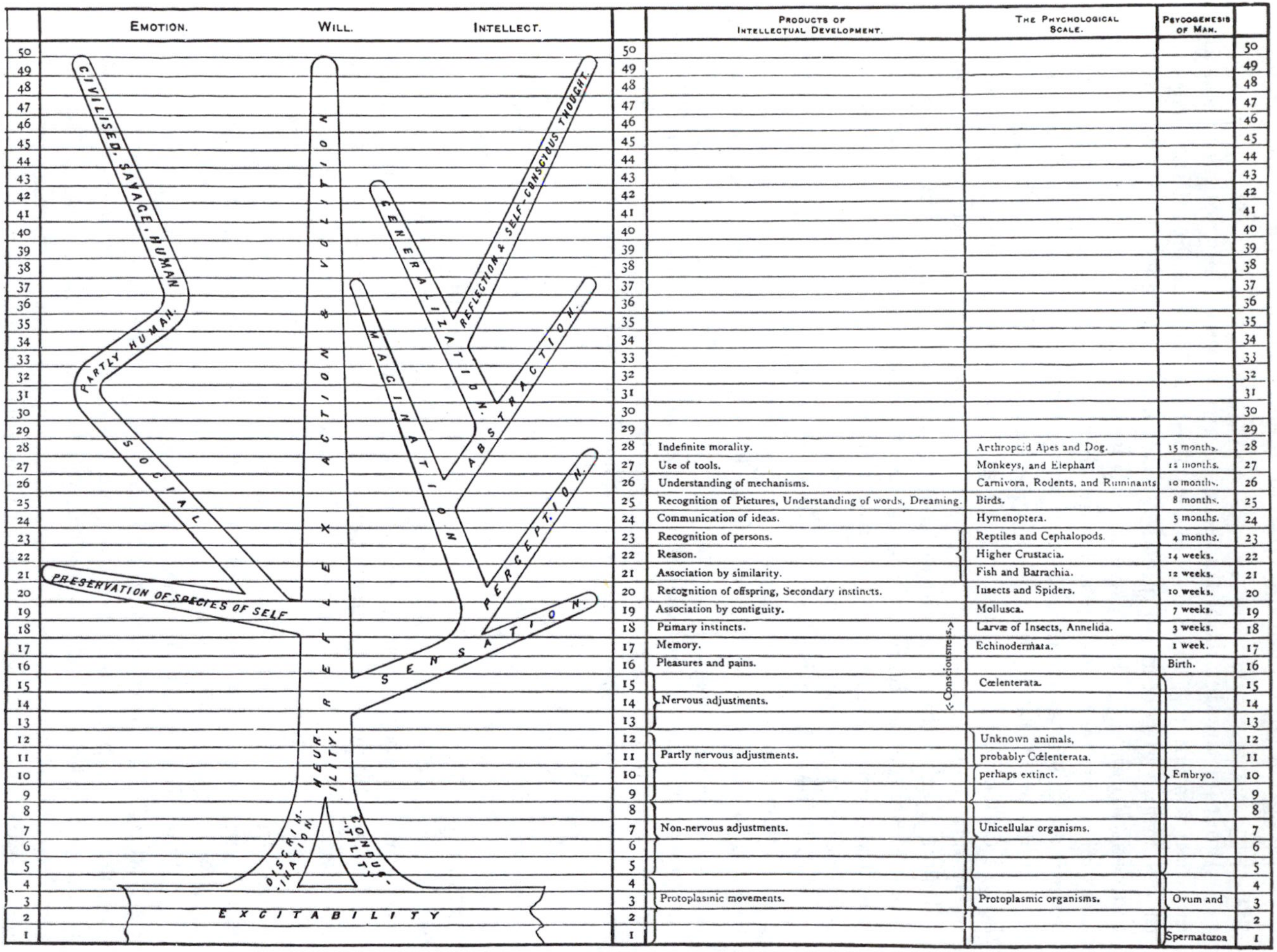

Figure 8–1 Romanes's Chart of the Evolution of Intelligence in Animal Species.

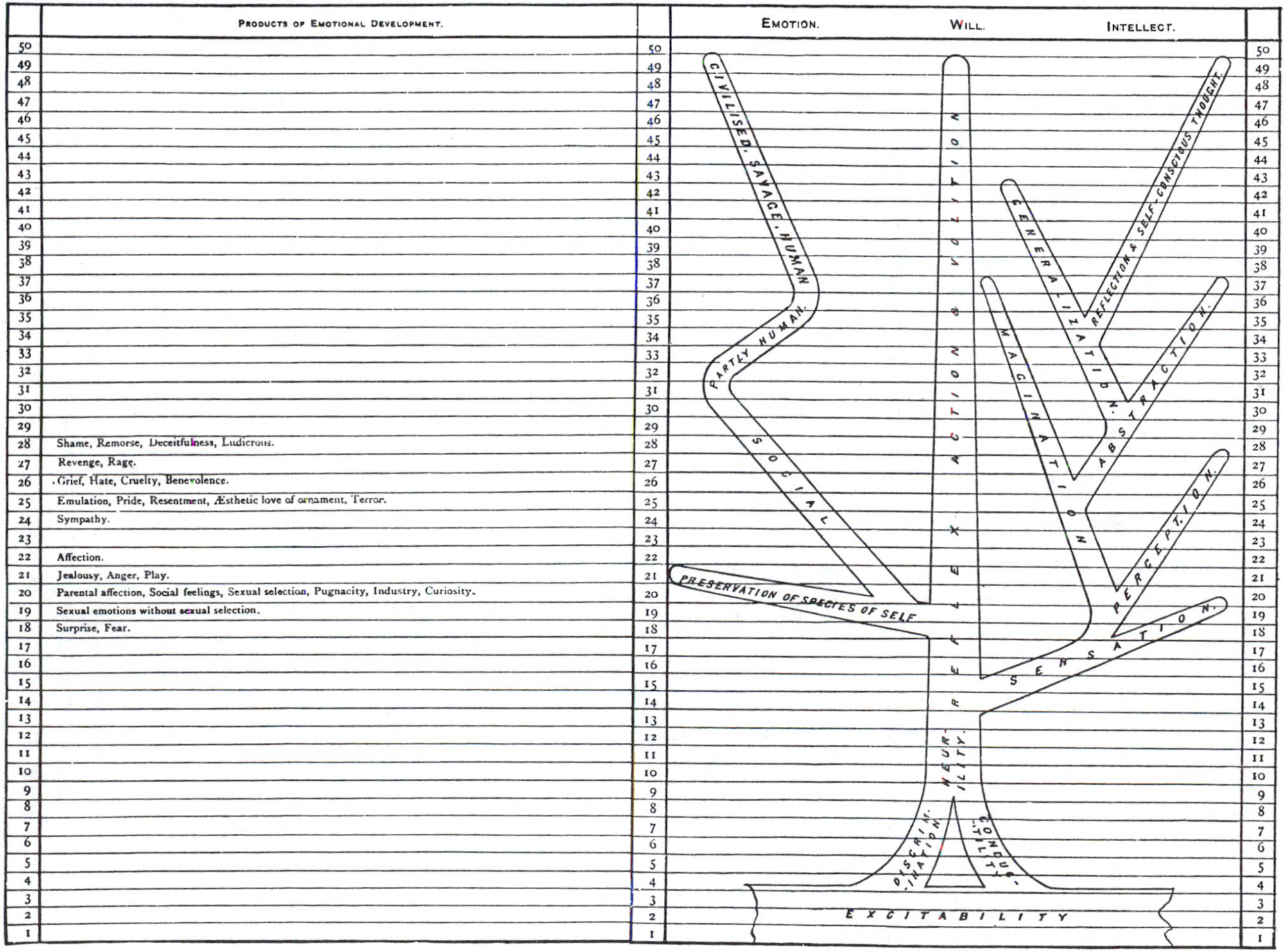

Figure 8-1 Continued

often imitate their elders in social situations and thus derive some of the behavior patterns and moral ideas necessary for successful operation in groups of people. By the time the individual is an adult, there will have been a "functional selection" of those habits that were successful in acquiring thinking skills and social behavior, an ontogenetic evolution.

On the other hand Baldwin believed that in phylogenetic evolution species adapted to their environments had evolved not only by natural selection and sexual selection, as Darwin had argued, but also by what he called *organic selection*. According to this those species that in the course of genetic variation may have been more able to accommodate their behavior to changes in the environment may have passed this ability on to their offspring and thus assured the perpetuation of individuals capable of modifying themselves in similar ways. In this context, in his third book, Baldwin criticized Romanes, who in his later works had suggested that adults might pass on *what* they had learned to their offspring. The theory that acquired characteristics might be inherited is known as Lamarckism; Baldwin contended that the theory of organic selection offered an alternative explanation of the evolution of intelligent behavior. Baldwin's theory of organic selection implies that the study of ontogenetic development is relevant to the study of phylogenetic development: A favorable evaluation of this claim has recently been given by Gottlieb (1979). In trying to show the importance of imitation in the origin of handwriting, Baldwin did some of the earliest experiments with very young children; these are described in his first book. Baldwin was thus a pioneer in comparative, developmental, and social psychology all at the same time.

Nevertheless, he was not the first evolutionist to do research with human infants: Charles Darwin himself had kept a diary of the progress of his own child, and William Preyer (1841–1897), a naturalist and physiologist who settled in Germany, studied the behavior of very young children in even finer detail. His *Mind of the Child* (1882) was at the time perhaps the most extensive account of the development of sensations, voluntary behavior, and speech over the first few years of life. He believed that many early aspects of behavior, including certain logical processes he considered to occur prior to the development of speech, emerged spontaneously—they were hereditary, though not inborn. In justifying his remarks, he made frequent reference to relevant findings by Spalding. Preyer's book is still a standard reference on early behavior and includes extensive information based on observation of infants and on studies of persons deprived of one or more senses relevant to the discussion of nativism versus empiricism in perceptual development.

It will be appropriate to conclude this account of the influence of Darwinism on psychology with Sir Francis Galton. Galton was a cousin of Darwin who, after giving up a career in medicine, traveled in Africa before settling down to the life of a gentleman scholar. From 1857 onwards he published more than two hundred books and articles on a wide variety of scientific topics: At the start of his life, he was responsible for pointing out the importance of high and low pressure systems in the weather, and his most famous discovery, the use of fingerprints as a means of identifying individuals, occupied him for the final years before his death in 1911.

Galton's main interest throughout his life, however, was the question of how much individual personality, character, and ability is inherited as opposed to acquired. With his enthusiasm for the theory of inherited characteristics propounded by Darwin, Galton himself favored the idea that ability in particular is largely inherited, but he was well aware of the importance of a favorable environment in encouraging talent. He used the phrase "nature and nurture" in 1874 to epitomize the struggle between the two influences, although there is some disagreement about whether he invented the term since something like it can be found in Shakespeare (see also Fancher, 1979a). Galton attempted to show through research that intelligence "ran in families": His book *Hereditary Genius* (1869) presented both qualitative and quantitative evidence that this might be the case by showing that persons eminent in some particular field of endeavor (e.g., judges, scientists, commanders) often had close relatives prominent in the same field. The book includes an analysis of examination results that indicates that these scores are spread about an average much as physical measurements such as height are spread. Using some tables published by the Belgian statistician Quetelet, Galton came close to showing in fact that examination results are what we would call "normally distributed."

This is one of the first instances of statistics being applied to a psychological characteristic. Galton used the term "law of deviation from an average" to refer to the fact that most scores in a set of scores cluster about the average with fewer and fewer examples being obtained of scores at the extreme ranges. In a later paper, Galton also showed, using anecdotal evidence, how twins might be similar in preferences and abilities. Persuaded, then, that ability could be the result of "nature" as well as of "nurture," Galton proposed the term *eugenics* to refer to a new science to encourage selective breeding among humans, thus ensuring the higher intellectual qualities of succeeding generations.

Many of Galton's beliefs on heredity now strike us as prejudiced or even racist, but it cannot be denied that he was among the first to raise the issue of how far intelligence could be "improved," nor can it be denied that his application of statistical methods to problems of psychological measurement was extremely influential. Moreover, he was not content simply to show how scores on tests might be distributed: In 1888 he proposed that a single number be used as an index of what he called *co-relation*. The number, which he designated as r, was between 0 and 1; a high value of r meant that two scores were highly related (e.g., as height and weight); an r of 0 meant that two scores were not related to each other (e.g., height and visual acuity). One could also have negative correlations, varying between 0 and -1: A high negative correlation meant that as one score increased, the other systematically decreased (e.g., visual acuity and the likelihood of wearing glasses). Later Karl Pearson (1857–1936) amended Galton's index somewhat and gave us the familiar r known as the *coefficient of correlation*. All subsequent analyses of the nature of intelligence, and of the question as to how far intelligence might be inherited, have made use of this measure.

Galton also wrote on a variety of other psychological topics. He invented the Galton whistle, which emitted sounds at a frequency higher than the human ear could detect but could nevertheless be heard by certain animals. He devised a set of weights in which each weight stood to its neighbor in a ratio determined by Fechner's Law; this allowed very rapid testing of weight discrimination. He developed a technique whereby a succession of photographs was superimposed in such a way as to yield a "composite portrait"—several members of a family might be photographed, for example, to form a composite portrait in which facial features particularly characteristic of that family would be salient. Some modern theorists of memory suggest that a similar process of development of a "prototype" might occur in our everyday experience (Posner and Shulman, 1979). He was a pioneer in the use of self-administered questionnaires to obtain information on subjective experiences—he used a questionnaire, for example, to discover how efficiently and how widely visual imagery was experienced. He discovered that scientists seemed to use little visual imagery whereas other persons were capable of extremely vivid and accurate imagery. He also discovered that individuals tend to think of the numbers (1, 2, 3, . . .) as being arranged in a sort of pattern he called a "number-form."

Last but not least Galton was perhaps the first to do an experiment on associations. In 1879 he reported that he took a number of words from a dictionary and wrote down other words they reminded him of. He was able to show that many associations derived from childhood rather than recent experience, and he suggested a classification of the associations into three kinds, those based on imagery (particularly visual), those based on verbal associations (such as names of persons, or phrases and quotations), and those that reminded him of activity of one kind or another (he called these "histrionic" associations). A stimulus word clearly falling into one of these classes showed a tendency to elicit responses from the same class. Galton's experiment was widely quoted by Wundt, Cattell, and others who did experiments on associations in the following decades. All of the research mentioned in this paragraph, as well as some important remarks on eugenics, will be found in the collection of essays entitled *Inquiries into Human Faculty and its Development* (1883/1907). Galton's life and work, it will be obvious, were fascinating: There is a large four-volume biography by his pupil Pearson (1914–1930); and a readable account of how his psychology developed at the various stages in his life is given in the chapter on Galton in Fancher (1979b). He also exercised a strong influence on Cattell, who propagated Galton's ideas of mental measurement from his department at Columbia.

The impact of the theory of evolution on the development of comparative psychology cannot be overestimated, and because of the interest in the general question of the evolution of intelligent behavior, a new impetus was also given to the study of developmental psychology. This would in turn lead to its being generally agreed that questions about human behavior could receive at least partial answers from studies of animal behavior: In fact the twentieth-century psychological laboratories where experiments with animals were carried out have been mainly concerned with testing predictions from theories about learning and problem solving rather than with native animal behavior (e.g., instinctive behaviors). Research on instinctive behavior has often been done under the aegis of departments of biology rather than psychology. The theory of evolution also led to the development of statistical techniques (such as those of correlation) that have found their application in psychology as well in the more traditional biological fields. And finally, the religious and philosophical implications of the idea that humans evolved from lower animals did much to enhance the naturalistic and humanistic tendencies psychology was adopting.

Act Psychology: The Würzburg School

In the previous chapter, we saw that Titchener, while differing from Wundt on introspection and other matters, nevertheless represented the conservative experimental Leipzig tradition at a time when many new factions were contending for the interests of psychologists. He represented, for example, a structuralist position against the functionalist who would broaden the scope of psychological enquiry. But in addition he came to grips with two other movements, both having their origin in German-speaking countries, and attempted to evaluate their contributions. First, a group of psychologists, mainly centered in Austria and southern Germany, were preoccupied with the fundamental question of the nature of psychological events: Many of the problems they discussed had been first raised by a contemporary of Wundt, Franz Brentano (1838–1917). Second, in the first decade of the twentieth century, a group of psychologists centered in Würzburg began to study thought processes by a mixture of experiment and introspection. Titchener found it necessary to criticize their work. Titchener's discussion of the former group will be found in his *Systematic Psychology* (1929); his evaluation of the work of the latter group is in his *Experimental Psychology of the Thought-Processes*. (1909). But these groups are of importance not only because they inspired Titchener to some of his most careful reasoning, but also because there is a direct line of influence from Brentano to the Gestalt school, the subject of our next chapter. Moreover the behaviorist movement arose partly in reaction against the Würzburg school with its emphasis on introspection and the "higher" processes thought of as conscious. It should be said, however, that in many ways—including the fact that very little of the writing produced by the two groups is available in English—these topics are the province of the specialist in the history of psychology, and we shall therefore be briefer on the topic than is perhaps warranted by the sheer prolixity of the material available.

Brentano entered the priesthood but also lectured on philosophy and psychology at Würzburg, where he taught, among others, Carl Stumpf, who was later to head the Berlin laboratory. Brentano was forced to resign from Würzburg in 1873 because he disagreed with the new doctrine of the infallibility of the Pope; the following year, however, he wrote his *Psychology from an Empirical Standpoint*. This was also the year of the publication of the first edition of Wundt's *Grundzüge*, and the two books are often contrasted for that reason. Brentano then obtained a lecturing position at Vienna, where he stayed for many years, thus influencing young thinkers in Austria. A useful summary of his life and philosophy is given by Sullivan (1968).

Brentano's psychology was concerned with the relationship between the act of thinking, the "content" of the thought, and the relation of the content of the thought to reality. He adopted a term used in the Middle Ages, *intentionality*, to refer to the fact that a thought had a content that bore a specific relation to reality: It reflected reality, or was isomorphic with it. Note that this meaning has nothing to do with "intending," referring to purposeful. If I think of a red square, this thought (whether I actually have an image of the red square or think of it in words) is determined by experiences with red objects and squares, and thus the thought cannot be divorced from what it represents. Thoughts, moreover, exist "in" the experience or the mind, or the soul, or the consciousness (depending on your metaphysics, you can select what you mean) and therefore our experience of mental events is characterized by *intentional inexistence*. It is this characteristic of reflecting an external reality in experiential form that makes psychological events different from physical events.

Brentano's book is perhaps the most conscientious and heart-searching effort in the literature to answer the question: What is the nature of a psychological event? A psychological event can be the experiencing of a sensation, a feeling, a thought, to name the typical elements of Wundt's *Outlines*, but Brentano was more concerned with what was common to all these three. He decided that every psychological event had three aspects: an image or sensory aspect; a judgment aspect, in which the person experiencing evaluated, among other things, the degree to which the experience reflected reality; and a feeling aspect—nearly all psychological experiences have overtones of pleasure or pain, what Brentano called love and hate. Another way of looking at the same problem is to say that a presentation is presented, cognized, and felt as well as known, all these four facets of experience being coincident. Brentano then went on to discuss in detail the experiences of having presentations, judgments, and feelings; in so doing he frequently referred to the writings of the British associationists and of medieval scholars. For Brentano psychology was the science of mental phenomena rather than the science of reflections of mental phenomena such as overt behavior.

Brentano's influence was far-reaching, and we may pick out three ways in which he affected later thought. First, his pupil Stumpf, whose main research, as we showed on p. 219, was on auditory perception, analyzed mental phenomena even further. In 1906 he published two papers in which he analyzed psychological experiences into four classes, which we present in a somewhat different order. First there would be *relations*, a feature ignored by the elementists (but soon to be stressed by the Gestalt school). Then there were *psychical functions* such as perceiving, desiring, and willing. Then there were the actual data of experience such as sounds, smells, and the like. These were called *phenomena*. Finally, since the red square in "I think of a red square" seems to be contained intentionally within the thinking act whereas the red square in "I want a red square" seems to have a different kind of existence, Brentano called the items such as the red square in the latter kind of experience *formations*.

This kind of analysis was taken up by Edmund Husserl (1859–1938), a pupil of Stumpf who had also previously studied with Brentano. In 1900–1901, Husserl published his *Logische Untersuchungen (Logical Investigations)*, following which came several writings all devoted to building a new branch of knowledge, *phenomenology*. Insofar as phenomenology encouraged the cultivation of new ways of looking at the objects of mental experience, it was influential on philosophers (particularly existentialists) rather than psychologists; but insofar as Husserl stressed that mental experience was a topic to be studied in its own right, and not necessarily to be reduced to trains of physical events, he gave an impetus to the examination of what is directly given in perception, an impetus that facilitated the progress of Gestalt psychology a few years later.

Second, Brentano's emphasis on the mental (as opposed to the physiological as stressed by Wundt) was echoed by various other Austrian writers whose indebtedness to Brentano was, however, less direct than that of Stumpf and Husserl. In particular, the eminent physicist Ernst Mach (1838–1916), who was influenced by Fechner's psychophysical philosophy, stressed that all our knowledge of the external world was given by sensation only. His analysis of the concepts of space and time in terms of our knowledge of the *sensations* they are associated with would later be acknowledged by Einstein. For Mach the study of sensations in themselves bore fruit in a number of important experimental studies. These were in part described in his *Contributions to the Analysis of Sensations* (1886). They include some of the first evidence that sensations of rotation are mediated by the semicircular canals of the inner ear and the discovery of Mach bands—bright or dark lines that appear if a black figure of a certain shape on a light background is revolved so rapidly that its visual appearance is of a blur of gradated grayness. The bands occur where there are sudden discontinuities in the outline of the black figure. These Mach bands are now thought to be the result of interactions between neurons at the retinal level (see Ratliff, 1965), but for Mach they were important because they illustrated that if there is a sharp deviation from the "mean of adjacent parts," as Mach called it, a new sensation could result. That is, sensations are relative rather than absolute: A point-by-point sensory mosaic of the kind that a simple-minded elementist *might* describe would be in error.

Mach also stressed that, while a Helmholtzian analysis of the perception of individual pitches or tones was probably correct, a complete account of sensation also had to make mention of the fact that we hear *relations* as well as individual tones. An interval of a third sounds like a third no matter what notes of the piano are chosen to play them; we can recognize a melody in any key. For Mach this remained an important unsolved problem. Shortly afterwards, Christian von Ehrenfels, in an article of 1890, proposed a new word for this extra quality of relationship that may be picked out in space (triangles remain triangles no matter how distorted) or in time (melodies in different keys): He said they had "Gestalt" quality. *Gestalt* means shape or form or configuration. Reminiscing in 1932 (see von Ehrenfels, 1937), he remarked that whereas Mach had left the riddle unanswered, he had derived his notion of Gestalt quality by assuming that a new idea *(Vorstellung)* of a melody could arise in consciousness from the comparison of memory images each involving different tone elements but common tone intervals. And then Alexius Meinong (1853–1920), who had been a pupil of Brentano, suggested that the elements in a tune could be thought of as founding a content, whereas the Gestalt quality derived from them was founded content. The combination of both founding and founded contents was a *complexion*— Meinong (1891) was writing a review of von Ehrenfels's article and suggested that in the study of the relations the elements of a complexion should nevertheless not be overlooked. Thus from Mach's stress on sensation we arrive at the concept of a Gestalt, soon to be emphasized (and changed somewhat) by a whole school of writers. It might be noted that many of Mach's ideas were paralleled in great measure in the difficult *Kritik der Reinen Erfahrung* (*Critique of Pure Experience,* 1888–1890) of Richard Avenarius (1843–1896). In particular Avenarius stressed the dependence of sensations on physical events. Moreover, Mach's influence on psychology has been interpreted in different ways by different writers: A general review of this question is given by Blackmore (1972, Chap. 5).

Third, Brentano had offered a particular analysis of assertions such as "I image red" or "I like red." By making the "red" exist within the "imaging," Brentano had encapsulated an experience into a single something that may best be characterized, as Boring (1950) says, as an *act.* Even though the word *act* is not mentioned in the index of the English translation of *Psychology from an Empirical Standpoint,* it may reasonably be argued that Brentano was the first to stress that an assertion such as "I image red" is only a roundabout way of saying that "I have a single experience that might be characterized as red-imaging," that is, an act is occurring. One immediate implication is that the "object" or content of consciousness so stressed by elementists such as Külpe in his *Outlines* or Titchener is perhaps, if not mythical, at least misleading.

Writers succeeding Brentano, rather than clarifying the matter, merely made it more and more complicated. Stumpf, we saw, preferred to think of "formations" and "phenomena." But essentially later writers preferred to retain the idea that there was a distinction between the act— the "imaging"—and the content—the "red." In particular Witasek, in his *Grundlinien des Psychologie* (*Groundwork of Psychology,* 1908), Messer in his *Psychologie* (1914), and finally Külpe in his posthumous *Vorlesungen über Psychologie* (*Lectures on Psychology,* 1920), all concluded that both *content* and *act* should be applied to propositions of the form "I image red." But there are broad differences among these authors on points of detail. In *Systematic Psychology,* Titchener (1929, p. 226) lists fourteen points of difference between Witasek and Messer: Witasek considers, for example, that acts and contents are inseparable, whereas Messer argues that "sensory contents may appear in the background of consciousness unaccompanied by acts." Much of Titchener's *Systematic Psychology* is an attempt to argue that, because of the divisiveness rather than the unifying properties of Brentano's approach, "these men will give us psychologies, but not (as Brentano hoped) psychology" (1929, p. 255). Finally, as Boring (1950, p. 451) describes in detail, Külpe at the end of his life was trying to reconcile his original Wundtian attachment to content with the new act psychology, as the followers of Brentano's lead came to know it. For Külpe, a thought act had a function as well as a content: One could successively perceive, recognize, and judge the same sensory content. Külpe therefore tried to analyze consciousness in terms of function and content. Why did

Külpe feel drawn towards the act psychologists? Partly because of the results of some experiments that had been carried out in his Würzburg laboratory, by Messer and others, on thought processes.

Külpe had left Wundt's laboratory to go to Würzburg in 1894. Here, while writing on philosophy and aesthetics, he encouraged many younger members of the Würzburg department to tackle a problem even Wundt had thought intractable, namely, the analysis of thought processes and problem solving. Between 1901 and 1908 a number of papers devoted to this topic appeared, all by members of Külpe's department, and Külpe's participation as a subject is acknowledged in many of them. These authors, along with Külpe, have come to be known as the members of the Würzburg school; they include Mayer, Orth, Marbe (late of Leipzig), Watt, Ach (later to succeed G. E. Müller at Göttingen), Messer, and Bühler. Before the rise of this group, simple association processes had been studied experimentally by Cattell and Galton, among others; but the Würzburg group was more interested in such sophisticated processes as judgment (e.g., how do I judge one thing to be bigger, or more beautiful, than another?), problem solving (such as in mental arithmetic), or what is now called divergent thinking (such as might be found in a difficult problem of philosophy to which there is no one accepted answer). The methods employed by the group were simple: Experienced observers such as Külpe and the members of the group themselves were asked questions and gave their answers verbally. At the same time they made introspections on how they arrived at their solutions and, in some experiments, measured reaction times.

Because of the detail of the protocols obtained, most of the monographs and articles published by the group are rather long, but Boring (1950) and Humphrey (1951) have offered excellent English summaries of the main findings of the school. In fact, by about 1908, a fairly coherent picture of the mechanism and nature of certain thought processes had emerged, one that included a number of terms coined by the group. Watt (1905) was the first in the group to divide the problem-solving process into four states: a preparatory "set," the actual cognition of the problem, the effortful and thoughtful attempt to solve the problem, and the eventual emergence and giving of the solution. Watt attempted to measure the time elapsing in each of these. In Figure 8–2 we show Watt's four stages. Above the four stages are what might be called *qualitative* aspects of certain of the stages stressed by the Würzburg group. The earliest paper of the series, that by Mayer and Orth (1901), had shown that associations could be given to stimulus words either immediately, with little conscious thought involved, or immediately after a conscious sequence of intervening thoughts. Under the latter category might come the familiar images and feelings of classical associationism, but sometimes a thought would appear to come from nowhere even though it clearly made sense in the context and could not be obviously linked with any visual or auditory image. Although rare—one later report gave the frequency of such imageless presentations as 3 percent, another as 11 percent—these events deserved a name of their own, so Mayer and Orth called them *states of consciousness*. The German word was *Bewusstseinslage* but because even *states of consciousness* or *conscious attitudes* is not precisely what is meant, the German word is often left untranslated or abbreviated as Bsl. In later papers from the Würzburg school, the introspecting observers frequently used this technical term in their reports, an indication of the kind of sophistication found in the subjects' protocols.

In view of the fact that a conscious experience could seem to have no image content and was at the same time a coherent link in a chain of thoughts, the final papers of the Würzburg school, those by Bühler (1907, 1908a, 1908b), attempted to analyze what is meant by the very word *thought* and to link thoughts with memories. In so doing Bühler concluded, to quote Humphrey, that a typical imageless thought was a "true, unanalysable unity . . . an irreducible fact of experience" (1951, p. 58). It was in part because of this somewhat negative conclusion that the Würzburg school did not really lead on to a fruitful approach to problem solving in the next decades of the twentieth century. Another instance of apparent irreducibility was found in the case of judgments. Marbe (1901) tried to pinpoint the various stages that presumably went in to a comparative judgment, such as judging that one thing was larger than another. Introspectively, he found none; the judgment seemed to be given directly.

Rather more promising, however, was the discovery by Watt (1905) and Ach (1905), using reaction time, that if one set oneself in advance to solve a problem of a given kind, one did better than if one was totally unprepared. Researchers on reaction times in Wundt's laboratory (see p. 220) had earlier shown the importance of "set"; Watt was a little more precise in his terminology and said that the task itself initiated the subject's set. The German for *task* is *Aufgabe:* the *Aufgabe* in turn works in such a way as to permit the subject to process only the most necessary portions of the task when the task is actually posed in detail: The thoughts one has during the attempted solution of a problem are not haphazard but are directed and relatively efficient. Ach put this down to *determining tendencies* in the subject, another word used by many of the Würzburg group. Finally Messer (1906), in a 224-page article full of details of introspective protocol, stressed that the determining tendencies operated unconsciously, a fact reflected in the subjective experience of the *Bewusstseinslage*. Although these various terms did not gain wide currency outside the Würzburg group, they clearly pointed to the importance of motivation in the determination of the content of the thought flow in task solution.

The writings of the group did not go unchallenged. Wundt (1907)

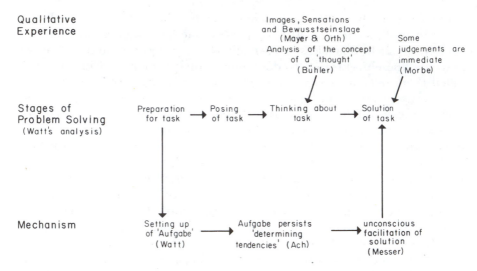

Figure 8–2 Schematic Representation of Some of the Terms Used by Members of the Würzburg School.

was incensed that the introspective method he thought he had been able to eradicate was being used to such effect by the group: His criticism, while directed particularly at the group, was a general condemnation of introspection. Titchener, in his *Experimental Psychology of the Thought-Processes* (1909), reviewed the findings of the group in detail and was, if anything, impressed with the sophistication of their introspection but could not be satisfied with irreducible or imageless thoughts. It seemed to him that a psychic experience that was not obviously a visual or auditory image could nevertheless be a kinesthetic image—that is, an image containing verbal content associated with feelings connected particularly with the vocal apparatus. He cited some research from American laboratories that supported his contention. It should be noted that Humphrey, in his detailed analysis of the critiques of the Würzburg school, considers that neither Wundt nor Titchener succeeded in rendering the conclusions of the school untenable. It should also be noted that it was the recognition that psychic experiences could consist of more than simple sensations or imagery that probably persuaded Külpe to reconsider Brentano's approach to psychic events rather than Wundt's, with results we saw earlier.

Gigerenzer and Murray (1987, p. 140) also claim that it was in part because the Würzburg school found that so many of the processes determining thought were unconscious that skepticism set in about the value of studying thought processes by examining conscious processes. There were competing answers to this dilemma. One group of psychologists, led by J. B. Watson in the United States, decided there was no point to further experimentation on "consciousness" using introspective methods, and that psychology could better advance by the study of overt behavior. This of course could be most easily investigated in animals and infants rather than in university professors, who had complicated chains of thoughts between receiving stimuli and giving responses. With Watson's 1913 plea began the movement of *behaviorism* that was to dominate much of twentieth-century psychology. At the same time, partly in opposition to behaviorism, but also partly in opposition to Brentano-type analyses of simple contents of consciousness without reference to the relations between the contents, there arose the *Gestalt* school, which stressed the need for a holistic analysis of perception and behavior. A third competing movement stressed what the Würzburg school had also discovered, the unconscious processes determining behavior. Sigmund Freud, working in the city of Vienna at the same time as Brentano and Mach, developed a large theory of how unconscious processes operated to determine adult thought and behavior. This theory he called *psychoanalysis*. Western psychology from about 1900 to 1940 was in part fractionated into these three movements, and to each we may now devote a chapter. At the same time physiological psychology and the study of individual differences in intelligence were advancing fairly independent of these movements; they will therefore be dealt with in a fourth chapter (Chap. 12) to follow our discussion of Gestalt psychology, behaviorism, and psychoanalysis.

Summary

This chapter discusses three developments important in psychological thinking that occurred contemporaneously with Wundt's tenure of the Leipzig chair.

1. Since the eighteenth century, there had been American writers on psychology, some influenced by the Scottish school of Reid and his successors. But the most eminent teacher of psychology in the United States in the late nineteenth century was William James. He studied medicine and psychology and underwent a mental crisis that made him particularly sensitive to the need to discuss the concept of will in psychology. His ideas were focused in his *Principles of Psychology* (1890). Among his more original contributions were his concepts of the stream of consciousness, his view that an emotion *consists* of physiological feelings, his distinction between primary and secondary memory, and his theory of the efficacy of religious conversion. Other American psychologists of note at this time were Ladd and Calkins.

2. A brief outline was given of Darwin's evolutionary theory, with particular emphasis on Darwin's belief that certain "instinctive" behavior patterns are the result of natural selection. Humans are placed on a

continuum of mental ability with the lower animals; this represents a reversion to the Aristotelean view. The facial and other expressions of emotions were also thought to reflect adaptive values. Darwin's ideas were to some extent foreshadowed by Spencer, who offered an associationist and empiricist theory of psychology with an evolutionist background. The instincts were studied experimentally by Spalding, Lubbock, and Romanes, the last of whom offered a substantial account of the intellectual capacities of various species insofar as these could be determined by experiment or observation. Baldwin also offered a theory to account for the natural selection of certain psychological dispositions. Galton developed statistical measures correlating physical or psychological propensities between parent and offspring and was an innovator in several other areas of experimental psychology.

3. In Austria and Germany a number of authors, notably Brentano, became intrigued with the question of how mental functioning should be described. One offshoot of this concern was a distinction between mental *acts* and mental *contents;* another was a concern, voiced particularly by Mach, that mental contents subsume not merely isolated entities but relationships between entities. The introspective work of the Würzburg group on thought processes also led some to believe in imageless contents of thought and in determining tendencies that dictate the flow of thought.

Gestalt
Psychology   9

The Origins of Gestalt Psychology

As the name suggests, Gestalt psychology has sometimes been considered a movement that arose in reaction to the notion that psychological experience can be seen as the result of the operations of many individual sensations and ideas somehow adding together in a simple way to yield an outcome. We may note immediately that it is hard to say exactly *who* was guilty of holding this elementaristic approach; we have seen that both Wundt and Helmholtz were well aware of the continuity of mental life and of the importance of contexts in determining how an individual object would be perceived. Sullivan (1968), however, suggests that some Gestalt psychologists may have reacted against the general viewpoint associated with Brentano, namely, that the task of psychology is to analyze single mental acts and not necessarily the relations between acts (or the relations between the contents of, say, an image). For this reason it is perhaps better to see Gestalt psychology not as a movement in reaction to current trends, but rather as a movement emerging from several different sources and crystallizing a point of view that had been in the air for several years.

The very notion of Gestalt quality, the quality that gives a melody its shape or figure such that the same melody can be recognized in any key, had been introduced by Von Ehrenfels in 1890. Meinong had elaborated the idea, and we may remark now that one of Meinong's students, Vittorio Benussi (1878–1927), had carried out a long series of experiments in the early years of the twentieth century in which he had tried to discover what subsidary processes of attention and discrimination might go into the formation of a Gestalt concept. Then again Wundt had suggested that individual elements could combine according to a principle of creative synthesis to yield a new combination, while Helmholtz had stressed the role of unconscious inference as a factor to be added to the raw mosaic of sensations in determining the final contents of perception. That perception should be studied in its own right and not analyzed into subelements, which themselves might be fictions of imagination, had been stressed by Husserl and other phenomenologists. And in the realm of thinking, it had been shown by the Würzburg school that each process in a chain of thought was determined by some original set the subject had adopted in attempting to solve the problem (Ach's "determining tendencies").

The Gestalt school was given its start and its individual identity by the meeting at Frankfurt, in 1911, of three persons all of whom remained in close contact for the rest of their lives and who were in substantial agreement as to the direction psychology should take in the future. These were Max Wertheimer (1880–1943), Kurt Koffka (1886–1941), and Wolfgang Köhler (1887–1967). Many others contributed to the development of the Gestalt movement, but these are the three names most usually associated with it.

Wertheimer obtained his Ph.D. with Külpe at Würzburg in 1904 and traveled to various departments before arriving in Frankfurt very keen to begin experimentation on the perception of movement. His interest in this topic stemmed from earlier research on music, problem solving in feeble-minded children, and number concepts in primitive people, where he had observed examples of conceptual structures that he felt could only be understood as complete entities in themselves: They were not divisible into separate parts. He sought to isolate such wholes experimentally and conceived the idea that he could do so by studying perceived movement. We shall return in a moment to Wertheimer's experimentation. He met Köhler, who was an assistant to Schumann in the psychology department at Frankfurt; and in 1910 they were joined by Koffka, who was also appointed as an assistant to Schumann. Wertheimer wrote his important paper on apparent movement; Koffka then contributed a number of articles following up on Wertheimer's work and critical of some of Benussi's attempts to analyze Gestalt qualities into isolated components. Köhler left Frankfurt in 1913 to become director of a research station the Prussian Academy of Sciences had established on Tenerife, an island off the northwest African coast. Here he studied problem solving and other capacities in apes and developed new principles that would become part of the Gestalt doctrine. Meanwhile, Koffka had received an appointment at a small university, Giessen, where he stayed until 1924. But Köhler came back to Germany in 1920 and was appointed head of the department at Berlin in 1922; Wertheimer had already gone to Berlin from Frankfurt in 1916. From 1922 to 1933 Köhler and Wertheimer were together at Berlin. With the rise of Nazism, it no longer became feasible to stay in Germany: Köhler, after showing considerable courage in the face of the threat to academic freedom (see Crannell, 1970), moved to Swarthmore College in the United States in 1934, and Wertheimer went to the New School for Social Research, in New York, in 1933. Koffka had moved to the United States in 1924, eventually receiving a full-time position at Smith College in 1927. Thus in their separate careers we see that the three men had the opportunity to meet regularly at various points in their lives and thus may genuinely be said to constitute a group. Figure 9–1 shows the above in a schematic form that may make it easier to follow the separate careers of Wertheimer, Koffka, and Köhler. Ash (1982) has written an as yet unpublished doctoral thesis on the origins of the Gestalt movement seen against the social and academic background of the German universities.

In treating of the substance of the movement we shall work in a chronological fashion showing how the general Gestalt theory was slowly widened and deepened as the result of individual experimental results. From the original Wertheimer paper, the movement grew until it had its own journal, the *Psychologische Forschung*, founded in 1922. The journal remained the central organ of the Gestalt movement until 1938, when it temporarily ceased publication. The journal was revived after the Second World War and now exists as *Psychological Research*.

Examining the experimental contributions of the Gestalt school, we might first note that most of the original research appeared in German,

Figure 9–1   The Careers of Wertheimer, Kohler, and Koffka.

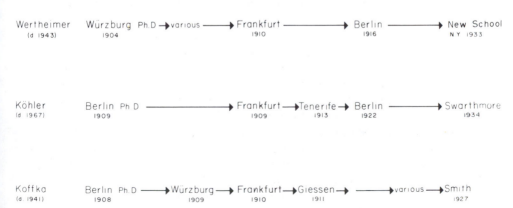

but Ellis (1938) provided translations of excerpts of most of the key articles, and a set of papers by Helson (1925, 1926) gave the main details of many of the earlier Gestalt contributions. Another invaluable source of information on the Gestalt experimentation was Hartmann's *Gestalt Psychology* of 1935. A second observation might be that, although the Gestalt psychologists themselves saw the movement as having implications for every branch of theoretical psychology (and even to some extent in applied psychology), the most convenient medium for demonstrating Gestalt principles was perception. As a result many of the studies now to be mentioned are concerned with perception. Perhaps the most convincing proof that the Gestalt movement took perception as its starting point is the fact that, if one analyzes the titles of the papers appearing in the *Psychologische Forschung* from 1922 to 1938, one finds 54.62 percent of the 249 papers (i.e., 136 papers) devoted to visual, auditory, or tactile perception; 10.84 percent (27 papers) are devoted to memory, thinking, and the like; and 6.43 percent (16 papers) to general Gestalt theory. The remaining papers (28.11 percent) range from anthropology through aesthetics to abnormal psychology, to mention only a few areas. There is a long series of contributions by various workers under Koffka's direction; and there is another series of papers, moving somewhat away from the original Gestalt position, by Kurt Lewin (1890–1947). Lewin's work will be discussed separately at the end of this chapter.

Early Gestalt Experiments: 1912–1929

If one is to show that perception involves more than just individual sensations, one should ideally find a situation with, say, two clearly definable objects of sensation and show that nevertheless one "sees" or "perceives" more than that. Just such a study is at hand in apparent movement. Wertheimer demonstrated that, in this case, the added element of "perception" is directly given and probably the result of the operation of a process in the brain. Wertheimer's 1912 paper opens with a description of the following situation: First a single stimulus, such as a vertical line, is shown for a short time. Then a second stimulus, such as a horizontal line lying in the same plane as the vertical line, is shown. If the interval between the two stimuli is not too short or not too long, one "sees" the vertical line "move" to a horizontal position. This apparent movement is not, Wertheimer showed, an artifact of eye movements or of afterimages: It seems to be a genuine third component in the total perception of the two stimuli. Wertheimer called the relation between the two stimuli *phi* and thus named the apparent movement the *phi phenomenon*.

Of course, apparent movement had long been known. It had been used in toy stroboscopes in the nineteenth century; in the twentieth century it forms the basis of cinema, where a sequence of static images projected at the appropriate rate, one by one, seems to have continuous movement. For Wertheimer, the importance of the phi phenomenon was that it demonstrated perception to be more than a single "and-combination," more than simply additive. At the end of his paper Wertheimer suggested that the origin of apparent movement lay in a brain process. To quote Helson:

> If a place *a* is excited, a circle of excitation arises spreading from *a*. If two places, *a* and *b*, are excited, the circular spread occurs from both. If *a* is excited before *b*, a short circuit takes place: the spread of excitation crosses from *a* to *b*. The direction of the current is determined by the part first stimulated. The nearer *a* and *b* are to each other, the more favourable are the conditions for the phi phenomenon. (1925, p. 516)

It has been argued by Carini (1970) that the real importance of Wertheimer's paper was not to found the notion of Gestalt theory as such—the term *Gestalt quality* is used very briefly by Wertheimer at one point only—but to make it plausible that no theory of perception can exist that leaves out brain processes acting on the raw data of sensation. Wertheimer's paper formed a focus from which other writers took their lead: Korte (1915) was able to specify how optimal phi movement related to the spacing between the two stimuli, the interval between them, and their respective intensities; Koffka (1913), describing work in part done by Kenkel, showed that apparent movement could occur if two lines which only *seemed* different in length were flashed rapidly one after the other to the same retinal location. The lines seemed to expand or contract depending on whether the background made them seem longer or shorter (the Müller-Lyer illusion).

The early Gestalt writing was also influenced by two contributions from the Göttingen laboratory. David Katz (1884–1953) wrote a most original work, *The World of Colour* (1911), in which he argued that, *phenomenologically*, color took various forms. The usual form was surface color, where a color seemed to inhere in a surface; but other forms were film color, as seen if one looked at a blue sky, or volume color, as when one looked through a glass vessel containing colored liquid. The book was particularly important for its analysis of how the surface color of an object appeared under various conditions of illumination. In particular, Katz was one of the first to point to the existence of brightness constancy. If a white disc is in shadow, the disc does not *look* as dark as objective measurement with a photometer would show it to be: Somehow the perceiver allows for the fact that the object is seen in shadow. Again, we have an instance of a perception being apparently unpredictable from a mere sensation. The other Göttingen contribution came from Edgar Rubin

(1886–1951). Rubin wrote a monograph in 1915 showing that, phenomenologically, the world is not seen as a flat array of interlocking surfaces all of equal importance in the visual field. Instead we organize the visual field into objects that are *figures* seen as set against a *ground*. Typically, an object with a strong contour, a moving object, or a brightly colored object might tend to be the figure, with the rest of the visual field serving as background. Sometimes a visual field can be organized in more than one way: Rubin's famous figure of a white vase on a black background, which can be seen also as two black faces on a white background, has become the standard example of a reversible figure-ground situation. Rubin's paper went into considerable detail on the importance of contour in determining figure-ground organization, but for the later Gestalt writers, the importance of Rubin's work was that it again suggested that the brain operates on the bare sensory contents to produce not a piecemeal but an organized totality in which the perception of a part (e.g., a figure) is dependent on the overall whole (the figure *and* its background).

In 1918 Köhler undertook to show that von Ehrenfels's Gestalt qualities could be demonstrated in animals, notably chimpanzees and chickens. If food is associated with a light gray but not with a medium gray, the animal can learn to choose the light gray. When this light gray is presented along with a still lighter gray, however, the animal now selects the latter instead of the former. Köhler argued that this was because the animal was not reacting to the particular stimulus "light gray" in the first instance but to the *total* stimulus configuration consisting of the two grays and choosing the lighter of the two. In the new situation the subject continues to choose the lighter of the two, therefore selecting the lightest gray of all. There is, as Köhler put it, an inner union between the two colors in the overall situation: The pairing attains Gestalt quality, and it is to this part the animal responds. Subsequent work has confirmed this relational responding by animals in a discrimination situation. Köhler himself also tested a child almost three years old: Two boxes were placed before the child, one with a darker cover, one with a brighter. The child learned that the brighter box contained candy—not too quickly; it took forty-five trials—and was then given the critical test of a new still brighter box paired with the old bright box. The child performed in the same way as the animals, responding to the relations of brightness between the boxes rather than to the absolute brightness. Once again the evidence is pointing against a piecemeal stimulus processing and in favor of a processing that takes into account the total situation, with each individual stimulus element being seen as part of a context.

But Köhler's major work on animal psychology was his book *The Mentality of Apes* (1917), in which he described the results of several years' work with the colony of chimpanzees kept on Tenerife. Köhler had spent the whole of World War I there and had concerned himself both with matters of detail, in his carefully demonstrated studies of how apes solved problems, and with matters of theory, for he also worked out a system relating perception to brain processes (see following). In the earlier perceptual work of Wertheimer, Rubin, and others we have seen how the contents of the total visual field determine how a part of that visual field will be perceived. In *The Mentality of Apes* Köhler's aim was to show that problem solving, even in animals, follows a similar pattern. In a problem, one is given many aids to the solution, but the final solution requires new steps using the usual rules of inference. This amounts, argued Köhler, to a reorganization or restructuring of the total array of stimuli available, one that may be preceded by intense thought and accompanied by an experience of elation or surprise. Moreover, once the moment of understanding has occurred, the completion of the solution follows smoothly and without hesitation. Köhler called the restructuring of the total array of stimuli *insight:* The criterion of insight, he wrote, was "the appearance of a complete solution with reference to the whole lay-out of the field" (1917, p. 164).

It was Köhler's achievement to show that insightful behavior of the kind just mentioned occurred in apes as well as humans. Köhler devised a large number of problems for the animals to solve, including detour problems where the subject had to circumvent an obstacle to obtain food; tool-using problems where the subject had to use sticks, boxes, or other implements to obtain food; and obstacle problems where the subject had to remove awkward obstructions to reach the food. Chimpanzees turned out to be very good at the first two kinds of problems but poor at the last. As for insight, we may quote one of Köhler's protocols describing how one ape, Sultan, used a short stick to obtain a long stick outside the cage and then used the long stick to obtain fruit also on the outside of the cage:

> Sultan is squatting at the bars, but cannot reach the fruit, which lies outside, by means of his only available short stick. A longer stick is deposited outside the bars, about 2 metres on one side of the objective, and parallel with the grating. It cannot be grasped with the hand, but it can be pulled within reach by means of the small stick. Sultan tries to reach the fruit with the smaller of the two sticks. Not succeeding, he tears at a piece of wire that projects from the netting of his cage, but that too is in vain. Then he gazes about him; (there are always in the course of these tests some long pauses, during which the animals scrutinize the whole visible area). He suddenly picks up the little stick once more, goes up to the bars directly opposite to the long stick, scratches it toward him with the "auxiliary," seizes it, and goes with it to the point opposite the objective, which he secures. From the moment that his eyes fall upon the long stick, his procedure forms one consecutive whole. (1917, p. 150)

Here we see evidence for apparent contemplation of the total situation and for the smooth carrying through of the solution once insight is achieved. But the reader should be cautioned that the chimpanzees failed to find solutions to many problems and that a great deal more trial-and-error behavior went on than the preceding extract suggests. Köhler, however, criticized certain authors who had argued that animals solve problems mainly by trial and error by asserting that, if an animal is to show insight, it has to have all the elements of the solution visible at the same time—it needs the whole in order to be able to relate the parts satisfactorily. "Insight learning," as Köhler called it, is still considered one of several kinds of learning of which the higher animals are capable.

In 1922 the first issue of *Psychologische Forschung* appeared. Among its contents were two more articles by Köhler on chimpanzees, a review by Rubin on figure-ground articulation, a long paper by Cermak and Koffa on the phi phenomenon, and the first of Lewin's papers. An article by Fuchs showed how persons with brain damage would develop a pseudofovea. If they could not use the center of their eye in the normal fashion because its function was deficient, they learned to structure their visual field by making a new part of the visual field the center of attention. There was also the first important Gestalt paper on memory. This was by Wulf, who presented shapes of different kinds to subjects and showed that when they later tried to recall the shapes, the recalled items seemed to involve exaggerating certain parts or making certain parts less salient than they had been in the original. Wulf called these different patterns of response *sharpening* and *leveling*, respectively. He argued that, just as in the visual field the various elements are subject to organizing forces by the whole, so in memory the memory traces are the target for forces that make the memories simpler and better articulated. It should be noted that Wulf's research has not been well confirmed; a review by Riley (1962) concludes that memory changes are far more idiosyncratic than Wulf's rather sweeping generalization would suggest.

In the following year, in Volume 4 of the journal, there appeared what was probably the best known of the various papers on perception by the Gestalt school, Wertheimer's paper entitled "Investigations of the Doctrine of Gestalt." In this paper he argued that when we survey the visual world, our perceptions are structured according to certain quite specificable principles (others later called them laws). For example, in the following pattern

. .   . .

I do not "see" a single dot followed by two widely spaced dots followed by a single dot and so on; I "see" a row of pairs of dots. A principle known as *grouping* based on the proximity of the elements has determined how I perceive the array. This in fact came to be known as the law of proximity.

Other such principles, described in detail by Wertheimer, included grouping by similarity, in which similar elements seem to cohere together, and grouping by continuity. If I superimpose a wavy line on a jagged line, the wave and the jagged line retain their identity, they do not fuse into an incoherent pattern. Finally, there is the principle of closure: If a contour encloses a complete space, this structures the visual field. If I superimpose a square on a circle, the square retains its squareness and the circle its circleness; the two do not fuse into a new whole unless some other principle of organization is brought into play. Patterns that form coherent, simple, unified structures came to be known as *good figures.* Wertheimer saw the act of perceiving as implying that the brain tried to impose "good-figuredness" on the elements in the field, thus reorganizing the field into a simple unity where the whole determined the parts. This was the essence of Gestalt *theory,* the theory that had started with von Ehrenfels's positing of Gestalt *qualities.* A good figure, in fact, came to be known as a good Gestalt.

Gestalt psychologists made a number of other important contributions over the next six years. Koffka gave an account of Gestalt theory in English in 1922 and wrote a book on the development of learning and thought in children, *The Growth of the Mind* (1921). This book is best understood in the light of its historical context, which includes the behaviorist movement: It represents one of the key works in which the Gestalt theory, with its emphasis on organizing forces and holistic structuring, clashes with a simple-minded learning theory with its emphasis on stimulus–response associations. Koffka reviewed much of the available evidence on the reflexes and abilities of children up to the age of six or so, but there are many digressions into discussions of instinct and learning in animals, the aim being to cast light on instinct and learning in human children. Koffka's most important point is that neither instinctive behaviors (in animals) nor learning (in animals and children) can be seen as the mechanical firing of a chain of responses by a stimulus. Instead, the organism is seen as trying to impose a pattern or configuration (something like the Würzburg school's "determining tendency") upon a set of movements so that a particular goal is achieved.

Köhler (1923) contributed to the notion that memory traces undergo spontaneous changes, due to forces acting on them, with his account of the "time error." If a stimulus of a certain brightness is perceived at time T_1 and then a similar stimulus is exposed shortly afterwards at time T_2, the second stimulus is sometimes reported to seem brighter than the first. This, argued Köhler, was because the second stimulus was being compared with the memory of the first stimulus, which had grown fainter in the interval between T_1 and T_2. Köhler's original view was that the growing fainter of the first stimulus was due to destructive forces, but Lauenstein (1933) later argued that the trace of the first stimulus was being assimilated into the general background of other traces, losing its figure quality, so to speak. A review of the time error and of its implication for modern short-term memory research is given by Tate and Springer (1971).

On perception, Gottschaldt (1926) argued that we do not perceive in a piecemeal fashion, familiar element by familiar element, but rather holistically. This was shown by the following experiment: A simple shape was exposed to a viewer as many as a few hundred times. Then it was shown embedded in a larger figure. Subjects never judged the latter as consisting of the familiar element plus other elements; they always saw the whole configuration and often failed to describe the familiar element as part of the whole configuration. Gottschaldt presented a variety of hidden figure patterns in which a familiar shape was camouflaged by other stimulus elements that formed a more coherent Gestalt in themselves.

Syntheses of Gestalt Psychology: 1929–1944

But the time had clearly arrived for Gestalt theory to be expounded in a single comprehensive work. It fell to Köhler to do this, in his *Gestalt Psychology* of 1929. We shall not attempt a summary of this work but rather shall point to certain new concepts that have not yet been stressed. First, just as Wertheimer had suggested in his pioneering paper on the phi phenomenon, Gestalt psychology argues that the various processes of organization that take place in perception and memory are mediated by processes in the brain substance. *Psychological isomorphism* is the name for the theory that, when a stimulus array effects the nervous system, automatic nervous processes are brought into play to determine the way the array will be perceived. To each shape, or Gestalt, associated with a brain process is a shape, or Gestalt, in the experience of the perceptual phenomenon. In particular, Köhler stressed that isomorphism implies that "experienced order in space is always structurally identical with a functional order in the distribution of underlying brain processes" (1929/1947). Later he added that experience of time followed a similar principle. But his ideas about isomorphism were not always properly understood, and Henle (1984) is essential reading for a clarification of this difficult issue.

Second, Köhler offered a more coherent picture than had hitherto been available of the forces presumed to operate in perception, memory, and thinking. The word *force*, of course, is essentially an analogy drawn from physics. If you put a magnet under a piece of paper covered with iron filings, the filings almost instantaneously jump into a pattern focused about the ends of the magnet: Magnetic forces have structured the field from a random one into a coherent one. Similarly, Köhler argued, the forces of good figure, figure-ground articulation, and Wertheimer's various principles instantaneously cause our visual experience to be structured and not consist of a random mosaic of color and lines. But, given the principle of isomorphism, one recognizes that the word *force* has an almost literal meaning in Gestalt psychology, for these forces are the result of brain processes presumed to be built into the organism from birth. From the time of the appearance of Köhler's book, there would be little hesitation on the part of Gestalt psychologists to evoke the notion of forces organizing the field of perception.

A third important focusing point of the book was Köhler's insistence that the Gestalt laws operate directly and are not the result of learning. At various places in the book he attacked simple empiricistic associationism on the grounds of its incompleteness. He asked two questions on which he finds associationism wanting (1929/1947, p. 258): First, "Is it really true that the mere repetition of two contiguous processes establishes an association between them?" and second, "Is an association a mere bond, which connects experiences in the way in which a string connects two objects?" To both questions, Gestalt psychology replies no. Acts may be repeated many times without being learned: What makes them learned is their being bound into a preexisting structure. Nor is an association a mere bond; when something is learned it is fitted into a more general scheme or pattern and does not exist in isolation. The "whole" determined by the subject's experiences determines how the "parts," the individual associations, are fitted in to the general structure. (Incidentally, the *self* for Gestalt psychology, is an important word signifying the totality of memories and tensions constituting the "whole" into which new memories and tensions must be integrated.) In discussing these general questions, Köhler extended Gestalt theory as originally derived from studies of sensation and perception to learning, memory, and thought in general: The book in fact closes with a discussion of insight.

Finally, Köhler's *Gestalt Psychology* played an important part in establishing the Gestalt movement as a school or group in its own right, to be distinguished from other movements such as the introspectionist movement epitomized by the Würzburg school or by the behaviorist movement, with which it was broadly contemporaneous. There are separate chapters criticizing behaviorism and introspection, and a discussion of the importance of establishing psychology, the young science, on a physicalist basis by incorporating the findings of brain research. In general, then, Köhler's *Gestalt Psychology* laid down a future terminology and crystallized the Gestalt movement as a unit in itself in the history of psychology.

In the following six years, more work flowed in from the German laboratories, and Helson, the chief interpreter of the Gestalt movement to English-speaking psychologists, was able to list as many as 114 Gestalt "laws" of perception (Helson, 1933). Duncker, in 1929, showed how the organization of the visual field into a figure and ground could be so strong as to induce illusionary movement. If you have an outlined frame with a spot of light within it, setting the frame moving makes the spot appear to move in the opposite direction even though it is stationary. We are so used to having the figure as the object of movement against a stationary background that we interpret many situations in this manner. The effect is related to the experience we have all had of sitting in a train stopped at a station and thinking we are moving when in fact it is another train alongside which is moving.

Another contribution to memory theory was made by von Restorff, who in 1933 described how an object isolated from others by having some peculiar characteristic was better retained than were the others: Von Restorff maintained that this argued for a figure-ground articulation in memory, where something standing out from the background is subject to strong unifying forces. A series of papers heavily invoking fields and forces came from J. F. Brown and his colleagues in the United States. They showed that when many stimuli were in motion, organizing forces, operating along lines similar to the way forces operate on natural objects, determine the direction of motion of individual elements in the array of stimuli.

However, the major event of the 1930s was the publication of Koffka's large *Principles of Gestalt Psychology* in 1935. If Köhler's book had been a focusing point, Koffka's book was the official systematization of the movement: Much more detailed and experimentally oriented than Köhler's work, it offered Gestalt accounts of many problems of perception (including the constancies), the nature of the self and voluntary action, memory and learning, and even society and personality. Of particular importance were the discussions of contemporary research not carried out under the aegis of the Gestalt writers themselves. It represents the highest point of the movement and should be consulted on almost all matters of detail concerning the experimental verification of the Gestalt principles. It is particularly notable that the doctrine of isomorphism, and the terms *forces* and *fields* are used extensively in the book. For example, in describing Wertheimer's law of proximity as referring to the pairs of dots (p. 288 above), Koffka remarks:

> We above . . . demonstrated that when the field contains a number of equal parts, those among them which are in greater proximity will be organized into a higher unit . . . we must think of our group formation as due to actual forces of attraction between the members of the group. This is not a mere hypothesis, much less a mere name, for these forces have demonstrable effects. (1935, p. 65)

An evaluation of the importance of Koffka's *Principles* in the light of subsequent research has been given by J. J. Gibson (1971).

In 1938 the *Psychologische Forschung* ceased publication, but in America the three main protagonists of the school did not stop writing in defense of the movement. Koffka continued to write, and in particular to lecture, at length on his reasons for maintaining his adherence to the movement (on this, see Harrower, 1971).

Wertheimer published a book in 1945 entitled *Productive Thinking*, in which he showed, by experiments in which he gave children tasks of arithmetic and geometry to solve, that there are different ways of solving problems, some of which are more efficient than others. It is an important book, partly because of its analysis of previous approaches to reasoning. The approach of the logicians, that of breaking down complex strings of reasoning into steps, said little about the psychological processes involved in real-life problem solving; the approach of the associationists left out the unconscious processes and the "insights" demonstrated by the Würzburg school and by Köhler. Wertheimer distinguished between rote and insightful understanding of a mathematical rule; for example, it is all very well to learn by heart that the sum of the first n numbers is $(n + 1)(n/2)$, but an insightful understanding would be to see why this equation is correct. (To give you an idea of this insight, consider that the sum of the first number, 1, and the last number, n, is $(n + 1)$; the sum of the second number, 2, and the next to the last number, $(n - 1)$, is $(2 + n - 1)$, i.e., $(n + 1)$ again; and there are $(n/2)$ such pairs in the whole list. Thus you multiply $(n + 1)$ by $(n/2)$ to get the sum of the whole list.)

Wertheimer's whole thrust was that insightful understanding of a problem was unlikely to be attained by a simple rambling of thought from one idea to another; insight was attained by seeing a particular connection in the total problem, and working from that connection to a "new look" or *restructuring* of the problem. Some of his most vivid examples of how science advances by leaplike restructurings included Galileo's restructuring of the problem of how forces operated, a restructuring that Newton would build on, and Einstein's restructuring of the notion of time that in turn led to a reappraisal of Newton's physics. Other examples of experiments showing the importance of restructuring were given in Wertheimer's seminars, reproduced by Luchins and Luchins (1970), and by Duncker (1945), who collected introspective reports of how students solved a problem in medicine, for example. Introspection as a means for collecting data on problem solving has never died out and is given approving treatment in such contemporary works as Newell and Simon's *Human Problem Solving* (1972).

Köhler concentrated on developing the theory of brain processes he had so long been interested in. In his *Dynamics in Psychology* (1942) he reexamined his old theory concerning electric potentials in the brain substance and first reported some experiments on a phenomenon he believed to demonstrate the validity of his theory, namely the figural aftereffect. A typical example of this kind of aftereffect is as follows: A point between two equally large squares is fixated for some time. Then the gaze is moved to a new fixation point lying between two small squares. The small square on the left occupies the place previously allocated to the large square on the right; the small square on the right is in a new location. This small square on the left seems to be smaller than its counterpart on the right and displaced away from the fixation point. Köhler explained this along the following lines: The first figure sets up electric currents in the brain substance, which, because of the prolonged inspection, becomes "satiated." When the second figure is presented to the same area, the satiated part of the brain can no longer process it, so the second figure is processed by an area of the brain that is not satiated. (This second brain area need not be *adjacent* to the original brain area, but the experiment is often interpreted as if it were.) According to isomorphic principles, this dictates that the second figure will have different relations within itself than the first figure had, so that the square on the left looks smaller and displaced from the square on the right.

In 1944 Köhler and Wallach wrote a major monograph dealing with this and other figural aftereffects, and Köhler insisted on the validity of his theory of brain currents for the rest of his life. But other theories of the figural aftereffect that involved far less speculation about brain currents were put forward (Osgood and Heyer, 1951), and on the whole physiologists have not been very receptive to the theory that electric currents spreading symmetrically about certain loci of the brain determine perceptual experience. A variety of views on synapses, single cells, and gross patterns of firing distributed over large areas have become more popular. A review of modern attitudes to Köhler's direct current theory is in part provided by the interchange between Henle (1984) and Pribram (1984). Pribram argues, it should be noted, that the Gestalt notion of isomorphism between perceptual experience and brain event can be preserved without accepting Köhler's specific neurophysiological account of it.

Koffka died in 1941; Wertheimer in 1943. Köhler remained the spokesman of the Gestalt movement until his death in 1967; in fact, his last work, published in 1969, was a short book entitled *The Task of Gestalt Psychology*. The first chapter was about the early history of the Gestalt movement, in which Wertheimer's role was clearly brought out; the second chapter discussed a theme always dear to Köhler, the relationship between psychology and the other sciences; the third chapter was an updated account of the progress of his theory of brain currents; the last chapter concerned the application of Gestalt theory to thought processes and added some new problems to those discussed in Wertheimer's *Productive Thinking*. The book closed with a question that reminds one of the very origins of Gestalt psychology: "Why do brain processes tend to produce perceptual organizations of remarkable clearness of structure?" Answers to this question may be given by theories such as that described by Hoffman and Dodwell (1985), according to which certain configurations act as invariants in the complicated train of events between stimulation in the eye and the conscious perception of an object.

In a curious way, Gestalt psychology has receded into a closed Gestalt itself, historically speaking. It flourished between 1910 and 1940; it influenced our thinking on perception as no other contemporary movement did. Although its influence on our thinking on learning and memory has been slight, its influence on our thinking on problem solving seems, in hindsight, greater than was at first conceived. There has been little since 1940 that could be called an addendum to or revision of Gestalt psychology as described in Köhler's *Gestalt Psychology* and Koffka's *Principles*. Helson, whose role as an expositer of Gestalt theory was most important, went on to produce his own *Adaptation Level Theory* (1964), in which individual percepts are related, in a quantitative manner, to the characteristics of the background and context in which they are perceived. But Gestalt psychology can never be said to have died; rather, it seems dormant. We shall see in the next chapter that the Gestalt movement was genuinely seen as an opponent by Pavlov and others concerned with learning theory in particular. Some later developments in Gestalt theory are mentioned in Chapter 13.

Kurt Lewin

It remains to deal briefly with the work of Kurt Lewin. Lewin studied at Berlin and was excited early in his career by the contributions of Köhler, Wertheimer, and Koffka on Gestalt principles. He was particularly impressed with the notion that the perceptual field is structured by forces. His own interests, however, lay more in questions concerning individual motivation and interpersonal relations, and he was therefore led to try to apply the holistic Gestalt terminology to problems concerning persons who are striving to achieve goals, either by themselves or with others. He formulated the notion that an individual could be represented as an element in a general field with the objects attracting or repelling the individual being seen as forces operating, within the field, on the individual. Each object, he believed, has a certain *valence* (a translation of *Aufforderungscharacter*), so that behavior could be seen as the result of competing valences operating on the person. In later developments of the theory, the person was seen as a unit capable of further analysis: Depending on the forces operating, he was in a state of equilibrium or tension. Any situation in which a goal was operating as a force put the individual into tension. This brief outline of the application of the Gestalt terminology to motivational studies was reinforced by the presentation, in *Psychologische Forschung,* of at least ten experimental studies from Lewin's laboratory all concerned with determining how subjects respond in tension-giving situations.

The most famous of these was that of Zeigarnik (1927/1938), who showed that, if subjects are given several tasks to carry out and are allowed to complete some but are interrupted before completing others, they reveal better recall of the interrupted tasks than of the completed tasks. This, Zeigarnik argued, was because when a task was interrupted, the tension to solve that task remained unresolved—there was a "quasi-need"—and this tension had the side effect of keeping alive the memory of the task. Over time, the "Zeigarnik effect" dissipated. There has been a great deal of further research on the effect, some of it reviewed by Van Bergen (1968).

Other aspects of need reduction studied by Lewin's students included the use of substitutes when one course of behavior was prevented (Mahler, 1933), and the influence of the subjects' own attitudes on their resolution to solve a problem. Hoppe (1931) was able to raise or lower what he called the level of aspiration of subjects by appropriate instructions and was then able to study how the level of aspiration apparently changed after success or failure. Most of these Berlin studies have been conveniently summarized by Marrow (1969, pp. 244–259).

On the outbreak of Nazism, Lewin, who was Jewish, came to North America, where over the succeeding years he worked at Cornell, Iowa, and the Massachusetts Institute of Technology. His theory, encapsulated in his *Principles of Topological Psychology* (1936), continued to be developed, but his interests turned increasingly to practical problems such as racial prejudice, industrial efficiency, and the behavior of small groups. At the various universities where he taught, he sponsored an enormous amount of research on social psychology, and at Iowa, on the behavior of children; Steiner, in his review of the history of social psychology in the century (1979) remarks that Lewin's influence was liberating because of the freshness of his ideas and stimulating because of the number of students he encouraged. Lewin remained on cordial terms with Köhler and other important Gestalt psychologists, but his later years may better be characterized as important for the history of social and developmental psychology rather than for a perpetuation of Gestalt beliefs.

Summary

Gestalt is the German word for "whole" or "configuration." Several psychologists prior to the beginnings of the Gestalt school had stressed that we perceive and think in terms of integrated units, which cannot always be analyzed into smaller units, and that relations between perceptual entities determine how we perceive those entities. Wertheimer, Köhler, and Koffka met at Frankfurt in 1911 and shared a common interest in this point of view. Wertheimer's studies of apparent movement indicated that one "sees" more than just two elements if one is presented rapidly after the other, and he initiated attempts to specify the brain processes underlying perceptual events. Other studies crucial to the development of the movement followed, including research on figure-ground organization, responses to relationships, the restructuring of the elements in a problem-solving situation (Köhler's apes), the introduction of the terminology of *fields* and *forces*, Wertheimer's laws of perceptual organization, and the time error. Köhler's *Gestalt Psychology* (1929) and Koffka's *Principles of Gestalt Psychology* (1935) were key works in presenting Gestalt psychology as a unified system. Köhler, Koffka, and Wertheimer moved to America in the 1930s and continued their works there; we note particularly Wertheimer's analysis of problem-solving processes in humans and Köhler and Wallach's analysis of figural aftereffects.

Lewin offered a system in which the individual was seen to be the object of forces acting on him or her to produce particular motives. He inspired a considerable amount of research on motivation and, later, in social psychology.

Behaviorism

10

The behaviorist movement, in contrast to the Gestalt movement, arose as a clear reaction against introspectionism as reflected in the works both of Titchener and of the Würzburg school. It was started almost single-handedly by J. B. Watson. Although others were thinking along similar lines in 1913, when Watson's first article on behaviorism appeared, he may be said to have encapsulated the general mood of the time and to have provided the leadership the movement needed.

Behaviorism had essentially two aspects, and it is, in some contexts, worth keeping the two separate. First, behaviorism was a methodological movement: It argued against the use of introspection and of the concept of consciousness in psychology generally and for a concentration on the study of behavior that could be objectively measured. To this extent it was almost inevitable that animal psychology, which so far had played a subsidiary role in the history of psychology, should now become a focus for experimental research. The behavior of animals could be controlled and measured to a greater extent than human behavior. Watson himself also inaugurated many studies of the behavior of infants. But second, Watson quickly incorporated into his system the notion that even the most complex of human behavior patterns could be reduced or analyzed into simpler elements. In particular, he chose to stress "conditioned reflexes" as the elements of his system. *Conditioned reflexes* was the name Pavlov gave to certain very simple forms of associative learning that had been demonstrated in higher animals. Clearly then, before we can discuss Watson's work, we must consider what was happening in animal psychology in the years preceding 1913 and also discuss the discovery of conditioned reflexes.

Animal Psychology Prior to 1913

We saw in Chapter 8 that the evolutionary movement had led Romanes and others to the detailed study of animal behavior and abilities. Spalding had stressed the apparently innate nature of many instinctive responses, and Romanes himself had attempted to show that, as one moved up the evolutionary scale, behavior became more and more complex and more and more indicative of what we commonly call intelligence. Baldwin had elaborated Darwin's theory with his theory of organic selection as a means whereby natural selection might operate to ensure the survival of those species equipped for certain forms of adaptive behavior, including the ability to learn.

But not all students of animal behavior in the 1890s were sympathetic to Romanes's methods of studying the subject. Nor were Spalding's sweeping assertions as to the innateness of certain responses in very young animals unquestioned. In particular Conwy Lloyd Morgan (1852–1936) queried the reliability of the anecdotal method used by Romanes and was less willing than Romanes to ascribe "higher" intellectual abilities even to mammals. The Canadian Wesley Mills (1847–1915) asserted that learning played a greater part in the adaptation of very young animals to their environment than Spalding had allowed. In 1885, Mills also founded a club at McGill University in Montreal for the study of *comparative psychology*, as the new topic came to be called. Moreover, there was a sudden outpouring of studies on the lowest organisms, down even to bacteria: Jacques Loeb (1859–1924) and H. S. Jennings (1886–1947), in particular, raised many questions about the application of such words as *learning* and *consciousness* to very simple creatures. Watson himself was a colleague of both Loeb and Jennings and was influenced by them. In discussing these various contributions, we may distinguish between two major questions, both of which were to be focal points of behavioristic doctrine: First, how broadly should the word *consciousness* be used in describing animal behavior? And second, what was the role of learning in the repertory of animal behavior?

Lloyd Morgan, in his youth, had worked under the Darwinian Thomas Huxley, and after spending five years in South Africa teaching various subjects, he was appointed to the chair of geology and zoology at University College, Bristol, in the south of England. He was also close to

Romanes, whose final papers he helped publish. Morgan wrote many books during his lifetime, including several on geology and the theory of evolution, but is now best remembered for a trio of works on animal behavior: *Animal Life and Intelligence* (1890–1891, revised in 1900 as *Animal Behavior); An Introduction to Comparative Psychology* (1895); and *Habit and Instinct* (1896). It is in the second of these books that the study of consciousness is made the target of a general inquiry. The question is whether animals can be said to have consciousness in the way humans have it. At the very outset of the work, Morgan asserts that one should adopt a certain principle in the study of animal behavior, a principle that has since become known as Lloyd Morgan's canon. It runs:

> In no case may we interpret an action as the outcome of the exercise of a higher psychical faculty, if it can be interpreted as the outcome of the exercise of one which stands lower in the psychological scale. (1895/1909, p. 53)

The canon is repeated in *Animal Behavior* (1900, p. 270) in the context of Morgan's discussion of the question of whether animals have aesthetic or ethical feelings. In his *Introduction to Comparative Psychology* Morgan went on to note that simple reflexes and simple associative learning seem adequate to explain even the complex tricks performed by pet dogs and that there is no reason to believe that they apprehend relationships with the facility or self-awareness possessed by humans. In this respect, he found himself in disagreement with Romanes. Later, Morgan was to make a break with the Lamarckism he had shared with Romanes and came to see instincts as having evolved by natural selection. Throughout the work, in fact, the contrast is made between human sophistication as reflected in consciousness and the more automatic or reflex behaviors presented by various species of animal.

That animal behavior was essentially mechanistic was argued in a series of papers in the late 1890s written by Loeb; a useful summary will be found in his paper, "The Significance of Tropisms for Psychology" (1909/1964). Loeb was among the first to notice that there seemed to be an analogy between the way plants grow towards the light and the way certain species of animals move towards (or away from) light and other stimuli. The tendency of plants to grow towards light had been called a *tropism* by the botanist Sachs, with whom Loeb worked at Würzburg, and Loeb began a series of studies on worms, insects, and other creatures to determine if their behavior might also be seen as tropistic. Loeb made the tropism the basis for a thoroughgoing mechanistic account of much behavior: The stimulus of light, say, acts on the receptors of the animal in such a way as to force it to move in such a direction that more light is received. The essential point is that such behaviors can be described without recourse to words such as *will* or *purpose:* The animal is a stimulus-driven machine. Loeb showed, in elegant experiments, that the degree to which a tropism shows itself might be a function of the level of growth of the animal, of the chemical constituents of the environment, and other variables.

Jennings, in his masterly *Behaviour of the Lower Organisms* (1906) agreed with Loeb that simple behavior can be ascribed to inbuilt stimulus–response mechanisms of the kind seen in tropisms. But, after extensive research, particularly on protozoa (amoebae, paramecia, etc.), Jennings came to the conclusion that the organism would rarely rest quiescent, awaiting, as it were, an appropriate stimulus to fire off a tropistic act; rather, any state of disequilibrium in the animal's physiological state or in the external environment would cause a succession of behaviors whose nature depended on whether a balance was restored. In a noxious environment, an animal would move away; a hungry animal would move in a variety of ways and if appropriate food was located it would stop to feed. If one mode of escape from a harmful situation was not effective, another would be adopted even by such simple one-celled animals as *Stentor.*

The amazing versatility of behaviors that Jennings clearly described in the protozoa led him to assert that, while it would be wrong to assume human emotional states to be present in these animals, it would not be wrong to assume that the variety of behaviors exhibited by these creatures was preserved and elaborated as one moved up the evolutionary scale. One of Jennings's most surprising discoveries, for example, was that there was little more in the way of adaptive, or "learned," behavior to be found in sea anemones and hydra as compared with the protozoa, even though the former have rudimentary nervous systems. Moreover, Jennings argued, it is possible that the word *consciousness could* be ascribed even to protozoa, for they show many behavior patterns similar to those of humans. However, he went on to remark, "such impressions and suggestions do not demonstrate the existence of consciousness in lower organisms" (1906/1962). Historically, Jennings's work served as a catalyst in exciting interest in the general issue of animal consciousness. Watson actually reviewed Jennings's book in 1907, somewhat negatively, because he felt Jennings to have courted anthropomorphism: Later, however, he came to know Jennings personally, and Jennings's skill as an experimenter may have convinced Watson of the potential fruitfulness (as opposed to sterility) of the analysis of animal behavior in terms of stimuli and responses.

Finally, the sociologist L. T. Hobhouse (1864–1929), in a rather neglected work *Mind in Evolution* (1901), attempted to show how consciousness in humans might have evolved as a series of stages. In simple animals there was a direct correlation between stimulus and motor experience. A tropism might be one example. In higher animals the motor response becomes the subject of conscious awareness, and gradually the animal comes to see relationships between percepts and memories of motor experiences. A higher development still, found in humans, involves the ability to correlate perceptual ideas and motor ideas, thus leading to abstract concepts. Hobhouse was led to stress the sophistication rather than the automatonlike nature of dogs and primates as a result of certain experiments he undertook; these will be mentioned again later.

By 1913, then, there was disagreement as to whether or not animals possessed consciousness, but the general trend was against the notion. The anecdotal method was being replaced by controlled experimentation and observation, and this is perhaps best seen if we turn to the second question of interest, learning in animals.

Comparative psychology to this time was mainly concerned with the instincts. But in the late nineteenth century it began to be realized that very rarely does an instinct show itself which is not in some way "plastic" or subject to modifications acquired by experience. That the importance of learning was beginning to be stressed was shown by the very title of Lloyd Morgan's third work of comparative psychology, *Habit and Instinct*. Here and elsewhere he argued that certain innate responses, such as pecking in chickens, was modifiable by experience. In a famous experiment Morgan demonstrated how chickens would learn not to peck at certain caterpillars, presumably because of their unpleasant taste, although they would still peck at other caterpillars. This went *against* instinct, as Morgan described it.

Other psychologists stressed the importance of learning in early infancy by keeping diarylike records of the progress of young animals. W. Mills (1898) kept track of the development of sensory and motor adaptations in puppies and kittens from the moment of birth; Small (1899) studied baby rats. Lloyd Morgan himself observed young poultry and described his findings in various places in his books. In essence all were agreed that the young of these various species had to find their way about in their world by a process of continual experimentation, learning by experience what was noxious and what was not. They soon began to suspect that taste preferences and fear of predators were not always inborn; in the latter case, what was innate seemed to be a fear of anything strange or unusual. Even behaviors such as drinking, which seemed basic in the animal's repertoire, were amenable to the effects of experience.

There were also the beginnings of experimentation into the learning capacities of full-grown animals. Small (1900a) studied how rats could find their way to food by gnawing or digging; Yerkes and Huggins (1903) showed that crayfish could learn to choose the correct one of two paths to food; and Jennings, at various places in his book, noted that one kind of very simple learning could be found in protozoa, hydra, and higher creatures. This kind of learning is now known as *habituation*. If a stimulus is suddenly delivered to a creature, its immediate reaction is to avoid the stimulus or withdraw from it. But, if no harm comes from the stimulus, the withdrawal response gradually drops out. Because of the general concern with conditioned reflexes in the following decades, the study of habituation was rather neglected, but it is now seen as central to an understanding both of behavior and of the physiology of learning (Kandel, 1979).

The most ambitious and influential study of learning in animals of this period was, however, the research undertaken by E. L. Thorndike (1874–1949). Thorndike first studied psychology at Wesleyan University but was inspired, by reading William James, to study with him at Harvard. Here Thorndike developed an interest in animal psychology and did some simple studies of the development of fear in chickens (he was one of those who disagreed with Spalding). He then started an extended series of studies at Columbia, under Cattell, with the aim of determining the course of learning in controlled situations; these were described in a monograph in 1898. He built a variety of boxes, large enough to hold a cat but small enough for it apparently to feel confined, that could be opened by a variety of means, such as pulling strings or pressing on buttons. Photographs of some of these boxes are given by Burnham (1972). When the cats were fairly hungry, food was placed outside the boxes. Thorndike then kept a record of the procedures the cats used to escape from their confinement and obtain the food. In general, he observed that they would try various means of escape but sooner or later would accidentally pull the correct string or whatever. When they were again put in the box, it usually took them less time to escape, and Thorndike published a series of curves showing how the escape latency decreased with the amount of experience the individual cats had with the individual boxes. In other studies, he showed that cats apparently did not learn to escape from a box the first time by watching another (experienced) cat escape from the same box, and if the experimenter passively manipulated the cat's paw to pull the correct string, the animal did not seem to benefit from this experience.

Thorndike came to a number of conclusions that at the time seemed outrageously bold. First, he argued that the cats, if anything, were stupid rather than intelligent. The anecdotes of Romanes and even of Lloyd Morgan intended to show the higher intelligence of pet animals could, he claimed, have been the result of chance; as Thorndike put it in his *Animal Intelligence:*

> It is then absolutely sure that a dog or cat can open a door closed by a thumb latch or button, merely by the accidental success of its natural impulses. If *all* cats, when hungy and in a *small* box, will accidentally push the button that holds the door, an *occasional* cat in a *large* room may very well do the same. If three cats out of eight will accidentally press down a thumb

piece and push open a small door, three cats out of a thousand may very well open doors or gates in the same way. (1898/1911, p. 73)

For Thorndike animal learning did not consist of an animal's surveying a situation and forming associative connections between ideas; it consisted instead of a trial-and-error procedure. During its somewhat undirected attempts at escape, the animal accidentally finds the correct solution. Thorndike went on to say that the experience of pleasure the cat then obtained on being released somehow caused the association between the accidental movement and the escape to be "stamped in."

Later, writing an addendum to his *Animal Intelligence,* Thorndike asserted that there were two laws that determined all learning. One, the Law of Effect, asserted that if a movement was followed by the experience of satisfaction or the removal of annoyance, that movement would tend to be firmly "connected" with the solution; upon reinstatement of the situation, the same movement would probably recur. The other law, about which a great deal more doubt was to be expressed in the following years, was the Law of Exercise. This may be quoted in full:

> Any response to a situation will, other things being equal, be more strongly connected with the situation in proportion to the number of times it has been connected with that situation and to the average vigor and duration of the connection. (1898/1911)

Thorndike's theory came to be known as *connectionism.*

When Thorndike's work appeared it was attacked by W. Mills (1899) on the ground that the unnatural situation of placing animals in boxes would limit their behavior to an unacceptable extent and that Thorndike's claims that his subjects lacked "reasoning" were therefore invalid. Thorndike (1899) replied by asserting that his subjects in fact rarely showed panic and argued against Mills's own interpretation of certain anecdotes apparently revealing reason and associative ideation in pets. Then Hobhouse (1901) gave a detailed critique of Thorndike's evidence, claiming, for example, that often a cat would learn to escape from a box after just one experience and that this showed evidence of learning of a rapidity Thorndike himself might have denied to his animals. Hobhouse was led to carry out a series of experiments, some with zoo animals such as a monkey and an elephant, which he believed showed evidence that the higher animals could learn merely by the perception of an event and its consequence. Much later, Köhler, in his *Mentality of Apes,* argued that Thorndike's confined cats had no opportunity to combine the various elements of the problem into a unified whole. If the elements of a problem were all available to the animal's perception, then, Köhler held, apes at least did show evidence of ideational association and inference.

To the earlier objections, Thorndike replied by doing a series of experiments with monkeys in which they tried to get food that was lying inside boxes that were difficult to open. In fact, his monkeys showed behavior quite similar to that of humans (and, we might add, Köhler's apes). Whereas Thorndike's cats, dogs, and chicks had shown evidence of *gradual* learning by trial and error, his monkeys showed evidence of "a process of sudden acquisition by a rapid, often apparently instantaneous, abandonment of the unsuccessful movements" (1898/1911, p. 189). Clearly then, the higher primates might indeed be capable of inference, although Thorndike also found them to be very slow at learning by imitation or by having their limbs passively manipulated. As for the lower animals, Small (1900b) studied rats in a maze situation and confirmed Thorndike's findings in many respects: The subjects showed little evidence of reasoning; rather, they stumbled across the solution by accident and then gradually became more and more skilled at traversing the maze.

The influence of Thorndike's research cannot be underestimated. It was the most telling blow against the use of anthropomorphism and anecdotalism in that era of comparative psychology. The Law of Effect revived the associationism of Bain and Spencer, who had also emphasized the importance of "pleasure" in causing the "stamping in" of a "connection" (to use Thorndike's terminology). It forced all workers on learning to take Lloyd Morgan's canon even more seriously than they had, and it revived a sort of elementalism in the study of learning: One now looked for stimulus–response connections in the analysis of even complex learning situations. In his later writing, Thorndike adopted the term *reinforce* instead of *stamp in*—a satisfying outcome reinforced a connection. This word would become standard in learning theory, although later writers varied to some extent in their exact usage of the term.

From Thorndike onwards the study of learning would involve animal experimentation to a great extent, and the concept of trial-and-error learning would become a basic notion in discussions of learning in situations of the kind described by Thorndike. Thorndike himself believed that the more sophisticated behaviors shown by primates and humans were the result of their having evolved brains in which the "increase in number, delicacy and complexity of cell structures is the basis for an increase in the number, delicacy, and complexity of associations" (1911, p. 287). It was against this rigorous and skeptical background that Watson was free to develop his belief that even consciousness should be dropped as a topic of scientific enquiry.

There were other important events in the area of comparative psychology during this period. In 1899 Beer, Bethe, and von Uexküll wrote an article in which they attempted to offer a standard nomenclature for various kinds of animal behavior. They wished to restrict the word *reflex* to cases of unlearned behavior of organisms with nervous systems; for unlearned behavior in animals without nervous systems, such as amoeba, they proposed the word *antitype*. For learned behavior in animals with nervous systems they proposed the word *antiklise*. Their nomenclature, however, was not widely adopted. They also proposed that the question of whether animals acted consciously should not be the concern of comparative physiology.

Then Yerkes, in his *The Dancing Mouse* (1907), published a detailed account of instinctive behavior patterns in this animal, along with evidence concerning its learning ability. In this book are to be found some of the earliest curves showing how errors were reduced as the mouse gradually learned its way through a maze. We must also mention the case of a horse which, when asked a mathematical question such as "What is two plus three?" would tap out the answer correctly with his foot; to the above question, the horse would tap five times. Even more complicated feats of arithmetic and spelling were apparently within the horse's capacity. It was shown that the horse was responding to slight movements on the part of its master: After five taps, for example, its master would straighten up slightly from the stooping position he had adopted to watch the horse's foot, and this would be a cue to the horse (Pfungst, 1907/1965). This monograph was effective in making comparative psychologists even more skeptical of claims of high intelligence in infrahuman species. Finally, a widely used textbook in comparative psychology, *The Animal Mind* by Margaret Washburn, appeared in 1908.

Russian Psychology

In the middle of the nineteenth century Russia was still a fairly backward country run by a powerful aristocracy where peasant workers sometimes lived frugal and hard lives under the whim of often tyrannical landowners. Reforms were gradually introduced, and towards the end of the nineteenth century a lively cultural milieu was to be found in the great centers of Moscow and St. Petersburg (now Leningrad). It was in this milieu that Tchaikovsky wrote his great ballets, such as *Nutcracker* and *Swan Lake*. It was customary, however, for scientists of talent to study in Germany and elsewhere before returning to Russia to continue their work. Such was the career of Ivan M. Sechenov (1829–1905). Having studied both engineering and medicine in Russia, he spent four postgraduate years learning physiology in Germany in the laboratories of J. Müller, du Bois-Reymond, Helmholtz, and others. His early research, on neurophysiology, concerned the effects of alcoholic intoxication on nervous functioning in animals; much of his later life was devoted to a long series of studies on carbon dioxide metabolism. But early in his career, while working with frogs, he discovered that if the brain were sectioned through at a certain level (in frogs, the level of the optic thalami), then stimulating the sectioned areas could suppress certain reflexes such as the scratch reflex. This was the first reported case of inhibition of a reflex: It raised the same excitement in physiological circles as had the demonstration, by the Webers, that the vagus nerve served in part to inhibit heartbeat.

Shortly after this Sechenov, in 1863, sixteen years before the founding of Wundt's laboratory, wrote a short monograph entitled *Reflexes of the Brain,* in which he tried to apply the concept of nervous inhibition of reflexes to the much broader problems of voluntary behavior and thought. His mechanistic account of these capacities was not viewed with favor by the Russian censors, and for some time the book was notorious because some believed that it argued that if voluntary behavior could be explained away in terms of reflexes, then no guilt could be attached to immoral actions.

Reflexes of the Brain is in two parts, the first concerned with involuntary reflexes, the second with voluntary behavior. At the outset Sechenov noted that in the normal adult, behavior does not seem to be an automatonlike sequence of responses to external stimuli because many of our natural reflexes, such as the investigatory reflex, are overridden by determination or habit. That is, we can inhibit certain reflexes or, alternatively, can be so preoccupied with habitual responses that we do not notice certain stimuli. In general, an unexpected stimulus can elicit, for example, a startle reflex, but expectation involves a new mechanism that can effectively inhibit startle reflexes and other inborn responses. The mechanism of this inhibition is assumed to be an elaboration of the same mechanism that inhibited reflexes in Sechenov's frogs. At the same time, the brain also has the power to intensify or elaborate reflexes; this elaboration underlies certain feelings we associate with certain reflexes, notably feelings of aversion and pleasure.

The picture Sechenov paints, therefore, is of a reflex machine in which the brain serves as a modifying or regulating device, sometimes inhibiting reflexes under the influence of learning, sometimes enhancing them, as when they are associated with aversion or pleasure. That learning can occur is shown by the existence of faint memory images from sensations and from the fact that, even in a decapitated frog, a leg that has been frequently moved can remain slightly bent. Learning takes place from infancy on and gradually many learned behavior patterns become quite habitual or involuntary—that is, they themselves become "reflexes." At first, infants learn to fixate and attend to stimuli that attract them, then they learn to reach for and grasp objects. Over the first few years of life the child develops not merely crude responses to particular stimuli but also notions of the stimuli. More and more complicated notions are gradually acquired, including those of time and size. As the faculty of mimicry emerges, much learning is by imitation. Speech is eventually acquired and becomes habitual.

In the adult, thought is held to consist of a series of reflex motor events associated with memories of sounds—that is, it consists of inner speech, which is not expressed but is inhibited. In a famous quotation, Sechenov describes thought as "the first two-thirds of a psychical reflex" (1863/1965a, p. 86). In other ways, children also learn to be skilled at inhibiting their reflex actions. They can acquire control over single muscle units, as in moving a single finger, and they learn not to express all their emotions—that is, their intensified reflexes. By way of a brain, therefore, the system, from being simply one in which all behavior was involuntary, became one in which the individual acquired control over various responses. But in principle the system was still dependent on reflexes. It was thus Sechenov who suggested that the word *reflex* could be attached to learned as well as unlearned behavior patterns and who built a psychological theory on the basis of the mechanisms of the reflex and of excitatory and inhibitory processes influencing the reflex. It may be asked if Sechenov owed these ideas to any predecessor: In his *Autobiographical Notes* (1905,1965b) he remarked that he was impressed by reading the ambitious system of Beneke, but his use of the reflex as the basic element of behavior appears to have been original. Boakes (1985) gives an interesting account of the development of Sechenov's ideas against the backgrounds of Berlin and Russia.

Sechenov's book had little influence on the psychologists who wrote in the last half of the nineteenth century; scarcely any of the writers we have so far discussed mention his name. But one young scientist in Russia, Ivan Petrovich Pavlov (1849–1936), did read Sechenov in his youth, and the experience left a lasting impression. Pavlov studied physiology at St. Petersburg University and early in his career did first-rate research on nervous influences on the circulation and on the pancreas. He studied in Germany from 1884 to 1886 and on his return to Russia was appointed professor of pharmacology at the Military Medical Academy in St. Petersburg and director of the physiology section of the Institute of Experimental Medicine. Here he started research on digestion in which he was able to clarify the roles of certain chemicals in the digestive process and, among other discoveries, was able to observe the stomach contractions we normally associate with hunger pangs. While studying these topics he invented new surgical techniques that allowed the stomach's contents to be easily collected; he also invented means of collecting the contents of the salivary gland and of the esophagus through tubes inserted into those regions. His *The Work of the Digestive Glands* (1897/1910) summarized his researches on digestion but is also notable for its reference to what Pavlov called *psychical secretions*. He observed that, while salivation is the normal response when dry food or distasteful substances are put in the mouth, an animal will also salivate if sights or sounds associated with these substances (the stimuli) are present. Pavlov therefore called the physiological reflex the *unconditional* reflex because all that is necessary to evoke it is the stimulus itself. If, on the other hand, the surroundings evoke salivation, this is a psychic reflex and is *conditional* because "it never occurs without perceptible stimulation of some sense-organ from without" (1897/ 1910, p. 84).

Pavlov restricted his discussion of psychic reflexes to a few pages, and in fact for his work on digestion itself Pavlov won the Nobel Prize in physiology in 1904. But clearly his interest was captured by the psychic reflex. At the academy, where Pavlov stayed until 1925, each medical student had to present a research thesis, and Pavlov readily found collaborators to write their thesis on psychic reflexes. The result was that Pavlov eventually concentrated all his attention on those phenomena and with his students was able to carry out an enormous amount of research on conditional reflexes. It may be noted, however, that in translations of Pavlov's later works, the word *conditional* was replaced by *conditioned*, and it is as *conditioned reflexes* that we now know these learned elements.

Among the earlier reports of research on conditioned reflexes was a lecture given in Madrid in 1903; the best single source for Pavlov's own account of them is his book *Conditioned Reflexes* (1927/1960); various other lectures both preceding and following the book are found in Pavlov's *Selected Works* (1955). At the end of his life Pavlov became particularly interested in the application of the theory of conditioned reflexes to abnormal psychology; he was also highly respected by the Soviet government and remains to this day the authority most highly regarded by Russian psychologists.

Many of the concepts of conditioned reflex theory were first identified and named by Pavlov. We may give a short account of these as shown by the types of experiments that were conducted in Pavlov's laboratory. First we note that Pavlov restricted most of his investigations to dogs, although some of his students worked on other animals. Typically, the dog would be placed on a stand in a harness that restricted its movements (if the dog were free to run around, it would be too distractible and focusing its attention on the relevant stimuli would be very difficult). Prior to the experiment, an operation had been carried out so that a tube led from the dog's salivary gland out to a measuring device. Typically, a stimulus would be presented followed very shortly afterwards by another stimulus designed to elicit salivation (either dry food or a weak solution of acid). The first stimulus could be visual (e.g., a square), or auditory (e.g., a bell or the sound of a metronome), or tactile (e.g., a touch to the animal's body), or even an odor. At first, this stimulus has little effect other than to arouse a mild investigatory reflex (sometimes

called an orienting reflex). The second stimulus, of course, elicits salivation. Pavlov typically measured the number of drops of saliva secreted.
But as the two stimuli continue to be paired, the first stimulus begins to
elicit salivation by itself, at first slightly but, on later pairings, more copiously. We thus have a previously neutral stimulus (say, the bell) now
eliciting a reflex response. Pavlov gave names to the various elements of
the experiment. The food or acid that originally elicited salivation was
called the *unconditioned stimulus;* the salivation it caused was called the
unconditioned response or *reflex.* The previously neutral stimulus (e.g., the
bell) was called the *conditioned stimulus,* and the salivation it eventually
evoked was called the *conditioned response* or *reflex.*

One of Pavlov's earliest concerns was with the timing of the pairing
of the two stimuli: He found that conditioning was often optimal if a
slight gap in time separated the conditioned stimulus from the unconditioned stimulus. Since the association of the salivation to the former must
be by way of memory of the former, Pavlov called such reflexes *trace*
conditioned reflexes. Another observation made early in Pavlov's career
was that a stimulus similar to the conditioned stimulus could also evoke
the conditioned response. In general, the more similar the new stimulus
to the original conditioned stimulus, the greater the probability of evok-
ing the response. This phenomenon was named *generalization.* For example, if the conditioned stimulus were a touch to the shoulder, a touch to
the upper leg might evoke a diminished conditioned response, whereas a
touch to the foot might be ineffective.

But, following Sechenov perhaps, Pavlov soon came to invoke the
concept of inhibition when referring to conditioned reflexes. In fact, he
argued that there were four kinds of inhibition whose interplay could
determine whether or not a subject would demonstrate a conditioned
response. First, there was external inhibition. Any sudden or intense
stimulus could disturb the animal and prevent its showing a particular
conditioned response. As Pavlov suggested, "the investigatory reflex is
excited and the conditioned reflex is in consequence inhibited" (1927/
1960, p. 44). Any stimulus that arouses an animal's instinctive responses,
such as the hunting instinct, will be particularly effective in disrupting
conditioned reflexes.

Second, there were three forms of internal inhibition. First, if a
conditioned stimulus was presented many times without presentation of
the unconditioned stimulus, the conditioned response gradually dropped
out. For example, a bell presented many times without food gradually
came to elicit no salivation. Pavlov called this phenomenon *extinction* and
used the word *reinforcement* in describing it: "This phenomenon of a rapid
and more or less smoothly progressive weakening of the reflex to a
conditioned stimulus which is repeated a number of times without reinforcement may appropriately be termed experimental extinction of con-

ditioned reflexes" (1927/1960 p. 49). Such extinguished responses are not forgotten; they can be readily restored if reinforcement is reintroduced into the experimental situation. Presenting a sudden and unexpected stimulus may also cause the original conditioned reflex to reappear. This phenomenon Pavlov called *disinhibition.*

A second kind of internal inhibition Pavlov named *conditioned inhibition.* Pavlov gave this example: A metronome has been paired with food until the animal salivates to the metronome. Then a new stimulus, a motor hooter, is sounded just before the metronome; at the same time an extinction procedure is begun, so that the hooter plus the metronome no longer signal food. After several unreinforced trials the pairing of hooter and metronome yields no salivation. But if the metronome is then sounded by itself, salivation returns. Thus, the combination of hooter plus metronome seems to be associated with lack of reinforcement and hence inhibits the response of salivation.

A third kind of internal inhibition was named *differential inhibition.* In this case, an animal can be taught to differentiate between two stimuli, for example, to salivate at the sight of a circle but to give no response to the sight of an ellipse. Such discrimination learning is accomplished by presenting the unconditioned stimulus (e.g., food) regularly with the circle but not with the ellipse. Pavlov did admit that differential inhibition could be regarded as a special case of conditioned inhibition.

We have stressed Pavlov's emphasis on inhibition because it shows the heritage of Sechenov. Pavlov, in fact, developed a rather complicated theory to account for these various phenomena of conditioning by assuming that in the brain, particularly in the cerebral cortex, areas stimulated could cause waves of excitation or inhibition, irradiating and concentrating in such a way as to yield such effects as generalization and extinction. Whether excitation or inhibition irradiates from a cortical point or concentrates on it is held to depend on the strength of the stimulus. Thus a complicated model is built up where it is possible for weak stimuli to have a strong effects and vice versa, where weak irradiation of inhibition is believed to result in various stages of hypnosis, where strong irradiation of inhibition is believed to result in sleep, and where irradiation can transform an inhibited area into an excited area, as in disinhibition. The model can be teased out of Pavlov's *Conditioned Reflexes* but is presented in more succinct form in a 1934 encyclopedia article reprinted in his *Selected Works* (1955, pp. 245–270).

Throughout his career Pavlov was anxious to show that the mechanism mediating conditioned reflexes was in the cortex. He labeled those areas of cortex underlying the sensations connected with unconditioned and conditioned stimuli *analyzers:* When a bell elicits salivation after being associated with food, activity in the auditory analyzer is presumed to have somehow been associated with activity in the food analyzer region. By dint of many associations acquired over a lifetime—including the association of the *sight* of food with salivation—the cortex builds up a signaling system in which the various analyzers contribute to the final repertory of conditioned reflexes (associations) possessed by the subject. In humans, conditioned reflexes linking sensations of sound and oral movement with other sensations are particularly predominant—we call this *language*. In humans, therefore, there is a second signaling system concerned with speech and abstract concepts. The similarity between this and Sechenov's concepts will be obvious.

So far we have written as if a dog in Pavlov's laboratory were an ideal subject, standing still when required to do so and somehow representative of all dogs in general. But of course this impression would be misleading. Early in his career Pavlov noticed that some dogs behaved differently from others in a conditioning situation; in particular, he observed that some dogs that were very excitable under normal circumstances become very lethargic when placed in the conditioning situation. He surmised that they had a surfeit of irradiation both of inhibition and of excitation. This observation was the first of a long series of attempts to classify dogs by types. Whereas most of Pavlov's ideas remained relatively unchanged during his lifetime, his typology underwent several modifications. The best-known typology was presented in *Conditioned Reflexes:* Dogs were divided into four groups depending on their degree of excitation/inhibition and the equilibrium between these. Dogs with an extreme predominance of excitation were called *sanguine,* following Hippocrates' nomenclature; those with a moderate predominance of excitation were called *choleric;* those with a moderate predominance of inhibition were called *phlegmatic;* and those with an extreme predominance of inhibition were called *melancholic.* But Pavlov later invoked the concept of the "strength" of the nervous system, being so precise as to denote by this the strength of "cortical cells" and also went back to his earlier observation concerning the degree of mobility or lability in his animals.

The final typology consisted of three types: excitatory, equilibrated, and inhibitory. Here the notion of equilibrium is preserved; the concept of the "strong" versus "weak" nervous system is that between the excitatory plus the equilibrated animals, and the inhibitory animals; and the lability or mobility dimension distinguishes the excitatory from the equilibrated animals. A full account of these various changes in Pavlov's beliefs is given by Teplov (in J. A. Gray, 1964). While speculating on the variables that contributed to his various types, Pavlov also speculated on the application of the theory to human abnormal behavior.

Pavlov's typology depended in part on his observation of individual dogs' reactions to conflict. We have already seen that a dog can be taught to salivate to a circle and not to an ellipse. What happens if the circle is made more and more elliptical? At a certain stage the dog shows signs of stress, and the individual dogs react differently. Pavlov labeled this behavior *experimental neurosis*. In the case of the circle/ellipse experiment, for example, one dog wriggled about and tore at the apparatus with his teeth; later, he barked violently when taken to the experimental room, contrary to his usual custom. Individual differences between dogs in their reactions to difficult problems of the kind just mentioned were noted and attempts were made to relate them to the current typology. Pavlov's pioneering work led to a great deal of later research, both in Russia and in the West, on experimental neurosis and the related topics of frustration, conflict, and aggression (see Chap. 13).

In the last decade or so of Pavlov's life, regular meetings were held in his laboratory every Wednesday morning and records were kept of the conversations. We should not leave Pavlov without noting that in these meetings he was very critical of Gestalt theory. For Pavlov, Köhler's apes were not "thinking" in those quiescent moments in their problem-solving activities; they were merely resting. Their behavior could be completely described in terms of trial and error and associations: For Pavlov all behavior, being essentially composed of conditioned reflexes elicited by external stimuli or by internal speech, had to be associative, and the Gestalt psychologists' attempts to overthrow associationism were seen as short-sighted.

But what of the Gestalt theories of holistic perception? Pavlov considered that they had not asked "what is perception?" For Pavlov: "Perception, if considered profoundly, is simply a conditioned reflex; however, since Helmholtz knew nothing of conditioned reflexes, he called them unconscious conclusions . . ." (1955, p. 574). It was Pavlov's opinion that the Gestalt psychologists had erected an unnecessary superstructure when an associationistic account both of problem solving and of perception would suffice. He accused them of ignoring Helmholtz and other associationists of the nineteenth century.

Pavlov was not the only major Russian researcher on conditioned reflexes. The physiologist Vladimir M. Bekhterev (sometimes spelled Bechterev) (1857–1927) became famous for his fundamental research on nervous anatomy and pathology. He at one time studied with Wundt and in 1907 wrote *Objective Psychology*, in which, like Sechenov, he stressed the importance of reflexes as a means of studying behavior and argued that learned reflexes could be elements of complex behavior, including speech. We know that this work was read by Watson, and it is of great interest to note that, like Watson, Bekhterev argued against the view that psychology was the study of consciousness. The book is remarkable for its heavy reliance on the new experimental evidence concerning such processes as learning and attention. Bekhterev argued that, just as a spinal reflex could be analyzed into "sensation—spinal interaction—reaction," so a "psychoreflex" could be analyzed into "reception—association—reaction."

In many ways the book is one Sechenov might have written had he known about conditioned reflexes and the "new psychology." Bekhterev preferred to call Pavlov's conditioned reflexes *associative reflexes* and studied them in some detail at the Psychoneurological Institute he had founded in St. Petersburg in 1907. Some of his research is described in his *General Principles of Human Reflexology* (1917). He objected to Pavlov's use of the salivation response on the grounds that presenting acid or meat powder to a dog involved the stimulation of various sense organs, so the response was too diffuse and variegated to be of value. Instead, he developed the following paradigm: A sound (or other conditioned stimulus) is presented, followed by a shock to a dog's paw. The shock causes the paw to be withdrawn. After several pairings, the sound elicits paw withdrawal, an example of an associative reflex that can be easily measured with appropriate equipment.

Bekhterev speculated, in more detail than had Pavlov, on how the development of human behavior depended on the development of associative reflexes; how imitative behavior might be reduced to a chain of associative reflexes; and how thought might represent inhibited speech. He labeled voluntary activity *aim reflexes,* a term he took from Pavlov, and argued that most of the Western research inspired by Thorndike was a study of highly evolved aim reflexes rather than of simpler associative reflexes. Unfortunately, he became engaged in a controversy with Pavlov: He believed he had identified a "salivary center" in the cortex, which, if extirpated, led to the abolition of previously established salivary conditioned reflexes: Pavlov was able to disconfirm this theory and accused Bekhterev of carelessness (the story is told by Babkin, 1949).

The work of Pavlov and his colleagues on conditioned reflexes was first described for American researchers by Yerkes and Morgulis (1909). When Watson came to develop his behaviorist theory, therefore, he was able to use the conditioned reflex as a weapon in his armory. It is sad to have to report that in 1902 the American E. B. Twitmyer independently discovered how to condition the knee jerk, but nobody paid much attention at the time to his finding (Coon, 1982).

J. B. Watson and Behaviorism

It is sometimes claimed that materialistically oriented philosophers such as La Mettrie (p. 99) anticipated the behaviorist position first adopted by John Broadus Watson (1878–1958). Verhave (1967) has shown that the pioneering American writer Joseph Buchanan (see p. 242) foreshadowed

Thorndike and Watson with his discussion of how performance improves with practice. Wesley (1968) claims that the ophthalmologist E. Raehlmann could be claimed as an early behaviorist because in 1890 he established color discrimination in infants under a year old. In Boring's *History of Experimental Psychology* (1950) the chapter on behaviorism shows Watson's indebtedness to Thorndike and to the Russian school but also mentions functionalism and positivism as related movements antedating behaviorism. The influence of Loeb and Jennings on Watson is not as clear as it might be, with Jensen (1962) claiming that Jennings was the first behaviorist and Burnham (1968) arguing that in fact there were many differences of opinion between Watson, Loeb, and Jennings. Although Watson knew Loeb personally at Chicago, and Jennings at Johns Hopkins, there seems to have been little important interchange between them. Watson himself was lecturing in 1908 as if he believed in some of the doctrines of behaviorism: Burnham contends that Watson's 1913 article "Psychology as the Behaviorist Views It" was in fact delayed because Watson had not as yet worked out a method for dealing with the higher thought processes.

Other psychologists such as Knight Dunlap (1875–1949) and Max Meyer (1873–1967) held views rather similar to Watson's at about the same time. Finally, we note that Leahey (1987, pp. 259–270) has argued that psychologists were receptive to Watson's explaining away of human consciousness as mere verbalization because there was intensive discussion between 1900 and 1915 about how far consciousness itself depended on movements (the *motor theory of consciousness*; see Scheerer, 1984, for a review). Leahey also stresses how writings on functionalism stemming from the controversy between Angell and Titchener (see Chap. 7 Appendix) served as a bridge in America between the influence of Wundt and the revolution of Watson. Nevertheless, the corpus of Watson's writing is fairly self-consistent and self-contained and we may therefore treat it as a unit in itself.

Watson was born in South Carolina and studied, with apparent lack of enthusiasm, at Furman University. But, we learn from his short autobiography (1936), he did become interested in philosophy. One of his professors recommended he might try to study with Dewey at Chicago: Once there, however, J. R. Angell captured his interest with his lectures on psychology. Here Watson also studied with Donaldson (see p. 225) and Loeb. His Ph.D. thesis concerned the correlation between the complexity of behavior in the white rat and the degree to which the nerve fibers were myelinated. He spent a further two years teaching at Chicago, during which time he carried out a detailed study of the kinds of cues rats use when learning a maze (this will be mentioned again later), studies of instinctive patterns in sea birds, and studies of color vision in various species. He also kept a diary of development in baby monkeys and had an invigorating correspondence with Yerkes on various problems of comparative psychology, including the role of imitation.

In 1908 Baldwin had to leave Johns Hopkins, and the young Watson took his place at that university. Also on staff were Dunlp, with whom he had many discussions and who later claimed to have been a cofounder of behaviorism, Jennings, and one of Jenning's students, Karl S. Lashley (1890–1958). Watson and Lashley became close friends, and both were to have illustrious careers, with Lashley in particular becoming one of the best physiological psychologists of his time (see Chapter 12). Watson formulated the basic ideas of behaviorism in an article published in the *Psychological Review* for 1913: We shall discuss it in more detail later. In 1914 he reproduced this article as the first chapter in a book called *Behavior*, in which a great deal of space was devoted to showing the success of observation and experiments in comparative psychology. It was about this time that Watson read Pavlov's work and Bechterev's *Objective Psychology*, and so became interested in conditioned reflexes. Interestingly, Watson's main question was whether conditioned reflexes could be established in humans. He and Lashley discovered that there were many practical difficulties in studying conditioning in humans: For example, they paired a sound with a bright light to see if the pupil of the eye would constrict to the sound alone. It did, after twenty minutes' training, but subjects complained their eyes hurt.

But the most important development of 1915 was that Watson obtained permission to build a laboratory associated with a psychiatric clinic headed by the psychiatrist Adolf Meyer (1866–1950), in which he would look after as many as forty children and study them daily from birth. This was the natural outcome of the diaries kept on animals by Mills and others, but the important point is that from now on Watson would be exclusively preoccupied with human rather than animal psychology. It was also at this time that Watson read Freud (see Chapter 11) and came to the conclusion that he and Freud, while differing greatly on the role to be played by conscious and unconscious factors in a scientific psychology, were fundamentally agreed on one point: Adult behavior and habits can be determined by love attachments (conditioned love) laid down in early childhood. It was by careful research in this clinic that Watson concluded the baby has three basic emotions, love, rage, and fear (see later). In 1915 he became president of the American Psychological Association; in his presidential address (published in 1916) he stressed the importance of studying conditioned reflexes in humans as well as animals.

In 1917 Watson was asked to cooperate on war work, a circumstance that reflects the fact that one of the most important developments in the history of psychology as a discipline was the way in which psychologists began to be recognized as "experts" who had a role to play in society outside the universities. As O'Donnell (1985) has shown, part of the reason behaviorism was so successful was that it offered an alternative to the tedium of introspective studies of human consciousness. But there was another and possibly more important reason for its spread: As far back as the 1890s, America had been deliberately striving for economic success, and one of its tasks was to provide the best possible education for its students, including the immigrants who were flooding into the country, particularly from continental Europe. The result of this heightened awareness of the importance of education was that many professors of psychology were asked to teach on the applications of psychology to education. Two areas of research in particular were well funded and offered potential jobs for graduates trained in the new psychology: the application of learning theory in the classroom and the development of procedures for helping learning-disabled children. For example, Thorndike soon left animal psychology for the study of educational psychology, a topic to which he devoted most of his life; and Lightner Witmer (1867–1956), who obtained his Ph.D. from Wundt, was at the University of Pennsylvania when, in 1896, he was asked for advice on how to help a poor speller. He discovered that the child needed glasses, but the scene was set for Witmer to switch out of experimental psychology and develop a "Psychological Clinic" devoted to the assistance of schoolchildren with learning problems. When Watson gave his speech on behaviorism in 1915, there was a huge ready-made audience in the educational field waiting for new guidance on human learning. And when Watson extended his theorizing to cover emotions, the audience swelled to clinical psychologists, psychiatrists, and the population at large, who wanted to know how to bring up their children free of emotional conflict.

One of the aspects of educational psychology most in demand was intelligence testing, a topic we shall discuss in more detail in Chapter 12. When World War I broke out, psychologists were called in to aid the armed forces in the selection of people for particular jobs, and Watson was one of those consulted. In particular, Watson was asked to do research on tests for the selection of airplane pilots, but his low opinion of the tests currently being used got him in trouble with his military superiors and he spent much of the war on trivial duties. Just after the end of the war, however, Watson and Lashley, because of their military contacts, received a grant to do a survey to evaluate the effectiveness of a film stressing the dangers of venereal disease; from this he was led to do questionnaire studies of attitudes to sex, which Cohen (1979) claims were the first studies of this kind. Of course, sexology is now an established branch of psychology; in Watson's time, however, such studies were daring, and Max Meyer was dismissed in Missouri for carrying out a similar study as late as 1930. It is important to note that Watson did not identify introspection with questionnaire studies: He felt that by asking questions one could in fact obtain data that were valid enough to be comparable with the "observation" data he had found so useful in animal studies.

Back at Johns Hopkins after the war, Watson plunged into further research into infants and put his findings into his next book, *Psychology from the Standpoint of Behaviorism* (Watson, 1919a). In 1919 he also claimed to have established that emotional responses could be conditioned (the "little Albert" study; see later); a film has been recently uncovered that in part records this experiment, as well as others from the child clinic (Watson, 1919b). Cohen (1979, p. 142) claims that this was probably the first psychological film ever made. Also in 1919, Rosalie Rayner, a student from Vassar, came to do graduate study under Watson and was the co-author of the paper on little Albert. But she and Watson fell in love; when the university discovered Watson's infidelity to his wife of many years, he was asked to resign. None of his friends seem to have stood up for him, and nobody else would offer him a position; it was an embittered Watson who found himself, for want of anything better, working for an ambitious young advertising company, J. Walter Thompson, who seemed to have been glad to attract the most famous psychologist in America to their staff. Watson was poor for a while—his wife sued for divorce with large alimony and child care payments—but in 1921, now living in New York, he married Rayner. The marriage lasted till Rayner's untimely death in 1936; there were two children, whose behavior Watson closely observed in much the same way Darwin and, later, Piaget observed their children; and Watson ultimately became very rich.

All this time, however, he had a hankering to get back to his psychological research with children and compensated for his lack of academic respectability by writing *Behaviorism* (1924, 2nd ed. 1930), which includes the best summary of his human psychology available; *The Psychological Care of the Infant and Child* (1928), a bestseller whose virtues are often underestimated by professional psychologists; and many popular articles on behaviorism. Like Skinner later, and Bertrand Russell in his own time, Watson believed that human happiness depended on habits acquired in infancy and childhood, and he gave prescriptions for these that were widely discussed in the 1930s. Perhaps he is best known for arguing that parents should not smother their children with physical affection, as this could cause a dependent and perhaps unstable adult personality; this is of course in agreement with the Freudian view that adult neuroses can be caused by overattachment to the parent(s). He also believed in a regular routine during the day for toilet, meals, naps and so on: this aspect of his child guidance program is not so popular nowadays.

At the end of his life in 1957, Watson, then living in retirement in Connecticut, received a Gold Medal from the American Psychological Association: he was probably too shy to appear in person to accept it, and his son accepted it for him. He died a year later, but the obituary notices from psychologists were lukewarm about the merits of his contributions to psychology. Watson was also important in the history of advertising; he was among the first to stress that advertisements should not simply shout that a particular product was the "best" but should appeal to the consumer's emotions, including love (he sold underarm deodorants on the basis of their sex appeal) and fear (all responsible mothers have a duty to use brand X baby powder). He also carried out research on product acceptability and on brand-name loyalty.

At the beginning of this chapter we remarked that behaviorism had two aspects, methodological and substantive. From the point of view of methodology, Watson argued that psychology had not yet escaped from the medieval position that humans were "central" with the other organisms somehow less important. Darwin had successfully effected a dethronement of humanity in the biological realm, but psychology still thought of humans as the prototype insofar as they had consciousness, were supposed to possess imagery of various kinds, and were capable of complex reasoning processes. The question then became whether animals had these capacities. Watson argued that the question should be stood on its head: What should be asked are questions concerning the basic capacities of animals and whether humans differ from them in these capacities. To answer this, we need a study method that can be applied to both animals and humans. What is needed, in fact, is a science based entirely on the observation of measurable behavior where such human-based concepts as consciousness and imagery become unnecessary.

In his 1913 article, Watson pointed to the inconsistencies of the Würzburg school and to the indefinite structuralism of Titchener as examples of the excesses that can result from a psychology based on the analysis of consciousness. He also pointed out that those branches of psychology not using introspection—for example, studies of efficiency in the classroom and in industry—were being more successful than traditional experimental psychology. Furthermore, a psychology in which consciousness was imputed to animals would necessarily be incomplete because it was based entirely on analogy and not on accurate knowledge. In the first chapter of *Behavior,* Watson also took Titchener to task for his talk of the affections: For Watson the emotions were visceral responses evoked, even if only faintly, by certain stimuli and should be measured objectively wherever possible. His final claim in his manifesto was that, having taken consciousness as its field, human psychology had failed to make good its claim as a natural science. The book *Behavior* was an attempt to show that comparative psychology could be successfully carried out without reference to consciousness and imagery. The behaviorist was to study problems related to the sensory organs, instinctive responses, habit formation, and three kinds of correlations: correlations among behavioral data, correlations of behavior with structure, and correlations among behavior, structure, and physicochemical processes.

It will be seen that Watson stressed the importance of physiological psychology. In his chapter on apparatus used in comparative psychology, Watson mentioned, very briefly, Pavlov's salivary conditioning technique, Thorndike's puzzle boxes, Yerkes's mazes, and other devices. In the chapter on habits, some stress was laid on the fact that learning can be facilitated not only by reward, as Thorndike had stressed with his Law of Effect, but also by punishment. Watson was particularly interested in the kind of information the rat apparently utilized when learning to run a maze: After showing that blind and/or anosmic rats were still capable of learning to run a maze, he argued that retention in rats was primarily of a kinesthetic kind. In support of this, he mentioned one of his experiments in which a rat first learned to run a maze of a certain layout. The alleyways in the maze were then shortened or lengthened. It was found that the rat would attempt to turn at those points that would have been correct in the original maze. This demonstration of the importance of retention based on cues from the muscles may have persuaded Watson of the feasibility of a theory of thought based on kinesthetic cues from the speech apparatus (see later). In other sections of *Behavior* Watson showed how instinctive behavior patterns could be modified by learning, made suggestions concerning the physiological mechanism underlying learning, and took the side of Thorndike against Hobhouse and others who were rather generous in their ascription of reasoning and other capacities to infrahuman animals.

On questions of substance, Watson came to view the conditioned reflex as the kind of simple learning on which all higher learning was based. This represented a shift of opinion. In earlier writings he had been critical of Pavlov (Herrnstein, 1969). His 1916 presidential address described both Pavlov's method of salivary conditioning and Bekhterev's method of motor conditioning and came to the conclusion that for much animal research the latter is more convenient. He was particularly enthusiastic about the value of differential conditioning for the study of animals' sensory capacities. In *Psychology from the Standpoint of a Behaviorist* (1919) he showed how the two methods could be applied to humans, using in part apparatus designed by Lashley, but reported little research applying the methods. Instead, he argued that infants acquired many habits they would preserve all their lifetimes through conditioning. According to Watson, the baby was born with a few instinctive responses such as grasping and reaching, sucking, and so on and also possessed three primitive kinds of emotion. Fear resulted when the infant was exposed to loud noises or to a loss of support. Rage was the result if the infant's natural movements were hampered in any way. Love, under which Watson included sexual responses, was evoked if the infant was stroked, cuddled, or otherwise gently handled.

These innate emotional responses could, however, become conditioned responses—Watson, possibly at Lashley's suggestion, called them *conditioned emotional responses* (CERs), a term still widely used. He and Rayner (1920) described an experiment on CERs that has since become notorious. It was established that banging an iron bar with a hammer caused a fear response in a nine-month infant (little Albert), whereas observing a number of live animals (including a rat, a rabbit, a dog, and a monkey) did not. Then, two months later, Watson and Rayner presented the child with a white rat followed immediately by a loud clang caused by beating the iron bar with the hammer. After seven such pairings, the infant began to cry and to show avoidance responses when the rat was presented without the noise. Five days later there was some evidence that Albert's fear generalized to other furry objects, and it seemed that this generalized fear persisted when the infant was tested again a month later. Partly because Albert left the clinic, partly because Watson left Johns Hopkins, it was not possible for Watson to embark on his next project, a study of how CERs could be extinguished. When he was in New York, however, a student named Mary Cover Jones asked him to supervise her on such a project, using children from a nearby clinic, and Jones (1924) describes the extinction of CERs in a child. The technique included presenting the fear stimulus a long way off and gradually bringing it nearer the child. It should, however, also be noted that attempts to replicate the little Albert experiment were not always successful (Harris, 1979).

Other instinctive responses, such as vocalization, were also held by Watson to be capable of conditioning: Learning speech, Watson argued, was essentially learning to substitute a sound for an external object. Many experiments on the development of reaching and other responses in infants were reported in the 1919 book. But the fullest account of how conditioning affects one's behavior was given in *Behaviorism*. In this work the earlier speculations as to the growth of adult behavior resulting from conditioned reflexes added to the corpus of innate reflexes and emotional responses were worked out in detail. Watson also emphasised that one's later personality can be influenced by the conditioning of sexual and "love" behavior even in infancy. Watson called this whole scheme the *activity stream*, a term deliberately chosen for its contrast to the Jamesian "stream of consciousness."

Watson's views on thinking, images, and memory deserve special mention. *Thought*, he believed, consisted simply of silent speech. While admitting that it was often difficult to measure the small laryngeal movements he considered to underlie the process of thinking, he nevertheless believed that if they could be measured, thought could be made the subject of behavioristic studies. He pointed out that in deaf persons finger movements could be observed while they silently thought. In *Behaviorism* he made an effort to show how the course of thought could be seen in a completely associationistic manner. But he never really came to grips with the problems of insight and solution discovery that were being raised by Gestalt psychologists at about the same time.

On the other hand, he did claim that some experiences of early childhood can affect later behavior, but, because they were never consciously verbalized, their effects were not always understood by the subject (Watson, 1924).

As for imagery, he felt that all cases of so-called visual imagery could be analyzed into cases of verbalization. Since this conflicts with the introspective experience of many persons, it has been suggested that Watson himself lacked visual imagery, and there have recently been many experimental studies that indicate that the rated visualizability of words and situations leads to enhanced retention, as does deliberate visualization (Paivio, 1971). But Watson remained convinced that images "remain unproven—mythological, the figment of the psychologist's terminology" (J. B. Watson, 1926/1930, p. 248). The result of Watson's denigration of the image concept was that research on imagery, a favorite topic from Galton to Titchener, almost vanished from the American scene until the late 1960s.

Since the human adult's behavior could be described entirely in terms of unlearned reflexes or conditioned reflexes, it became a matter of words as to what was meant by a person's "character" or "personality." In *Behaviorism* Watson expressed his belief that adult personality was almost entirely a matter of nurture rather than nature in the famous words:

> Give me a dozen healthy infants, well-formed, and my own specific world to bring them up in and I'll guarantee to take any one at random and train him to become any type of specialist I might select—doctor, lawyer, artist, merchant-chief and yes, even beggar-man and thief, regardless of his talents, penchants, tendencies, abilities, vocations, and race of his ancestors. (1924/1930, p. 104)

This cohered well with the belief of many that each of us is the master of our own destiny, and Watson reinforced his stance with the various books and articles on child raising mentioned earlier. Similarly, he believed that so-called mental illness was nothing but the development of acquired emotional habits and suggested, at the end of *Behaviorism,* that therapy in many cases might consist of the extinction of such acquired habits (particularly fears). This foreshadowed the beginnings of modern behavior therapy. He argued that one of the goals of psychology was to permit organized society to predict and control the behavior of its members in such a way as to maximize the usefulness and happiness of each person.

There is no doubt that Watson was a polemic crusader with an axe to grind, but there is equally no doubt that the discipline of psychology has been more directly influenced by behaviorism than by any other movement. The study of personality and individual differences in ability has shaken itself free of the nineteenth-century belief that much of our adult makeup is the result of inheritance; the study of human and animal learning is still fundamentally based on the notion of the conditioned reflex, though neobehaviorism (see later) has, of course, added much to our conceptualization of the learning process; behavior therapy is now assiduously studied in most academic departments concerned with clinical pyschology. On the other hand, the study of human cognition was undoubtedly retarded by Watson's denial of imagery and of thought processes other than those yielded by a simple associative chain of subvocal responses mediating between stimulus and final overt response. Behaviorism has been thought to be shallow by those taking the view that human behavior is influenced by unconscious memories and conflicts. We shall turn to Freud and other representatives of this position in the following chapter.

We should not, however, leave the impression that behavioristic doctrine was accepted by the majority of experimental psychologists in the early decades of the century. Watson's denial of the value of introspection was criticized by Titchener (1914b); his theory that all learning could be reduced to chains of associations was contested in Koffka's *Growth of the Mind;* and even young psychologists interested in learning theory were not all impressed with the idea that thought is only subvocal speech or that the notion of purpose, with its overtones of consciousness, could be ignored (Woodworth, 1959). Nevertheless behaviorism did have a strong influence on learning theory in the 1930s, and it was by this route, now known as neobehaviorism, that behaviorism's influence has persisted, in admittedly diluted form, to the present day.

Neobehaviorism

It will only be possible to give a brief introduction to those theories of the 1930s that are often grouped under the general title of neobehaviorism. For a fuller secondary account, the best source is probably Hilgard and Bower (1966), though many other books on learning cover the experimental evidence put forward by the various neobehavioristic writers. They are called *neobehavioristic* chiefly because their psychology eschewed such terms as *consciousness* and *imagery* and adopted concepts directly from the Pavlovian terminology, just as Watson had done. The individuals concerned are E. L. Thorndike (1874–1949), Edwin Ray Guthrie (1886–1959), Clark Leonard Hull (1884–1952), B. F. Skinner, Edward Chace Tolman (1886–1959), Edward Stevens Robinson (1893–1937), and John Alexander McGeoch (1897–1942). Thorndike, Guthrie, Hull, Skinner, and Tolman all put forward learning theories of their own; Robinson, in his *Association Theory Today* (1932), performed a valuable duty in showing the continuity of and commonality between concepts of the nineteenth-century associationists and concepts of the twentieth-century learning theorists; and McGeoch, who has been characterized as a functionalist, reviewed the available evidence on human learning and memory in *The Psychology of Human Learning* (1942). Here we shall give a brief indication of the features of the work of the five main learning theorists.

After publishing his monograph on animal learning in 1899, Thorndike obtained a position at Teachers College, Columbia University, in New York, where he remained for the rest of his life. His duties brought him increasingly into contact with educational psychologists, and his contributions to that discipline were many. They included writing a widely adopted textbook in arithmetic, compiling a list of the most commonly used words (this with the aim of facilitating the teaching of reading and writing), and devising a number of intelligence and aptitude tests for use both in schools and in the armed services. A full account of Thorndike's career as an educational psychologist is given by Joncich (1968). Moreover, Thorndike tried to apply his Law of Effect and Law of Exercise in the context of human learning. His efforts in this direction were described in *The Psychology of Learning* (1914) and *The Fundamentals of Learning* (1932), both of which are replete with experimental data derived from observations of human subjects carrying out various learning tasks.

We may quickly summarize later developments in Thorndike's thinking as follows: On the Law of Effect, which holds that a satisfying situation "stamps in" or "reinforces" a "connection," Thorndike later added that the reinforcing situation could have its effect not only on the immediately preceding action but on actions prior to and following that. He called this a "spread of effect" and showed that if one connection in a task being learned by an adult were reinforced by the word *right,* neighboring connections, both preceding and following the reinforced connection, were also well retained. This claim engendered a controversial literature, reviewed by Hilgard and Bower (1966, pp. 29–44), and the matter is still unresolved. Thorndike also stressed that neighboring connections could be reinforced by virtue of what he called their *belongingness.* Thus, in the sentences "John is a carpenter. Bill is a professor," the connection of *John* with *carpenter* is stronger than the connection of *carpenter* with *Bill* even though these two terms are closer together in the sequence than are the former two. The reason is that *John* and *carpenter* are made to belong together by being in the same sentence.

For Thorndike, the human psyche consisted of a multitude of bonds originally established by reinforcement and held together by belongingness. What of the Law of Exercise, according to which bonds should be strengthened by practice? In the *Fundamentals of Learning* Thorndike described some experiments that he claimed indicated that the simple use of a connection over and over again did not seem to make the connection any more circumscribed or integrated than it originally had been. He therefore asserted that the importance of the Law of Exercise was less than he had claimed in his original *Animal Intelligence* (1911). He was led to state:

> All psychological and educational doctrines which rely upon experience as such, in disregard of its consequences, are now less acceptable than ever. If a certain state of affairs acts upon a man a thousand times a week for a year, he will, so far as the mere repetition of that state of affairs is concerned, probably respond no better the last week than the first. (1932, p. 63)

Thorndike's stress on reinforcement and his skepticism concerning mere repetition as an aid to learning had many supporters.

The learning theorist closest to Watson in his emphasis on the simplicity of learning was Guthrie. In *The Psychology of Learning* (1935, 2nd ed., 1952) Guthrie asserted a basic principle that he held to underlie even complex learning: "A combination of stimuli which has accompanied a movement will on its recurrence tend to be·followed by that movement." Nothing was said about reinforcement, and to that extent Guthrie's theory resembled that of Pavlov, who also stressed that in conditioning, one stimulus, simply by being accompanied by a response, could, after appropriate pairing, come to elicit the response.

The next question, then, is how Guthrie handled the evidence for the Law of Effect. He believed that the function of reward was not to stamp in a connection but to prevent its being "unlearned." Suppose an animal does something ineffective in helping it to escape from confinement. That action is not accompanied by a new situation, so it is not made prepotent in any way—the next action replaces it, and it may not be retained. But a successful act leads to a new situation, one of escape, with the effect that the new situation—escape—is associated with the movement: The memory of the movement remains salient. As evidence supporting this kind of analysis, Guthrie and Horton (1946) made films of cats escaping from puzzle boxes and showed how the cat would tend to repeat its behavior in the box after each successful escape. In the theory, however, the new situation of escaping could have sensory cues associated with it, which are also conditioned to the escape movement, so that the role of reward may be greater than just that of preventing unlearning (on this, see Hilgard and Bower, 1966, p. 82). In his book, Guthrie attacked Thorndike for being overspeculative in his assessment of the function of reward in the learning process. Guthrie's theory has been called a contiguity theory of learning.

Hull attempted to integrate Pavlov's concept of classical conditioning with Thorndike's evidence for the importance of reward. Hull's theory, the most elaborate of all the learning theories of this period, in part arose from his own fascination with the power of axiomatic systems in science. Hull saw how, in ancient times, Euclid had based a system of geometry on a few axioms; how Newton had based a system of physics on axioms, in the *Principia*; and, in his own time, how Russell and Whitehead had based a system of logic on axioms. Hull wanted to do the same with learning theory, and above all he wanted that theory to be mechanical, that is to say, one could put a stimulus into the system and, from a knowledge of the organism's past coupled with postulates about how the stimulus interacted with the system, could predict the next response.

In 1936 Hull began his program for predicting behavior by a preliminary exercise with a model devoted exclusively to the way humans learn nonsense material by heart: This resulted in his first model based on postulates, the *Mathematico-Deductive Theory of Rote Learning* (Hull et al., 1940). In this book Hull suggested that an association between a stimulus and a response had to have a certain "strength" composed of excitatory tendencies (so that when a cue or earlier stimulus in the list is presented, this "excites" the desired response) that are competed with by inhibitory tendencies. An association between S_1 and R_1 may be formed with a certain strength that is insufficient for S_1 to excite R_1 on a subsequent trial, but by repeating the pairing of S_1 and R_1 the excitation can summate until eventually the strength of the association is sufficient for S_1 to lead to the subject's giving the response R_1. However, the inhibitory tendencies, related to such subjective phenomena as fatigue and the desire of the subject *not* to repeat actions also summate. In between trials, both excitatory and inhibitory tendencies die away, but the inhibitory tendencies die away faster than the excitatory. In this way Hull was able to explain Ebbinghaus's finding that learning a list in a series of trials massed together is not so effective as learning with rests in between trials: When the trials are massed, the inhibitory tendencies do not have time to die away, so slow down learning. This model was also able to account for a number of other phenomena, including the facts that the middle of a list is the hardest part to learn and that sometimes memory after a long interval is better than memory after a short interval, particularly for middle items of a list.

Hull's book was received with great attention because it seemed to embody so well the superficial appurtenances of the respectable sciences like geometry and physics. Anything that could get psychology off the hook of being "unscientific" was welcomed, and Hull was encouraged to go on to develop a similar system to cover learning in general. The advantage of studying human verbal learning was that the dynamics of excitatory and inhibitory tendencies could be demonstrated without worrying too much about motivation: The human student was at a fairly consistent level of motivation, so this factor could be controlled. But when we turn to learning in general, particularly learning in animals, we know that it is very much more a function of reinforcement, and that reinforcement in turn is only effective insofar as it satisfies an animal's wants. I have used the word "want" deliberately, because one of the most important outcomes of Hull's research on motivation and learning was that a distinction came to be made between an animal's *needs* (such as food or liquid for survival) and an animal's *likings* (such as a taste for sweetness; saccharin, even though it has no food value, can still serve as a reinforcer for a rat running a maze). It was mainly as a result of Hull's work that learning theorists began to talk of reinforcement as an event that was effective in relation to an animal's *drive*; a valuable summary of the impact of Hull's theory on our understanding of drive is given by J. S. Brown (1979).

Between his first statement of the learning model in *Principles of Behavior* (1943) and his last, *A Behavior System* (1952), a change took place: Initially, Hull believed that a reinforcer had to reduce an animal's primary drive such as hunger. Later he came to see that a reinforcer could be effective because it pleased the animal or was *associated* with a reinforcer that reduced a primary drive (was a *secondary reinforcer*). In the first model, Hull had sixteen postulates: The gist of the model was that a rat could learn a sequence of movements through a maze because each movement became associated with the next, with the last movement associated with reward. The association between the last movement and getting reward was learned first, with the early movements appended over a sequence of trials. As in the earlier model, an association was held to have a strength that was given by a combination of excitatory and inhibitory tendencies. This strength had to reach a certain level before it could release a measurable response, and it could be related, by simple mathematical equations, to such factors as the number of trials, the animal's drive strength, and inhibition arising from competing response tendencies. From a theoretical point of view, the issue that has most interested mathematical modelers of memory and learning since Hull's time was the question of whether repeated trials actually do add to the "strength" of an association; other evidence has suggested that an association is formed in a single moment as an all-or-none event. Those interested in this important question should consult Restle and Greeno (1970, Chaps. 1 and 2).

Hull's theory dominated research on learning until the middle 1960s. One of the reasons it is no longer such a topic of interest is that it was very unwieldy from a mathematical point of view (D. J. Murray, 1987), even though some of the more general questions it raised, such as the question of whether a reinforcer had to reduce a drive, could be easily tested. Some personality theorists such as E. J. Eysenck (1974) argued that the difference between introverts and extraverts could be seen in terms of the balance of excitatory and inhibitory tendencies, and there were also attempts to relate the notion of inhibitory tendencies to human anxiety (Spence and Taylor, 1962). Although there is little research now on Hull's theory as to how animals learn, his ideas will probably survive in psychology in general because of these attempts by some of his followers, notably Kenneth J. Spence (1907–1967), to extrapolate his theory to areas outside learning.

When planning his ambitious project, Hull (1936) had stated that his aim was to produce a psychology that explained "purpose." As far as Hull was concerned, he succeeded, he thought, in producing a reductionist argument according to which a valid psychology of animal learning can be produced *without* the need for the word "purpose."

Hull had acted as if learning a maze were a matter of strengthening connections between movements, but for Tolman, there were two aspects to this vague word *learning*: a problem-solving aspect and a retention aspect. Hull's theory may be on the right lines for explaining how habits were retained and strengthened from trial to trial, but learning a maze also presents a problem to the rat. Tolman, in his *Purposive Behavior in Animals and Man* (1932), argued that a rat learns a maze partly by setting himself the goal of attaining food and adapting his behavior accordingly. The start box of a maze sets up a *means-end readiness* in the animal that directs the solution of the problem in finding his way to the foodbox. That the animal did have some sort of internal representation or *cognitive map* (a term dating to Tolman, 1948) of the maze was shown by ingenious experiments: A rat blocked from using a path to a goalbox will choose an alternative path he has not necessarily traversed before; a rat that has a visual cue of the rough direction of the goalbox will adapt its behavior accordingly and not follow old turning habits; a rat that is allowed time to explore a maze before food is put into the goalbox will learn the maze more rapidly than one not allowed any preliminary exploration. The most important result of Tolman's work was that even animals were conceived of as experiencing a cognitive state we now call *expectation*. And the implications of this for our understanding of Pavlov's classical conditioning are theoretically interesting, for it now becomes conceivable that a bell elicits salivation (after conditioning) not by a passive mechanism, but by a mechanism that involves the dog's *expecting* food and preparing himself for it by salivating. Whether purposive or expectant cognitive states can be eliminated in a true psychology of learning is now a much less clear-cut question than it was for Hull.

Skinner, in his *The Behavior of Organisms* (1938), adopted from Pavlov the notion that the word *reflex* could be applied to learned behavior patterns and from Thorndike the concept of reinforcement. But he was concerned that many types of learned behavior did not seem to be elicited by any identifiable stimulus; instead, the organism seemed to emit the behavior spontaneously. Skinner invented a device whereby spontaneous behavior patterns could be reinforced at the experimenter's will and at the same time a record could be kept of the animal's response. Now known as a Skinner box, the device consisted of an enclosed area with a lever and food tray. When the lever was pressed (at first accidentally) by the animal (in Skinner's early work, rats; in later work, pigeons), food would be automatically delivered. Thereafter, the rat would spontaneously press the lever when put back into the box. By attaching the lever to an external recording device, a continuous record could be kept of the animal's lever-pressing behavior. Skinner called this kind of learning *operant conditioning* and the Pavlovian kind *respondent conditioning* and stated that "the conditioning of an operant differs from that of a respondent by involving the correlation of a reinforcing stimulus with a response" (1936/1966, p. 21).

Skinner went on to show that lever pressing could be obtained even though the reinforcement was not given on every trial and he was able to demonstrate differential conditioning to separate stimuli. He also discussed the role of drive in influencing lever-pressing behavior. At a more theoretical level, Skinner argued that a science of behavior could consist entirely of inferences based on experimenter-controlled contingencies of reinforcement and need not involve physiological speculation or the discussion of such concepts as consciousness. Skinner's work has been vital insofar as it extended learning theory to include operant, or spontaneously emitted, behavior; it also formed the basis of the field of behavior therapy, in which Watson's idea that inappropriate behavior patterns could be extinguished by appropriate methods of reinforcement has reached contemporary fruition. It should be noted that in Poland in the 1930s, following a more Pavlovian tradition, Konorski had also discussed conditioned reflexes in which spontaneous movements were reinforced by reward (Konorski, 1948).

We restrict what we say here to Skinner's work before 1940, but we shall return to modern applications of operant conditioning theory in Chapter 13. It should be noted, however, that one reason so much more attention is paid nowadays to Skinner's paradigm of lever pressing than to Hull's paradigm of maze learning is that the former is much easier to investigate, using modern apparatus, than the latter.

By 1940 considerable information had been collected about learning in both human beings and animals. The literature on human learning was reviewed in detail by McGeoch (1942): Most of the work elaborated on the original findings of Ebbinghaus and G. E. Müller, but a great deal of new research investigated such matters as practice, interference in learning, and the variables that determined the ease of learning serial lists of paired associates. In Britain Bartlett (1932) argued that the Ebbinghaus paradigm of learning lists of nonsense syllables by heart was too artificial to reveal much about human memory as it ordinarily functions.

He investigated, instead, the recall of stories and showed that much recall activity consists of an attempt to reconstruct the details of a story from key elements that were easily recalled. He also proposed that, instead of talking of static memory traces, memories should be seen as fluid, constantly changing schemata in which each individual element was enmeshed with many other elements. His book *Remembering* (1932), neither behavioristic nor Gestalt in orientation, was to be influential. In America Melton and Von Lackum (1941) argued that when one list is learned, then another, the second list causes retroactive inhibition of the first, partly because there is confusion between the elements of the two lists, but also because the subject actively unlearns or deliberately suppresses the associations from the first list while learning the second list.

In the area of animal learning, a large amount of new information was amassed on Pavlovian conditioning (or *classical conditioning,* as it came to be known) and the variables that influenced both it and operant conditioning and trial-and-error learning. In particular, the technique of eyelid conditioning was widely used to study classical conditioning in humans. In this technique a neutral stimulus is followed by a puff of air directed at the side of the eye; this causes the subject to blink. After successive pairings, the neutral stimulus comes to elicit the eye blink. Much of this research was reviewed by Hilgard and Marquis (1940).

At this point we shall be content to note that a rigorous experimental approach to animal learning became the norm after the onset of behaviorism. The study of human learning progressed with little reference to subjective states of consciousness or to imagery. Only since the 1960s has a more cognitive approach been adopted by many experimental psychologists. This has been partly in reaction to the limits imposed by a strict behaviorism.

Summary

Two questions that particularly interested psychologists at the turn of the century were whether the word *consciousness* should be used in describing animal behavior and what role learning—as opposed to instinct—played in determining animal behavior. Lloyd Morgan insisted that anthropomorphic accounts of animal behavior be avoided, and Loeb and Jennings, in their studies of invertebrates, insisted on mechanistic accounts of their behavior. There was thus a move against the use of the words based on conscious experience. As to the role of learning, several authors stressed that learning was important in infant development and animals; Thorndike, following his studies of cats escaping from boxes, stressed that their behavior should be described as trial-and-error learning rather than intelligent learning; moreover, successful outcomes were the result of the behaviors' being reinforced by rewards (the Law of Effect). Even so, some authors maintained that animals should be seen as being more intelligent than Thorndike maintained.

Meanwhile, very simple forms of learning were being investigated in Russia. In the nineteenth century Sechenov had argued that even learned behaviors could be described in a language based on reflexes and inhibition; later Pavlov, who had observed psychic reflexes during his studies of digestion, mapped out the course of what is now called classical conditioning. *Conditioning* was described in the terminology of *stimulus, response, extinction, generalization,* and *inhibition.* Bekhterev, who had followed Sechenov in his belief that complex human behavior could be reduced to sequences of psychoreflexes, also developed experimental paradigms for studying conditioning.

The person who pulled these various lines of thought together was J. B. Watson. He argued explicitly, in 1913, that a scientific psychology should be based on the observation of behavior only and that it could do without the concept of consciousness. The introspection method was also invalid, he claimed—a direct challenge to Titchener and to the Würzburg psychologists. He later investigated conditioned reflexes and claimed that adult personality could be seen as the result of many instances of individual conditioning superimposed on a basic set of innate behavior patterns. Watson propagated his behaviorism for many years, even after leaving the academic world.

In the 1930s a number of learning theorists tried to elaborate on Watson's view and produce systematic accounts of conditioning and higher learning. Thorndike studied his Law of Effect in more detail; Guthrie studied the role of contiguity in learning; Hull constructed a large system based on axioms concerned with stimulus–response events; Skinner explored operant conditioning, where habits are formed after spontaneous actions are systematically rewarded; and Tolman discussed the more cognitive aspects of learning in animals. These authors formed the nucleus of the neobehaviorist movement.

Psychoanalysis

11

The History of Psychiatry

The third great school or movement of psychology in the early part of the twentieth century was psychoanalysis, founded by Sigmund Freud (1856–1939). Psychoanalysis did not arise out of the mainstream of psychology, however, but from developments in psychiatry during the late nineteenth century. To place psychoanalysis in its proper perspective, therefore, we shall first give a quick sketch of developments in psychiatry up to that time. It is of note that so far, with few exceptions, we have been able to discuss the history of psychology with little reference to abnormal psychology; of the major figures in the history of psychology, few attempted to offer a system of psychology that took account of abnormal as well as normal behavior. Freud was one of these.

From the beginning of time it has been recognized that the emotionally disturbed have unusual states of consciousness and strange behavior patterns. Some primitive societies insisted that their witch doctors or medicine men undergo what we would now consider a mental illness. Many peoples, including the Babylonians, Egyptians, and ancient Hebrews, believed mental illness to be caused by evil spirits, and incantations designed to ward off the spirits have been found in their extant writings. Epilepsy was also thought to be caused by an evil demon "possessing" the patient: We saw that one of Hippocrates' great insights (Chap. 1) was to realize that epilepsy might be the result of brain disease. Hysteria, in which psychological stress is associated with apparent physiological dysfunctions such as anesthesia of a limb, paralysis of a limb, mutism, or even blindness, was thought to be restricted to women. In the classical period it was believed that the uterus wandered about and a paralysis of, for example, the arm resulted when the uterus invaded the arm region.

Cures for mental illness in ancient times ranged from physical methods such as use of the purgative hellebore to psychological methods such as a stay in a temple of healing. In these temples the priests may have pretended to be gods visiting the patients to heal them; perhaps patients may have been put into trancelike states to make them believe in this deception. In classical Greece temple healing was widespread, but it also came to be believed that mental illness could be caused by an imbalance of the humors. *Melancholia*, for example, was supposed to be caused by a surfeit of black bile; *mania*, by a surfeit of yellow bile. But the words *melancholia* and *mania* were used much more widely then than now, and cannot be identified with the "depressive" and "manic" phases of the modern manic-depressive psychosis; instead, melancholia included withdrawn states as well as depression, and both states included what we now call paranoid symptoms.

In Roman times the theory of humors was elaborated to include the notion that the various "pores" of the body might become congested, preventing fluids from circulating properly, a theory known as *methodism*. One of its first practitioners was the Greek Asclepiades (b. 124 B.C.), who brought the idea to Rome. Physical therapy and the application of heat or cold to the patient's body to open or close the pores became fashionable methods of treatment. Most doctors and thinkers, including Cicero, were sympathetic to patients with mental illness, but the influential Celsus (25 B.C.–A.D. 50) advocated harsher treatments to make the patient want to get better more quickly, and he began a long tradition of punitive "therapy" that has only recently disappeared from Western psychiatry.

Galen wrote extensively on mental changes caused either by illness (as in fevers or during intoxication) or from emotional stress. Siegel (1973) is essential reading on Galen's theory of psychopathology, for he shows how certain words that were used in Galen's time have changed their meanings during the intervening centuries. Galen's treatment of mental illness included psychotherapy—his book *The Passions of the Soul* (see Chapter 1) is in part a book of self-education on how to control the passions—blood-letting, purgatives and, for the well-educated, intellectual activity.

During the Dark Ages of Europe, Arab physicians gave special care to cases of mental illness and developed the beginnings of psychotherapeutic measures. In Baghdad the hospital had a ward devoted to the care of the mentally ill as early as the ninth century. In the West the sick were often cared for in monasteries and institutions associated with them. But demonology as an explanation for mental illness made a comeback in the Middle Ages. In particular, probably because many celibate Christian males felt that women posed a particular threat to their moral principles, there arose the misogynous belief that some women were in consort with demons. Such women were known as witches. Following Biblical injunctions (see Exodus 22:18; Leviticus 20:27; Galatians 5:20–21) the Church mounted a campaign against witchcraft, and there is no doubt that many hysterical women and other mentally disturbed persons fell victim to this persecution. The witch hunts were given official Catholic approval in the *Malleus Maleficarum* (1487–1489), a guide to the detection and punishment of witches: It is clear from the cases described that many of the women so categorized suffered from emotional disturbances. At the same time special hospitals were built for the insane, the best-known being that of Bethlehem (Bedlam) founded in London in 1547; these were often more like prisons and the patients suffered from cruelty and neglect. Exceptions were found in Spain, where in the Valencia hospital (founded 1409) and elsewhere patients were given freedom and exercise and decent therapy.

But it has also been pointed out by Foucault (1965), who has written a history of how the mentally ill have been regarded in modern Western history, that the mentally ill became particular outcasts at this time: In the late Middle Ages they seemed to replace lepers, who were becoming rare, as feared persons. Almost up to the present a stigma has been attached, in the predominantly Christian West, to mental illness; at various times the mentally ill have been persecuted, sometimes for political or religious reasons. For example, in the seventeenth century the mentally ill were accused of the sin of idleness and became considered as animals because they were not productive in society; "madhouses" were built to contain them. The early nineteenth century witnessed the growth of a great public fear that madness was a sort of contagion that could spread into the community, and there was an enthusiastic building of "asylums," as the new madhouses were called, which were seen essentially as services to keep society uncontaminated by mental illness rather than as curative hospitals. Some of the more enlightened doctors, who saw mental illness as a matter for medicine rather than for moral outrage, are listed here.

During the sixteenth century several courageous individuals defied the Church and argued that "witches" were suffering from emotional disorders and not the incursion of demons. Paracelsus (1493–1541), for example, claimed that hysteria might be of sexual origin and that mania was the result of bodily substances influencing the brain. In particular, he thought that one such substance was a "natural spirit" made up of mercury, sulphur, and salts; Paracelsus represented the transition between medieval alchemy and modern biochemistry. Although Paracelsus frequently inveighed against authority, he was apparently well liked by the patients who consulted him. He prescribed medicines in small exact dosages for various ailments, including mental afflictions. Agrippa (1486–1535) also spoke out against the witch hunts and saved many women from persecution. His pupil Johann Weyer (1515–1588) published *De Praestigiis Daemonum* (*The Deception of Demons*) in 1563, a book in which he claimed that most victims of the witch hunts were merely deranged or deluded. He investigated many cases of alleged witchcraft and in some cases was able to help the victims in question. Many of Weyer's views were espoused by Reginald Scot (1538?–1599), who in 1584 pleaded the case against witchcraft in *The Discoverie of Witchcraft*. Weyer was also a fine observer and delineated many clinical symptom patterns.

The final great psychiatrist of the late Renaissance was the Swiss Felix Platter (1536–1614). Platter wrote a *Practice of Medicine*, extracts from which have been recently translated by Diethelm and Heffernan (1965). He outlined various symptoms of mental abnormality, including lethargy, convulsions, mental weakness, consternation, delirium, hallucination, melancholy, foolishness, drunkenness, mania, hypochondria, and disturbances of sleep and unusual dreams; however, even he included demoniacal possession as a class of mania. He recognized that these symptoms often occurred as a result of emotional trauma such as bereavement or unrequited love.

In the seventeenth century the situation became a little better for the mentally ill. In 1682 Louis XIV abolished the death penalty for witches in France; the great British physician Thomas Sydenham (1624–1689) noted that males as well as females could suffer from hysteria and wrote extensively on hysterical symptoms; and Thomas Willis (see pp. 87 and 100), in his *Two Discourses concerning the Soul of Brutes,* decried the belief that hysteria resulted from a wandering uterus. For melancholia he prescribed occupational therapy conducive to cheerfulness, but for mania he urged punishment as well as medicine. One book that did much to bring about the recognition that mental illness can be a direct outcome of straightforward emotional upset was the scholarly *The Anatomy of Melancholy* (1621), written by an English clergyman, Robert Burton (1577–1640). In this book Burton analyzed the many manifestations of the vague disease entity melancholia, devoting particular attention to demonstrating how emotional illness could result from unrequited love and from religious conflict.

In the first part of the eighteenth century William Battie (1704–1776) wrote one of the first textbooks of psychiatry, his *Treatise on Madness* (1738), and he is sometimes credited with being the first to make psychiatry a full-time profession. William Cullen (1710–1790), known for his classification schemes in general medicine, suggested that illness without an obvious origin in fever or local pathology be called "neurosis"; he included, however, such physical ailments as stroke and epilepsy, and it is not until the late nineteenth century that the word *neurosis* was used to refer to obsessions, anxiety attacks, hysteria, and similar complaints. Psychiatry was also given added status when George III of England showed signs of insanity related to a disease we now know as porphyria (Macalpine and Hunter, 1969).

An especially noteworthy contribution to psychiatry was the attempt by Erasmus Darwin to devise a classification for all diseases, including mental illnesses, in his *Zoonomia* (1796). Avoiding the old classifications, he preferred instead to treat mental illness as cases of "decreased" or "increased" volitions.

It was not until the last decade of the eighteenth century that we see the beginning of true psychiatric reform in the figures of Philippe Pinel (1745–1826) in France, William Tuke (1732–1822) in Britain, and Vincenzo Chiarugi (1759–1822) in Italy. Pinel studied medicine in his youth but apparently only became interested in mental illness in his forties. Following the French Revolution in 1789, Pinel was put in charge of two of the largest mental hospitals in France, the Bicêtre Asylum in 1793 and the Salpêtrière, a hospital for women, in 1795. In both these hospitals he insisted, against the advice of many, on releasing the patients from their chains. At about the same time in Italy Chiarugi was put in charge of a new hospital where the "moral" treatment of the insane was encouraged, and in 1792 the Quaker William Tuke founded the York Retreat in Britain, where equally enlightened principles of care for the patients were put into practice.

Pinel, however, did more than just "liberate the insane" in Paris. In 1801 he wrote an extremely influential book, *A Treatise on Insanity*, which brings us directly into the modern period of psychiatry. He outlined various causes, including hereditary predisposition, that he thought led to mental illness. He classified mental illness into four main kinds: mania, melancholia, dementia, and idiocy; mental aberrations due to fevers were classified separately. His treatment involved many innovations. He segregated the different types of patient, advised against restraint unless absolutely necessary, encouraged occupational therapy, wrote against any form of punishment or exorcism, and favored bathing, mild purgatives, and opium as physical treatments. He was one of the first psychiatrists to keep careful case histories and statistics on his patients, including a record of cure rates.

In America, Benjamin Rush advocated similar reforms in his *Medical Inquiries and Observations upon the Diseases of the Mind* (1812): Although he was in favor of a "tranquilizing" chair treatment, he also called for humanitarian care of the insane and was one of the first to campaign for hospital treatment for alcoholics. His book is notable for its wealth of observations on individual cases. In Germany J. C. Reil promoted hospital reform and stressed the value of psychotherapy over physical treatments.

Pinel was the first of an illustrious line of French psychiatrists that included J. E. D. Esquirol (1772–1840), a pioneer in problems of forensic psychiatry who stressed the importance of emotional trauma in the genesis of much mental illness, and G. Ferrus (1784–1861), who inaugurated a system of occupational therapy at the Bicêtre. It was also at about this time that systematic efforts to care for the mentally retarded were begun in France and in Switzerland: One spur to this movement was the discovery of a boy aged about ten who had been abandoned by his parents and left to "grow wild" until he was found and brought to Paris. Pinel considered him to be simply retarded, but a young doctor, J. M. G. Itard (1775–1838), rose to the challenge of trying to educate the boy. The story is told in two memoirs of 1801 and 1806, translated as *The Wild Boy of Aveyron*. Humphrey, one of the translators, notes:

> Of the immediate success of Itard's work there is no question. In place of the hideous creature that was brought to Paris, there was to be seen after two years' instruction an "almost normal child who could not speak" but who lived like a human being; clean, affectionate, even able to read a few words and to understand much that was said to him. (Itard, 1801 and 1806/ 1962, p. xii)

In Switzerland, J. Guggenbühl (1816–1863) founded a home for the care of those suffering from cretinism, a common condition in parts of that country, and in France Edward Séguin (1812–1880) began the teaching of mentally retarded children at the Bicêtre in 1842. He emigrated to the United States in 1848, where he was responsible for encouraging the founding of special schools for the retarded. At the beginning of the nineteenth century a group of psychiatrists also arose who anticipated psychoanalysis in their stress on the fact that patients could be at the mercy of emotional conflicts whose source they were not aware of: Among these were J. Moreau de Tours (1804–1884), a pupil of Esquirol, and the Germans J. C. Heinroth (1773–1843) and K. G. Carus (1789–1869).

The main trend in orthodox psychiatric circles of the middle nineteenth century, however, was a belief that mental illness had some physiological origin of an as yet undetermined nature. In Germany, W. Griesinger (1817–1868) had the title of Professor of Psychiatry and Neurology at the University of Berlin. In his *Mental Pathology and Therapeutics* (1845) he argued that, just as cretinism had recently been discovered to be due to a deficiency of iodine, so there might be some metabolic, vascular, or neurological abnormalities in the brains of the insane. He was humane in his treatment of his patients and was well aware of the importance of the threat to self-esteem brought on by serious disappointment. He stressed the concept of the *ego,* which had to be kept intact despite the inroads on it from psychological or neurological trauma. In his book he gave special attention to individual symptoms such as anomalies of emotion, reasoning, and will. The three main forms of mental illness for Griesinger were states of depression, states of mental exaltation, and states of mental weakness such as found in dementia or retardation.

In Britain, Henry Maudsley (1835–1918) upheld the same medical model as Griesinger: *The Physiology and Pathology of the Mind* (1867) advocated treating of mental illness as if it were a physical illness. At the same time, however, he emphasized the importance of sexual conflict, social pressure, and childhood experiences in the etiology of mental disorder. Like many others in the nineteenth century he believed that there was hereditary predisposition to mental illness.

Another popular text of the time in Britain was the *Manual of Psychological Medicine* (1858) of J. C. Bucknill (1817–1897) and D. M. Tuke (1827–1895). This book is noteworthy for its compilations of statistics on insanity, the denial of the value of restraint, and its many case histories. Again, the physiology of the nervous system was given particular emphasis. That the psychiatrists of the late nineteenth century had good reason to adopt this neurological stance was demonstrated by the frequency of cases of insanity brought on by syphilis—"general paralysis of the insane." The discovery of the bacterium that caused this disease and of drugs for alleviating it belongs, however, to the early twentieth century.

The modern classification of mental illness into the psychoses, in which the patient seems divorced from reality, and the neuroses, in which the patient seems more in command of his faculties, is due mainly to Emil Kraepelin (1856–1926). Kraepelin, after graduating in medicine from Würzburg, studied for a short period under Wundt. He was almost tempted to enter what we would now call experimental psychopathology—in Wundt's laboratory he studied the effects of alcohol, caffeine, and other drugs on mental and physical work—but Wundt persuaded him to return to psychiatry. It was Kraepelin who, in studying various forms of psychosis, made the widely adopted distinction into (1) catatonic dementia praecox, a condition in which the patient, often a young person, seems mute and often remains for long periods in one position, (2) hebephrenic dementia praecox, in which the patient's behavior is characterized by inappropriateness of word and deed, and (3) paranoia, in which the patient has a system of delusions, usually of persecution and/or grandeur. Separate from the categories of dementia praecox were the manic-depressive psychoses.

Kraepelin was skeptical about the outcome of dementia praecox—many young patients were doomed to lives on closed wards as a result of this attitude—but Eugene Bleuler (1857–1939) insisted that the illness was of psychological origin and could respond, admittedly not always easily, to psychotherapy. Bleuler disagreed with Kraepelin in the use of the word *dementia* to refer to the syndrome, instead suggesting that it be called *schizophrenia,* the word now commonly used. *Schizophrenia* means "split" or "divided" personality; Bleuler believed that morbid thought processes disturbed the emotional integrity of the self in this disease. Schizophrenia is, of course, to be distinguished from "multiple personality," in which a person seems to have two or even three distinct selves that may or may not intercommunicate.

The above is a summary of the events in orthodox psychiatry prior to Freud's time. But running like an undercurrent through the nineteenth century was the realization that the mind, and particularly the emotional facets of psychological functioning, can be more complicated than the neurological model would permit. In particular, altered states of consciousness such as are found in hypnosis or certain forms of hysteria seem to demand a concept of mental functioning that stresses its vulnerability rather than its integrity, its conflicts rather than its stability. Freud's speculations began when he came to study hysteria: But in his time the current theory of hysteria related it to hypnotizability, so we must briefly turn back to the late eighteenth century to describe this byway of psychological history.

Hypnosis and Hysteria Before Freud

There is little doubt that some mentally ill people *felt* cured or had their hysterical symptoms alleviated by the practice of exorcism. One of the most famous exorcists of the late eighteenth century was the Austrian Father J. V. Gassner (1727–1779). Gassner had great success in "casting out devils," but in 1775 he was challenged by a young doctor named Franz Anton Mesmer (1734–1815). Mesmer had written a thesis claiming that the planets exerted an influence on human diseases. He later developed this theory so that in its final version, Mesmer suggested that a "gravitational fluid" emanated from the stars and planets and that certain individuals could harness this fluid and use it to control the course of events inside other people's bodies. This power he called *animal magnetism.* The gifted individual—and, of course, Mesmer claimed that he was one himself—could, by merely touching a person, cause the fluid to bring about the disappearance of such symptoms as paralysis. Mesmer argued that Gassner's exorcistic "cures" were simply manifestations of animal magnetism. In the heated controversy on the matter, Mesmer won, and exorcism henceforward played a vanishing role in the history of psychotherapy.

Mesmer himself left Austria two years after his bout with Gassner and arrived in Paris in 1778. Here he turned animal magnetism into a sort of fashionable game. In a luxurious apartment he arranged a large tub, the *baquet,* which was supposed to collect the magnetic fluid and discharge it through the bodies of those who sat around it holding the iron rods that projected from the *baquet.* To the sound of strange music, Mesmer would appear in a lilac robe. Quite often the subjects would go into a sort of convulsive crisis and have to be removed from the room; others claimed that their ailments, many of which we should now describe as hysterical, vanished. Mesmer's fame grew until 1784, when a Royal Commission was appointed to investigate his theory. The commission members included the great chemist Lavoisier and Benjamin Franklin; they concluded there was no good evidence to support the notion of a magnetic fluid, and the cures reported were probably due to "imagination." However, this verdict scarcely discountenanced Mesmer; it was because of a number of disagreements with his disciples and other critics that he eventually left Paris in 1785. He apparently lived as a recluse for the remainder of his years. But *mesmerism,* as his theory of harnessing the fluid via touch was called, continued to survive.

The most important convert to the theory was de Chastenet, Marquis de Puységur (1751–1825). Puységur tried his mesmeric passes on a young peasant, but instead of showing the convulsive behavior characteristic of others the peasant fell into a sort of sleep state in which he nevertheless remained aware and to some extent hypersensitive. Soon Puységur was putting many persons into magnetic sleep. Other practitioners of mesmerism also were able to induce this sleep state in their patients. It was discovered that the subjects could be put into the state by the command to sleep (rather than by touch or passes) and that during the sleep subjects could be given suggestions, which they would later obey after coming out of the sleep, unaware of why they were doing this task. The name mesmerism was also applied to Puységur's sleep state, and interest in his phenomenon spread across Europe, especially to Germany. Because of its associations with Mesmer, most medical people considered mesmerism quackery. This attitude changed slightly when two British doctors became persuaded of the value of magnetic sleep as an anaesthetic device (Elliotson, 1843/1977; Esdaile, 1846/1977) and another English physician, James Braid (1795?–1860), became persuaded of the reality of the unusual phenomena associated with the sleep state. He renamed the sleep state *neurypnology,* a word that gradually changed to *hypnotism; hypnotism* has now almost completely replaced *mesmerism* and *animal magnetism* as the general term. Nevertheless, hypnotism remained in general disrepute, and after the discovery of chloroform in 1847 it was used only rarely as an anaesthetic. Braid also expressed his disbelief that hypnotic phenomena had anything to do with mysterious fluids passing between the hypnotist and the subject.

The situation changed in the second half of the century when it began to be realized that some hypnotic phenomena resembled hysterical phenomena, and the question was raised as to the relationship between them. There were two schools of thought, the so-called Nancy school represented by A. A. Liébault (1823–1904) and H. Bernheim (1840–1919), and the Salpêtriére school, represented by Jean-Martin Charcot (1835–1893) and his pupils.

Liébault had long believed that in a state of hypnotic trance ill subjects could be given suggestions that would apparently alleviate their symptoms. He practiced his hypnotic therapy without fees and was ignored for many years until the eminent physician Bernheim became persuaded of the validity of some of Liébault's claims and recognized that the kind of illness most likely to be helped by hypnotic treatment was of the kind we now call *psychosomatic*. It was Bernheim who argued that the subject in a hypnotic trance was rendered more "suggestible": In fact, Bernheim in his later career successfully used suggestion with persons in a waking state as well as those hypnotized. Bernheim also noted that by skillful questioning a person could sometimes be brought to recall what had happened in a hypnotic state.

Quite different, more erratic, and yet more influential were the views of Charcot and his pupils. Charcot was the most eminent neurologist of his time. He will always be remembered for his pioneering and competent research on multiple sclerosis, Parkinson's disease, tabes dorsalis, and other diseases of the brain and spinal cord. Charcot had been put in charge of the Salpêtriére, which by the middle 1800s contained as many as five thousand women, most destitute and very many suffering from nervous or mental disease. It was to Charcot's credit that he recognized the value of the Salpêtriére for neurological and psychiatric research. He studied epilepsy—he set aside a special ward for epileptic patients—and distinguished between *grand mal* epilepsy, involving severe seizures, and *petit mal* epilepsy, involving momentary losses of consciousness. But certain hysterical patients housed with the epileptics began to imitate them and go into apparent convulsions themselves. This led Charcot to make the analogous distinction between a *grande hystérie*, characterized by convulsions, large movements, and delirium, and *la petite hystérie*, where only minor bodily symptoms, such as tics or isolated paralysis, were observed.

At this point Charcot's reasoning took an interesting turn. He discovered that certain patients, when hypnotized, could be induced to demonstrate their hysterical symptoms (including convulsions) on command. Furthermore, posthypnotic suggestion could be used to elicit such behavior. It was suggested to one patient, for example, that she would undergo a paralysis of the arm after being slapped on the back when she emerged from the trance, and this posthypnotic suggestion was successfully demonstrated to a crowd of eager medical students and others. Charcot believed, in fact, that hypnotizability was a symptom of hysteria, and he thought of it as something like a syndrome. He characterized "*le grand hypnotisme*" as having three stages: cataleptic, during which the subject was relaxed and insensitive; lethargic, during which movements would occur; and somnambulic, during which the subject could carry out complex movements at the physician's suggestion.

The immediate quarrel with the Nancy school arose because Bernheim contended that hypnotizability characterized everybody, not just hysterical patients, and because he and others simply failed to obtain a standard pattern corresponding to Charcot's grand hypnotism. In the long run, Bernheim's theories won out over Charcot's. Many of Charcot's demonstrations were on favorite hysterical subjects who knew what was demanded of them and who may have been coached by assistants without Charcot's awareness; for some historians of science, Charcot's dabbling in hypnosis and hysteria detracts from his greatness as a neurologist.

Furthermore, one of Charcot's pupils, Pierre Janet (1859–1947), was able to show that Charcot's choice of three stages of hypnotism might have derived from accounts of the old magnetizers, whose aim was often to inculcate a state of automatism or somnambulism in their subjects. Nevertheless, because of his prestige, Charcot made hypnotism a respectable tool for psychiatrists; among his pupils were many who saw that the phenomena of hypnotism and hysteria were *somehow* related, even if not as Charcot believed, and Charcot's work gave the death knell to old theories about hysteria being confined to women and having something to do with the uterus. Charcot, however, did express the view that hysteria might be related to a disturbance of sexual function. Interested readers are advised to consult Veith (1965) for a history of theories and treatments of hysteria and for an evaluation of Charcot's theories; Charcot's career is traced in detail by Owen (1971).

We must say more, however, about Janet. Janet had originally taught philosophy in the small northern French town of Le Havre, but partly because he became involved in hypnotism, he developed a strong interest in psychopathology. Eventually he decided to take up medicine as a career, and in 1889 he studied with Charcot before settling down for the rest of his long life as a physician with a private practice in Paris. While at Le Havre, he studied the behavior of a young woman named Léonie, who possessed the unusual facility of entering hypnotic trances very easily. In fact, she had been hypnotized previously by members of the old magnetic school. Janet observed that Léonie seemed to show different aspects of personality in different levels of hypnotic trance. In other patients, he also saw how new facets of the individual revealed themselves in such phenomena as automatic writing, and Janet eventually concluded that certain memories or desires that were "split off" from the normal waking personality could make their presence known in altered states of consciousness such as hypnotic trance. That is, facets of the person were "dissociated" from the main body of the subject's memories and desires.

Following his move to Paris and his experience with many other patients on Charcot's wards, Janet came to recognize that hysterical symptoms might be the result of the "subconscious" influence of these dissociated aspects of personality; in particular, he discovered that in many cases of hysteria the dissociated memories that set up the disturbance were of an unpleasant or traumatic nature. Such memories he called "subconscious fixed ideas"; he came to believe that the aim of the therapist was to use hypnosis or any other means to ferret out the fixed ideas. Janet felt that the hysterical symptoms should abate when the patient was made aware of the ideas. In fact, individual patients reacted in a variety of ways to the recollection of their trauma: Sometimes Janet aimed at a reeducative process; at other times, he tried to encourage the patient to ignore or transform the unpleasant memory.

All this work was carried out in the late 1880s and early 1890s, antedating some of Freud's discoveries on the importance of trauma in the origin of hysteria. Janet went on to develop his notions into a large and ambitious system based on a division of behavior tendencies into various levels, ranging from reflexive behavior to the formulation of abstract goals; the fullest account of this system in English will be found in Ellenberger (1970, Chap. 6). Janet's late system never attained the influence of Freud's later systems. However, there is no question that some of Freud's earlier ideas were anticipated by Janet, whose work Freud acknowledged in passing, but with which he did not entirely agree. Janet's method for unearthing subconscious traumatic memories was called psychological analysis: Freud deliberately chose a new word, *psychoanalysis*, to stress the differences between his ideas and those of Janet. To the development of these ideas we now turn.

Freud

Sigmund Freud was born at Freiberg in Czechoslovakia in 1856, but at the age of four his family moved to Vienna. As a member of a devout Jewish family, he experienced some anti-Semitism, but on the whole his childhood and adolescence years were spent peacefully. He was a good scholar and in his teens developed an interest in zoology. He therefore decided on a medical career and entered Vienna University in 1873. He spent eight years studying and doing research before finally graduating, and it was during this time that he was influenced by the physiologist E. W. von Brücke (1819–1892) and made the acquaintance of Joseph Breuer (1842–1925), with whom he later collaborated. His translation of a volume of John Stuart Mill's works attests to his interest in psychology and philosophy during this period; he also published a paper on the male sex organs of the eel and undertook research on methods of staining the brain for neurological purposes.

In 1882 Freud began work as an intern in medicine, possibly because he needed a larger income to marry his fiancee, Martha Bernays. It was while he was in his middle twenties that he began research on cocaine, not only as a medication and analgesic, but also for the relief of mental tension. The "cocaine episode," as it is called, is strange because Freud himself took cocaine with no obvious harmful effects, whereas one of his coworkers became seriously addicted to the drug. For a while Freud championed cocaine as a medicine and achieved some fame in the Viennese medical community as a result, but when the addictive properties of cocaine became more widely known, his reputation was rather tarnished. At the same time, however, it is possible that this episode helped to switch his interests from purely physiological matters to more psychological matters.

The great center of psychiatry at the time was Charcot's department in Paris, so Freud went there and stayed from October 1885 to February 1886. Here he translated some of Charcot's lectures into German, and here, according to Sulloway (1979, p. 34), he formulated the notion that a hysterical symptom, such as a paralysis, might be the result of some sort of traumatic memory persisting in the unconscious. According to Masson (1984), he also became acquainted with a growing literature on child abuse, including child sexual abuse, that may also have influenced his thinking.

Back in Vienna, Freud opened a private practice and, on October 15, 1886, gave a lecture entitled "On Male Hysteria." Earlier accounts of Freud's life suggested that his lecture was a failure because Freud described one of Charcot's cases of male hysteria to a Viennese audience that still believed in the notion that hysteria was restricted to females. Later accounts of Freud's life, however, such as those by Ellenberger (1970) and Sulloway (1979), suggest that it was not a great success because male hysteria was already known about in Vienna, but in a new context. There had been several cases of railway and industrial accidents affecting males that had left symptoms such as paralysis, which may have been nonorganic and caused by psychological shock. Because these cases were sometimes called "hysterical," to report a male case of "hysteria" was therefore not very new. Furthermore, Freud presented many of Charcot's ideas uncritically, and the Viennese doctors had already heard the charges that some of Charcot's patients were putting on an act. In other words, Freud's initial paper on hysteria seems to have been received courteously but somewhat unenthusiastically. At the same time, in his own private practice he continued to use hypnotism despite its controversial reputation and, keeping up with the changing views on the subject, he visited Bernheim and Liebault in Nancy in 1889. During these years— from 1886 to about 1890—his medical research was focused particularly on neurology, however, and he wrote on aphasia and various forms of paralysis caused by cerebral injury in children.

It was during this period that Freud made contact with another doctor, Josef Breuer, who was to play an important role in his career. In 1868 Breuer, who had met Freud when they were students, had made a fundamental discovery about the reflexes involved in breathing; in 1873 he had discovered, simultaneously with Mach and A. C. Brown, how the semicircular canals operated to control balance. Breuer helped Freud financially during his medical studies, and when Freud married in 1886 the Breuer and Freud families made frequent contact. But Breuer's real influence on Freud was to show Freud that hysterical systems could indeed have their root in earlier traumatic experiences, as Freud had suspected. Breuer based these inferences on his experiences with a patient, Anna O., whom he had started treating in 1880; Freud made similar observations on several other cases; and their collaboration culminated with the publication of *Studies in Hysteria*, in which Breuer and Freud each had separate chapters discussing their individual patients, Breuer offering a chapter on the theory of hysteria and Freud a chapter on its treatment.

The Breuer-Freud theory can be stated, oversimply, as follows: An unhappy experience, which could be sexual or nonsexual, left a strong memory that caused so much disturbance to the conscious self that it was pushed down into the unconscious. But because it contained so much "energy," this memory could not be completely pushed down and manifested itself in the form of physical complaints. In the case of Anna O., for example, a number of quite separate incidents in her life left distinct memories, each of which was reflected in a hysterical symptom: For example, under hypnosis, or by putting the patient into a relaxed state where she talked freely, Breuer discovered that Anna O.'s fear of drinking water went back to a time when she saw a dog drinking water out of a glass, which disgusted her. This is an example of a nonsexual trauma; the example in the book of a sexual trauma concerns one of Freud's cases (Katherina) in which the patient kept losing her breath and felt "buzzing" in her head and something "crushing" her chest. Freud tracked these down to memories of a time two years earlier, when the patient was in her teens, when her father had made sexual advances to her. Breuer, in his chapter on theory, offered an account in purely physiological terms of how the organism arrived at preserving a constant state of "excitation";

threatening memories disrupted this state and, in defense, were re-pressed into the unconscious (the words *defense* and *repression* both occur in this book).

It was really Freud, however, who went a step further and stressed that sexual, rather than nonsexual, traumata were the causes of most, if not all, hysteria—and, he added in other writings about this time, anxiety neuroses were the result of sexual frustration in both males and females. Over the course of the next few years an estrangement gradually occurred between Breuer and Freud. One reason was that Breuer found that he was getting into deeper waters than he intended when Anna O. became emotionally involved with him; he also found that the sheer length of time it took to deal with a patient such as Anna O. made it impossible for him to carry out his other medical duties.

From 1894 to 1897, Freud continued to ponder the theory that hysteria was caused by traumatic memories but became more and more convinced that the traumas in question were sexual. During this time he corresponded intensively with a Berlin physician, Dr. Wilhelm Fliess. Fliess had attended some of Freud's lectures on neurology as early as 1887 and they had corresponded since then, but the letters in the period 1894 to 1900 have turned out to be a particularly fruitful source of information about the changes that took place in Freud's thinking about neuroses after his break with Breuer. After Freud's death about half of his letters to Fliess were published in a book entitled *The Origins of Psychotherapy* (Bonaparte, A. Freud, & Kris, 1954); the full set has recently been published by Masson (1985). The importance of Fliess in the development of Freud's ideas has been traced more fully by Sulloway (1979), who gives a detailed account of Fliess's system of psychophysiology; more will be said on this later.

Essentially the main change that took place in Freud's view, in the two or three years following the 1895 publication of *Studies in Hysteria*, was that the sexual traumas many of his hysterical patients reported had not really happened, but only represented secret wishes or fantasies: He claimed that hysterical symptoms could indeed be the result of real psychological injuries, but that many symptoms reflected a secret desire on the part of the patient to be seduced. The change appears rather suddenly in Freud's published writings: We quote here an essay written by Freud in 1898 entitled "My Views on the Part Played by Sexuality in the Aetiology of the Neurosis." Between 1895 and 1898 he had treated a number of patients, including many whose case histories could not be reported publicly, he said, because of their private nature, and the following passage is Freud's own description of his change of heart:

> At that time my material was still scanty, and it happened by chance to include a disproportionately large number of cases in which sexual seduction by an adult or by older children played the chief part on the history of

the patient's childhood. I thus overestimated the frequency of such events (though in other respects they were not open to doubt). Moreover, I was at that period unable to distinguish with certainty between falsification made by hysterics in their memories of childhood and traces of real events. Since then I have learned to explain a number of phantasies of seduction as attempts of fending off memories of the subject's own sexual activity (infantile masturbation). When this point had been clarified, the "traumatic" element in the sexual experiences of childhood lost its importance and what was left was the realization that infantile sexual activity (whether spontaneous or provoked) prescribes the direction that will be taken by later sexual life after maturity. (1898/1953–74, Vol. 7, p. 274)

Here he is saying that the repressed content underlying the neurosis was not a memory of a real trauma and may be related to psychological conflict over masturbation, particularly in childhood years. The change was also documented in a letter to Fliess (September 21, 1897), in which Freud wrote that among his reasons for abandoning the theory that his patients really had been seduced, apart from his frequent therapeutic failures, was "the surprise that in all cases, the *father*, not excluding my own, had to be accused of being perverse." He also realized that in the unconscious no distinction might be made between a content that consisted of a memory and a content that consisted of a wish.

From now on, Freud's theory would be determined and guided by the notion that, in childhood, each of us secretly wishes for sexual contact with others (including parents), and that the desires are repressed into the unconscious, where they can have unexpected effects on our conscious behavior. That this is a major change of opinion can be seen if we compare it with a lecture Freud gave a year earlier (1896) entitled "The Aetiology of Hysteria," in which he claimed that "whatever case and whatever symptom we take as our point of departure, *in the end we infallibly come to the field of sexual experience*" (quoted in Masson, 1984, p. 267) and, since he based this article on a sample of at least eighteen cases, "in all eighteen cases (cases of pure hysteria and of hysteria combined with obsessions, and comprising six men and twelve women) I have, as I have said, come to learn of sexual experiences of this kind in childhood" (Masson, 1984, p. 276). The kind of sexual abuse he refers to could be carried out by strangers, family, servants, siblings, or parents. We have already mentioned that he read books on the incidence of child sexual abuse during his stay in Paris. His change of heart, in turning away from the theory that his patients had been *really* abused, is surprising by its suddenness.

Once again, we find a controversy in the literature on Freud. Earlier writers, including Ernest Jones, whose *Life of Freud* (1953) had long been treated as authoritative, and Bonaparte, A. Freud, and Kris (1954), simply accepted Freud's own words as they were quoted here. But Masson (1984) has created considerable animosity in the modern psychoanalytic community by arguing that Freud changed his mind on the seduction theory, not because he disbelieved it as he said, but because it would damage his reputation if he claimed that parents and others were guilty of sexual abuse. He preferred to argue that hysterical patients were fantasizing as opposed to remembering. Masson's evidence includes (1) the evidence from contemporary books that child sexual abuse was indeed quite frequent, (2) quotations from later letters of Freud which indicate that Freud still believed to some extent in the seduction theory, and (3) the suggestion that Freud wished to make himself more "respectable" in Viennese medical circles following a crisis in which he and Fliess were involved.

This crisis concerned one of Freud's patients (not mentioned in the book with Breuer), named Emma Eckstein, who had been treated by Freud for various hysterical symptoms. At Freud's request, she was operated on by Fliess; Fliess bungled the operation, and Freud narrowly averted a medical scandal.

The story of how contemporary historians of psychoanalysis rejected this claim of Masson is told by Malcolm (1984). The present writer has two remarks to make. First, child sexual abuse does seem to be more common than has been accepted in the past. For example, in Kingston, Ontario, the small town where this is being written, reported cases of child sexual abuse to the Children's Aid Society rose from 11 in 1980 to 95 in 1985. This might be because people are *reporting* it more frequently, though there are no hard statistics on the incidence of real abuse as contrasted with reported abuse. (There is also a school of thought that says children are prone to make up stories about having been abused.) Second, if it is true that the childhood *fantasy* of being abused is not as common as Freud claimed it was (after 1897), then our thinking about mental illness will have to undergo even another revision, given that Freud's theories have been so widely promulgated. As a historian, however, I must now go on to describe Freud's later theories as he wrote them.

It is common to think of Freud as the pioneer in the discovery that not only mental illness, but also personality development, is in large part shaped by the way we develop our own sexual instincts. One of the major achievements of Sulloway's (1979) research was to show how, in the later nineteenth century, Freud was not the only one to write about sex and sexuality. He was probably strongly influenced by Fliess and by other sexologists, and he was also strongly influenced by Darwin. We may briefly outline Sulloway's arguments.

Sulloway points out that, far from merely being a sounding board for Freud's ideas, Fliess actually developed a system that in many ways paralleled Freud's and that greatly influenced Freud. Fliess constructed a theory that, despite having pockets of new truths in it, is nowadays considered mainly fallacious. The gist of the theory was that, since human beings evolved from lower animals, certain characteristics of the lower animals were perpetuated across the many species that evolved between primitive sea creatures and humankind. Just as in such primitive animals both male and female sex organs are present, in the human embryo, before it changes into the fetus after a "critical period" of about forty-six days and becomes recognizably male or female, we see a recapitulation of the primitive organization: Both male and female reproductive organs are present. This means that humans "start" life after conception as essentially bisexual beings. One of Fliess's strongest beliefs was that this bisexuality can show itself in sexual preferences even in infancy, after the child is born. The bisexuality is hidden as the child grows and—in part because of physical development, in part because of socialization—by the time the child is a teenager he or she usually evinces heterosexual preferences. In the correspondence between Freud and Fliess during the crucial years between 1896 and 1900, we see Freud's intense preoccupation with the notion that very young children can be bisexual; it is, of course, a short step from this to the notion that both homosexual and heterosexual preferences coexist in young children. But, taking the notion of "repression" from the Breuer and Freud study, Freud came to believe that certain sexual desires, including homosexual desires, were "repressed" into the unconscious during childhood, forming the nucleus for later psychoneurotic conflicts.

Fliess also believed, as did Darwin, that primitive creatures such as the seasquirt adapted their physiology to match the rhythm of the tides, which, in later species, was reflected in the time course of growth and development of the species, both in the womb and afterward. The rhythm that most fascinated Fliess was the female menstruation cycle, in which the beginning of the menstrual period is followed about 28 days later by the beginning of the next period. The *end* of the first period is followed by the beginning of the next period by about 23 days. A Scottish professor, John Beard, had speculated that it was of evolutionary adaptive value to have the critical period (duration of embryo) and the gestation period (time between conception and birth) as strict multiples of the 23-day ovulation cycle. So, in humans, the gestation period (276–280 days, or about nine months) is about twelve times the ovulation cycle. So far the argument is reasonable, but Fliess extended the use of the numbers 23 and 28 to predict the ratio of male to female births (the argument is given in Sulloway, 1979, pp. 164–165) and gradually developed the notion that there are two chemical substances in the (bisexual) human, one with a 23-day cycle and one with a 28-day cycle. This led gradually to a "numerology" according to which general states of mind and times of maximum productivity are related to these two cycles; matters were made worse by the addition of a third cyclical period by later writers. In our time, therefore, the Fliessian numerology has been classified as a fallacious pseudoscience (Gardner, 1966). Freud himself took it seriously at first, however; in particular he was influenced by the notion that at certain periods in the growth of the child there is a "thrust" of growth, the most striking example being the onset of puberty. In Freud's writings after 1900 little is left of Fliess's numerology, but Sulloway gives evidence that when Freud was developing his ideas of different sexual *stages* in early childhood, it was in the context of his discussions with Fliess about periodicity in the life cycle.

Finally, as mentioned earlier, Fliess believed that the nose, which plays an important part in animal sexuality because of the sexually exciting nature of certain animal odors, retained some of its characteristics as a sexual organ even in humans. He agreed with Darwin that one of the consequences of humans having adopted an upright stature on two legs was that the nose was so far off the ground that smell attractions had lost their importance over millions of years of human evolution. Nevertheless, Fliess claimed there were unrecognized relationships between the nose and the genitalia. But in a letter to Fliess (November 14, 1897) Freud links Fliess's theorizing about the loss of the importance of the nose to the notion that within our own lives erogenous feelings associated with nongenital regions (such as the mouth and anus) are also "lost" to some extent; in his elaboration of the theory of repression, he came to the idea that the different sexual stages of development are linked to erogenous feelings in particular body zones.

During the years of correspondence with Fliess, 1887–1904, Freud wrote a number of key works that established the basis for the movement he himself called *psychoanalysis*. In 1895, the *Studies in Hysteria* with Breuer showed the importance of trauma in determining hypnotic symptoms; then, in 1895, Freud wrote a book he took a great deal of trouble with, and which, when he had completed it, left him with a sense of relief and completion as if he had made a major breakthrough. The book was only published in 1950, after Freud's death. The English translation was given the title *Project for a Scientific Psychology* and is published in the Standard Edition of Freud's works (edited by J. Strachey), Vol. 1. It is essentially a neurological model that gives an account both of repression and of the relation between the emotions and the higher-order thought processes. It is summarized in Fancher (1973), and its arguments are related to modern research by Pribram and Gill (1976).

The period from 1896 to 1905 was filled with intense work by Freud; it is in this period that he follows through on the model suggested by the *Project* and it is also in this period that his emphasis on unpleasant memories as causes of psychoneurosis shifts to an emphasis on repressed wishes. The move towards the main psychoanalytic theory can be seen as having two stages: First, Freud proved to his own satisfaction that unconscious wishes can influence conscious experience by devious routes, such as dreams, slips of the tongue, forgetting, and jokes. This stage was represented by the publication of *The Interpretation of Dreams* (1900), *The Psychopathology of Everyday Life* (1901), and *Jokes and Their Relation to the Unconscious* (1905), whereas the focus on sexuality as the chief characteristic of unconscious wishes was found most explicitly in *Three Essays on Sexuality* (1905).

The Interpretation of Dreams is a very long book and does indeed contain dozens of dreams—some of them Freud's own, including dreams he had as a child, and some of them reported by colleagues and patients. After slowly working his way through the evidence suggesting that dreams represent the breaking through of ideas into conscious imagery from unconscious wishes, Freud reiterates the model of the *Project* in simpler form. He argues that in childhood a memory system is laid down consisting of individual memory traces associated, or *cathected*, with events representing the relief of desire, or with events associated with physical or psychological pain. But now Freud distinguishes between two classes of memories, those in the *unconscious*, which are hardly accessible to the conscious retrieving person, and those in the *preconscious*, which are accessible (often with difficulty). The preconscious acts as a screen between the conscious and the unconscious. When the conscious mind is relaxed, as in sleep, it is possible for repressed wishes from the unconscious to form connections with memories laid down recently, which are easily available to the preconscious. The two fuse in a "dream-work" that gives rise to the experience of a dream. In the dream, we have the *manifest content*, that which is reported (not always reliably) by the observer, but this manifest content merely disguises the *latent content*, or the real meaning of the dream. The mixture of memories from the unconscious and the preconscious allow memories to be *condensed* so that, for example, two separate people may be fused into one person in the dream. There may also be *displacement* so that emotions associated with one person or event are focused onto another person or event in the dream. From the theory of hysteria, Freud says, we know that repressed wishes can find their outlet in physiological symptoms; now, he argues, even in normal people repressed wishes can find their outlet in dreams, which form a sort of safety valve. In the *Interpretation of Dreams* Freud notes a particular kind of dream sometimes reported where boys dream of killing or hurting their father, and girls their mother: It is here that we get Freud's first mention of child-parent conflict, and he likens this situation to that of the hero of Greek legend, Oedipus, who, without realizing what he was doing, killed his father and married his mother. But this line of thought is not pursued at any length in the book, and in a footnote Freud also says he avoids amassing evidence that the unconscious wishes are sexual in nature; to do this, he says, he would need a theory of "perversion and bisexuality" that deserves an extended treatment in a different work. Nevertheless, there is no question that many of the dreams reported in the book reflect sexual conflicts, and Freud explicitly suggested that many common objects reported in dreams were symbols of the sexual organs and that certain common experiences in dreams (such as running without moving forward, or flying) are symbols for sexual activities.

Freud's next book, *The Psychopathology of Everyday Life*, argued that forgetting of names, events, and intentions, and lapses of attention such as shown in slips of the tongue (*parapraxes*), are rarely caused by pure chance. Usually there is some unconscious motivation—as Freud put it, we can always "refer the phenomena to unwelcome, repressed, psychic material, which, though pushed away from consciousness is nevertheless not robbed of all capacity to express itself" (p. 279). This book appeared shortly after *The Interpretation of Dreams*, and Freud shows that some misprints in that book passed unnoticed in the editing stage because of unconscious factors on his part. There is little about sex in this work, but, like *The Interpretation of Dreams*, there is so much observational material that it is hard to imagine a charge being brought against Freud that he based his arguments on too little evidence.

In 1905 he also described a famous case, that of Dora, in which he claimed that some of Dora's hysterical reactions to a present conflict had their origin in a repressed love for her father. Dora's case involved the analysis of dreams, jokes, and parapraxes. However, the time was clearly ripe for Freud to give a more detailed account of sexuality in itself, and this he did in his *Three Essays on Sexuality* (1905).

At the time sexuality was a topic of considerable interest in both medical and lay circles. Even psychiatrists following the medical model of Griesinger and Maudsley were well aware of the importance of sexual conflict in determining various forms of mental illness. The sexual customs of peoples around the world were being described by comparative anthropologists, and sexual deviations had been described in detail, in a medical context, by R. von Krafft-Ebing (1840–1902) in his *Psychopathia Sexualis* (1886/1928). Freud's work on sex was innovative because it suggested how personality was based on sexual feelings present in very young children, but even this theory had been foreshadowed by such sexologists as Albert Moll (1862–1939) and Havelock Ellis (1859–1939). A detailed account of sexology as it existed at the turn of the century is given by Sulloway (1979, Chap. 8). Sulloway points out that at the end of the nineteenth century many psychiatrists viewed mental illness, and sexual deviations, as signs of an inherited "degeneracy"; but by 1905, when Freud wrote his *Three Essays on Sexuality*, it was becoming recognized that sexual feelings could sometimes be explained in terms of associations with particular events; for example, *fetishism*, a word invented by the French psychologist Alfred Binet (see Chap. 12), could arise if a neutral stimulus was associated with a sexual event. It was also known from observations of both young children and young animals that children enjoyed touching themselves sexually, or being touched. The old degeneracy theory died a natural death, and it should be stated that one of Freud's greatest achievements was to have demonstrated that mental illness could be considered as a *natural* outcome of the laws of association operating in conjunction with the development of sexual emotions. Words like "unnatural" and "degenerate" vanished from psychiatric literature, though not from the popular mind. It should be noted that some of those psychiatrists who viewed sex as "unnatural," particularly in female patients, were guilty of cruel treatments for clients who masturbated, for example; the role of orthodox psychiatry in keeping sex a "shameful" subject at the end of the nineteenth century has been discussed by Masson (1986).

In the *Three Essays* Freud attempted to chart the course of infantile sexuality. First, he argued that by *sexuality* or *libido* he meant something quite broad—the desire to be touched and stimulated. But he also accepted that certain parts of the body were more sensitive to touch than others and that libido therefore might focus on certain erogenous zones. Using a word that had played an important part in the neurological model of the *Project,* Freud considered that libido was *cathected* onto certain erogenous zones at various phases of the infant's development. At the same time, of course, Freud's recognition that the points of cathexis of libido could change from time to time indicated that infantile sexuality was not necessarily focused in the genitals but was capable of taking various forms; that is, it was "polymorphous." The sexual perversions were therefore to be seen as exaggerations of quite normal tendencies, and thus in one sweep Freud offered an etiology of sexual deviation as well as an account of normal heterosexual development. For Freud, the baby was born bisexual, with no particular innate preference for a member of the same sex or a member of the opposite sex: Heterosexual development would come later and be in part a function of experience, in part a function of psychological development at puberty.

At first libido is cathected onto the mouth region because that is where the child gains nourishment and tactile pleasure. The child also learns that the mother is associated with oral gratification, and this is the beginning of the cathexis of libido onto external objects. Even after the child has stopped breast-feeding or bottle-feeding, oral pleasure remains desirable and the child must compensate, in infancy, by thumb-sucking or, in adulthood, by smoking or chewing gum.

At about the age of two, the center of tactile gratification shifts from the oral to the anal region as the child begins the stormy period of toilet-training. Many are still surprised or disgusted at the notion that there is an anal phase of libido cathexis, but Freud marshaled many arguments to buttress his belief that, at about this age, the child develops a fixation on, or concern with, defecation. The anal stage is a complicated one, for Freud believed that, depending on the strictness and/or success of toilet-training, different personality characteristics could be developed at this stage. For the child, having a successful bowel movement, which is praised by the parents, is almost like giving them a gift. Since the child is learning to control the sphincter movements, he or she has a choice as to whether to give the parent the gift or not. It is as if he or she had the ability to hoard material. Freud therefore argued that the character traits of mean-ness and obstinacy might have their origin at this stage. He also argued that a very strict toilet-training procedure will make the child obsessed with cleanness and tidiness. At the same time, the child, for the first time in his or her life, acquires a certain amount of control over the parent's behavior, and in the 1905 version Freud surmised that the origins of cruelty might be found at some stage before the genitals have taken on their later role.

The third stage of libidinal development concerns the cathexis of libido onto the genitals. This occurs in part because the focus is no longer exclusively on the mouth or anus, but also relates to the discovery by the child of the pleasure of manipulating his or her own genitals; to the discouragement by the parents of any interest in excremental functions; and to the growth of physical control by the child. This stage is usually called the phallic stage but Freud meant it to apply to girls too. He recognized that in many children there is a fascination at this age with the genital structure of the opposite sex. The phallic stage coincides with the oedipal stage, the period when the child must make the break from tactile association with the mother, a break made particularly difficult because of possible new associations formed between phallic libido and the mother. The subject must also rechannel libido to some extent as he or she learns the arts of socialization at kindergarten or school. If they learn about the reproductive act at this age, they may imagine it consists of a sort of fighting, and Freud believed that the intense curiosity of children at this age about where they came from, combined with the difficulty they have of understanding the nature of insemination, could, if discouraged, lead to a lasting injury to the desire for knowledge.

Following the phallic stage, Freud assumed that there was a fourth stage, a latent period during which the child showed little interest in sexual matters. This lasted until the onset of the fifth stage—puberty, or the genital stage. At puberty the child's sexual interests, including the desire to masturbate, are reawakened, and the final essay argued that, while in most children libido would be successfully cathected onto a mem-ber of the opposite sex, regressions to or fixations at infantile levels of sexuality could lead to sexual deviation. At puberty the boy or girl must at first indulge only in fantasy, and this can arouse the dormant memories of infantile sexuality, particularly the cathexis of libido onto the mother or the father. Such feelings are repressed, but with mixed success, particularly if the oedipal conflict has not been resolved. Thus, boys might often fall in love with girls who remind them of their mother, and girls might become infatuated with older, authoritative men who remind them of their father.

However, the reader should realize that in the *Three Essays* there is some ambiguity as to the exact relationship between fixation of libido on a particular zone (e.g., the phallic zone) and the fixation of libido onto external objects such as might be found in an oedipal conflict. Such questions would be dealt with by Freud and others in later developments of psychoanalysis. For example, in the *Introductory Lectures on Psychoanalysis* (1915–1917) Freud noted that the object love for the mother engendered at the oral stage never really vanished. But as the phallic stage is associated with the child's being forced to repress the libidinal urge, this is the stage at which the boy must also repress his desire for the mother and the concomitant jealousy of the father. In this work Freud believed that the solution was equivalent for the little girl, who had to repress her feelings for the father. There is, however, a jump in logic here: Suppose that for most children, libido by the age of five is cathected onto the mother, because she nurtured the child; why should this not be true of girls, too? Why should girls have *any* libido cathected onto the father? Freud's treatment of the Oedipus complex changed throughout his career: Here, at midcareer, he seems to have assumed that, just as boys must repress a longing for the mother at about the age of five, girls must also repress their longing for the father, but this assumption does not necessarily follow from his earlier theorizing. We might also note that Ellenberger (1970, pp. 502–507) points out that Freud had precursors in almost all of these ideas, but it was clearly Freud's originality to synthesize the concepts into a general system that would account for deviations and neuroses as well as normal personality development.

Freud had by no means finished elaborating his theory at this point. Two problems were left unanswered in the *Three Essays*. First, although Freud argued that during the anal stage the child first learned that he could to some extent control his parents and that this might be the origin of a drive to control others, maybe even to the extent of sadistically wielding power over them, he was not satisfied that sadism could be explained entirely by a fixation at or regression to this stage. Second, although he had demonstrated that there was an oedipal conflict, he did not spell out the details of how the conflict was resolved in individual cases. On the matter of sadism, it was fifteen years before Freud in his *Beyond the Pleasure Principle* (1920) elaborated the theory of instincts to include a closer account of sadism and its related deviation, masochism. On the question of the Oedipus complex, Freud finally offered one solution in his *The Ego and the Id* (1923), eighteen years after the *Three Essays*.

During this period Freud wrote many individual papers, some based on case histories (including the famous case of "little Hans," a child with a quite overtly expressed fear of castration linked with a fear of his father). Another change in his theory of the Oedipus complex comes in a paper in 1931 (see later).

At the same time psychoanalysis began to be propagated around the world. Ever since 1902 a group of individuals favoring Freud's approach, the Vienna Psychoanalytic Society, had been holding regular meetings in Vienna. Some remained faithful Freudians, such as Karl Abraham (1877–1925), Sandor Ferenczi (1873–1933), and A. Ernest Jones (1879–1958). Others, such as Carl Gustav Jung (1875–1961), Alfred Adler (1870–1937), and Otto Rank (1884–1939), while retaining a belief in the unconscious origins of mental disturbance, broke away from the movement in dissatisfaction with some of Freud's ideas, particularly the notion that sexuality underlay all psychological disturbances, and possibly in dissatisfaction with his somewhat authoritarian attitude to their suggestions.

In 1909, when Freud was fifty-three, he received an invitation from Stanley Hall to give a series of lectures at Clark University. He traveled there with Jung, and the lectures were later expanded into his *Introductory Lectures on Psychoanalysis* (1915–1917). Bleuler and many of his staff at the famous Swiss hospital named the Burghölzli were also keenly interested in the new psychoanalytic movement. Some psychiatrists, however, felt that psychoanalytic doctrine was as yet unproven, lacked statistical evidence, and was too heavily based on subjective opinion concerning individual case histories (on this, see Ellenberger, 1970, p. 802). They also objected to being told, as was often the case, that their resistance to the theory itself originated in an unconscious fear of learning the truth about their own unconscious sexual conflicts, and some felt that psychoanalysis, by subjecting the patient to emotional distress, could actually be harmful. Nevertheless, the movement spread; by 1910 Freud was famous, and though the later elaborations of the theory met with mixed success, there is no doubt that many psychiatrists both in Europe and in North America welcomed psychoanalysis.

In *Beyond the Pleasure Principle* Freud drew together various strands that had become more dominant in his thinking since the *Three Essays*. First, like Breuer, Freud became aware that the therapist's own self began to play a part in his neurotic patients' fantasies. He came to recognize that the transference phenomenon represented a repetition in microcosm of the patient's original neurosis. He also came to recognize that many patients had a compulsion to repeat even erroneous actions of a kind that had led to their becoming ill in the first place. He came to the conclusion that there was some sort of new instinct here, one that "seems more primitive, more elementary, more instinctual than the pleasure-principle which it overrides" (1953–1974, p. 23). Furthermore, Freud was impressed with the severity of "traumatic neurosis" found in soldiers who had become ill after frightening experiences in the trenches of World War I; there was no reason to believe that this neurosis was the result of repressed infantile sexuality.

Freud's eventual answer was to argue that there were two main instincts inherent, not merely in humans, but in all living matter: an instinct for pleasurable stimulation (which he called *Eros*) and death instinct (which others called *Thanatos*). It was the death instinct that impelled individuals to be destructive towards themselves (as in the compulsion to repeat errors) and to be destructive towards others (as in wars or individual cases of sadism). Masochism was not just inturned sadism, but a reflection of a basic drive. The importance of war neuroses was that they too forced Freud to go against his theory that libidinal pleasure seeking is the sole aim of the individual. Instead, he suggested that the individual had to develop a protective shield against the bombardment of stimuli both from the inner instincts and from the external world. In a case of intense fright, the protective shield was broken down. The tendency for persons suffering from war neurosis to relive their experience in fantasy and even in dreams was itself a reflection of the compulsion to repeat. We should note, however, that the concepts of Eros and Thanatos were not as widely accepted as Freud had hoped.

On the other hand, *The Ego and the Id* offered a number of new constructs that received acclaim from analysts and nonprofessionals alike. In the *Three Essays* Freud had stated that the oedipal conflict in boys consisted of a fear of the father because he represented a stronger rival for the attentions of the mother. Coinciding as it did with the phallic stage of sexual development, the fear was crystallized in boys as a castration anxiety. But it will be recalled that for Freud infantile sexuality was polymorphous, which implied that a little boy could have both male and female components in his sexuality. According to *The Ego and the Id* the resolution of the Oedipus complex depended in part on which aspect of the boy's sexuality was dominant. If the male component was dominant, he resolved the conflict resulting from hating and fearing his father by actually identifying with the father and taking in, or "introjecting," the father's characteristics.

The picture then emerging was of three structures in the personality, what Freud called the id, the pleasure-seeking, unconscious, sex-dominant part; the ego, the protective part, mainly conscious, which tried to control the id even though it originally developed from the id; and now the introjected ego-ideal deriving from the father, the *superego*. The superego was also in part unconscious and was responsible both for the origins of morality in the child and for a certain amount of conflict: The harshness of the superego in suppressing desires arising from the id could often result in excessive feelings of guilt. But all of this happens only in the little boy whose male sexual component is dominant. If his female component is dominant, he is likely to identify with the mother rather than the father.

As for little girls, Freud assumed that, because they did not suffer a castration anxiety (since they did not have penises) the oedipal conflict was less severe. On the other hand they sometimes felt that, because they did not have a penis, that in some way they had already been punished. The effect according to Freud was the females grew up with a less harsh superego; their behavior was also more passive than that of males partly because they envied the male penis and saw themselves as somehow inferior. However, Freud always felt that he had less of a grasp on female as opposed to male psychological dynamics; other analysts such as Helene Deutsch in her *Psychology of Women* (1944) have attempted to clarify points on which Freud was less confident.

The idea of the resolution of the Oedipus complex by the formation of the superego was readily adopted by Freud's followers, but it should be clear that its application in practice is subtle. With eight possible combinations of the three variables of boy/girl, male/female principle, and father/mother identification, it is little wonder that there is no simple answer to the problem of why the superego is more developed in some persons than in others. Furthermore Freud, in *The Ego and the Id*, argued that each of these constructs played a part in combining and fusing the demands of both Eros and Thanatos; in particular, the superego was supposed to inhibit repetition-compulsive and suicidal drives by redirecting energy from Thanatos to Eros. It should be mentioned that Freud also saw the origins of melancholia, obsessional neurosis, and anxiety neurosis in the three-way struggle between ego, id, and superego. Three years later, in his *Inhibitions, Symptoms and Anxiety* (1926), he elaborated particularly on the notion that anxiety results from the threat to the ego of the demands of both the id and the superego. This denoted a marked change from an early theory of anxiety in which free-floating anxiety was seen as the expression of a dammed-up libido associated with an unsatisfactory sex life.

In view of the importance for normal adjustment of protecting the ego against the forces of the id, we may very briefly mention some of the defense mechanisms postulated by Freud. The list changed over the years, but among the various ego-defending methods that Freud speculated were used to ward off the sexual and aggressive urges of Eros and Thanatos, respectively, were:

1. *Sublimation.* Libidinal and aggressive energies are rechanneled into harmless activities. Art represents the more typical kind of sublimation; it is also reflected in hobbies, intellectual interests, and sports.
2. *Projection.* Feelings unacceptable to oneself are ascribed to others. The mechanism of projection was held to play a major role in paranoia, where

hostile and destructive desires in oneself are transferred to others, with the resulting delusions that others are particularly hostile towards oneself.

3. *Reaction formation.* In order to compensate for a feeling unacceptable to the ego, its opposite feeling is cultivated. A repressed hatred of somebody may be accompanied by an overt tenderness towards them.

4. *Introjection.* This defense mechanism is important in the formation of the superego. Hostile feelings towards another are overridden when the individual consciously imitates or identifies with the person in question.

5. *Rationalization.* Here unacceptable events or impulses are made less harmful by being given a gloss of respectability and reasonability. An example might be a soldier who excuses a wartime atrocity he has committed by arguing that he was just obeying orders.

6. *Displacement.* Here hostile and libidinous desires originally directed towards object X are channeled onto object Y so as to allow their expression without too serious consequences. The husband who comes home angry about work and shouts at his family is showing displacement behavior.

The important thing to remember about these defense mechanisms is that they represent compromises that allow the ego, somewhat uncomfortably, to adjust itself to reality. Defense mechanisms sometimes operate consciously, but more often they operate unconsciously. Underlying many of these defense mechanisms is the most fundamental one of repression, which is usually unconscious.

In 1931, when Freud was seventy-five, a paper appeared entitled "Female Sexuality" that is worth special mention because it returned to the Oedipus complex and seems to offer a more cogent account of the development of female libido than that Freud had offered in mid-career. According to this late theory, most little girls *do* have their libido cathected onto the mother more than the father at about the age of five. This means that some girls are more likely to be attached to females rather than to males from that age onward, and that when they reach puberty they may have unusual difficulty in transferring libidinal affection onto males, the opposite sex. Many women never make this shift satisfactorily, and Freud believed that women were more prone to have lesbian feelings than men were to have homosexual feelings. At the same time, Freud recognized that in many families the girl's relations with her mother were not always satisfactory (see later), and that some marital unhappiness occurs because the women brings into the marriage hostile attitudes toward her own mother which are then directed to her husband. Another sign of the little girl's identification with her mother is seen in her playing with dolls: "The little girl's preference for dolls is probably evidence of the exclusiveness of her attachment to her mother, with complete neglect of her father-object" (p. 237). From a historical point of view, Freud abandoned his old notion that girls are libidually attracted to their father in an "Electra complex":

We have an impression here that what we have said about the Oedipus complex applies with complete strictness to the male child only and that we are right in rejecting the term "Electra complex" which seeks to emphasize the analogy between the attitude of the two sexes. It is only in the male child that we find the fateful combination of love for the one parent and simultaneous hatred for the other as a rival. (p. 229)

At the same time, the woman *does* have a conflict at about the age of five that corresponds to the Oedipus complex in males. This conflict was discussed in Freud's *New Introductory Lectures on Psychoanalysis* (1933). The little girl is deeply attached by nurture to the mother, but, partly in dissatisfaction with the fact that she had to be weaned, partly in dissatisfaction with the fact that she does not have a penis and feels envious about this, a hostility towards the mother develops that is sometimes deflected into excessive love for the father. Moreover, Freud retained his mid-career view that the boy develops a superego because of his fear of castration, whereas the girl (already "castrated," symbolically speaking) does not develop such a strong superego. For Freud, the adult solution to the problem of lack of a penis, for many women, was the having of a boy child, and Freud noted that very often this solution led to the woman's giving all her affection to her son and taking away some of her affection from her husband. For Freud, how a woman felt in the marriage relationship was very much a reflection of how far she had resolved her struggle between affectionate and hostile feelings to her own mother. It is clear that in this late work of Freud we are moving to a discussion of how a little girl's childhood affects not only her personality but also her further role as a wife and mother. In these lectures, Freud acknowledged the help that some female analysts had given him, and we shall see that women have played important roles in the history of the psychoanalytic movement. It should also be said that some modern feminists have objected to Freud's theory of femininity on a number of grounds, including his claim that women have less "conscience" than men.

Most of Freud's later writings concerned the application of psychoanalysis to sociocultural affairs. In *Totem and Taboo* (1913) he argued that in ancient times the Oedipus complex had been resolved when the young men of the tribe actually killed the older fathers. They still revered the memory of the fathers, however, in the form of totems; later, taboos prevented incest and patricide as solutions to the Oedipus conflict. In *Group Psychology and the Analysis of the Ego* (1921) Freud argued that individuals lost their identity in a crowd: Their ego ideal was, for a time, no longer the introjected father but the crowd leader himself, who could persuade the crowd to do immoral deeds if he so desired. Religion was attacked in *The Future of an Illusion* (1927) as being nothing more than a defense mechanism in which a nonthreatening father figure, God, was taken into the ego system as an added defense against the threatening forces of the id. For Freud civilization was a fragile means of channeling the ego into socially acceptable modes of behavior: His fear that it could break down, as expressed in *Civilization and its Discontents* (1930), nearly came to be realized in the growth of Nazism in Central Europe.

Moses and Monotheism (1934–1938) was an attempt to delve into the origins of the Judaic belief in one God. This was the last book Freud wrote. In 1938 the German Nazis succeeded in annexing Austria, but, aided by friends, Freud was able to escape to Britain just before the outbreak of World War II. He died of cancer of the mouth, which he had had for some thirteen years, in London on September 23, 1939, at the age of eighty-three. At his funeral, the International Psychoanalytic Association, which had by then been in existence for nearly thirty years, was represented by Ernest Jones, who later wrote what has become a classic biography of Freud (E. Jones, 1953).

Developments Related to Freud's Theory

From the first meetings of the Vienna Psychoanalytic Society in Freud's house in 1902, the psychoanalytic movement spread rapidly. In 1907 psychoanalysis was one of many new therapies discussed at the First International Congress of Psychiatry and Neurology in Amsterdam. In 1908 the first International Congress of Psychoanalysis was held in Salzburg, with forty-two persons present, most Austrians. In 1910 the International Psychoanalytic Association was founded with Jung as its first president. In 1911 Abraham A. Brill (1874–1948) founded the New York Psychoanalytical Society, and Ernest Jones, who at the time was in Toronto, founded the American Psychoanalytic Association. But Adler resigned from the Viennese Society in 1911, and Jung resigned from the International Association in 1913. Despite these defections, the movement continued to grow. Max Eitingon (1881–1943) opened a Psychoanalytic Institute in Berlin in 1919. This was particularly important, for here the principles were laid down according to which analysts themselves should be taught. Eitingon insisted, and Freud agreed, that the practicing analyst should himself undergo rigorous analysis while receiving instructions in analytic technique and receiving supervision in his own first attempts at analysis.

In 1925 the International Training Commission was organized to supervise the education of analysts. In the late 1930s, however, some disagreement arose between the members of the American Psychoanalytic Association, who wished psychoanalytic training to be restricted to persons with a medical degree, and the members of the International Training Commission, who were willing to train laypeople. This rift is still not fully healed, and in the United States courses organized by the American Association are still restricted to physicians, usually psychiatrists. Before

World War II psychoanalysis was mainly a European movement; after World War II, partly because of the forced exodus of many psychoanalysts, the center of psychoanalytic activity became the United States, particularly New York City. As the societies were being founded, so were journals for the dissemination of psychoanalytic therapy. *Imago* was founded in 1912, the *International Journal of Psychoanalysis* in 1920, and the *Psychoanalytic Quarterly* in 1932.

Progress along the lines Freud had indicated consisted partly of extending his theories to cover illness other than neurosis. In the United States, Harry Stack Sullivan (1892–1949) argued that schizophrenia could be treated by psychoanalysis and claimed some success in this endeavor. In Britain Anna Freud and Melanie Klein (1882–1960) did extensive work with very young children using observations of their play behavior to identify sources of conflict. Klein in particular believed that the origins of the superego went back further than the oedipal conflict; in fact, she argued that the very young infant learns the concepts of *good* and *bad* from experience at the breast and that the processes of introjection of the mother and projection of feelings onto the mother occur prior to the development of the oedipal stage. Klein's emphasis on the infantile origins of the moral feelings is now widely accepted, even by orthodox Freudians. After World War II much interest was generated by the notion that personality characteristics and neurotic or psychotic behavior did not necessarily originate in the family circle alone: The socioeconomic, ethnic, and cultural backgrounds were also important. These points of view were espoused by such analysts as Karen Horney (1885–1952) and Erich Fromm (1900–1980).

We cannot leave psychoanalysis, however, without special mention of Jung and Adler. We should note immediately of both psychologists that they formulated some of their own ideas before collaborating with Freud and that the break with Freud was not therefore as surprising as it might seem. In fact, the word *psychoanalysis* is no longer applied to their theories: For Adler's, one refers to *individual psychology* and for Jung's *analytical psychology*.

Like Freud, Adler was of Viennese Jewish background. After finishing medical school, he did some research on occupational hazards to health and practiced medicine in a Vienna neighborhood of lower socioeconomic status than that of Freud. Partly as a consequence of this experience, he felt that psychoanalysis should be made available to a wide public, and his writing was therefore addressed to the layperson as well as the professional therapist. He soon developed an interest in psychiatry and, after six years in private practice, he met Freud in 1901. He eagerly embraced the notion of the subconscious origins of the neuroses but was particularly intrigued by the idea that in many neurotics there is a sense of deficiency in one or other organ of the body—he called it an organ inferiority. The aim of the person thus becomes to compensate for the inferiority, using whatever resources of courage he or she can command. Children feel inferior because of their small size, and on two related issues Adler came to differ from Freud. First, he believed that the conflicts at about age five resulted not simply from oedipal sources but also from the child's situation with respect to other children, notably older or younger siblings. Adler himself was the middle child and experienced illness and sibling rivalry in his own childhood: Middle children, he believed, suffered from the double pressure of having to measure up to the oldest child and having to fend off competition from the youngest child. Second, he believed that the child had a persistent striving for superiority in society: Unlike Freud, he did not stress libidinal urges, but did claim that the child had strong competitive aggressive urges. (Later Freud would accept that aggressive urges had to be added to libidinal urges, but before the break with Adler in 1911, he was adamant on the salience of libidinal urges.)

Adler went on to develop his theory that the child must strive to compete at all ages; he developed a psychology that stressed commonsense much more than that of Freud. His main work was his *Understanding Human Nature* (1927): The title indicated that Adler took a practical view of human conflicts, far removed from Freud's view that only extended psychoanalysis could unearth the secrets causing neurotic conflicts. Adler did a great deal of counseling in the Vienna school system and was eventually appointed a professor at the Pedagogical Institute there in 1924. He also gave special attention to the psychopathology of criminals, many of whom, he believed, became criminal because of neglect in childhood or because they had the misfortune to be ugly. Either circumstance would hamper the child in a struggle for superiority in his or her social stratum. Adler emigrated to the United States in the early 1930s. In 1934 the *Journal of Individual Psychology* was founded to propagate Adlerian views. Adler died in 1937 while on a lecture tour of Scotland. His influence on later psychoanalysts, particularly of the "cultural" school, was quite marked, and the term *inferiority complex* is now well rooted in the English language.

Jung's father was a Protestant minister in Switzerland, and Jung's lifelong interest in religion may therefore owe something to his background. He studied medicine at Basel from 1895 to 1901 and was appointed a resident in Bleuler's hospital, the Burghölzli, in 1900. He spent the winter of 1902 to 1903 studying with Janet. One of the first pieces of research Jung undertook was on the application of Galton's word association test in the study of psychosis. Galton, it will be recalled, had taken key words and analyzed the associations they evoked in him; several other writers, including Wundt and Kraepelin, had used the test to study associative processes. At Bleuler's suggestion, Jung gave the test to psychotic patients in the hope that their responses would reveal something of their underlying *complexes,* as Jung came to call individual constellations of ideas held together by an underlying emotional tone. The tests were fairly successful, and there was a flurry of excitement after it was discovered that unusually long reaction times to give an association could indicate lying. For example, somebody guilty of the theft of a jewel box might be unusually slow to give a response to a key word such as *jewel.* Little came of this but the research established Jung's reputation as an experimentalist.

Jung first visited Freud in 1907 and rapidly became an enthusiast for the new psychology of the unconscious. But he gradually grew unhappy with Freud's stress on sexuality and preferred to use the word *libido* to refer to general psychic energy rather than to restrict it to sexual urges alone. Moreover, he did not agree on the sources of the Oedipus complex; it has even been suggested that because Jung's own mother was not very attractive, he failed to find in himself any vestige of desire for his mother (Ellenberger, 1970, p. 662). Jung and Freud corresponded extensively on the substance of psychoanalysis, and there is no doubt that Freud was disappointed to see Jung's ideas take the directions they did.

After the final break with Freud in 1913, Jung embarked on a period of self-analysis, using dreams, diaries, and other means at his disposal for unearthing his own unconscious life. One of the outcomes of this work was *Psychological Types* (1921), his most widely read work. He continued to write and teach and travel widely throughout the world for the remainder of his long life, and he wrote copiously on the elaboration of his theory of the unconscious to cover such topics as religion, parapsychology, the occult, and the history of alchemy. His aim was to show that throughout history individuals' unconscious strivings and conflicts have been reflected in their creations, myths, and beliefs, but Jung himself was accused of being a mythologist, and his late works are certainly obscure even if impressively scholarly. His last work was an illustrated account, written with others, of *Man and His Symbols* (1964): What Freud had done for dreams, Jung tried to do for symbols such as crosses, mandalas, and the like, arguing that they reflected unconscious elements common to all men and women.

For Freud the unconscious life consisted of the struggle between the libidinous and aggressive forces of the id and the restraining forces of the ego and superego. Jung, however, took the position that all men and women share a collective unconscious substrate transmitted by heredity and that the constructs of the collective unconscious are symbolized in primordial images, or archetypes, that can be found in all societies. Of these, one of the most primitive and central is that of the self, the unified integrated element of the psyche, which has to be sought for and developed. Over one's lifetime one goes through various stages of individuation, each bringing one closer to the self. These stages are often crisis periods: the crisis of weaning, the crisis of starting school, the crisis of finding a marriage partner, the crisis of finding a career, and the crisis of midlife, when one surveys one's achievements and one's goals, not always with satisfaction. One's success at overcoming these various crises is in part a function of one's personality, and Jung developed a personality theory as a consequence.

In general there were, for Jung, two ways of apprehending the external world: One was to take everything as given in a quick apprehension, either of raw sensations or of rapid inferences of which one was scarcely aware. These were the irrational means of sensations and intuitions. The other was to evaluate the external world more rationally and more self-consciously by way of thinking and feeling. All persons possess a modicum of sensation, intuition, thinking, and feeling, but usually one predominates. At the same time, not only is the world apprehended by one of these means, but the person also presents a particular side of himself or herself to the world. This is the "persona," and it is generally sex-linked in the sense that men will stress their masculine qualities and women their female qualities. The psychic energy of the libido is also concentrated either on the external world or on one's internal thought life. Possibly adopting the terms from a distinction made by Alfred Binet, Jung referred to those persons whose libido was focused on the objects and persons of the external world as extraverted and to those whose lives were determined by contingencies of their own beliefs and ideals as introverted. Combining extraversion and introversion with the four function types of sensation, intuition, thinking, and feeling yields eight personality types, each of which is described in detail in *Psychological Types*.

But this description remained, for Jung, essentially superficial, for it concerned the conscious mind only. He argued in fact that extraverts were unconsciously introverted and vice versa, and that those with a strong masculine persona had strong feminine elements in their unconscious (the anima) while those with a strong feminine persona had strong masculine elements in their unconscious (the animus). Hysteria was a reaction of the extravert under the stress of a crisis, and dementia praecox represented a breakdown in the functioning of the introvert. Critics have not always been kind to Jung's plethora of characteristics with their unconscious opposites. Alexander and Selesnick remark:

> Psychotherapy—that is, Jungian "analytical psychology"—attempts to bring this "play of opposites" into harmonious integration by evaluating the polar opposites residing in the unconscious, both collective and personal, and in the consciousness. How the therapist can discriminate between the multiple antitheses and assess their relative importance becomes, however, a matter of conjecture; and furthermore it is well-nigh impossible to detect a major and nuclear conflict in this bewildering maze of opposing interests. (1966, p. 247)

However, Jung's followers believe he made substantial contributions to our understanding both of the development of an integrated personality throughout the course of life and of the symbols that permeate religion, mythology, and the writings and dreams of psychotic patients. Training centers for Jungian analysts were set up, and in contrast to the view taken by the American Psychoanalytic Association, laypersons were allowed to receive training in analytical psychology. It should perhaps be added that although the vast majority of practicing psychologists probably do not believe in the concept of a collective unconscious, the concepts of introversion and extraversion have been widely accepted and made the focus of experimental investigation (Eysenck, 1973). Many also believe that Jung's theory has been misunderstood. In particular, Jung may have been correct in stressing that pathology could result if there were an imbalance between the urges of anima and animus: An overtly masculine person could be upset if he found feminine emotional qualities influencing his behavior and vice versa. Jung was among the first to recognize the importance of how one views one's own sex role in determining mental health.

In this chapter we have only been able to skim the surface of a tortuous and fascinating subject. The most scholarly history of the psychoanalytic movement and its precursors is probably Ellenberger's masterly *Discovery of the Unconscious* (1970). For an account of the development of Freud's theory in particular, we may recommend Fancher's *Psychoanalytic Psychology* (1973) and of course Ernest Jones's biography (1953) and Sulloway (1979). For developments in psychoanalysis since Freud, Adler, and Jung, the reader should consult J. A. C. Brown's *Freud and the Post-Freudians* (1961) and Fine's *History of Psychoanalysis* (1979). The story of the origins of American psychoanalysis is given in Hale's *Freud and the Americans* (Vol. 1, 1971).

It is important to realize that psychoanalysis was by no means adopted by all or even the majority of psychiatrists in the early decades of this century. Doubts as to the truth of its doctrines, coupled with the expense and time involved in analysis, made it only rarely useful in hospital settings. Custodial care was still widely resorted to in the 1920s and 1930s; one of the major breakthroughs in therapy for general paralysis of the insane was the development of a malarial treatment by J. von Wagner-Jauregg (1857–1940), an opponent of psychoanalysis; and in the 1930s such physical methods of treatment as insulin therapy for schizophrenia and surgical procedures for severe psychosis were advocated. Electroconvulsive therapy was also first used in the 1930s. These physical treatments were preferred to psychoanalysis in many mental hospitals in the years that followed.

Summary

The history of psychiatry is traced from the temple healing in ancient Greece through the witch hunts of the late Middle Ages to the growth of the medical model in the eighteenth and nineteenth centuries. Pinel played a role as scientist and as liberator of the insane. During the nineteenth century, however, studies of hypnosis led some psychologists, such as Charcot and Janet, to realize that some mental illnesses, particularly cases of hysteria, might be the result of psychodynamic forces working on the unconscious in such a way as to cause conflicts which interfered with normal conduct.

The founder of the psychoanalytic school, Sigmund Freud, had studied with Charcot and initially used hypnosis to try to unearth unconscious conflicts in his patients. Gradually, he came to use free association instead. He formulated and elaborated a scheme in which he tried to list the unconscious conflict laid down in all of us as the result of experiences in infancy and childhood. These conflicts, argued Freud, mainly concern the sexual domain: Sexual energy, or libido, is focused on various bodily zones in a fixed order at various stages in development. By the time the child is about five, libido cannot focus on the original love object, the mother, and must be directed elsewhere. Successful behavior in maturity depends on the successful redirection of libido: Hindrances to this can result in conflicts severe enough to cause a clinical neurosis. In later developments of the theory, he argued that there was an instinct towards self-destruction as well as a love instinct; he also conceived of the constructs of id, ego, and superego as conflicting entities, each with unconscious and conscious components. The need to reconcile unconscious desires with conscious moral demands also led to Freud's describing a number of defense mechanisms.

Some colleagues of Freud broke away from the movement in its early years: Adler, for example, laid more stress on conflicts within the family than did Freud, and Jung laid less emphasis on sexuality and more on self-development.

1879 to 1940:
New Directions

12

In this chapter we shall review progress in various areas of psychology that are only indirectly related to the three movements we have just examined. In particular, we shall consider developments in physiological psychology, psychometrics, social psychology, and applied psychology.

Physiological Psychology

In 1866 J. Bernstein had proposed that nervous conduction consisted of an electrical change propagated down the nerve. This was well known in 1879, when Wundt was writing, and Bernstein himself developed apparatus for demonstrating the change. But a true understanding of the propagation of the impulse had to wait for the invention of better recording apparatus, and such devices became available only in the first decade of the twentieth century. In the meantime, however, H. P. Bowditch (1840–1911) had discovered, in 1871, that if stimuli of various intensities excited the heart muscle, the muscle gave an either-or response: Either it contracted or it did not. Skeletal muscle was later shown to have this all-or-nothing property, and with the development of the new recording devices, it became possible to demonstrate that the nerve also reacted in all-or-nothing fashion.

368

The pioneers of nervous physiology at this period included Francis Gotch (1853–1913), Keith Lucas (1879–1916), and E. D. Adrian (1889–1977). The material that follows is based on Adrian's summaries in his *The Basis of Sensation* (1928) and *The Mechanism of Nervous Action* (1932). First, means were devised of dissecting out single fibers or single sensory end organs, which could then be stimulated. By the time Adrian's books were published, the invention of the vacuum tube allowed extremely sensitive and rapid recording. It was discovered that too weak a stimulus would not evoke a nerve impulse; the stimulus had to be above a certain strength to give rise to an impulse. One measure of the size of an impulse is the voltage developed at the point the impulse passes a measuring device. It was discovered that the voltage did not vary with the intensity of the stimulus. Thus, it seemed that the impulse in the nerve reached its full strength immediately in an all-or-nothing fashion. Following the transmission of the impulse, the nerve failed to respond to stimulation for a short while: The nerve fiber was said to be refractory at this time. After the refractory period, the fiber would once again respond to stimulation, and it was discovered that the intensity of the stimulation was reflected in the frequency of discharges down the fiber. Adrian was aware at this time that ions probably flowed across the membrane of a nerve fiber during an impulse, but the actual details were worked out later, in the 1940s, by such physiologists as A. F. Huxley and A. L. Hodgkin. Adrian received the Nobel Prize in 1932 for his contributions to our understanding of nerve impulse propagation.

When this work was being done, it was well known that the unit of the nervous system was an entity consisting of a cell body with a nucleus and various appendages, the dendrites and the axon. But back in 1879 it was not known for certain whether these units were joined, forming a reticulum, or net, or whether the units were discretely spaced apart from each other. The answer came when new methods of staining the various parts of the nervous system were made available. C. Golgi (1843–1926) used a new staining method to show how the cell body gave rise to the axon and dendrites, some of which traveled for long distances in the brain. S. Ramon y Cajal (1852–1934) modified Golgi's method and came to the conclusion that the dendrites were not interconnected but were separated by small gaps. Golgi and Cajal shared a Nobel Prize in 1906, but Golgi was still an adherent of the reticulum theory and attacked Cajal's arguments for discrete nervous units. Cajal also showed that impulses traveled inwards from the dendrites to the cell body: This was the first evidence of directionality of impulse propagation within the nerve cell. The word *neuron*, used to refer to the single nerve cell, was coined by H. W. G. Waldeyer (1837–1921) in 1891: The gaps between the neurons were called *synapses* by Sherrington in 1897. Both words are now standard usage.

The question of how an impulse crossed the synapse remained open for many years: Did the impulse traverse the gap by purely electrical means, or was some sort of chemical mediation necessary? The clue was revealed initially by research, not on synapses in the brain or spinal cord, but on the junctions between nerve endings and motor units in muscles innervated from the autonomic nervous system. The autonomic nervous system comprises those parts of the central nervous system not normally under voluntary control. The system had been mapped out mainly by W. H. Gaskell (1847–1914), who had suggested that the individual involuntary (smooth) muscles could be either excited or inhibited by antagonistic parts of the system, and by J. Langley (1852–1925), who suggested the distinction between two parts of the system, the sympathetic part, which originated in the central region of the spinal cord, and the parasympathetic part, which derived from the upper and lower regions of the cord.

The first insight that chemical mediation might be involved in the working of the system was yielded by the discovery that a smooth muscle could contract, even when deprived of sympathetic nervous input, if the chemical adrenalin were applied to the muscle. Adrenalin is normally produced by the adrenal glands, situated just above the kidneys. In 1914, H. H. Dale found that the drug acetylcholine seemed to have effects that mimicked the action of the parasympathetic system. That acetylcholine was the chemical mediator at parasympathetic nerve-muscle junctions turned out to be a useful generalization, although later research has shown that some junctions in the sympathetic system involve adrenalin rather than acetylcholine. Following the establishment of chemical mediation at nerve-muscle junctions, it was possible to show that these chemicals might also mediate transmission at synapses in the brain: Much more recent research has shown that neurotransmitters in the brain may comprise more than just acetylcholine and adrenalin.

The study of reflexes and the operation of the spinal cord was revolutionized by the extensive work of Sir Charles Sherrington (1857–1952). Sherrington studied in Cambridge, London, and Germany before taking up a position in the physiology department at Liverpool (1895–1913). Here he was instrumental in founding a psychology department. In 1913 he moved to Oxford, where he was professor of physiology until 1935. He shared the Nobel Prize with Adrian in 1932 and wrote not only on reflexes but also on binocular vision and on the history of physiology. Sherrington's most influential work was his *The Integrative Action of the Nervous System* (1906/1961), a book that, despite its early date, is still a valuable source of information on the topic of reflexes.

Sherrington's first task was to show how the extent of a reflex varied quantitatively with the intensity of the stimulus that initiated it. Using as subjects dogs in which the brain had been prevented from influencing the spinal cord because of a transection of the cord at an appropriate level, Sherrington stimulated muscles with electrical impulses and recorded the size of the resulting movement. He found that as stimulus intensity increased, so did the size of the movement; the movement also began more quickly, and after large movements, there was frequently spasmodic movements of the same limb, which Sherrington denoted as afterdischarges. He also showed that stimuli too weak to elicit a reflex could nevertheless summate, so that two weak shocks could elicit a reflex whereas one was inadequate. Just after a reflex movement was given, the muscle was refractory to further stimulation. Sherrington also mapped out the receptive field of various reflexes, showing how stimulation yielded reflex responses only if the stimulation was within an area served by the appropriate sensory nerves. In so doing he mapped the dermatomes, or areas supplied by each of the various sensory nerves emerging from individual spinal roots.

Reflex responding, however, involved more than pure excitation; inhibition was also a factor. Sherrington analyzed what he called reciprocal inhibition in detail: This is the mechanism whereby, if I bend my arm so that the biceps muscle is contracted, a reflex inhibition prevents a possible damaging contraction of the muscle underneath the upper arm (i.e., the muscle antagonistic to the biceps). Reciprocal inhibition was shown to be the result of inhibition at synapses in the spinal cord. Other reflexes involving reciprocal inhibition were described by Sherrington, some quite complicated and all involving multisynaptic functioning within the cord. Sherrington also analyzed the nature of the stimuli that would elicit reflexes. He distinguished between exteroceptive receptors, such as those on the skin, which detected changes on the outer surface of the body, and interoceptive receptors, such as those in the abdomen, which detected changes in internal organs; he invented a new word, *proprioceptive*, to refer to those receptors he discovered in muscles. Prior to Sherrington's time it had been unclear whether any sort of sensations were unique to muscles; Thomas Brown, E. H. Weber, and others had suggested the existence of sensory receptors in the muscles, but it was Sherrington who correctly identified the "muscle spindles" as detectors of the degree of muscle contraction. Clearly, the spindles play an important part in the feedback system that lets one know just how far one can contract a muscle without damaging it and allows for fine voluntary control of a muscle contraction.

Many other reflex phenomena are described in *The Integrative Action of the Nervous System,* but it will be clear from the above summary that Sherrington's contributions were manifold. In his later career he explored the interactions between excitatory and inhibitory mechanisms in more detail and was able to show how gravity could serve as a stimulus for the reflexes involved in standing. The analysis of the events at synapses in the spinal cord when reflexes were elicited were largely carried out by Sherrington's students, such as J. C. Eccles.

In 1915 another work of importance for our understanding of involuntary behavior appeared. This was the *Bodily Changes in Pain, Hunger, Fear, and Rage* of Walter B. Cannon (1871–1945). In this work Cannon showed that, in an emergency reaction, such as one caused by pain or fear, the adrenal glands released adrenalin, which mobilized the body's reserves for sudden intense exercise, as in fighting or fleeing. When the adrenalin is released, blood is diverted from the internal organs to the skeletal muscles; blood coagulates more quickly, reducing bleeding from wounds; the number of blood cells is increased so that by-products of muscular exercise can be burned off more quickly; and blood sugar is increased, sending more energy to the muscles. We have already seen that adrenalin simulates the sympathetic nervous system, although Cannon, while he describes the sympathetic system, is not so explicit on the relationship between sympathetic activity and emergency reactions. On the other hand, he showed—as had Sherrington before him—that animals deprived of their sympathetic nervous system survive quite well and apparently register emotion. Cannon interpreted this finding as going against the James-Lange theory of emotions. Cannon also demonstrated that sensations of hunger were related to stomach contractions (a fact not known for certain prior to 1915) and that the trigger for thirst was a sensation of dryness in the mouth and throat.

For psychologists with physiological interests, however, the most exciting developments of the 1800s concerned the brain. Successive editions of Wundt's *Principles of Physiological Psychology* (1894–1911) devoted more and more space to the discussion of the role of the cerebral hemispheres in determining behavior, and in particular to the question of localization of functions in the hemispheres. Flourens, at the beginning of the century, and Goltz, in the middle of the century, had shown that animals without a cerebral cortex seemed lacking in intention and initiative, although reflex and autonomic functioning appeared intact. The first suggestion that particular functions might be localized in certain cerebral areas had come from Broca, with his demonstration that speech deficit was associated with lesions of the left temporal cortex. But other workers thought that there was little localization of functions in the cortex because quite severe lesions of the cortex could be carried out on animals with no immediately obvious defect and, more importantly, because stimulation of the cortex with electric currents led to no observable response. However, clinical neurologists were well aware that damage to the cortex in humans could be associated with sensory, motor, or intellectual deficit, though again the evidence was tenuous.

It was John Hughlings Jackson (1835–1911) who, on the basis of his wide clinical experience, suggested a resolution of the paradox that such a large area of the brain as the cerebral hemispheres seemed to be lacking in obvious functions. In the study of epilepsy he described how frequently a seizure could start, say, in the hand, move up to the shoulder, and then spread to the leg or the face on the same side. This "march of symptoms" characterized what is now known as Jacksonian epilepsy and seemed to Jackson to be the result of discharge in the brain spreading from one brain area subserving the hand to other brain areas subserving the other regions. To this theory the immediate rejoinder was that damage to the cortex did not necessarily result in the patient's losing the use of the hand or other region. Jackson's reply was that the brain might be organized in a series of levels, each level probably corresponding to a stage in the evolution of the species. At the lowest level were the reflex systems mediated by the spinal cord and brain stem. At a middle level were systems of coordinate movements mediated by those areas of the cerebral hemispheres that Jackson presumed to subserve motor functioning. At the highest level were systems characterized by intelligence: Jackson later thought these might be associated with the frontal lobes. In an epileptic discharge, neurons at one level involving motor regions presumably sent impulses that affected the activity of lower levels, and a seizure was observed. But removing an area at the same level might have little effect. To explain this, Jackson drew the analogy between the brain and a committee, such as the Navy Board, which gave out orders to lower echelons. Any order from on top was carried out. On the other hand, a single member of the board could be removed with relatively little effect on the functioning of the team. This analogy was given by Jackson in 1884, but his surmises on the march of symptoms date to the 1860s (see his *Selected Writings*, 1958).

It was some years before Jackson's speculation that there might be special motor areas in the cortex was confirmed. In 1870 Fritsch and Hitzig found a method of electrical stimulation that successfully elicited movements when applied to the cortex of a dog. In the following few years, Sir David Ferrier (1843–1928) perfected the method of stimulation and was able to map the cortex in a number of species: Stimulation of one cortical area might cause a limb to move, stimulation of a different area might cause a different limb to move, and so on. He found that the motor areas were concentrated just anterior to the fissure of Rolando in the species he studied. He also explored the effects of ablating large areas of cortex, not only on motor functioning but on sensory functioning, and was able to show that the area of cortex at the back of the head (the occipital region) was associated with vision, an area in the temporal region was associated with audition, and excision of regions of the frontal lobes was sometimes associated with difficulties in eye movement control but was more often related to increased apathy in his subjects. Ferrier's

The Functions of the Brain (1st ed., 1876; 2nd ed., 1886/1978) describes this epoch-making research.

Other pioneers of the study of cerebral localization were also active at the time, notably Goltz, who studied the behavior of decerebrate dogs, and H. Munk (1830–1920), who mapped out the part of the cortex subserving tactile and bodily sensations. This is located just posterior to the Rolandic fissure. He also studied the visual deficits caused by lesions of the occipital cortex. Mapping of cortical centers in the human brain was mainly achieved by Wilder Penfield in the 1940s and 1950s: He was able to stimulate the cortex in conscious patients, who then reported that they felt sensations, or alternatively gave movements, which allowed localization of function to be ascribed to the pre- and post-Rolandic areas. It was also in the 1940s that it became possible to detect electrical activity in the sensory cortex evoked when different parts of the body were stimulated.

At the same time, there was considerable controversy about extending the notions of cerebral localization to linguistic functioning. Broca, it will be recalled, had shown that lesions of the left temporal area might be associated with some forms of aphasia. Other students of aphasia were even more ready to localize speech functions in particular parts of the left hemisphere: H. C. Bastian (1837–1915) thought, for example, that there were separate centers for speech performance based on visual, auditory, or kinesthetic impressions. But P. Marie (1853–1940) took a much more global view of aphasia and was even critical of Broca's claims. The history of these conflicting views on aphasia is given in the *Aphasia and Kindred Disorders of Speech* (1926) of Sir Henry Head (1861–1940). The extent to which the various speech functions are localized in the cortex remains controversial, but we may note that most proposed sites lie at the junction of those motor and sensory areas concerned with the oral region and the areas of the temporal lobe that probably subserve audition.

Apart from the question of cerebral localization, there was considerable interest at this time in how the brain mediated memory and learning. T. A. Ribot (1839–1916), in his *Diseases of Memory* (1881/1977) showed that memory loss followed a progression from the least stable memories—recent ones—to the most stable, or older, ones. Then S. S. Korsakoff (1853–1900) in 1889 described the syndrome now known as Korsakoff's psychosis, a disease characterized by the inability to acquire new information even though memory for information learned before the onset of the disease is fairly intact. Modern research has indicated that clinical amnesia is often associated with subcortical lesions near the third ventricle. Nevertheless, most research of the earlier period was devoted to the investigation of the role of the cerebral cortex in learning and memory. Pavlov and Bechterev, for example, believed that conditioning involved associations being formed between sensory and motor "analyzers" in the cortex.

The most extensive research on the relationship between the brain and the phenomena of learning was carried out by Karl S. Lashley (1890–1958). Lashley's technique was to remove a particular area of the brain in the rat and then determine how far the rat's ability to learn a particular task was affected. Alternatively, the rat might learn a task and then Lashley would ablate a given region with the aim of determining whether the rat could still retain the task. Much of Lashley's early work was summarized in his *Brain Mechanisms and Intelligence* (1929). Using mazes of three levels of difficulty (corresponding to one, three, or eight cul-de-sacs), Lashley found that the difficulty of learning was directly associated with the amount of cortex removed from the rat. It mattered little from what area the cortex was removed: In the rat even a large part of the occipital region could be ablated with little effect on maze-learning, although in other research Lashley showed that ablation of this area could effect some kinds of visual discrimination learning. Lashley was led to the view that any given area of the brain might have the property of equipotentiality, by which he designated "the apparent capacity of any intact part of a functional area to carry out with or without reduction in efficiency, the functions which are lost by destruction of the whole" (1929, p. 25).

In later research Lashley attempted to isolate different parts of the brain one from another by severing "association pathways," but was not successful in disturbing acquisition or retention of even simple discriminations. In his 1950 review article titled "In Search of the Engram," Lashley concluded that memories were not localized in any particular area of the cortex, but that somehow the cortex acted *en masse* to facilitate learning. He expressed his skepticism as to whether the conditioned reflex was the simple unit of learning some had thought it to be and favored a view more akin to that of Gestalt psychology. A memory, he believed, could be seen as a vast pattern of firing that could involve neurons in almost any part of the brain. Modern research has done little to disconfirm this conjecture.

By 1940, then, a great deal was known about nervous functioning, reflex action, and the function of the cerebral cortex. Much less was known about the subcortical regions and the structures of the midbrain: Our modern knowledge of the hypothalamus, reticular formation, hippocampus, and related areas dates to the years after World War II. Since these regions are particularly important in the mediation of instinctive and emotional behavior, little has been said about them here, although the importance of hormones in reproductive behavior was recognized in the 1930s. "Brain waves," as reflected in the electroencephalograph

(EEG), were first reported by Hans Berger (1873–1941) in 1929: His discoveries were at first greeted by disbelief, but after Adrian lent his support to the cause, the EEG was rapidly established as a useful clinical and research tool. A valuable guide to current research was provided in 1943 by the first edition of C. T. Morgan's *Physiological Psychology,* a book showing that the discipline had come of age.

We conclude this section by examining some of the main developments in sensory physiology during this period. The most ardent student of olfaction at the turn of the century was H. Zwaardemaker (1857–1930). He invented an olfactometer that presented odors of controlled intensity to the nostrils and with it studied differential thresholds for smell and the course of adaptation to odors. He discovered that odors can mask each other to varying extents. He offered a nine-item classification of odors. The first major attempt to relate odors to chemical properties of the stimuli was made by H. Henning (1885–1946) in 1916, a system which has since been superseded. Henning also offered a tentative chemical account of the fact that tastes could generally be classified into four kinds, sweet, sour, salt, and bitter, but our understanding of the chemistry of taste is still in its infancy. It was in the 1930s, however, that Carl Pfaffmann began his extensive research on the nature of the nervous messages conveying taste information.

Several important developments in our understanding of touch took place during these years. These were mainly based on the discovery that separate points on the skin are associated with separate sensations of pressure, warmth, cold, and pain: Blix in 1882, Goldscheider in 1884, and Donaldson in 1885 reported punctate sensitivity independently of each other. The next step was obviously to try to relate these four kinds of sensation to special receptor organs in the skin. Max von Frey (1852–1932) argued that pressure was mediated by free endings clustered around the roots of the hairs or in hairless regions by Meissner corpuscles, cold by the Krause bulbs, warmth by the Ruffini endings, and pain by free nerve endings. These various microscopic structures had been isolated and described in the middle of the nineteenth century. We now know the system to be more complicated, but von Frey's scheme was widely reported in early psychological texts. Von Frey, with Alrutz, also put forward evidence that heat was a sensation elicited by the combined stimulation of warm and cold spots.

Another interesting discovery of the early years of this century resulted from an experiment carried out by Rivers and Head (1908). A nerve was severed in Head's arm, and he and Rivers studied the return of sensitivity in the arm as the nerve regenerated. They distinguished between a very crude and rather undifferentiated kind of sensation, the first to return, which they called *protopathic* sensation, and a finer kind of sensation, allowing for the discriminations of pressure, warmth, and cold, which they called *epicritic* sensation. The exact relationship between Head's system and von Frey's system remains somewhat enigmatic; others have confirmed Head's experiences but did not agree with the inferences he drew from them.

In hearing, Helmholtz's resonance theory remained supreme, and in the early years of this century localization of pitch sensation with respect to specific areas in the cochlea were carried out using animals. At the end of the last century, however, Rutherford and others proposed that a pitch was encoded in terms of the frequency of firing within specific fibers. Such a mechanism could of course be set alongside a place theory of pitch perception, although many experts on hearing saw the place theory and the frequency theory as somehow contradictory. After the all-or-nothing law had been discovered, however, it was found that the maximum frequency of firing in an auditory fiber was of the order of hundreds of impulses per second, whereas the human ear could detect frequencies of up to about 20,000 cycles per second. Clearly the frequency of a vibration could not be translated directly into a frequency of firing for higher pitches in a single fiber. A possible solution to this dilemma was offered by Wever and Bray (1930), who showed how systems of fibers firing in volleys could encode higher pitch frequencies without equivocation.

The first research of Bekesy into the mode of vibration of the basilar membrane also took place in the 1930s. Other researchers of this period were concerned with the anatomy of the cochlea, the determination of thresholds of pitch and loudness in persons with various hearing disabilities, and tonal masking. There was considerable research on the analysis of speech sounds and in the localization of sound. After a time when most proponents favored one or other of the various means whereby sound might be localized, it was recognized that we know the direction of a sound by a combination of cues from time differences in the arrival of the sound at the two ears, phase differences, and intensity differences. Of these the first is believed to be prepotent by most modern theorists.

The most important advance in our understanding of vision, following Helmholtz, was the development of the duplicity theory by J. von Kries (1853–1928) in 1894. The rods and cones had been anatomically distinguished in the 1860s, and it had shown that the cones were concentrated near the center of the retina while the rods predominated at the periphery of the retina. It was also known that color discrimination was most acute if the stimulus was viewed with the center of the eye; at the periphery there was a loss in color discrimination. Finally, several careful studies at the end of the century examined how, when a person was introduced into a dark room, his or her eyes gradually adapted to the darkness. Color vision in darkness always remained poor, however. But if the subject saw colors in light and then the room was gradually made darker, there was a shift in the colors he could best discriminate, from the red region to the blue region (the Purkinje shift, see p. 189).

Von Kries combined these various items of evidence to offer the theory that the cones were specially adapted for color vision—indeed, there might be three kinds of cones, one for each of the Young-Helmholtz primary colors of red, green, and blue—and the rods were specially adapted for brightness discrimination. The process of dark adaptation would involve an increasing sensitivity on the part of the rods, and curves of intensity discrimination during dark adaptation did indeed show a sudden jump after about eight minutes of adaptation, suggesting that this was the point at which rod vision took over from cone vision. Later development of the theory brought (1) increasing evidence that the cones, which were packed densely together, also mediated vision of finer acuity than the rods; (2) an understanding of the fact that interactions between cells interposed between the retina and the brain were greater for rods than for cones, with many implications for the detection of contours; and (3) the gradual discovery of the processes of visual chemistry. In the nineteenth century "visual purple" had been isolated from the rods, but our understanding of how light serves to break down molecules of rhodopsin, as the rod chemical is now called, belongs to the 1930s and 1940s.

With respect to color vision, the modern classifications of types of color blindness were made in the 1890s and discussed in the light of the conflicting theories of Helmholtz and Hering; detailed descriptions of the absolute thresholds of hue detection at various levels of intensity were made at the turn of the century. With respect to vision in three dimensions, there was a renewed emphasis on the convergence of the two eyes as a cue to distance additional to that of accommodation; size constancy was measured and discussed in great detail in the 1920s and 1930s. This last phenomenon was considered by Gestalt psychologists to indicate the importance of global as opposed to piecemeal perception of the environment: The size of an object was judged not simply in terms of the size of its retinal projection but also in terms of its presumed size, given its apparent distance as inferred from other environmental cues.

Psychometrics

Psychometrics is a name given to that branch of psychology concerned with the measurement of individual abilities and propensities. In the period with which we are dealing, psychometric research was largely concerned with the examination of differences in intelligence, but differences in personality traits, such as extroversion, were also examined. The first scientifically oriented tests of individual differences were given by psychiatrists and neurologists in the nineteenth century to detect simulation, brain damage, aphasia, and similar dysfunctions (Bondy, 1974).

The word *intelligence* was rarely used to refer to human ability in texts such as those of James or Wundt. The concern in these works was to characterize what is common to different persons rather than what is different. Galton, however, was convinced that intellectual ability was inherited, and he was anxious to show correlations between the performance of parents and the performance of their offspring. He also made extensive anthropometric measurements of such variables as height and weight in large samples of the population. In the middle 1880s Galton set up an "Anthropometric Laboratory" at a large museum in London: In exchange for a small fee, a visitor could have various measurements taken of himself, including measurements of sensory acuity and reaction time. A great many statistics were collected, though not much use seems to have been made of them. At the same time, the young J. McK. Cattell was in Leipzig, but in 1886 he obtained a two-year research fellowship that allowed him to study at Cambridge, where he was treated as an expert on the new psychology. More importantly, Galton contacted him and as a result Cattell set up a small anthropometric laboratory at Cambridge. Again, nothing much seems to have come out of this, but in 1890 Cattell published a list of tests that he assumed would measure individual characteristics related to intelligence. The tests included strength of grip, speed of arm movement, two-point threshold, reaction time to sound, and six other functions. Upon receiving his first position in America, at the University of Pennsylvania, Cattell did extensive studies on these ten tests, plus as many as forty others largely concerned with sensory acuity.

In 1901, however, Clark Wissler, one of Cattell's own students, discovered, using the new technique of correlation, that intellectual achievement as measured by class standing bore no significant correlation to any of these tests. Moreover, the correlations between the tests themselves were very low, as if they were not measuring any common ability. The effect of Wissler's findings was to cause the rapid demise of this "anthropometric" approach to intelligence testing.

In France a different approach was taken. The leader of the testing movement in that country was Alfred Binet, the most prolific French psychologist of his era. His early research had been with Charcot at the Salpêtrière. Binet had claimed that he could influence subjects in hypnotic trance by moving magnets on or near their body: After a bitter controversy with members of the Nancy school as supported particularly by the Belgian J. R. L. Delboeuf (1831–1896), Binet had to concede defeat and turned from hypnotism to other fields. He studied the intellectual growth of his two daughters in detail and came to the conclusion that intelligence necessarily was concerned with abstract reasoning and other complex kinds of mental functioning. It was in studying his daughters that he also made a distinction between introverted and extroverted persons. Other researches at this time included investigations of skilled chess players and persons with unusual ability at mental arithmetic; and he worked with V. Henri (1872–1940) on memory in schoolchildren. With Henri, he published a "programme" for the study of individual differences that in many ways foreshadowed his later achievements.

In 1899 Theodore Simon (1873–1961), an intern at a colony for retarded children, approached Binet with a proposal to collaborate on a program of research on children. At about the same time Binet joined a society for the psychological study of the child and edited its bulletin. Both doctors and teachers at the time were concerned with the poor educational opportunities offered to retarded children, and as a result of the protestations of the society, the French Government instituted a commission for the study of the instruction of retarded children. Binet was appointed to the commission, and he soon realized that there was an urgent need for a means of separating retarded children from normal children if the former were to receive the special education they needed. With Simon he worked out, essentially by trial and error, a list of tasks that children at various ages could effectively perform; in so doing he was influenced by a similar study carried out by Blin and Damaye at Simon's hospital. Binet and Simon published successive versions of the test in 1905, 1908, and 1911. Binet then went on to write extensively on mental illness and on pedagogy; most of his research was published in a journal he himself edited, *L'Année Psychologique*. Nevertheless, he did not have a professorship at the Sorbonne, where he had been director of the Laboratory of Physiological Psychology since 1895. He died prematurely in 1911. A full biography has been given by T. H. Wolf (1973).

The 1905 scale consisted of thirty tasks ranging in difficulty from simple eye movements to abstract definitions and was based on a sample of fifty normal children aged three to twelve and an unknown number of mentally retarded children. In 1908 the list was extended, and it stipulated the age at which children could first effectively perform each task. This was the first mention of the concept of mental age. For example, a normal four-year-old child can copy a square; most children cannot copy a diamond before the age of seven. For each age group there were different numbers of tasks, but in the final 1911 version five tasks were named for each group. The child's mental age could then be given in more precise terms. The difference between the child's mental age and his chronological age was used as an index of advancement or retardation. However, this led to anomalies: A child of six with a mental age of three offers greater educational problems than does a child of twelve with a mental age of nine even though both are "retarded" by three years. It was Stern (1912) who proposed instead that a mental quotient be used in which the child's mental age was divided by his chronological age, yielding a score of unity if the two coincided. Nowadays it is customary to multiply the mental quotient by 100, yielding the so-called intelligence quotient, or IQ.

The Binet-Simon tests were rapidly translated into other languages; in the United States, H. H. Goddard (1865–1957) propagated their use, at the same time asserting his Galtonian belief that intelligence was mainly inherited. Goddard had previously made his name by a study of a family that descended from a man who had fathered one child by an uneducated mistress and another by an educated wife. The descendants of the former child included many retarded or criminal persons; the descendants of the latter child tended to be pillars of respectability. One of the direct results of this book was that several states passed laws allowing involuntary sterilization of retarded persons. Goddard himself was the director of research at a training school for the developmentally handicapped in New Jersey; after writing his two books on the Kallikak family (a fictional name) in 1912, he became convinced of the usefulness of the Binet tests in classifying degrees of retardation, and in 1916 he supervised the English translation of Binet's tests.

It was, however, Lewis M. Terman (1877–1956) who revised and standardized the test for American children in 1916. He studied some 2300 subjects to obtain the data and was able to report that the distribution of IQs seemed to be statistically normal. For Terman, an IQ above 140 represented "near genius or genius"; and an IQ below 70 represented "definite feeble-mindedness." When the correlations between IQ and class grades were found wanting, he blamed the schools for promoting children by age rather than by ability. Terman's revision came to be known as the Stanford-Binet; it included six tests for each mental age for the years three to fifteen as well as six tests for "average" adults and six tests for "superior" adults. The Stanford-Binet test was revised again by Terman and Merrill in 1937. Terman went on to do a follow-up study on children who scored highly on the tests: In 1922 he found a sample of 1500 children who had IQs of about 140 and followed their careers from then on; the study is still continuing. Most went on to successful careers, and in 1960 it was discovered that if the most successful were compared with the least successful, the latter had higher rates of alcoholism and divorce than the former (see Savage, 1975).

The Binet tests are often inconvenient for large-group testing, and in World War I a team headed by Yerkes devised two widely used new paper-and-pencil tests, the Army Alpha for those who could read and write and the Army Beta, which required no reading or writing; these tests are reproduced in Jenkins and Paterson (1961, pp. 140–172). The Army Alpha was administered to about 1,700,000 men, the Army Beta to about 100,000. An analysis of these scores indicated that persons from cities tended to perform better than persons from rural areas and that there were regional discrepancies in the scores. These results afforded some ammunition for those who argued for environmental influences on intelligence test scores. The Alpha tests included questions on arithmetic, definitions, analogies, and general information; the Beta tests included mazes, block-counting, pattern completion, and geometrical construction.

Many other tests were devised prior to 1940, but the most influential were the tests constructed by David Wechsler (1958) known as the Wechsler Adult Intelligence Scale (WAIS) and the Wechsler Intelligence Scale for Children (WISC). These are still widely used, particularly in clinical practice, and are noteworthy because they are specific about the fact that scores on various kinds of test do not remain constant after the age of twenty but often decline in a way that was not taken into account by the Binet tests.

At the same time as intelligence tests were being developed the nature of "intelligence" itself was the subject of considerable controversy. As early as 1904 C. E. Spearman (1863–1945) argued that the score on any test reflected the operation of two factors: one specific to the test itself and one that reflected a general ability, which Spearman labeled simply g, but which is often interpreted as a general intelligence factor. Spearman's evidence depended on a mathematical analysis of a table of correlations. If a number of tests are given—Spearman himself used tests of ability in school subjects such as classics and mathematics and also tests of sensory discrimination—a correlation can be obtained between scores on each test and scores on each of the others. If these correlations are then placed in a table, it will generally be found that all correlations are positive. Spearman then showed that a certain pattern known as "hierarchical order" held for tables derived in actual practice and argued that this pattern was *consistent* with the notion of a single general function underlying all the correlations. In fact, he showed how one might derive correlations between each test and that general function. One cannot do justice to the matter in less than several pages; Thomson (1939, Chap. 1) gives a clear account of what led Spearman to this conclusion. Unfortunately, Thomson himself showed that the presence of hierarchical order was equally consistent with a model according to which each test sampled a number of associative bonds in random fashion, so that there was no need to assume a single kind of intelligence denoted by g. Moreover, Thorndike, Lay, and Dean (1909) obtained results conflicting with some of Spearman's conclusions relating intelligence as judged by performance on intellectual tasks to performance on sensory discrimination tasks. This conflict led Thorndike, Lay, and Dean to assert that Spearman's assertions of a general factor g were "extravagant" and that they were tempted to replace it by the statement that there is "nothing whatever common to all mental functions."

However, Spearman continued to assert that there was a single *g* factor in his later books *The Nature of "Intelligence" and the Principles of Cognition* (1923) and *The Abilities of Man* (1927). In the former he put forward certain principles that he believed underlay most higher-order cognitive performance: Whenever two or more characters were presented together, he believed, the subject automatically experienced a knowing of the relation between them. This evocation of knowledge Spearman labeled *eduction,* and he argued that whenever a single character was presented the subject would immediately be reminded of its educed correlates. In the latter book, after rejecting many psychological and physiological accounts of *g*, he came to the conclusion that *g* reflected the subject's ability to educe relationships.

On the other hand, L. L. Thurstone (1887–1955) found that Spearman's "hierarchical order" was in fact a special case of a more general phenomenon. Thurstone was the first important mathematical psychologist of the present century. He worked on an equation for the learning curve and on methods for making mental tests more reliable and more valid; he made valuable contributions to psychophysics, including the development of a theory to account for choices in various kinds of situations; but in his lifetime he received most credit for his work on the analysis of tables of correlations (Adkins, 1964). The method he developed is known as "factor analysis," and Spearman's kind of analysis represents one level. By making use of all the data in the table of correlations, and by certain mathematical manipulations, which are in part optional, factor analysis allows the investigator to tease out those factors accounting for most of the variability in the data. Using his new methods, Thurstone (1938) analyzed a table of correlations of scores between as many as fifty-seven mental tests and came to the conclusion that there were at least nine different factors underlying his results, with four other minor factors present that could not be positively identified. These nine factors were visual-spatial ability, facility in finding particular items in a perceptual field, numerical judgment, verbal relations, verbal fluency, memory, inductive rule finding, and, more tentatively, deductive reasoning, and the "successful completion of a task that involves some form of restriction in the solution" (1938, p. 88). Thurstone remarked, "So far in our work we have not found the general factor of Spearman, but our results do not preclude it" (1938, p. vii).

Thorndike (1927) also argued, without using factor analysis, that an intelligence test should be considered to measure only what it purports to measure (e.g., deduction, comprehension) and that hasty generalizations about the relationship of the test to an amorphous "general factor" should be avoided. In general, the multifactor viewpoint has won the day, and in our own time Guilford (1967) has presented a scheme with as many as 120 factors arranged in a systematic fashion. R. B. Cattell (1957), however, has suggested that *g* can be divided into two kinds of abilities: "fluid" versus "crystallized"—the former largely innate, the latter the result of culturalization.

More detailed historical accounts of intelligence testing and intelligence theory will be found in Tuddenham (1962) and Matarazzo (1972). A particularly useful book is Fancher's *The Intelligence Men* (1985), a readable account of the history of intelligence testing, including an account of the contemporary controversy over whether intelligence is innate or acquired (see also Chapter 13). Another book that is essential reading is S. J. Gould's *The Mismeasure of Man* (1981). Gould takes the position that much of the so-called evidence for innate intelligence differences between individuals, and between groups such as men and women, or whites and other races, is based on extremely shaky evidence. He shows how Broca and other nineteenth-century researchers came to wrong conclusions by measuring brain sizes; and contends that in the twentieth century similar wrong conclusions have been arrived at by overreliance on intelligence tests. He is particularly critical of Goddard's work, stressing that little reliability can be placed on the massive data collected in World War I with the Army Alpha and Beta tests because they were administered under grossly unfair conditions. Gould also reviews the general problem of the interpretation of the results of factor analysis, stressing how contrary conclusions can be arrived at by different and equally plausible mathematical operations, and is critical of any attempt to "reify" *g*, that is, make *g* into a real object called "intelligence." The factor *g* should only be considered a mathematical expression, and there are alternative interpretations, such as Thomson's, which deny that *g* is a measure of "intelligence" at all.

Although there is currently considerable controversy over the extent to which intelligence is innately determined, some of the data on which the controversy is based were collected prior to 1940. These included studies of IQ scores in twins, IQ scores in foster children, and IQ scores in different races living in different environments; a summary of these early findings is given in Murphy, Murphy, and Newcomb (1937, Chap. 2).

Although personality theories based on factor analysis emerged after the period in question, there were some early attempts to scale various personality attributes by asking subjects to fill in questionaires. G. W. Allport offered a test for ascendance-submission in 1928, and G. W. Allport and P. E. Vernon presented a test concerned with personal values in 1931. The most widely used personality test in these early years was the Bernreuter Personality Inventory of 1931, which purported to measure introversion, neurotic tendency, dominance, and self-sufficiency. In 1930 Thurstone and Thurstone prepared an inventory to measure neuroticism. Also explored in this period were projective tests in which the subject can interpret a situation in his or her own way. The hope here is that aspects of personality that may not otherwise be obvious will be revealed. The two best-known projective tests date from our period: The famous "inkblot test" was described by H. Rorschach (1884–1922) in 1921, and Henry A. Murray described the Thematic Apperception Test in 1938, in which the material to be interpreted consists of drawings showing individuals in various somewhat ambiguous situations.

Social Psychology

Almost all of the research we have reviewed so far was concerned with finding generalizations about the reactions of the individual to stimuli from the environment. We have had occasion to mention the interactions between individuals in discussing, for example, imitation learning. But in general we have said little about what has come to be known as social psychology, the branch of psychology concerned with the responses of individuals to other individuals. However, writers on politics, economics, sociology, and anthropology in the nineteenth century all touched on the behavior of individuals in groups, so that one finds that G. W. Allport (1968), in his review of the early history of social psychology, discusses the writings of John Stuart Mill, Spencer, and others on the means of improving society. In fact, three separate disciplines—anthropology, sociology, and psychology—arose at the end of the nineteenth century, each of which fed the others to a small extent but then quickly went its separate way. In France Auguste Comte (1798–1857) coined the term *sociology* in 1839, and the famous sociologist Emile Durkheim (1858–1917) corresponded with Wundt on the tricky question of whether sociology can do without psychology because individual behavior is so excessively influenced by social pressures and the imitation of others that a separate science is needed to deal with the topic. In Germany M. Lazarus (1824–1903) and H. Steinthal (1823–1899) were responsible for a journal on *Völkerpsychologie* that appeared in 1860: Wundt adopted this term. *Völkerpsychologie* largely corresponded to what we now call cross-cultural psychology, and the first occurrence of the term *social psychology* in a book title may have been in a book by Vierkandt (1896), a pupil of Wundt. In America, particularly at the University of Chicago, there was pressure in the 1890s, to formulate a separate study of social psychology, but little actual experimentation was done (Rudmin, 1985). At the end of the century two works by a French writer appeared that are frequently cited as important in the development of modern social psychology.

Gustave Le Bon (1841–1931) had an adventurous life as an explorer and natural scientist. During his travels he was struck by the differences among individuals of different races and cultures, and after he had settled down in France in his middle age, he wrote two books which became very popular, *The Psychology of Peoples* in 1895 and *The Crowd* in 1895. At the time he wrote these, Charcot's influence was still strong and Le Bon adopted the idea that cultural characteristics were essentially ingrained in the individuals' unconscious minds. Normally the conscious dominated and the individual was well behaved and independent in thought, but given a crisis, coupled with the encouragement of a leader, the individual in a crowd could lose his or her sense of conscious identity, and the unconscious, and less moral, side of the cultural heritage would come to the fore. In *The Crowd* Le Bon described the methods of demagogues for swaying the crowd's ideas and actions and indicated that, just as the hypnotized subject would obey without question the suggestions of the hypnotist, so the individual "lost" in the crowd would also obey the commands of lower instincts as appealed to by the crowd leaders. The importance of this contribution to social psychology was both positive and negative: On the positive side it led scientists to ask how the behavior of the individual changed as a result of contact with other individuals; on the negative side it caused some to believe in a "group mind" or other unclear concepts of this kind. It was only in the 1930s that notions of a group, or collective, mind vanished from the literature.

The other development at the end of the nineteenth century was the beginning of experimentation into social factors affecting the performance of individuals. In 1898 Norman Triplett of Indiana University described the results of a survey he undertook concerning the effects of "pacing" on the speeds attained by bicycle racers. He found that riders who were paced outperformed riders who were not paced. He then investigated this effect in the laboratory, using a reel-winding task with various subjects, including children, either working alone or in competition with each other. Performance was better in the competitive situation. Triplett concluded that "the sight of the movements of the pacemakers or leading competitors, and the idea of higher speed, furnished by this or some other means, are probably in themselves dynamogenic factors of some consequence" (1898, p. 533). This study would form a start from which, in the course of the next forty years, would be built a large corpus of research on the effects of groups on the performance of individuals within the group. In fact, by 1940 this was the most solidly founded body of experimentation in social psychology; many other areas now widely studied (e.g., attitude change) were barely touched in the early decades. It should be noted, however, that Haines and Vaughn (1979) consider the impact of Triplett's study on the general development of social psychology in the early years to have been exaggerated.

The catalytic force that brought social psychology to public attention as an area in its own right was probably *Social Psychology* (1908) by William McDougall (1871–1938). McDougall had a medical degree, had done anthropological research in the East Indies, had worked with G. E. Müller in Göttingen, and promised to be a prominent exponent of early British experimental psychology. He carried out some competent work on color contrast, in which he invoked a concept of central inhibition to account for the way in which one color could dominate another. But he felt that experimental psychology as he knew it was too narrow a field, and he soon turned his mind to social psychology and abnormal psychology.

In *Social Psychology* McDougall attempted a synthesis of social behavior in terms of functions of the individuals within society. Each individual, argued McDougall, had a repertoire of basic instincts; life was a continuous striving as the individual's instincts led him or her in one direction or another; and many of these instincts had social origins—for example, pugnacity, which involves fighting with others, and a gregarious instinct, the desire for company. McDougall's early list of instincts in fact totaled eleven—flight, repulsion, curiosity, pugnacity, self-abasement, self-assertion, parental, reproductive, gregarious, acquisitive, and constructive. Later lists were even longer, and others of this period vied in producing rival lists (Krantz and Allen, 1967). In describing each, and the emotions and sentiments associated with them, McDougall in fact gave a broad view of behavior within society. But many felt his book, despite its title, to be but a prolegomenon to a true social psychology. His later writings on such subjects as vitalism, telepathy, and Lamarckism also made him unpopular with many scientists, particularly in the United States, his country of adoption since 1920. His position in the history of psychology is therefore insecure, with many believing that his instinct theory, which was attacked so broadly in the 1920s as to be almost forgotten nowadays, was to the good insofar as it stressed motivation but detrimental insofar as the concept itself was amorphous and lacking in explanatory power. McDougall's psychology came to be called *hormic* psychology, after a Greek word for striving, and was given equal prominence with behaviorism, Gestalt psychology, and psychoanalysis in many psychological works of the 1930s.

McDougall gave social psychology an identity, but it was F. H. Allport (1890–1978), who gave it a status. Strongly influenced by the behaviorist movement, Allport's *Social Psychology* of 1924 set forth a survey of the capacities of the individual, but at the same time stressed how the individual's behavior in groups was influenced by such factors as sympathy, imitation, suggestion, and laughter. He distinguished between two kinds of small groups, co-acting groups in which the main results might be social facilitation of performance, and face-to-face groups such as are found in discussion groups. He discussed the literature arising from Le Bon's work on crowds and stressed how conflict situations in the family group had been described by the psychoanalysts. Post (1980) also stresses Allport's importance in launching experimentation in social psychology.

Another work strongly influenced by behaviorism was the posthumous *Mind, Self and Society* (1934) by G. H. Mead (1863–1931). Mead argued that J. B. Watson's theory had been applied mainly to children and animals and that it needed elaboration to account for social influences on the growing child. He believed that simple vocal gestures and sounds, which were at first the only means of communication for the child, were transformed as he learned language into "significant symbols." At the same time the child built up, by learning from others and from a growing facility with language, the concept of a self that could become a focus of thought, "me." This reflexiveness of thought, Mead asserted, resulted from social contact and could be considered as a sophisticated construct built up originally from simple conditioned reflexes.

F. H. Allport himself had contributed to research on social facilitation. The following years showed an increasing amount of experimental investigation into such groups. We may pick out three studies as being particularly revealing and influential. Shaw (1932) gave a number of reasoning problems to individuals by themselves and to the same individuals acting in groups. Performance in groups was far superior, and Shaw, by an analysis of protocols, was able to indicate that the group was readier to reject wrong steps or answers than was the individual. This study has since been criticized because the same results could have been obtained if the groups' results were determined by one or two particularly clever individuals, but it led to a great deal of further research on cooperation and the mechanisms of decisions by committees.

Then Sherif (1936) showed that an individual can be very strongly influenced by decisions and promptings from other members of a group. Using the fact that a spot of light in a dark room seems to move even though it stays stationary (the autokinetic effect), Sherif showed that individual decisions as to the light's "movements" were greatly influenced by the individual's knowledge of the decisions made by others. This research opened the way for many subsequent studies of conformity and peer pressure. Finally, Gurnee (1937) showed that maze learning based on a group decision was superior to maze learning by individuals, but he was also able to show that individuals within a group would tend to focus on particular problems and leave others to other members of the group. This study was among the first to indicate the importance of role taking within a group.

By 1937 enough data had been collected for Murphy, Murphy, and Newcomb to offer a major summary, *Experimental Social Psychology*, which had over a thousand references. Their definition of *social psychology* seems to us rather broad, for the book included much information on intelligence testing, personality, and child development. The authors' position was that the influence of groups of various kinds showed itself in different ways at different ages; the order imposed on social psychology by this developmental approach has dissipated to some extent in our own day. But Murphy, Murphy, and Newcomb were able to offer excellent syntheses of the evidence then available on such topics as aggressiveness, cooperation, attitude formation (particularly racial prejudice), and attitude change as a result of education, all of which would become the focus for intensive research efforts after the 1940s.

Another event of importance in the 1930s was the arrival of refugees from Central European Nazism, including Fritz Heider (b. 1896), who formulated the theory that we try to balance our attitudes so that they seem to be self-consistent; Egon Brunswik (1903–1955), who developed the theory that perception and judgment involve the formulation of enlightened guesses or "hypotheses" about the world, a forerunner of modern views about perception; Kurt Lewin (see Chapter 9), who became very active in social psychology on arriving in North America; and G. Ichheiser (1897–1969), who wrote on many of the misperceptions and misapprehensions we have about other people's personalities and achievements. The story of the exodus from Europe has been briefly outlined by Mandler and Mandler (1968) and Wellek (1968); its impact on American psychology is still being studied. But there is no doubt that many topics of concern to social psychologists after 1940, in particular the topic of attitudes people hold to one another, were raised by persons who had themselves experienced what it was like to be the object of prejudice and persecution.

A frequently quoted history of social psychology is given by G. W. Allport (1968); Steiner (1979) has more on experiments. Hilgard (1987) has a useful history of American social psychology, and the 1983 volume of the *British Journal of Social Psychology* has a collection of articles on the subject, including articles by Jaspars (1983) on the historical relationships between psychology and sociology, and articles by Farr (1983) and Danziger (1983) on the historical role played by Wundt's *Völkerpsychologie*.

Applied Psychology

"Applied" psychology has many branches, including industrial psychology, clinical psychology, counseling psychology, and psychology concerned with crime and law. One might be tempted to think of applied psychology as being a relatively new branch of the subject, but in fact some of its pioneers were Wundt students: Münsterberg, Scott, and Witmer (see following) all studied at Leipzig. The development of applied psychology can best be traced if we focus first on industrial psychology, for considerable progress was made in this area between 1900 and 1940. There were important concurrent developments in America and Britain, but for convenience the history of industrial psychology in the two countries will be sketched separately.

In America, the best-known pioneers of industrial psychology were Hugo Münsterberg and W. D. Scott (1869–1955). In Chapter 7 we mentioned Münsterberg's efforts in establishing psychology as a *useful* discipline, and his main work in industrial psychology, *Psychology and Industrial Efficiency* (1913), laid out the groundwork of the psychologist's tasks: He or she should help in job placement and in making sure a worker was fitted for his job; should attempt to make the job itself as comfortable to carry out as possible and should have some input into the design of equipment or machinery so as to make it "user compatible," as we would now say; and, once the product was manufactured, should try to contribute to our understanding of sales success. Münsterberg described some small experiments on selecting persons for particular tasks, using tests that seemed to examine the abilities needed for the job in question. Nearly all of Münsterberg's ideas were to be followed up on by contemporaries or later psychologists.

W. D. Scott started in experimental psychology, but Ferguson (1961) tells how he was approached in 1901 by the advertising manager of a chain of magazines who persuaded him to do research on the efficacy of advertising. Scott was at first reluctant, but he rapidly made a name for himself for his skill at research in applied psychology, publishing, for example, *The Psychology of Advertising* in 1900. In 1915 he was appointed the first professor of applied psychology in the new Division of Applied Psychology at the Carnegie Institute of Technology. Here he was responsible for setting up a Bureau of Salesmanship Research and later became a leading expert on personnel selection and management. In 1917 Scott did original research on the selection of sales personnel: This set common standards for the use of application blanks, letters of reference, interviews, and certain psychological tests. We may note here that it was Thorndike (1920) who contributed the term *halo effect* to the artifact whereby personnel selection is often biased by perhaps trivial initial impressions.

It was also in 1917 that America entered World War I. Yerkes, the president of the American Psychological Association, organized a Committee on the Psychological Examination of Recruits: It was at this committee's request that the Army Alpha and Beta tests mentioned on p. 381 emerged. We may note now that one use made of these tests was to obtain an estimate of the kinds of intelligence needed for various occupations in the armed services. These formed a guideline for future research guiding individuals to appropriate careers. Scott himself was responsible for setting up a Committee on the Classification of Personnel, which was one of the first systems employed by a government agency for allocating men and women to particular jobs.

After the war, Scott founded a company to develop tests to business clients' specifications, and at various universities bureaus were set up to conduct research into sales training for specific industries. Increasingly, businesspeople turned to the universities for guidance in the selection of personnel for particular positions. One of the earliest examples was in 1920 when a Milwaukee company approached Morris S. Viteles of the University of Pennsylvania's psychology clinic to develop a test for the selection of streetcar operators. The test he devised involved the construction of a machine that simulated the operator's task in a streetcar; Viteles also developed a methodology for describing job specifications in "psychographs."

Another American development of the decade between 1910 and 1920 was the time and motion study. This method of trying to improve job efficiency by analyzing, in fine detail, the motions made in a task was originated by Frederick Taylor (who wrote a best-selling *Principles of Scientific Management* in 1911) and Frank B. Gilbreth. Gilbreth, for example, was able to analyze the process of brick laying in such a way as to reduce the number of movements in laying a brick from eighteen to five. By 1920 in America, then, the task of improving job efficiency was being approached from several directions, including better selection of personnel, better analysis of what the job involved, and improvement of the actual performance of certain jobs by time and motion study. However, the reader should not have the impression that these contributions by psychologists to the increase of productivity were welcomed by the workers: The psychologists were felt to be intrusive and the workers disliked being "under the thumb" of somebody telling them how to do their jobs (Hilgard, 1987, p. 702).

World War I was also the impetus for the development of industrial psychology in Great Britain, but there it took a slightly different direction. Munitions factories were working around the clock, causing serious health problems for fatigued workers. The study of the effects of fatigue and monotony on mental work went back to Oehrn (1895), but Münsterberg, in his influential *Psychology of Industrial Efficiency* (1913), pointed out that laboratory studies on mental work often had little relevance to industrial situations involving physical work. He pointed to the advantages of detailed study of the kind carried out by Taylor and Gilbreth for the reduction of fatigue and the improvement of efficiency and pay. Hearnshaw (1964) stresses the influence of Münsterberg's book on British psychologists of the time. Another stimulus was a book by the Australian Bernard Muscio, *Lectures on Industrial Psychology* (1917). This work particularly attracted the attention of C. S. Myers (1873–1947): Myers had written a widely used *Textbook of Experimental Psychology* (1909) and had been associated with the laboratory of experimental psychology at Cambridge. In 1918 Myers's suggestion that institutes of applied psychology be set up in the United Kingdom was supported by members of the industrial community, and the National Institute of Industrial Psychology (NIIP) was founded in 1921 with Myers as its director. Over the years the institute published many research reports, mainly concerned with ways of improving the environment and conditions of the industrial worker. The British government sponsored another group, the Industrial Fatigue Research Board, in 1919. Under the aegis of these two bodies, important studies were done on the reduction of fatigue by the introduction of appropriate rest periods; there were studies on the improvement of output by noise reduction, better ventilation and heating, and bonus and piecework rates of pay. H. M. Vernon, one of the most active applied psychologists of this period, wrote a scholarly book, *Accidents and Their Prevention* (1936), which was influential in pinpointing sources of accidents both in the factory and the home and in transportation. The NIIP also devised tests of its own for use in vocational guidance.

Viteles's *Industrial Psychology* of 1933 summarized research as it then stood and was widely read as a standard reference work. The book included a historical introduction dealing with the rise of industrial psychology in Germany, Russia, and other countries as well as the United States and Great Britain.

Progress in testing the effects of environmental conditions, in job analysis and personnel selection, and in studying management-worker interactions—a task psychology was beginning to tackle—continued until the outbreak of World War II. The war led to increased study of human-machine interactions in particular and gave an impetus to the new science of cybernetics.

Psychology was also viewed as an important adjunct to education during this period, and many educators tried to incorporate psychology into their works on effective teaching. Thorndike tried to help children to learn to read by giving them first common words, then rare words as listed in his *Teacher's Word Book of 30,000 Words* (Thorndike and Lorge, 1944); he also wrote a popular arithmetic textbook and an elaborate book entitled *The Psychology of Arithmetic* in which he tried to show the relative roles of drill (learning the tables by heart) and reason (as seen in understanding fractions) in the way the child learns this topic. His theory was based on his notion that associative bonds need to be stamped in by appropriate satisfiers. Huey (1908) and Judd (see Chapter 7) carried out extensive studies of the processes of reading, a task which is still not very well understood. The intelligence test movement rapidly entered the school system and the work of Thorndike and Terman in particular was widely discussed. But there was relatively little concern for the emotional well-being of schoolchildren, and counseling as we now know it in the school system was rather rare.

One topic deserving special mention was vocational guidance. The first book dedicated to expounding methods of vocational guidance was Frank Parsons's *Choosing a Vocation,* published in 1909. The development of several new tests facilitated educational and vocational guidance. In America, the Strong Vocational Interest Blank (see Strong, 1943) was devised after a long series of trial studies in 1927 (on the form for men) and 1933 (on the form for women). Another popular test was the Kuder Preference Record (Kuder, 1934–1956). Thurstone (1931) factor-analyzed scores on the Strong test and found interests divisible into four main kinds: interest in science, in language, in people, and in business. He showed how different vocations catered in different proportions to these interests.

The growth of the profession of *clinical psychology* as we now know it had separate roots in education and psychiatry. The first psychological clinic, as noted on p. 317, was founded by Lightner Witmer to help children having difficulties at school. When vocational guidance became prominent, however, schools began to employ more counselors, who soon, of course, came to be involved in adjustment problems, particularly the problems of juvenile delinquents. Many women, such as Grace M. Fernald (1879–1950), became involved in remedial work: She first assisted W. Healy (1869–1963), who directed an institute in Chicago for the help of juvenile delinquents, and later she joined the University of California in Los Angeles. Simultaneously, a growing need was felt for consultants who would assist mentally disturbed adults who were not so ill as to require hospitalization; an important boost was given to this opinion by the missionary work of Clifford Beers (1876–1943), a former mental patient who founded the National Committee on Mental Hygiene in 1908. This was a group that argued strongly for patients' rights and the need for consultation facilities before an illness got out of hand. The public attention this movement received led directly to the growth of child guidance clinics, which in turn led to the development of clinics for adults in which psychiatric social workers were employed in addition to psychiatrists and psychologists. Although these clinics for adults were not widespread before World War II, as they are now, it was at this time that clinical psychologists such as David Shakow (1901–1981) began their efforts to increase the number of facilities available for adults with emotional problems. One of the main impacts of these patterns of growth was that an increasing number of psychologists were employed outside of universities, a phenomenon recognized in 1937 by the founding of the American Association of Applied Psychologists (AAAP). At first this society was separate from the American Psychological Association (APA), but in 1945 the APA was reorganized into divisions, some of which were suitable for members of the AAAP, and the two societies were reamalgamated. Equally interesting is an analysis of membership interests in APA in 1939: Clinical psychologists form the majority of members, followed by research workers, school psychologists, guidance and personnel workers, and industrial psychologists (Hilgard, 1987, Chap. 20).

The study of psychology as it relates to legal matters has beginnings as early as the turn of the century. William Stern developed the *Aussage* experiment, in which an incident is unexpectedly staged and the witnesses are asked to describe the incident as accurately as possible. The witnesses usually make so many errors that the observer can lose considerable faith in the reliability of eye-witness testimony. There were also studies during this period on "lie detection" by means of word association tests and changes in autonomic functioning, particularly blood pressure and breathing rate. Later research focused on the psychogalvanic reflex (change in electrical conductance of the skin as perspiration occurs). The behavior of judges and juries was subjected to various forms of statistical analysis. A great deal of applied research investigated characteristics supposedly related to the propensity to criminal behavior, such as low intelligence or coming from broken homes. An excellent summary of research in this period is Burtt's *Legal Psychology* (1931).

A single work giving an overall view of the progress of applied psychology in the early 1940s was Poffenberger's *Principles of Applied Psychology* (1942). This work discusses the previously mentioned issues concerned with industrial efficiency, guidance, advertising, and legal psychology but is also noteworthy for the inclusion of a chapter on aging as it relates to adjustment and skill and three chapters on psychology as related to disease. A list of key dates in the history of applied psychology will be found in Fryer and Henry (Vol. I, 1950).

Summary

This chapter reviews progress in physiological psychology, psychometrics, social psychology, and applied psychology in the period from 1879 to 1940.

Physiological Psychology. Adrian's work on nervous action was reviewed, followed by a discussion of how the modern concepts of the neuron and the synapse were arrived at. Sherrington was the main figure to do research on reflex behavior, and Cannon did pioneering research on drives and emotions. Discoveries about localization of function in the brain were summarized; the main figures included Hughlings Jackson, Ferrier, and Lashley. The section concluded with a discussion of discoveries of this period concerned with the special senses.

Psychometrics. Mental testing had its origins in the nineteenth century but was initially not very successful. The breakthrough came with the work of Binet, who was able to list tasks that children who developed normally were able to perform at different ages. Binet's work led directly to the concept of the intelligence quotient and later to the development of tests that could be administered to groups. Spearman also developed a theory based on a concept of general intelligence; controversy over the theory led later to the notion of different group and specific factors in intelligence as well as to the development of the technique of factor analysis by Thurstone.

Social psychology. Social psychology had its beginnings in a variety of disciplines, but its modern identity was established with F. M. Allport's *Social Psychology* of 1924, which stressed the scientific study of ways in which individual behavior is influenced by the behavior of others. Typical early research on social psychology included studies of group decision making, group pressure, and role taking in groups. This period also saw the beginnings of research into attitude change and prejudice.

Applied Psychology. Applied psychology began when industrial leaders in North America approached individual psychologists with problems of advertising and personnel selection. In Britain industrial efforts in World War I focused attention on the problem of fatigue at work. Gradually some psychologists came to specialize in research on these and related matters. The course of early developments in school coureling, vocational guidance, clinical psychology, and legal psychology was also traced.

1940 to 1985:
Eclectic Psychology 13

At this point in our progress, we are forced to make a choice. Writing in the late 1980s it would seem that a history of psychology could reasonably stop at 1940 and refer the reader to up-to-date texts for a summary of contemporary developments in the subject. But the reader might then have a feeling of being left high and dry. Or we could continue at the same level of detail and bring the history up to 1985, but to do this properly would really demand a book-length work along the lines of Hearst (1979) or Koch and Leary (1985), who survey the first one hundred years of experimental psychology. Or finally, we could try to give a bird's-eye view of the major developments over the last forty years, with the proviso that this can be nothing more than a sketch whose main purpose will be to orient rather than instruct. Recognizing that the latter solution must, of necessity, be unsatisfactory, but that the reader might nevertheless find it helpful, we here offer a brief overview of events in psychology in the past forty-five years.

The period from 1940 has been marked by a move towards a more eclectic psychology. By *eclectic* we mean that few psychologists now adhere to a single line of thought as propounded by the leaders of a single school. Rather, they prefer to absorb the best ideas of all schools. In their teaching they try to present a rounded and fairly complete picture of what is now known about behavior in its various aspects, including cognitive facets; in their research, they focus on particular issues and try to develop models directly relevant to these issues. In some cases, however, this research does have close affinities with the viewpoints of one or another school of the 1930s, as will be made clearer later.

There are now few all-encompassing schools of the kind represented by Gestalt psychology, behaviorism, or psychoanalysis. The main findings of the Gestalt psychologists have been integrated into perceptual theory, learning theory, and studies of thinking processes. The legacy of the behaviorists primarily consists in a rigorous experimental method and an avoidance of anthropomorphism, but there is now less confidence that a simple stimulus-response analysis of individual behavior patterns is adequate for a comprehensive psychology of learning. And psychoanalysis, as Freud taught it, has been subject to a great deal of criticism. His basic view that mental illness has its roots in childhood sexuality has not so much been disproved—it is very difficult to disprove—as simply overlooked in favor of more direct attempts to cure the symptoms causing the most immediate distress to the patient. In this chapter we shall first elaborate on certain developments in the classical schools within recent years and then spend the larger part of the chapter reviewing current progress in the acquisition of psychological knowledge that is relatively independent of any framework specific to a particular school.

Gestalt Psychology

Although Köhler kept Gestalt notions in the forefront of his theorizing up to his death in 1967, it would be exaggerating to say that there was an active Gestalt school after the outbreak of World War II. Nevertheless, the influence of Gestalt concepts remained pervasive and students of perception still quote Wertheimer's laws; students of thinking acknowledge their indebtedness to the Gestalt concept of a "set," which provided a framework for more fine-grained cognitive actions; and students of animal learning still try to understand "insightful" behavior in their subjects. Some examples of Gestalt-influenced research since 1940 may be given.

Luchins (1942) encapsulated the importance of the concept of set in his water-jar problems. Each problem asks the subject to use imagined water jars, each of a given capacity, to measure out a specific amount of water. Following a series of problems that can be solved using a particular fixed pattern, the researchers pose a much simpler problem, which can be solved without using the fixed pattern. But subjects persist in employing the fixed pattern and do not adapt their strategy. This has become a classic example of a failure to restructure a pattern of actions in order to achieve a new goal.

Also in America, Hans Wallach continued to study a variety of perceptual problems, including color and brightness perception, motion perception, the constancies, perceptual learning, and compensation for movement-produced visual stimulation. A selection of his papers is reprinted in Wallach (1976). In all of these areas, Wallach stressed how the perception of a given unit is dependent on the relationship between that unit and surrounding units.

A new development in Gestalt thinking took place in Germany in 1954: Following the revived publication of the *Psychologische Forschung*, Tausch offered a general theory of the illusions. The argument ran that, whenever we peruse a two-dimensional configuration, processes that normally help us to interpret three-dimensional configurations are called into play. For example, if we see this shape/ \, Tausch argued that it reminds us of two parallel lines, like railway tracks, receding into the distance. Since the upper half of the display is interpreted as being further away then the lower half, a size constancy mechanism ensures that objects placed within the upper half are seen as larger than objects placed within the lower half. Many two-dimensional illusions were interpreted by Tausch in terms of this model, and Gregory, in his influential *Eye and Brain* (1966), gave it favorable treatment. However, the theory has also met with some opposition. E. L. Brown and K. Deffenbacher (1979) prefer a theory in which subjects are held to be unable to ignore the elements surrounding a particular detail in a visual display. And Witkin and others, in their book *Personality through Perception* (1954), argued that some individuals are less able than others to ignore the influence of the total field on a given detail. These authors therefore distinguish field-dependent from field-independent persons. During these years, Helson was working on a theory according to which all our perceptions are evaluated against a baseline that is itself a function of the total perceptual surround; the details of the system are given in his *Adaptation Level Theory* (1964).

The above are examples of how Gestalt relationism has continued to influence studies of perception. In Germany, Gestalt psychology remains a potent force. Metzger, the foremost later exponent of Gestalt theory, edited with Erke the encyclopedic *Allgemeine Psychologie (General Psychology)* in many volumes; the first volume (1966) contained several contemporary accounts of how Gestalt attitudes towards perception continue to dominate certain topics. More recently Ertel, Kemmler, and Stadler (1975) have produced another survey of the influence of Gestalt concepts on modern psychological theorizing.

Behaviorism

Behaviorism has gone through an upheaval. Insofar as the early behaviorists were the founders of modern learning theory and insofar as learning theory is still an active area of investigation, there is no question as to the indebtedness of the contemporary learning theorist to Thorndike, Pavlov, and Watson. But some of Watson's principles are beginning to lie like withered flowers along the pathway of history. He argued that *consciousness* should be banished from the vocabulary of the dedicated psychologist, but most introductory textbooks of the 1980s have chapters on altered states of consciousness. Moreover, current theorists of cognitive processes are deeply concerned with the distinction between automatic, or unconscious, processes, as opposed to conscious processes, particularly following the publications of Posner and Snyder (1975) and Schneider and Shiffrin (1977). Watson argued there was no such thing as imagery, but starting with Paivio's *Imagery and Verbal Processes* (1971), there are now many articles and books devoted to the experimental study of imagery, and the question of how imagery can be represented in a computer model is currently receiving attention (Cunningham, 1980). Watson believed that all behavior could be seen in terms of stimulus-response associations, but modern theorists of human memory and language behavior are highly skeptical of the value of static associations. They prefer to write of more complex units—known by such names as "scripts"—that represent programs of actions such as are involved in a visit to a restaurant or in dressing oneself, or of "schemata," following Bartlett (1932). These concepts, incidentally, have much in common with Gestalt concepts.

The history of the erosion of pure behaviorism by attacks from cognitive theorists and also by those who have argued for certain innate principles of behavior has been traced by Gardner (1985) and Leahey (1987). The landmark events include a growing stress on internal covert mental processes by traditional learning theorists, the criticism of the "dehumanizing" aspects of behaviorism by clinical psychologists such as Carl Rogers, a controversy between Skinner and Noam Chomsky on the question of how far language behavior can be analyzed in terms of fixed stimulus-response chains, the discovery in the early 1960s that some examples of animal behavior seem to be determined by unlearned tendencies rather than by learning, and the development of cognitive psychology, which was in part the result of a viewpoint known as the cybernetic viewpoint, founded in the war years. According to this viewpoint, the organism should be seen as a communication system processing information much as a mechanical system such as a radio or a telephone grid can be said to process information. More will be said later on these developments. But though it would seem that behaviorism and neobehaviorism have been superseded, there is a growing feeling that cognitive science has not made good its promise, and, as we shall see, many psychologists have been sidetracked away from conducting experiments into engaging in sophisticated arguments. Skinner (1985) has accused cognitive psychologists of making exactly the same mistake as Watson accused the introspectionists of making, and in particular Skinner criticizes the cognitive theorists for misusing the word "purpose," wrongly assuming that in our heads we have "representations" of reality, and of bringing psychology back into the old metaphysical ways.

Learning theory, the branch of psychology about which the behaviorists had most to say, has, however, shown steady advances from the 1930s onward. Attempts to provide systems of axioms from which predictions about learning behavior could be made did not die out with Hull; in the 1950s Estes offered a new system according to which the organism could be seen as "sampling" the environment and making responses to a subset of stimuli, these responses being given with experimentally determinable finite probabilities.

One of the most interesting extensions of learning theory to human learning came in the 1960s, after it was shown by Rock (1957) that a new association might be learned in one trial, and that learning therefore did not necessarily consist of an accumulation of "habit strength" over several trials, as Hull had suggested. A number of writers, starting with Bower (1961), were able to predict how quickly human subjects could learn paired associate lists using as the basic factor to be determined by experiment the "probability of forming an association in one trial." Many of these papers were reported in the new *Journal of Mathematical Psychology*, and although models of the learning process are not so popular now as they were in the 1960s, there is no question of the impetus these models gave to the development of mathematical psychology. The rise of this subdiscipline has also given new life to the old subject of psychophysics (see, e.g., Falmagne, 1985).

The work of Tolman in the 1930s was neglected for some time, but at the beginning of the 1970s it was increasingly recognized that cognitive psychology might offer some concepts of value to theorists of animal learning, and Tolman's "cognitive maps" came to be looked at in a more favorable light. Moreover, many learning theorists had assumed that animals behaved like automata: One inserts the stimulus and the response follows with a certain probability. But a stimulus can also be seen as a signal that elicits not simply an overt response but a covert expectation on the part of the subject; increasingly, the notion that even a conditioned stimulus can serve as a medium for eliciting a particular expectation has come to pervade learning theory. A good example of this shift from the view that animals are S–R automata to the view that they in some way evaluate *contingencies* may be seen in Gleitman's *Psychology* (1986), which introduces expectancy theory as a clear alternative to traditional S–R mechanistic models and in turn stresses Tolman's role as a forerunner of this approach.

The most influential learning theorist of the 1930s was probably Skinner, for although Skinner was very behavioristic in his emphasis that a science of behavior—one that said little about the physiological or cognitive processes underlying behavior—was a goal in its own right, the techniques he developed for studying simple behavior patterns of an operant kind led to a close evaluation of the role of reinforcement in learning. In the 1940s Skinner and his colleagues worked out the behavior patterns resulting from various schedules of reinforcement in rats and pigeons, and they also began to ask whether human behavior patterns could perhaps also be influenced by appropriate schedules of reinforcement.

It was at this time that a few individuals began to inquire whether abnormal behavior could be viewed as a complex of learned, if not necessarily adaptive, behavior patterns. The psychoanalysts, with their emphasis on unconscious dynamics, had long preempted the field of abnormal psychology, but after Pavlov had demonstrated that dogs show maladaptive behavior patterns when confronted with insoluble problems in a classical conditioning situation, others such as Gantt (1942), H. S. Liddell (1938), and Masserman (1943) in the United States were able to demonstrate "experimental neurosis" in animals. This, in turn, raised the question of how such emotionally charged behavior patterns could be extinguished, leading in the 1950s to the pioneering work of Wolpe and others on the extinction of learned fears in humans.

Joseph Wolpe had become disillusioned with traditional psychotherapy of a psychoanalytic bias and turned to learning theory as an alternative. Impressed with the work of Masserman, who had produced experimental neurosis in cats by forcing them to sustain a shock in order to procure food, Wolpe (1952) was able to induce neurosis in cats in the same way, but he then went on to explore means whereby the neurotic behaviors could be reduced. In particular, he devised a method based on what he called reciprocal inhibition: The fear the animal shows in the surroundings associated with the food plus shock stimulation can be reduced if a competing response not involving anxiety can be substituted for the fear response. Wolpe's method, known as desensitization, involved giving the animal food in a room remotely resembling the original room in which the fear response was elicited. When that feeding response was well established, the animal would be fed in a room yet more similar to the original room; gradually the animal could be enticed to eat in the original room without showing symptoms of fear by being brought through a succession of rooms that became more and more similar to the original room. The desensitization technique adapted to individual human cases has been used increasingly by therapists to reduce phobias of various kinds.

Another technique for changing undesirable behaviors, also based on the general notion of substituting a socially acceptable response for a maladaptive one, is based on systematically rewarding desired behaviors until they become habitual. First Skinner and Lindsley at Harvard, and later Ayllon in Canada and Azrin in Illinois, introduced systems of rewards and incentives in psychiatric wards mainly populated with psychotic patients who were greatly withdrawn and showed little interest in appropriate social behaviors or interactions with staff and other patients. By rewarding small positive actions, such as voluntarily attending meals, these researchers were able to instigate behavior that was judged to be more acceptable. The general name for the use of extinction and reinforcement techniques in applied settings such as schools and hospitals is *behavior modification* or *behavior therapy*. It is now a major branch of clinical psychology in its own right and considerable research effort has been devoted to setting up therapeutic situations and evaluating the consequent results. A full and fascinating history of behavior modification, including an account of its roots in behaviorism and an account of how behavior therapists are trying to cope with the charge that behavior control infringes on the rights of patients, is given by Kazdin (1978). There are now several journals devoted to behavior modification, of which we may single out the *Journal of Applied Behavior Analysis* (founded in 1968), which was a direct offshoot of the *Journal of the Experimental Analysis of Behavior* (founded in 1958), the major vehicle for publications on operant conditioning. More recently, the term *cognitive therapy* has come into vogue to describe forms of psychotherapy based on the premise that the aim of therapy is to extinguish bad habits, and that this aim can be achieved by appropriate verbal communication.

Another development arising from Skinner's concern with schedules of reinforcement has been the application of reinforcement in educational contexts. In the 1920s Pressey had devised machines for self-scoring test materials, but the machines also presented material to be learned. These early "teaching machines" were ignored until the 1950s when Skinner (1957) stressed that operant conditioning could be invaluable in a classroom situation. A child can be rewarded simply by seeing that he or she obtains the correct answer to a question. By offering questions of increasing difficulty interspersed with instructions that progress one step at a time the child (or even the adult) can gradually acquire a corpus of information at a rate that suits his or her own abilities. The material can be presented either by machine or in book form; research evaluating the merits of this *programmed instruction,* as it came to be called, is published in such journals as the *Journal of Programmed Instruction* (founded in 1962).

Programmed instruction is used quite widely not only in schools but also in universities, in the military, and in job training. One can acquire the rudiments of operant conditioning theory, for example, through the programmed text of Geis, Stubbins, and Lundin (1965); and knowledge of a computer programming language, LISP, frequently used by modelers of human cognitive processes, can be acquired through the programmed text of Friedman (1974). More recently, a system known as personalized instruction (Keller, 1968) has appeared as an alternative to programmed instruction. The student works through a course by accomplishing a fairly large number of small exercises, at his own rate, with guidance from an instructor available each time he completes an exercise. There are, of course, many variations on this basic procedure: The *Journal of Personalized Instruction* (founded in 1977) serves as a forum for research on this method. Again, the key to success would appear to depend on the judicious application of reinforcement at key stages in the acquisition phase. However, Skinner (1985) has complained that programmed learning has not been exploited as fully as it should, because the influence of Gestalt and cognitive psychologists led educational authorities to stress "understanding" and "the discovery of principles" as essential to the learning process. Skinner asserts that after twenty-five years of following these guidelines, "American students are no better in science and mathematics than they were before" (p. 299).

Psychoanalysis

In a work of this length it is impossible to discuss in detail the many amendments to Freud's theory that have been suggested by his followers. These include elaborations of the role played by the family and the sociological subculture in determining the emotional growth of the child; the extension of psychoanalytic theory to cases of psychosis and other emotional illnesses in addition to the neuroses; the incorporation of findings in experimental psychology into psychoanalytic theory (e.g., the results of research on infants' behavior or on dreaming); and attempts to be more precise than Freud was on emotional development in the female. These developments are discussed in Fine's *A History of Psychoanalysis* (1979). One's main impression from reading this book is to have confirmed one's estimation of Freud as having built the superstructure as well as the foundations of the psychoanalytic edifice, with others essentially adding the final touches. On the other hand, there have been a number of attempts to evaluate critically the scientific status of psychoanalysis and to estimate its therapeutic efficiency. We shall give a brief account of these.

Shortly after Freud's death, R. R. Sears was commissioned by a subcommittee of the Social Sciences Research Council, an American government body, to survey the evidence for and against psychoanalytic doctrine. His report appeared in 1943 and covered experimental evidence that seemed relevant to Freudian doctrine as well as the results of sociological surveys on such matters as child-rearing and sexual practices in a large number of families. He did not give a blanket opinion as to whether psychoanalysis was "right" or "wrong" but rather dealt with the matter issue by issue. He concluded, for example, that Freud's stress on infantile sexuality was supported by evidence for sexual interests in very young children, but he was skeptical about the value of the view that sexuality was focused on different bodily zones in a set sequence. He agreed with Freud's opinion that sex was associated with shame and guilt at a very early age but could find no evidence that children had a particular fear of being castrated. His comments on the Oedipus complex stressed the enormous variability of relationships that could be found between parents and offspring of the age of five or so in different families and different cultures and implied that Freud's rather restricted view of love-hate bonds at this age would have to be amplified. He was quite favorable to Freud's view that neurotic disturbances were the result of a fixation at, or a regression to, a particular stage in emotional development; evidence was reviewed from animal studies and studies of children at play that strongly supported the notion that such behavior patterns as aggression or regression were associated with emotional frustration.

These studies, incidentally, also played a part in persuading learning theorists that their discipline could make a contribution to clinical psychology: Many of them were done by Neal Miller and other students of Hull at Yale. Sears, in fact, believed that animal studies were the most fruitful of the various studies of psychoanalytic phenomena he examined. But Sears was less optimistic that Freud's postulated defense mechanisms could be examined in the laboratory because one simply could not reproduce the strong emotions underlying the mechanism of repression or projection. Despite many attempts to reproduce repressive mechanisms in studies of the memorization of "pleasant" or "unpleasant" material, these efforts seemed to Sears unproductive because they never dealt with the truly ego-threatening forces against which regression served as a defense. The sheer difficulties of experimentally testing Freudian hypotheses have been dealt with at book length by Sarnoff (1971).

After Sears's report, studies continued to appear that seemed on the surface to offer some confirmation of some of Freud's ideas. Relationships were found between the duration of breast-feeding and the development of oral habits such as thumb-sucking and smoking; attempts were made to use questionnaires to delineate personality traits based on Freud's oral or anal stages of sexuality; the contents of dreams were enumerated with a view to determining how far they reflected apparent oedipal fears; and further attempts were made to demonstrate repression in artificial experiments. Kline (1972) reviewed many of these studies and came out with the positive verdict that many of Freud's ideas had been confirmed. But Eysenck and Wilson (1973) reprinted some of these same studies in full and were able to show in each case that alternative nonpsychoanalytic explanations could account for the data. They also reprinted two earlier studies heavily critical of psychoanalysis. One was a survey by Eysenck (1952), who argued, among other things, that there was no convincing evidence that psychoanalytic treatment was more effective than any other kind of psychotherapy. He asserted, moreover, that the rate of spontaneous remission of symptoms was such as to raise the question of the efficacy of *any* kind of psychotherapy. The other was an examination by Wolpe and Rachman (1960) of Freud's case history of the child "little Hans" where they persuasively show that Freud and the patient's father tended to ask the patient questions that obliged him to reply in a way that made an explanation of the patient's symptoms in terms of the Oedipus complex appear valid, when in fact a much more straightforward account in terms of learned fears was equally appropriate.

The charge that Freud "persuaded" his patients to make statements in line with his theory has been made by others (see Leahey, 1987, p. 211). Eysenck and Wilson felt that Kline, in his review of these studies, was not sufficiently critical. Eysenck and Wilson also found that quite often, if Freud predicts X and the opposite result appears in the experimental results, then the author argues that this is because the subjects have developed a reaction formation that can explain the contradiction. This convenient out, argued Eysenck and Wilson, makes it even more difficult to evaluate the virtues of Freud's suggestions.

Fisher and Greenberg (1977) made an extremely comprehensive survey of evidence for and against Freudian theory, and their conclusion, like Kline's, was that Freud's conjectures were often supported by the evidence. In particular, following an evaluation of evidence based on questionnaires, they decided that there were indeed "clusters of traits in children and adults corresponding to the core qualities associated with the oral and anal concepts" (1977, p. 393). They believed that there was fairly firm support for Freud's view that paranoia was an outcome of repressed homosexuality and that homosexuality could be the result of conflict with the father figure at the oedipal stage. In contrast to Sears, Fisher and Greenberg believed that they had found experimental confirmation of the castration fear. But other findings led them to cast doubt on some of Freud's suggestions. The true meaning of a dream was not necessarily completely disguised, as Freud had thought, and revealing the patient's unconscious to him or her did not necessarily have a therapeutic effect. The superego—that is, the construct held to underly the development of moral standards—may develop not as a result of a fear of the father so much as a desire to please the father; there is quite good evidence that "the boy's masculine identification and development of moral standards are most facilitated by a positive, nurturant attitude on the part of father" (1977, p. 395). There seemed, to Fisher and Greenberg, no evidence to support the view that females have a more inferior concept of their bodies than males or have less well-developed superego standards than males.

Fisher and Greenberg conclude that Freud had "fared rather well. But like all theorists, he has proved in the long run to have far from a perfect score" (1977, pp. 395–396). It should be said that even this verdict should be judged carefully, for Fisher and Greenberg, in reviewing some of the evidence also in the Eysenck and Wilson book, do not discuss some of the criticisms raised by these last authors.

Psychoanalysis has by no means been superseded as the most detailed account of emotional development in the individual, even though psychoanalytic treatment is rarely given if a mentally disturbed person goes to a hospital or health clinic for treatment. Freud's emphasis on childhood sexuality as the origin of many of our most profound feelings is still maintained by many, and his account of the defense mechanisms is generally given, in somewhat watered-down form, as "accepted terminology" in most introductory textbooks of psychology. But psychoanalysis is now peripheral, rather than central, as a topic in many accredited university courses that train students to be clinical psychologists; behavior therapy and an acquaintance with chemotherapy are usually considered more useful assets in the treatment of mentally disturbed persons, at least in the early 1980s. Nevertheless, there are signs that Freud's concept of the unconscious is receiving renewed attention on the part of researchers in more traditional areas of experimental psychology: There are now neurological models of disassociation, reappraisal of the role of unconscious factors in perception, and analyses of how the Freudian "unconscious" relates to changes in "consciousness" caused by drugs or strong emotions (see Bowers and Meichenbaum, 1984). But psychoanalysis is still receiving strong criticism, one of the latest being a challenge on various philosophical grounds by Grünbaum (1984).

Apart from developments within psychoanalysis and attempts to verify its postulates, psychoanalytic theory had a considerable impact on the broader branch of psychology known as personality theory. In the 1930s Henry A. Murray led a group of researchers at Harvard in a very extensive study of fifty students whose life histories were taken, whose attitudes were sampled by questionnaire, and who were given various tests including the now famous Thematic Apperception Test, developed by Murray and Christiana D. Morgan. In the resulting book, *Explorations in Personality* (1938), Murray offered a broad framework intended as an organizational device for integrating findings on personality as derived from these various sources. Much of it was concerned with listing and analyzing a large number of needs the subject has and with listing the various pressures a subject comes under at different stages of his or her life. Still, Murray's indebtedness to psychoanalysis is clear. The concepts of id, ego, and superego are retained and considerable emphasis is placed on the child's needs associated with feeding, excretion, and tactile stimulation. The Thematic Apperception Test itself was devised as a means of eliciting the subject's *unconscious* fears and feelings, and it is clear that psychoanalysis was the major starting point for Murray's experimental research on personality.

Finally, in contrast to the stress placed by Murray on critical stages in the development of the adult personality, we should note that another prominent personality theorist, Gordon Allport (1897–1967), has argued that one's personality at a given phase of life might be viewed as independent of early childhood experiences, a feature Allport denotes as the functional autonomy of the personality characteristic. This in turn led Allport to a consideration of the exact meanings of terms frequently used by personality theorists, such as *trait* and *disposition*. Allport's critical evaluation of the success of personality theory, put forward in his *Pattern and Growth in Personality* (1961), placed personality theory in perspective and stressed in passing both the positive and negative aspects of the indebtedness of personality theorists to Freud and his successors. Allport also wrote on various topics concerned with the interaction of persons, such as prejudice and humor.

Another personality theorist highly skeptical of psychoanalytic doctrine is H. J. Eysenck. His use of factor analysis as applied to questionnaire answers has confirmed his belief that personality can in part be described in terms of a person's ranking on each of two dimensions, which he labeled *neuroticism* and *introversion-extraversion*. He arrived at this view after many years of research, during which he shifted opinion on such matters as whether there is another factor that can be labeled *psychoticism*. The relationship between Eysenck's view that there are few factors that can represent variations in personality and the view of others, such as Guilford and Cattell, that many factors or clusters of traits are required, is put forward most succinctly in Eysenck and Eysenck's *Personality Structure and Measurement* (1969).

As the schools of the 1930s waned in importance, new approaches to the problems of psychology emerged, until eventually they came to appear as strong elements in the eclectic psychology of the 1980s. We may trace in particular the development of cognitive psychology and humanistic psychology.

Cognitive Psychology

The "cognitive revolution" represented a breakaway from S–R psychology to a psychology of human mental processes that assumed that it was once again acceptable to talk of consciousness (and the unconscious); to do research on images (which many people never doubted existed); and to define human behavior as guided by goals and purposes (as the Gestalt and Würzburg schools had insisted). Moreover, the researchers in the new vein explored tasks such as the identification of verbal material presented tachistoscopically, the memorization of stories rather than lists of nonsense syllables, and the solution of tricky problems of reasoning and calculation that did not lend themselves readily to analysis in S–R terms. And finally, if S–R psychology is one based on the mechanical analogy of a "chain" of conditioned reflexes, the new cognitive psychologists drew their analogies from different types of technological systems, some of which may now be listed.

For example, behavior was seen as "controlled" because if it got out of hand it could be brought back to a stable level much as an automatic pilot brings a ship back on course if it veers too much in one direction. Such a correction involves *feedback* into the system of information about what the system was doing, and this word was frequently used to refer to the fact that subjects monitor their own responses and adjust their behavior accordingly. The pioneer of this new view was Wiener (1948), and much of the evidence for feedback came from studies of the skilled behavior of pilots and gunners during World War II.

Or again, the human operator was thought of as an active processor of *information*: A rare event tells you more than something you are expecting, so information can be measured in terms of the probability of the various stimuli you encounter. In the 1950s there was some hope that by measuring human efficiency in terms of how much information could be processed in acts of perception and memory, new light would be shed on how we operate (Attneave, 1958; Garner, 1962). One important discovery that came out of this work was that there is a limit on how many distinct categories of a particular kind of stimulus one can "hold in one's head" at a time: It is very much fewer than the number that can be distinguished by the senses. Another important discovery was that the ability to make discriminations was facilitated if elements in the stimuli were "redundant" or repeated. But information theory has only been used occasionally since the early 1960s.

A third analogy to come out of the 1950s compared a human mind with a detection system such as a radar network that can discern whether, say, an aircraft enters a particular area. The immediate context of this analogy was psychophysics, where the task of finding an absolute threshold, for example, was restated in terms of detection. If a person is in a dark room, fixating a particular spot, and has to detect whether a dim light is present, that person will experience a number of states of consciousness and must determine whether a given state comes from a set of possible states associated with the presence of a stimulus or whether it comes from a set of possible states associated with the absence of a stimulus. This is a *decision* the observer has to make, and we note immediately the strong contrast here with the vocabulary of S–R theory: S–R theory postulates a response competition in which the stronger response will win, with no need for the word "decision" except to describe what the observer concurrently feels. Signal detection theory, rather than offering an S–R account of what occurs (which, by the way, might be possible though as yet unattempted), states that the decision is based on the subject's setting himself a certain standard or *criterion*: If there are no serious costs to making an error, one may well say "Yes, the stimulus is there" even at the risk of being wrong, whereas if one is penalized for error one will adopt a more cautious criterion.

This adoption of a criterion, and the relative weights of the various feeling states associated with "stimulus" and "no stimulus," can be modeled mathematically. The important outcome for psychologists was the acknowledgment that the old notion of a fixed threshold might have to be reviewed: The "threshold" as measured in different experiments will vary with the observer's sensitivity, certainly, but also with the criterion for responding that the observer adopts. Signal detection theory was extended to cover not only psychophysical problems, but also problems in recognition memory (have you seen this stimulus before, yes or no?) and it is routinely applied to experimental situations where we wish to know the effects of subjects' biases, which will affect the criterion setting. An evaluation of the historical importance of signal detection theory is given by Gigerenzer and Murray (1987); a good representative paper from the early years of this tradition is that of Swets, Tanner, and Birdsall (1961).

The most important analogy of all for the cognitive psychologists was with the computer. Computers have always been of importance to psychologists, at first because they greatly facilitated the computation of statistics such as factor analysis and the analysis of variance. (The latter is a technique introduced in the 1930s for suggesting whether differences between scores obtained under different conditions are greater than chance would lead us to expect.) It was soon discovered, though, that computers could be used to run experiments: They could be turned into high-powered tachistoscopes, for example, that not merely presented verbal material for fractions of a second, but also measured and scored the subject's responses. Many experiments on human memory that had been tedious to carry out by conventional means such as slide presentations now became easy with the aid of a computer screen. A third use of computers was in the *simulation* of models of human behavior: The idea was that if a given theory was any good, it could be programmed on the computer and the behavior generated would mimic what humans actually do.

A final consequence of the invention of computers was that many psychologists began to wonder if human minds were like computer "minds" and, vice versa, if computers could be designed to do what human minds could do. These two questions, which should be clearly differentiated, formed the basis for an interest in what became known as *artificial intelligence* in the 1970s and 1980s. However, the origins of the cognitive revolution have been dated to the year 1956 in particular, the year of the first computer program for solving problems and a year of important progress in understanding memory, language, and thinking (see Simon, 1980, p. 34).

Since the 1960s the "cognitive revolution" seems to have bifurcated into two groups of researchers. One group consists of experimentalists, the group that originally got the movement going by its new look at problems of memory and word identification; this group remained relatively unified and still publishes research in such journals as *Memory and Cognition* (founded in 1972). The other group, which has stronger links with computer science and artificial intelligence, tends to have turned its back on what it sees as slowpoke experimentation; this group included many members of the Cognitive Science Society, and some of its goals were outlined in an inaugural address to that society (Simon, 1980). The question is, which group has contributed most to our understanding of psychology in the last twenty years? In the author's view, the experimentalists are making slow and steady steps forward, whereas the artificial intelligence group produces the occasional flash of insight that deserves further exploration. We shall now examine selected examples of both kinds of contribution.

The study of human memory is now very intensive, and we know much more now than was available to Hull in the 1930s. The major change away from S–R analysis of verbal learning came when Broadbent (1958) suggested that information was received in parallel at the senses, was processed item by item in a short-term memory store that could be seen as having two aspects, sensory and internal speech, and that the result of this processing was that *some* information was stored in long-term memory. This series of events can be modeled by a flowchart showing separate boxes for the different kinds of memory (Broadbent's model started a fashion for flowchart models); an important mathematical version of the sequence was given by Atkinson and Shiffrin (1968). Equally important was the exploration of short-term recognition memory by signal detection methods, and Wickelgren and Norman's (1966) model demonstrated how recognition ability was a function both of the attention given to the stimulus as it was encoded and of a weakening of memory for the target item as new items arrived after the target item. The first of these aspects of memorization has received extensive treatment since; Cermak and Craik (1979) have reviewed accumulated evidence that one retains material best that one has encoded into a context provided by previously existing memories ("levels of processing"). There are now several studies showing how retention is poor if the subject is prevented from articulating the material as it is presented ("articulatory suppression," D. J. Murray, 1966). There is less consistent opinion on the nature of forgetting.

Another major contribution to memory theory was the establishment by Tulving and his colleagues that any memory theory as to describe not only the setting up of a trace and its vanishing from consciousness, but also the relationship between a successful retrieval cue and the trace. In a word, the best retrieval cue is one that was associated with the target item at the time the latter was encoded into memory. Tulving's theory had many similarities with a theory put forward by Richard Semon (1859–1918). Semon's theory was neglected partly because it involved an unusual vocabulary, including the word *engram* to refer to the physiological representation of a memory, and partly because Semon had no university position in Germany in the first decades of the century. Schacter (1982) has written a biography of Semon that attempts to analyze why some good scientific theories are overlooked in their time. Tulving describes the new work on retrieval in his *Elements of Episodic Memory* (1983), a book in which he also makes the distinction between memories for events that happened to us and can be located in time (*episodic* memory) and memory for knowledge in general that seems to form an autonomous system separate from episodic memory (*semantic* memory).

Finally, there is an ongoing movement, led by Murdock (1982), to pull memory theory together in one comprehensive model that takes as its starting point the notion that items entering memory can be seen as bundles of features and that these bundles become interfused with each other in a particular way. Retrieval involves the "unfusing" of individual bundles of features from these fusions. Because it is not always an accurate replica of the original that is unfused, the observer must make a decision (as in signal detection theory) about whether the retrieval is accurate or not. According to this model, retrieval does not involve a chain of reflexes culminating in a reevocation of the original trace; every memory we ever had is fused with all the rest and is "distributed" rather than localized in a particular place in the brain (or in a box in a flowchart). Murdock is making rapid strides in extending this model to the process of learning material over a series of trials; he has made extensive use of computer simulation in testing whether the model is mathematically plausible. In some ways, the model with which this is best contrasted is that of Anderson and Bower (1973), the first major model of memory to be tested by computer simulation. Anderson and Bower's model is essentially an elaboration of S–R association theory with the complication that the model is being applied to *propositions*. The representation of associations in a proposition is by fanlike structures (several associations leading from a single node) rather than a chainlike structure (association

1 leading to association 2, leading to association 3, and so on). This model was also of historical importance in encouraging the growth of the artificial intelligence movement.

Another task explored by the experimentalists was human *problem solving*. The two main contributions of the last twenty years have both aroused controversy. First, Newell and Simon in their *Human Problem Solving* (1973) reviewed evidence that certain kinds of problems could be solved by computers. These problems involved *algorithms*, the routine application of some procedure over and over again until the problem is cracked. Examples are chess problems, proofs of certain propositions in symbolic logic, and cryptarithmetic (e.g., where $AB + C = AC$, what numbers can replace A, B, C? There are several possible answers, e.g., $A = 1, B = 0$, and $C = 2: 10 + 2 = 12$). But many problems solved by humans involve the discovery of *heuristics*, systematized ways of looking at the total problem and seeing the elements in a new light. Newell and Simon discussed how far heuristics can be programmed into computers, and their work was an essential starting point for modern research in which computers are programmed to be "expert systems." Since 1973, however, this work has been mainly carried out in computer science departments or in private industry, which likes to keep its findings secret. At the risk of sounding pessimistic, we must regard progress in this area as slow despite all the publicity surrounding the development of computers that can "think" like humans.

Also controversial were a number of studies, summarized in Kahneman, Slovic, and Tversky (1982), in which difficult problems involving the calculations of probabilities were given to educated subjects to solve mentally. This work is usually reported as indicating that even highly intelligent subjects are prone to biases that distort their rationality: They are biased, for example, to give responses that come readily to mind (the "availability" bias) or to make judgments depending on how "representative" a stimulus is of a certain class. For example, if there is a series of coin tosses (heads, H; tails, T), many persons predict that the series *HHHTTT* is less likely to occur than the series *HTHHTT*, because the latter corresponds to a stereotype of "randomness." In fact, the two series are equally probable. Nevertheless this work has received some criticism on the grounds that often the problems set were ambiguous and that the evidence for "irrationality" is not so convincing as it seems (see Gigerenzer and Murray, 1987, Chap. 5).

Turning to contributions from the artificial intelligence group, we divide the topic into two issues: (1) whether the human mind is like a computer's, and (2) whether computers can do what human minds can do.

1. An enormous amount of heartsearching has resulted from the question of what makes the human mind unique. Brentano's concept of

"intentionality" has been revived, although sometimes intentionality in its original meaning—the intrinsic property mind has of reflecting external reality—seems to have been stretched to include purposiveness in general. Pylyshyn (1984) has argued that any system, computer or human, consists of a functional architecture that is hardwired in and cannot be altered—the human equivalent is the nervous system—and an alterable or programmable part. Pylyshyn maintains that many aspects of perception, memory, and thought can only be understood if we include reference to the factors other than the functional architecture. Such factors suggest that a proper explanation of perception, memory, and thought will have to include reference to cognition, so that there is a valid justification for a separate branch of enquiry known as *cognitive science*.

In this new science, we have to be clear about the way in which the mind "represents" reality, and an issue of some importance is whether we represent reality entirely in systems of words or "propositions," or whether it is also represented by visual and other sensory images. The idea that there is a "dual coding" system, verbal and visual, was first stressed strongly by Paivio (1971), and increasing evidence since then suggests that we do use more visual images in a variety of tasks (for the newer evidence, see Paivio, 1986). Pylyshyn, however, though not denying that we do *experience* images, is skeptical about whether the *storage* of information is in a "visual" form and thus queries whether our "representations" of reality are encoded in any form other than propositionally.

There are also problems with arguing that human memory is like a computer memory. Among the differences are the following: You can revive a computer's memory by accessing an address, then revive it again at a later time and get the same "content." But it seems that every revival of a human memory subtly changes the content, as Semon's model and Murdock's model can predict. It is therefore probably wrong to think of a human memory as being a "content" with an "address." Second, access to a computer's memory is probably by a series of switches, whereas access to human memory might be more like a sympathetic resonance: Just as, if you sing to a piano, one piano string will resonate to the frequency you are singing, so one retrieval cue may serve to access one pattern of firing that is distributed throughout the brain. Third, some people believe that human memory is characterized by the fact that being reminded of part of a total scenario that took place in the past is enough to evoke a memory of the total scenario. This part-whole kind of association is not normally built into computers, though I believe that it could be programmed in if it were found useful. Fourth, if *x* is entered into a computer's memory and the same content *x* is entered at a later time, the two may be entered into different addresses. But in human memory there is sometimes an association formed between the two automatically: The second *x* "reminds" you of the first *x*. Again, even though this could be programmed into a computer, in the human it might be part of the functional architecture for one stimulus to evoke a memory of a similar stimulus that occurred in the past. In general, then, any attempt to show that the human mind is a model of the computer mind will not necessarily fare very well.

2. On the other hand, some progress has been made at programming computers so that they imitate humans. In particular, as Gardner (1985) outlines in detail, progress has been made in the area of modeling visual identification and even the manipulation of visual stimuli. There are programs that can "discriminate" between squares and triangles, and programs that can "pick up" blocks of different shapes and build them into structures. Progress has also been made in modeling human decision making: Programs are currently being used, for example, for selecting medical diagnoses or stock market investments on the basis of evidence fed into the computer. It is trite to say that these programs are only as good as their programmer's minds, but they can work faster than humans and take into account more information and more possibilities than the average human. These are the "expert systems" yielding most easily to investigation. Not so easy to devise are expert systems that will *understand, translate, learn,* and *adapt their reasoning to new problems.* There are many collaborations between computer scientists and psychologists working to overcome these problems: I have the impression that the computer scientists are not very impressed with the efforts of psychologists so far to unravel higher-order cognitive processes.

Finally, there has been a general discussion on whether computers can only successfully imitate human minds if a great deal of computation goes on in parallel. Not all cognitive scientists are convinced this is so: Simon (1980) stresses the need for serial processes, for example. Humans can do many things at once, and the process of reading, for example, illustrates just how complex the interaction of sensation with memory and thought can be. A recent book that has attracted much attention is a volume entitled *Parallel Distributed Processes* (Vol. 1: Rumelhart and McClelland, 1986; Vol. 2: McClelland and Rumelhart, 1986). In this book, a number of discrete problems in cognitive psychology are approached via a mix of general principles concerning the activation of large systems of neurons all working in parallel. Such models have been called *connectionist,* an unfortunate choice of word as it already has been used to refer to seventeenth-century learning theory (p. 92) and Thorndike's system (p. 304). The book includes a neurological model of how, from a series of individual exemplars of a concept, we derive a final prototype—for example, from a Cocker spaniel, a Labrador retriever, and a Cairn terrier we can derive a general concept of "dog." It also involves models of speech perception and reading, and includes a neurological model of memory consolidation.

In summary, the cognitive revolution has focused extensively on higher-order human mental processes, is heavy on speculation, and makes use of concepts unwelcome to Skinner and other neobehaviorists, such as images, representations, and goals. It was mentioned earlier that Skinner (1985) himself believes that the cognitive revolution was a backward, rather than a forward, step in the history of psychology. Neisser, the author of the first modern book with the title *Cognitive Psychology* (1967), is also of the opinion that the contemporary mélange of computer science and psychology is retrogressive; like the theories of neobehaviorism, it is restricted to the analysis of simple artificial tasks that bear little relation to real life. Instead, Neisser prefers an "ecological" approach, and he himself has contributed to the study of memory in actual life situations by a collection of studies of memory in very gifted persons, memory by professional storytellers, and recall for vivid historical events (Neisser, 1982).

Humanistic Psychology

In the 1940s a movement emerged that presented itself as a third force in psychology, an alternative to psychoanalysis and behaviorism. It is now known mainly under the name *humanistic psychology* and is associated not so much with a type of explanation of human behavior as with the assertion that the task of the psychologist is to encourage the development of a new set of positive outlooks for the individual. In part, this movement had its roots in a disenchantment with the results of traditional psychoanalysis, but it also had origins in the philosophical movement known as existentialism and in the work of Kurt Goldstein (1878–1965), a great neurologist strongly influenced by the Gestalt movement.

The existentialist philosophers ranged from S. A. Kierkegaard (1813–1855), a Christian philosopher who saw a possible escape from a despair at humanity's helplessness in the adoption of a God, to J. P. Sartre (1905–1980), a modern philosopher who claimed in his atheism that one's only escape from the despair at knowing one will eventually be confronted with death—that is, nothingness—was to develop one's own abilities and will power. What they have in common is a concern with how the individual should "face up to" a feelingless universe. These remarks give nothing of the searching detail of the existentialist quest, but they do lead us to note that some psychiatrists, trained in orthodox psychoanalysis, were led by contemporary existentialists to become critical of psychoanalysis. Psychoanalysis, they argued, was too deterministic: It saw the individual as a machine at the mercy of memories left by childhood fixations. Therefore they argued, therapy aimed simply at revealing the "complexes" was of necessity inadequate if the person were to become a happier and more integrated individual. The word *become* is significant in existentialist thought: It stresses the notion that a person's goal in life should not be merely to survive in a biological sense but rather to develop a positive attitude to his or her own self and make the best of his or her talents. To use the terminology of the thinker most influential on psychologists, Martin Heidegger, one must establish an authentic "existence" and take responsibility for achieving this state of being. Heidegger had studied under Husserl (Brentano's student, see p. 273) and in turn influenced the Swiss psychiatrist Medard Boss. In Boss's *Psychoanalysis and Daseins-analysis* (1963) the contrast is clearly drawn between the therapist who treats a patient's fears and emotions as essentially the negative results of child-hood traumata and the more enlightened therapist who sees a patient's symptoms as expressions of the patient's search for a more satisfactory mode of being *(Dasein* is the German for *existence* in the positive sense outlined before).

A similar emphasis on the virtues of self-development came from a more unexpected source, in the work of Goldstein. Goldstein had made his reputation with his studies of the effects of brain injuries in World War I, and his contacts with the Gestalt psychologists were strong. His book *The Organism* (1939) was an attempt to change the way people thought about the brain. In contrast to the view that a reflex was an isolable unit of behavior and that the brain was simply a more complex unit influencing the efficiency of reflex behavior, Goldstein stressed that even a reflex affects all parts of the body via the brain. He argued that only a holistic, Gestaltlike view of the brain's mechanism could explain some of his findings on brain injuries. For example, if movement in the right hand is impaired, the patient can readily learn to use the left hand for tasks previously allotted to the right hand, such as writing. But the left hand does not have to acquire its new capabilities step by step: There seems to be a transference of many modes of use from right to left hand, and this "adjustmental shift," as Goldstein called it, can even be seen in the lower animals after experimental amputation of a limb. The brain has been functioning as a whole, a view then quite in fashion partly because of the research findings of Lashley (see p. 375). But Goldstein noted— almost casually—that no "motivated" behavior could be isolated from the total behavior of the organism. Food seeking, maternal behavior, and sexual behavior were all part of a general propensity on the part of the organism not merely to survive but to improve its lot. Goldstein gave the name *self-actualization* to this general tendency, and the word was readily adopted by other psychologists in such a way as to become the focus of their interests.

Perhaps the best-known of these was Goldstein's student, Abraham

H. Maslow (1908–1970). Maslow surveyed *not* persons who were psychologically depressed or otherwise disturbed, but rather those who were successful and had well-integrated personalities, broad interests, and a realistic view of themselves and others. Such persons, he argued, had achieved self-actualization, they had gone beyond the mere satisfaction of survival needs to the satisfaction of their needs as growing individuals. Often such persons had what Maslow called peak experiences, sensations of joy and completion in their own achievements. The goal for the therapist, he argued, was to help the patients build on their abilities so as to become more satisfied with themselves. His *Toward a Psychology of Being* (1968) is an account of what it is like to be self-actualized; it generously acknowledges that Goldstein and the existentialists were precursors of this view.

In the early 1960s this new emphasis on the positive role to be played by the therapist—one that, it is fair to add, had been anticipated by others, particularly Adler—led to the mushrooming of many new forms of psychotherapy. What they have in common is the belief that psychotherapy, if properly applied, can help the patient to a more positive and happier outlook on life. Where they differ is in the significance they attribute to individual symptoms. For some, such as A. Ellis, many symptoms are the results of false beliefs, and the aim of the therapy is to change those beliefs to a more rational view of the world. Others believe that the patient needs to be educated in socialization techniques, and they often advocate group therapy as a means for expressing and confronting self-damaging emotions.

An important forerunner of these various therapies stressing the growth of the individual was the "client-centered therapy" of Carl Rogers. As the name suggests, the therapist does not view the patient as another "subject" in a grand experiment where stimuli influence the organism to respond, but rather he tries to help the patient in his or her search for self-respect and self-regard. Like Maslow and Goldstein, Rogers stresses the concept of actualization, but he is also concerned to demonstrate, using scientific methods, that this form of therapy is actually effective. Thus, in both his *Client-Centered Therapy* (1951) and his *The Therapeutic Relationship and Its Impact* (1967), he emphasizes statistical evidence showing the improvement of the patients. In the latter work, Rogers repeats that the therapist should always try to understand the client's "self-meaning" and to communicate to the client the therapist's understanding of that meaning, even with patients as disturbed as schizophrenics.

Useful reviews of the plethora of new psychotherapeutic methods that are challenging psychoanalysis are given by Corsini (1973) and Harper (1975). In 1972 the American Psychological Association formed a special division for humanistic psychology. The impact of this movement had been felt mainly by psychologists concerned with counseling and therapy; psychologists concerned with the scientific explanation of behavior have remained relatively untouched by it.

Other Advances in Psychology

In the above account, we have stressed progress in relation to the evaluation of the various schools of the 1930s and added short accounts of the developments in cognitive and humanistic psychology. But the real progress in psychology has been in the amassing of data concerning behavior, both human and animal. The problem is how—within the span of a few pages—to give a diorama of this data base without tediously listing facts or simply giving a series of useful references. One solution is to stand back from the overview of the history of psychology and ask, "What are the main questions psychologists have posed?" Without doubt, one question that is highly central to the psychological thinking is how information is gathered, stored, and retrieved by an organism that has within it, from the time of its birth, the potential for certain kinds of behavior. The question can be refocused by use of the term *tabula rasa,* a concept that has preoccupied psychologists from the time of Plato: Is the organism indeed a blank tablet from birth, or is there innate knowledge in it? We may give a continuity to the flow of the argument in these last pages by attempting to outline the discoveries of modern psychology that would be of interest to a *tabula rasa* theorist such as Locke or an empiricist such as Helmholtz.

Acquisition of Information
by the Developing Child

We may begin with the human baby. James thought of the baby's world as a "blooming buzzing confusion." Gradually, because the brain is able to correlate visual sensations with movements, the baby was assumed to differentiate individual sense data from the confusion and over time to build up an understanding of how to relate to the external world. For Helmholtz, all that was needed was a brain capable of the retention of associations; Hering demanded more in the way of innate mechanisms. The modern psychologist, however, is apt to be more nativistic than Helmholtz, more empiristic than Hering, and still confess there is a long way to go in understanding the mechanisms of adaptation to a sensory environment.

Hebb, in his influential *The Organization of Behavior* (1949), offered a neuropsychological theory that attempted to bring some accord out of the dispute between the nativists and the empiricists. The nervous system, he argued, is so structured that certain aspects of the environment are processed immediately. For example, the Gestalt notion of an innate figure-ground organization may have some merit, according to Hebb, for the brain might immediately be able to react to certain dominant, homogenous elements of the environment. Furthermore, certain salient features of the environment such as corners and angles might receive special attention: As the child's eye focuses on such key features, associations are learned between these sensory features and the movements made by the child's eyes and head in reaching them. This nativistic element in the build-up of what Hebb called cell assemblies in the brain has received some support in recent years from studies showing that, when presented with a complex display, newborn children will often stare longest at angles and at curves rather than at simple straight lines. They will also often focus on details and only after two months or so learn to look at the total configuration in which these details are contained. Moreover, the claim made by some nativists that newborns possess a shape or size constancy mechanism is still not validated by a consensus of opinion. There is some evidence that depth perception may be available to a child at a very early age: Children will crawl over a sheet of glass to a point where the surface on which the glass is laid seems to drop away. They will not crawl out over the apparent drop, and even children who cannot crawl will respond differently to the solid surface than to the drop (E. J. Gibson and R. R. Walk, 1961).

As the infant matures, he or she progresses from the possession of a few innate reflexes to voluntary control over the muscles of the limbs, the sphincter, and so on. It might be thought that all such later behavior is therefore a matter of learning and experience, but one of the major discoveries of the 1940s and 1950s was the finding that in various species many motor responses to specific stimuli seem to be unlearned. Spalding had shown in the nineteenth century that perhaps flying is an unlearned response in birds; in the twentieth century Konrad Lorenz and others showed that, in the very young of many species, unlearned responses are made to particular stimulus configurations. One of the most striking of these is the phenomenon known as imprinting: A young goose, for example, will follow not only its mother but any moving object it makes contact with during a particular *critical period* in the first few days of its life.

The study of behavior in natural settings came to be known as ethology, and a great deal of research on "instinctive" behavior has been carried out in psychology and biology departments over the past few decades. Following Tinbergen's important book *The Study of Instinct* (1951), certain key terms came to be used in describing unlearned animal behavior. Take, for instance, the pattern of response in the feeding behavior of the herring gull chick: Experiments have shown that it is most likely to peck at a model of a gull's head that is long and thin with a red patch at its tip. The red patch forms part of a stimulus configuration that may be called the *innate releasing stimulus*. When the young chick sees this stimulus, a *fixed action pattern* of pecking is *released*. Much more complex fixed action patterns are seen in nest-building and courtship behavior in fish, birds, and other species. However, various criticisms were made of this vocabulary by Lehrman (1953), and the present state of affairs in ethology seems to be that more stress is now laid on the role of maturation and experience in determining even what seem on the surface to be unlearned behavior patterns (Gottlieb, 1979).

The human child, however, is more adaptable and flexible in his or her behavior than are many young animals. Over the first year of life it is probable that he or she begins to form symbolic representations of external objects. If a ball rolls under a sofa, a very young child will behave as if it had vanished from his or her thoughts; an older child will reach under the sofa, as if he or she had formed the notion that the ball somehow continued to exist even though it was absent from sight. Just when the symbolic, or memorial, representation of objects takes place is a question currently under intensive investigation. The matter is complicated, as can be seen from the following example: A child three or four months old will attend for some time to a mask of a human face; between six and nine months he or she will stare less at the mask; then from nine to twelve months the child will show a renewed interest in it. It has been suggested that this renewal of interest reflects a particular cognitive activity on the part of the child—a comparison of the mask with his or her memory of, say, a parent's face. Similarly, children of this age show fear of strange objects, which, again, may be the result of their comparing the objects with memories of familiar objects. Support for this notion comes from studies of short-term memory in infants: By the age of one year, a child can find a toy that has been hidden for three seconds, a task an eight-month-old cannot accomplish. Shortly after the first year the child can probably represent to itself events that might or could happen in the near future. Perhaps children of this age can also form primitive concepts such as that of "animal." Experimental evidence supporting these remarks is given in Mussen, Conger, and Kagan (1979, Chap. 3).

During the second year, the child begins to master the rudiments of language. Traditional S–R theorists have taken the view that language acquisition was mainly a matter of the child's being reinforced for making certain sounds, these sounds being produced chiefly by imitation of the parent. In an attempt to bring some order into the discussion of complex language acquisition, Skinner, in his *Verbal Behavior* (1957), had proposed that each emission of a word could be categorized either as a response from which a particular outcome was anticipated (as when a child says *please*, expecting to receive something) or a verbal symbol representing an object (as when a child says *cat* on seeing the household pet). Emissions of the first kind were called *mands* and emissions of the second kind were called *tacts*. Skinner went on to show how even the most complex linguistic utterances, such as those in prose or in poetry, could be discussed in terms of stimulus, response, and reinforcement.

Chomsky, reviewing Skinner's book in 1959, argued that Skinner's analysis could only be accepted if the words *stimulus, response,* and *reinforcement* were so stretched and malleable that they could be used as the author saw fit. No pretense could be made, argued Chomsky, at a scientifically rigorous theory of language if these terms were all that were allowed to the scientist. Chomsky was more impressed with the evidence that young children seem to acquire language spontaneously and derive the rules of grammar as the result of inductive processes rather than as the result of some sort of drill procedure based on reinforcement. He even suggested that language ability involved innate capacities and quoted ethological evidence in favor of this concept. That thought or symbolic representation preceded the ability to express one's ideas in words seemed to him likely, and he accused Skinner of overlooking the covert formulation of yet-to-be-phrased propositions.

Chomsky's review was one of the most telling critiques of behaviorism in recent decades; one of its effects was to turn the attention of students of language development to the close examination of what the child says spontaneously and away from attempts to squeeze the phases of language development into rigid S–R frameworks. A great deal is now known concerning the way in which the child makes the best use of his available vocabulary to express his often sophisticated ideas in a few words. On the other hand, Chomsky's view that the human child is perhaps unique in possessing an innate tendency to acquire language has been criticized on the grounds that certain apes can act as if they had acquired primitive languages. One chimpanzee has been taught the rudiments of American sign language, and another can spell out simple requests and commands by pressing buttons marked with visual symbols (Gardner and Gardner, 1969; Premack, 1976).

But the growth of intellect in the child cannot be described adequately by an account of the development of memory capacity and a listing of the linguistic skills. Overshadowing these, so to speak, are the growth of reasoning powers and increased flexibility of adaptation to the external environment. A normal child of five has developed incredible facility at making his or her way through the world, interacting with others, and understanding the basic rules that govern the behavior of objects. The awesome task of trying to bring order into a scientific description of the growth of cognitive skills has been undertaken particularly by Jean Piaget (1896–1980). Piaget's ideas are still open to investigation, but the terminology in which he phrased them appears to be widely accepted. At any given age the child shows a certain pattern of adaptation to the environment, which is based on *structures* the child is said to have acquired over the years preceding that particular age. In order to cope with this environment, the child must learn to make certain changes in his or her behavior, so-called *accommodations* to the environment, and at the same time he or she must integrate new incoming information into whatever cognitive structures have been acquired up to that time. The integration of new information into preexisting cognitive structures is called *assimilation*. The processes of repeating actions, of recognizing stimuli, of comparing stimuli, of generalizing from stimuli, and of combining information from separate senses concerning a particular object or configuration are all examples of assimilation processes. At the same time the child begins to make plans that determine the course of his or her actions: Piaget calls such plans *schemata*.

Piaget spelled out in detail the cognitive structures he associated with different phases in the child's development, which he calls *stages*. Each stage is defined in terms of the structures associated with it but also in terms of "operations" the child can perform at that stage. An operation is a rule that the child has so well grasped that he or she can carry out not only a single operation but also its reverse. Thus a child might grasp that adding two sticks to three sticks will yield five sticks, but also that the operation can be reversed: The two sticks can be taken away to give the original three sticks. Up to the age of seven or so, the child is thought to be "preoperational," not to understand the reversibility of certain operations. After the age of seven, the child begins to grasp the concept of reversibility and to make progress in such topics as mathematics. The child will understand that matter can preserve its quantity even though it changes in shape: Two pieces of clay of equal volume, one a sphere and the other flattened and shaped like a disc, will be judged to have the same volume, whereas a younger child would probably insist that the disc had more clay in it. Thought is less egocentric and more capable of including correct inferences about relationships, parts and wholes, and the ordering of objects according to certain specifications. A further stage of thought is said to evolve around the age of twelve, when the child begins to understand the formal rules governing appropriate reasoning. An adolescent can detect logical inconsistencies and reason validly about hypothetical situations.

There are many books available on Piaget's system (e.g., Ginsburg and Opper, 1969), and most introductory texts now include a brief description of it. Evaluations of its validity, however, are constantly changing. Some have asserted, for instance, that precursors of cognitive capacities Piaget supposes to develop relatively late are in fact evident at earlier stages in the child's development. Some of Piaget's demonstrations of errors in children's thinking can be shown to be in part the result of the particular instructions given and questions asked. The border-lines between the various stages of development he postulated are likely to be less sharp than he imagined. But nobody doubts that Piaget was the foremost child psychologist—or, as he preferred to call himself, "genetic epistomologist"—of recent decades, and his scheme will probably form the basis of any future outlines of the development of reasoning capacities.

A child's personality will clearly be influenced by those with whom he or she comes in contact. That normal social development might in part depend on an infant's experiencing close bonds with its mother or other nurturant adult was suggested by Harlow, who in a number of studies showed that young monkeys deprived of maternal care experi-enced difficulties in social and sexual behavior in later life. However, more recently, Suomi, Harlow, and McKinney (1972) have indicated that appropriate social stimulation from monkeys who do not pose a threat to the deprived youngster can undo some of the damage resulting from being reared in isolation. The deleterious effects of maternal deprivation in human children have been closely analysed by Bowlby (1973).

More generally, social learning has received a great deal of attention in recent decades, particularly following the publication of Bandura and Walters's *Social Learning and Personality Development* (1963). Experimental evidence exists concerning the ways in which children will model their behavior on that of adults and peers, and it has been shown that some undesirable behavior patterns, such as aggression, are often the result of copying models, including models seen on the TV screen. The growth of concepts of morality in the child is also a function of interactions with parents and peers. Kohlberg (1963), who was influenced by Piaget, has analyzed the ways in which the various stages of moral development the child goes through are affected by contingencies of reward and punish-ment on the part of others. Children will also learn more positive skills by imitation, and a desire to emulate models they admire, including parents, will often be reflected in a strong need for achievement. The strength of a child's desire to succeed, and his or her choice of areas in which to excel, are strongly determined by parental aspirations and the sociocul-tural milieu, as McClelland in particular has shown in his *The Achieving Society* (1961).

The child's perception of his or her own role as a boy or girl, and of course later preoccupations with masculinity and femininity, have been shown to depend on societal demands as well as on purely physiological factors, although the phenomenon of sex typing is still a controversial issue; psychoanalysts stress the importance of identification mechanisms, whereas those concerned with social learning stress the importance of such variables as parental and peer pressure. As children grow older they develop an increasing understanding that their behavior vis-a-vis model figures such as teachers and parents can differ from the behavior they show to their peers, and the process of growing up reflects an increasing independence from the former. The social learning theorists stress that this growing independence need not have its roots solely in psychosexual conflicts, as the psychoanalysts had suggested.

Development Beyond Childhood

When the child reaches sexual maturity in the early teens, many new problems arise, partly because of the new demands made on the adolescent in terms of the need to find a sexual partner and the need to choose a vocation. Probably because many problems of theoretical interest to the psychologist translate directly into a need for research on infancy and childhood—for example, the roles of nature versus nurture as determinants of cognitive abilities—it is only relatively recently that much attention has been paid by psychological researchers to the problems of adolescence, adulthood, and old age. True, Stanley Hall had been a pioneer of research into both adolescence and aging at the beginning of the century, but until very recently most textbooks paid little attention to the attempts to bring scientific order to the discussion of the psychological problems associated with maturity. The result is that most recent work on these topics relies heavily on the results of questionnaires and statistical surveys and is less geared to theory. Whether teenage promiscuity or crime have increased, whether working women feel a conflict between their roles in the labor force and their roles as wives or mothers, whether there is a "mid-life crisis" in the early forties, whether older persons are adversely affected by menopause or diminishing sexual powers, whether the aged see retirement as a negative or a positive circumstance, and the attitudes of the dying to their situation—all these questions and many others are the focus of much current research, but this is a very recent development in terms of the long history of psychology. In discussing such matters, concepts are drawn eclectically from the writings of various earlier psychologists.

Obviously, Freud had much to say on adolescent sexuality, but writers on adolescence and maturity draw equally from others such as Jung or Erikson in trying to delineate the problems associated with the various life stages the individual passes through. There are also methodological problems concerned with longitudinal studies of development. Often the feelings described by people of different ages relate to the political and social circumstances of their past and cannot be adequately described without reference to these. For example, persons who grew up in the Great Depression tend to think of themselves as relatively well off now, whereas persons who were young more recently have somewhat different standards for "well off." Persons who were adolescent during the Vietnam era have a more skeptical attitude towards political, military, and financial institutions than many older persons. Current economic problems are causing high unemployment, particularly among teenagers, and this gives rise to problems of loss of self-esteem and a sense of aimlessness. Changes in attitudes to sexual morality have made it easier to be involved sexually but have also led to a rise in unwanted pregnancies. Moreover, since about 1983 there has been a change of attitude to casual sex because of the rise of the disease AIDS. Similarly, a greater tolerance for divorce has brought with it the economic and psychological stress of single parenthood, and some evidence suggests that boys reared in single-parent homes without their fathers are less masculine and more dependent than boys from two-parent homes (Mussen, Conger, and Kagan, 1979, p. 375). Another important change in society, in part necessitated by the high cost of housing, is that in many more families both parents now work outside the home, and children have to be left with babysitters or at daycare centers. A number of studies have tried to determine whether leaving children in day care has any detrimental effects on their emotional or intellectual development; so far the evidence seems to be that it does not, and it may even enhance social skills in preschool children (Liebert, Wicks-Nelson, & Kail, 1986, pp. 138–139). Many of the problems associated with old age are the direct result of poverty quite as much as of physical or psychological failings.

But changes of the kind that interest the theoretical psychologist and are less tied to the vagaries of political or social circumstances, such as changes in memory or in problem-solving ability as age increases, have been fairly well documented (Birren and Schaie, 1977). Among the deficits associated with the aging process are a general slowing down of motor responses and reaction times and some deficits in memory performance whose explanation is still controversial. On the other hand, verbal skills remain surprisingly intact, and intellectual skills do not necessarily decrease with age to the extent that earlier surveys suggested. To be more precise, it was shown years ago that typical IQ scores for the aged are lower than for younger persons given the same test, but recent studies also indicate that IQ scores for an individual may actually increase over the course of many years. The general conclusion is that cross-sectional studies underestimate true performance and longitudinal studies overestimate it. For example, the longitudinal do not take into account evidence that IQ scores generally increased between the 1930s and the 1960s.

A discussion of this intriguing problem will be found in Kimmel (1980, p. 34), whose book we may recommend as an introduction to this new research on adulthood and aging. Kimmel's final chapter deals with recent research on dying and bereavement. In this context we should note the pioneering research of Kübler-Ross (1969), whose analysis of the various reactions of the dying patient—anger, resignation, and so on—is forming a basis on which future work can build. Apart from the study of psychological changes over the lifespan, there have been great advances in our understanding of the physiological processes of sexual maturation and sexual functioning and, to a lesser extent, the physiology of aging. Kimmel's book includes a review of these: As a historical point, we must make special mention of the fundamental research of Masters and Johnson (1966) on sexual responses.

Apart from studies based on a developmental approach, two topics concerned with the heredity versus environment question have received special attention in the decades since 1940. One concerns the degree to which intelligence is inherited; the other, whether a predisposition to mental illness has a genetic origin.

Heredity and Environment:
Intelligence and Mental Illness

With respect to the heritability of intelligence, it may be stated at the outset that the opinions of psychologists have definitely exerted an influence on educational and other practices in the countries concerned. Galton's belief that intelligence ran in families led directly to his espousal of a eugenic program. In the United States in the early twentieth century the results of IQ tests carried out on World War I army recruits by Terman and others led Brigham (1923) to assert that immigrants from some European countries had a lower level of intelligence that did immigrants from other countries. But instead of inferring that this might be because of differences between the cultures of these countries and the United States, Brigham concluded that the differences were due to inborn characteristics. One outcome was that in 1924 an act of Congress limited immigration from those countries.

In the United Kingdom, Sir Cyril Burt (1883–1971) produced evidence from studies comparing the IQ of different members of the same family, particularly twins, to argue that the IQ was determined by inherited factors; his findings were partly influential in persuading the British to adopt an educational system, put into effect just after World War II, in which children were "streamed" on the basis of tests of IQ, English, and arithmetic given at the age of eleven. Burt himself, however, had doubts as to the wisdom of this scheme. During these years literally hundreds of studies collected evidence thought to be related to the question of whether there was a genetic influence on the IQ. Some assumed the validity of Spearman's notion of a general intelligence factor *g;* others tried to determine whether Thurstone's specific factors could be influenced by familial background or environment. In particular, studies were carried out using populations from different races, populations of related family members, and populations of adopted children. A large number of surveys of different races indicated that the average IQ of blacks was lower and less variable than the average IQ of whites in the United States. Surveys of related family members found positive correlations between the IQs of members of the same family, with the correlations tending to decrease as the family members became more "removed" from each other—particularly high correlations were found between monozygotic twins. Some important studies, notably that of Skodak and Skeels (1949) found that while the average IQ of adopted children was higher than that of nonadopted children, there were stronger correlations between the IQ of the child and that of its biological mother than that of its adoptive mother. Evidence was also obtained in the 1930s and 1940s that animals, including laboratory rats, could be bred selectively for problem-solving ability: One could obtain strains of rats that were bright or dull at solving mazes, for example. All of this evidence tilted the balance in favor of the view that intelligence could be genetically determined.

The egalitarian attitude of the American public, however, favored an environmentalist approach, as did the behaviorists in general. The view that all are equal in the eyes of the law was associated with an adoption of educational policies that insisted on equal opportunities for all, and in particular on special enriching educational programs for the underprivileged. Some experimental support for this environmental position was forthcoming from animal studies, clearly influenced by Hebb's writing, which showed that animals deprived of a stimulating environment or of particular kinds of experience (e.g., visual experience), in comparison with animals with natural or enriched environments, were poor at solving problems or at coping with unfamiliar aspects of their surroundings. Other research surveys indicated that IQ scores might rise when individuals moved to better neighborhoods or other more rewarding environments, and still other surveys showed that measures of IQ could vary considerably within an individual's lifetime and that the usual correlation between the IQs of twins was lowered if the twins were reared apart. Much of the evidence for the environmentalist position was summarized in Hunt's valuable *Intelligence and Experience* (1961), which also incorporated an account of Piaget's notions concerning the development of intellect. By the late 1960s the older evidence for a genetic influence on IQ was often ignored or discounted.

Then in 1969 Arthur Jensen was invited by the *Harvard Educational Review* to summarize developments in research on intelligence, particularly with a view to assessing the usefulness of programs designed to help the underprivileged. The review, which was over one hundred pages long, concluded that these programs were not very effective and that among the possible reasons for this was the likelihood that some kinds of intelligence performance were genetically determined. Some of Jensen's arguments relied on a 1966 paper by Burt, in which the latter claimed that twins reared in different environments nevertheless showed a strong correlation between their IQs. Jensen also offered suggestions that cognitive or abstract thought, which is often examined in IQ tests, might be primarily genetically determined but that the ability to learn might be a different "capacity," underestimated in conventional IQ tests. He claimed that the available evidence on IQ differences between blacks and whites, while not excluding the influence of environment or its interaction with genetic factors, was less consistent with a strictly environmentalist hypothesis than with a genetic hypothesis. (That genetic and environmental influences could interact was a thesis supported in part by the results of experiments in which maze-bright or maze-dull rats were reared in improved or enriched environments; both genetic and environmental influences were shown to affect performance.)

Jensen's modestly asserted claims were greeted by an outcry that reflected badly on the good manners of his attackers; more serious challenges were, however, soon forthcoming. Probably the best-known of these was Kamin's *The Science and Politics of IQ* (1974), which argued essentially that great care had to be taken in inferring, from family studies and the studies of twins, that environmental influences were in fact discounted. More surprising was the charge that Burt's data on twins were carelessly reported, a charge that was substantiated in that some of Burt's data have now been demonstrated to be fraudulent (Hearnshaw, 1979). Kamin's conclusion was that there was not enough good evidence available to support the genetic hypothesis. Meanwhile, further studies were being carried out: We may note particularly that Horn, Loehlin, and Wellerman (1979) found little difference in the correlations between the IQs of mother and biological child as compared with mother and adopted child, whereas the correlation between the IQ of the father and that of the biological child was higher than that for the adopted child.

These data and others have been considered in books by Jensen (1981) and Kamin (in Eysenck versus Kamin, 1981). Jensen has been forced to revise his earlier high estimate of the degree to which intelligence is inherited (from about 80% down to 50–70%); Kamin stresses, among other evidence, the fact that the Horn et al. study provided so little evidence for inheritance of IQ from the mother's side. Furthermore, Kamin (in a 1979 talk quoted by Fancher, 1985, p. 224) cites evidence that in general correlations between the IQs of close relatives seem to be lower now than they were in earlier studies, and suggests that the reason is that we are now using better controlled and larger studies. But the matter is still not resolved. Jensen and others are currently investigating whether

IQ scores are correlated with rapid reaction times in making *choices* between stimuli, an interesting variant on Galton and Cattell's old program of research.

When the "experts" disagree to this extent, it is difficult for the historian to do much more than chronicle the dispute and deliver no final verdict. But there is probably no other single issue in the history of psychology that leaves the nonexpert feeling such a sense of insecurity and a consequent determination to be skeptical of wide-sweeping claims. A useful collection of articles for and against the genetic argument has been compiled by Block and Dworkin (1976).

Extensive research has also been undertaken on the question of whether mental illness, particularly schizophrenia, has a genetic origin. The best-known early study was that of Kallmann (1938); Slater and Cowie (1971) provided a useful overview of later evidence. The methods used to investigate whether mental illness has a genetic origin have included studies of twins, including twins reared apart; the examination of the likelihood that relatives of different degrees of kinship will develop similar illnesses; and studies relating the incidence of mental illness in foster children to the incidence of mental illness in their biological as opposed to adoptive families. In the case of schizophrenia, the evidence from all these sources concurs on there being a genetic factor involved, but it is also clear that environment plays an important part. New evidence supporting this statement comes from Davison and Neale (1982), who show that although first-degree relatives share about 50 percent of their genes with a person diagnosed as schizophrenic, they are only at about 5–16 percent at risk themselves of developing the condition.

Schizophrenia is the mental illness whose genetic origins have been most intensively investigated, partly because it has been felt that the illness has its inception not merely in psychodynamic conflicts, as the psychoanalysts suggested, but in some sort of biological abnormality. Over the years a number of investigations found a variety of chemicals in the brain and elsewhere that seemed to be more prevalent in schizophrenics than in normals, but few of these claims have been properly substantiated. On the other hand it was observed in the late 1960s that a surfeit of amphetamines could cause paranoid symptoms. Since amphetamines can enhance the activity of neurotransmitters in the brain, the possibility was raised that in some forms of schizophrenia there is overactivity of some neurotransmitter substance. The current favorite candidate is dopamine, a neurotransmitter found mainly in the brainstem. There was also increasing evidence that phenothiazine drugs such as chlorpromazine, which had been found effective in therapy, acted to block dopamine release. This theory is relevant here because it seems likely that, if a physiological abnormality is found to be at least partly the cause of a psychosis, it could be genetically determined. But it cannot be emphasized strongly enough that the actual breakout of a psychosis usually coincides with psychological stress: For example, it is widely thought that one side effect of overactivity of the dopamine system is that the subject cannot handle the overstimulation resulting from manifold sensory inputs, and this makes him or her more vulnerable to stress.

But the genetic component is still strongly emphasized by some writers; indeed, Slater and Cowie are able to contrast the evidence that schizophrenia might be associated with the joint effect of many genes with the evidence that there is one particular gene, a theory these authors prefer. Slater and Cowie also assert that there is evidence for some hereditary predispositions towards other forms of behavior (such as anxiety neurosis, manic-depressive psychosis, and alcoholism), but they admit that environmental factors can account for much of the variance in the available data. It should also be borne in mind that reactivity to stress is in part a function of the responsivity of the autonomic nervous system, and there is no *a priori* reason why the latter should not in part be influenced by genetic factors (Jost and Sontag, 1944). On the other hand some forms of breakdown, including schizophrenic responses, probably result from being reared by parents who themselves have dispositions towards abnormal behavior, and evidence for a concordance in illness propensity between parents and offspring might therefore often reflect environmental factors quite as much as genetic factors. As much caution must be exercised in interpreting evidence of hereditary predispositions towards psychological illness as was needed in interpreting evidence of a genetic basis for intelligence.

Other Influences on the Developing Individual

When we move away from the nature versus nurture question, we must admit that there are three sources of influence on the growing individual that deserve separate mention: his or her reactions to stress, the effect of others on attitudes and beliefs, and the possession of a properly functioning ability to conform in society. Recognizing the wide individual differences in how each of these factors will be effective, we shall nonetheless briefly discuss progress in our understanding of these three topics in the years following 1940.

The problem of stress has always concerned psychiatrists, educational counselors, social workers, and others, and the treatment of stress has been closely bound to developments in psychotherapy and, more recently, chemotherapy. In 1939 a group associated with Hull at Yale attempted to account for some forms of stress by showing that frustration in the attainment of a goal often resulted in aggression: This claim was supported by a small amount of experimental evidence and a larger amount of sociological evidence (Dollard, Doob, Miller, Mowrer, and Sears, 1939). Subsequently, stress due to conflict was analyzed by Miller (1944), whose division of conflict situations into approach/approach conflicts, approach/avoid conflicts, and avoid/avoid conflicts, with the extra hypothesis that the tendencies to avoid or approach objects become stronger the nearer one is to them, is still quoted widely in the 1980s. Maier (1949) analyzed various kinds of reaction to frustration in experiments with rats, noting in particular that frustration can lead to the adoption of "fixations," or stereotyped patterns of responding. Besides aggression and fixation, frustration can lead to regressed behavior and, when stress or frustration is unavoidable, there may be a diminution of self-initiated acts and a general reduction in the motivation to solve problems ("learned helplessness," Seligman, 1975).

Apart from these laboratory studies of stress behavior, Selye (1976) has described what he called the "general adaptation syndrome," or set of physiological responses to stress, including alarm reactions with increased autonomic activity, attempts to resist or cope with this stress, and, sometimes, final exhaustion. These physiological changes can ultimately lead to a variety of psychosomatic illnesses such as hypertension, stomach ulcers, or asthma, but we do not as yet understand the details of these physiological interactions. In response to the variety of complaints brought about by stress, psychiatrists have become increasingly ready to prescribe drugs first found to be successful in the relief of psychotic symptoms. Amongst these are the phenothiazenes such as chlorpromazine, developed in the 1950s, and antidepressant drugs. These drugs probably act to control the release of certain neurotransmitters in the brain, but again, the fine details of how they affect physiological and psychological processes in the patient are not understood. There is little doubt, however, that they "tone down" strong emotional responses and this helps the patient to be more rational in his or her approach to the frustration or conflicts in question.

The study of social interactions was given impetus by World War II when a number of problems that had been briefly discussed by social psychologists in the 1930s came into prominence because of their practical importance. Among such problems were the nature of leadership, the determination of the effectiveness of propaganda, the degree to which problem-solving efficiency varied with the structure of the group, and the importance of the group in determining the extent to which an individual conformed with its desires. In the years following the war social psychology became a distinct area of specialization. A major influence on its development was Lewin, whose emphasis on the individual as an acting entity in a "field" that exerted its influence on him or her made it easy for social interactions to be treated as an integral part of the field. Lewin numbered among his students such influential social psychologists as Festinger, Kelley, and Schachter. We may briefly outline the contributions of these three individuals.

Leon Festinger developed a theory of cognitive dissonance, which held that individuals will change their attitude towards something or somebody if there is a discrepancy between their beliefs and either the evidence for these beliefs or their own behavior with respect to those beliefs. If such dissonance arises, the subject will alter his or her attitudes or opinions, not necessarily in the direction corresponding to greater rationality, but in a direction such as to reduce the dissonance. For example, a group of religious believers were persuaded that the world would end on a particular day. When the day passed uneventfully, they were able to resolve their feelings of dissonance by asserting that their prayers had persuaded God to postpone the day of reckoning. The theory of cognitive dissonance, expounded by Festinger (1957), is only one of a number of theories of attitude change, including some based on traditional S–R concepts and others stressing the need to achieve a balance between our beliefs and the beliefs of those with whom we are in close contact. A critical review of these various theories is given by Kiesler, Collins, and Miller (1969).

Another influential student of Lewin was H. H. Kelley, who worked on various aspects of interpersonal psychology and is perhaps best known for his 1967 analysis of the ways we attribute beliefs and characteristics to others. Among the criteria used when we make inferences about other people's motives are our understanding of how the majority of people react in a given situation, the extent to which the other person's response remain consistent, and the degree of distinctiveness of the behavior in question. A number of experimental studies have confirmed the broad lines of this analysis, and one study (McArthur, 1972) indicated that we tend to judge others in terms of what we perceive to be their personality characteristics rather than to infer that their behavior is simply a pattern or responses to a given social situation.

The third of our Lewin students, Stanley Schachter, has worked on a variety of problems. In one well-known study (Schachter and Singer, 1962) subjects were given injections of adrenalin, which increased the degree of autonomic arousal they felt. But the emotions they reported were consistent with the social situation they found themselves in: Subjects in the company of an irritating stranger reported anger, and those in the company of an amusing stranger reported euphoria. It thus seems that we are less capable of judging the true cause of an emotional feeling than might be expected, a finding which is in some ways consistent with the James-Lange theory that we first feel bodily symptoms, then ascribe a reason for them.

Schachter has also worked on the problem of conformity in small groups. As mentioned on p. 388, Sherif in the 1930s had shown that subjects who find themselves deviating from the opinion of a group will often change their report, even of a sensory event, in such a direction as to make it less deviant from the group norm. During the 1940s many other studies on conformity were reported, and in 1951 Schachter showed that if a person does not bow to group pressure but continues to deviate from it, the group will tend to give such persons less attention than formerly, assign them less rewarding tasks, and even attempt to exclude them. When deviating persons are excluded they will tend to meet with others of like opinion and form a new group, or "outgroup." The tendency of individuals to conform to what they observe to be the behavior of others has been shown, in some rather dramatic experiments, to lead to unethical behavior. Milgram (1974) demonstrated that if subjects are ordered by a person they perceive to be authoritative to do something immoral, such as giving a painful shock to another person, they will often comply; Latané and Darley (1970) showed that the likelihood of a bystander's coming to the aid of a distressed person depends largely on the behavior of other bystanders. If other bystanders do nothing, the newcomer is likely to conform and also do nothing; but the newcomer's seeing that others are helping a victim will increase the chances that the newcomer will in turn go to the aid of a victim later. A third contribution of Schachter's was his book *The Psychology of Affiliation* (1959), in which he showed that the likelihood of a person's seeking out the company of others depends in part on his or her level of anxiety—an anxious person likes to meet others in the same position, possibly because they can provide not only comfort but also practical advice. In the last decade an increasing amount of research has also been done on the variables that make individuals attractive to each other.

The above account does not begin to exhaust the range of questions asked by social psychologists. Their investigations have included attempts to analyze patterns of cooperation and competition; studies of the effect of population density on behavior; analysis of patterns of responding based on the societal norms of the individual's immediate relatives and colleagues (cross-cultural psychology); and attitudes of particular groups towards others, including the origins and functions of stereotyping and prejudice, a research topic in which Lewin had been a pioneer. Kelley's ideas have led to the development of a separate branch of social psychology, *attribution theory* (for a review, see Kelley and Michela, 1980). N. H. Anderson (1981) has developed a theory that attempts to quantify how we integrate various kinds of information, especially information about other persons.

Physiological Psychology

These observations bring us to our last main point concerning discoveries made in the field of psychology in the last forty-five years. While the evidence cited above will have left the reader with a perhaps depressing sense of the slowness of progress in the solution of the tabula rasa problem, progress in physiological psychology and in the study of the special senses has not lost any of the impetus that existed prior to 1940.

In physiological psychology the greatest progress has probably been in our understanding of the lower parts of the cerebrum, the brainstem, cerebellum, hypothalamus, and limbic systems. Before 1940 it was known that these areas subserved instinctive and emotional behavior, but our detailed understanding of localization of function within the core of the brain has advanced enormously since then. In the brainstem there is a netlike block of cells known as the reticular formation, and this has been shown to influence the rest of the brain by arousing it, a function reflected in the fact that stimulation of the reticular formation can block the flow of ongoing waves in the EEG. The reticular formation has therefore been thought of as the power source of the rest of the brain, highly active when the subject is alert, less active when the subject is more passive. Specific areas in the brainstem are also known to be involved in the various stages of sleep. The hypothalamus is divided into various nuclei, and close relationships have been shown between the activity of these nuclei and the onset or cessation of such life-preserving functions as eating, drinking, mating, sweating, and shivering. Other centers in the brainstem near the hypothalamus give rise to the sensation of pleasure or pain if stimulated, a finding with implications for theories relating learning to reinforcement. Certain long pathways arching up from the hypothalamus into the lower central cerebral hemispheres are known to be active in aggressive self-defensive behavior, predatory hunting behavior, and mating behavior in animals; many emotional responses are linked with this limbic system, and it is possible that it plays a part in determining learning, though the matter remains controversial. Control of the autonomic system is mediated in part by the hypothalamus and limbic system and in part by centers in the cerebral cortex. A great deal of research is being done on the chemistry of the control of the autonomic nervous system and on the roles of various neurotransmitters (such as dopamine) in different kinds of behavior; in fact, the student of physiological psychology is increasingly obliged to have a command of brain biochemistry.

Studies of the cerebral hemispheres continues; two major areas of current research are: (1) studies of the functioning of the two sides of the brain when the corpus callosum, the fiber bundle linking the two hemispheres, is severed, and (2) studies of lateralization, the different roles played by the two halves of the brain. Evidence is accumulating that the two sides of the brain can function independently; and there is increasing evidence that the left cerebral cortex is specialized, in adults, for verbal behavior and possibly more logical, or closed-ended, kinds of thinking, whereas the right side subserves the perception of holistic relationships in time (including the perception of music) and space (coordination of movements with visual conceptualization, as in drawing). There is a suggestion that the male sex hormone, testosterone, can inhibit the development of the left hemisphere in males, leading to a possible explanation of the frequent finding that females score higher on many tasks of verbal ability than do males. Inglis and Lawson (1984) present a review of evidence showing differences between men and women in the degree to which verbal and other skills are localized in the left temporal lobe. The old controversy between Lashley, with his emphasis on mass action, and those who sought for very precise localization of function has abated to a great extent, although some evidence from research on aphasia suggests that certain areas in the left temporal lobe are specialized for particular tasks in the processes of reading, writing, understanding, and speaking.

Our knowledge of the special senses has advanced to the point where most new information on seeing, hearing, and so on is so technically advanced that the average student of psychology cannot easily understand it. The biochemistry of the retina, the mathematical analysis of visual configurations, the mathematics of cochlear functioning, and the anatomy of the receptors of the skin are all areas on which a great deal is known, but it is beyond the domain of the average psychologist. At a simpler level, the most important advances in vision have concerned (1) convincing new evidence that although there might be three kinds of color receptors in the retina, the cells behind the retina, which relay the visual images to the brain, act to modify the messages so profoundly that the resulting visual perceptions are much as Hering predicted on the basis of his opponent-processes theory (see p. 190); and (2) evidence from recordings in the visual cortex that individual cells respond differentially to stimuli of particular orientations or moving in particular directions.

In the case of hearing we now know much more about how the movements of the basilar membrane are related to the sensation of particular tones and about the complex pathways linking the inner ear to the brain; there is some evidence that particular areas of the auditory cortex mediate the perception of particular tones. The perception of taste and smell is better understood now than it was forty-five years ago, and there is increased evidence that molecules of a particular shape are preferentially sensed by particular receptors. Certain chemicals sensed by smell, known as pheromones, play an important part in animal reproductive behavior. The old idea that there were specific receptors for pressure, pain, and touch, each of which could be clearly described and located, has had to be replaced by a vaguer picture that allots a certain amount of flexibility to the various skin receptors in their likely role in mediating specific sensations.

A useful up-to-date summary on the latest ideas in sensation and perception is given by E. L. Brown and K. Deffenbacher (1979); for recent research on the brain, we recommend Carlson (1986), who includes an account of contemporary research on the physiology of memory. As a historical note we may observe that there seems to be a move towards the institution of new disciplines known as the neurosciences, or visual science, to which psychologists are contributing along with physiologists, anatomists, biochemists, and engineers.

Final Note

Quite apart from the explosion in research, there has been a massive growth in the number of persons employed as psychologists. In 1945, the American Psychological Association undertook a radical revision of its bylaws, one result of which was to break membership up into divisions: Of the divisions formed in 1945, eighteen were still in operation in 1980 and included a total of 38,821 members, with the largest divisions being those concerned with clinical psychology, psychotherapy, and other applied areas. Since 1945 a further twenty divisions had been added by 1980, including 17,354 members as of that date. Of these newer divisions, the largest were the division for the psychology of women and the division for the experimental analysis of behavior (devoted largely to Skinnerian psychology). A division for the history of psychology, with 470 members in 1980, was added in 1966. A history of the APA and of other American societies, including the Psychometric Society (largely concerned with the mathematics of test theory) and the Psychonomics Society (largely concerned with experimental psychology), will be found in Hilgard (1987, Chap. 20). These figures indicate the attractiveness of applied psychology for the great majority of psychologists. Moreover, by 1982 there were over forty thousand clinical psychologists in the world, most of them in the United States, and "by 1980 applied psychologists made up about 61 percent of all doctoral psychologists, while traditional experimentalists constituted but 13.5 percent" (Leahey, 1987, p. 477). The Canadian Psychological Association had 1,066 members in the Applied Division and 427 members in the Experimental Division as of March 1987. It is plain that there has been a massive shift away from the hard core of academic experimental psychology into applied areas. In part, this may be related to a shortage of jobs and funding in university environments.

In line with this increase in the number of psychologists now working actively to help others, research has begun to accelerate into the three areas identified in the preface as underinvestigated, considering the long history of psychology. There is now a great deal of research on mental illness and emotional stress, and we also have the historically unique circumstance that enormous numbers of college graduates in North America have taken courses in introductory psychology, including a fair amount on the nature and treatment of mental illness. Even though we shall never eradicate schizophrenia in the way we have eradicated small-pox, less of a stigma is now attached to emotional illness than in the past and many active self-help organizations are available for persons who have schizophrenia or alcholism, as well as organizations for their friends and relatives. On the question of sex differences, progress is less certain: A great deal of heat has been generated about whether the personality stereotypes of "maleness" and "femaleness" are inborn or merely the result of socialization. It is worth recalling that Freud himself disliked the notion of "male" versus "female" characteristics, but the new work on possible differences in cerebral lateralization between men and women (see p. 435) is bringing in its train new controversy, including disagreements among feminists themselves. Salamon and Robinson (1987) have collected a number of articles representing various points of view on gender roles: A review of sex differences and sex stereotyping will be found in Liebert, Wicks-Nelson, and Kail (1986, Chap. 12). Finally, though it is true that theology dominated psychological theorizing in the Middle Ages, and still does in certain Church circles, there is little doubt that the psychological study of religious emotion has been rather neglected since the pioneer work of James. But there is a revival of interest in this topic; since 1976 the APA has had a Division for Psychologists Interested in Religious Issues. A useful recent work is an annotated bibliography of books relating religion to psychology published before 1965 (Vande Kemp, 1984). This book also includes a listing of institutions and professional societies concerned with relating psychological knowledge to pastoral problems; and a listing of journals, including the *Journal for the Scientific Study of Religion*, founded in 1961. As we move toward the twenty-first century, public discussions of mental illness, sex differences, and religion will probably accelerate, and there will be an increased demand for the informed professional opinions of psychologists on these matters.

Summary

In an overview of research in psychology between 1940 and 1985, we see that Gestalt psychology pursues a flickering existence, particularly in Germany. Although behaviorism as a movement has been offset by the growth of cognitive psychology, it has exerted important influences in the areas of learning theory, behavior therapy, and instructional techniques. The case for psychoanalysis remains unproven, but its influence on personality theories such as H. A. Murray's is unquestioned. New movements include cognitive psychology, which has been greatly influenced by various analogies between the human organism and mechanical systems, and humanistic psychology, a movement that stresses the self-actualization of the individual.

Research done without any particular leanings towards the above schools was summarized within the framework of the question "How much of our adult behavior is learned and how much is the result of inborn dispositions?" The neuropsychologist Hebb attempted to bring accord out of the dispute on this question; Skinner and Chomsky disagreed on whether language acquisition is basically learned or innate; Piaget developed a theory of the development of various thought processes in the growing child. Problems currently concerning psychologists involve the behavior of adolescents, adults, and the aged. Researchers have long been interested in whether there are genetic contributions determining intelligence and the disposition to mental illness: The history of such research efforts is briefly considered. The chapter closes with a survey of recent research on stress, social psychology, and psychophysiology.

References

ABRAMOV, I. Retinal mechanisms of color vision. In M. G. F. Fuortes (Ed.), Physiology of photoreceptor organs, *Handbook of Sensory Physiology* (Vol. 8/2). New York: Springer Verlag, 1972.

ACH, N. *Uber die Willenstätigkeit und das Denken*. Göttingen: Vandenhoeck & Ruprecht, 1905.

ADKINS, D. C. Louis Leon Thurstone: Creative thinker, dedicated teacher, eminent psychologist. In N. Frederiksen & H. Gulliksen (Eds.), *Contributions to mathematical psychology*. New York: Holt, Rinehart & Winston, 1964.

ADLER, A. *Understanding human nature*. New York: Greenberg, 1927.

ADRIAN, E. D. *The basis of sensation*. New York: Hafner Publishing Co., 1964. (Originally published, 1928.)

ADRIAN, E. D. *The mechanism of nervous action*. Philadelphia: University of Pennsylvania Press, 1932.

AFNAN, S. M. *Avicenna: His life and works*. London: George Allen & Unwin, 1958.

ALEXANDER, F. G., & SELESNICK, S. T. *The history of psychiatry*. New York: Harper & Row, 1966.

ALLEN, G. W. *William James*. New York: Viking Press, 1967.

ALLISON, H. E. Locke's theory of personal identity: A re-examination. *Journal of the History of Ideas*, 1966, 27, 41–58.

ALLPORT, F. H. *Social psychology*. New York: Houghton Mifflin, 1924.

ALLPORT, G. W. A test for ascendance/submission. *Journal of Abnormal and Social Psychology*, 1928, 23, 118–136.

ALLPORT, G. W. The productive paradoxes of William James. *Psychological Review*, 1943, 50, 95–120.

ALLPORT, G. W. *Pattern and growth in Personality* (2nd ed.). New York: Holt, Rinehart & Winston, 1961.

ALLPORT, G. W. William James and the behavioral sciences. *Journal of the History of the Behavioral Sciences*, 1966, 2, 145–147.

ALLPORT, G. W. The historical background of modern social psychology. In G. Lindzey & E. Aronson (Eds.), *Handbook of social psychology* (2nd ed., Vol. 1). Reading, Mass.: Addison-Wesley, 1968.

ALLPORT, G. W., & VERNON, P. E. A test for personal values. *Journal of Abnormal and Social Psychology,* 1931, *26,* 231–248.

AMERIKS, K. *Kant's theory of mind: An analysis of the paralogisms of pure reason.* Oxford: Clarendon Press, 1982.

ANDERSON, J. R., & BOWER, G. H. *Human associative memory.* Washington, D.C.: Winston, 1973.

ANDERSON, N. H. *Foundations of information integration theory.* New York: Academic Press, 1981.

ANGELL, J. R. The relations of structural and functional psychology to philosophy. *Philosophical Review,* 1903, *12,* 243–271.

ANGELL, J. R. *Psychology.* New York: Henry Holt & Co., 1904.

ANGELL, J. R. The province of functional psychology. *Psychological Review,* 1907, *14,* 61–91. Also reprinted in E. R. Hilgard (Ed.), *American Psychology in Historical Perspective: Addresses of the Presidents of the A. P. A.* Washington: American Psychological Association, Inc., 1978. (Originally published, 1906.)

ANNAS, J. Classical Greek philosophy. In J. Boardman, J. Griffin, & O. Murray (Eds.), *The Oxford history of the classical world.* New York: Oxford University Press, 1986.

AQUINAS, THOMAS. *Summa Theologica* (3 vols. Fathers of the English Dominican Province, trans.). New York: Benziger Brothers, 1948.

AQUINAS, THOMAS. *Aristotle's De Anima in the version of William of Moerbeke and the commentary of St. Thomas Aquinas* (K. Foster and S. Humphries, trans.). London: Routledge & Kegan Paul, 1951.

AQUINAS, THOMAS. *The Soul: A translation of St. Thomas Aquinas' De Anima* (J. P. Rowan, trans.). St. Louis: B. Herder Book Co., 1951.

ARDAL, P. S. *Passion and value in Hume's Treatise.* Edinburgh: University Press, 1966.

ARISTOTLE. See SMITH, J. A., & ROSS, W. P.

ARMSTRONG, A. H. *An introduction to ancient philosophy* (3rd ed.). London: Methuen & Co., 1957.

ARNHEIM, R. The other Gustav Theodor Fechner. In S. Koch & D. E. Leary (Eds.) *A century of psychology as science.* New York: McGraw-Hill, 1985.

ARNOBIUS. The seven books of Arnobius against the heathen. In *The Ante-Nicene Fathers,* (Vol. 6). Buffalo: Christian Literature Company, 1886.

ASH, M. G. *The emergence of Gestalt theory: Experimental psychology in Germany 1890–1920.* Unpublished Ph.D. thesis, Harvard University, 1982.

ATKINSON, R. C., & SHIFFRIN, R. M. Human memory: A proposed system and its control processes. In K. W. Spence & J. T. Spence (Eds.), *Advances in the psychology of learning and motivation: Research and theory.* New York: Academic Press, 1968.

ATTNEAVE, F. *Applications of information theory to psychology.* New York: Holt, Rinehart & Winston, 1959.

AUGUSTINE. *Confessions.* In *The Nicene and Post-Nicene Fathers* (Vol. 1). Buffalo: Christian Literature Company, 1886. (a)

AUGUSTINE. Letters. In *The Nicene and Post-Nicene Fathers* (Vol. 1). Buffalo: Christian Literature Company, 1886. (b)

AUGUSTINE. *On the Holy Trinity.* In *The Nicene and Post-Nicene Fathers,* (Vol. 3). Buffalo: Christian Literature Company, 1887.

AUGUSTINE. *Homilies on the Gospel of St. John.* In *The Nicene and Post-Nicene Fathers* (Vol. 7). Buffalo: Christian Literature Company, 1888.

AUGUSTINE. *On Free Choice of the Will* (A. S. Benjamin & L. H. Hockstaff, trans.). New York: Bobbs-Merrill, 1964.

AVENARIUS, R. *Kritik der reiner Erfahrung* (2 vols.). Leipzig: O. R. Reinsland, 1888–90; 2nd ed., 1907.

AVERROES. *Epitome of Parva Naturalia* (H. Blumberg, trans.). Cambridge, Mass.: Medieval Academy of America, 1961.

BABKIN, B. P. *Pavlov: A biography.* Chicago: University of Chicago Press, 1949.

BACON, R. *The opus majus of Roger Bacon* (2 vols.) (R. B. Burke, trans.). New York: Russell & Russell, 1962.

BAIN, A. *The senses and the intellect* (3rd ed.). London: Longmans, Green, 1868. (Originally published, 1855.)

BAIN, A. *The emotions and the will* (3rd ed.). London: Longmans, Green, 1880. (Originally published, 1859).

BAINTON, R. *Penguin History of Christianity* (2 vols.). Harmondsworth, Middlesex: Penguin Books, 1967.

BALDWIN, J. M. *Handbook of psychology,* Vol 1. *Senses and intellect* (1889); Vol 2. *Feeling and will* (1891). New York: Henry Holt & Co.

BALDWIN, J. M. *Mental development in the child and the race.* New York: Macmillan, 1895.

BALDWIN, J. M. *Social and ethical interpretation in mental development.* New York: Macmillan, 1897.

BALDWIN, J. M. (Ed.). *Dictionary of philosophy and psychology* (3 vols.). New York: Macmillan, 1901–1902.

BALDWIN, J. M. *Development and evolution.* New York: Macmillan, 1902.

BALDWIN, J. M. *History of psychology.* London: Watts & Co., 1913.

BALDWIN, J. M. *The story of the mind.* New York & London: D. Appleton & Co., 1916.

BALME, D. M. Aristotle's use of differentiae in zoology. In J. Barnes, M. Schofield, & R. Sorabji (Eds.), *Articles on Aristotle,* Vol. 1. *Science.* London: Duckworth, 1975.

BANDURA, A., & WALTERS, R. H. *Social learning and personality development.* New York: Holt, Rinehart & Winston, 1963.

BARNES, J. Hellenistic philosophy and science. In J. Boardman, J. Griffin, & O. Murray (Eds.), *The Oxford history of the classical world.* New York: Oxford University Press, 1986.

BARTLETT, F. C. *Remembering: A study in experimental and social psychology.* Cambridge: Cambridge University Press, 1932.

BATTIE, W. *A treatise on madness.* New York: Brunner/Mazel, 1969. (Originally published, 1738.)

BAUMRIN, J. M. Aristotle's empirical nativism. *American Psychologist,* 1975, *30,* 486–494.

BEARE, J. I. *Greek theories of elementary cognition from Alcmaeon to Aristotle.* Oxford: Clarendon Press, 1906.

BECHTEREV, V. M. *General principles of human reflexology* (E. Murphy & M. Murphy, trans.). London: Jarrolds, 1933.

BECHTEREW, W. *La psychologie objective.* Paris: Librairie Felix Alcan, 1913.

BEER, G. DE. Darwin, Charles Robert. In *Dictionary of scientific biography* (Vol. 3). New York: Scribner's, 1971.

BEER, T., BETHE, A., & VON UEXKÜLL, J. Vorschläge zu einer objektivierenden Nomenklatur in der Physiologie des Nervensystems. *Biologisches Zentralblatt,* 1899, *19,* 517–521.

BEKHTEREV, V. M. See *Bechterev* and *Bechterew.*

BENEKE, F. E. *Lehrbuch der Psychologie als Naturwissenschaft,* Berlin: E. S. Mittler & Sohn, 1877. (Originally published, 1833.)

BERGEN, A. VAN. *Task interruption.* Amsterdam: North Holland, 1968.

BERKELEY, G. *Essay towards a new theory of vision.* (Originally published, 1709); *Treatise concerning the principles of human knowledge* (1710); *Dialogues between Hylas and Philonous* (1713). In *Berkeley: A new theory of vision and other writings.* London: J. M. Dent & Sons Ltd., 1954.

BERNREUTER, R. G. *The Personality inventory.* Stanford, Calif.: Stanford University Press, 1935.

BINET, A., & SIMON, T. The development of intelligence in the child (E. S. Kite, trans.). In D. N. Robinson (Ed.), *Significant contributions to the history of psychology, 1750–1920* (Series B, Vol. 4). Washington, D.C.: University Publications of America Inc., 1977. (Originally published, 1908.)

BIRREN, J. E., & SCHAIE, K. W. (Eds.). *Handbook of the psychology of aging.* New York: Van Nostrand Reinhold, 1977.

BLACKMORE, J. T. *Ernst Mach: His works, life and influence.* Berkeley: University of California Press, 1972.

BLOCK, N. J., & DWORKIN, G. *The IQ controversy.* New York: Pantheon, 1976.

BLUMENTHAL, A. L. A reappraisal of Wilhelm Wundt. *American Psychologist,* 1975, *30,* 1081–1088.

BLUMENTHAL, A. L. Wilhelm Wundt—Problems of interpretation. In W. G. Bringmann & R.

D. Tweney (Eds.), *Wundt studies*. Toronto: C. J. Hogrefe, 1980.

BLUMENTHAL, H. J. *Plotinus' psychology: His doctrines of the embodied soul*. The Hague: M. Nijhoff, 1971.

BOAKES, R. *From Darwin to behaviourism*. New York: Cambridge University Press, 1984.

BOETHIUS. *The consolation of philosophy* ("I. T.," trans.; revised by H. F. Stewart). Loeb Classical Library. London: William Heinemann; New York: Putnam's, 1918.

BOETHIUS. *The theological tractates* (H. F. Stewart & E. R. Rand, trans.). Loeb Classical Library. London: William Heinemann; New York: Putnam's, 1918.

BONDY, M. Psychiatric antecedents of psychological testing (before Binet). *Journal of the History of the Behavioral Sciences*, 1974, *10*, 180–194.

BONNET, C. *Essai analytique sur les facultes de l'ame*. Hildesheim, West Germany, and New York: Georg Olms Verlag, 1973. (Originally published, 1760.)

BORING, E. G. *Sensation and perception in the history of experimental psychology*. New York: D. Appleton Century Co., 1942.

BORING, E. G. *A history of experimental psychology* (2nd ed.). Englewood Cliffs, N.J.: Prentice-Hall, 1950. (1st ed., 1929.)

BORING, E. G. A note on the origin of the word *psychology*. *Journal of the History of the Behavioral Sciences*, 1966, *2*, 167.

BORING, E. G. Titchener's experimentalists. *Journal of the History of the Behavioral Sciences*, 1967, *3*, 315–325.

BOSS, M. *Psychoanalysis and Daseinsanalysis*. New York: Basic Books, 1963.

BOURGEY, L. Observation and experiment in analogical explanation. In J. Barnes, M. Schofield, & R. Sorabji (Eds.), *Articles on Aristotle*, Vol. 1. *Science*. London: Duckworth, 1975.

BOWER, G. H. Application of a model to paired-associate learning. *Psychometrika*, 1961, *26*, 255–280.

BOWERS, K. S., & MEICHENBAUM, D. (Eds.). *The unconscious reconsidered*. New York: Wiley, 1984.

BOWLBY, J. *Attachment and loss*. New York: Basic Books, 1973.

BRENNAN, R. *Thomistic psychology*. New York: Macmillan, 1941.

BRENNAN, R. *History of psychology from the standpoint of a Thomist*. New York: Macmillan, 1945.

BRENTANO, F. *Psychology from an empirical standpoint* (A. C. Rancurello, D. B. Terrell, & L. L. McAlister, trans.). London: Routledge & Kegan Paul, 1973. (Originally published, 1874.)

BRETT, G. S. *A history of psychology, Vol 1. Ancient and patristic*. London: George Allen & Co., 1912.

BRETT, G. S. *A history of psychology, Vol. 2. Mediaeval & early modern period*. London: George Allen and Unwin, 1921. (a)

BRETT, G. S. *A history of psychology*, Vol. 3. London: George Allen and Unwin, 1921. (b)

BRIGHAM, C. C. *A study of American intelligence*. Princeton, N.J.: Princeton University Press, 1923.

BRINDLEY, G. S. *Physiology of the retina and visual pathway*. London: Edward Arnold, Publishers, 1960.

BRINGMANN, W. G., BALANCE, W. D. G., & EVANS, R. B. Wilhelm Wundt, 1832–1920: A brief biographical sketch. *Journal of the History of the Behavioral Sciences*, 1975, *11*, 287–297.

BRINGMANN, W. G., BRINGMANN, N. J., & UNGERER, G. A. The establishment of Wundt's laboratory: An archival and documentary study. In W. G. Bringmann & R. D. Tweney (Eds.), *Wundt studies*. Toronto: C. J. Hogrefe, 1980.

BRINGMANN, W. G., & TWENEY, R. D. (Eds.). *Wundt studies: A centennial collection*. Toronto: C. J. Hogrefe, 1980.

BRINGMANN, W. G., UNGERER, G. A., & GANZER, H. Illustrations from the life and work of Wilhelm Wundt. In W. G. Bringmann & R. D. Tweney (Eds.), *Wundt studies*. Toronto: C. J. Hogrefe, 1980.

BROADBENT, D. E. *Perception and communication*. New York: Pergamon Press, 1958.

BROOKS, G. P. The faculty psychology of Thomas Reid. *Journal of the History of the Behavioral Sciences*, 1976, *12*, 65–77.

BROWN, E. L., & DEFFENBACHER, K. *Perception and the senses*. New York: Oxford University Press, 1979.

BROWN, J. A. C. *Freud and the post-Freudians*. London: Penguin Books, 1961.

BROWN, J. F., & VOTH, A. C. The path of seen movement as a function of the vectorfield. *American Journal of Psychology*, 1937, *49*, 543–563.
BROWN, J. S. Motivation. In E. Hearst (Ed.), *The first century of experimental psychology*. Hillsdale, N.J.: Lawrence Erlbaum Associates, 1979.
BROWN, T. *Lectures on the philosophy of the human mind*. Edinburgh: William Tait, 1830. (Originally published, 1820.)
BUCKNILL, J. C., & TUKE, D. H. *A manual of psychological medicine*. New York: Hafner Publishing Co., 1968. (Originally published, 1858.)
BUDGE, E. A. *The book of the dead*. London: Kegan Paul, Trench, Trubner & Co., 1898.
BÜHLER, K. Tatsachen und Probleme zu einer Psychologie der Denkvorgänge. 1. Über Gedanken (a); 2. Über Gedankenzusammenhänge (b); 3. Über Gedankenerinnerungen (c). *Archiv für die gesamte Psychologie*, 1907, *9*, 297–365 (a); 1908, *12*, 1–23 (b); 1908, *12*, 24–92 (c).
BURNHAM, J. C. On the origins of behaviorism. *Journal of the History of the Behavioral Sciences*, 1968, *4*, 143–151.
BURNHAM, J. C. Thorndike's puzzle boxes. *Journal of the History of the Behavioral Sciences*, 1972, *8*, 159–167.
BURNHAM, W. H. Memory, historically and experimentally considered. *American Journal of Psychology*, 1888–1889, *2*, 39–90; 225–270; 431–464; 568–622.
BURT, C. The genetic determination of differences in intelligence: A study of monozygotic twins reared together and apart. *British Journal of Psychology*, 1966, *57*, 137–153.
BURTON, R. *Anatomy of melancholy* (3 vols.) New York: Dutton, 1964–1968. (Originally published, 1621.)
BURTT, H. E. *Legal psychology*. Englewood Cliffs, N.J.: Prentice-Hall, 1931.
CABANIS, P. J. G. Rapports du physique et du moral de l'homme. In *Oeuvres philosophiques de Cabanis* (Vol. 1). Paris: Presses Universitaires de France, 1956. (Originally published, 1799.)
CALKINS, M. W. Association (Part 1). *Psychological Review*, 1894, *1*, 476–483.
CANNON, W. B. *Bodily changes in pain, hunger, fear and rage*. New York: Harper & Row, 1963. (Originally published, 1915; 2nd ed., 1929.)
CARINI, L. A reassessment of Max Wertheimer's contribution to psychological theory. *Acta Psychologica*, 1970, *32*, 377–385.
CARLSON, N. R. *Physiology of behavior* (3rd ed.). Boston: Allyn & Bacon, 1986.
CARPENTER, W. B. *Principles of mental physiology*. London: C. Kegan Paul, 1874.
CARTER, R. B. *Descartes' medical philosophy: The organic solution to the mind-body problem*. Baltimore: The Johns Hopkins University Press, 1983.
CARUS, F. A. *Geschichte der Psychologie*. Leipzig: I. A. Barth & P. G. Kummer, 1808.
CASTONGUAY, J. *Psychologie de la mémoire*. Montreal: Les éditions du lévrier, 1963.
CATTELL, J. McK. Mental tests and measurements. *Mind*, 1890, *15*, 373–381.
CATTELL, J. McK. The advance of psychology. *Science*, 1898, *8*, 533–541.
CATTELL, J. McK. Early psychological laboratories. In M. L. Reymert (Ed.), *Feelings and emotions*. The Wittenberg Symposium. Worcester, Mass.: Clark University Press, 1928.
CATTELL, R. B. *Personality and motivation structure and measurement*. New York: Harcourt Brace Jovanovich, 1957.
CHESTERTON, G. K. *St. Thomas Aquinas*. London: Hodder & Stoughton, 1933.
CHOMSKY, N. Review of Skinner's *Verbal behavior*. *Language*, 1959, *35*, 26–58
CLARKE, E., and O'MALLEY, C. D. *The human brain and spinal cord: A historical study illustrated by writings from antiquity to the twentieth century*. Berkeley and Los Angeles: University of California Press, 1968.
CLEMENTS, R. D. Physiological-psychological thought in Juan Luis Vives. *Journal of the History of the Behavioral Sciences*, 1967, *3*, 219–235.
COHEN, D. *J. B. Watson: The founder of behaviorism*. London: Routledge & Kegan Paul, 1979.
CONDILLAC, E. B. DE. *Treatise on the sensations* (G. Carr, trans.). Los Angeles: University of Southern California School of Philosophy, 1930. (Originally published, 1754.)
CONDILLAC, E. B. DE. *Essai sur l'origine des connaissances humaines*. Auvers-sur-Oise, France: Editions Galilée, 1973. (Originally published, 1746.)
COON, D. J. Eponymy, obscurity, Twitmyer and Pavlov. *Journal of the History of the Behavioral Sciences*, 1982, *18*, 255–262.
COOTER, R. *The cultural meaning of popular science: Phrenology and the organization of consent in*

nineteenth-century Britain. New York: Cambridge University Press, 1984.

CORBET, H., & MARSHALL, M. E. The comparative anatomy of angels: A sketch by Dr. Mises: 1825. *Journal of the History of the Behavioral Sciences,* 1969, *5*, 135–151.

CORSINI, R. (Ed.). *Current psychotherapies.* Hasca, Ill.: F. E. Peacock Publishers, 1973.

COSSLETT, T. (Ed.). *Science and religion in the nineteenth century.* New York: Cambridge University Press, 1984.

COX, C. *The early mental traits of three hundred geniuses.* Stanford, Calif.: Stanford University Press, 1926.

CRAIK, F. I. M., & CERMAK, L. S. *Levels of processing in human memory.* Hillsdale, N.J.: Lawrence Erlbaum Associates, 1979.

CRANEFIELD, P. F. On the origin of the phrase *Nihil est in intellectu quod non prius fuerit in sensu. Journal of the History of Medicine and Allied Sciences,* 1970, *25*, 77–80.

CRANEFIELD, P. F. *The way in and the way out: Francois Magendie, Charles Bell and the roots of the spinal nerves.* New York: Futura Publishing Company, 1974.

CRANNELL, C. W. Wolfgang Köhler. *Journal of the History of the Behavioral Sciences,* 1970, *6,* 267.

CROMBIE, A. C. Early concepts of the senses and the mind. *Scientific American,* May 1964, *210,* 108–116.

CUNNINGHAM, J. P. Trees as memory representations for simple visual patterns. *Memory and Cognition,* 1980, *8,* 593–605.

DANZIGER, K. The positivist repudiation of Wundt. *Journal of the History of the Behavioral Sciences,* 1979, *15,* 205–230.

DANZIGER, K. The history of introspection reconsidered. *Journal of the History of the Behavioral Sciences,* 1980, *16,* 241–262.

DANZIGER, K. Mid-nineteenth-century British psycho-physiology: A neglected chapter in the history of psychology. In W. R. Woodward & M. G. Ash (Eds.), *The problematic science: Psychology in nineteenth-century thought.* New York: Praeger, 1982.

DANZIGER, K. Origins and basic principles of Wundt's *Völkerpsychologie. British Journal of Social Psychology,* 1983, *22,* 303–313.

DANZIGER, K. The origins of the psychological experiment as a social institution. *American Psychologist,* 1985, *40,* 133–140.

DANZIGER, K. Statistical methods and the historical development of research practice in American psychology. In L. Kruger, G. Gigerenzer, & M. S. Morgan (Eds.), *The probabilistic revolution.* Vol. 2: *Ideas in the sciences.* Cambridge, Mass.: MIT Press, 1987.

DARLEY, J. M., GLUCKSBERG, S., KAMIN, L. J., & KINCHLA, R. A. *Psychology.* Englewood Cliffs, N.J.: Prentice-Hall, 1981.

DARWIN, C. *The descent of man* (2 vols.). New York: D. Appleton & Co., 1871.

DARWIN, C. *The expression of the emotions in man and animals.* London: John Murray, 1904. (Originally published, 1872.)

DARWIN, C. *The origin of species.* London: John Murray, 1911. (Originally published, 1859; 6th ed. 1872.)

DARWIN, E. *Zoonomia,* Part II. London: Printed for J. Johnson in St. Paul's churchyard, 1796.

DASTON, L. J. The theory of will versus the science of mind. In W. R. Woodward & M. G. Ash (Eds.), *The problematic science: Psychology in nineteenth-century thought.* New York: Praeger, 1982.

DAVIES, J. B. *The psychology of music.* London: Hutchinson, 1978.

DAVISON, G. C., & NEALE, J. M. *Abnormal psychology.* New York: Wiley, 1982.

DAWKINS, R. *The blind watchmaker.* New York: W. W. Norton, 1986.

DESCARTES, R. *Philosophical works* (2 vols., E. S. Haldane & G. R. T. Ross, trans.). The first volume contains *The Discourse on the Method of Rightly Conducting the Reason, Meditations on first Philosophy, The Principles of Philosophy, The Passions of the Soul,* and *Notes directed against a certain Programme.* New York: Dover, 1955.

DESCARTES, R. *On man. Le traité de l'homme,* in *Oeuvres philosophiques* (Vol. 1). Paris: Editions Garnier Freres, 1963. (Originally published, 1618–1637.)

DESSOIR, M. *Geschichte der neueren deutschen Psychologie,* Vol. 1. Berlin: C. Duncker, 1894 (2nd ed., 1897).

DESSOIR, M. *Outlines of the history of psychology* (D. Fisher, Trans.). New York: Macmillan, 1912.

DEUTSCH, H. *The Psychology of women: A psychoanalytic interpretation.* New York: Grune & Stratton, 1944.

DEWEY, J. *Psychology.* New York: Harper & Brothers, 1886.

DEWHURST, K. *John Locke (1632–1704) physician and philosopher.* London: Wellcome Historical Medical Library, 1963.

DIAMOND, S. Marin Cureau de la Chambre (1594–1669). *Journal of the History of the Behavioral Sciences,* 1968, *4,* 40–54.

DIAMOND, S. Seventeenth century French "connectionism": La Forge, Dilly, and Regis. *Journal of the History of the Behavioral Sciences,* 1969, *5,* 3–9.

DIAMOND, S. The debt of Leibniz to Pardies. *Journal of the History of the Behavioral Sciences,* 1972, *8,* 109–114.

DIDEROT, D. *Lettre sur les aveugles.* In Diderot, *Oeuvres philosophiques.* Paris: Editions Garnier Frères, 1964. (Originally published, 1749.)

DIETHELM, O., & HEFFERNAN, T. F. Felix Platter and psychiatry. *Journal of the History of the Behavioral Sciences,* 1965, *1,* 10–23.

DIETZE, G. Untersuchungen über den Unfang des Bewusstseins bei regelmässig aufeinander folgenden Schalleindrucken. *Philosophische Studien,* 1884, *2,* 362–393.

DIOGENES LAERTIUS. *Life of Zeno.* In M. Hadas (Ed.), *Essential works of stoicism.* New York: Bantam Books, 1961.

DODDS, E. R. *The Greeks and the irrational.* Berkeley: University of California Press, 1951.

DOLLARD, J., DOOB, L. W., MILLER, N. E., MOWRER, O. H., & SEARS, R. R. *Frustration and aggression.* New Haven: Yale University Press, 1939.

DONALDSON, H. H. *The growth of the brain: A study of the nervous system in relation to education.* New York: Scribner's, 1895.

DONDERS, F. C. Two instruments for determining the time required for mental processes. English translation in *Acta Psychologica,* 1969, *24,* 432–435. (Originally published, 1867–1869.) (a)

DONDERS, F. C. On the speed of mental processes. English translation in *Acta Psychologica,* 1969, *24,* 412–431. (Originally published, 1868.) (b)

DONDERS, F. C. A short description of some instruments and apparatus belonging to the collection of the physiological laboratory and the Dutch Ophthalmic Hospital. English translation in *Acta Psychologica,* 1969, *24,* 436–438. (Originally published, 1876.) (c)

DUNCKER, K. Über induzierte Bewegung (Ein Beitrag zur Theorie optisch wahrgenommener Bewegung). *Psychologische Forschung,* 1929, *12,* 180–259. (Excerpts in English in Ellis (1938), pp. 161–172.)

DUNCKER, K. On problem solving (L. S. Lees, trans.). *Psychological Monographs,* 1945, *58,* (5, Whole No. 270). (Originally published, 1935.)

DUNKEL, H. B. *Herbart and Herbartism: An educational ghost story.* Chicago: University of Chicago Press, 1970.

DUNS SCOTUS. *Philosophical Writings* (A. Walter, trans.). London: Thomas Nelson & Sons, 1962.

EBBINGHAUS, H. *Grundzüge der psychologie.* Vol. 1, 1897–1902; 2nd ed. of Vol. 1, 1905; Vol. 2, 1908. Leipzig: Verlag von Veit & Comp.

EBBINGHAUS, H. *Abriss der Psychologie.* Translated as *Psychology: An elementary textbook.* Boston: D. C. Heath, 1908.

EBBINGHAUS, H. *Über das Gedächtnis* (trans. by H. A. Ruger & C. E. Bussenius as *Memory.*) New York: Dover, 1964. (Originally published, 1885.)

EHRENFELS, C. VON. Über Gestaltqualitäten. *Vierteljahrschrift für wissenschaftliche Philosophie und Soziologie,* 1890, *14,* 249–292.

EHRENFELS, C. VON. On Gestalt-qualities. *Psychological Review,* 1937, *44,* 521–524.

ELLENBERGER, H. F. *The discovery of the unconscious.* New York: Basic Books, 1970.

ELLIOTSON, J. Numerous cases of surgical operations without pain in the mesmeric state. Reprinted in D. N. Robinson (Ed.), *Significant contributions to the history of psychology 1750–1920* (Series A, Vol. 10). Washington, D.C.: University Publication of America, 1977. (Originally published, 1843.)

ELLIS, W. D. *A source book of Gestalt psychology.* London: Routledge & Kegan Paul, 1938.

EPICURUS. *The extant remains* (C. Bailey, trans.). Oxford: Clarendon Press, 1926.

ERIKSON, E. H. *Childhood and society.* New York: W. W. Norton & Co., 1963.

ERTEL, S., KEMMLER, L., & STADLER, M. *Gestalttheorie in der modernen Psychologie.* Darmstadt: Steinkopff, 1975.

ESDAILE, J. Mesmerism in India. Reprinted in D. N. Robinson (Ed.), *Significant contributions to the history of psychology, 1750–1920* (Series A, Vol. 10). Washington, D.C.: University Publications of America, 1977.

ESPER, E. A. *A history of psychology.* Philadelphia: Saunders, 1964.

EVANS, E. C. Physiognomics in the ancient world. *Transactions of the American Philosophical Society* (Vol. 59, Part 5), 1969.

EVANS, R. B. E. B. Titchener and his lost system. *Journal of the History of the Behavioral Sciences,* 1972, *8,* 168–180.

EYSENCK, H. J. The effects of psychotherapy: An evaluation. *Journal of Consulting Psychology,* 1952, *16,* 319–324.

EYSENCK, H. J. Principles and methods of personality description, classification and diagnosis. *British Journal of Psychology,* 1964, *55,* 284–294.

EYSENCK, H. J. *Eysenck on extraversion.* New York: John Wiley & Sons, 1973.

EYSENCK, H. J., and EYSENCK, S. B. G. *Personality structure and measurement.* London: Routledge & Kegan Paul, 1969.

EYSENCK, H. J., and WILSON, G. D. *The experimental study of Freudian theories.* London: Methuen, 1973.

EYSENCK, H. J., versus KAMIN, L. *The intelligence controversy.* New York: Wiley, 1981.

FALMAGNE, J-C. *Elements of psychophysical theory.* New York: Oxford University Press, 1985.

FANCHER, R. E. *Psychoanalytic psychology.* New York: W. W. Norton & Co., 1973.

FANCHER, R. E. A note on the origin of the term "nature and nurture." *Journal of the History of the Behaviorol Sciences,* 1979, *15,* 321–322. (a)

FANCHER, R. E. *Pioneers of psychology.* New York: W. W. Norton & Co., 1979 (b)

FANCHER, R. E. *The intelligence men: Makers of the IQ controversy.* New York: W. W. Norton, 1985.

FARR, R. M. Wilhelm Wundt (1832–1920) and the origins of psychology as an experimental and social science. *British Journal of Social Psychology,* 1983, *22,* 289–301.

FAY, J. W. *American psychology before William James.* New York: Octagon Books, 1966. (Originally published, 1939.)

FEARING, F. *Reflex action: A study in the history of physiological psychology.* New York: Hafner Pub. Co., 1964. (Originally published, 1930.)

FECHNER, G. T. *Nanna: Oder ueber das Seelenleben der Pflanzen (Nanna, or On the soul-life of plants).* Leipzig: L. Voss, 1848.

FECHNER, G. T. *Zend-Avesta: Oder Über die Dinge des Himmels und des Jenseits (Zend Avesta, or On the things of heaven and the beyond).* Leipzig: L. Voss, 1851.

FECHNER, G. T. *Vorschule der Aesthetik.* Leipzig: Breitkopf and Härtel, 1876.

FECHNER, G. T. *Revision der Hauptpunkte der Psychophysik.* Leipzig: Breitkopf und Härtel, 1882.

FECHNER, G. T. *Elemente der Psychophysik* (2 vols.) Amsterdam: E. J. Bonset, 1964. An English translation of Vol. 1 is: Fechner, Gustav: *Elements of Psychophysics,* Vol. 1 (H. E. Adler, trans.). New York: Holt, Rinehart, & Winston, 1966. (Originally published, 1860.)

FEINSTEIN, H. M. William James on the emotions. *Journal of the History of Ideas,* 1970, *31,* 133–142.

FEINSTEIN, H. M. *Becoming William James.* Ithaca, N.Y.: Cornell University Press, 1984.

FERGUSON, L. W. The development of industrial psychology. In B. von Haller Gilmer, *Industrial psychology.* New York: McGraw-Hill, 1961.

FERRIER, D. *The functions of the brain.* In: D. N. Robinson (Ed.), *Significant contributions to the history of psychology 1750–1920* (Series E, Vol. 3). Washington, D.C.: University Publications of America, 1978. (Originally published, 1876; 2nd ed., 1886.)

FESTINGER, L. *A theory of cognitive dissonance.* Evanston, Ill.: Row, Peterson, 1957.

FINE, R. *A history of psychoanalysis.* New York: Columbia University Press, 1979.

FISHER, S., & GREENBERG, R. P. *The scientific credibility of Freud's theories and therapy.* New York: Basic Books, 1977.

FISHMAN, S. M. James and Lewes on unconscious judgment. *Journal of the History of the Behavioral Sciences,* 1968, *4,* 335–348.

FORREST, G. Greece: The history of the archaic period. In J. Boardman, J. Griffin, & O.

Murray (Eds.), *The Oxford history of the classical world*. New York: Oxford University Press, 1986.

FOTINIS, A. P. *The De Anima of Alexander of Aphrodisias*. Washington, D.C.: University Press of America, Inc., 1979.

FOUCAULT, M. *Madness and civilization: A history of insanity in the age of reason* (R. Howard, trans.). New York: Random House, 1965. (First published as *Histoire de la folie*, Paris, Librairie Plon, 1961.)

FREDERICK II. *De Arte venandi cum avibus (The art of falconry)* (T. A. Wood and F. M. Fyfe, trans.). Stanford Calif.: Stanford University Press, 1943.

FREDERICK II. *Das Falkenbuch Kaiser Friedrichs II*. Dortmund: Harenberg Kommunikation, 1980.

FREEMAN, K. *Ancilla to the pre-Socratic philosophers*. Oxford: Basil Blackwell, 1948.

FREUD, S. All works mentioned in the text will be found in J. Strachey (Ed.), *The complete psychological works of Sigmund Freud* (24 vols.). London: Hogarth Press and the Institute of Psychoanalysis, 1953–1974.

FREUD, S. *Project for a scientific psychology* (C. Mosbacher & J. Strachey, trans.). In S. Freud, *The origins of psychoanalysis: Letters to Wilhelm Fliess, drafts and notes, 1887–1902*, M. Bonapart, A. Freud, & E. Kris, Eds. New York: Basic Books, 1954.

FRIEDMAN, D. P. *The Little LISPer*. Chicago: Science Research Associates, Inc., 1974.

FRYER, D. H., & HENRY, E. R. *Handbook of applied psychology*. New York: Holt, Rinehart & Winston, 1950.

FUCHS, W. Eine Pseudofovea bei Hemianopikern. *Psychologische Forschung*, 1922, *1*, 157–186. Excerpts in English in Ellis (1938), pp. 357–361.

FURUMOTO, L. Mary Whiton Calkins (1863–1930): Fourteenth president of the American Psychological Association. *Journal of the History of the Behavioral Sciences*, 1979, *15*, 346–356.

GALEN. *On the natural faculties* (A. J. Brock, trans.). Loeb Classical Library. London: William Heinemann, 1916.

GALEN. *On anatomical procedures* (Books 1–9, C. Singer, trans.). London: Oxford University Press, 1956.

GALEN. *On anatomical procedures: The later books* (W. L. H. Duckworth, trans.). Cambridge: Cambridge University Press, 1962.

GALEN. The diagnosis and care of the soul's passions. In *Galen on the passions and errors of the soul* (P. W. Harkins, trans., with an introduction and interpretation by W. Riese). Columbus, Ohio: Ohio State University Press, 1963.

GALEN. *On the usefulness of the parts of the body* (2 vols., M. T. May, trans.). Ithaca, N.Y.: Cornell University Press, 1968.

GALILEO GALILEI. *The Assayer*. In S. Drake & C. D. O'Malley, *The controversy on the comets of 1618*. Philadelphia: University of Pennsylvania Press, 1960.

GALTON, F. Psychometric experiments. *Brain*, 1879, *2*, 149–162.

GALTON, F. *Hereditary genius*, new and revised edition, with an American preface. New York: D. Appleton & Co., 1881. (Originally published, 1869.)

GALTON, F. Co-relations and their measurements, chiefly from anthropometric data. *Proceedings of the Royal Society*, 1888, *45*, 135–145.

GALTON, F. *Inquiries into human faculty and its development*. London: J.M. Dent & Sons (Everyman edition), 1907. (Originally published, 1883.)

GANTT, W. H. The origin and development of nervous disturbances experimentally produced. *American Journal of Psychiatry*, 1942, *98*, 475–481.

GARDNER, H. *The mind's new science*. New York: Basic Books, 1985.

GARDNER, R. A., & GARDNER, B. T. Teaching sign language to a chimpanzee. *Science*, 1969, *165*, 664–672.

GARNER, W. R. *Uncertainty and structure as psychological concepts*. New York: Wiley, 1962.

GARVEY, C. R. List of American psychology laboratories. *Psychological Bulletin*, 1929, *26*, 652–660.

GAY, P. *The Enlightenment: An interpretation*. New York: Knopf, 1966.

GEIS, G. L., STEBBINS, W. C., & LUNDIN, R. W. *Reflex and operant conditioning*. New York: Appleton-Century-Crofts, 1965.

GESCHEIDER, G. A. *Psychophysics: Method and theory*. Hillsdale, N.J.: Lawrence Erlbaum Associates, 1976.

GIBSON, E. J., & WALK, R. R. The "visual cliff." *Scientific American*, 1960, *202*, 64–71.

GIBSON, J. J. The legacies of Koffka's *Principles. Journal of the History of the Behavioral Sciences*, 1971, *7*, 3–9.

GIGERENZER, G., & MURRAY, D. J. *Cognition as intuitive statistics*. Hillsdale, N.J.: Erlbaum Associates, 1987.

GINSBURG, H., & OPPER, S. *Piaget's theory of intellectual development: An introduction*, 2nd ed. Englewood Cliffs, N.J.: Prentice-Hall, 1979.

GLANVILLE, A. D., & DALLENBACH, K. M. The range of attention. *American Journal of Psychology*, 1929, *41*, 207–236.

GLEITMAN, H. *Psychology* (2nd ed.). New York: Norton, 1986.

GODDARD, H. H. *The Kallikak family: A study in the heredity of feeble-mindedness*. New York: Macmillan, 1912.

GOETHE, J. W. VON. *Theory of colors* (C. L. Eastlake, trans.). London: John Murray, 1840. Reprinted, New York: Dover Press, 1970. (Originally published, 1810.)

GOLDSTEIN, K. *The organism*. New York: American Book, 1939.

GOTTLIEB, G. Comparative psychology and ethology. In E. Hearst (Ed.), *The first century of experimental psychology*. Hillsdale, N.J.: Lawrence Erlbaum Associates, 1979.

GOTTSCHALDT, K. Über den Einfluss der Erfahrung auf die Wahrnehmung von Figuren. I. Über den Einfluss gehäufter Einprägung von Figuren auf ihre Sichtbarkeit in umfassenden Konfigurationen. *Psychologische Forschung*, 1926, *8*, 261–317. Excerpts in English in Ellis (1938), pp. 109–122.

GOULD, S. J. *The mismeasure of man*. New York: Norton, 1981.

GRAHAM, C. H. Color mixture and color systems. In C. H. Graham (Ed.), *Vision and visual perception*. New York: John Wiley & Sons, 1965. (a)

GRAHAM, C. H. Color: Data and theories. In C. H. Graham (Ed.), *Vision and visual perception*. New York: John Wiley & Sons, 1965. (b)

GRAY, J. A. (Ed.). *Pavlov's typology: Recent theoretical and experimental developments from the laboratory of B. M. Teplov*. New York: Macmillan, 1964.

GRAY, P. H. Spalding and his influence on research in developmental behavior. *Journal of the History of the Behavioral Sciences*, 1967, *3*, 168–179.

GREGORY, R. L. *Eye and brain*. New York: McGraw-Hill, 1966.

GRIESINGER, W. *Mental pathology and therapeutics*. (C. L. Robinson & J. Rutherford, trans., 1867). New York: Hafner Publishing Co., 1965. (Originally published, 1845.)

GRÜNBAUM, A. *The foundations of psychoanalysis: A philosophical critique*. Los Angeles, Calif.: University of California Press, 1984.

GRUNER, O. M. *A treatise on the Canon of Medicine of Avicenna, incorporating a translation of the first book*. M. Kelley, 1970. (Originally published London: Luzac & Co., 1930.)

GUILFORD, J. P. *The nature of human intelligence*. New York: McGraw-Hill, 1967.

GURNEE, H. Maze learning in the collective situation. *Journal of Psychology*, 1937, *3*, 437–443.

GUTHRIE, E. R. *The psychology of learning* (rev. ed.). New York: Harper & Row, 1952. (Originally published, 1935.)

GUTHRIE, E. R., & HORTON, G. P. *Cats in a puzzle box*. New York: Holt, Rinehart & Winston, 1946.

HACKING, I. Individual substance. In H. G. Frankfurt (Ed.), *Leibniz: A collection of critical essays*. Garden City, N.Y.: Doubleday, 1972.

HALDANE, E. S. *Descartes: His life and times*. London: John Murray, 1905.

HALE, M. *Human science and social order: Hugo Münsterberg and the origins of applied psychology*. Philadelphia: Temple University Press, 1980.

HALE, N. G. *Freud and the Americans: The beginnings of psychoanalysis in the United States, 1876–1917*. New York: Oxford University Press, 1971.

HALL, G. S. Review of G. T. Ladd's *Elements of physiological psychology. American Journal of Psychology*, 1887, *1*, 159–164.

HALL, G. S. *Adolescence* (2 vols.). New York: D. Appleton & Co., 1904.

HALL, G. S. *Senescence: The last half of life*. New York: D. Appleton & Co., 1922.

HALL, G. S. *Life and confessions of a psychologist*. New York: D. Appleton & Co., 1923.

HALLER, A. VON. *Elementa physiologiae corporis humani*. Lausanne: Bousquet et Sociorum, 1757–1766.

HAMILTON, W. *Lectures on metaphysics*. Edinburgh and London: William Blackwood and Sons, 1859.

HARPER, R. A. *The new psychotherapies*. Englewood Cliffs, N.J.: Prentice-Hall, 1975.

HARRIS, B. Whatever happened to little Albert? *American Psychologist,* 1979, *34,* 151–160.

HARROWER, M. A note on the Koffka papers. *Journal of the History of the Behavioral Sciences,* 1971, 7, 141–153.

HARTLEY, D. *Observations on man, his frame, his duty and his expectations.* London: Thomas Tegg & Sons, 1834. (6th ed., 1749).

HARTMANN, G. W. *Gestalt psychology.* New York: Ronald Press, 1935.

HARVEY, E. R. *The inward wits: Psychological theory in the Middle Ages and the Renaissance.* London: Warburg Institute, 1975.

HARVEY, W. *The works of William Harvey, M. D.* (R. Willis, trans.). London: Sydenham Society, 1847.

HAZARD, P. *La pensée européene au XVIIIeme siecle.* Paris: Boivin, 1946. Translated as *European thought in the eighteenth century* (J. L. May, trans.). Gloucester, Mass.: Peter Smith, 1973.

HEAD, H. *Aphasia and kindred disorders of speech* (2 vols). Cambridge University Press, 1926.

HEARNSHAW, L. S. *A short history of British psychology.* London: Methuen, 1964.

HEARNSHAW, L. S. *Cyril Burt: Psychologist.* Ithaca, N.Y.: Cornell University Press, 1979.

HEARST, E. (Ed.). *The first century of experimental psychology.* Hillsdale, N.J.: Lawrence Erlbaum Associates, 1979.

HEBB, D. O. *The organization of behavior.* New York: John Wiley & Sons, 1949.

HELMHOLTZ, H. VON. *Treatise on physiological optics* (3 vols.). (English translations of 3rd edition edited by J. P. C. Southall in three volumes bound as two, 1925.) New York: Dover, 1962. (Originally published, 1856–1866.)

HELMHOLTZ, H. VON. On the physiological causes of harmony in music. In H. von Helmholtz, *Popular scientific lectures.* New York: Dover, 1962. (Originally published, 1857.)

HELMHOLTZ, H. VON. *On the sensations of tone.* New York: Dover, 1954. (Originally published, 1863; English translation of the 4th edition of 1877 with additional notes by A. J. Ellis, 1885.)

HELSON, H. The psychology of *Gestalt. American Journal of Psychology,* 1925, *36,* 342–370, 494–526; 1926, *37,* 25–62, 189–223.

HELSON, H. The fundamental propositions of Gestalt psychology. *Psychological Review,* 1933, *40,* 13–32.

HELSON, H. *Adaptation level theory.* New York: Harper & Row, 1964.

HELVÉTIUS, C. A. *De l'esprit; or, Essays on the mind, and its several faculties.* London: Albion Press, 1810. (Originally published, 1758.)

HELVÉTIUS, C. A. *A treatise on man; his intellectual faculties and his education* (2 vols., W. Hooper, trans.). New York: Burt Franklin, 1969. (Originally published, 1772–1773.)

HENLE, M. Isomorphism: Setting the record straight. *Psychological Research,* 1984, *46,* 317–327.

HENLE, M. E. B. Titchener and the case of the missing element. *Journal of the History of the Behavioral Sciences,* 1974, *10,* 227–237.

HERBART, J. F. *A textbook in psychology* (M. K. Smith, trans.). New York: D. Appleton & Co., 1891. (Originally published, 1816.)

HERBART, J. F. *Psychologie als Wissenschaft neu gegründet auf Erfahrung, Metaphysik und Mathematik.* In K. Kehrbach (Ed.), *J. F. Herbart's sämtliche werke* (Part I is in Vol. 5, 177–434; Part II is in Vol. 6, 1–340). Langensalza: H. Beyer & Söhne, 1892. (Originally published, 1824.)

HERING, K. E. K. *Outlines of a theory of the light sense* (L. M. Hurvich & D. Jameson, trans.). Cambridge, Mass.: Harvard University Press, 1964. (Originally published, 1920.)

HERING, K. E. K. *The theory of binocular vision* (B. Bridgeman & L. Stark, Ed. and trans.). New York: Plenum Press, 1977. (Originally published, 1868.)

HERRNSTEIN, R. J. Behaviorism. In D. L. Krantz (Ed.), *Schools of psychology.* New York: Appleton-Century-Crofts, 1969.

HILGARD, E. R. *Psychology in America: A historical survey.* New York: Harcourt Brace Jovanovich, 1987.

HILGARD, E. R., & BOWER, G. H. *Theories of learning* (3rd ed.) Englewood Cliffs, N.J.: Prentice-Hall, 1966.

HILGARD, E. R., & MARQUIS, D. G. *Conditioning and learning.* New York: Appleton-Century-Crofts, 1940.

HIPPOCRATES. *The genuine works of Hippocrates* (2 vols., F. Adams, trans.). London: Sydenham Society, 1849.

HIPPOLYTUS. The refutation of all heresies. In *The Ante-Nicene Fathers,* (Vol. 5). Buffalo: Christian Literature Company, 1886.

HISPANO, PEDRO. *Scientia libri de anima.* Consejo Superior de Investigaciones Cientificas, Instituto Filosofico "Luis Vives" (Series A, No. 1). Madrid: Bolanos y Aguilar, S. L., 1941.

HISPANO, PEDRO. *The Summulae Logicales of Peter of Spain* (J. P. Mullaly, trans.). Notre Dame, Ind.: University of Notre Dame Press, 1945.

HOBBES, T. *Leviathan.* In Sir W. Molesworth (Ed.), *The English works of Thomas Hobbes* (Vol. 3). London: John Bohn, 1839. (Originally published, 1651.)

HOBBES, T. *Human nature.* In Sir W. Molesworth (Ed.), *The English works of Thomas Hobbes* (Vol. 4). London: John Bohn, 1840. (Originally published, 1651.)

HOBHOUSE, L. T. *Mind in evolution.* London: Macmillan, 1901.

HOFFMAN, W. C., & DODWELL, P. C. Geometric psychology generates the visual Gestalt. *Canadian Journal of Psychology,* 1985, *39,* 491–528.

D'HOLBACH (PAUL HENRY THIRY). *The system of nature* (H. D. Robinson, trans.). New York: Burt Franklin, 1970. (Originally published, 1770.)

HOPPE, F. Erfolg und Misserfolg. *Psychologische Forschung,* 1931, *14,* 1–62.

HORN, J. M., LOEHLIN, J. C., & WELLERMAN, L. Intellectual resemblance among adoptive and biological relatives: The Texas Adoption Project. *Behavior Genetics,* 1979, *9,* 177–208.

HUARTE, J. *The examination of men's wits.* Gainesville, Fl: Scholar's Facsimiles and Reprints, 1959. (Originally published, 1575; trans. by R. Carew, 1594.)

HUEY, E. B. *The psychology and pedagogy of reading.* New York: Macmillan, 1908.

HULL, C. L. *Principles of behavior.* New York: Appleton-Century-Crofts, 1943.

HULL, C. L. *A behavior system.* New Haven: Yale University Press, 1952.

HULL, C. L., HOVLAND, C. I., ROSS, R. T., HALL, M., PERKINS, D. T., & FITCH, F. B. *Mathematico-deductive theory of rote learning.* New Haven: Yale University Press, 1940.

HUME, D. *A treatise of human nature.* (L. A. Selby-Bigge, Ed.). Oxford: Clarendon Press, 1955. (Originally published, 1739–1740.)

HUME, D. *Enquiry concerning human understanding.* In D. Hume, *Essays and treatises on several subjects* (Vol. 1). Edinburgh: Bell and Bradfute, 1800. (Originally published, 1748.)

HUME. D. *Enquiry concerning principles of morals.* In D. Hume, *Essays and treatises on several subjects* (Vol. 1). Edinburgh: Bell and Bradfute, 1800. (Originally published, 1751.)

HUMPHREY, G. *Thinking: An introduction to its experimental psychology.* London: Methuen & Co.; New York: John Wiley & Sons, 1951.

HUNT, J. McV. *Intelligence and experience.* New York: Ronald Press, 1961.

HURVICH, L. M. Hering and the scientific establishment. *American Psychologist,* 1969, *24,* 497–514.

HURVICH, L. M., and Jameson, D. Some quantitative aspects of an opponent-colors theory. II. Brightness, saturation, and hue in normal and dichromatic vision. *Journal of the Optical Society of America,* 1955, *45,* 602–616.

HUSSERL, E. *Logische Untersuchungen.* Halle: M. Niemeyer, 1900.

INGLIS, J., & LAWSON, J. S. Sex, intelligence and the brain. *Queen's Quarterly,* 1984, *91,* 37–54.

IRWIN, J. R. Galen on the temperaments. *Journal of General Psychology,* 1947, *36,* 45–64.

ITARD, J. M. G. *The wild boy of Aveyron* (G. Humphrey & M. Humphrey, trans.). Englewood Cliffs, N. J.: Prentice-Hall, 1962.

JACKSON, J. H. *Selected writings of John Hughlings Jackson* (2 vols., J. Taylor, Ed.). New York: Basic Books, 1958.

JACKSON, S. W. Melancholia and partial insanity. *Journal of the History of the Behavioral Sciences,* 1983, *19,* 173–184.

JACOBS, J. Experiments on "prehension." *Mind,* 1887, *12,* 75–79.

JAMES, W. On some omissions of introspective psychology. *Mind,* 1884, *9,* 1–26. (The section on structure and function is quoted in James's *Principles of Psychology,* Vol. 1, p. 478). (a)

JAMES, W. What is an emotion? *Mind,* 1884, *9,* 188–205. (b)

JAMES, W. *The principles of psychology* (2 vols.). New York: Dover, 1950. (Originally published, 1890, Henry Holt & Co.)

JAMES, W. *Psychology: Briefer course.* New York: Crowell-Collier Publishing Co., 1962. (Originally published, 1892, Henry Holt & Co.)

JAMES, W. The physical basis of emotion. *Psychological Review,* 1894, *1*, 516–529.

JAMES, W. *Talks to teachers on psychology: And to students on some of life's ideals.* New York: Henry Holt & Co., 1899.

JAMES, W. *The varieties of religious experience.* New York: New American Library, 1958. (Originally published, 1902.)

JASPARS, J. M. F. The task of social psychology: Some historical reflections. *British Journal of Social Psychology,* 1983, *22,* 277–288.

JAYNES, J. The problem of animate motion in the seventeenth century. In M. Henle, J. Jaynes, and J. J. Sullivan (Eds.), *Historical conceptions of psychology.* New York: Springer, 1973.

JAYNES, J. *The origin of consciousness in the breakdown of the bicameral mind.* Boston: Houghton Mifflin, 1977.

JAYNES, J. Consciousness and the voices of the mind. *Canadian Psychology,* 1986, *27,* 128–148.

JAYNES, J., & WOODWARD, W. R. In the shadow of the enlightenment. I. Reimarus against the Epicureans. *Journal of the History of the Behavioral Sciences,* 1974, *10,* 3–15. (a)

JAYNES, J., & WOODWARD, W. R. In the shadow of the enlightenment. II. Reimarus and his theory of drives. *Journal of the History of the Behavioral Sciences,* 1974, *10,* 144–159. (b)

JENKINS, J. J., & PATERSON, D. G. (Eds.). *Studies in individual differences: The search for intelligence.* New York: Appleton-Century-Crofts, Inc., 1961.

JENNINGS, H. S. *Behavior of the lower organisms.* Bloomington: Indiana University Press, 1962. (Originally published, 1906.)

JENSEN, A, R. How much can we boost IQ and scholastic achievement? *Harvard Educational Review,* 1969, *39,* 1–123.

JENSEN, A. R. *Straight talk about mental tests.* New York: Mathuen, 1981.

JENSEN, D. D. Introduction to H. S. Jennings, *Behavior of the lower organisms.* Bloomington: Indiana University Press, 1962.

JOHN OF DAMASCUS. *Exposition of the orthodox faith.* In *The Nicene and Post-Nicene Fathers* (Vol. 9). New York: Scribner's, 1899.

JONCICH, G. *The sane positivist: A biography of Edward L. Thorndike.* Middletown, Conn.: Wesleyan University Press, 1968.

JONES, E. *Sigmund Freud: Life and work* (3 vols). London: Hogarth Press, 1953.

JONES, M. C. The elimination of children's fears. *Journal of Experimental Psychology,* 1924, *7,* 383–390.

JOST, A. Die Assoziationsfertigkeit in ihrer Abhängigkeit von der Verteilung der Wiederholungen. *Zeitschrift für Psychologie,* 1897, *14,* 346–472.

JOST, H., & SONTAG, L. W. The genetic factor in autonomic nervous system function. *Psychosomatic Medicine,* 1944, *6,* 308–310.

JOWETT, B. *The Dialogues of Plato translated into English* (2 vols.). New York: Random House, 1937.

JUDD, C. H. The relation of special training to general intelligence. *Education Review,* 1908, *36,* 28–42.

JUHASZ, J. B. Greek theories of imagination. *Journal of the History of the Behavioral Sciences,* 1971, *7,* 39–58.

JUNG, C. G. *Psychological types* (H. G. Baynes, trans.; revised, R. F. C. Hull). In H. Read, M. Fordham, G. Adler, & W. McGuire (Eds.), *The collected works of C. G. Jung* (Vol. 6). London: Routledge & Kegan Paul, 1971.

JUNG, C. G., FRANZ, M. L. VON, HENDERSON, J. L., JACOBI, J., & JAFFE, A. *Man and his symbols.* London: Aldus Books, 1964.

KAHNEMAN, D., SLOVIC, P., & TVERSKY, A. (Eds.). *Judgments under uncertainty: Heuristics and biases.* Cambridge: Cambridge University Press, 1982.

KALLMANN, F. J. *The genetics of schizophrenia.* New York: Augustin, 1938.

KAMIN, L. J. *The science and politics of I. Q.* Hillsdale, N.J.: Lawrence Erlbaum Associates, 1974.

KANDEL, E. R. Small systems of neurons. *Scientific American,* 1979, *241,* 67–76.

KANT, I. *Critique of pure reason* (J. M. D. Meiklejohn, trans.). New York: Colonial Press, 1900. (Originally published, 1781.)

KANT, I. *Anthropology from a pragmatic point of view* (M. J. Gregor, trans.). The Hague: Martinus Nijhoff, 1974. (Originally published, 1798.)

KANTOR, J. R. *The scientific evolution of psychology* (Vol. 1). Chicago: Principia Press, 1963.

KATZ, D. *Der Aufbau der Farbwelt* (*The world of color,* R. B. MacLeod & C. W. Fox, trans.). London: Kegan Paul, Trench, Trubner & Co., 1935. (Originally published, 1911; 2nd ed., 1930.)

KAZDIN, A. E. *History of behavior modification: Experimental foundations of contemporary research.* Baltimore: University Park Press, 1978.

KELLER, F. S. "Good-bye, teacher . . ." *Journal of Applied Behavior Analysis,* 1968, *1*, 79–89.

KELLEY, H. H. Attribution theory in social psychology. In D. Levine (Ed.), *Nebraska Symposium on Motivation,* 1967, *15*, 192–238.

KELLEY, H. H., & MICHELA, J. L. Attribution theory and research. *Annual Review of Psychology,* 1980, *31*, 457–501.

KEPLER, J. *Ad Vitellionem Paralipomena.* (German translation by F. Plehn as *J. Keplers Grundlagen der geometrischen Optik (im Anschluss an die Optik des Witelo.)* Leipzig: Akademische Verlagsgesellschaft M.B.H., 1922. (Originally published, 1604.)

KEPLER, J. *Dioptrice.* Cambridge: W. Heffer and Sons, 1962. (Originally published, 1610.)

KIESLER, C. A., COLLINS, B. E., & MILLER, N. *Attitude change: A critical analysis of theoretical approaches.* New York: John Wiley & Sons, 1969.

KIMMEL, D. C. *Adulthood and aging* (2nd ed.). New York: John Wiley & Sons, 1980.

KLINE, P. *Fact and fantasy in Freudian theory.* London: Methuen, 1972.

KOCH, S., & LEARY, D. E. (Eds.). *A century of psychology as science.* New York: McGraw-Hill, 1985.

KOFFKA, K. (with F. KENKEL). Beiträge zur Psychologie der Gestalt und Bewegungserlebnisse. *Zeitschrift für Psychologie,* 1913, *67*, 353–449.

KOFFKA, K. *The growth of the mind* (R. M. Ogden, trans.). London: Kegan Paul, Trench, Trubner & Co. Ltd., 1924. (Originally published, 1921.)

KOFFKA, K. Perception: An introduction to the Gestalt-theorie. *Psychological Bulletin,* 1922, *19*, 531–585.

KOFFKA, K. *Principles of Gestalt psychology.* London: Routledge & Kegan Paul, 1935.

KOHLBERG, L. Development of children's orientation towards a moral order. 1. Sequence in the development of moral thoughts. *Vita Humana,* 1963, *6*, 11–36.

KÖHLER, W. Nachweis einfacher Strukturfunktionen beim Schimpansen und beim Haushuhn. Über eine neue Methode zur Untersuchung des bunten Farbensystems. *Abhandlungen der königliche Preussische Akademie der Wissenschaften Phys-Math. Klasse,* 1918, Nr 2, 1–101. Excerpts in English in Ellis (1938), pp. 217–227.

KÖHLER, W. Zur Theorie des Suksessivvergleichs und der Zeitfehler. *Psychologische Forschung,* 1923, *4*, 115–175.

KÖHLER, W. *Dynamics in psychology.* London: Faber & Faber, 1942.

KÖHLER, W. *Gestalt psychology.* New York: Liveright Publishing Corp, 1947. (Originally published, 1929.)

KÖHLER, W. *The mentality of apes* (Ella Winter, trans.). London: Penguin, 1957. (Originally published, 1917.)

KÖHLER, W. *The task of Gestalt Psychology.* Princeton, N.J.: Princeton University Press, 1969.

KÖHLER, W., & WALLACH, H. Figural after-effects. *Proceedings of the American Philosophical Society,* 1944, *88*, 269–357.

KONORSKI, J. *Conditioned reflexes and neuron organization* (S. Garry, trans.). Cambridge: Cambridge University Press, 1948.

KORTE, A. Kinematoskopische Untersuchungen. *Zeitschrift für Psychologie,* 1915, *72*, 194–296.

KOVACH, F. J., & SHAHAN, R. W. (Eds.). *Albert the Great: Commemorative essays.* Norman, Oklahoma: University of Oklahoma Press, 1980.

KRAFFT-EBING, R. VON. *Psychopathia sexualis.* (C. G. Chaddock, trans.). Philadelphia: F. A. Davis Co., 1928. (Originally published, 1886.)

KRANTZ, D. L., & ALLEN, D. The rise and fall of McDougall's instinct doctrine. *Journal of the History of the Behavioral Sciences,* 1967, *3*, 326–338.

KRISTELLER, P. O. *Renaissance thought.* New York: Harper Torchbooks, 1961.

KROHN, W. O. Faculties in experimental psychology at the various German universities. *American Journal of Psychology,* 1892, *4*, 585–594.

KROHN, W. O. The laboratory of the Psychological Institute at the University of Göttingen. *American Journal of Psychology,* 1893, *5*, 282–284.

KÜBLER-ROSS, E. *On death and dying.* New York: Macmillan, 1969.

KUDER, G. F. *Kuder Preference Record—Vocational.* Chicago: Science Research Associates, 1934–1956.

KÜLPE, O. *Grundriss der Psychologie (Outlines of psychology,* E. B. Titchener, trans.). New York: Macmillan, 1895.

KÜLPE, O. *Vorlesungen über Psychologie.* Leipzig: S. Hirzel, 1920.

KUO, Z. Y. Ontogeny of embryonic behavior in *aves:* III. The structural environmental factors in embryonic behavior. *Journal of Comparative Psychology,* 1932, *13,* 245–271.

LADD, G. T. *Elements of physiological psychology.* New York: Scribner's, 1887. Rev. ed., G. T. Ladd & R. S. Woodworth, New York: Scribner's, 1911.

LA FORGE, L. de. *Traité de l'esprit de l'homme.* In P. Clair (Ed.), *Oeuvres philosophiques.* Paris: Presses Universitaires de France, 1974. (Originally published, 1665.)

LAMBERT, W. G. *Babylonian wisdom literature.* Oxford: Oxford University Press, 1960.

LA METTRIE, J. O. DE. *Traité de l'âme.* In M. Tisserand (Ed.), *La Mettrie: Textes choisis.* Paris: Editions sociales, 1954. (Originally published, 1745.)

LA METTRIE, J. O. DE. *Man a machine.* (G. C. Bussey, trans.; revised by M. W. Calkins). Chicago: Open Court Publishing Co., 1927.

LANGE, C. G., & JAMES, W. The emotions. In K. Dunlap (Ed.), *The emotions.* Baltimore: Williams and Wilkins Co., 1922.

LANGE, L. Neue Experimente über den Vorgang der einfachen Reaction auf Sinnesein-drücke. I. *Philosophische Studien,* 1888, *4,* 479–510.

LAPOINTE, F. H. Who originated the term "psychology"? *Journal of the History of the Behavioral Sciences,* 1972, *8,* 328–335.

LASHLEY, R. S. *Brain mechanisms and intelligence.* Chicago: University of Chicago Press, 1929.

LASHLEY, K. S. In search of the engram. In F. A. Beach, D. O. Hebb, C. T. Morgan, & H. W. Nissen (Eds.), *The neuropsychology of Lashley.* New York: McGraw-Hill, 1960.

LATANÉ, B., & DARLEY, J. M. *The unresponsive bystander: Why doesn't he help?* Englewood Cliffs, N.J.: Prentice-Hall, 1970.

LAUENSTEIN, O. Ansatz zu einer physiologischen Theorie des Vergleichs und der Zeitfehler. *Psychologische Forschung,* 1933, *17,* 130–177.

LAVATER, J. C. *Essays on physiognomy* (T. Holcroft, trans.). London: Ward, Lock & Co., n.d. (Originally published, 1775–1778.)

LAVER, A. B. Precursors of psychology in ancient Egypt. *Journal of the History of the Behavioral Sciences,* 1972, *8,* 181–195.

LAYCOCK, T. *Mind and brain: or, the correlations of consciousness and organization; with their applications to philosophy, zoology, physiology, mental pathology, and the practice of medicine.* Edinburgh: Sutherland and Knox, 1860. Reprinted New York: Arno Press, 1976.

LEAHEY, T. H. The mistaken mirror: On Wundt's and Titchener's psychologies. *Journal of the History of the Behavioral Sciences,* 1981, *17,* 273–282.

LEAHEY, T. H. *A history of psychology: Main currents in psychological thought* (2nd ed.). Engle-wood Cliffs, N.J.: Prentice-Hall, 1987.

LEARY, D. E. The philosophical development of the conception of psychology in Germany, 1780–1850. *Journal of the History of the Behavioral Sciences,* 1978, *14,* 113–121.

LEARY, D. E. The historical foundation of Herbart's mathematization of psychology. *Journal of the History of the Behavioral Sciences,* 1980, *16,* 150–163.

LE BON, G. *The crowd.* London: Ernest Benn Ltd., 1952. (Originally published, 1895.)

LE BON, G. *The psychology of peoples: Its influence on their evolution.* New York: Arno Press, 1974. (Originally published, 1895.)

LEHRMAN, D. S. A critique of Konrad Lorenz's theory of instinctive behavior. *Quarterly Review of Biology,* 1953, *28,* 337–363.

LEIBNIZ, G. W. *New essays concerning human understanding* (A. G. Langley, trans.). La Salle, Ill.: Open Court Publishing Company, 1949. (1700–1705; first published in 1765.)

LEVI, A. *French moralists: The theory of the passions, 1585 to 1649.* Oxford: Clarendon Press, 1964.

LEWES, G. H. *The life and work of Goethe.* London: J. M. Dent & Sons Ltd. (Everyman's Library), 1930. (Originally published, 1855.)

LEWES, G. M. *Problems of life and mind.* London: Trubner & Co., 1872–1879.

LEWIN, K. *Principles of topological psychology.* New York: McGraw-Hill, 1936.

LIDDELL, E. G. T. *The discovery of reflexes.* Oxford: Clarendon Press, 1960.

LIDDELL, H. S. The experimental neurosis and the problem of mental disorder. *American Journal of Psychiatry,* 1938, *94,* 1035–1042.

LIEBERT, R. M., WICKS-NELSON, R., & KAIL, R. V. *Developmental psychology* (4th ed.). Englewood Cliffs, N.J.: Prentice-Hall, 1986.

LINDBERG, D. C. *John Pecham and the science of optics: Perspectiva communis.* Madison: University of Wisconsin Press, 1970.

LINDBERG, D. C. *Theories of vision from Al-kindi to Kepler.* Chicago: University of Chicago Press, 1976.

LOCKE, J. *An essay concerning human understanding* (2 vols.). London: J. M. Dent & Sons Ltd., 1961. (Originally published, 1690.)

LOEB, J. The significance of tropisms for psychology. In J. Loeb, *The mechanistic conception of life.* Cambridge, Mass.: Belknap Press of Harvard University Press, 1964. (Originally published, 1909.)

LOTZE, R. H. *Medicinische Psychologie oder Physiologie der Seele.* Leipzig: Weidmann, 1852.

LOTZE, R. H. *Outlines of psychology* (G. T. Ladd, trans.). Boston: Ginn & Co., 1886.

LUBBOCK, J. *Ants, bees and wasps.* London: Kegan Paul, Trench & Co., 1882.

LUCE, A. A. *Berkeley and Malebranche: A study in the origins of Berkeley's thought.* Oxford: Clarendon Press, 1934.

LUCHINS, A. J. Mechanization in problem solving: The effect of *Einstellung. Psychological Monographs,* 1942, *54,* 6 (Whole No. 248).

LUCHINS, A. S., & LUCHINS, E. H. *Wertheimer's seminars revisited: Problem solving and thinking.* Albany: Faculty-Student Association, State University of New York at Albany, 1970.

LUCRETIUS. *De rerum natura* (R. C. Trevelyan, trans.). Cambridge: University Press, 1937.

MACALPINE, I., & HUNTER, R. *George III and the mad-business.* London: Allen Lane, Penguin Press, 1969.

MACH, E. *Contributions to the analysis of the sensations* (C. M. Williams, trans.). Chicago: Open Court Publishing Co., 1897. (Originally published, 1886.)

MAHLER, V. Ersatzhandlungen verschiedenen Realitätsgrades. *Psychologische Forschung,* 1933, *18,* 26–89.

MAIER, N. R. F. *Frustration: The study of behavior without a goal.* Ann Arbor: University of Michigan Press, 1949.

MALCOLM, J. *In the Freud archives.* New York: Knopf, 1984.

MALEBRANCHE, N. *De la recherche de la vérité.* In *Oeuvres de Malebranche* (Vol. 2). Paris: Charpentier, 1855. (Originally published, 1674.)

MANDLER, G. Emotion. In E. Hearst (Ed.), *The first century of experimental psychology.* Hillsdale, N.J.: Lawrence Erlbaum Associates, 1979.

MANDLER, J. M., & MANDLER, G. The diaspora of experimental psychology: The Gestaltists and others. In D. Fleming & B. Bailyn (Eds.), *The intellectual migration: Europe and America, 1930–1960.* Cambridge, Mass.: Harvard University Press, 1968.

MARBE, K. *Experimentell-psychologische Untersuchungen über das Urteil: Eine Einleitung in die Logik.* Leipzig: W. Engelmann, 1901.

MARROW, A. J. *The practical theorist: The life and work of Kurt Lewin.* New York: Basic Books, 1969.

MARSHALL, M. E. Gustav Fechner, Dr. Mises, and the comparative anatomy of angels. *Journal of the History of the Behavioral Sciences,* 1969, *5,* 39–58.

MARSHALL, M. E. G. T. Fechner: Premises toward a general theory of organisms (1823). *Journal of the History of the Behavioral Sciences,* 1974, *10,* 438–447.

MARSHALL, M. E. Physics, metaphysics and Fechner's psychophysics. In W. R. Woodward and M. G. Ash (Eds.), *The problematic science: Psychology in nineteenth-century thought.* New York: Praeger, 1982.

MARTINEZ, J. A. Galileo on primary and secondary qualities. *Journal of the History of the Behavioral Sciences,* 1974, *10,* 160–169.

MASLOW, A. H. *Toward a psychology of being* (2nd ed.). New York: Van Nostrand Reinhold, 1968.

MASSERMAN, J. H. *Behavior and neurosis: An experimental psychoanalytic approach to psychobiologic principles.* Chicago: University of Chicago Press, 1943.

MASSON, J. M. *The assault on truth: Freud's suppression of the seduction theory.* New York: Farrar, Straus & Giroux, 1984. Published with a new preface and afterword, Penguin Books, 1985.

MASSON, J. M. (Trans. and Ed.). *The complete letters of Sigmund Freud to Wilhelm Fliess 1887–*

1904. Cambridge, Mass.: The Belknap Press of Harvard University Press, 1985.

MASSON, J. M. *A dark science: Women, sexuality and psychiatry in the nineteenth century*. New York: Farrar, Straus & Giroux, 1986.

MASTERS, W. H., and JOHNSON, V. E. *Human sexual response*. Boston: Little, Brown, 1966.

MATARAZZO, J. D. *Wechsler's Measurement and appraisal of adult intelligence* (5th and enlarged ed.). Baltimore: Williams & Wilkins, 1972.

MAUDSLEY, H. *The physiology and pathology of the mind*. In D. N. Robinson (Ed.), *Significant contributions to the history of psychology, 1750–1920* (Series C, Vol. 4). Washington, D.C.: University Publications of America, 1977.

MAYER, A., & ORTH, J. Zur qualitativen Untersuchung der Associationen. *Zeitschrift für Psychologie*, 1901, *26*, 1–13.

MCARTHUR, L. A. The how and what of why: Some determinants and consequences of causal attribution. *Journal of Personality and Social Psychology*, 1972, *22*, 171–193.

MCCLELLAND, D. C. *The achieving society*. New York: D. Van Nostrand, 1961.

MCCLELLAND, J. L., & RUMELHART, D. E. *Parallel distributed processing: Explorations in the microstructure of cognition*. Vol. 2. *Psychological and biological models*. Cambridge, Mass.: MIT Press, 1986.

MCDERMOTT, J. J. *The writings of William James*. New York: Random House, 1967.

MCDOUGALL, W. *Social psychology*. London: Methuen & Co., 1908. (This work went into a 22nd ed. in 1931).

MCGEOCH, J. A. *The psychology of human learning*. New York: Longmans, Green, 1942.

MCHENRY, L. C. *Garrison's history of neurology*. Springfield, Ill: Chas. C Thomas, 1969.

MCRAE, R. *Leibniz: Perception, apperception and thought*. Toronto: University of Toronto Press, 1976.

MCREYNOLDS, P. The motivational psychology of Jeremy Bentham: I. Background and general approach. *Journal of the History of the Behavioral Sciences*, 1968, *4*, 230–244. (a)

MCREYNOLDS, P. The motivational psychology of Jeremy Bentham: II. Efforts towards quantification and classification. *Journal of the History of the Behavioral Sciences*, 1968, *4*, 349–364 (b)

MEAD, G. H. *Mind, self and society: From the standpoint of a social behaviorist*. Chicago: University of Chicago Press, 1934.

MEINONG, A. Zur Psychologie der Komplexionen und Relationen. *Zeitschrift für Psychologie* 1891, *2*, 245–265.

MELTON, A. W., & VON LACKUM, W. J. Retroactive and proactive inhibition in retention: Evidence for a two-factor theory of retroactive inhibition. *American Journal of Psychology*, 1941, *54*, 157–173.

MERCIER, CARDINAL. *The origins of contemporary psychology*. New York: P. J. Kenedy & Sons, 1918.

MESSER, A. Experimentell-psychologische Untersuchungen über das Denken. *Archiv für die gesamte Psychologie*, 1906, *8*, 1–224.

MESSER, A. *Psychologie*. Stuttgart & Berlin: Deutsche Verlagsanstalt, 1914.

METZGER, W., & ERKE, H. (Eds.). *Allgemeine Psychologie* (Vol. 1). Göttingen: Verlag für Psychologie Dr. C. J. Hogrefe, 1966.

MEUMANN, E. *The psychology of Learning* (J. W. Baird, trans.). New York: D. Appleton and Co., 1913. (Originally published, 1903.)

MICHAUD-QUANTIN, P. *La psychologie de l'activité chez Albert le Grand*. Paris: J. Vrin, 1966.

MICHOTTE, A. *The perception of causality* (1946) (T. R. Miles & E. Miles, trans.). London: Methman & Co. Ltd., 1963. (Originally published, 1946.)

MILGRAM, S. *Obedience to authority*. New York: Harper & Row, 1974.

MILL, JAMES. *Analysis of the phenomena of the human mind* (New ed. with notes by A. Bain, A. Findlater, & G. Grote. Edited with additional notes by J. S. Mill). London: Longmans, Green, Reader, and Dyer, 1869.

MILL, J. S. *A system of logic*. London: Longmans, Green, 1893.

MILL, J. S. *An examination of Sir William Hamilton's philosophy* (6th ed.). London: Longmans, Green, 1889. (Original ed., 1865.)

MILL, J. S. *Autobiography*. New York: Columbia University Press, 1960. (Originally published, 1873.)

MILLER, N. E. Experimental studies of conflict. In J. M. Hunt (Ed.), *Personality and the behavior disorders*. New York: Ronald Press, 1944.

MILLS, E. S. *George Trumbull Ladd, pioneer American psychologist.* Cleveland: Press of Case Western Reserve University, 1969.

MILLS, W. *The nature and development of animal intelligence.* London: T. Fisher Unwin, 1898.

MILLS, W. The nature of animal intelligence and the methods of investigating it. *Psychological Review,* 1899, *6,* 262–274.

MISCHEL, T. Wundt and the conceptual foundations of psychology. *Philosophy and Phenomenological Research,* 1970–1971, *31,* 1–26.

MORA, G. Book review of Huarte, J. *The examination of men's wits (1575). Journal of the History of the Behavioral Sciences,* 1977, *13,* 67–78.

MORA, G. Mind-body concepts in the Middle Ages: Part I. The classical background and its merging with Judeo-Christian tradition in the early Middle Ages. *Journal of the History of the Behavioral Sciences,* 1978, *14,* 344–361.

MORGAN, C. L. *Animal life and intelligence* (revised as *Animal Behavior).* London: Edward Arnold, 1900. (Originally published, 1890–1891.)

MORGAN, C. L. *An introduction to comparative psychology* (2nd ed.). London: Walter Scott Publishing Co., 1909.

MORGAN, C. L. *Habit and instinct.* London: Edward Arnold, 1896.

MORGAN, C. T. *Physiological psychology.* New York: McGraw-Hill, 1943.

MORGAN, M. J. *Molyneux's question: Vision, touch, and the philosophy of perception.* Cambridge, Mass.: Cambridge University Press, 1977.

MORRIS, J. Pattern recognition in Descartes' automata. *Isis,* 1969, *60,* 451–460.

MOUNTJOY, P. T., BOS, J. H., DUNCAN, M. D., & VERPLANK, R. B. Falconry: Neglected aspect of the history of psychology. *Journal of the History of the Behavioral Sciences,* 1969, *5,* 59–67.

MÜLLER, G. E. *Die Gesichtspunkte und die Tatsachen der psychophysischen Methodik.* Printed separately. Wiesbaden: J. F. Bergmann, 1904.

MÜLLER, G. E. Zur Analyse der Gedächtnistätigkeit und des Vorstellungsverlaufes. Part I: *Zeitschrift für Psychologie, Ergänzungsband* No. 5, 1911; Part III: No. 8, 1913; Part II: No. 9, 1917.

MÜLLER, G. E. Über die Farbenempfindungen: Psychophysische Untersuchungen, I and II. *Zeitschrift für Psychologie, Ergänzungsbande* Nos. 17 and 18, 1930.

MÜLLER, G. E., & PILZECKER, A. Experimentelle Beiträge zur Lehre vom Gedächtniss. *Zeitschrift für Psychologie, Ergänzungsband* No. I, 1900.

MÜLLER, G. E., & SCHUMANN, F. Experimentelle Beiträge zur Untersuchung des Gedächtnisses. *Zeitschrift für Psychologie,* 1893, *6,* 81–190, 257–339.

MÜLLER, J. *Handbuch der Physiologie des Menschen für Vorlesungen.* Coblenz: J. Holscher, 1833–1840.

MÜNSTERBERG, H. *On the witness stand: Essays on psychology and crime.* New York: McClure, 1908.

MÜNSTERBERG, H. *Psychology and industrial efficiency.* Boston: Houghton Mifflin, 1913.

MÜNSTERBERG, H. *Psychology and social sanity.* New York: Doubleday, Page & Co., 1914.

MÜNSTERBERG, H. *The film: A psychological study.* New York: Dover, 1970. (Originally published as *The photoplay: A psychological study,* 1916.)

MÜNSTERBERG, M. *Hugo Münsterberg: His life and work.* New York: Appleton, 1922.

MURDOCK, B. B., JR. A theory for the storage and retrieval of item and associative information. *Psychological Review,* 1982, *89,* 609–626.

MURPHY, G. William James on the will. *Journal of the History of the Behavioral Sciences,* 1971, *7,* 249–260.

MURPHY, G., & KOVACH, J. K. *Historical introduction to modern psychology* (3rd ed.). New York: Harcourt Brace Jovanovich, 1972.

MURPHY, G., MURPHY, L. B., & NEWCOMB, T. M. *Experimental social psychology.* New York: Harper & Brothers, 1937.

MURRAY, D. J. Research on human memory in the nineteenth century. *Canadian Journal of Psychology,* 1976, *30,* 201–220.

MURRAY, D. J. The role of speech responses in short-term memory. *Canadian Journal of Psychology,* 1967, *2,* 1263–1276.

MURRAY, D. J. A perspective for viewing the integration of probability theory into psychology. In L. K. üger, G. Gigerenzer & M. S. Morgan (Eds.), *The probabilistic revolution.* Vol. 2: *Ideas in the sciences.* Cambridge, Mass.: MIT Press, 1987.

MURRAY, D. J., & ROSS, H. E. Vives (1538) on memory and recall. *Canadian Psychology,* 1982, *23,* 22–31.

MURRAY, H. A. *Explorations in personality: A clinical and experimental study of fifty men of college age.* New York: Oxford University Press, 1938.

MUSCIO, B. *Lectures on industrial psychology.* Sydney: Angus and Robertson, 1917.

MUSSEN, P. H., CONGER, J. J., & KAGAN, J. *Child development and personality* (5th ed.). New York: Harper & Row, 1979.

MYERS, C. S. *A text-book of experimental psychology.* Cambridge: Cambridge University Press, 1909.

MYERS, F. W. H. *Human personality and its survival of bodily death* (2 vols.). New York: Longmans, Green & Co., 1903.

MYERS, G. E. *William James: His life and thought.* New Haven: Yale University Press, 1986.

NAHM, M. C. *Selections from early Greek philosophy* (4th ed.). Englewood Cliffs, N.J.: Prentice-Hall, 1964.

NEISSER, U. *Cognitive psychology.* Englewood Cliffs, N.J.: Prentice-Hall, 1967.

NEISSER, U. *Memory observed: Remembering in natural contexts.* San Francisco: W. H. Freeman, 1982.

NEISSER, U. Toward an ecologically oriented cognitive science. In T. M. Schlecter & M. P. Toglia (Eds.), *New directions in cognitive science.* Norwood, N.J.: Ablex, 1984.

NEMESIUS (see TELFER, W.)

NEWELL, A., & SIMON, H. A. *Human problem solving.* Englewood Cliffs, N.J.: Prentice Hall, 1972.

NEWTON, I. *Opticks.* New York: Dover, 1952. (Originally published, 1704.)

NEWTON, I. *The mathematical principles of natural philosophy.* New York: Citadel Press, 1964. (Originally published, 1687.)

NOBLE, C. E. Measurements of association value (a), rated associations (a′) and scaled meaningfulness (m′) for the 2100 CVC combinations of the English alphabet. *Psychological Reports,* 1961, *8,* 487–521.

OATES, W. J. (Ed.). *Basic writings of Saint Augustine* (Vol. 1). New York: Random House, 1948.

OEHRN, A. Experimentelle Studien zur individual Psychologie. *Psychologische Arbeiten,* 1895, *1,* 92–151.

O'DONNELL, J. M. *The origins of behaviorism: American psychology, 1870–1920.* New York: New York University Press, 1985.

O'LEARY, DE L. *How Greek science passed to the Arabs.* London: Routledge & Kegan Paul, 1949.

ORIGEN. *On first principles* (G. W. Butterworth, Ed.). New York: Harper & Row, 1966.

OSGOOD, C. E. The nature and measurement of meaning. *Psychological Bulletin,* 1952, *49,* 197–237.

OSGOOD, C. E., & HEYER, A. W. A new interpretation of figural aftereffects. *Psychological Review,* 1951, *59,* 98–118.

OWEN, A. R. G. *Hysteria, hypnosis and healing: The work of J.-M. Charcot.* New York: Garrett Publications, 1971.

PAIVIO, A. *Imagery and verbal processes.* New York: Holt, Rinehart & Winston, 1971.

PAIVIO, A. *Mental representations: A dual encoding approach.* New York: Oxford University Press, 1986.

PARSONS, F. *Choosing a vocation.* New York: Agathon Press, 1967. (Originally published, 1909.)

PASTORE, N. William James: A contradiction. *Journal of the History of the Behavioral Sciences,* 1977, *13,* 126–130.

PAVLOV, I. P. *The work of the digestive glands* (W. H. Thompson, trans.). London: Charles Griffin & Co., 1910. (Originally published, 1897.)

PAVLOV, I. P. *Selected works* (S. Belsky, trans.). Moscow: Foreign Language Publishing House, 1955.

PAVLOV, I. P. *Conditioned reflexes* (G. V. Anrep, trans.). New York: Dover, 1960. (Originally published, 1927.)

PEARSON, K. *The life, letters, and labours of Francis Galton* (3 vols. in 4). Cambridge: Cambridge University Press, 1914–1930.

PERRY, R. W. *The thought and character of William James* (2 vols.). London: Humphrey Milford; New York: Oxford University Press, 1935.

PETERS, F. E. *Greek philosophical terms: A historical lexicon.* New York: New York University Press, 1967.

PFUNGST, O. *Clever Hans: The horse of Mr. van Osten* (Carl C. Rahn, trans.). New York: Holt, Rinehart & Winston, 1965. (Originally published, 1907).

PINEL, P. *A treatise on insanity* (D. D. Davis, trans.). New York: Hafner Publishing Co., 1962. (Originally published, 1801.)

PLATO (see JOWETT, B.)

PLINY THE ELDER. *Natural History* (10 vols.). The Loeb Classical Library. London: William Heinemann, 1938–1963.

PLISKOFF, S. S. Antecedents to Fechner's Law: The astronomers J. Herschel, W. R. Davies and N. R. Pogson. *Journal of the Experimental Analysis of Behavior,* 1977, *28,* 185–187.

POFFENBERGER, A. T. *Principles of applied psychology.* New York: D. Appleton-Century Co., 1942.

POPKIN, R. H. *The history of scepticism from Erasmus to Descartes.* Assen, Netherlands: Koninklijke Van Gorcum & Comp., 1960.

PORTERFIELD, W. *A treatise on the eye, the manner and phaenomena of vision.* Edinburgh: printed for A. Miller of London, and for G. Hamilton and J. Balfour at Edinburgh, 1759.

POSNER, M. I., & SHULMAN, G. L. Cognitive science. In E. Hearst (Ed.), *The first century of experimental psychology.* Hillsdale, N.J.: Lawrence Erlbaum Associates, 1979.

POSNER, M. I., & SNYDER, C. R. R. Attention and cognitive control. In R. Solso (Ed.), *Information processing and cognition: The Loyola Symposium.* Hillsdale, N.J.: Lawrence Erlbaum Associates, 1975.

POST, D. Floyd H. Allport and the launching of modern social psychology. *Journal of the History of the Behavioral Sciences,* 1980, *16,* 369–376.

PREMACK, D. *Intelligence in ape and man.* Hillsdale, N.J.: Lawrence Erlbaum Associates, 1976.

PREYER, W. *Die Seele des Kindes* (1882). Translated by H. W. Brown as *Mind of the child* (2 vols.). New York: D. Appleton & Co., 1909.

PRIBRAM, K. H. What is iso and what is morphic in isomorphism? *Psychological Research,* 1984, *46,* 329–332.

PRIESTLEY, J. *The history and present state of discoveries relating to vision, light and colors.* London: Printed for J. Johnson, 1772.

PRITCHARD, JAMES B. *The ancient Near East: An anthology of text and pictures.* Princeton, N.J.: Princeton University Press, Vol. 1, 1958. Vol. 2, 1975.

PROCHASKA, G. (see UNZER, J. A.)

PYLYSHYN, Z. W. *Computation and cognition: Toward a foundation for cognitive science.* Cambridge, Mass.: MIT Press (Bradford Books), 1984.

QUINTILIAN. *Institutes of oratory* (2 vols., J. S. Watson, trans.). London: George Bell & Sons, 1899.

RADNER, D. Descartes' notion of the union of mind and body. *Journal of the History of Philosophy,* 1971, *9,* 159–170.

RAHMAN, F. *Avicenna's psychology.* London: Oxford University Press, 1952.

RAHMANI, L. *Soviet psychology.* New York: International Universities Press, 1973.

RAMUL, K. Some early measurements and ratings in psychology. *American Psychologist,* 1963, *18,* 633–659.

RAPHAEL, B. *The thinking computer: Mind inside matter.* San Francisco: W. H. Freeman & Co., 1976.

RATLIFF, F. *Mach bands.* San Francisco: Holden Day, 1965.

RAUE, G. *The elements of psychology on the principles of Beneke* (4th edition, altered, improved, and enlarged by J. G. Dressler; trans. from the German). Oxford and London: James Parker and Co., 1871.

REID, T. *Inquiry into the human mind* (1764); *Essays on the intellectual powers of man* (1785); *Essays on the active powers of the human mind* (1788). All in Sir William Hamilton (Ed.), *The works of Thomas Reid* (3rd ed.). Edinburgh: Maclachlan and Stewart, 1852.

RESTLE, F., & GREENO, J. G. *Introduction to mathematical psychology.* Menlo Park, Calif.: Addison-Wesley, 1970.

RESTORFF, H. VON. Über die Wirkung von Bereichsbildungen in Spurenfeld. *Psychologische Forschung,* 1933, *18,* 294–342.

Rhetorica ad Herennium (ascribed to Cicero, M. Caplan, trans.). The Loeb Classical Library. London: William Heinemann, 1958.

RIBOT, T. *Diseases of Memory* (W. H. Smith, trans.). In D. N. Robinson (Ed.), *Significant contributions to the history of psychology 1750–1920* (Series E, Vol. 1). Washington. D.C.: University Publications of America, 1977. (Originally published, 1881.)

RICHARDS, R. J. Christian Wolff's prolegomena to empirical and rational psychology: Translation and commentary. *Proceedings of the American Philosophical Society*, 1980, *124*, 227–239. (a)

RICHARDS, R. J. Wundt's early theories of unconscious inference and cognitive evolution in their relation to Darwinian biopsychology. In W. G. Bringmann & R. D. Tweney (Eds.), *Wundt studies*. Toronto: C. J. Hogrefe, 1980. (b)

RIEBER, R. W. (Ed.) *Wilhelm Wundt and the making of a scientific psychology*. New York/London: Plenum Press, 1980.

RILEY, D. A. Memory for form. In L. Postman (Ed.), *Psychology in the making*. New York: Knopf, 1962.

RIVERS, W. H. R., & HEAD, H. A human experiment in nerve-division. *Brain*, 1908, *31*, 323–450.

ROBERTS, A., & DONALDSON, J. (Eds.). *The Ante-Nicene Fathers* (9 vols.). Buffalo: Christian Literature Publishing Co., 1885–1896. See also: *A select library of the Nicene and Post-Nicene Fathers of the Christian Church*, 1st series (ed. P. Schaff), New York: The Christian Literature Co., 1886–1890; 2nd series (eds. P. Schaff and H. Wace), 1890–1900.

ROBINSON, D. N. *An intellectual history of psychology* (rev. ed.). New York: Macmillan, 1981.

ROBINSON, E. S. *Association theory today: An essay in systematic psychology*. New York: Appleton-Century-Crofts, 1932.

ROBINSON, T. M. *Plato's psychology*. Toronto: University of Toronto Press, 1970.

ROCK, I. The role of repetition in associative learning. *American Journal of Psychology*, 1957, *70*, 186–193.

ROGERS, C. R. *Client-centered therapy*. Boston: Houghton Mifflin, 1951.

ROGERS, C. R. (Ed.). *The therapeutic relationship and its impact: A study of psychotherapy with schizophrenics*. Madison: University of Wisconsin Press, 1967.

ROMANES, G. J. *Animal intelligence*. London: Kegan Paul, Trench & Co., 1882.

ROMANES, G. J. *Mental evolution in man*. London: Kegan Paul, Trench & Co., 1888.

ROMANES, G. J. *Mental evolution in animals*. New York: AMS Press, 1969. (Originally published, 1883.)

RORSCHACH, H. *Psychodiagnostics* (4th ed.). New York: Grine and Shalton, 1942.

ROSENFIELD, L. C. *From beast-machine to man-machine*. New York: Octagon Books, 1968.

ROSS, D. G. *Stanley Hall: The psychologist as prophet*. Chicago: The University of Chicago Press, 1972.

RUBIN, E. *Synsoplevede Figurer* (trans. into German as *Visuell wahrgenommene Figuren*). Copenhagen: Gyldendalsde Boghandel, 1921.

RUDMIN, F. William McDougall in the history of social psychology. *British Journal of Social Psychology*, 1985, *24*, 75–76.

RUMELHART, D. E., & McCLELLAND, J. L. *Parallel distributed processing: Explorations in the microstructure of cognition*. Vol. 1. *Foundations*. Cambridge, Mass.: MIT Press, 1986.

RUSH, B. *Medical inquiries and observations upon the diseases of the mind*. New York: Hafner Publishing Co., 1962. (Originally published, 1812.)

RUSSELL, B. *A critical exposition of the philosophy of Leibniz*. London: George Allen & Unwin, 1900.

RUSSELL, B. *A history of Western philosophy*. New York: Simon & Schuster, 1945.

SAHAKIAN, W. S. *History and systems of psychology*. New York: John Wiley, 1975.

SALAMON, E. D., & ROBINSON, B. W. *Gender roles: Doing what comes naturally*. Methuen, 1987.

SARNOFF, I. *Testing Freudian concepts: An experimental social approach*. New York: Springer, 1971.

SCHACTER, D. L. *Stranger behind the engram: Theories of memory and the psychology of science*. Hillsdale, N.J.: Lawrence Erlbaum Associates, 1982.

SCHACHTER, S. Deviation, rejection, and communication. *Journal of Abnormal and Social Psychology*, 1951, *46*, 190–207.

SCHACHTER, S. *The psychology of affiliation*. Stanford, Calif.: Stanford University Press, 1959.

SCHACHTER, S., & SINGER, J. E. Cognitive, social and physiological determinants of emotional state. *Psychological Review,* 1962, *69,* 379–399.

SCHEERER, E. Motor theories of cognitive structure: A historical review. In W. Prinz & A. F. Sanders (Eds.), *Cognition and motor processes.* Heidelberg: Springer, 1984.

SCHNEIDER, W., & SHIFFRIN, R. M. Controlled and automatic human information processing: I. Detection, search and attention. *Psychological Review,* 1977, *84,* 1–66.

SCHÜLING, H. *Bibliographisches Handbuch zur Geschichte der Psychologie des 17. Jahrhundert.* Giessen: Universitätsbibliothek, 1964.

SCHÜLING, H. *Bibliographie der psychologischen Literatur des 16. Jahrhunderts.* Hildesheim: Georg Olms, 1967.

SCHUMANN, F. Über das Gedächtnis für Komplexe regelmässig aufeinander folgender gleicher Schalleindrucke. *Zeitschrift für Psychologie,* 1890, *1,* 75–80.

SCOT, R. *The discoverie of witchcraft.* Carbondale, Ill.: Southern Illinois University Press, 1964. (Originally published, 1584.)

SCOTT, J. F. *The scientific work of René Descartes .* London: Taylor & Francis, 1952.

SCOTT, W. D. *The psychology of advertising.* Boston: Small Maynard, 1908.

SCRIPTURE, E. W. *The new psychology.* New York: Scribner's, 1897.

SEAGOE, M. V. *Terman and the gifted.* Los Altos, Calif.: W. Kaufmann, 1975.

SEARS, R. R. *Survey of objective studies of psychoanalytic concepts.* New York: Social Science Research Council, 1943.

Secreta Secretorum (three prose versions). Early English Text Society, Extra Series, No. 74. London: Kegan Paul, Trench, Trubner & Co., 1898.

SECHENOV, I. M. *Reflexes of the brain* (S. Belsky, trans.). Cambridge, Mass.: M.I.T. Press, 1965. (Originally published, 1863.) (a)

SECHENOV, I. M. *Autobiographical notes* (K. Hanes, trans.). Washington D.C.: American Institute of Biological Sciences, 1965. (Originally published, 1905.) (b)

SELIGMAN, M. E. P. *Helplessness: On depression, development and death.* San Francisco: W. H. Freeman & Co., 1975.

SELYE, H. *The stress of life* (2nd ed.). New York: McGraw-Hill, 1976.

SHARPE, W. D. Isidore of Seville: The medical writings. *Transactions of the American Philosophical Society,* 1964, Vol. 54, Part 2, pp. 1–75.

SHAW, M. E. A comparison of individuals and small groups in the rational solution of complex problems. *American Journal of Psychology,* 1932, *44,* 491–504.

SHERIF, M. *The psychology of social norms.* New York: Harper & Row, 1936.

SHERRINGTON, C. S. *The integrative action of the nervous system.* New Haven: Yale University Press, 1961. (Originally published, 1906; 2nd ed., 1947.)

SHIELS, D. A cross-cultural study of beliefs in out-of-the-body experiences. *Journal of the Society for Psychical Research,* 1978, *49,* 697–741.

SHIPLEY, T. (Ed.). *Classics in psychology.* New York: Philosophical Library, 1961.

SIEGEL, R. E. *Galen on sense perception.* New York: S. Karger, 1970.

SIEGEL, R. E. *Galen on psychology, psychopathology and function and diseases of the nervous system.* New York: S. Karger, 1973.

SIMON, H. A. Cognitive science: The newest science of the artificial. *Cognitive Science,* 1980, *4,* 33–46.

SINGER, B. R. Robert Hooke on memory, association and time perception. *Notes and Records of the Royal Society of London,* 1976, *31,* 115–131.

SINGER, C. *A short history of anatomy and physiology from the Greeks to Harvey.* New York: Dover, 1957.

SINGER, C. *A short history of scientific ideas to 1900.* Oxford: Clarendon Press, 1959.

SKINNER, B. F. The science of learning and the art of teaching. *Harvard Educational Review,* 1954, *24,* 86–97.

SKINNER, B. F. *Verbal behavior.* Englewood Cliffs, N.J.: Prentice-Hall, 1957.

SKINNER, B. F. *The behavior of organisms.* Englewood Cliffs, N.J.: Prentice-Hall, 1966. (Originally published, 1938.)

SKINNER, B. F. Cognitive science and behaviorism. *British Journal of Psychology,* 1985, *76,* 291–301.

SKODAK, M., & SKEELS, H. A final follow-up study of children in adoptive homes. *Journal of Genetic Psychology,* 1949, *75,* 85–125.

SLATER, E., & COWIE, V. *The genetics of mental disorders.* London: Oxford University Press, 1971.

SMALL, W. S. Notes on the psychic development of the white rat. *American Journal of Psychology,* 1899, *11,* 80–100.

SMALL, W. S. An experimental study of the mental processes of the rat. *American Journal of Psychology,* 1900, *11,* 131–165. (a)

SMALL, W. S. Experimental study of the mental processes of the rat, II. *American Journal of Psychology,* 1900, *12,* 206–239. (b).

SMITH, J. A., & ROSS, W. D. (Eds.). *The works of Aristotle translated into English* (12 vols.). Oxford: Clarendon Press, 1910–1952.

SOKAL, M. M. The unpublished autobiography of James McKeen Cattell. *American Psychologist,* 1971, *26,* 626–635.

SOKAL, M. (Ed.). *An education in psychology: James McKeen Cattell's journal and letters from Germany and England, 1880–1888.* Cambridge, Mass.: MIT Press, 1981.

SOLMSEN, F. Greek philosophy and the discovery of the nerves. *Museum Helveticum,* 1961, *18,* 150–167, 169–197.

SPALDING, D. A. On instinct. *Nature,* 1872, *6,* 485–486.

SPALDING, D. A. Instinct and acquisition. *Nature,* 1875, *12,* 507–508.

SPEARMAN, C. E. "General intelligence," objectively determined and measured. *American Journal of Psychology,* 1904, *15,* 201–292.

SPEARMAN, C. E. *The nature of "intelligence" and the principles of cognition.* London: Macmillan, 1923.

SPEARMAN, C. E. *The abilities of man.* London: Macmillan, 1927.

SPENCE, K. W., & TAYLOR, J. A. The relation of conditioned response strengths to anxiety in normal, neurotic and psychotic subjects. *Journal of Experimental Psychology,* 1952, *45,* 265–272.

SPENCER, H. *Social statics.* New York: D. Appleton & Co., 1875. (Originally published, 1851.)

SPENCER, H. *Principles of psychology* (3rd ed.). London: Williams and Norgate, 1890. (Originally published, 1855.)

SPILLANE, J. D. *The doctrine of the nerves: Chapters in the history of neurology.* Oxford: Oxford University Press, 1981.

SPINOZA, B. *Ethics.* In J. Wild (Ed.), *Spinoza: Selections.* New York: Scribner's, 1930. (Originally published, 1677.)

SPOERL, H. D. Faculties versus traits: Gall's solution. *Character and Personality,* 1935, *4,* 216–231.

SPURZHEIM, J. G. *Phrenology: In connexion with the study of physiognomy.* Boston: Marsh, Capen & Lyon, 1834.

STEINER, I. D. Social psychology. In E. Hearst (Ed.), *The first century of experimental psychology.* Hillsdale, N.J.: Lawrence Erlbaum Associates, 1979.

STERN, L. W. The psychological methods of testing intelligence. In D. N. Robinson (Ed.), *Significant contributions to the history of psychology, 1750–1920* (Series B, Vol. 4). Washington, D.C.: University Publications of America, 1977. (Originally published, 1912.)

STEVENS, J. C., & GREEN, B. G. Temperature-touch interaction: Weber's phenomenon revisited. *Sensory Processes,* 1978, *2,* 206–219.

STEVENS, G., & GARDNER, S. *The women of psychology.* Vol. 1. *Pioneers and innovators.* Vol. 2. *Expansion and refinement.* Cambridge, Mass.: Schenkman, 1982.

STEVENS, S. S. The direct estimation of sensory magnitude—loudness. *American Journal of Psychology,* 1956, *69,* 1–25.

STEWART, D. *Elements of the philosophy of the human mind* (Vol. 1, 1792; Vol. 2, 1814; Vol. 3, 1827.) Reprinted as the first three volumes of *The Works of Dugal Stewart* (7 vols.). Cambridge: Hilliard and Brown, 1829.

STIGLER, S. M. Some forgotten work on memory. *Journal of Experimental Psychology: Human Learning and Memory,* 1978, *4,* 1–4.

STOUT, G. F. The Herbartian psychology. *Mind,* 1888, *13,* 321–338; 473–498.

STOUT, G. F. Herbart compared with English psychologists and with Beneke. *Mind,* 1889, *14,* 1–26.

STRATTON, G. M. Vision without inversion of the retinal image. *Psychological Review,* 1897, *4,* 341–360; 463–481.

STRATTON, G. M. *Theophrastus and the Greek physiological psychology before Aristotle.* New York: Macmillan, 1917.

STROMBERG, R. N. *An intellectual history of modern Europe* (2nd ed.). Englewood Cliffs, N.J.: Prentice-Hall, 1975.

STRONG, E. K. *Vocational interests of men and women.* Stanford, Calif.: Stanford University Press, 1943.

STROUT, C. William James and the twice-born sick soul. *Daedalus,* 1968, *97,* 1062–1082.

STRUNK, O., JR. The self-psychology of Mary Whiton Calkins. *Journal of the History of the Behavioral Sciences,* 1972, *8,* 196–203.

STUMPF, C. *Tonpsychologie.* Leipzig: S. Hirzel, Vol. 1, 1883; Vol. 2, 1890.

STUMPF, C. Erscheinungen und psychische Funktionen (a); Zur Einteilung der Wissenschaften (b). *Abhandlungen der preussichen Akadamie der Wissenschaften Berlin (philosophischehistorische Klasse),* 1906, No. 4(a), No. 5(b).

SULLIVAN, J. J. Franz Brentano and the problem of intentionality. In B. B. Wolman (Ed.), *Historical roots of contemporary psychology.* New York: Harper & Row, 1968.

SULLOWAY, F. J. *Freud, biologist of the mind: Beyond the psychoanalytic legend.* New York, Basic Books, 1979.

SUOMI, S. J., HARLOW, H. F., & McKINNEY, W. P. Monkey psychiatrists. *American Journal of Psychiatry,* 1972, *128,* 927–932.

SWEDENBORG, E. *The brain, considered anatomically, physiologically and philosophically* (2 vols., R. L. Tafel, trans.). London: James Speirs, 1882.

SWEDENBORG, E. *The soul or rational psychology* (F. Sewall, trans.). New York: New Church Board Publication, 1890. [The book was written at some unknown date between 1700 and 1750.]

SWETS, J. A., TANNER, W. P., JR., & BIRDSALL, T. G. Decision processes in perception. *Psychological Review,* 1961, *68,* 301–304.

TATE, J. D., & SPRINGER, R. M. Effects of memory time on successive judgments. *Psychological Bulletin,* 1971, *76,* 394–408.

TATON, R. *Ancient and medieval science.* London: Thames and Hudson, 1963.

TAUSCH, R. Optische Täuschungen als artifizielle Effekte der Gestaltungsprozesse von Grössen- und Formenkonstanz in der natürlichen Raumwahrnehmung. *Psychologische Forschung,* 1954, *24,* 299–348.

TAYLOR, E. *William James on exceptional mental states. The 1896 Lowell lectures.* New York: Charles Scribners' Sons, 1982.

TAYLOR, F. W. *The principles of scientific management.* New York: Harper, 1911.

TELFER, W. (Ed.). *Cyril of Jerusalem and Nemesius of Emensa* (includes annotated translation of Nemesius's *Of the nature of man*). London: SCM Press, 1955.

TERMAN, L. M. *The measurement of intelligence.* New York: Houghton Mifflin, 1916.

THOMSON, G. *The factorial analysis of human ability.* London: University of London Press, 1939.

THORNDIKE, E. L. A reply to "The nature of animal intelligence and the methods of investigating it." *Psychological Review,* 1899, *6,* 412–420.

THORNDIKE, E. L. Animal intelligence. Psychological Review Monograph, 1898, supplement No. 2. Reprinted with other articles in *Animal Intelligence.* New York: Macmillan, 1911.

THORNDIKE, E. L. *The psychology of learning* (Vol. 2 of *Educational Psychology*). New York: Teacher's College, Columbia University, 1914.

THORNDIKE, E. L. A constant error in psychological ratings. *Journal of Applied Psychology,* 1920, *4,* 25–29.

THORNDIKE, E. L. *The psychology of arithmetic.* New York: Macmillan, 1923.

THORNDIKE, E. L. *The measurement of intelligence.* New York: Teacher's College, Columbia University, 1927.

THORNDIKE, E. L. *The fundamentals of learning.* New York: Teacher's College, Columbia University, 1932.

THORNDIKE, E. L., & LORGE, I. *The teacher's word book of 30,000 words.* New York: Teachers College, Columbia University, 1944.

THORNDIKE, E. L., LAY, W., & DEAN, P. R. The relation of accuracy in sensory discrimination to general intelligence. *American Journal of Psychology,* 1909, *20,* 364–369.

THUMB, A., & MARBE, K. *Experimentelle Untersuchungen über die psychologischen Grundlagen der sprachlichen Analogiebildung.* Amsterdam: John Benjamins B.V., 1978. (Originally published, 1901).

THURSTONE, L. L. A multiple factor study of vocational interests. *Personnel Journal,* 1931, *10,* 198–205.

THURSTONE, L. L. *Primary mental abilities.* Chicago: University of Chicago Press, 1938.

THURSTONE, L. L., & THURSTONE, T. G. A neurotic inventory. *Journal of Social Psychology,* 1930, *1,* 3–30.

TINBERGEN, N. *The study of instinct.* Oxford: Clarendon Press, 1951.

TINKER, M. A. Wundt's doctorate students and their theses 1875–1920. *American Journal of Psychology,* 1932, *44,* 630–637.

TITCHENER, E. B. *An outline of psychology.* New York: Macmillan, 1896; 2nd ed., 1902; 3rd ed., 1907.

TITCHENER, E. B. *A primer of psychology.* New York: Macmillan Co., 1898. (a)

TITCHENER, E. B. The postulates of a structural psychology. *Philosophical Review,* 1898, *8,* 449–465. (b)

TITCHENER, E. B. Structural and functional psychology. *Philosophical Review,* 1899, *8,* 290–299.

TITCHENER, E. B. *Lectures on the elementary psychology of feelings and attention.* New York: Macmillan, 1908.

TITCHENER, E. B. *Lectures on the experimental psychology of the thought-processes.* New York: Macmillan, 1909. (a)

TITCHENER, E. B. *A textbook of psychology.* New York: Macmillan Co., 1909. (Enlarged editions were printed in 1910 and 1911.) (b)

TITCHENER, E. B. A historical note on the James-Lange theory of emotion. *American Journal of Psychology,* 1914, *25,* 427–447. (a)

TITCHENER, E. B. On psychology as the behaviorist views it. *Proceedings of the American Philosophical Society,* 1914, *53,* 1–17. (b)

TITCHENER, E. B. Wilhelm Wundt. *American Journal of Psychology,* 1921, *32,* 161–178. (a).

TITCHENER, E. B. Functional psychology and the psychology of act: I. *American Journal of Psychology,* 1921, *32,* 519–542. (b)

TITCHENER, E. B. *Systematic psychology: Prolegomena.* New York: Macmillan, 1929.

TITCHENER, E. B. *Experimental psychology: A manual of laboratory practice.* Vol. I, *Qualitative:* Part I, Student's Manual, Part II, Instructor's Manual, 1901; Vol. 2, *Quantitative:* Part I, Student's Manual, Part 2, Instructor's Manual, 1905. New York: Macmillan. Reprinted, New York: Johnson Reprint Corporation, 1971.

TITCHENER, E. B., & GEISSLER, L. R. A bibliography of the scientific writings of Wilhelm Wundt. *American Journal of Psychology,* 1908, *19,* 541–556.

TOLMAN, E. C. A new formula for behaviorism. *Psychological Review,* 1922, *29,* 44–53.

TOLMAN, E. C. *Purposive behavior in animals and man.* New York: Appleton-Century-Crofts, 1932.

TOLMAN, E. C. Cognitive maps in rats and man. *Psychological Review,* 1948, *55,* 189–208.

TRIPLETT, N. The dynamogenic factors in pacemaking and competition. *American Journal of Psychology,* 1898, *9,* 507–533.

TUDDENHAM, R. D. The nature and measurement of intelligence. In L. Postman (Ed.), *Psychology in the making.* New York: Knopf, 1962.

TULVING, E. *Elements of episodic memory.* New York: Oxford University Press, 1983.

TURNER, R. S. Hermann von Helmholtz and the empiricist vision. *Journal of the History of the Behavioral Sciences,* 1977, *13,* 48–58.

TURNER, R. S. Helmholtz, sensory physiology, and the disciplinary development of German psychology. In W. R. Woodward & M. G. Ash (Eds.), *The problematic science: Psychology in nineteenth-century thought.* New York: Praeger, 1982.

TWENEY, R. D., & YACHANIN, S. A. Titchener's Wundt. In W. G. Bringmann & R. D. Tweney (Eds.), *Wundt studies.* Toronto: C. J. Hogrefe, 1980.

UNZER, J. A. *The principles of physiology.* London: Sydenham Society, 1851. (Also contains Prochaska, G., *A dissertation on the functions of the nervous system.*)

VANDE KEMP, H. *Psychology and theology in Western thought 1672–1965: A historical and annotated bibliography.* Millwood, N.Y.: Kraus International Publications, 1984.

VEITH, I. *Hysteria: The history of a disease.* Chicago and London: University of Chicago Press, 1965.

VERHAVE, T. Contributions to the history of psychology. IV. Joseph Buchanan (1785–1829) and the "Law of Exercise" (1812). *Psychological Reports,* 1967, *20,* 127–133.

VERNON, H. M. *Accidents and their prevention.* Cambridge: Cambridge University Press, 1936.

VIERKANDT, A. *Naturvölker und Kulturvölker. Ein Beitrag zur Sozialpsychologie.* Leipzig: Duncker & Humbolt, 1896.

VITELES, M. S. *Industrial psychology.* London: Jonathan Cape, 1933.

VIVES, J. L. On the soul and on life. In Spanish in J. L. Vives, *Obras completas* (trans. into Spanish by L. Riber). Madrid: M. Aguilar, 1948. In Latin in J. L. Vives, *Opera omnia,* as published by B. Monfort, 1745; republished London, The Gregg Press, 1964.

VLEESCHAUWER, H. J. DE. *The development of Kantian thought: The history of a doctrine* (A. R. C. Duncan, trans.). New York: T. Nelson, 1962. (Originally published, 1939.)

WADE, N. (Ed.). *Brewster and Wheatstone on vision.* New York: Academic Press, 1984.

WALLACH, H. *On perception.* New York: Quadrangle/ The N.Y. Times, 1976.

WARREN, H. C. *A history of the association psychology.* London: Constable and Co., 1921.

WARREN, R. M., & WARREN, R. P. *Helmholtz on perception: Its physiology and development.* New York: John Wiley & Sons, 1968.

WASHBURN, M. F. *The animal mind.* New York: Macmillan, 1908. *Psychological Review,* 1915, *22,* 333–353.

WASHBURN, M. *Movement and mental imagery: Outlines of a motor theory of the complexer mental processes.* Boston: Houghton Mifflin, 1916.

WATSON, F. The father of modern psychology. *Psychological Review,* 1915, *22,* 333–353.

WATSON, J. B. Review of H. S. Jennings: *The behavior of the lower organisms. Psychological Bulletin,* 1907, *4,* 288–291.

WATSON, J. B. Psychology as the behaviorist views it. *Psychological Review,* 1913, *20,* 158–177.

WATSON, J. B. *Behavior: An introduction to comparative psychology.* New York: Henry Holt & Co., 1914.

WATSON, J. B. The place of the conditioned reflex in psychology. *Psychological Review,* 1916, *23,* 89–116.

WATSON, J. B. *Psychology from the standpoint of a behaviorist.* Philadelphia: Lippincott, 1919. (a)

WATSON, J. B. *Studies upon the behavior of the human infant.* (Film.) From the Psychological Laboratories, Johns Hopkins University. Baltimore, Md.: Eagle Film Productions, 1919. (b) (Obtainable from the Society for Research on Child Development.)

WATSON, J. B. *Behaviorism.* Chicago: University of Chicago Press, 1st ed., 1924; 2nd ed., 1930.

WATSON, J. B. Memory as the behaviorist sees it. *Harper's Magazine,* 1926, *153,* 244–250.

WATSON, J. B. The unverbalized in human behavior. *Psychological Review,* 1934, *31,* 273–280.

WATSON, J. B. Autobiography. In C. Murchinson (Ed.), *A history of psychology in autobiography* (Vol. 3). Worcester, Mass.: Clark University Press, 1936.

WATSON, J. B., & RAYNER, R. Conditioned emotional reactions. *Journal of Experimental Psychology,* 1920, *3,* 1–14.

WATSON, R. I. *The great psychologists from Aristotle to Freud* (2nd ed.). New York: Lippincott, 1968.

WATSON, R. I. A prescriptive analysis of Descartes' psychological views. *Journal of the History of the Behavioral Sciences,* 1971, *7,* 223–248.

WATT, H. J. Experimentelle Beiträge zu einer Theorie des Denkens. *Archiv für die gesamte Psychologie,* 1905, *4,* 289–436.

WAUGH, N. C., & NORMAN, D. A. Primary memory. *Psychological Review,* 1965, *72,* 89–104.

WEBER, E. H. *The sense of touch.* Contains *De Tactu* (1834), trans. H. E. Ross; and *Der Tastsinn und das Gemeingefühl* (1846), trans. D. J. Murray. New York: Academic Press, 1978.

WECHSLER, D. *The measurement and appraisal of adult intelligence* (4th ed.). Baltimore: Williams & Wilkins, 1958.

WELLEK, A. The impact on the German immigration on the development of American psychology. *Journal of the History of the Behavioral Sciences,* 1968, *4,* 207–229.

WERTHEIMER, M. Experimentelle Studien über das Sehen von Bewegungen. *Zeitschrift für Psychologie,* 1912, *61,* 161–265.

WERTHEIMER, M. Untersuchungen zur Lehre von der Gestalt. *Psychologische Forschung,* 1923, *4,* 301–350. Excerpts in English in Ellis (1938), pp. 71–88.

WERTHEIMER, M. *Productive thinking* (1945). Enlarged edition edited by Michael Wertheimer: New York: Harper & Brothers, 1959.

WESLEY, F. Was Raehlmann the first behaviorist? *Journal of the History of the Behavioral Sciences,* 1968, *4,* 161–162.

WEST, M. Early Greek philosophy. In J. Boardman, J. Griffin & O. Murray (Eds.), *The Oxford history of the classical world.* New York: Oxford University Press, 1986.

WEVER, W. G., & BRAY, C. W. Present possibilities of auditory theory. *Psychological Review,* 1930, *37,* 365–380.

WEYER, J. See WIER, J.

WHITEHEAD, T. N. *The industrial worker* (2 vols). Cambridge, Mass.: Harvard University Press, 1938.

WHITELY, P. L., & BLANKENSHIP, A. B. The influence of certain conditions prior to learning upon subsequent recall. *Journal of Experimental Psychology,* 1936, *19,* 496–504.

WICKELGREN, W. A., & NORMAN, D. A. Strength models and serial position in short-term recognition memory. *Journal of Mathematical Psychology,* 1966, *3,* 316–347.

WIENER, N. *Cybernetics.* New York: John Wiley & Sons, 1948.

WIENER, P. P. *Leibnitz: Selections.* New York: Scribner's, 1951.

WIER, J. *De praestigiis daemonum.* Basel: Per Joannem Oporinum, 1563.

WILLIS, T. *The anatomy of the brain and nerves* (2 vols., W. Feindel, Ed.). Montreal: McGill University Press, 1965.

WILLIS, T. *Two discourses concerning the soul of brutes.* Gainesville, Fla: Scholars' Facsimiles and Reprints, 1971. (Originally published, 1672.)

WISSLER, C. The correlation of mental and physical tests. *Psychological Review Monograph,* Supplement 3, No. 6, 1901.

WITASEK, S. *Grundlinien der Psychologie.* Leipzig: F. Meiner, 1908.

WITKIN, H. A., LEVIS, H. B., HERTZMAN, M., MACHOVER, K., MEISSNER, P. B., & WAPNER, S. *Personality through perception.* New York: Harper & Row, 1954.

WOLF, A. *A history of science, technology and philosophy in the sixteenth and seventeenth centuries.* London: George Allen & Unwin, 1935.

WOLF, T. H. *Alfred Binet.* Chicago: University of Chicago Press, 1973.

WOLFF, C. *Preliminary discourse on philosophy in general* (translated with an introduction and notes by R. J. Blackwell). New York: Bobbs-Merrill, 1963.

WOLFF, C. *Psychologia empirica.* In J. Ecole (Ed.), *Christian Wolff: Gesammelte Werke,* Part II, Vol. 5. Hildesheim: Georg Olms, 1968.

WOLFF, C. *Psychologia rationalis.* In J. Ecole (Ed.), *Christian Wolff, Gesammelte Werke,* Part II, Vol. 6. Hildesheim: Georg Olms, 1972.

WOLFSON, H. A. *The philosophy of Spinoza* (2 vols.). Cambridge, Mass.: Harvard University Press, 1934.

WOLFSON, H. A. The internal senses in Latin, Arabic and Hebrew philosophic texts. *Harvard Theological Review,* 1935, *28,* 69–133.

WOLPE, J. Experimental neuroses as learned behavior. *British Journal of Psychology,* 1952, *43,* 243–268.

WOLPE, J., & RACHMAN, S. Psychoanalytic "evidence": A critique based on Freud's case of Little Hans. *Journal of Nervous and Mental Disease,* 1960, *130,* 135–148.

WOODWARD, W. R. Fechner's panpsychism: A scientific solution to the mind-body problem. *Journal of the History of the Behavioral Sciences,* 1972, *8,* 367–386.

WOODWORTH, R. S. *Experimental psychology.* New York: Holt, Rinehart & Winston, 1938.

WOODWORTH, R. S. John Broadus Watson: 1878–1958. *American Journal of Psychology,* 1959, *72,* 301–310.

WOODWORTH, R. S., & SCHLOSBERG, H. *Experimental psychology.* New York: Holt, Rinehart & Winston, 1954.

WULF, F. Über die Veränderung von Vorstellungen (Gedächtnis und Gestalt). *Psychologische Forschung,* 1922, *1,* 333–373. Excerpts in English in Ellis (1938), pp. 136–148.

WUNDT, W. Über der gegenwärtigen Zustand der Tierpsychologie. *Vierteljahrschrift für wissenschaftliche Philosophie,* 1878, *2,* 137–149. Recast in *Essays* (1885).

WUNDT, W. Der Spiritismus. An open letter to Prof. Ulrici of Halle. Leipzig: W. Engelmann, 1879. Reprinted in *Essays* (1885).

WUNDT, W. *Logik* (3 vols.). Stuttgart: Ferdinand Enke, 1880–1883.

WUNDT, W. *Essays.* Leipzig: W. Engelmann, 1885.

WUNDT, W. *Ethik.* Stuttgart: Ferdinand Enke, 1886. The 2nd edition of 1892 was translated by E. B. Titchener, J. H. Gulliver, and M. F. Washburn as *Ethics: An investigation of the facts and laws of the moral life.* New York: Macmillan, 1897.

WUNDT, W. Selbstbeobachtung und innere Wahrnehmung. *Philosophische Studien*, 1887, *4*, 292–310.

WUNDT, W. Über die Einteilung der Wissenschaften. *Philosophische Studien*, 1888, *5*, 1–55.

WUNDT, W. *System der Philosophie.* Leipzig: W. Engelmann, 1889.

WUNDT, W. *Hypnotismus und Suggestion.* Leipzig: W. Engelmann, 1892.

WUNDT, W. Über psychische Causalität und das Princip des psychophysischen Parallelismus. *Philosophische Studien*, 1894, *10*, 1–124.

WUNDT, W. *Völkerpsychologie. Eine Untersuchung der Entwicklungsgesetze von Sprache, Mythus und Sitten.* Vol. 1. *Die Sprache*, 1900. Vol. 2. *Mythus und Religion:* Part I, 1905; Part II, 1906; Part IV, 1909. Leipzig: W. Engelmann, 1900–1909.

WUNDT, W. *Einleitung in die Philosophie.* Leipzig: W. Engelmann, 1901.

WUNDT, W. *Grundriss der Psychologie.* Leipzig: W. Engelmann, 1896. The 4th revised edition was translated by C. M. Judd as *Outlines of Psychology.* Leipzig: W. Engelmann; London: William & Norgate; New York: Gustav E. Stechart, 1902.

WUNDT, W. *Vorlesungen über die Menschen- und Tierseele.* (2 vols.). Leipzig: L. Voss, 1863. The second edition of 1892 was translated by J. E. Creighton and E. B. Titchener as *Lectures on human and animal psychology.* London: Swan Sonnenschein & Co., 1901.

WUNDT, W. *Grundzüge der physiologischen Psychologie* (1st ed., Leipzig: W. Engelmann, 1874. 2nd ed., 1880; 3rd ed., 1887; 4th ed., 1893; 5th ed., 1902–1903; 6th ed., 1908–1911). Vol. I, Part I of the 5th ed. was translated by E. B. Titchener as *Principles of physiological psychology.* London: Swan Sonnenschein and Co., 1904.

WUNDT, W. Über Ausfrageexperimente und über die Methoden zur Psychologie des Denkens. *Psychologische Studien*, 1907, 3, 301–360.

WUNDT, W. Das Institut für experimentelle Psychologie zu Leipzig. *Psychologische Studien*, 1910, *5*, 279–293.

WUNDT, W. *Einführung in die Psychologie.* Leipzig: W. Engelmann, 1911. Translated by R. Pintner as *Introduction to Psychology,* London: Allen, 1912.

WUNDT, W. *Beiträge zur Theorie der Sinneswahrehmung.* Leipzig: C. F. Winter, 1862. The introduction, titled "On the methods of psychology," is translated in T. Shipley (Ed.), *Classics in psychology.* New York: Philosophical Library, 1961.

WUNDT, W. *Erlebtes und Erkanntes.* Stuttgart: A. Kroner, 1920.

YATES, F. A. *The art of memory.* London: Routledge & Kegan Paul, 1966.

YERKES, R. M. *The dancing mouse.* New York: Macmillan, 1907.

YERKES, R. M., & HUGGINS, G. E. Habit formation in the crawfish Cambarus affinis. *Harvard Psychological Studies*, 1903, *1*, 565–577.

YERKES, R. M., and MORGULIS, S. The method of Pavlov in animal psychology. *Psychological Bulletin*, 1909, *6*, 257–273.

YOLTON, J. W. *John Locke and the way of ideas.* Oxford: Clarendon Press, 1956.

YOUNG, P. T. *Motivation and emotion.* New York: John Wiley & Sons, 1961.

YOUNG, R. M. *Mind, brain and adaptation in the nineteenth century.* Oxford: Clarendon Press, 1970.

YOUNG, T. On the theory of light and colours. In Peacock, G. *Miscellaneous works of the late Thomas Young* (Vol. 1). London: John Murray, 1855. (Originally published, 1802.)

ZEIGARNIK, B. Über das Behalten von erledigten und unerledigten Handlungen. *Psychologische Forschung*, 1927, *9*, 1–85. Excerpts in English in Ellis (1938), 300–314.

Name Index

Abelard, P., 60
Abraham, K., 356
Abramov, I., 163
Ach, N., 276ff., 282
Adkins, D.C., 383
Adler, A., 356, 361, 362ff., 417
Adrian, E.D., 369, 370, 376
Aeschylus, 23
Afnan, S.M., 56
Agassiz, L., 244
Agricola, G., 72
Agrippa, 335
Akhnaton, 2
Albertus Magnus, 60ff, 64, 76
Alcmaeon, 18, 20, 21
Alcuin, 55
Alexander, 3, 23
Alexander, F.G., 365
Alexander of Aphrodisias, 58
Al-Farabi, 57
Alhazen, 65
Alison, A., 141
Al-Kindi, 65
Allen, G.W., 247
Allen, S.D., 387

Allison, H.E., 99
Allport F.H., 387
Allport, G.W., 248, 252, 384, 389, 407
Alrutz, S., 376
Ameriks, K., 133
Amos, 15
Anaxagoras, 20, 22, 24
Anaximander, 16, 17
Anaximenes, 16, 17, 29
Anderson, J.R., 411
Anderson, N.H., 433
Angell, F., 229, 234
Angell, J.R., 230, 236ff., 315
Aquinas, St. Thomas, 4, 48, 60ff., 72, 76,
    82, 94
Ardal, P.S., 115
Aristophanes, 23
Aristotle, xvi, 20, 23, 27ff., 32, 33, 35, 42,
    49, 57, 58, 59, 63, 64, 65, 66, 70, 72,
    74, 76, 77, 80, 81, 85, 94, 97, 100,
    104, 123, 124, 148, 257
Armstrong, A.H., 27
Arnheim, R., 184
Arnobius, 46, 49, 51, 117
Artemidorus, 74

Subject Index

Purkinje cells, 169
Purpose, 400
Puzzle boxes, 303

Questionnaires, 317

Rational psychology
  Wolff's concept, 129
Rationalization, 359
Rats, 302, 305, 320, 329
Reaction formation, 359, 405
Reaction times
  apparatus, 220
  Donders, 195 ff.
  "sensorial" versus "muscular," 220, 231
Reading, 392, 414
Reasoning, Piaget's theory of, 422
  Taine on, 161
Recapitulation in evolution, 265
Reciprocal inhibition
  Sherrington's use, 371
  Wolpe's use, 401
Recognition, 410
Redintegration
  Hamilton, 151
  Wolff, 130
Reflexes
  Carpenter, 157
  Descartes, 82
  eighteenth-century research, 105
  Goldstein, 416
  Hall's research, 171
  implying "unlearned," 305
  La Mettrie, 117
  Laycock, 157
  reflex movement in dead animals, 89,
    105
  Sechenov, 306 ff.
  Sherrington, 370
Reformation, 1, 4
Refractory period, in nerves, 369
Regression, 355, 404
Rehearsal, 410
Reinforcement, 305, 324, 327, 401 ff., 420
Religious belief, 251, 360, 437
Renaissance, 1, 4, 69
Repression, 346 ff., 404
Resistance, muscular, 152
Response
  in context of language, 420
  first usage, 105
  unconditioned and conditioned, 309
Restructuring, 293

Rete mirabile, 40, 67, 71, 75
Reticular formation, 375, 434
Reversible figures, 286
Revolutions, 5, 7
Rhetorica ad Herennium, 35, 75
Rhodopsin, 378
Ribot's law, 374
Rods and cones, 187, 232, 377, 378
Roman period, 3, 28 ff., 333
Romantic movement, 6
Rorschach Test, 385
Ruffini endings, 376
Russia, 7, 306

Sadism, 355
Salpêtrière Hospital, 336, 341
Schema
  Bartlett's use, 330, 399
  Piaget's use, 422
Schizophrenia, 339, 362, 366, 417, 429
Schwann cells, 169
Science, 227
Scientific Monthly, 227
Scientific societies, 86
Scottish school, 140 ff., 243
Scripts, 399
Secreta Secretorum, 74
Self
  Cabanis, 106
  Calkins, 254
  Condillac, 119
  Gestalt concept, 291
  Herbart, 166
  Hume, 116
  James, 251
  Jung, 364
  Kant, 134
  Locke's analysis, 98
  Mead, 388
  Reid, 122
Self-actualization, 416 ff.
Senescence, 225
Sensation, 435
  Aristotle, 28
  Avicenna, 57
  Bonnet, 110
  contrasted with perception by Reid, 123
  Ebbinghaus, 215
  Fechner, 181 ff.
  Gestalt psychology, 284
  Hartley, 109
  Helmholtz, 158 ff.
  Kant, 131 ff.